INTRODUCTION TO STATISTICS

This book is dedicated to the memory of my father, Malcolm, and my brother, Robert. Both were outgoing, inquisitive, supportive, energetic, intelligent, and hardworking. They were devoted to their families, and each embraced life to the fullest. Tragically, each died much too young. They are greatly missed. And the book is dedicated to my mother, Jeannette, whose love, support, and kindness are a blessing to all who know her.

INTRODUCTION TO STATISTICS

Fundamental Concepts and Procedures of Data Analysis

Howard M. Reid

SUNY Buffalo State

+ I like this book
+ It uses pretty much the same symbols I use

Los Angeles | London | New Delhi
Singapore | Washington DC

Los Angeles | London | New Delhi
Singapore | Washington DC

FOR INFORMATION:

SAGE Publications, Inc.
2455 Teller Road
Thousand Oaks, California 91320
E-mail: order@sagepub.com

SAGE Publications Ltd.
1 Oliver's Yard
55 City Road
London EC1Y 1SP
United Kingdom

SAGE Publications India Pvt. Ltd.
B 1/I 1 Mohan Cooperative Industrial Area
Mathura Road, New Delhi 110 044
India

SAGE Publications Asia-Pacific Pte. Ltd.
3 Church Street
#10-04 Samsung Hub
Singapore 049483

Acquisitions Editor: Vicki Knight
Assistant Editor: Kalie Koscielak
Editorial Assistant: Jessica Miller
Production Editor: Stephanie Palermini
Copy Editor: QuADS Prepress (P) Ltd.
Typesetter: C&M Digitals (P) Ltd.
Proofreader: Barbara Johnson
Indexer: Marilyn Augst
Cover Designer: Candice Harman
Marketing Manager: Nicole Elliott
Permissions Editor: Karen Ehrmann

Printed in the United States of America

Library of Congress Cataloging-in-Publication Data

Reid, Howard M.

Introduction to statistics : fundamental concepts and procedures of data analysis / Howard M. Reid.

pages cm
Includes bibliographical references and index.

ISBN 978-1-4522-7196-5 (paperback : acid-free paper)
ISBN 978-1-4833-0157-0 (web PDF)

1. Statistics—Textbooks. I. Title.

QA276.12.R45 2013
519.5—dc23   2013006445

This book is printed on acid-free paper.

Certified Chain of Custody
SUSTAINABLE   Promoting Sustainable Forestry
FORESTRY   www.sfiprogram.org
INITIATIVE   SFI-01268
SFI label applies to text stock

13 14 15 16 17 10 9 8 7 6 5 4 3 2 1

BRIEF CONTENTS

DETAILED CONTENTS

ABOUT THE AUTHOR

Howard M. Reid is a professor at State University of New York, Buffalo State. He received his doctorate in experimental psychology from the University of Maine and followed it by postdoctoral study in behavior genetics at The Jackson Laboratory. He is currently conducting studies examining perception of art, is directing a variety of undergraduate student research projects, and is chairing the College senate. He has been an active researcher with broad interests, including published work in operant analysis of behavior, animal models of epilepsy, links between ADHD (attention-deficit/hyperactivity disorder) and laterality, as well as construction of a scale measuring student appreciation of the liberal arts. He has also directed numerous undergraduate research projects. He is the recipient of a number of prestigious awards, including the SUNY Chancellor's Awards in Teaching and Faculty Service and the BSC President's Award for Excellence as an Undergraduate Research Mentor.

ABOUT THE AUTHOR

PREFACE

There are many fine introductory statistics books that have been written for undergraduate students. Yet these students often continue to view statistics courses negatively, and many fear they will be unable to master the basic level of understanding that is essential to progress in their majors. The present text is an attempt to rethink what students need to learn in an introductory statistics course and how best to organize the presentation of this material to assist them in acquiring the competence necessary to succeed in their chosen field of study.

Every book is written from some perspective. This book is written from the perspective that a first course in applied statistics is an introduction to a form of critical thinking as much as it is an introduction to a mathematically based discipline. And this book emphasizes what a student will need to remember in future semesters, even years, rather than focusing on a cursory introduction to numerous techniques, many of which will soon be forgotten. Finally, this book is designed to provide a foundation on which students can build as they take further statistics or methodology courses.

As a consequence, while this book covers many of the same topics as in other texts, the presentation, and in some cases the content, differs in significant ways. First, the text is organized to assist students in understanding the logic of statistical procedures and how they are related to each other. And the material is presented so that students gain confidence in their ability to master this subject. Simple concepts and procedures are presented before difficult ones, and concepts build so that by the end of the book readers have gained a clear comprehension of the goals, basic techniques, and the limitations of statistical analysis. Second, an aim of the text is to have the reader not only be exposed to fundamental concepts such as variability but also come to appreciate that these concepts re-occur in a variety of contexts. Repetition and an emphasis on the use of definitional equations enhance students' gaining a deeper understanding. For instance, the reader repeatedly sees that statistical measures of variability are based on deviations, something that can be lost when computational equations are used. Of course, researchers don't commonly employ definitional equations in statistical calculations. (They no longer turn to computational equations either.) Instead, they turn to statistical packages to conduct analyses of their data. Accordingly, a third major thrust is that this text emphasizes the mastery of SPSS through the use of step-by-step directions and numerous figures, all integrated into the chapters. As a result, students see how mastery of SPSS complements their learning of statistical procedures. Fourth, a concerted effort has been made to integrate the study of statistics with numerous disciplines as well as by including brief historical sections and incorporating relevant quotations. While it is unlikely that every example will resonate with every reader, the goal is to present statistics in a manner that appeals to students coming to the course with diverse backgrounds and interests.

The result is, I believe, a text that will assist students in being able to understand the proper uses, and limitations, of a set of commonly employed statistical procedures. By incorporating progress checks, lists of assumptions, consequences of violating the assumptions, and referral to an overview table of statistical procedures (Appendix K), I have found that my students are better able to match the correct procedure with a research design. This is often a difficult challenge for students. Consequently, one of the goals while writing this text was to present the material in such a way that students would be better able to correctly identify the appropriate procedure to use, not just be able to calculate an answer when told what test to employ.

The book's organization differs significantly from what is commonly seen in other introductory statistics texts. Instead of the almost universal order of presentation which relegates nonparametric tests, seemingly as an afterthought, to a final chapter, the current book is organized so that the procedures that employ nominal data, and which are also the easiest for students to calculate, are presented before the procedures that employ ordinal or interval and ratio data. The resulting presentation is, by design, somewhat repetitious, but it allows for positive transfer among the commonly used procedures that are reviewed. For instance, important statistical concepts, including significance, effect size, and use of post hoc tests, are introduced with the review of the chi-square test of independence. Students see these concepts again when the procedures that employ interval and ratio data are discussed. The goal is for students to experience important concepts repeatedly and to understand how the different statistical procedures are related.

A final note for instructors:

I am fully aware that this book presents a different approach to teaching introductory statistics. And a new approach can be challenging, particularly for those of us who have always viewed the discipline of statistics from a particular perspective. All I can say is that, for me, this system works. My students are learning more material. They are learning more easily. And they are better prepared and more confident going into my department's subsequent methodology course. I know that no single approach to teaching statistics will work for everyone, but I encourage you to consider the difficulties that many students currently have with mastering this subject and whether they would find the approach taken by this text beneficial.

ACKNOWLEDGMENTS

A list of everyone whose contribution to this book could appropriately be acknowledged would be quite long. However, the contributions of three individuals were so significant that I would be particularly remiss if they were not recognized:

I want to especially thank my wife, Dr. Susan E. Mason. The book was greatly strengthened by her insights on teaching statistics and her amazing talents as an editor, and it might not have come about without her encouragement and support. I will always be grateful to her.

I also want to thank Dr. Robert L. Collins, a very close friend, who first introduced me to the field of statistics and who has taught me so much over many years.

And I would like to thank Ms. Kelly Boos, an extraordinary secretary, who contributed in many ways to creating this finished product.

I would also like to acknowledge the constant support and advice of everyone at Sage, particularly Vicki Knight, Rajasree Ghosh, and Stephanie Palermini. Finally, I would like to acknowledge the numerous contributions of the Sage reviewers. They provided invaluable suggestions for the improvement of this text:

Michael A. Bock, American International College

C. A. Brooks, Bowie State University

Ngoc H. Bui, University of La Verne

Christy Miller Cowan, Lincoln Memorial University

Marilyn Dantico, Arizona State University

Johnathan D. Forbey, Ball State University

Henry Gorman, Austin College

Michele S. Hirsch, St. Francis College

Matthew Jerram, Suffolk University

Joseph G. Johnson, Miami University

Elizabeth Kudadjie-Gyamfi, Long Island University, Brooklyn

Veena S. Kulkarni, Arkansas State University

Sean Laraway, San Jose State University

Kristi Lemm, Western Washington University

Michael A Mangan, University of New Hampshire, Durham

Nanette Silverman, Dowling College

May Takeuchi, University of North Alabama

Thomas Uttaro, College of Staten Island, City University of New York

Amy Wagler, The University of Texas at El Paso

INTRODUCTION

Why You Need to Understand Statistical Reasoning

Few things mislead us more than failure to grasp simple statistical principles.

—Sharon Begley

S tatistics is a general term for a variety of procedures that have been found to be helpful, even essential, in fields such as psychology, economics, biology, and political science, as well as many others. Newspapers are filled with statistical statements. Politicians turn to statistics for support of their policies as well as to attack their opponents. What would sports be without statistical analyses? Our high standard of living would not be possible without the use of statistics in business and finance. Our health has been immeasurably enhanced by employing statistical procedures. And, when we die, though it is a time of sadness and reflection for family and friends, we will become another statistic in census books. You cannot avoid statistics and you should not try to. Statistics are useful and ubiquitous.

A LITTLE HISTORY

Statistics is an example of a field that has had an impact far beyond what any of its founders could have imagined. Before the late 19th century, there was no recognizable discipline of statistics. Now, knowledge of statistical procedures is seen as essential for undergraduates majoring in any of the natural or social sciences, and specialized statistics courses are offered in most college mathematics departments. For many careers, a knowledge of statistics is essential.

The field of statistics began with the study of probabilities in games of chance. Gerolamo Cardana (1501–1576), in the first book on probability, noted that if a die (singular of dice) is fair, then each face will have an equal chance of occurring. Jacques Bernoulli (1654–1705) showed that the greater the number of times a die is tossed, the more closely the results come to the predicted probabilities. This understanding of probability was first put to practical use by wealthy aristocrats who wanted to optimize their chances of success in games of chance. However, the field quickly expanded into other areas. For instance, John Graunt (1620–1674) estimated the population of London based on mortality figures in a 1662/1981 book titled, *Natural and Political Observations Upon Bills of Mortality*. He checked his predictions by collecting data from three parishes. This was the first instance of representative sampling, a technique still in widespread use. In another example, in 1854, John Snow (1813–1858) noted a relationship between the source of a family's drinking water in London and their likelihood of contracting cholera. As a result of this finding, steps were taken that may well have hastened the end of the epidemic.

The field of statistics really took off in the late 19th and early 20th centuries. Florence Nightingale (1820–1910), a widely known reformer, employed statistics to support her campaign to improve hospital care. Francis Galton (1822–1911) introduced the concept of the correlation, though it was his student Karl Pearson (1857–1936) who developed the equation that is used to this day. In honor of Pearson's accomplishment, this procedure is known as the Pearson r correlation. You will learn about this procedure in Chapter 14. Pearson also developed what is known as the chi-square (pronounced ki square) goodness-of-fit test, a major topic of Chapter 7, and he was the first to use the term *standard deviation*, a concept reviewed in Chapter 3. During the same period, William Gosset (1876–1937) proposed the t test, a procedure covered in Chapters 9 and 10, to assist in making decisions based on small samples. At the time, Gosset worked for the Guinness brewery in Dublin and was prevented from publishing the procedure under his own name. As a result, he published his article using the name "Student," and to this day, the procedure is sometimes referred to as Student's t test. While this review of the history of statistics is obviously brief, even a brief survey should not omit Sir Ronald Fisher (1890–1962). Fisher is famous for numerous contributions to the field of statistics. He is probably most famous for his foundational work leading to the analysis of variance. Much of the latter part of this book (Chapters 11–13) is devoted to describing this set of useful procedures.

THE TWO USES OF STATISTICS

Today, statistics continue to be used to enhance the quality of decisions. Specifically, statistical procedures are used in two related ways—they assist us in seeing the world more clearly and in thinking more clearly.

Seeing Clearly Is Harder Than It Appears

We tend to be confident that we can rely on our vision. After all, we are able to recognize our friends, we can drive our cars without hitting anything, and we can tell when someone is hurt or sad. Unfortunately, while each of these is usually true, we all know that there are exceptions. Sometimes, we have difficulty recognizing people we know. Sometimes, due to rain, snow or fog, we cannot see well enough to drive safely. And sometimes, we are mistaken when we try to read another person's emotions.

A famous example of inaccurate perception is what psychologists call the attractiveness bias—we have a tendency to attribute good qualities to attractive people and bad qualities to unattractive people. This is certainly not a new situation, for the witches in folktales are always ugly, and the hero and heroine are attractive. What you may not be aware of is how pervasive this bias is. For instance, research has indicated that attractive defendants are less likely to be found guilty by a jury, and if they are convicted, they receive lighter sentences! That is wonderful news for those of you who are good looking but not so good for the rest of us.

Thinking Clearly Is Also Harder Than It Appears

Psychologists have also found that people don't think as accurately as they suppose they do. For instance, when people estimate risks, they frequently rely on personal experience, especially recent news reports. Thus, when asked which is more dangerous, taking a trip by flying in a plane or riding in a car, many people base their judgment on what they have heard in the news and respond that flying in a plane is more dangerous. Actually, riding in a car is much more dangerous, but car accidents are less likely to be reported in the news. This is known as the availability bias.

Knowledge of Statistics Can Help You See and Think More Accurately

We have mentioned only a few examples of not seeing or thinking effectively. Cognitive scientists have demonstrated many ways that we tend to make errors. Fortunately, there are a variety of statistical procedures to help us see and think more clearly and accurately. Since no one wants to be wrong, these are very valuable techniques indeed.

So why aren't you thinking statistically now? Perhaps you *never had an opportunity to learn to use statistics*. Then this is your lucky day! You are beginning a field of study that has many rewards. Perhaps you have avoided learning statistics because you think that *statistics are scary*. Actually, the vast majority of students are able to master the statistical procedures covered in this text in one semester, and many come to appreciate the logic of these procedures. Of course, there are lots of numbers, but if you apply yourself, you will do fine. You may also fear that *statistics are boring*. However, since the procedures you will be learning will help you gain a better understanding of the world and the people in it, statistics will make your life more interesting, not less.

PLAN OF THIS BOOK

This book is designed to assist you in *using statistics, first to see more clearly and then to think more clearly*. Using statistics to see information more clearly is called **descriptive statistics**. Specifically, descriptive statistics are the techniques that enable you to summarize a set of numbers clearly and accurately. In the study of statistics, factual information, often in the form of numbers, is called **data (plural of datum)**. So the earlier part of this book will teach you to "see" a set of data more accurately by summarizing it more succinctly.

Descriptive statistics: techniques that are used to summarize a set of numbers.

Data (plural of datum): factual information, often in the form of numbers.

Inferential statistics: techniques that are used in making decisions based on data.

The remainder of the book will show you how to use statistics to think more clearly about data. This is called **inferential statistics**. When you make an inference, you are making a decision based on your data. Specifically, in this part of the book, you will learn how to recognize whether there are relationships in your data. For instance, you will discover how we can be confident with the conclusion that attractive people are treated differently by juries than are unattractive people.

Descriptive statistics and inferential statistics—that's all there is to this book and to the field of statistics. What could be simpler?

Goal of This Book

In life, most of us find that it is a good idea to have both *breadth and depth of knowledge*. It is important to know some area or skill well (depth), but it is also important to have some knowledge of many things (breadth). For instance, in college, you select a major that will provide you with the depth of knowledge necessary for your chosen career. At the same time, you are expected to take a variety of other courses to broaden your education. It is the goal of this book to introduce you to the breadth and depth of statistics. As with home or auto repair, you will need to be able to pick the right "tool" (breadth) and know how to use it well (depth).

Taking a Step at a Time

The techniques and logic of statistics cannot be mastered all at once. Instead, this book is designed to provide a progressive process so that you can learn statistics in as efficient a manner as is possible. It is also my goal to make this process fun and entertaining. So let's get started!!!

PROGRESS CHECK

1. The two uses of statistics assist us in _____ and _____ more clearly.

2. Using statistics to see more clearly is called _____ statistics.

3. Using statistics to assist us in making decisions is called _____ statistics.

Answers: 1. Seeing; thinking. 2. descriptive. 3. inferential.

A Brief Review of Mathematics

This book's goal is to assist you in understanding and learning how to use statistics. Thus, you will be reading about a variety of procedures that have been found to be useful in a range of settings. The book will not be explaining how these procedures were developed or why they take the specific form that they do. Thus, this book, though mathematical, will likely have a very different focus from any mathematical book you have previously read. Obviously for most people, including me, the manipulation of numbers is not a favorite pastime. In fact, it is even possible that at least some readers may find mathematics to be aversive, and you may be concerned about the prospect of learning about this mathematical discipline. If you are one of these readers, you should know that it is a major goal of this text to alter that view. By the end of this book, you should feel a sense of pride in mastering an introduction to a mathematical discipline, and further, you should have gained an appreciation for the usefulness of this field. You may even find that your view of mathematics in general has changed!

No doubt about it, statistics is mathematical. If you leaf through the pages of this, or any, statistics text, you will see graphs, tables filled with numbers, and some very impressive-looking equations. You may even feel intimidated. Do not be. You will see that the only background in mathematics you need is knowledge through basic algebra. Even if that knowledge is quite "rusty," you will do fine. In case it has been some time since you have used much mathematics, we will now turn to a brief review of the procedures required for this book, which you will see are quite modest.

The Need for Math to Follow Rules

Numbers are simply symbols. They take the place of something else. For instance, if you were asked how many newspapers or magazines you have read in the last year, by using mathematics you do not have to actually produce each of them. Instead, you just state a number. Clearly, saying a number is much more convenient than carting around a load of old newspapers. Furthermore, just as we can manipulate another type of symbol—the letters of the alphabet— to make words, we can also manipulate numbers. In both cases, however, we must follow rules to be understood. It would not be helpful to you if I had used my own, unique system for spelling when this book was written. Similarly, it would not be helpful if each of us followed our own unique system for manipulating numbers. There have to be some agreed-on rules. Fortunately, to master the material of this book, there are surprisingly few mathematical rules. However, they will be used repeatedly, and thus, it is critical that you understand them.

Numbers frequently signify the magnitude of something. For example, we all know that 10 apples are more than 5 apples. This concept of magnitude can be linked to what is called a number line. A number line is simply a line on which all possible numbers can be located. It stretches from negative infinity ($-\infty$) through 0 to positive infinity ($+\infty$, commonly symbolized as just ∞), which is shown in Figure 1.1. It should be clear that the farther to the right of 0 one goes, the larger the positive number, and the farther to the left of 0 one goes, the larger the negative number. The line is thus symmetrical. For every possible positive number, there is a corresponding negative number. When a pair of numbers that are identical, except for their sign, are added together, the result is 0. For instance, the sum of positive 7 and negative 7 is 0. And if you sum negative 7 and positive 3, the answer would be negative 4. You should also remember that if you multiply or divide two positive numbers, the result is a positive number. Thus, 6 divided by 3 equals 2. If you multiply or divide two negative numbers, the result is also positive. For instance, $(-3) \times (-4)$ equals 12, not -12, and $(-8) \div (-4)$ equals 2. Finally, the result of multiplying or dividing one number that is positive and another number that is negative is a negative number. Thus, $(-3) \times (2)$ is equal to -6, not 6, and $(-4) \div (2)$ equals -2.

You also need to remember that when you square a number, you are multiplying the number by itself. Thus, 7 squared, which is written as 7^2, is equivalent to 7×7, which equals 49. Similarly, the square root of a number is the number that when multiplied by itself would equal the number with which we are concerned. This course will only be dealing with the

Figure 1.1   The Number Line

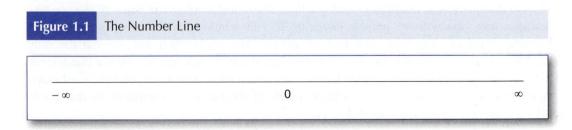

$-\infty$ 0 ∞

positive square roots. Therefore, the square root of 49, which is written $\sqrt{49}$, is equivalent to 7. To check this, 7×7 equals 49. As we will frequently be squaring and finding the square root of numbers, it is essential that you have a calculator with these functions. However, to use this book, it is not necessary that you have a sophisticated statistical calculator.

Finally, it is important that you remember the order in which mathematical operations are performed: Begin with items within parentheses, then exponents and roots, then multiplication and division, and finally addition and subtraction. Thus, $(2 + 3)^2$ is equal to 5^2, which is 25, but $2 + 3^2$ is equal to $2 + 9$, which is 11.

It Is Time to Learn Some Greek

Many of the mathematical procedures that you will see in this text involve adding numbers together and then manipulating the total in some manner. For instance, we could add all of the heights of the members of a softball team and then divide by the number of players. This would give us what you probably learned is called the average of the heights. In statistics, this is called the **mean** of the heights. It is the same procedure, with a different name. Unfortunately, describing how to calculate a mean takes a lot of words. To keep the length of this text tolerable, we need to agree on some simple definitions. Instead of "add all of the

> *Mean: sum of the scores divided by the total number of scores.*

heights" or "add all of the scores," we will write ΣX. The symbol Σ (the summation symbol, which resembles the Greek letter capital sigma) indicates that we are to add all the examples of something, and the X stands for a single score or datum (datum is the singular of data, which is always plural). Thus, ΣX says the same thing as "sum each of the scores," but it takes less space. It is read as "sum of X." And the mean can be written as $\Sigma X/N$, where N is the total number of scores. Similarly, ΣX^2 says the same thing as "sum each of the squared scores." It is read as "sum of X squared." But be careful, in mathematics, the precise symbols and the order in which they occur are important. Just as "Susan, please give the paper to Howard" does not mean the same thing as "Howard, please give the paper to Susan," ΣX^2 is not equivalent to $(\Sigma X)^2$. In the case of ΣX^2, we are being told to sum all of the X^2 values. In other words, we first square each score and then add the resulting numbers together. This is illustrated with a set of numbers given in Table 1.1. Note that ΣX^2 is equal to 110. On the other hand, the expression $(\Sigma X)^2$, which is read as "sum of X, quantity squared," indicates that we are first to sum all of the X scores and then square the result. In our case, this would be 18^2, which equals 324. Obviously 110 is not the same as 324! It will be important to remember as you read this text that ΣX^2, which can also be written as $\Sigma(X^2)$, is not the same thing as $(\Sigma X)^2$.

Two additional mathematical concepts that you need to understand are the inequalities "less than" and "greater than." These concepts are symbolized by $<$ and $>$, respectively. Writing $X < 10$ indicates that the value of X must be less than 10. It might be 9.99, 0, -20, or any other number less than 10. We do not know the precise value of X, but we know that it must be

| Table 1.1 | Computing $(\Sigma X)^2$ and ΣX^2 |

X	X^2
5	25
6	36
7	49
$\Sigma X = 18$	$\Sigma X^2 = 110$
$(\Sigma X)^2 = (18)^2 = 324$	

less than 10. Similarly, to write $X > 4$ indicates that X must have a value greater than 4. We do not know what this value is, but we do know that it cannot be 4 or less than 4.

The next mathematical concept in this brief review is the **absolute value**. The absolute value is the magnitude of a number irrespective of whether it is positive or negative. Thus, the absolute value of -3 is 3, and the absolute value of $+3$ is also 3.

Absolute value: the magnitude of a number irrespective of whether it is positive or negative.

In concluding this brief review of mathematics, it is important to point out that you also need to be familiar with the manipulations conducted with algebraic equations. For instance, if you are given the rather impressive equation $r_s = 1 - [(6\Sigma D^2)/n(n^2 - 1)]$ and are told that ΣD^2 equals 10, and n equals 5, you should be able to determine the value of r_s. To do so, simply substitute the value 10 where ΣD^2 appears in the equation and substitute the value 5 where n appears in the equation:

$$r_s = 1 - \frac{6\Sigma D^2}{n(n^2 - 1)}$$

$$= 1 - \frac{6(10)}{5(5^2 - 1)}$$

$$= 1 - \frac{6(10)}{5(25 - 1)}$$

$$= 1 - \frac{60}{5(24)}$$

$$= 1 - \frac{60}{120}$$

$$= 1 - 0.5$$

$$= 0.5.$$

If you successfully followed this calculation, the algebraic expressions in this book should not be a problem. By the way, you just calculated your first Spearman *r* correlation, a statistic reviewed in Appendix B. Congratulations!

CONCLUSION

To be proficient with statistics, you need to understand which statistical procedure to utilize and why. This book is designed, therefore, to focus on the ideas that are essential to the understanding of statistical reasoning. Exposure to the calculations used in statistical tests is clearly important but, as you will see, much of the tedium of number crunching can be eliminated by utilizing SPSS, a powerful statistical computer package.

Chapter Resources

GLOSSARY OF TERMS

Absolute value: the magnitude of a number irrespective of whether it is positive or negative.

Data (plural of datum): factual information, often in the form of numbers.

Descriptive statistics: techniques that are used to summarize a set of numbers.

Inferential statistics: techniques that are used in making decisions based on data.

Mean: sum of the scores divided by the total number of scores.

Questions: Chapter 1

(Answers to odd-numbered items are provided in Appendix I.)

1. The field of statistics began with the study of probabilities in _____.

    a. Scientific studies

    b. Growing crops

    c. Games of chance

    d. Voting in elections

2. The field of statistics "took off" in the _____ centuries.

    a. Late 17th and early 18th

    b. Late 18th and early 19th

    c. Late 19th and early 20th

    d. Late 20th and early 21st

3. Basing decisions on limited exposure to the relevant information is known as the _____ bias.

   a. Availability

   b. Probability

   c. Limited exposure

   d. Information

4. You collect data on the heights of students taking a statistics course to determine whether they are taller than students taking some other course. This is an example of _____.

   a. Inferential statistics

   b. Descriptive statistics

5. What does $2X + Y^2$ equal if X is 3 and Y is 6?

   a. 21

   b. 28

   c. 42

   d. 95

6. What does $-2\ (36)$ equal?

   a. -72

   b. -18

   c. 34

   d. 118

7. I have a large set of data and wish to present it to an audience in a form that is easy for them to understand. This is an example of _____.

   a. Inferential statistics

   b. Descriptive statistics

8. What is ΣX and ΣX^2 for the set of numbers consisting of 2, 3, and 4?

   a. 9 and 81

   b. 24 and 29

   c. 9 and 29

   d. 9 and 9

9. What is ΣX and ΣX^2 for the set of numbers consisting of -2, 3, and 4?

   a. -9 and 81

   b. 5 and 29

   c. 9 and 29

   d. -9 and -9

10. The procedures that are used to describe large amounts of data in quickly understandable ways are called _____.

    a. Inferential statistics

    b. Descriptive statistics

11. What does $(-2)/4$ equal?

    a. .5

    b. 8

    c. −.5

    d. −8

12. What does $(-3) - (-5)$ equal?

    a. −8

    b. −2

    c. 2

    d. 15

13. What does (-6) (-3) equal?

    a. 18

    b. −9

    c. −3

    d. −18

14. What is the positive square root of 144?

    a. 10

    b. 11

    c. 12

    d. 13

15. Which of the following statements is equivalent to $X > 6$ and $Y < 22$?

    a. X is less than 6; Y is greater than 22

    b. X is greater than 6; Y is less than 22

    c. X is less than 6; Y is less than 22

    d. X is greater than 6; Y is greater than 22

16. The equation for the variance of a population (this will be covered in Chapter 3—don't worry about the definition of the symbols) is $\sigma^2 = \Sigma(X - \mu)^2/N$. If $\Sigma(X - \mu)^2$ is equal to 8, and N is equal to 3, what does σ^2 equal?

    a. 2.67

    b. .375

    c. 24

17. What does (−6)/(−3) equal?

    a. −2

    b. −18

    c. 18

    d. 2

18. What does 36/(−2) equal?

    a. −2

    b. −18

    c. 18

    d. 2

19. The absolute value of 36 is _____.

    a. $\sqrt{36}$

    b. 36^2

    c. 36

    d. −36

20. The absolute value of −14 is _____.

    a. $\sqrt{14}$

    b. 14^2

    c. 14

    d. −14

Part I

Descriptive Statistics

Seeing Clearly With Data

DESCRIBING NOMINAL AND ORDINAL DATA

The Descriptive Statistics Used With Nominal and Ordinal Data

Whenever you can, count.

—Sir Francis Galton

ALL NUMBERS ARE NOT EQUAL

We are all familiar with measuring things. In the United States, the gas you use to fill the tank of your car is measured in gallons. Your height is measured in feet and inches. Your weight is measured in pounds. In most of the world, you would have used liters, centimeters, and kilograms for these measurements. Regardless, you probably have not given much thought to the implications of how we measure things. For instance, does it matter at the Olympics if we know precisely how quickly three runners completed a race? As long as we know their order of finishing we can hand out the medals properly. Actually, for statistics, it matters a great deal. Whether you simply measure order, or instead elapsed duration, has implications for the proper choice of statistical technique to employ.

Sometimes a Number Is Just a Name or Category

The **nominal scale of measurement** provides the least amount of information. As the word nominal implies, with a nominal scale of measurement, we are using a number in place of a name. In other words, the number serves as a label. Put another way, with a nominal scale of measurement, we are using numbers to assign individuals to categories. For instance, each adult is either a man or a woman. We could arbitrarily assign the number 1 to each man and the number 2 to each woman. In this case, the number simply indicates the group to which each individual belongs. The only data that are meaningful would be how many individuals are members of each group. Thus, it might be important for a college to know how many men and how many women are enrolled in each semester. Notice that it makes no sense to argue that because a man is a "1" and a woman is a "2," a woman is twice what a man is. In other words, multiplication or division, for instance, cannot be used with these data. The labels of the groups were assigned arbitrarily. Obviously, we could have assigned the number "1" to each woman and the number "2" to each man. Alternatively, we could have given each man a label of "0" and each woman a label of "9." It does not matter. With a nominal scale of measurement, the number is just a label; the magnitude of the actual label is not meaningful. All that is meaningful is the frequency of individuals in each group.

Nominal scale of measurement: a measurement scale in which numbers serve as names of categories. In this level of measurement, the magnitude of the number is arbitrary.

Sometimes a Number Tells Us the Order of Events

With the **ordinal scale of measurement**, we know the order in which events occurred. Thus, we have more information than with a nominal scale. For instance, where a person places at the conclusion of a footrace is an example of ordinal data. With ordinal data, we know that whoever came in first had to get to the finish before whoever came in second. What we do not know is how much sooner the first place finisher completed the race compared with the second place finisher. It might have been a photo finish, or there may have been enough time for the first place runner to shower and go home before the runner in second place completed the race. In other words, with ordinal data, we know the order of events, but we do not know the magnitude of the difference between events.

Ordinal scale of measurement: a measurement scale in which the magnitude of the numbers indicates the order in which events occurred. In this level of measurement, the magnitude of the number is meaningful.

Sometimes We Can Add and Subtract Numbers

Data on an **interval scale of measurement**, in contrast, indicate the magnitude of the difference between events, as well as the order in which they occurred. As a result, interval data provide more information than ordinal data. It is now appropriate, for the first time, to use addition and subtraction. For instance, we can now say not only that one day is colder than another day, we can subtract their temperatures to find how many degrees colder. However, with data measured on an interval scale, it is still not appropriate to multiply or divide the scores.

> *Interval scale of measurement: a measurement scale in which the magnitude of the difference between numbers is meaningful, and thus, addition and subtraction are possible. However, there is no true zero, and thus, multiplication and division are not meaningful.*

The two most popular temperature scales, Fahrenheit and Centigrade, are examples of interval scales of measurement. A characteristic of interval scales is that though they may have a 0 point, this does not indicate the complete absence of whatever is being measured. Thus, there is a 0°F, but it does not indicate that this is the coldest possible temperature. I live near Buffalo, New York, and can attest to the fact that it may drop below 0°F during the winter. On those occasions, the temperature is measured in negative numbers. The same situation occurs for the Centigrade scale. In the Centigrade scale, 0°C is defined as the freezing point of water. Your refrigerator's freezer should have a temperature below 0°C. Since there is no absolute zero point in either the Fahrenheit scale or the Centigrade scale, it is not appropriate to multiply or divide these numbers. Thus, a day with a temperature of 90°F is not three times as hot as a day that is 30°F. However, as it is appropriate to add or subtract with an interval scale of measurement, we can say that the 90°F day is 60°F warmer than the 30°F day.

Some Numbers Can Be Multiplied and Divided

The last of the four scales is the **ratio scale of measurement**. It differs from an interval scale by having an absolute zero point. Those of you who have taken chemistry may recall that with the Kelvin scale, there is a true zero point below which it cannot get colder. Therefore, the Kelvin scale is a ratio scale. Time is another example of a ratio scale. A race starts at time zero and proceeds to the finish. Since there is a true zero with time, we can not only subtract runners' times to look at differences, we can also meaningfully multiply and divide their times. If one runner completes a race in 2 minutes and another finishes in 4 minutes, we can say that the

> *Ratio scale of measurement: a measurement scale in which the magnitude of the difference between numbers is meaningful, and there is a true zero. Thus, multiplication and division as well as addition and subtraction are meaningful.*

first runner was twice as fast as the second. It is only with data on a ratio scale that we can meaningfully say that one number is a multiple of another.

THE BIG PICTURE

We have just learned that there are four measurement scales: (1) nominal, (2) ordinal, (3) interval, and (4) ratio. From our perspective, this distinction between scales of measurement is important because the statistical procedures that are appropriate depend on the scale of measurement that was utilized. Thus, the statistical procedures utilized with nominal data differ from those used with ordinal data. And while the same statistical procedures are used with interval and ratio data, these procedures are distinct from those used with either nominal or ordinal data. Also, in Chapter 1, you learned that the two major functions of statistics are to assist you in seeing and thinking about data more clearly. You will recall that these are referred to as descriptive and inferential statistics. This is important because the question you are asking—Are you trying to see or think about data more clearly?—is also important in determining the appropriate statistical procedure. How the question you are asking (descriptive or inferential statistics) and the measurement scale you utilized interact can easily be illustrated (Table 2.1) and would provide a logical basis for coverage of topics in an ideal statistics course. Unfortunately, time constraints require that some topics be omitted in a one-semester course. As a result, the coverage in this text is illustrated in Table 2.2.

Table 2.1 Order of Coverage of Topics in an Ideal Plan for a Statistics Course

		Type of Data		
		Nominal	**Ordinal**	**Interval/Ratio**
Type of statistics	Descriptive	1	2	3
	Inferential	4	5	6

Table 2.2 Actual Order of Coverage in This Course

		Type of Data		
		Nominal	**Ordinal**	**Interval/Ratio**
Type of statistics	Descriptive	1	2	3
	Inferential	4	Appendix	5

SEEING CLEARLY WITH NOMINAL DATA: AN INTRODUCTION TO DESCRIPTIVE STATISTICS

It's Time to Begin Learning to See Better

We will now begin to learn how to see more accurately. We will start with nominal data, those data that are used as names or categories. We are, therefore, beginning with position "1" in Table 2.2—the descriptive statistics of nominal data. Remember, with these data, you cannot meaningfully add, subtract, multiply, or divide.

Let's assume that we have asked the members of a class to identify their political party affiliation. The students are found to be Democrats (D), Republicans (R), Libertarians (L), Socialists (S), or to have no party affiliation (N). The results for the 25 students are indicated in Table 2.3.

In this form, it is not easy to quickly understand the students' party affiliations. All that one can rapidly discern is that most students appear to be Republicans (R), Democrats (D), or they have no party affiliation (N). If the data are organized so that the frequency of each party affiliation is recorded, we have what is called a **frequency distribution** (Table 2.4). With a frequency distribution, the outcome is much clearer.

I think you will agree that simply organizing the scores into a frequency distribution aids in the rapid understanding of the data. In other words, you are beginning to see the data more clearly.

Once a frequency distribution has been constructed, it is then easy to determine the **relative frequency** for any category. To do so, we divide the frequency for the category by the total frequency. Referring to Table 2.4, the relative frequency of Republicans would be 5/25, which is equivalent to 1/5 or .20.

Frequency distribution: a listing of the different values or categories of the observations along with the frequency with which each occurred.

Relative frequency: the frequency of a category divided by the total frequency.

Table 2.3	Data of Students' Political Party Affiliations			
N	R	D	D	N
L	N	N	R	D
R	N	D	S	N
N	D	R	N	D
R	N	L	N	D

Table 2.4	Frequency Distribution of Students' Political Party Affiliation

Party Affiliation	Frequency
No affiliation	10
Democrat	7
Republican	5
Libertarian	2
Socialist	1
Total	25

Using Graphs and Charts to See Nominal Data More Clearly

Bar graph: a graph in which the frequency of each category or class of observation is indicated by the length of its associated bar.

For nominal data, two of the most commonly used techniques for summarizing findings are the bar graph and the pie chart. With a **bar graph**, each category of response is usually identified on the X-axis, and the frequency with which it occurred is usually noted on the Y-axis. As we are dealing with separate categories, in the bar graph the "bars" representing the frequencies are drawn so that they do not touch each other. A bar graph for our hypothetical political affiliation scores is indicated in Figure 2.1.

Figure 2.1	Bar Graph of Student Political Party Affiliation

Note. N, no affiliation; D, Democrat; R, Republican; L, Libertarian; S, Socialist.

With a bar graph, the reader can quickly "see" the political party preferences of the students. Because bar graphs are an effective way to present summary data, you will commonly see them in newspaper articles as well as in magazines. However, the bar graph is not the only method to represent a set of nominal data.

The **pie chart** is also frequently used to summarize nominal data. With a pie chart, the frequency of responses is first converted into percentages. This is accomplished by dividing the frequency for each category of response by the total number of responses (the total of all of the frequencies for all of the categories), in our case 25. For instance, 10 students indicated that they do not have a party affiliation. To find the percentage of the total that these 10 students represent, we would divide 10 by 25, the total number of responses. This would be .40, which is equivalent to 40%. The result of the calculations for each category is shown in Table 2.5.

Pie chart: a presentation of categorical data in which the area of a slice of a circle is indicative of the relative frequency with which the category occurs.

Once the percentages are calculated, the area of a circle is divided into slices. There are as many slices as there are categories of response in the frequency distribution, and the size of each slice corresponds to the percentage each category represents (Figure 2.2).

Measure of central tendency: a single number that is chosen to best summarize an entire set of numbers.

The pie chart can be a very effective way to describe the data. However, its effectiveness is compromised if there are too many categories. Remember, the goal is to convey information efficiently, not to create a visually impressive, but overwhelming, presentation.

We have just reviewed how bar graphs and pie charts can be beneficial in summarizing a set of nominal data. In addition to these depictions of the frequency distribution, a reader can benefit from a single measure that summarizes the entire set of responses. This would be what statisticians call a **measure of central tendency**.

Table 2.5	Frequency Distribution of Student Political Party Affiliation With Associated Percentages	
Party Affiliation	**Frequency**	**Percentage**
No affiliation	10	40
Democrat	7	28
Republican	5	20
Libertarian	2	8
Socialist	1	4
Total	25	100

| **Figure 2.2** | Pie Chart of Student Political Party Affiliation |

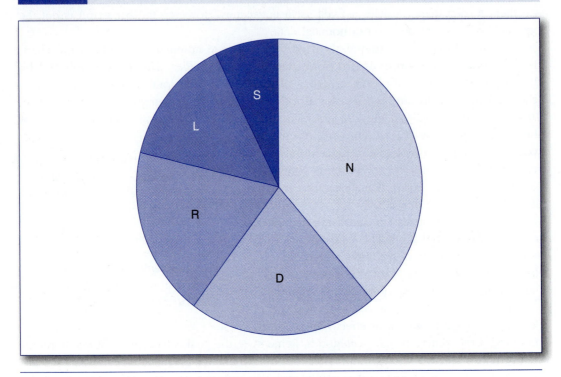

Note. N, no affiliation; D, Democrat; R, Republican; L, Libertarian; S, Socialist.

With nominal data, the **mode** is the appropriate measure of central tendency. The mode is simply the category with the highest frequency in the frequency distribution. With our data of student party affiliations, the "no affiliation" response would be the mode, as more of our hypothetical students chose this option than any other. The mode has the advantage that it is very easy to calculate and understand. However, it has a major limitation; it is very **unstable**. In many instances, if only a few responses were to change, then the mode would change to a different category. Thus, if only two of the students who had indicated that they did not have a party affiliation had, instead, chosen Democrat, then the mode would have shifted to this new category.

It is also possible that two, or more, categories will have the highest, tied frequency. If two categories

Mode: a measure of central tendency. It is the most common category or score.

Unstable: a term used to describe a measure, such as of central tendency, that can vary significantly with only a few changes to the original set of data. This is seen as an undesirable quality.

are tied for the highest frequency, both categories would be modes and the distribution would be said to be **bimodal**. If three categories were tied for the highest frequency, the distribution would be said to be tri-modal, and so on.

> *Bimodal: a descriptive term for a distribution that has two modes.*

There is no measure of **variability** for use with nominal data. Variability refers to how much scores differ or deviate from each other. The closest you could come with nominal data would be to simply

> *Variability: how much scores differ or deviate from each other.*

indicate how many response categories the subjects in a sample had either chosen or been assigned to. With our example, students identified five political party affiliations.

Summary

From this brief review, it should be evident that there is nothing challenging about the descriptive statistics of nominal data. Once a frequency distribution is constructed, a bar graph or pie chart and the mode(s) are easy to obtain.

Table 2.6 clarifies what you have learned so far in this chapter.

Table 2.6 Descriptive Statistics of Nominal Data

Descriptive Statistics (Summarizing Data)	Type of Data Nominal
Frequency distribution	Bar graph or pie chart
Central tendency	Mode
Variability	—

PROGRESS CHECK

1. In this measurement scale, all that is meaningful is the frequency of events or individuals in each category.

2. In this measurement scale, there is a zero, but it is not a true or absolute zero.

3. When you list the frequency associated with each value or category, you have created a _____.

Answers: 1. Nominal.   2. Interval.   3. Frequency distribution.

SEEING CLEARLY WITH ORDINAL DATA: CONTINUING WITH DESCRIPTIVE STATISTICS

First, Second, Third, I See a Pattern

With ordinal data, you are able to rank a set of data along some dimension. For instance, you might know the order in which runners finished a race, or it might be possible to rank 25 students from most to least outgoing. Thus, you know who is first, second, and so on, but with data in this form, there is nothing further that can be done to increase a reader's understanding. All that is known, or knowable, is the ranking of the runners or that there were a total of 25 students and they were ranked on how outgoing they were. However, if instead of being ranked individually each of the 25 students was assigned to one of five ranked levels, from "very shy" to "very outgoing," we could create a frequency distribution as shown in Table 2.7.

Table 2.7	Frequency Distribution of Being Outgoing
Very outgoing	5
Somewhat outgoing	8
Neither outgoing nor shy	6
Somewhat shy	4
Very shy	2

This allows us to "see" the data more clearly.

Just as was the case with nominal data, with ordinal data, it is simple to create a bar graph once a frequency distribution has been made. However, while the order in which the categories are presented is arbitrary with nominal data, the order is meaningful with ordinal data. Therefore, when ordinal data are assigned to ranked categories, in our case from "very shy" to "very outgoing," the bar graph should be organized to reflect this order, as is shown in Figure 2.3.

Clearly, a properly constructed bar graph permits a rapid understanding of the data.

With ordinal data, a pie chart is not appropriate. The problem with using a pie chart with ordinal data is that the categories would wrap around the circle so that those that are most extreme would end up side by side. Thus, the "very shy" category would be next to the "very outgoing" category, which would make it more difficult to recognize the order in the responses.

Figure 2.3   Bar Graph of Ratings of How Outgoing Students Are

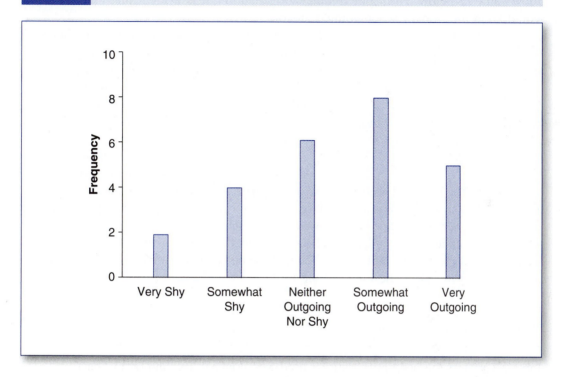

As ordinal data involve ranks, it is now possible to specify relative standings. The **percentile rank** is the percentage of the distribution within or below a category. For instance, referring to Table 2.7 will indicate that 20 of the 25 coworkers, or 80%, indicated that they were either "somewhat outgoing" or less than "somewhat outgoing." And the percentile rank for "neither outgoing nor shy" would be almost 50% (12/25 = 48%).

The **median** is the measure of central tendency employed with ordinal data. The median can be defined in a number of ways. Perhaps the simplest is that the median is the value that has as many scores above it as below it. In other words, it is the value that divides the distribution into two equal halves; it is the middle of the distribution; it has a percentile rank of 50% and thus is at the 50th percentile. In our example with 25 subjects, the median value would be the value associated with the 13th individual from either end

Percentile rank: the percentage of the data at or below a category or score.

Median: a measure of central tendency. It is the midmost score in a distribution. In other words, the median splits a distribution in half, with just as many scores above it as below it. It is at the 50th percentile.

of the distribution. This individual is at the midpoint of the distribution, with 12 entries above, and 12 below. From our frequency distribution, it is evident that this individual would be in the "somewhat outgoing" category.

If the distribution had an even number of scores, the procedure is slightly different. For instance, in the distribution 2, 4, 6, 9, there is no score at the midpoint. In such a situation, the median would be the value associated with the mean of the two midmost scores. These scores are 4 and 6 and their mean, and thus, the median is 5. (Calculation of the median when used with interval or ratio data is discussed in Chapter 3.)

Range: a measure of variability for ordinal data.

Unlike the case with nominal data, with ordinal data, there are measures of variability. The simplest is the **range**. The range is based on the two most extreme data points. For the data provided in Table 2.7, each student was assigned to one of five categories, with the range being from "very shy" to "very outgoing." If there was another set of data that consisted of the ranks in an athletic contest, the range would be determined by finding the difference between the lowest and the highest ranks. Thus, if a high school swimming team obtained the ranks of 2, 4, and 12 in a race, the range would be $12 - 2 = 10$.

CONCLUSION

Table 2.8 reviews the descriptive statistics used with nominal data and ordinal data.

Table 2.8   Descriptive Statistics of Nominal and Ordinal Data

Descriptive Statistics (Summarizing Data)	Type of Data	
	Nominal	Ordinal
Frequency distribution	Bar graph or pie chart	Bar graph
Central tendency	Mode	Median
Variability	—	Range

Hopefully, you will agree that there is nothing challenging about these descriptive statistics. Once a frequency distribution is made, appropriate measures of central tendency and variability (for ordinal data) are easy to obtain.

GLOSSARY OF TERMS

Bar graph: a graph in which the frequency of each category or class of observation is indicated by the length of its associated bar.

Bimodal: a descriptive term for a distribution that has two modes.

Frequency distribution: a listing of the different values or categories of the observations along with the frequency with which each occurred.

Interval scale of measurement: a measurement scale in which the magnitude of the difference between numbers is meaningful, and thus, addition and subtraction are possible. However, there is no true zero, and thus, multiplication and division are not meaningful.

Measure of central tendency: a single number that is chosen to best summarize an entire set of numbers.

Median: a measure of central tendency. It is the midmost score in a distribution. In other words, the median splits a distribution in half, with just as many scores above it as below it. It is at the 50th percentile.

Mode: a measure of central tendency. It is the most common category or score.

Nominal scale of measurement: a measurement scale in which numbers serve as names of categories. In this level of measurement, the magnitude of the number is arbitrary.

Ordinal scale of measurement: a measurement scale in which the magnitude of the numbers indicates the order in which events occurred. In this level of measurement, the magnitude of the number is meaningful.

Percentile rank: the percentage of the data at or below a category or score.

Pie chart: a presentation of categorical data in which the area of a slice of a circle is indicative of the relative frequency with which the category occurs.

Range: a measure of variability for ordinal data.

Ratio scale of measurement: a measurement scale in which the magnitude of the difference between numbers is meaningful, and there is a true zero. Thus, multiplication and division as well as addition and subtraction are meaningful.

Relative frequency: the frequency of a category divided by the total frequency.

Unstable: a term used to describe a measure, such as of central tendency, that can vary significantly with only a few changes to the original set of data. This is seen as an undesirable quality.

Variability: how much scores differ or deviate from each other.

Questions: Chapter 2

(Answers to odd-numbered items are provided in Appendix I.)

1. The number of correct answers on an exam with 50 items would be an example of which scale of measurement?
   a. Nominal
   b. Ordinal
   c. Interval
   d. Ratio

2. In a history course, you learn that World War II began in 1939. The year is an example of which scale of measurement?
   a. Nominal
   b. Ordinal
   c. Interval
   d. Ratio

3. Over a summer, a tourist travels 3,000 miles visiting national parks in the Western United States. Miles are an example of which scale of measurement?
   a. Nominal
   b. Ordinal
   c. Interval
   d. Ratio

4. At a car show, awards are given for the best, the second best, and the third best automobiles. This is an example of which scale of measurement?
   a. Nominal
   b. Ordinal
   c. Interval
   d. Ratio

5. A bar graph is used with _____ and _____ data.
   a. nominal and ordinal
   b. ordinal and interval
   c. interval and ratio
   d. nominal and ratio

6. A pie chart is used with _____ data.
   a. nominal
   b. ordinal
   c. interval
   d. ratio

7. For ordinal data, the _____ is the measure of central tendency.

   a. mean

   b. median

   c. mode

8. If we graphed the heights of a large group of men and women, we might expect to find a distribution with two peaks, one corresponding to the most frequent height of men and the other corresponding to the most frequent height of women. This would be an example of a _____ distribution.

   a. unimodal

   b. bimodal

   c. trimodal

9. In addition to giving a measure of central tendency, such as the median, a measure of how much a set of scores differ is also commonly provided. This second piece of information is called a measure of _____.

   a. variability

   b. indecisiveness

   c. incompleteness

10. Do nominal data have a measure of variability?

    a. Yes

    b. No

11. The measure of central tendency for nominal data is the _____.

    a. mean

    b. median

    c. mode

12. This is the only scale in which multiplication and division are meaningful.

    a. Nominal

    b. Ordinal

    c. Interval

    d. Ratio

13. The only information provided with nominal data is _____.

    a. the frequency of events within each category

    b. the order that events occurred, such as in an athletic competition

    c. greater than, or less than, but not by how much

14. A measure of variability for ordinal data is the _____.

    a. range

    b. mode

    c. median

    d. There isn't a measure of variability for ordinal data.

15. A measure, such as the range, which can vary substantially when only a few scores' values change is _____.

    a. preferable to a measure which doesn't vary substantially

    b. never to be used

    c. unstable

16. The median of the ranks 1, 4, 5, 6, 17 is _____.

    a. 4

    b. 5

    c. 5.5

    d. 6

17. The range of the ranks in Question 16 is _____.

    a. 4

    b. 5

    c. 16

    d. 17

18. The median of the ranks 4, 5, 6, 17 is _____.

    a. 4

    b. 5

    c. 5.5

    d. 6

19. The range of the ranks in Question 18 is _____.

    a. 3

    b. 4

    c. 13

    d. 17

20. Which measurement scale provides the *least* information?

    a. Nominal

    b. Ordinal

    c. Interval

    d. Ratio

DESCRIBING INTERVAL AND RATIO DATA—I

An Introduction to the Descriptive Statistics Used With Interval or Ratio Data

Statistical thinking will one day be as necessary for efficient citizenship as the ability to read and write.

—H. G. Wells

With data measured at the interval level or the ratio level, the magnitude of the difference between scores is known as well as their order. For instance, as this chapter is being written, the deadline for filing taxes is fast approaching. The Internal Revenue Service could compare the individual tax returns it receives and determine not only whether one person makes more than another but how much more. This is because income is measured on a ratio scale. For instance, let's assume that Table 3.1 lists the hypothetical incomes of 10 students in a college class, rounded to the nearest thousand dollars.

In this form, the data are hard to understand. However, they can be converted into a frequency distribution, as shown in Table 3.2.

Once a frequency distribution has been created, it is easy to graph the data. With interval or ratio data, the graph we would use is either a histogram or a frequency polygon. A **histogram** for the data in Table 3.2 is shown in Figure 3.1. Clearly, a histogram looks very much like a bar graph. On both a bar graph and a histogram, the values of the responses are usually depicted on the *X*-axis and the frequencies of the responses are on the *Y*-axis. However, there are some important differences between the two types of graphs. First, the vertical "bars" in a

Table 3.1	Income of 10 College Students

Student	Income in Dollars
1	20,000
2	3,000
3	1,000
4	2,000
5	4,000
6	3,000
7	10,000
8	3,000
9	4,000
10	7,000

Table 3.2	Frequency Distribution for Student Income Data

Income	Frequency
20,000	1
10,000	1
7,000	1
4,000	2
3,000	3
2,000	1
1,000	1

bar graph are separated, while the vertical bars in a histogram are positioned side by side so that they touch. Furthermore, on the X-axis of a bar graph there are distinct categories, while the intervals on the X-axis of a histogram are specified by what are called the **real limits**. The income labeled $2,000, for example, has the lower real limit of $1,500 and the upper real limit of $2,500, because we rounded off to the nearest $1,000 and any value from $1,500 to $2,500 was included in the $2,000 category. When there are scores that have the same value as a real limit, the scores should be randomly assigned to one of the two intervals associated with that limit. In our example, an income of exactly $2,500 could be included in the interval from $1,500 to $2,500, or the interval from $2,500 to $3,500, depending on the flip of a coin. Finally, for some intervals, such as from $8,500 to $9,500, there were no student incomes, and thus, there is no vertical "bar."

It would also be appropriate for these data to be graphed with a **frequency polygon**. A frequency polygon of the data in Table 3.2 is shown in Figure 3.2. As with a histogram, a frequency polygon is quite easy to construct once a frequency distribution has been constructed. Though a frequency polygon looks somewhat different than a histogram, they are actually closely related. In fact, a frequency polygon can be constructed by simply connecting the center points of each of the vertical "bars" in a histogram, as is shown in Figure 3.3. With a set of data that has a large number of possible X values, a frequency polygon will be easier to construct and read than a histogram.

Histogram: a graph used with interval or ratio data. As with the bar graph, frequencies are indicated by the length of the associated bars. However, as there are no distinct categories in a histogram, the bars are positioned side by side.

Real limits: with interval or ratio data, the actual limits used in assigning a measurement. These are halfway between adjacent scores. Each score thus has an upper and a lower real limit.

Frequency polygon: a graphic presentation for use with interval or ratio data. It is similar to a histogram except that the frequency is indicated by the height of a point rather than the height of a bar. The points are connected by straight lines.

| Figure 3.1 | Histogram of the Student Income Data |

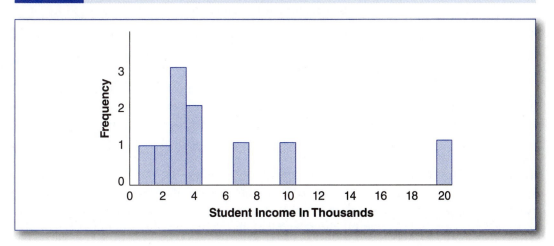

| Figure 3.2 | Frequency Polygon of the Student Income Data |

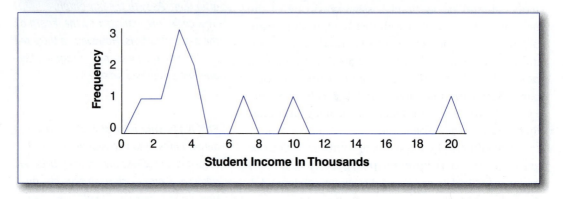

| Figure 3.3 | Comparison of a Histogram and a Frequency Polygon |

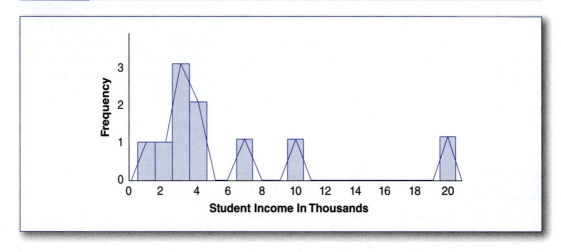

We have seen that, with interval or ratio data, constructing either a histogram or a frequency polygon is a straightforward and useful way to summarize a set of data. Calculating a measure of central tendency is also easy. *The mean is generally the preferred measure of central tendency when there are interval or ratio data.* Recall that the mean is what most people call an average. To calculate a mean, we add the scores and then divide by the number of scores. This is symbolized by $(\sum X)/N$, where N equals the total number of scores. The mean for our 10 student incomes would be $57,000/10, which equals $5,700.

The mean is not as easy to conceptualize as the mode or the median. The mean is the balance point of a distribution. In other words, if you made a copy of the frequency polygon in Figure 3.2 out of metal or wood, the point along the *X*-axis where it would balance would be the **mean**. The mean is the most frequently used measure of central tendency. It has the advantage that it is used in further statistical procedures that you will learn in later chapters. One unfortunate characteristic, however, is that the mean can be greatly affected by extreme scores. In our set of income data, for instance, the $20,000 response is $10,000 higher than the next highest income. Removing this one income would have a dramatic effect on the mean. The mean of all of the 10 incomes was $5,700. Without the $20,000 income, the mean would be $37,000/9, or only $4,111. Thus, removing one extreme score results in the mean dropping by more than $1,500, or about 28%.

Mean: a measure of central tendency for use with interval or ratio data. It is what is commonly called an average, but in statistics, the term average can refer to a mean, median, or mode. The mean is the sum of the scores divided by the number of scores.

This limitation of the mean can be further understood by looking at either the histogram (Figure 3.1) or the frequency polygon (Figure 3.2). The mean does not appear to be a particularly good single measure of these data. Most of the scores are grouped around $3,000 and $4,000, not around the mean value of $5,700. The extreme score of $20,000 is pulling the mean toward a higher value. This effect of an extreme score will happen whenever the frequency polygon is not symmetrical. In a **symmetrical distribution**, the right half of the distribution is the mirror image of the left half. Figure 3.4 is an example of a symmetrical distribution. In a symmetrical distribution, there is a low score that balances the effect that each high score has on the mean.

Symmetrical distribution: a distribution in which the right half is the mirror image of the left half. In such a distribution, there is a high score corresponding to each low score.

The curve depicted in Figure 3.4 is a special type of symmetrical distribution referred to as a **bell-shaped curve**. It is high in the middle, and scores become progressively less

---

Figure 3.4 Graph of a Symmetrical Distribution

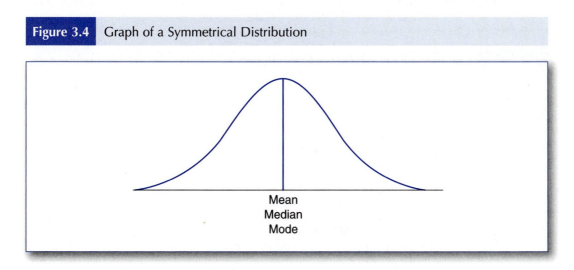

Mean
Median
Mode

Bell-shaped curve: a symmetrical distribution in which the highest frequency scores are located near the middle, and the frequency drops the farther a score is from the middle.

Positively skewed: a nonsymmetrical distribution in which the tail pointing to the right is larger than the tail pointing to the left.

Negatively skewed: a nonsymmetrical distribution in which the tail pointing to the left is larger than the tail pointing to the right.

frequent the farther they are from the middle. One of the characteristics of a bell-shaped distribution is that the balance point (mean), the middle score (median), and the most frequent score (mode) all have the same value.

The data in Table 3.2 do not form a symmetrical distribution. Instead, the distribution appears to look more like Figure 3.5, a nonsymmetrical distribution that points to the right. Such a distribution is called **positively skewed**. The word "positive" in this context does not indicate "good," just as the "positive" terminal of a battery is not "good." In both cases, "positive" is simply being used to identify an option. In the case of a battery, it is a particular electrical charge. In the case of a graph, it is a direction.

In a positively skewed distribution, the mean, the median, and the mode do not all fall at the same point. Instead, there is characteristic pattern, as indicated in Figure 3.5. The mode is at the point on the *X*-axis where the frequency is greatest, the mean is "pulled" to the right by the extreme scores, and the median is located between the mode and the mean. The income distribution in America is an example of a positively skewed distribution. Many people have modest incomes; and a few have very large incomes.

It is also possible for a distribution to be negatively skewed, as is shown in Figure 3.6. In a **negatively skewed** distribution, the mean is again "pulled" by the extreme scores, except this time to the left; the mode is at the highest frequency score; and the median is between the mean and the mode. The distribution of scores on an easy exam is an example of a negatively

---

Figure 3.5   Graph of a Positively Skewed Distribution

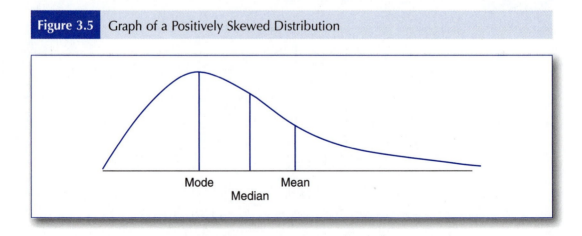

Figure 3.6 Graph of a Negatively Skewed Distribution

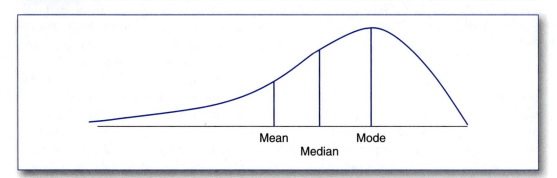

skewed distribution. Many students will do very well, but a few still find the exam to be difficult.

The distributions that have been reviewed thus far are all **unimodal**; in other words, they have only one mode. A symmetrical, bimodal distribution is depicted in Figure 3.7. In a symmetrical, bimodal distribution, there are two modes, and the mean and the median are located at the same point between the two modes. A distribution of heights might be an example of a bimodal distribution, with one mode indicating the most common height for women and the other mode indicating the most common height for men.

Unimodal distribution: A distribution with only one mode.

We have seen that with interval or ratio data, the graph of the frequency distribution can take a number of forms. Whether it is symmetrical or skewed is important, for it affects our choice of the statistical procedure. Some statistical procedures assume that the data form a

Figure 3.7 Graph of a Symmetrical, Bimodal Distribution

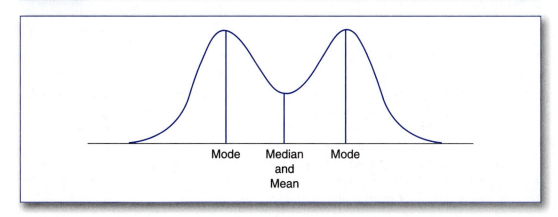

Normal distribution: a specific, bell-shaped distribution. Many statistical procedures assume that the data are distributed normally.

specific bell-shaped curve called a **normal distribution**. With interval or ratio data that are normally distributed, the mean is the optimal measure of central tendency. We will see later in the book that the mean has the advantage that it can be used in a variety of flexible statistical procedures. However, when the distribution is not normal but is skewed in one direction, we have seen that the mean is "pulled" by the extreme scores. In that case, the mean would be a poor choice as the measure of central tendency. The median, defined as the midmost score, is less affected by extreme scores and would be a better choice with skewed data. For example, the data presented in Table 3.2, and graphed in Figure 3.1, are skewed. This is evident as there is a distinctive tail pointing to the right. With these data, even though they were collected at the ratio level, you would probably want to calculate a median rather than a mean as a measure of central tendency.

Calculation of the median with interval or ratio data is straightforward:

$$\text{Median} = \text{the value of the score at the } \frac{N+1}{2} \text{ position.}$$

If a distribution has an odd number of entries, this equation will result in the median being the middle number in the distribution. For instance, if there were income data from 9 workers, the median would be equal to the income of the worker in the (9 + 1)/2 position. This would be 10/2, which equals 5. In other words, the median would be the income of the fifth worker from the bottom, or top, of the distribution.

The situation is somewhat more complex if there is an even number of entries. With our data, there were incomes from 10 students. The median would be the value associated with the (10 + 1)/2 position. This equals 11/2, or 5.5. Obviously, there is no 5.5th subject. However, we proceed as if there were. The income of the 5th subject was $3,000. The income of the 6th subject was $4,000. We calculate the *mean* of these two incomes to find the income of the 5.5th subject. In our case, this would be ($3,000 + $4,000)/2. Thus, the *median* income of the 10 students is $3,500.

SUMMARY TO THIS POINT

I think you will agree that this introduction to the descriptive statistics of interval and ratio data is not any more challenging than the descriptive statistics of nominal or ordinal data. Once a frequency distribution is made, the histogram or frequency polygon, and the mean (or median if the data are skewed) are easy to obtain.

Reviewing Table 3.3 may make what you have learned in this chapter clearer, as it shows a comparison of the descriptive statistics used with nominal data and ordinal data with those we have just reviewed for interval and ratio data.

Table 3.3	Descriptive Statistics Discussed Thus Far

Descriptive Statistics (Summarizing Data)	Type of Data		
	Nominal	**Ordinal**	**Interval Ratio**
Frequency distribution	Bar graph or pie chart	Bar graph	Histogram or frequency polygon
Central tendency	Mode	Median	Mean
Variability	—	Range	*Standard deviation* (discussed below) and *z score* (discussed in Chapter 4)

PROGRESS CHECK

1. To graph the frequency distribution of interval or ratio data, we would use either a _____ or a _____.

2. If we measure the duration of a foot race in seconds, then the real limits for a time of 36 seconds would be _____ and _____ seconds.

3. In most soccer games, even the winning team ends with a modest score. However, there are exceptions where the winning team has a high score. This is an example of a _____ skewed distribution.

Answers: 1. Histogram; frequency polygon. 2. 35.5; 36.5. 3. Positively.

MEASUREMENT OF THE VARIABILITY OF INTERVAL AND RATIO DATA

We focus in this text on two descriptive measures of variability that are used with interval and ratio data that are normally distributed. These are the standard deviation and the z score. Each is based on the mean. This chapter introduces the standard deviation; Chapter 4 will describe the z score.

When the Data Are Skewed

We just reviewed that when the data are obviously skewed, we do not use the mean as the measure of central tendency. Instead, the preferred measure of central tendency for a skewed distribution is the median, not the mean, even though we are dealing with interval or ratio data. A similar situation occurs for the measure of variability.

As was just noted, with normally distributed interval or ratio data, the standard deviation and z score are used. When the data are strongly skewed, the **range** should instead be chosen. We have briefly discussed the range previously. It is simply the spread of the scores. More specifically, *with interval or ratio data, the range is the difference between the upper real limit of the highest score or category and the lower real limit of the lowest score or category.* In the case of our income data (Table 3.2), the highest value that was reported was $20,000. We only recorded to the nearest thousand dollars, so the $20,000 value that was recorded could have been for an actual income anywhere from the lower real limit of $19,500 to the upper real limit of $20,500. Similarly, the lowest recorded income of $1,000 could have been for an actual income anywhere from $500 to $1,500. The range of the incomes, therefore, is the difference between the upper real limit of the highest value and the lower real limit of the lowest value. For our example, the range is $20,500 to $500, which equals $20,000. This is all that is involved with calculating the range of skewed data.

> *Range: a measure of variability. With interval or ratio data, it equals the difference between the upper real limit of the highest score or category and the lower real limit of the lowest score or category.*

When the Data Are Normally Distributed

Much of this text deals with interval or ratio data that are normally distributed. A critical concept with these data is deviance. In everyday use, deviant indicates that there is a difference, and the word has a rather bad connotation. In statistics, it just indicates a difference, usually from the mean. There isn't any value judgment. In fact, we are all deviant. No one has the mean score for all traits. Each of us is a little heavier, or shorter, or smarter, or quieter, or happier than the mean.

A related concept, the standard deviation, can be thought of as the amount that scores are *expected to vary.* While it is difficult to verbally define this term in an easy-to-grasp manner, this is not a cause for concern. The situation is, in fact, somewhat analogous to what we found with the mean. The mean is a very useful statistic, though it is not the easiest concept to explain. It just seems easy because you are familiar with it. You will find that the same is true for the standard deviation. However, before proceeding, we need to make a short detour to understand the difference between a population and a sample.

Population and Sample: Statisticians' Way of Saying "All" and "Some"

In statistics, the entire group that is of interest is called a **population**. A part or subset of a population is called a sample. An example should make the distinction clear. Assume that you are a teacher. If the entire group that is of interest to you consists of the members of your class, then the members of your class would be a population and any subset of it, such as the students who are sitting in the front row, would be a **sample**. However, if all of the students who attend your school are the group that is of interest, then your class would now be a sample of this much larger group. In other words, whether you are dealing with a population or a sample depends on the specific situation.

> *Population: the entire group that is of interest.*

> *Sample: a subset of a population.*

> *Then there is the man who drowned crossing a stream with an average depth of six inches.*
>
> —W. I. E. Gates

Now we can return to our discussion of the standard deviation. This will at first seem strange, but the best way to introduce the standard deviation is to begin with a discussion of a closely related measure, the **variance**. Both the standard deviation and the variance are measures of variability. The variance is defined as the average of the squared deviations from the mean. This is, admittedly, not a particularly enlightening definition. Fortunately, this is a case where the mathematical equation is much clearer than the verbal definition, even though the symbols may appear peculiar at first. For a population (not a sample), the equation for the variance is as follows:

$$\text{Variance of a population} = \sigma^2 = \frac{\sum (X - \mu)^2}{N}.$$

Hopefully, you recognize that this is actually a very simple equation. It is just necessary to break it down into its parts and learn the meaning of the new symbols. First, the symbol σ^2 (pronounced sigma squared) is just another way of saying that we are dealing with a variance of a population. (Note that σ is lower case Greek letter sigma.) Next, the $(X - \mu)$ section indicates that we are to take a score, symbolized by the letter X, and subtract the population mean, symbolized by the Greek letter μ (pronounced mu). This difference between a score and its mean is called a **deviation**. The $(X - \mu)^2$ part of

> *Variance: a measure of variability; the average of the sum of the squared deviations of scores from their mean. The symbol for the population variance is σ^2.*

> *Deviation: the difference between a score and some measure, usually the mean. Thus, with population data, the deviation equals $X - \mu$.*

the equation indicates that we are to square this deviation. Next, the $\Sigma(X - \mu)^2$ indicates that we are to sum the squared deviations of all of our scores. This term is called, appropriately, the *sum of the squared deviations*. Finally, the $/N$ indicates that we are to divide the sum of the squared deviations that we just found by the total number of scores. This is a lot of vocabulary for one paragraph, but an example will make the steps clear.

Let us assume that you are a member of a very select group that has only three members. Someone is interested in determining how the group is doing and collects data on a quiz. The scores are listed in Table 3.4. As this is the only group that is of interest, the three members constitute a population, not a sample.

We can now proceed to calculate the variance. The first step is to calculate the population mean. The sum of the three scores is 24. To find the mean, we divide the sum of the scores by the total number of scores, which in this case is 3. The mean equals 24/3, which is 8. We now turn to finding the deviations. The deviation of the first quiz score, symbolized by $(X - \mu)$, would equal 6 – 8. This is –2, and it is indicated in the first entry of the third column by being bolded. When we square –2, we obtain 4, the deviation squared, which is the first entry in the fourth column. We would then proceed to the second and third quiz scores.

Calculating the variance is now just a matter of substituting into the equation:

$$\text{Variance of a population} = \sigma^2 = \frac{\Sigma(X-\mu)^2}{N}.$$

$$= \frac{8}{3}$$

$$= 2.67.$$

The good news is that we have just calculated a variance. Unlike the range, which is based solely on the two most extreme scores and is thus unstable, the variance is affected by all of the scores. This is a good feature. The bad news is that the variance is not a particularly useful descriptive statistic. The reason is that the variance is measured in squared units, as is indicated by the symbol σ^2. In other words, the variance is providing a measure of variability, but in this case, it is 2.67 points squared, probably not the easiest concept to grasp.

Table 3.4   Initial Steps in Calculating the Variance

Subject	Score	Deviation $(X - \mu)$	Deviation Squared $(X - \mu)^2$
1	6	**–2**	4
2	8	0	0
3	10	2	4
Sum	24	0	8

There are two obvious solutions to the problem of the variance being measured in squared units. First, you might suggest that we simplify the entire process and base our measure of variability on the deviation scores. In other words, if we do not square the deviations, then our measure of variability will not be in squared units. It is true that you will have solved one problem, but you will have created another. If you refer to Table 3.4, you will see that the sum of the column of deviations equals zero. This will always be the case. No matter what set of numbers is being examined, the sum of the deviations from the mean will always equal zero. Clearly, the sum of the deviations from the mean will not work as a measure of variability.

The other obvious solution to our problem with the squared units of the variance is to simply take the square root. This puts the measure of variability back into the original units. The result is a measure of variability known as the **standard deviation**, which has the symbol σ. In other words:

$$\text{Standard deviation} = \sqrt{\text{Variance}}.$$

and

$$\text{Variance} = (\text{Standard deviation})^2.$$

Referring to our example with a variance equal to 2.67 points squared, the standard deviation would equal the square root of 2.67, which is 1.63 points. This measure of variability is back in the original units of measurement, points on the quiz. We can, therefore, succinctly summarize the central tendency and variability of a set of interval or ratio scores by providing the mean and the standard deviation. With our example of the test scores, the mean is 8 points and the standard deviation is 1.63 points.

You will see in this text that with interval and ratio data, the standard deviation is the most frequently used measure of variability with descriptive statistics, while the variance is the most frequently used measure of variability with inferential statistics.

A few more symbols are as follows.

We have just learned that the difference between a score and its population mean $(X - \mu)$ is called a deviation. This concept is used so commonly in statistics that it is given its own symbol, x. (Note that a capital X is used to represent a score and a lower case x is used to represent a deviation.) Similarly, the **sum of the squared deviations** $[\Sigma(X - \mu)^2]$ is used so commonly that it has its own abbreviation, SS. It should be clear that another way to express SS is Σx^2.

Standard deviation: a measure of variability—the average deviation of scores within a distribution. It is defined as the square root of the variance. The symbol for the population standard deviation is σ.

x: the symbol for a deviation. Thus, $x = (X - \mu)$ if we are dealing with a population.

Sum of the squared deviations: for a population, it is equal to $\Sigma(X - \mu)^2$ or Σx^2. It is often abbreviated as "sum of squares" which is shortened even further to SS.

Since the sum of the squared deviations can be abbreviated in a variety of ways, it follows that the equation for the variance can also be written in a number of forms. We have already seen that the variance of a population has the symbol σ^2, and is defined as $(\Sigma(X - \mu)^2)/N$. In addition, it was just pointed out that the sum of the squared deviations $[\Sigma(X - \mu)^2]$ is abbreviated as SS. Therefore, the population variance also could be written as SS/N. Furthermore, as $\Sigma(X - \mu)^2$ is also abbreviated as Σx^2, the population variance can be written as $\Sigma x^2/N$. And the standard deviation is equal to the square root of each of these forms of the variance equation, as is indicated in Table 3.5.

Table 3.5 Equations for the Population Variance and Standard Deviation

Variance	Standard Deviation
$\sigma^2 = \dfrac{\Sigma(X-\mu)^2}{N}$	$\sigma = \sqrt{\dfrac{\Sigma(X-\mu)^2}{N}}$
$\sigma^2 = \dfrac{SS}{N}$	$\sigma = \sqrt{\dfrac{SS}{N}}$
$\sigma^2 = \dfrac{\Sigma x^2}{N}$	$\sigma = \sqrt{\dfrac{\Sigma x^2}{N}}$

A further example may assist in clarifying the use of these equations.

Let us assume that we have an interest in the heights of basketball players on a college team. Specifically, we want to determine the mean and standard deviation of the heights of the five starting players. Their heights in inches are listed in Table 3.6. As these are all of the players that we are interested in, this group of five individuals is a population.

Table 3.6 Heights of Five Basketball Players in Inches

	70
	72
	76
	80
	81
Sum	379

The mean of the five heights would be found using the following equation:

$$\text{Mean} = \frac{\Sigma X}{N}.$$

$$\mu = \frac{379}{5}.$$

$$\mu = 75.8 \text{ inches.}$$

We can now use the equation, $\sigma = \sqrt{\Sigma(X-\mu)^2/N}$ from Table 3.5, to find the standard deviation. The first step is to find the deviation, $X - \mu$ which can also be written as x, for each of the five heights. We then square these values. This outcome can be written as $(X - \mu)^2$ or x^2. These steps are illustrated in Table 3.7.

As a check on our arithmetic, we confirm that the sum of the deviations, $\Sigma(X - \mu)$, which can also be written as Σx, is zero. Having obtained this, we proceed to find the sum of the squared deviations, $\Sigma(X - \mu)^2$, which can also be written as Σx^2 or SS. This is equal to 92.80 inches squared.

The next step, as is evident from Table 3.5, is to divide 92.80 by N. As a result, we find that $\Sigma(X - \mu)^2/N$ (which is equivalent to SS/N or $\Sigma x^2/N$) is equal to 92.80 divided by 5, which in turn equals 18.56 inches squared. We have just found the variance of the heights of the basketball players. Notice again that the variance is measured in inches squared. This is not a particularly meaningful number, so we now take the square root, which will give us the standard deviation of 4.31 inches.

We have just used the three equations for the variance and standard deviation in Table 3.5. They are simply different ways to write the definitional equations for the variance and standard deviation.

Table 3.7 Initial Steps in Calculation of the Standard Deviation

X	$(X - \mu)$ or x	$(X - \mu)^2$ or x^2
70	$(70 - 75.8) = -5.8$	33.64
72	$(72 - 75.8) = -3.8$	14.44
76	$(76 - 75.8) = 0.2$	0.04
80	$(80 - 75.8) = 4.2$	17.64
81	$(81 - 75.8) = 5.2$	27.04
Sum = 379	= 0	= 92.80

REPORTING THE CALCULATED VALUES OF THE MEAN AND STANDARD DEVIATION

If we wanted to report the results, we would say, "The mean of the heights of the basketball players, in inches, as well as the standard deviation were calculated ($\mu = 75.8$, $SD = 4.31$)." This would indicate to the reader that the players were tall, 75.8 inches or almost 6 feet 4 inches on average, and that the "standard" difference between their heights was slightly more than 4 inches. A great deal of information has been conveyed with only two numbers. This efficient summary of data is the goal of descriptive statistics.

PROGRESS CHECK

Assuming the goals scored by a population consisting of four soccer players during a season are 6, 8, 9, and 12.

1. What is the mean?

2. What is the variance?

3. What is the standard deviation?

Answers: 1. 8.75 goals.   2. 6.5 goals squared.   3. 2.55 goals.

There are times when a constant number is added to every score in a set of data, such as when a professor curves the scores on a test. It is important to understand how adding a constant will affect the mean and standard deviation of the set of scores. In our example, imagine that each basketball player started playing on stilts that were 12 inches high; then each player's height would increase by 12 inches. This would, in turn, increase the mean height by 12 inches. But how would it affect the standard deviation? The situation is summarized in Table 3.8.

The original mean height was 379/5, or 75.8 inches. The mean of the new heights is 439/5 or 87.8 inches, 12 inches more than the original mean. We confirm, using the new mean, that $\Sigma(X - \mu)$ equals zero. Next, we note that the sum of $(X - \mu)^2$, which can also be written as $\Sigma(X - \mu)^2$, Σx^2 or SS has not changed. It is still equal to 92.80. Since the N, which is 5, has not changed, this will lead to a variance and standard deviation that are also the same as was calculated with the previous example. In other words, if you add a constant value to every score in a set of data, the mean will increase by this constant but the standard deviation and variance will not change. All that you have done by adding a constant value to every score is to shift the distribution to the right on the number line, as is indicated in Figure 3.8. The mean

Table 3.8	Illustration of the Effect of Adding a Constant to Every Score		
Original Score (OS)	**OS + 12 = X**	**(X − μ) or x**	**(X − μ)² or x²**
70	82	(82 − 87.8) = −5.8	33.64
72	84	(84 − 87.8) = −3.8	14.44
76	88	(88 − 87.8) = 0.2	0.04
80	92	(92 − 87.8) = 4.2	17.64
81	93	(93 − 87.8) = 5.2	27.04
Sum = 379	= 439	= 0	= 92.80

of the distribution increases by the constant, but as the shape of the distribution and the spread of the scores do not change, neither do the standard deviation or the variance.

Similarly, if you subtract a constant value from every score in a set of data, the mean will decrease by the amount of the constant but, once again, the shape of distribution as well as the standard deviation and variance will not be altered. You can verify that the variance and standard deviation do not change by using the data for basketball players' heights and subtracting a constant. But what happens if you multiply or divide each score by a constant?

The situation that would result from multiplying each basketball player's height by 3 is indicated in Table 3.9. (This would result in a very tall team!)

The new mean of the heights would be found by dividing the total of the heights, 1,137 inches, by 5. This would equal 227.4 inches, three times the original mean, which was 75.8 inches. In other words, multiplying each player's height by 3 also results in a mean height that is three times as large as the original mean height. To find the effect on variability

Figure 3.8	Effect of Adding a Constant to Each Score

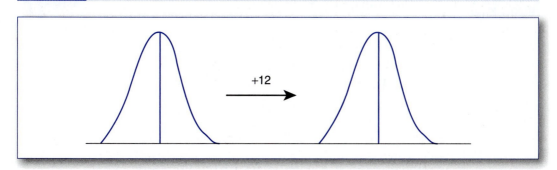

Table 3.9   Illustration of the Effect of Multiplying Each Score by a Constant

Original Score (OS)	3(OS) = X	(X − μ) or x	(X − μ) or x^2
70	210	(210 − 227.4) = −17.4	302.76
72	216	(216 − 227.4) = −11.4	129.96
76	228	(228 − 227.4) = 0.6	0.36
80	240	(240 − 227.4) = 12.6	158.76
81	243	(243 − 227.4) = 15.6	243.36
Sum = 379	= 1,137	= 0	= 835.20

of multiplying each height by 3, we need to find the sum of the squared deviations which, you recall, can be written as $\Sigma(X − μ)^2$, Σx^2 or SS. Before doing so, we check that $\Sigma(X − μ)$, which can also be written as Σx, is zero. Having determined this, we proceed to find that $\Sigma(X − μ)^2$ equals 835.20 inches squared. Substituting into the equation $\sigma^2 = (\Sigma(X − μ)^2)/N$ from Table 3.5, we obtain our variance, which equals 835.20/5, or 167.04 inches squared. The standard deviation is the square root of the variance, which in this case would be $\sqrt{167.04}$, or 12.92 inches. This is, except for a small rounding difference, three times the standard deviation of 4.31 inches that we obtained previously. In other words, if all of the scores in a set of data are multiplied by a constant, the standard deviation (but not the variance) will also be multiplied by that constant. This can be illustrated in Figure 3.9, which shows that the distribution will not only move to the right, it will also become three times as spread out. You are encouraged to divide each member of a set of data and verify that in this case the mean and the standard deviation (but not the variance) will each be divided by your constant.

Figure 3.9   Effect of Multiplying Each Score by Three

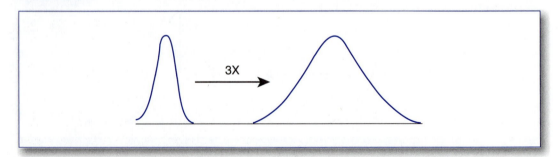

CONCLUSION

This chapter has begun the review of the descriptive statistics utilized with interval or ratio data. If the data are skewed, the measures for central tendency and variability would be the median and the range, respectively. However, as this text will be emphasizing the analysis of normally distributed data, the measures for central tendency and variability that we will most commonly be using will be the mean and the standard deviation. The relation between these statistics and the statistics utilized with nominal and ordinal data are summarized in Table 3.3. Though the calculations are somewhat more involved when there are interval or ratio data, as you will see in the next chapter, the amount of information gained is also greater.

Chapter Resources

GLOSSARY OF TERMS

Bell-shaped curve: a symmetrical distribution in which the highest frequency scores are located near the middle, and the frequency drops the farther a score is from the middle.

Deviation: the difference between a score and some measure, usually the mean. Thus, with population data, the deviation equals $X - \mu$.

Frequency polygon: a graphic presentation for use with interval or ratio data. It is similar to a histogram except that the frequency is indicated by the height of a point rather than the height of a bar. The points are connected by straight lines.

Histogram: a graph used with interval or ratio data. As with the bar graph, frequencies are indicated by the length of the associated bars. However, as there are no distinct categories in a histogram, the bars are positioned side by side.

Mean: a measure of central tendency for use with interval or ratio data. It is what is commonly called an average, but in statistics, the term *average* can refer to a mean, median, or mode. The mean is the sum of the scores divided by the number of scores.

Negatively skewed: a nonsymmetrical distribution in which the tail pointing to the left is larger than the tail pointing to the right.

Normal distribution: a specific, bell-shaped distribution. Many statistical procedures assume that the data are distributed normally.

Population: the entire group that is of interest.

Positively skewed: a nonsymmetrical distribution in which the tail pointing to the right is larger than the tail pointing to the left.

Range: a measure of variability. With interval or ratio data, it equals the difference between the upper real limit of the highest score or category and the lower real limit of the lowest score or category.

Real limits: with interval or ratio data, the actual limits used in assigning a measurement. These are halfway between adjacent scores. Each score thus has an upper and a lower real limit.

Sample: a subset of a population.

Standard deviation: a measure of variability—the average deviation of scores within a distribution. It is defined as the square root of the variance. The symbol for the population standard deviation is σ.

Sum of the squared deviations: for a population, it is equal to $\Sigma(X - \mu)^2$ or Σx^2. It is often abbreviated as "sum of squares," which is shortened even further to *SS*.

Symmetrical distribution: a distribution in which the right half is the mirror image of the left half. In such a distribution, there is a high score corresponding to each low score.

Unimodal distribution: a distribution with only one mode.

Variance: a measure of variability—the average of the sum of the squared deviations of scores from their mean. The symbol for the population variance is σ^2.

x: the symbol for a deviation. Thus, $x = (X - \mu)$ if we are dealing with a population.

Questions: Chapter 3

(Answers to odd-numbered items are provided in Appendix I)

1. A frequency polygon is preferred to a histogram when there are a _____.
   a. small number of possible *X* values
   b. many values of *Y* for each value of *X*
   c. large number of possible *X* values
   d. few values of *Y* for each value of *X*

2. If a person reports that his or her height is 5 feet 8 inches, the "real limits" were actually _____ and _____.
   a. 5 feet 7½ inches; 5 feet 8½ inches
   b. 5 feet 7 inches; 5 feet 9 inches
   c. 5 feet 8 inches exactly

3. The most obvious difference between a bar graph and a histogram is that _____.
   a. the bars touch in a bar graph but are separated in a histogram
   b. the bars touch in a histogram but are separated in a bar graph
   c. a bar graph is used for interval or ratio data, whereas a histogram is only used with nominal data
   d. a bar graph will always have more bars than a histogram will have

4. What is the mean of 96, 92, 98, and 90?
   a. 93
   b. 93.5
   c. 94.5
   d. 94

5. A serious problem with the mean as a measure of central tendency is that _____.

   a. it is too difficult to calculate

   b. it cannot be used if the set of numbers is large

   c. it is affected by extreme scores

6. The two most commonly used measures of variability with normally distributed interval and ratio data are _____ and _____.

   a. standard deviation; variance

   b. range; standard deviation

   c. variance; range

7. In a distribution, the sum of the deviations from the mean will always equal _____.

   a. 3

   b. 0

   c. 6.5

   d. It varies depending on the set of numbers.

8. If you have a distribution consisting of 13 scores, the median would be the _____ score.

   a. 1st

   b. 3rd

   c. 7th

   d. 13th

9. What are the median and range for temperatures of 91, 92, 93, and 94?

   a. 92; 2

   b. 92.5; 3

   c. 92.5; 4

   d. 93; 5

10. If I am solely interested in the views of my statistics class, I am considering the class to be a _____. However, if I am interested in using the statistics students' views to learn about all college students' opinions, I am considering the class to be a _____.

    a. population; sample

    b. sample; population

11. We use the _____ or _____ to graph interval or ratio data.

    a. histogram; pie chart

    b. bar graph; frequency polygon

    c. pie chart; bar graph

    d. histogram; frequency polygon

12. The concept of "real limits" occurs with _____ and _____ measurement scales.
    a. nominal; ordinal
    b. interval; ratio
    c. nominal; interval
    d. ordinal; ratio

13. A bell-shaped curve is _____ and _____.
    a. bimodal; symmetrical
    b. unimodal; skewed
    c. bimodal; skewed
    d. unimodal; symmetrical

14. The mean is the most common measure of central tendency for _____ and _____ measurement scales.
    a. interval; ratio
    b. nominal; interval
    c. ordinal; ratio
    d. nominal; ordinal

15. The difference between a score and its mean is called a _____.
    a. range
    b. real limit
    c. deviation
    d. modality

16. A distribution that is nonsymmetrical and has a tail that points to the left is called _____.
    a. negatively skewed
    b. positively skewed
    c. bimodal

17. The variance for the population consisting of the scores 2, 4, 6, 3, and 5 is _____, and the standard deviation is _____.
    a. 4; 2
    b. 1.4; 2
    c. 20; 4.5
    d. 2; 1.4

18. Adding or subtracting a constant (such as 5) to every score in a distribution will change the _____ but not the _____ or _____.

    a. mean; mode; median

    b. mean; variance; standard deviation

    c. standard deviation; variance; mean

    d. variance; mean; standard deviation

19. If all of the scores in a distribution are multiplied by 10, the mean will be _____ times larger and the standard deviation will be _____ times larger.

    a. 5; 10

    b. 10; 5

    c. 10; 10

    d. 5; 5

20. The standard deviation will equal 0 when _____.

    a. the range is less than 20

    b. every score in the distribution is the same

    c. the mean is negative

    d. the variance is greater than 6

21. If the mean of a distribution is to the right of the median, the distribution is probably _____.

    a. negatively skewed

    b. positively skewed

    c. symmetrical

    d. Any of the above are equally likely

22. The more varied the scores in a distribution, _____.

    a. the larger the standard deviation will be

    b. the smaller the standard deviation will be

    c. variation of scores does not affect the standard deviation

23. For a football team, if the mean yards gained per play were the same for their running and passing plays, but the standard deviation was greater for the passing plays, then _____.

    a. they would have a greater chance of making a large gain with a running play

    b. they would have a greater chance of making a large gain with a passing play

    c. the chance of making a large gain would be the same for a running or a passing play

24. The variance is equal to (the) _____.

    a. square root of the standard deviation

    b. standard deviation

    c. square of the standard deviation

    d. none of the above

25. What is the median and range of heights, measured in inches, of 72, 81, 85, and 91?

    a. 83; 19

    b. 83; 20

    c. 81; 19

    d. 85; 20

DESCRIBING INTERVAL AND RATIO DATA—II

Further Descriptive Statistics Used With Interval or Ratio Data

The most important questions of life are, for the most part, really only problems of probability.

—Pierre-Simon, marquis de Laplace

In Chapter 3, we dealt with the variance and standard deviation (*SD*) of a population. Fortunately, the situation is virtually identical if you are dealing with a sample. As you recall, a sample is a subset of a population. In our example with the basketball players that began with Table 3.6, we were only interested in the heights of the five starting players. They thus constituted a population. Let us assume, instead, that there were 20 basketball players and our 5 players were chosen from this group. Our 5 players would now constitute a sample of this population of 20 basketball players. If we remain interested in simply summarizing the data by calculating the mean, variance, and standard deviation, very little changes.

Nevertheless, when discussing data, it is important to keep the distinction between a population and a sample clear. Measures of characteristics of a population, such as its mean and standard deviation, are called **parameters**. Measures of characteristics of a sample, such as its mean and standard deviation, are called **statistics**. As this book deals with a discipline called statistics, not parameters, it should be obvious that we will be working with samples much more

Parameter: a measure of a characteristic of a population, such as its mean or its variance.

Statistic: a measure of a characteristic of a sample, such as it mean.

often than populations. To assist the readers (and writers) in keeping the distinction between a population and a sample clear, different symbols are used. Table 4.1 lists some of the common symbols.

In Chapter 3, we defined the deviation of a score from the population mean as $X - \mu$. From Table 4.1, the symbol for the mean changes when we are dealing with a sample. Consequently, the deviation of a score from the sample mean would be written as $X - M$. Similarly, from Table 3.5, you will see that the equation for the population variance is $\sigma^2 = \Sigma(X - \mu)^2/N$. By substituting the symbols listed in Table 4.1, we find that the equation for the sample variance is $s^2 = \Sigma(X - \mu)^2/n$. Clearly, the sample standard deviation would be $s = \sqrt{\Sigma(X-\mu)^2 / n}$. To assist you in comparing the equations for the standard deviation, they are provided for both populations and samples in Table 4.2.

Table 4.1   Symbols Used When Describing Population Parameters and Sample Statistics

	Population Parameter	Sample Statistic
Size of data set	N	n
Mean	μ	M
Variance	σ^2	s^2
Standard deviation	σ	s

Table 4.2   Equations for the Standard Deviation for Describing Populations and Samples

Population	Sample
$\sigma = \sqrt{\dfrac{\Sigma(X-\mu)^2}{N}}$	$s = \sqrt{\dfrac{\Sigma(X-M)^2}{n}}$
$\sigma = \sqrt{\dfrac{SS}{N}}$	$s = \sqrt{\dfrac{SS}{n}}$
$\sigma = \sqrt{\dfrac{\Sigma x^2}{N}}$	$s = \sqrt{\dfrac{\Sigma x^2}{n}}$

It is important to note that while the symbols used in the equations have changed, the calculations and the values obtained will not change. In other words, the standard deviation describing a set of data will be the same regardless of whether we are dealing with a population or a sample. Later in the text, you will see that with inferential statistics there is a minor change to the equations. However, with descriptive statistics, the equations lead to identical outcomes. The symbols are different solely as a reminder of whether you are dealing with a population or a sample.

In Chapter 3, we learned that the standard deviation is the most commonly used descriptive measure of variability for interval or ratio data that are normally distributed. We have also seen how to find the value of the standard deviation for both populations and samples. In addition, it was noted that unlike the range, the standard deviation makes use of all of the data and will, therefore, tend to be more stable. There are other characteristics of the standard deviation that make it particularly useful as a descriptive statistic.

We previously noted that if interval or ratio data are normally distributed, they form a symmetrical, bell-shaped distribution, as is shown in Figure 4.1. If you start at the far left on the graph and follow it to the right, you will see that the direction of the curve changes at point "a." To the left of point "a" the curve is concave, like the inside of a circle; to the right of point "a" the curve is convex, like the outside of a circle. As you continue to the right from point "a," the line continues to form a convex curve until you get to

> *Inflection point: a point on a graph where the curvature changes from concave to convex or from convex to concave.*

point "c." At point "c," the direction changes again and the line begins to form another concave curve. Point "a" and point "c" are what are called **inflection points**.

It should be evident from examining Figure 4.1 that point "b" is the mean of the distribution and that points "a" and "c" are equidistant from point "b." It is also the case that with a normal distribution, point "a" is located 1 *SD* below the mean (point "b") and point "c" is

Figure 4.1 Inflection Points on a Normal Curve

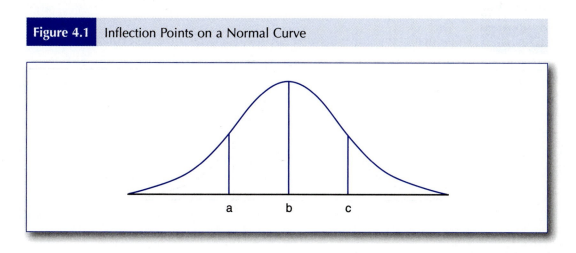

located 1 *SD* above the mean. Furthermore, it has been found that the proportion of the curve between points "a" and "b" is 0.3413 or about 34%. Similarly, since the curve is symmetrical, the proportion of the curve between points "b" and "c" is also 0.3413 or about 34%. Put another way, if there is a normal distribution of scores for 10,000 individuals, then 3,413 subjects will be in the region between the mean and 1 *SD* below the mean (point "a") and another 3,413 individuals will be in the region between the mean and 1 *SD* above the mean (point "c"). In other words, slightly more than 68% of the total cases will fall within ±1 *SD* of the mean when we are dealing with a normal distribution. This relationship between proportions or areas and the normal distribution is illustrated in Figure 4.2.

WHAT YOU ALWAYS WANTED TO KNOW ABOUT INTELLIGENCE QUOTIENT BUT NO ONE TOLD YOU

The critical concept to recognize is that regardless of what the specific data are, if they are normally distributed, there is a relationship between the magnitude of the standard deviation and corresponding proportions of the distribution. For instance, the intelligence quotient (IQ) test is normally distributed and has a mean of 100 and a standard deviation of 15. You now know that if 10,000 people took the test, then we expect that 3,413 will score between 85 (1 *SD* below the mean) and 100 (the mean). Another 3,413 will score between 100 (the mean) and 115 (1 *SD* above the mean). Thus, 6,826, or approximately two thirds of the individuals, will have IQ scores between 85 (1 *SD* below the mean) and 115 (1 *SD* above the mean).

Fortunately, through calculus, we also know what the proportion of the distribution will be between the mean and either plus or minus two 2 *SD*. This proportion is 0.4772, which is shown in Figure 4.3. Using our IQ example, 4,772 of the 10,000 individuals who took the test would be expected to fall between 70 (2 *SD* below the mean) and 100 (the mean). Similarly, 4,772 of the 10,000 individuals who took the test would be expected to fall between 100 (the

Figure 4.2 Proportion of the Curve Between the Mean and the Inflection Points

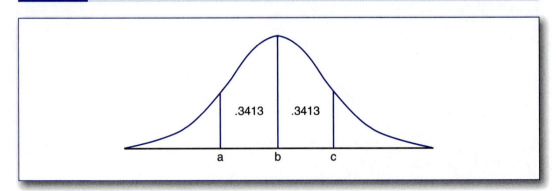

mean) and 130 (2 *SD* above the mean). In other words, 9,544 of the 10,000 people who took the IQ test would be expected to have scores between 70 and 130. Converting to percentages, slightly more than 95% of the cases will fall within 2 *SD* of the mean. What this indicates is that for *any* normal distribution, there is less than a 5% chance that a score will be more than 2 *SD* from the mean. Later in this book, you will learn that the areas associated with all the standard deviations, not just for 1 and 2 *SD*, have been calculated. For now, we will continue to deal with the values that we have already described.

By drawing a figure and referring to Figures 4.2 and 4.3, it is easy to determine the answers to a number of additional questions. For instance, how many of the 10,000 individuals would be expected to have IQ scores that would fall below 85? To determine this number, the first step would be to draw a figure indicating what is being asked. This is shown in Figure 4.4. We recognize that an IQ of 85 is equivalent to 1 *SD* below the mean. By referring to Figure 4.2, we note that 0.3413 of the total area falls between the mean and 1 *SD* below the mean. What we are looking for, however, is the region more than 1 *SD* below the mean. Since the normal distribution is symmetrical, the entire area below the mean represents 50%, or 0.5 of the curve. The region that we seek is thus 0.5 − 0.3413, which equals 0.1587. Since we were asked how many individuals out of 10,000 would be in this region of the distribution, we multiply 0.1587 × 10,000 and obtain 1,587. I hope you agree that as long as you draw a figure, working with the proportions associated with the standard deviations is not particularly difficult.

For our final example, let us find what proportion of the IQ scores would be less than 130. The first step, as always with these problems, is to draw a figure showing the area that is of interest. This is shown in Figure 4.5. Next, we recognize that an IQ of 130 is 2 *SD* above the mean. From Figure 4.3, we find that the area between the mean and a point 2 *SD* above

Figure 4.3	Proportion of the Curve Between the Mean and Plus or Minus Two Standard Deviations

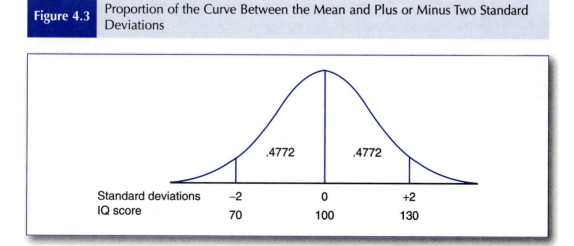

Note. IQ, intelligence quotient.

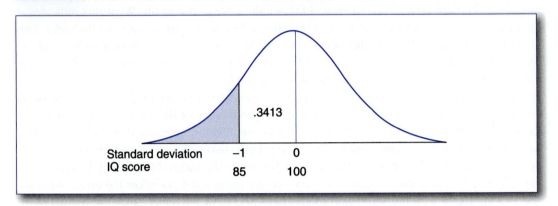

Figure 4.4   Region of the Curve Below an IQ Score of 85

Note. IQ, intelligence quotient.

the mean is 0.4772 or about 48% of the area under the curve. Since half, or 0.5, of a symmetrical distribution is below the mean, the region that we are searching for would be equal to 0.4772 plus 0.5, or 0.9772.

As an alternative for finding the proportion of scores less than 130, we could have found the proportion of scores more than 130 and subtracted that amount from the total area under the curve. To do this, we could have subtracted 0.4772 from the total area to the right of the mean, which is 0.5. This would give us 0.0228. We could then subtract this proportion from the total area of the curve, which is 1.0 or 100%. This would give us 1.0 − 0.0228 or 0.9772,

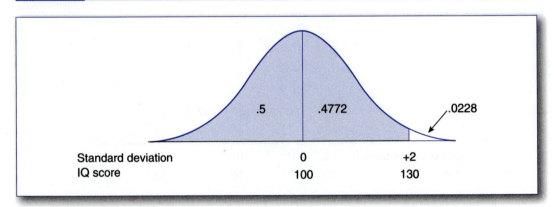

Figure 4.5   Region of the Curve Below an IQ Score of 130

Note. IQ, intelligence quotient.

the same value we obtained previously. What this shows is that there may be more than one way to find the desired answer. What is critical is that you draw the area you are seeking and, when you finish, you check to make certain that you have provided the answer in the desired form. If the question asks for a proportion, be certain that you gave the proportion. On the other hand, if the question requests a number of subjects, be sure to provide the number.

It should be evident that the standard deviation can be particularly useful when you are dealing with a normal curve. Once the standard deviation is determined, the probabilities associated with different outcomes can be determined. However, the verbal descriptions that we have been using are rather awkward. Expressions such as "2 *SD* below the mean" or "the area between the mean and 1 *SD* above the mean" require some careful attention to be understood. Fortunately, the field of statistics has developed an alternative, a simple unit known as the *z* score.

Later in this chapter, you will be given the mathematical definition of a *z* score. For now, just think of it as the number of standard deviations. For example, an IQ score of 115 is 1 *SD* above the mean. Because it is 1 *SD* above the mean, it is equivalent to a *z* score of 1. Similarly, an IQ score of 70 is 2 *SD* below the mean, which is the same as saying an IQ of 70 has a *z* score of −2. Thus *the magnitude of the z score is simply the number of standard deviations you are away from the mean and the sign, either positive or negative, indicates the direction*. For instance, a *z* score of −1 indicates that the point is 1 *SD* below the mean. In terms of IQ scores, this would be a score of 85. Furthermore, just as the area between the mean and 1 *SD* above the mean is equal to 0.3413 (Figure 4.2), the area between the mean and a *z* score of +1 is also 0.3413. The other areas in Figures 4.2 and 4.3 would also correspond to the associated *z* scores. Remember, the *z* score is simply a shorthand way of indicating the number of standard deviations from the mean and the direction from the mean (Figure 4.6).

Figure 4.6 Relationship Between Standard Deviations, IQ Scores, and *z* Scores

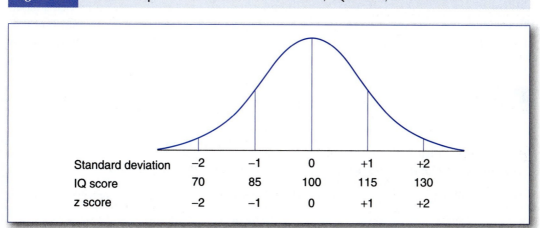

Standard deviation	−2	−1	0	+1	+2
IQ score	70	85	100	115	130
z score	−2	−1	0	+1	+2

Note. IQ, intelligence quotient.

DESCRIPTIVE STATISTICS: THE *z* SCORE

We will now be focusing on a further discussion of the descriptive measure known as the **z score**. The relation of the *z* score to other descriptive statistics is illustrated in Table 4.3.

A Little History and a Very Impressive Equation

z score: a conversion of raw data so that the deviation is measured in standard deviation units and the sign, positive or negative, indicates the direction of the deviation.

As Table 4.3 shows, the *z* score is used when there are interval or ratio data. In addition, you have seen that the *z* score is particularly useful in those situations in which the data are normally distributed.

The concept of a normal curve was developed when it was noticed that many, but certainly not all, variables tend to exhibit what we call a bell-shaped distribution. For instance, if we were to plot the weights of adult males, we would find that many have moderate weights and that progressively fewer have either extremely low or

Table 4.3   Summary of Descriptive Statistics

Descriptive Statistics (Summarizing Data)	Type of Data		
	Nominal	**Ordinal**	**Interval Ratio**
Frequency distribution	Bar graph or pie chart	Bar graph	Histogram or frequency polygon
Central tendency	Mode	Median	Mean
Variability	—	Range	Standard deviation and z score

extremely high weights. This pattern, with a high frequency of events surrounding the mean and progressively fewer occurrences as you move in either direction, attracted the interest of mathematicians. In 1733, Abraham De Moivre proposed an equation for the normal distribution. It is not something that is likely to be appreciated when first encountered:

$$P(x) = \frac{1}{\sigma\sqrt{2\pi}} e^{-(x-\mu)^2/2\sigma^2}.$$

Fortunately, it is not necessary for you to memorize or even be able to work with this equation. What is important is that you have a modest understanding of the pieces that make up the equation for the normal distribution.

The equation indicates that the likelihood of a score ($P(X)$) is dependent on two constants as well as three variables. You may be familiar with the two constants, the natural logarithm "e," which is approximately 2.178, and π, which is approximately 3.146 (Don't worry, you won't be using these numbers. Remember, we're keeping things simple). The three variables were introduced previously in this text and are the population mean, μ; population standard deviation, σ; and the population variance, σ^2. As there are an infinite number of possible combinations of μ and σ, there are also an infinite number of normal curves. However, they all share a number of characteristics, some of which were introduced in Chapter 3:

1. *Unimodal:* all normal curves have a single peak or mode.

2. *Symmetrical:* all normal curves have mirror image shapes to the left and right of the mean.

3. *Bell-shaped:* all normal curves have shapes that can be described as resembling a bell.

4. All normal curves can be transformed into what can be called a standard normal curve. The standard normal curve has a μ of 0 and a σ of 1. In addition, as was discussed previously, the inflection point of this curve occurs exactly 1 *SD* above and below the mean.

5. When dealing with the standard normal curve, we utilize what are called z scores.

The Standard, Very Important, z Score

The z score was defined as the number of standard deviations that a score differs from its mean. We are now ready for the equation for the z score, which is, $z = (X - \mu)/\sigma$. This equation is quite simple. It indicates that to find what z score corresponds to an individual score (signified with the letter X), we subtract the population mean, μ, from the X score and then divide this difference by the population standard deviation, σ. From Chapter 3, you will also recall that the numerator ($X - \mu$) is an example of a deviation. It is the difference between a score and its population mean.

The equation for z indicates that a deviation, the difference between an individual score and its mean, is to be divided by the standard deviation, σ. What this last step accomplishes is to convert a deviation, which was measured in units such as feet or the number of correct answers in an exam, into standard deviation units. You are familiar with doing similar transformations. For instance, if you find that the length of a rug is 15 feet, and then divide it by 3 feet, you will convert the length into yards. Dividing by the standard deviation, σ, is converting the original measurement into standard deviation units. Thus, regardless of what the original measurement units were, by dividing by σ all of the deviations between the original scores and the population mean are converted into standard deviations. Because of this uniformity of measurement, the z score is also called a standard score.

As an example, consider the most commonly used IQ tests, which have a mean of 100 and a standard deviation of 15. Remember, the equation is $z = (X - \mu)/\sigma$. If an individual obtained an IQ score of 145, that person's deviation from the mean would be $145 - 100$. The z score would then equal $(145 - 100)/15$. This is $45/15$, or 3. Thus, an IQ score of 145 is 3 SD above the mean and is equivalent to a z score of $+3$. An IQ of 70 would be equal to $(70 - 100)/15$. This is $-30/15$, which equals -2. This indicates that an IQ of 70 is 2 SD below the mean.

It is important to note the positive or negative sign of the z score. Whenever the z score is positive, we are dealing with an original score above, or greater than, the mean. Whenever the z score is negative, we are dealing with an original score that is below, or less than, the mean. Thus, an IQ of 145 results in a positive z score because 145 is greater than the mean of the IQ distribution, which is 100. Similarly, we found that with an IQ of 70, the z score is negative because 70 is less than the mean of 100. To reiterate, the magnitude of the z score is simply the number of standard deviations that a score falls from the mean, and its sign indicates the direction of this difference.

Who Says You Can't Compare Apples and Oranges?

Converting our initial data, which are called **raw scores**, into z scores permits us to make comparisons that would otherwise not be meaningful. For instance, if you scored 9 out of 10 on a music audition and 85 out of 100 on a statistics exam, on which test did you do better? To answer this question, your first step might be to convert one of the scales so it had the same upper limit as the other. For instance, you could multiply your music audition score by 10 so it was on a 100-point scale. Then, you might conclude that you did better on the music audition since your transformed score, which is now 90, is higher than the statistics score of 85. However, it might also occur to you that this is not a very satisfactory solution. What if most of the scores on the music audition tended to be very high and most

Raw score: your data as they are originally measured, before any transformation.

of the scores on the statistics exam tended to be lower? In this case, it is possible that you had the lowest score on the music audition but the highest score on the statistics exam. Of course, the opposite is also possible. Your score of 90 on the audition might have been the highest score obtained, while your score of 85 on the statistics exam might have been the lowest grade on the exam. As the original measurement scales were different, you are now in the situation where you are comparing apples to oranges. What is needed is a standard measurement scale, and this is where the *z* score can be of great value.

If you know the mean and standard deviation of the music audition and statistics exam and that both sets of data are normally distributed, you can convert each of the raw scores into *z* scores and then make a meaningful comparison. For instance, if the mean of the music audition scores was 8 and the standard deviation was 0.5, while the mean of the statistics scores was 81 and the standard deviation was 4, then the *z* scores could be calculated as shown below:

$$z \text{ for music audition} = \frac{(X - \mu)}{\sigma}$$

$$= \frac{(9 - 8)}{0.5}$$

$$= \frac{1}{0.5}$$

$$= 2.$$

$$z \text{ for statistics exam} = \frac{(X - \mu)}{\sigma}$$

$$= \frac{(85 - 81)}{4}$$

$$= \frac{4}{4}$$

$$= 1.$$

These results show that you had a *z* score of +2 for the music audition and a *z* score of +1 for the statistics exam. In both cases, the *z* scores are positive, so in each situation, you were above the mean. However, you did better on the music audition, for you scored 2 *SD* above the mean on the music audition and only 1 *SD* above the mean on the statistics exam.

Clearly, by standardizing the scores, in other words by converting the raw scores into *z* scores, you are able to make comparisons that would otherwise not be meaningful. Put differently, with *z* scores, you actually can compare apples to oranges!

Just as you can convert a raw score into a z score, it is also possible to do the reverse. For instance, you can find the raw score that is equivalent to a z score of +1.5 on the music audition. This can be accomplished using the original equation for the z score:

$$z \text{ for music audition} = \frac{(X - \mu)}{\sigma}.$$

Substituting the value we are given for the z score, plus the mean and standard deviation from before leads to the following equation:

$$1.5 = \frac{(X - 8)}{0.5}.$$

Multiplying each side of the equation by 0.5 gives us

$$0.75 = X - 8.$$

Adding 8 to each side of the equation leads to the following answer:

$$8.75 = X.$$

We conclude that a raw score of 8.75 is equivalent to a z score of +1.5.

If solving this type of equation is awkward for you, the original equation for z can be rearranged so that the X value is presented alone on the left. This is shown below:

$$X = z\sigma + \mu.$$

Substituting the values for z, μ, and σ from the previous example, would give us

$$X = (1.5) \times (.5) + 8$$

$$= 0.75 + 8$$

$$= 8.75.$$

This is the same outcome as we obtained before.

To be certain that you feel comfortable converting from z scores to raw scores, we will do one more example. What raw score is equivalent to a z score of −3 on the statistics exam? Using the definitional equation for z, we would have the following:

$$z \text{ for statistics exam} = \frac{(X - \mu)}{\sigma}.$$

Substituting the values that we know leads to

$$-3 = \frac{(X - 81)}{4}.$$

We then multiply by 4 to give

$$-12 = X - 81.$$

To find X, we now add 81 to both sides:

$$69 = X.$$

Alternatively, we could use the version of the equation that has X on the left side of the equation. In this case, we have

$$X = z\sigma + \mu.$$

Substituting the values that we know leads to

$$X = (-3) \times (4) + 81$$
$$= -12 + 81$$
$$= 69.$$

The answer is the same. You can choose whichever equation you find easier to use.

To this point, we have converted a raw score into a z score, and we have converted a z score into a raw score. In addition, we have seen that converting raw scores into z scores permits us to make comparisons that would not otherwise be meaningful. We will now see that it can be very useful to convert an entire distribution of raw scores into z scores. Before we do, it is important to understand that transforming raw scores into z scores does not change the shape of the distribution of your scores. If your original data formed a positively skewed distribution, then the distribution of their z scores will remain positively skewed. The same will happen for negatively skewed distributions, or normal distributions. Converting all of the scores to z scores does not affect the shape of the distribution. This is important, for if your data are positively or negatively skewed, you should generally not convert the distribution to z scores. However, if the data are normally distributed, then converting the distribution into z scores permits some valuable comparisons and insights.

Let's return to the example of the IQ test. The IQ test is normally distributed with a mean of 100. Converting the mean of 100 to a z score is accomplished using the same equation used previously:

$$z \text{ for mean IQ} = \frac{(X - \mu)}{\sigma}.$$

Substituting the known quantities leads to

$$z = \frac{(100 - 100)}{15}.$$

This, in turn, leads to

$$z = \frac{0}{15}.$$

$$z = 0.$$

Therefore, the mean of the z distribution is 0. This outcome will occur regardless of the variable being considered, for when we are dealing with the mean, $X - \mu$ will always be 0, and thus, z for the mean of the distribution will be 0.

Previously in this chapter, it was pointed out that the standard deviation of the common IQ test is 15. Thus, if we calculated the z score equivalent of an IQ of 115, we would obtain an answer of +1 (you are encouraged to do this calculation). In other words, an IQ of 115 is 1 SD above the mean. In fact, the standard deviation of a distribution of raw scores will always be converted to 1, when the raw scores are converted into z scores. Furthermore, as we found in the previous paragraph, the mean of a distribution of z scores will always be 0, regardless of the original measurement scale. In other words, *regardless of whether we are dealing with the IQ distribution, the distribution of points on an exam, or any other distribution, when it is converted to z scores, the mean of the new distribution will be 0 and the standard deviation will be 1*. This is very important to remember!

The z Table: Who Would Have Thought That a Few Numbers Could Be So Much Fun?

We just discussed that with a normal distribution there is a relationship between how many standard deviations a score is from its mean and its precise location on the normal curve. For instance, the inflection point of the normal curve occurs at precisely 1 SD from the mean. Furthermore, it was noted that the proportion of the normal curve between the mean and a standard deviation of 1 is always 0.3413. We will now see that once any score's location on the normal curve is determined, it is possible to specify a series of proportions or probabilities.

In our IQ example, it was noted that a test score of 115 is equivalent to a z score of +1. By referring to the z table (Appendix J, Table J.1), you will see that there are two entries associated with a z score of 1. The first entry is 0.3413, the proportion of the curve between the mean and a z score of 1.00. This indicates that 34.13% or 3,413 people out of 10,000 will score between the mean z score, which is 0, and the z score of +1. This is equivalent to saying that 34.13% or 3,413 people out of 10,000 will score between the mean IQ score, which is 100, and the IQ that corresponds to a z score of +1, which is 115.

Of course, 50% of the distribution falls below the mean. In other words, 84.13% of individuals (50% + 34.13%) or 8,413 people out of 10,000 would be expected to have a z score below +1 (equivalent to an IQ below 115). As you learned in Chapter 2, this percentage, the percentage of scores at or below a particular value, is called the percentile rank.

It should also be evident that 0.50 − 0.3413, which is 0.1587, is the proportion of the curve that is above our z score of +1. This is the second entry in the table for a z of 1. In other words, we would expect 15.87% or 1,587 people out of 10,000 to have IQ scores greater than 115. Clearly, if you are dealing with a normal distribution, once the z score is known, a great deal of additional information is easily obtained.

To be certain that you understand how the z table works, let's review the entries for the z score associated with an IQ of 70 that we calculated previously. In this case, the z score is −2, because an IQ of 70 is equivalent to scoring 2 *SD below* the mean. By referring to the z table, you will see that there is no row of entries associated with a z score of −2. Instead, you look up a z score of 2 and mentally flip it to the left side of the curve (drawing a normal curve and shading in the relevant area is a very good idea). The entry is 0.4772, the proportion of the curve between the mean and the z score. This indicates that 47.72% or 4,772 people out of 10,000 will score between the mean IQ score, which is 100, and the IQ that corresponds to a z score of −2, which is 70. As 50% of the distribution lies below the mean, then 0.50 − 0.4772 or 0.0228 is the proportion of the curve below the z score of −2 (this value is listed in column C of the table). In other words, only 2.28% of individuals, or 228 people out of 10,000 would be expected to have an IQ below 70. Of course, then 0.9772 is the proportion of the curve that is above our z score of −2. In other words, we would expect 97.72% or 9,772 people out of 10,000 to have IQ scores greater than 70. This last proportion is found by adding the proportion of the curve that is above the mean, which is 0.5, to the proportion of the curve that is located between the mean and the z score, which we found was 0.4772. (Or you could subtract 0.0228, the proportion expected to score below an IQ of 70, from 1.0, the proportion equivalent to the entire distribution.)

We have limited our discussion to z scores of +1 or −1, or +2 or −2. However, it should be evident that you can convert any raw score into a z score. In addition, we have seen how you can easily find three proportions associated with a z score, if it is part of a normal distribution. These are the proportion of the curve below the z score, the proportion of the curve between the mean and the z score, and the proportion of the curve above the z score. Once a proportion is known, the percentage is also known, and the number of individuals out of the total can also be determined.

With this information, it is also possible to find the proportion or percentage of the distribution that is between two z scores. For instance, what is the proportion of the distribution that is between a z score of +1 and a z score of +2? To solve this problem, it is best to draw what you are looking for. This is shown in Figure 4.7.

There are several ways to solve this problem. One way is to begin with the z score of +1. We know that the proportion of the curve that is located between the mean and this z is 0.3413. From the z table, we can find that the area above this z is 0.1587. This can also be found by subtracting 0.3413 from 0.5. This area is illustrated in Figure 4.8.

Of course, this is not the proportion that we seek, for it includes the region above a z score of +2. The solution, obviously, is to subtract the proportion of the curve that is located above a z score of +2. We previously found that this was equal to 0.0228, which is illustrated in Figure 4.9.

Figure 4.7   Region Between z Scores of 1 and 2

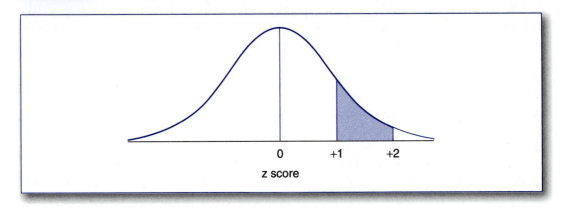

Figure 4.8   Region Above a z Score of 1

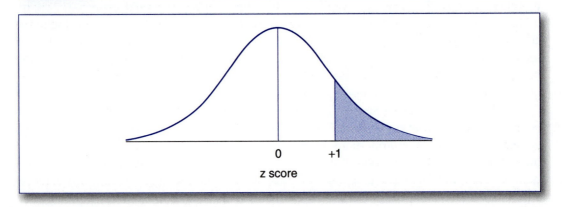

We finish by subtracting the proportion of the curve located above a z score of +2, which is equal to 0.0228, from the proportion of the curve that is located above a z of +1, which is equal to 0.1587. These proportions are illustrated in Figures 4.8 and 4.9. The difference, 0.1587 − 0.0228, is 0.1359.

Alternatively, we could have begun by finding the proportion of the curve below our z of +1. This is 0.5 + 0.3413, which equals 0.8413. This region is illustrated in Figure 4.10.

We would then find the proportion of the curve below our z of +2. This is 0.5 + 0.4772, which equals 0.9772. This region is illustrated in Figure 4.11.

The difference of these two areas would be the region we are interested in. It is 0.9772 − 0.8413, which is 0.1359, the same outcome as we found previously.

In the example we just completed you were given the z scores. Let's now do a complete example, beginning with the raw scores. The scores on the SAT exam are normally distributed

Figure 4.9 Region Above a *z* Score of 2

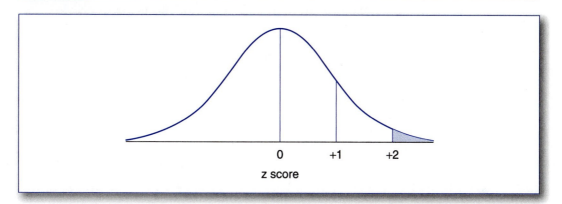

Figure 4.10 Region Below a *z* Score of 1

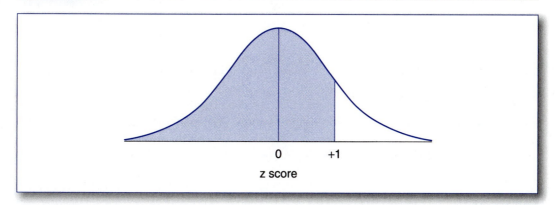

Figure 4.11 Region Below a *z* Score of 2

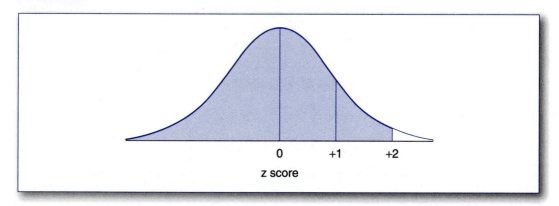

and have a mean of 500 and a standard deviation of 100. How many people, out of 1,000, would be expected to score between 350 and 575?

The first step is to convert the two raw scores into z scores. This is shown below:

$$z = \frac{(X - \mu)}{\sigma}$$

$$z \text{ for a SAT score of } 350 = \frac{(350 - 500)}{100}$$

$$= -\frac{150}{100}$$

$$= -1.5.$$

$$z \text{ for a SAT score of } 575 = \frac{(575 - 500)}{100}$$

$$= \frac{75}{100}$$

$$= +0.75.$$

We can now draw the region of the normal curve, in SAT as well as z scores, that is of interest to us. This is shown in Figure 4.12.

Once the z scores that are equivalent to SAT scores of 350 and 575 have been calculated, there are a variety of ways to find the desired region. Perhaps the easiest is to first find the proportion of the curve that lies between a z score of −1.5 and the mean of the z distribution, which is always 0. This region is illustrated in Figure 4.13.

Figure 4.12   Region Between SAT Scores of 350 and 575

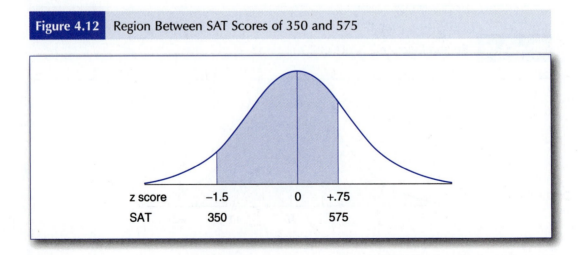

| Figure 4.13 | Region Between the Mean and a z Score of −1.5 |

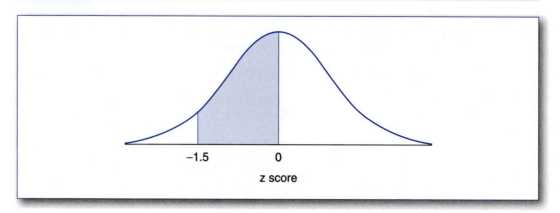

Using the *z* table, the proportion is found to be 0.4332. To complete the problem, the next step is to find the proportion of the curve that lies between a *z* score of 0 and a *z* score of +0.75. This region is illustrated in Figure 4.14.

From the *z* table, this is found to be 0.2734. We now add 0.2734 to 0.4332 to get 0.7066. This is the proportion of the curve that falls between *z* scores of −1.5 and +0.75, the *z* scores equivalent to the SAT scores of 350 and 575. While essential to finding the answer, this is not what the question asked us to find. The problem was to find *how many people*, out of 1,000, would be expected to have SAT scores between 350 and 575. To find this, we must multiply our proportion of 0.7066 by 1,000, the total number of people. This results in 706.6. As 0.6 of a person is not realistic, we round off to obtain the answer that 707 people out of 1,000 are expected to have SAT scores between 350 and 575.

| Figure 4.14 | Region Between the Mean and z Score of 0.75 |

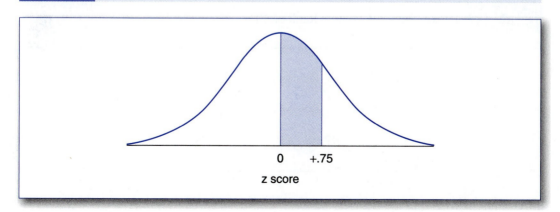

PROGRESS CHECK

1. The magnitude of a z score is the number of _____ that a score falls from the mean, and the _____ indicates whether the score is larger or smaller than the mean.

   As noted previously, SAT exam scores are normally distributed. The mean is 500 and the standard deviation is 100.

2. What is the z score that is equivalent to a SAT score of 700?

3. What proportion of SAT scores would fall below a score of 350?

Answers: 1. standard deviations; sign. 2. +2. 3. 0.0668.

There is one last type of problem we will cover using z scores. It deals with finding the raw score that is associated with a particular proportion of the curve. Remember that a z score of 0 is at the mean and, since the normal distribution is symmetrical, half of the area is below the mean and the other half of the area is above the mean. But what about other proportions, such as 0.40? What z score has 0.40 of the curve below it? In other words, what z score has a percentile rank of 40%? The region of the distribution that we are interested in is illustrated in Figure 4.15.

The solution is found by first noting that if 40% of the distribution falls below our z score, then 10% of the distribution falls between the z score and the mean. We now refer to the body of the z table and look for the proportion closest to 0.10 for the area between the mean and z or 0.40 for the area beyond z in the tail. The proportions 0.10 and 0.40 do not occur in the z table. The closest values are 0.0987 and 0.4013, which are associated with a z score of −0.25. (Remember, we are to the left of the mean, so the z score is negative.) In other words, approximately 0.40, or 40%, of the distribution occurs below a z score of −0.25. Alternatively, we could say that the percentile rank of a z score of −0.25 is 40%.

Figure 4.15   Region With a Percentile Rank of 40%

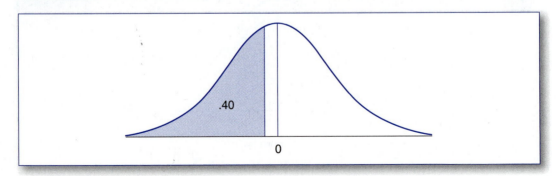

In some cases, a problem might ask for the answer to be converted to a raw score. This requires some additional calculation, but it is not difficult. For instance, using the example of SAT scores, it is easy to convert the z score with a percentile rank of 40% (which we just determined was −0.25) into a SAT score. To do this, we use either the definitional equation for the z score or the rearranged equation that was illustrated earlier. The solution, using both forms of the equation, is presented below:

$$z = \frac{(X - \mu)}{\sigma}$$

$$-0.25 = \frac{(X - 500)}{100}$$

$$-25 = X - 500$$

$$475 = X,$$

or

$$X = z\sigma + \mu$$

$$X = (-0.25) \times (100) + 500$$

$$X = -25 + 500$$

$$X = 475.$$

For our second example, what IQ score would have 80% of the population above it? This is equivalent to asking what score would have 0.80 of the distribution above it. The first step is to identify the appropriate region of the normal curve (Figure 4.16).

Note that as only 50% or 0.50 of the population scores above the mean, we must include an additional 30% or 0.30 that is below the mean to have a total of 80%. The next step is to

Figure 4.16 An Example With 80% of the Distribution Scoring Above *X*

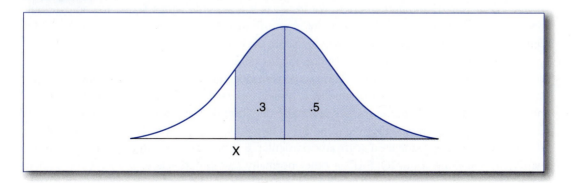

refer to the body of the z table and look for the proportion closest to 0.30. This is 0.2995, which is associated with a z score of –0.84. (The point we are dealing with is to the left of the mean, so the z score is negative.) To find the IQ score that is equivalent to a z score of –0.84, we substitute into the definitional equation (or the rearranged equation given previously):

$$z = \frac{(X - \mu)}{\sigma}$$

$$-0.84 = \frac{(X - 100)}{15}$$

$$-12.6 = X - 100$$

$$87.4 = X,$$

or

$$X = z\sigma + \mu$$

$$X = (-0.84) \times (15) + 100$$

$$X = -12.6 + 100$$

$$X = 87.4.$$

CONCLUSION

This chapter focused on a measurement of variability for use with interval or ratio data, the z score. The z score is known as a standard score. It is used when a normal distribution is converted into a standard normal curve. The standard normal curve is unimodal, symmetrical, and bell-shaped and has a mean of 0 and a standard deviation of 1. The z score is defined as the number of standard deviations that a score differs from its mean. The equation for the z score is, therefore, $z = (X - \mu)/\sigma$.

Converting raw scores into z scores can be very useful, for it makes it possible to compare outcomes measured on different scales. For instance, it is possible with z scores to compare outcomes on a 10-point quiz and a 100-point exam, even though the measurement scales differ dramatically. It is also possible to convert a z score back to a raw score.

We found that converting a distribution into z scores results in a distribution with a mean of 0 and a standard deviation of 1. This conversion does not change the distribution's shape. If the distribution was skewed originally, it remains skewed. If the original distribution was normal, then it remains normal. Once normally distributed scores are converted to z scores, it is possible, using the z table (Appendix J, Table J.1), to ascertain the proportions of the distribution that are associated with any particular z score. This is valuable in answering a variety of questions about IQ, SAT, or other normally distributed sets of scores. For instance, we found that we could easily find the proportion of the curve located between two scores, as well as the percentile rank of a score.

It should come as no surprise that the z score is a commonly used descriptive measure of variability.

GLOSSARY OF TERMS

Inflection point: a point on a graph where the curvature changes from concave to convex or from convex to concave.

Parameter: a measure of a characteristic of a population, such as its mean or its variance.

Raw score: your data as they are originally measured, before any transformation.

Statistic: a measure of a characteristic of a sample, such as it mean.

z score: conversion of raw data so that the deviation is measured in standard deviation units and the sign, positive or negative, indicates the direction of the deviation.

Questions: Chapter 4

(Answers to odd-numbered items are provided in Appendix I.)

1. A z score of −2 indicates that the point is _____.
    a. 2 standard deviations below the mean
    b. 2 standard deviations above the mean
    c. twice the mean
    d. half the mean

2. A "standard" normal curve has a mean of _____ and a standard deviation of _____.
    a. 1; 0
    b. 100; 10
    c. 0; 1
    d. 10; 100

3. In a normal curve, the inflection points occur at _____ standard deviation(s) from the mean.
    a. ±10
    b. ±1
    c. 0
    d. depends on the specific curve

4. Another name for the z score is the _____ score.

   a. normal

   b. special

   c. independent

   d. standard

5. If a distribution of scores is positively skewed, converting each score into a z score will result in a distribution which is _____.

   a. positively skewed

   b. negatively skewed

   c. normal

   d. cannot be answered without additional information

6. What percentage of scores fall below an IQ of 85?

   a. 8

   b. 10

   c. 16

   d. 25

7. On the IQ test, what percentage of people score below 90?

   a. 14.22

   b. 16.31

   c. 21. 06

   d. 25.14

8. On the IQ test, what percentage of people score between 90 and 130?

   a. 82.33

   b. 72.58

   c. 61.04

   d. 50

9. On the IQ test, what percentage of people score between 110 and 145?

   a. 25.01

   b. 27.66

   c. 29.46

   d. 31.27

10. Out of a population of 1,000 individuals, how many would you expect to have an IQ greater than 85?

   a. 670

   b. 734

   c. 803

   d. 841

11. Assuming a normally distributed population with a mean of 50 and a standard deviation of 5, how many people, out of 100, would you expect to score higher than 58 or lower than 48?

   a. 30

   b. 40

   c. 50

   d. 60

12. What IQ score results in 20% of the population scoring above it?

   a. 100

   b. 130

   c. 112.6

   d. 119.2

13. What score results in 40% of the population scoring below it, assuming a mean of 25 and a standard deviation of 4?

   a. 21

   b. 22

   c. 23

   d. 24

14. What score results in 65% of the population scoring below it, assuming a mean of 10 and a standard deviation of 5?

   a. 11.95

   b. 10.55

   c. 11.26

   d. 12.72

15. On any normal distribution, the 50th percentile corresponds to a z score of _____.

   a. 0

   b. +2

   c. +1

   d. −1

16. A z score of +2 indicates that _____.

    a. the raw score is 2 standard deviations below the mean
    b. the raw score is 2 percentage points below the mean
    c. the raw score is 2 standard deviations above the mean
    d. the raw score is 2 percentage points above the mean

17. With a normal curve, the probability of a score occurring above the mean (is) _____.

    a. 0
    b. 0.5
    c. .75
    d. cannot be determined

18. On an exam, a student would prefer an outcome equivalent to a z score of _____.

    a. −1
    b. +1
    c. +0.25
    d. 0

19. With a normal distribution, how many people, out of 100, would you expect to score *between* −1 and +2 standard deviations from the mean?

    a. 82
    b. 16
    c. 66
    d. 84

20. The SAT exam has a mean of 500 and a standard deviation of 100. What is the z score for a SAT exam score of 415?

    a. +0.15
    b. −0.15
    c. +0.85
    d. −0.85

Part II

Computer Assisted Statistical Analysis

5

USING SPSS

The saddest aspect of life right now is that science gathers knowledge faster than society gathers wisdom.

—Isaac Asimov

The calculations involved in solving statistical problems can become tedious, particularly if there is a large set of data. The initial response in the field of statistics was to derive a series of what are called **computational equations**. These equations make analyzing large data sets somewhat easier, and they still are given a prominent role in many undergraduate statistics books. This text relegates them to the appendices. This is because during the past few decades the availability of computers and powerful statistical software has become ubiquitous. The result has been a revolution in how statistics are actually practiced. Though it is still important for statistics students to learn how to calculate answers (this book emphasizes the use of definitional equations, so that you understand what you are calculating), it is also important for students to learn to use a statistical software package. One of the most widely used of these software packages is called **SPSS** (this originally stood for Statistical Package for the Social Sciences). When IBM acquired SPSS, it was renamed PASW, but recently the name has reverted back to SPSS (the official name is IBM SPSS Statistics).

SPSS has undergone numerous revisions over the past several decades. The result is a flexible, user-friendly program. In this chapter, you are introduced to this very important tool. More specifically, we utilize examples from previous chapters so that you can become acquainted with labeling variables,

Computational equations: equations developed to aid in statistical calculations. They were particularly useful with large data sets, but now researchers would employ computer software packages instead.

SPSS: a powerful, commonly used statistical computer package.

entering data, and creating bar graphs, pie charts, and histograms. In subsequent chapters, you will learn additional features of SPSS. Do not be concerned if you are not a computer expert, for basic SPSS is very easy to master.

SPSS is organized so that each column is a variable and each row consists of a subject's data (Figure 5.1). There can be as many variables (columns) or subjects (rows) as desired. You do not need to worry about having too many of either.

OUR FIRST EXAMPLE USING SPSS

To Begin SPSS

Step 1: The first step is to activate the program. You can accomplish this by double clicking on the SPSS icon on the computer's desktop or, if this icon is not evident, by clicking on "Program" and then on SPSS. If you have the PASW version of SPSS, you will then see the window displayed in Figure 5.2. (Other versions of SPSS will have a very similar window.) At this point, you have a number of options. If you click on "Run the tutorial" and then click "OK," you will be guided through a very informative, general introduction to using SPSS. The current chapter's goal is more limited—you will learn how to define variables, enter data by hand, and conduct the descriptive statistics that you have learned in Chapters 1 to 4.

Data view: SPSS window in which the data are displayed.

Step 2: Click on "Type in data" and then click on "OK." The blank screen shown in Figure 5.3 appears. SPSS utilizes two windows. At the bottom left of the current window are two "switches," one labeled **Data View** and the other **Variable View**. As the name suggests, the Data View window

Variable view: SPSS window in which experimental variables are defined.

| Figure 5.1 | Organization of Data in SPSS |

Figure 5.2 The Initial SPSS (PASW) Window

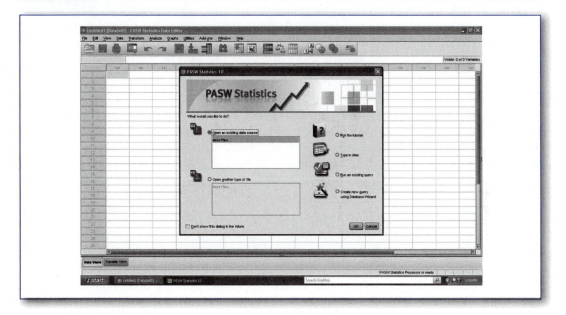

Figure 5.3 The Data View Window

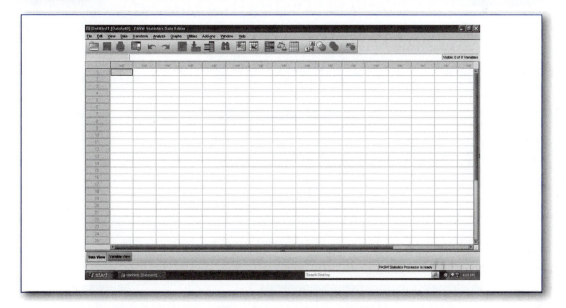

shows the data that the SPSS program is currently using. The Variable View window provides information concerning the variables that are listed in the Data View window.

Step 3: Click on "Variable View." This brings up a window that superficially looks like the Data View window (you can switch back and forth between them). Near the top of this page is a row of column headings, beginning with "Name," then "Type," and proceeding to "Role." For the present, we will only be dealing with the columns headed by "Name," "Label," "Values," and "Measure."

Step 4: Click on the first empty rectangle (called a "cell") under the column heading "Name." The upper left "cell" will turn yellow. You now type the name of the first variable for which you have data. We are going to utilize the same data and labels as were previously used in Table 2.3. As these data dealt with the political preferences of a group of hypothetical subjects, we have only one variable that I call "polparty." SPSS has a series of limitations in choosing variable names—must begin with a letter, no spaces, and certain symbols are not permitted. If you choose an incorrect variable name, you will be alerted with an error message.

Step 5: Click on the first empty "cell" under the column heading "Label." In this cell, you can type a more extensive description of your variable. In our case, type "Political Party Affiliation." Note that to see the entire label you may need to expand the size of this cell by placing your cursor on the right border of the Label heading and moving to the right.

Step 6: Click on the first empty "cell" under the column heading "Values." Then, click on the small blue square. A box will appear as in Figure 5.4. For most analyses, SPSS utilizes

Figure 5.4   The Value Labels Box of the Variable View Window

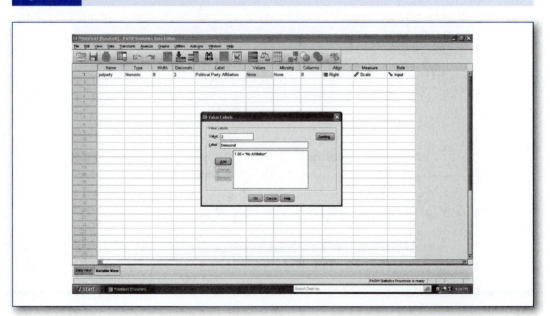

numbers. Thus, we will need to assign a number for each political party affiliation. In the blank space to the right of "Value," type the number "1." Then, type a brief description of this value of the variable in the blank space to the right of "Label." In our case, type "No Affiliation." Finally, click on "Add." Your label for a value of 1 will appear in the large white region in the center of the window. Now repeat the above steps in this section for each of the values in the data set as listed in Table 2.4. Figure 5.5 illustrates what you will see immediately before clicking on "Add" after defining all of the values of the data set. At this point, click on "OK."

Step 7: Click on the first empty "cell" under the column heading "Measure." As we are dealing with nominal data, select "Nominal" as is shown in Figure 5.6. You have now completed the "Variable View" window for the data we are interested in.

Step 8: Click on the "Data View" option at the lower left corner of the window. The label "polparty" will be present in the first variable column.

Step 9: Click on the first empty "cell" under "polparty," and while referring to Table 2.3, type in the number corresponding to the political affiliation of the first subject, in this case 1 as they did not indicate a party affiliation. Continue adding data by clicking on the next empty "cell" in the column under "polparty" until all 25 values have been entered (Figure 5.7). (Note that only values 4 to 25 are visible in this figure. Also, I entered the data by going down the columns in Table 2.3, but entering the data by going across the rows in Table 2.3 would have worked just as well.) You are now ready to use SPSS to describe the data you have entered.

| **Figure 5.5** | The Assignment of Value Labels |

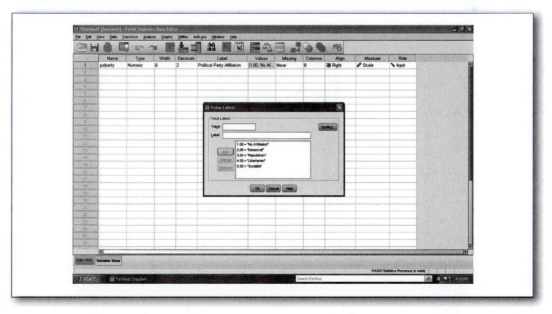

Figure 5.6 The Completed Variable View Window

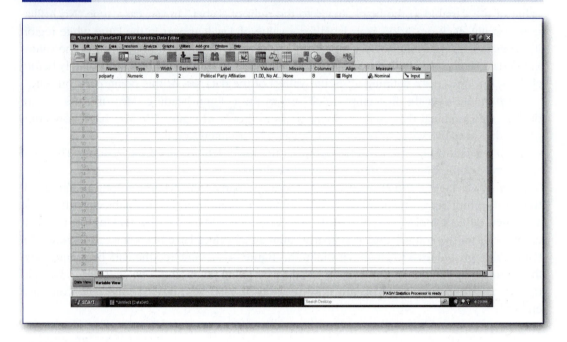

Figure 5.7 The Data View Window

To Find Frequencies

Step 1: Click on "Analyze" at the top of the window as is shown in Figure 5.8.

Figure 5.8 The Analyze Function

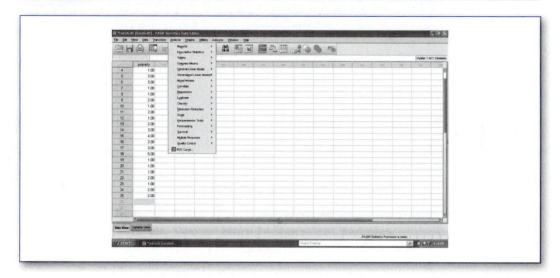

Step 2: Move your cursor down to "Descriptive Statistics." When you do so, an additional window will appear (Figure 5.9).

Figure 5.9 The Descriptive Statistics Function

Step 3: Click on "Frequencies" and the window shown in Figure 5.10 will appear.

Figure 5.10   The Frequencies Window

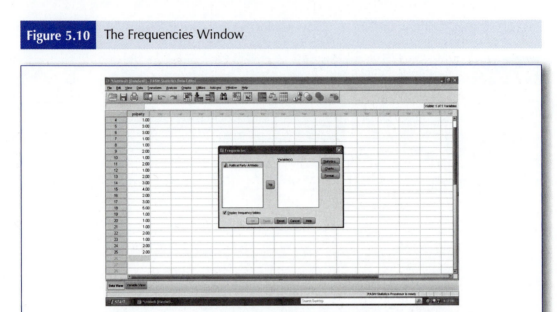

Step 4: Click on the arrow symbol pointing to the right to move the variable label, "Political Party Affiliation" to the rectangle with the heading "Variable(s)" (Figure 5.11). (As we only

Figure 5.11   Using the Frequencies Window

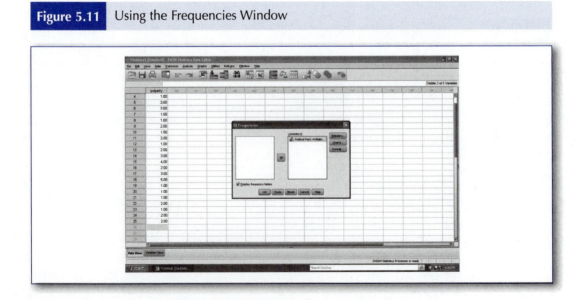

have one variable, this may seem unnecessary, but when you have numerous variables, this is how to indicate to SPSS which variables are currently of interest.)

Step 5: Click on "OK." The result is the output shown in Figure 5.12, which includes the frequencies previously shown in Table 2.4 as well as additional information that may be of interest. This output can be printed and/or saved, if desired.

Step 6: Exit from this output by clicking on the X in the upper right corner. You will be prompted whether you want to save the output. As this is just an exercise, you do not have to save it.

Figure 5.12	An Example of SPSS Output

Frequencies

Statistics

Political Party Affiliation

N	Valid	25
	Missing	0

Political Party Affiliation

		Frequency	Percent	Valid Percent	Cumulative Percent
Valid	No Affiliation	10	40.0	40.0	40.0
	Democrat	7	28.0	28.0	68.0
	Republican	5	20.0	20.0	88.0
	Libertarian	2	8.0	8.0	96.0
	Socialist	1	4.0	4.0	100.0
	Total	25	100.0	100.0	

To Create a Bar Graph

Step 1: You will have been returned to the "Data View" window. Once again, click on "Analyze" at the top of the window, move your cursor down to "Descriptive Statistics," and then click on "Frequencies." You should return to the window shown in Figure 5.11. Click your cursor on "Charts," and indicate which of the charts or graphs is wanted. As we desire a bar graph, "Bar charts" has been selected in Figure 5.13.

Figure 5.13   Selecting a Bar Graph

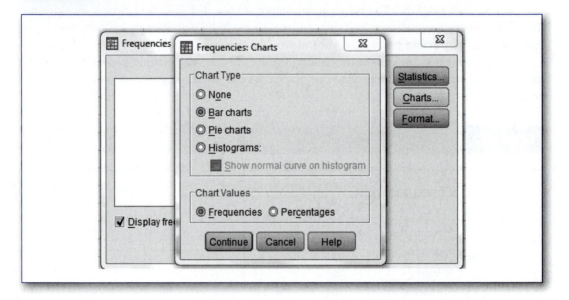

Step 2: Click on "Continue." If you do not want to see the frequency distribution again, click on the check box in front of the phrase "Display frequency tables," and then "OK," and you will see just the bar graph shown in Figure 5.14.

Step 3: Exit from this output by clicking on the X in the upper right corner. You will be prompted whether you want to save the output. As this is just an exercise, you do not have to save this graph.

To Create a Pie Chart

Step 1: To create a pie chart of your frequencies, we repeat the steps used for creating a bar graph except that when we reach Figure 5.13, we select "Pie charts."

Step 2: Click on "Continue." If you do not want to see the frequency distribution again, click on the check box in front of the phrase "Display frequency tables," and then click "OK," and you will see just the pie chart shown in Figure 5.15.

Step 3: Exit from this output by clicking on the X in the upper right corner. You will be prompted whether you want to save the output. Once again, as this is just an exercise, you do not have to save this chart. (You may want to practice making additional bar graphs and pie charts.) If you continue exiting, you will return to the Data View window. Exiting from this window will result in another prompt asking if you want to save the data. As this is just an example, there is no need to save the data unless you feel you might want to practice making bar graphs and pie charts using these data in the future.

Figure 5.14	The Bar Graph

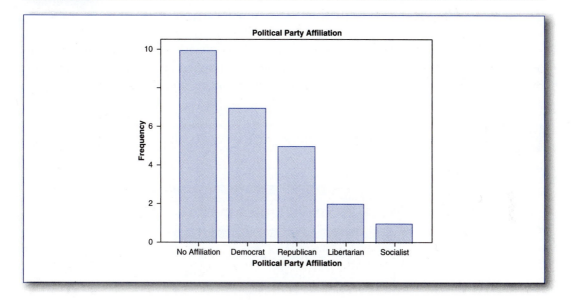

Figure 5.15	The Pie Chart

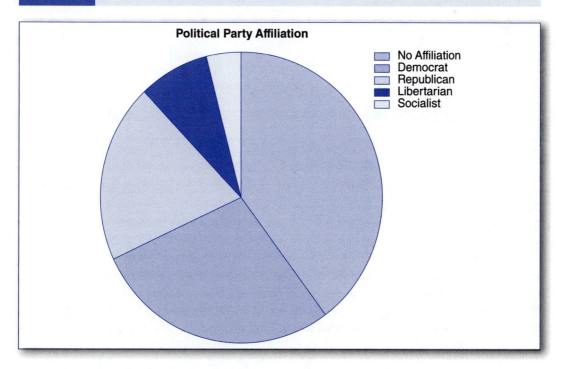

A SECOND EXAMPLE USING SPSS

To Begin SPSS Proceed as in the Previous Example

Step 1: Activate the program by double clicking on the SPSS icon on the computer's desktop or, if this icon is not evident, by clicking on "Program" and then on SPSS. At this point, you will see a window, and you will be given a number of options (Figure 5.16).

Figure 5.16   The Initial SPSS (PASW) Window

Step 2: Click on "Type in data" and then click on "OK." The blank screen shown in Figure 5.17 appears.

Step 3: Click on "Variable View." This brings up the Variable View window (Figure 5.18).

Step 4: Click on the first empty cell under the column heading "Name." We are going to utilize the same data and labels as were previously used in Table 3.1. As these data dealt with the incomes of 10 hypothetical students, we have only one variable which I call "income." Note that this variable name is appropriate for SPSS—it begins with a letter, there are no spaces, and it does not include any disallowed symbols.

Figure 5.17 The Data View Window

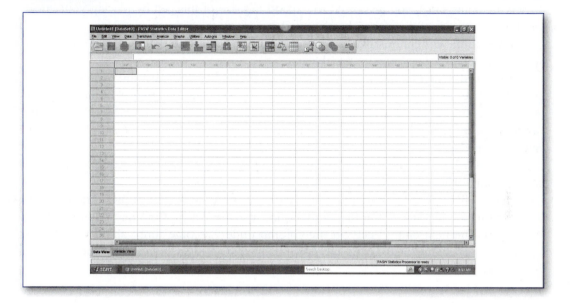

Figure 5.18 The Variable View Window

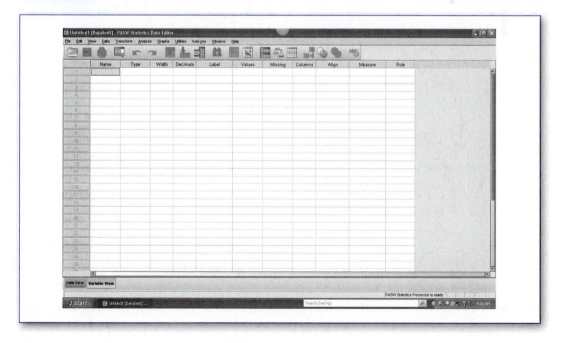

Step 5: Click on the first empty "cell" under the column heading "Label." In this cell, I have typed "Income of College Students" as a more extensive description of our variable. Note that to see the entire label, you may need to expand the size of this cell by placing your cursor on the right border of the "Label" heading and moving to the right.

Step 6: In the current example, all of the data are expressed in dollars. Therefore, there is no need to label "Values" of your variable.

Step 7: Check that in the first "cell" under the column heading "Measure," you see "Scale." In SPSS, "Scale" indicates that the data are at either the interval or ratio level of measurement. As our data are measured in dollars, and this is a ratio level of measurement, "Scale" is the appropriate entry. You have now completed the "Variable View" window for the data we are interested in (Figure 5.19).

Step 8: Click on the "Data View" option at the lower left corner of the window. The variable "income" will now be present.

Step 9: Click on the first empty "cell" under "income" and type in the number corresponding to the income of the first student, in this case 20000. Continue adding data by clicking on the next empty "cell" in the column under "income" until all 10 values have been entered (Figure 5.20). You are now ready to use SPSS to describe the data you have entered.

Figure 5.19   Defining a Label Within the Variable View Window

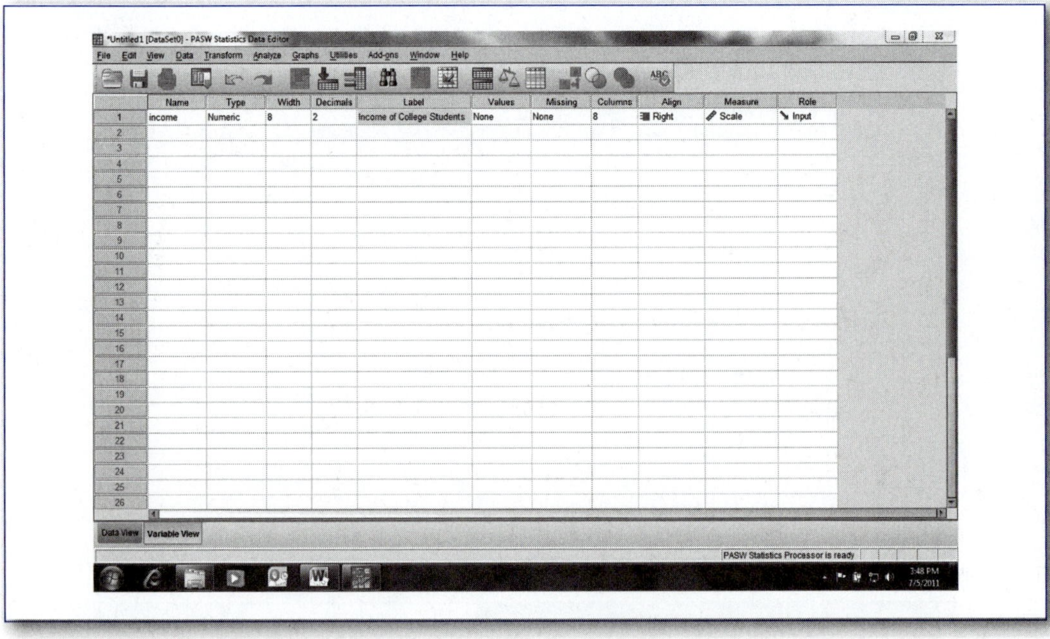

Figure 5.20	Entering Data in the Data View Window

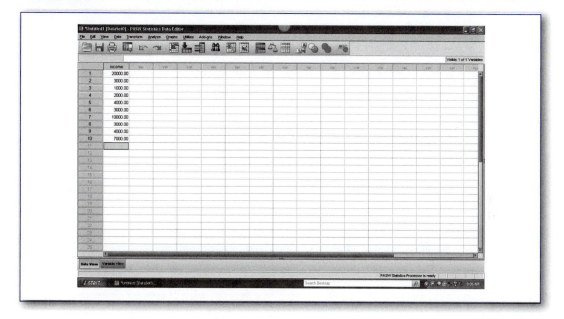

To Find Frequencies

Step 1: Click on "Analyze" at the top of the Data View window.

Step 2: Move your cursor down to "Descriptive Statistics." When you do so, an additional window will appear (Figure 5.21).

Step 3: Click on "Frequencies" and the window shown in Figure 5.22 will appear.

Step 4: Click on the arrow symbol pointing to the right to move the variable label, "Income of College Students," to the rectangle with the heading "Variable(s)" (Figure 5.23).

Step 5: Click on "OK." The result is the output shown in Figure 5.24, which includes the frequencies previously shown in Table 3.2 as well as additional information that may be of interest. This output can be printed and/or saved, if desired.

Step 6: Exit from this output by clicking on the X in the upper right corner. You will be prompted whether you want to save the output. As this is just an exercise, you do not have to save this output.

To Create a Histogram

Redo the most recent Steps 1, 2, and 3 above. You will have been returned to the window shown in Figure 5.23.

Figure 5.21 The Descriptive Statistics Function

Figure 5.22 The Frequencies Window

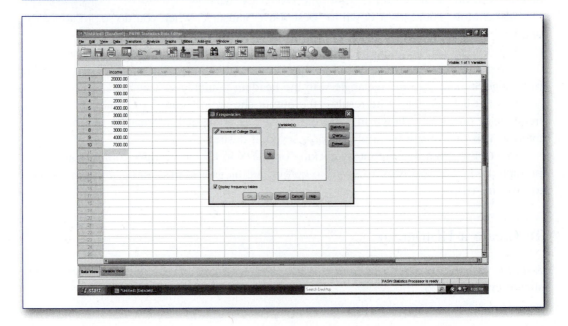

Figure 5.23   Using the Frequencies Window

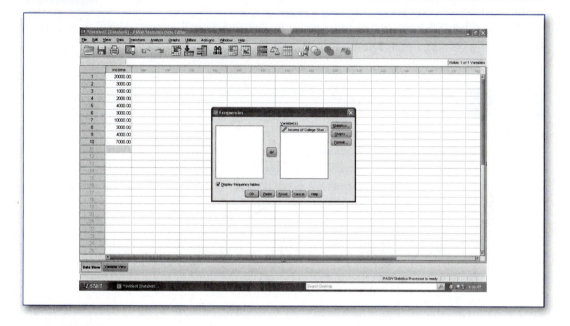

Figure 5.24   An Example of SPSS Output

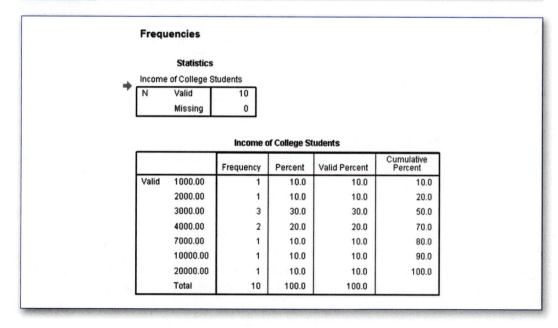

Frequencies

Statistics

Income of College Students

N	Valid	10
	Missing	0

Income of College Students

		Frequency	Percent	Valid Percent	Cumulative Percent
Valid	1000.00	1	10.0	10.0	10.0
	2000.00	1	10.0	10.0	20.0
	3000.00	3	30.0	30.0	50.0
	4000.00	2	20.0	20.0	70.0
	7000.00	1	10.0	10.0	80.0
	10000.00	1	10.0	10.0	90.0
	20000.00	1	10.0	10.0	100.0
	Total	10	100.0	100.0	

Step 4: Click on "Charts" and then "Histograms" and then "Continue." If you do not want to see the frequency distribution again, click on the check box in front of the phrase "Display frequency tables."

Step 5: Click "OK" and just the histogram in Figure 5.25 will appear. This is a somewhat condensed version of the histogram in Figure 3.1.

Figure 5.25   The SPSS Histogram

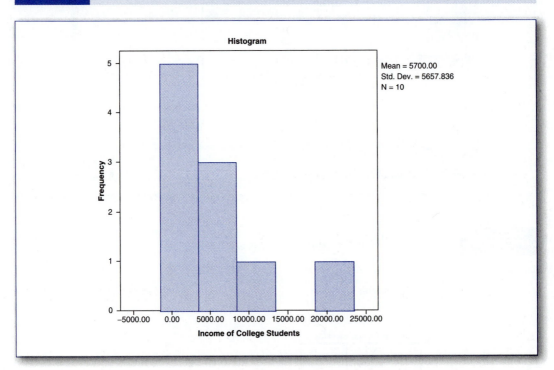

Step 6: Exit from this output by clicking on the X in the upper right corner. You will be prompted whether you want to save the output. As this is just an exercise, there is no need to save this output.

CONCLUSION

Hopefully, you will agree that there isn't anything difficult about creating frequencies, bar graphs, pie charts, or histograms with SPSS. The important points to remember are as follows:

1. Each column in SPSS is a different variable.

2. Each row is a different subject.

3. Use the "Variable View" window to name and label variables.

4. Use the "Data View" window to enter data.

5. Use "Analyze" to find descriptive statistics.

6. Use "Charts" to create bar graphs, pie charts, and histograms. But remember, we use bar graphs with nominal or ordinal data, pie charts with nominal data, and histograms with interval or ratio data.

Chapter Resources

GLOSSARY OF TERMS

Computational equations: equations developed to aid in statistical calculations. They were particularly useful with large data sets, but now researchers would employ computer software packages instead.

Data view: SPSS window in which the data are displayed.

SPSS: a powerful, commonly used statistical computer package.

Variable view: SPSS window in which experimental variables are defined.

Questions: Chapter 5

(Answers to odd-numbered items are provided in Appendix I.)

1. To make calculation of large data sets easier, statisticians created _____.

    a. a special, easily read type

    b. computational equations

    c. a unique form of slide rule

    d. a rule to round off all decimals to whole numbers

2. If you were using SPSS and wanted to enter data to an already existing data file, you would go to the _____ window to enter a subject's responses.

    a. variable

    b. output

    c. data

    d. graphing

3. If you had already entered your data and now wanted to create a pie chart, which SPSS command would you begin with if you were at the data view window?

   a. Analyze

   b. Graphs

   c. Compute

   d. Pie chart

4. Each column in the SPSS Data View window signifies a _____.

   a. subject

   b. experimental condition

   c. different type of statistical analysis

   d. variable

5. Each row in the SPSS Data View window signifies a _____.

   a. subject

   b. experimental condition

   c. different type of statistical analysis

   d. variable

6. To provide labels to clarify the meaning of the data, you would go to the _____.

   a. data View window

   b. variable View window

   c. analyze function

   d. graphs function

SPSS Problems: Chapter 5

1. Twenty students take an exam in statistics and receive the following grades:

B	B	B	C
A	A	B	A
C	C	E	B
A	D	A	B
B	C	C	D

Enter these data in SPSS (using A = 4, B = 3, C = 2, D = 1, and E = 0), and then find the frequencies and make a bar graph.

2. Twenty-five students report how many movies they have seen in the last week:

5	4	2	0	4
10	2	1	1	0
0	2	3	3	1
6	0	4	2	3
3	5	8	1	2

Enter your data in SPSS and then find the frequencies and make a histogram.

Part III

Inferential Statistics

Thinking Clearly About Data

THE LOGIC OF INFERENTIAL STATISTICS

The Distinction Between Difference and Association Questions

By a small sample, we may judge of the whole piece.

—Miquel de Cervantes from *Don Quixote*

WHERE WE HAVE BEEN

To this point in the book, we have dealt with descriptive statistics, the procedures used to summarize data. More specifically, we have reviewed frequency distributions, as well as the measures that are employed for central tendency and variability. As you will recall, the frequency distribution provides a rapid view of the entire set of data, while the measures of central tendency and variability are single numbers that best summarize the location and spread of data, respectively. As Table 6.1 indicates, the specific procedure chosen depends on whether you are dealing with nominal, ordinal, or interval/ratio data. With the procedures that have been reviewed, you are in an excellent position to communicate a maximum amount of information in an efficient manner.

WHERE WE ARE GOING

The remainder of the text deals with inferential statistics. These procedures are used when making data-based decisions. Specifically, we will be concerned with whether the evidence for

Table 6.1	An Overview of Descriptive Statistics

Descriptive Statistics (Summarizing Data)	Type of Data		
	Nominal	Ordinal	Interval Ratio
Frequency distribution	Bar graph or pie chart	Bar graph	Histogram or frequency polygon
Central tendency	Mode	Median	Mean
Variability	—	Range	Standard deviation and z score

a relationship or pattern that is observed in a sample is sufficient to warrant concluding that the same relationship also exists in a population. In other words, we will be dealing with the question of whether a finding is likely to generalize. By the end of the book, it will be evident that inferential statistics are very powerful tools that can be used in a wide variety of situations.

Before beginning our discussion of inferential statistics, it may be helpful to briefly review the distinction between a sample and a population. Recall that a population consists of all of the individuals that are potentially of interest. For instance, if we were interested in the effectiveness of a cancer therapy, the population would be all of the individuals who have cancer. Clearly, it is impractical to conduct a study that would examine every member of such a large population. Instead, we commonly select a subset of a population to examine. This subset is called a sample.

The sample should be chosen carefully. The goal is to select the members of the sample in such a way that any observed relationship can be generalized to the population that is of interest.

Random sample: a sample in which every member or subset of the population has an equal chance of being chosen.

For instance, let us assume that we are interested in what effect reducing legroom will have on passenger satisfaction on intercontinental airline flights. If the sample consists only of basketball players, then it is questionable whether the findings will generalize to the population of all passengers. Usually, the optimal procedure for choosing an appropriate sample is to randomly select the subjects. In a **random sample**, every member or subset of the population has an equal chance of being chosen to be in the sample.

Decisions, Decisions, Decisions

For the remainder of the book, you will be using samples to make decisions concerning populations. More specifically, you will be learning a set of agreed-on procedures for making these decisions. Which procedure is appropriate depends on the type of research design employed, as well as the type of data collected. As Table 6.2 indicates, there are, fundamentally, two types of research questions, and therefore two types of research designs. **Difference designs** examine whether an observed difference is likely to have been the result of chance or, instead, provides

> Difference designs: research undertaken to determine whether an observed difference is likely to generalize.

Table 6.2	An Overview of Inferential Statistics

	Type of Data			
	Nominal (Frequency)		**Ordinal** (Ranked)	**Interval/Ratio** (Continuous Measure)
Inferential Statistics (Finding Relationships)				
Statistical procedures for difference and interaction designs				
One variable with at least two outcomes	Goodness-of-fit chi-square	**One IV with one sample—one DV**		One-sample z score or one-sample t test
		One IV with two or more independent samples—one DV	*Kruskal–Wallis H*[a]	One-way between-subjects ANOVA (only two independent samples—independent samples t test)
		One IV with one sample having two or more repeated measures—one DV		One-way within-subjects ANOVA (only two repeated measures—dependent samples t test)
Two variables, each with at least two outcomes	Chi-square test of independence	**Two IV each with two or more independent samples—one DV**		Two-way between-subjects ANOVA
Statistical procedures for association designs				
Correlation	Phi		*Spearman r*[b]	Pearson r
Regression				Linear regression *Multiple regression*[c]

Notes. IV, independent variable; DV, dependent variable; ANOVA, analysis of variance. Research designs are shown in boldface. Italicized items are reviewed in the following appendixes:

a. Appendix A.

b. Appendix B.

c. Appendix C.

evidence of a real or systematic effect. The research undertaken to determine whether an observed difference is likely to generalize is called a difference design. If the experiment is properly designed and conducted, findings will generalize to the population. This means that conclusions can be drawn regarding the population based on sample data. There are a large number of difference designs. In addition, some difference designs provide a measure of interaction. We will be discussing this concept later.

Association designs are the other major type of research design. They *examine whether an association between variables is likely to have been the result of chance or, instead, provide evidence of a systematic effect.* Once again, if the research is properly designed and conducted, the findings based on samples will generalize to the corresponding populations.

> *Association designs: research undertaken to determine whether an observed association is likely to generalize.*

As Table 6.2 indicates, the choice of the appropriate statistical procedure is not only dependent on the research design (bolded descriptions in Table 6.2), it is also a function of the measurement scale that was utilized. In other words, for inferential statistics, as for descriptive statistics, whether the data are nominal, ordinal, or interval/ratio is important in choosing the appropriate statistical procedure.

You may feel intimidated by Table 6.2. Don't be. The remainder of this book will walk you through each test in turn. You mastered descriptive statistics, and you will master inferential statistics. The goal of the remainder of this book is to assist you in understanding when it is appropriate to use each test and how to conduct each of them and to show how these procedures are related.

A Little History

To appreciate why we use what may seem like an unnecessarily complex decision-making system, it is important to recognize that it is part of a many centuries–long process that has culminated in what we call the scientific method. Before the scientific method was developed, there were other approaches for making decisions. Probably the most common was tradition, you do what has been done in the past. A major advance occurred when the ancient Greeks employed what is sometimes called **intrinsic plausibility**. In this system, alternative explanations were identified and then the explanation that was judged to be the most plausible was accepted as being true. We continue to use this approach, and in many cases, it is effective. Unfortunately, it is also likely that incorrect decisions will be made using this method. One of the major problems is that this method is susceptible to bias. At one time it was "known" that the earth was the center

> *Intrinsic plausibility: decision-making process in which the alternative that seems most reasonable is accepted as being true.*

of the universe and that the sun went around it. This was the most plausible explanation for the observation that the sun rose in the east every morning and set in the west every evening. Unfortunately, though plausible, it was incorrect. In addition, views of racial and sexual superiority and inferiority were, in the not too distant past, almost universally accepted. Those views seemed plausible to most people at the time. We no longer accept those views as logically defensible, and they are not supported by the relevant data. Numerous other examples could be cited.

By the end of the 17th century, a different approach to finding truth was evident in western Europe. It is what we now call the **scientific method.** It has been refined into such a powerful approach that it may well be the most significant Western contribution to world civilization. The scientific method seeks to identify relationships and express them mathematically. It relies on a foundation of rigorous logic, but careful observation is the ultimate authority for determining truth. In other words, no matter how elegant the idea, if observations of nature do not provide support for it, the idea is rejected.

Scientific method: an approach to understanding that emphasizes rigorous logic and that careful observation is the ultimate authority for determining truth. It is a self-correcting approach that limits bias.

The scientific method does not ensure that every conclusion will be correct. However, a defining feature of the scientific method is that it is self-correcting. What this means is that even if a conclusion is incorrect, or only partially correct, the process of scientific inquiry will, in time, provide a more adequate explanation. An example of this is the revolution that occurred in physics early in the 20th century. Newton's laws of motion had been proposed in the 17th century. They adequately accounted for everyday experience. However, the behavior of events at very high speeds, such as the speed of light, required a different explanation. This was provided by Einstein. Clearly, Einstein's theory is able to account for more than Newton's. However, neither Newton's nor Einstein's theory can account for the behavior of very small, subatomic particles. As a result, a great deal of effort is currently being devoted to developing an even more general theory.

Along with being self-corrective, the scientific method is efficient. One of the greatest advantages of this approach is that a researcher does not have to start from scratch. Instead, new research builds on what has already been discovered. Research directions that are not productive are not pursued. Thus, effort is focused on areas with the greatest potential for success. It is this economy of effort that has led to our increasingly rapid technological advances, increased life spans, higher standards of living, and, unfortunately, the threat of nuclear war and global warming.

How Science Works

A critical component of the scientific method is making a comparison. To make a comparison, there must either be at least two groups, or one group versus some standard. For instance, if we wanted to know if a coin was fair, we would compare the results of tossing it a number of times with the expected outcome of an equal number of heads and tails. In this case, there would be only one set of data, and we would compare it against what the data would be expected to be if the coin was fair.

It is important to note that some difference from the expected 50:50 ratio of heads and tails might have occurred even with a fair coin. After all, by chance we would expect to see some deviation from the predicted ratio. So how can we determine whether a difference that we observe in this ratio is the result of an unfair coin or is simply due to chance variation? One clue would be how great this difference is. Differences in ratios of heads and tails due to chance alone would be expected to be small. On the other hand, it is at least possible that an unfair coin would lead to a ratio of heads and tails that is substantially different from the expected 50:50 ratio.

Alternatively, if we were interested in learning whether listening to a motivational speech would affect listeners' scores on an exam, we could randomly select two samples of subjects. Then, we could have the subjects in only one of the samples listen to the motivational speech. Finally, we would determine the scores on the exam for all of the subjects and check to see if there was a difference between the two groups. In this situation, there would be two sets of data that would be compared. This experimental design can be summarized as the following:

Control group: in a between-groups design, the group of subjects that does not receive the treatment.

Group 1: no treatment

Group 2: treatment

The group of subjects that does *not* receive the treatment is called the **control group**. The group of subjects that does receive the treatment is called the **experimental group**. While some difference between the two groups would be expected by chance, a large difference in the exam scores of the two groups would be evidence that the treatment had an effect.

Experimental group: in a between-groups design, the group of subjects that does receive the treatment.

In this example, the researcher is in control of who listens to the motivational speech. The researcher then examines the subsequent exam scores. Thus, two things are varying in this simple experiment. One variable, who listens to the motivational speech, is controlled or manipulated by the experimenter and is called the **independent variable (IV)**. The experimenter wishes to determine whether the magnitude of the other variable, exam scores, is dependent on the value of the IV that the subject receives. This is called the **dependent variable (DV)**.

Independent variable (IV): in an experiment, the variable the experimenter manipulates or directly controls.

Dependent variable (DV): in an experiment, the variable whose value is not directly controlled by the researcher. Its value may be changed by the independent variable.

MAKING AN EXPERIMENTALLY BASED DECISION

The only relevant test of the validity of a hypothesis is comparison of its predictions with experience.

–Milton Friedman

We just noted that an outcome might, or might not, be what was expected, and that a treatment might, or might not, have an effect. Scientists refer to these two possible outcomes as hypotheses. Thus, with a difference design, the **null hypothesis**, symbolized as H_0, is usually either that the situation is as expected (the coin is fair), or that the treatment does *not* have an effect (the motivational speech does not have an effect). The **alternative hypothesis**, symbolized as H_1, is that the situation is not as expected (the coin is not fair), or that the treatment does have an effect (the motivational speech changes exam scores). The goal of an experiment is to permit the researcher to distinguish between these two possible alternatives.

> *Null hypothesis (H_0): when used with a difference design, the statement that the treatment does not have an effect.*

> *Alternative hypothesis (H_1): when used with a difference design, the statement that the treatment does have an effect.*

To understand how a statistical procedure can assist in determining whether the null or alternative hypothesis is supported, let us return to our example of the experiment examining the effect of a motivational speech on exam scores. As explained previously, we would not be surprised if the mean exam scores of the control and experimental groups differed slightly. The question remains, how discrepant do the two means have to be to reject the null hypothesis that any difference is due to chance variation? In other words, how large a difference must be observed to conclude that the treatment had an effect on the exam scores? There is no absolute answer to this question. Statisticians provide an answer based on the likelihood or probability of the null hypothesis being true. In most fields, it has come to be accepted that if an outcome would be expected to occur, by chance, less than 1 time in 20 if the null hypothesis were true, then we reject the null hypothesis and accept the alternative hypothesis. One time in 20 is equivalent to .05 or 5%. There is nothing magical about .05. A different criterion such as .01 can be, and sometimes is, chosen. A criterion of .01 is equivalent to an outcome occurring only 1 time in 100 by chance. If a criterion of .01 is chosen, then we retain the null hypothesis unless an outcome is so unlikely that it would be expected to occur in less than 1 out of 100 cases by chance. We will discuss the reasons for using different criteria shortly. For now, it is important to understand that choosing a probability to differentiate between the null and alternative hypotheses is a critical part of experimentation. In fact, it is so important that the exact value that is chosen is given a name, the **alpha level**. Its symbol is the Greek letter alpha (α). As was just pointed out, the alpha level is commonly set at .05, but it could be some other value, such as .01.

> *Alpha level: criterion set for rejecting the null hypothesis. This is usually .05.*

In the example just given, the null hypothesis was that the treatment would not have an effect. The alternative hypothesis was that the treatment would have an effect. The null hypothesis would be rejected, therefore, if the mean for the experimental group's exam scores was either very high or very low. If we reject the null hypothesis, the alternative hypothesis will be accepted. However, if the mean of the experimental group is not so different from the mean of the control group, the null hypothesis will be retained.

Whew, That Was a Lot to Remember

Summarizing to this point, when conducting an experiment we define a null hypothesis and an alternative hypothesis. These are mutually exclusive views of what the true situation is. We tentatively accept that the null hypothesis is true unless there is sufficient evidence from the experiment to indicate that this is unlikely. The criterion for deciding how unlikely the outcome must be to reject the null hypothesis is set by the experimenter when the alpha level is chosen. If the null hypothesis is rejected, we then tentatively accept that the alternative hypothesis is correct. We use the word *tentatively* because it is important to recognize that with statistics we do not "prove" that a difference exists. Remember, in science we can make errors. However, further experiments would detect the error, and thus, the procedure is self-correcting.

PROGRESS CHECK

1. In an experiment, the variable that the experimenter directly controls or manipulates is called the _____.

2. The possible outcome of an experiment that indicates that the treatment does have an effect is called the _____.

3. The criterion the experimenter sets for rejecting the null hypothesis is called the _____, and it is usually set at 1 chance in 20, or .05.

Answers: 1. independent variable.   2. alternative hypothesis.   3. alpha level.

PROBABILITY, ERROR, AND POWER

Absolute certainty is a privilege of uneducated minds—and fanatics. It is, for scientific folk, an unattainable ideal.

—Cassius J. Keyser

The decision-making process that we have been reviewing is based on the probabilities of outcomes. If an outcome is unlikely to have happened by chance, we reject the null and accept the alternative hypothesis. By rejecting the null hypothesis, we have not proven that it is incorrect. We are simply stating that, assuming alpha was set to .05, the odds are less than 5% that the observed difference happened by chance. It is possible, therefore, that we could be making an error when we reject the null hypothesis. In fact, we know the probability of rejecting the null hypothesis when it is true. That probability is **alpha**, which is usually 5%. In other words, if alpha is set at .05, then in 1 comparison out of 20 we will reject the null hypothesis when it is in fact true. This is called **Type I error**.

> *Alpha: another term for Type I error. Its symbol is α.*

No one likes to make errors. It might occur to you that it would be possible to reduce the probability of making a Type I error by simply reducing the size of alpha from .05 to .01. It is true that this step would reduce the Type I error rate. Unfortunately, it would also have the unintended effect of increasing the probability of another type of error. By decreasing the Type I error rate, such as by setting alpha to .01 instead of .05, you make it harder to reject the null hypothesis. This is good if the null hypothesis is true. However, by decreasing alpha to .01 you simultaneously increase the likelihood that you will fail to reject the null hypothesis when it is in fact false. Failing to reject the null hypothesis when it is false is

> *Type I error: the probability of rejecting the null hypothesis when it is in fact true. This probability is equal to alpha, α, which is usually 5%.*

> *Type II error: the probability of retaining the null hypothesis when it is in fact false. This probability is equal to beta, β, which is usually not known.*

known as **Type II error**. Thus, as the probability of making a Type I error decreases, the probability of making a Type II error increases. The choice of the alpha level, therefore, will reflect which of these two types of error is felt to be most critical. Clearly, the consequences of failing to detect that a nuclear plant is unsafe are quite different than failing to detect that a new method of teaching chess is effective.

The probability of making a Type II error is called beta, and its symbol is the Greek letter β. The exact value of beta is not usually known. As was just discussed, what is known is that assuming nothing else in the experiment changes, if you reduce Type I error, you will increase Type II error. The reverse is also true.

The relationship between Type I and Type II errors is shown in Table 6.3.

Table 6.3   Relationship Between Type I and Type II Errors

		Actual Truth of the Null Hypothesis (which, of course, you do not know)	
		Null Is True	**Null Is False**
Decision from the experiment	**Null is true**	Correct decision	Type II error
	Null is false	Type I error	Correct decision

Power: the probability of correctly rejecting a false null hypothesis. The probability is $1 - \beta$.

We are thus faced with a dilemma. We want to make the correct decision, of course, but if we reduce one type of error, we simultaneously increase the probability of the other type. Is there anything that can be done? When statisticians address this issue, they introduce the concept of **power**. Power is simply the probability of correctly rejecting a false null hypothesis. Fundamentally, *the goal of experimentation is to conduct as powerful a study as possible.*

The probability of power is $1 - \beta$. Of course, we just learned that we rarely know the precise probability of β, so we usually do not know the probability of $1 - \beta$ either. However, the concept of power is still very useful. Even though we usually do not know its probability, we can take steps to increase the power of our study. Some of these steps are listed in Table 6.4.

As Table 6.4 indicates, one step that the researcher can take to increase the power of an experiment is to choose a treatment level that is likely to cause a noticeable effect. In some cases, this can be determined from previous, successful studies. In other cases, the researcher will have to make an educated guess. For instance, if you are studying the effect of sleep deprivation on ability to do math calculations, it is not likely that you will find an effect if the sleep deprivation consists of only a loss of 15 minutes of sleep a night. You would be more likely to find an effect if the size of this intervention were much greater. Perhaps a deprivation of 2 or 3 hours would be a wiser choice.

A second step that you may be able to take is to choose a measure that uses interval or ratio data. The statistical tests that are employed with interval or ratio data are more efficient than those that use ordinal or nominal data. This means that you will not need as many subjects to detect the same size effect if you use interval or ratio data. If you cannot use interval or ratio data, your next best choice would be to use ordinal rather than nominal data.

Choosing alpha to be .05 rather than .01 will also increase the likelihood of rejecting the null hypothesis when in fact it is false. Of course, by taking this action you will increase the probability of making a Type I error, but 5% is usually an acceptable level for this type of error. Remember, the scientific method is self-correcting, so if an error is made, future research will tend to correct it.

Table 6.4	Some Steps That Will Increase Power
1	Pick a treatment that is likely to have a large effect
2	Choose a measurement scale that has as much information as possible
3	Increase the alpha level (e.g., from .01 to .05)
4	Increase the sample size
5	Conduct the study so that sources of error are minimized

All else being equal, having larger samples will make rejecting the null hypothesis easier. For instance, with interval or ratio data, the means of larger samples are expected to vary less from each other by chance than the means of smaller samples. As a result, with large samples you do not need as large a difference between the experimental and control groups to reject the null hypothesis.

Finally, any steps that you can take to reduce error while conducting the study will increase the power of your study. Among the steps to be considered are using consistent procedures with all of the subjects and controlling conditions such as temperature and humidity during testing.

Real-World Limitations

As the previous overview of the scientific method indicated, the optimal features of an experiment are random assignment of subjects and manipulation of the IV. When both random assignment and manipulation of the IV have occurred, we have what is called a **true experiment**. And assuming the research has been carefully conducted, the experimenter is justified in rejecting the null hypothesis and accepting the alternative hypothesis based on the outcome of the study. More specifically, the researcher can come to what is called a cause and effect conclusion; the change in the value of the IV resulted in a change in the value of the DV. Of course, as was noted previously, this is a probabilistic decision. It is always possible that a Type I error has occurred. However, the probability of making a Type I error, called alpha, is known and is small.

True experiment: an experiment in which the researcher randomly assigns the subjects and also manipulates the value of the independent variable. As a result, at the conclusion of the study, the researcher is justified in reaching a cause and effect conclusion concerning the relationship between the independent and dependent variables.

An example of a true experiment is the classic Bobo doll research begun by Bandura, Ross, and Ross (1961). This research, which has involved a number of studies, examined imitation of aggression in children. In these studies, subjects were randomly assigned to either the control group or one of several experimental groups. The experimenter controlled whether the subject observed aggressive or nonaggressive behavior (there were a number of conditions). Then, the number of aggressive responses made by each child was recorded. It was found that when they were frustrated, many of the children imitated the specific aggressive behavior they had previously witnessed. This is an example of a true experiment for there is random assignment of the subjects and experimenter control of the IV.

However, in many real-world situations, it is not possible for an experimenter to randomly assign subjects and manipulate the variable that is of interest. In these cases the scientific method can still be employed, but the strength of the conclusion that the researcher is justified in making is reduced. For instance, if the researcher can manipulate the IV but cannot randomly assign the subjects, then the study has some, but not all, of the character-istics of a true experiment. Accordingly, it is called a **quasi-experiment**. Compared with a true experiment, we are now less confident that a difference found at the conclusion of the study is due to the manipulation of the IV. For example, in a classic series of studies Gazzaniga (1967) examined people whose corpus callosum (a band of neurons connecting the two hemispheres of the brain) had been surgi-cally cut to prevent the spread of seizure activity. These subjects were asked to identify objects placed in either of their hands, while they were prevented from looking. Briefly, when the object was placed in the right hand, the subjects could name it. How-ever, when the object was placed in the left hand, they could not name it. As the neural inputs cross, this is evidence that the ability to verbally name objects is lateralized to the left hemisphere. You should recognize that this is a quasi-experimental design. The subjects are not being randomly assigned. Instead, they come to the study with or without having had the corpus callosum cut. How-ever, the experimenter is in control of the IV, the placement of the objects to be named. The results of these studies are dramatic. And no one is going to seriously suggest that a researcher should instead conduct a true experiment, for this would require random assignment of subjects to undergo surgery!

Quasi-experiment: an experiment in which the researcher manipulates the value of the independent variable but does not randomly assign the subjects. As a result, at the conclusion of the study, the researcher has less confidence in concluding that there is a cause and effect relationship between the independent and dependent variables than with a true experiment.

Correlational study: a study in which the researcher does not randomly assign the subjects and does not manipulate the value of a variable. As a result, at the conclusion of the study, the researcher has little confidence that there is a cause and effect relationship between the variables.

Alternatively, it may not be possible for the researcher to randomly assign the subjects or to manipulate a variable. This is a **correlational study**. Due to the lack of control, we have even less confidence concerning the strength of the obtained relationship. All that can be stated is that the variables are related. As the researcher did not manipulate a variable, there is neither an IV nor a DV. Either variable could be causing a change in the other, both could be affecting each other, or some other variable(s) could be affecting them both. For example, it is commonly noted that football teams that have a propen-sity to turn the ball over to the other team are also more likely to lose the game. This may seem to be an obvious cause and effect relationship—repeatedly giving the ball to the opponent causes an increase in the likelihood of losing the game. However, it is important to recognize that this is a correlation, for there is neither random assignment nor experimenter control of a variable. And on closer inspection, the interpretation of the relationship becomes somewhat less certain. For instance, the likelihood of turnovers increases if a team is passing rather than running when they have possession of the ball. And teams that are already far behind are more likely to rely on passing the ball as a desperate means to score quickly. In other words, what seemed initially like an obvious cause and effect relationship, turnovers cause teams to lose, is more complex for teams that are already losing are also more likely to have turnovers!

CONCLUSION

The first section of this book dealt with descriptive statistics. These are the procedures that we use to summarize a set of data. This chapter is an introduction to inferential statistics. Inferential statistics are a set of procedures that assist us in determining whether a relationship or pattern observed with a sample(s) is likely to generalize to a population(s). The remainder of the book will be dealing with inferential statistics.

No new statistical procedures were introduced in this chapter. Instead, the emphasis was on reviewing the logic of hypothesis testing. The remainder of the text will build on this foundation. It is important, therefore, that you master the concepts and the associated terms described in this chapter. Specifically, the null and alternative hypotheses were defined in the context of a between-groups experiment. Then, the rationale for making probabilistic decisions, and thus the necessity of choosing an alpha level, was covered. It was noted that statistical procedures assist in the decision-making process but do not ensure that every conclusion will be correct. This led to a discussion of Type I and Type II errors. The steps that a researcher can take that will increase the power of a study were then briefly described. Finally, the distinctions between a true experiment, quasi-experiment, and a correlational study were introduced.

It should be noted that the logic of hypothesis testing applies equally well to studies that employ nominal, ordinal, or interval/ratio measurement scales. In Chapters 7 and 8, we turn our attention to the inferential procedures that are used with nominal data. Subsequent chapters describe the procedures utilized with interval and ratio data (the procedures utilized with ordinal data are reviewed in the appendixes). We are, therefore, continuing with the same general organization that we did with our discussion of descriptive statistics.

Chapter Resources

GLOSSARY OF TERMS

Alpha: another term for Type I error. Its symbol is α.

Alpha level: criterion set for rejecting the null hypothesis. This is usually .05.

Alternative hypothesis (H_1): when used with a difference design, the statement that the treatment does have an effect.

Association designs: research undertaken to determine whether an observed association is likely to generalize.

Control group: in a between-groups design, the group of subjects that does not receive the treatment.

Correlational study: a study in which the researcher does not randomly assign the subjects and does not manipulate the value of a variable. As a result, at the conclusion of the study, the researcher has little confidence that there is a cause and effect relationship between the variables.

Dependent variable (DV): in an experiment, the variable whose value is not directly controlled by the researcher. Its value may be changed by the IV.

Difference designs: research undertaken to determine whether an observed difference is likely to generalize.

Experimental group: in a between-groups design, the group of subjects that does receive the treatment.

Independent variable (IV): in an experiment, the variable the experimenter manipulates or directly controls.

Intrinsic plausibility: decision-making process in which the alternative that seems most reasonable is accepted as being true.

Null hypothesis (H_0): when used with a difference design, the statement that the treatment does not have an effect.

Power: the probability of correctly rejecting a false null hypothesis. This probability is $1 - \beta$.

Quasi-experiment: an experiment in which the researcher manipulates the value of the independent variable but does not randomly assign the subjects. As a result, at the conclusion of the study, the researcher has less confidence in concluding that there is a cause and effect relationship between the independent and dependent variables than with a true experiment.

Random sample: A sample in which every member or subset of the population has an equal chance of being chosen.

Scientific method: an approach to understanding that emphasizes rigorous logic and that careful observation is the ultimate authority for determining truth. It is a self-correcting approach that limits bias.

True experiment: an experiment in which the researcher randomly assigns the subjects and also manipulates the value of the independent variable. As a result, at the conclusion of the study, the researcher is justified in reaching a cause and effect conclusion concerning the relationship between the independent and dependent variables.

Type I error: the probability of rejecting the null hypothesis when it is in fact true. This probability is equal to alpha, α, which is usually 5%.

Type II error: the probability of retaining the null hypothesis when it is in fact false. The probability is equal to beta, β, which is usually not known.

Questions: Chapter 6

(Answers to odd-numbered items are provided in Appendix I.)

1. In an experiment, the group that does not receive the treatment is called the _____ group.

   a. alpha

   b. benign

   c. control

   d. critical

2. The probability of correctly rejecting a *false* null hypothesis is called _____.
    a. alpha
    b. beta
    c. error rate
    d. power

3. The essential feature of random assignment is that _____.
    a. every member of a population has an equal probability of being chosen
    b. no one knows who will be chosen
    c. subjects are clueless as to the purpose of the experiment
    d. only volunteers take part in a study

4. In an experiment, the _____ is that the treatment *does* have an effect and the _____ is that it *does not* have an effect.
    a. null hypothesis; alternative hypothesis
    b. alternative hypothesis; null hypothesis

5. The experimenter sets the size of _____ but usually does not know the size of _____.
    a. alpha; beta
    b. Type II error; Type I error
    c. beta; alpha
    d. Type I error; alpha

6. If you reject the null hypothesis when in fact it is true, you have _____.
    a. made a Type I error
    b. broken the law and will need a lawyer
    c. made a Type II error
    d. shown that you have mastered experimental methodology

7. To increase power, an experimenter would _____.
    a. decrease the sample size
    b. choose a nominal rather than an interval measurement scale
    c. increase the alpha level (e.g., from .01 to .05)
    d. not use any of the above options

8. The criterion for rejecting the null hypothesis is set by the experimenter and is usually equal to _____.
    a. .10
    b. .05
    c. .01
    d. .001

9. Critical features of the scientific method include all of the following except _____.

    a. ultimately relies on observation

    b. requires careful, rational thought

    c. never is in error

    d. often makes use of experiments

10. The experimenter usually will not know which of the following?

    a. Criterion for rejecting the null hypothesis

    b. Alpha level

    c. Value of beta

    d. The number of subjects in the experiment

11. There are, fundamentally, two types of research questions and, therefore, two types of research designs. These are called _____ and _____ designs.

    a. error prone; truthful

    b. small-scale; large-scale

    c. plausible; implausible

    d. difference; association

12. The ancient Greeks generally employed _____ to determine truth.

    a. intrinsic plausibility

    b. the scientific method

    c. statistical analysis

    d. difference designs

13. The probability of making a Type II error is _____.

    a. alpha

    b. the criterion set by the experimenter

    c. equal to the region of rejection

    d. beta

14. A basic goal of experimentation is to conduct _____.

    a. as complex a study as possible

    b. as powerful a study as possible

    c. a study with a criterion of .10.

    d. a study where Type I error has been eliminated

15. A teacher is interested in improving her students' grades and tests whether having the students engage in light exercise will be beneficial. In this example, the independent variable is _____ and the dependent variable is _____.

    a. students' grades; exercise

    b. exercise; students' grades

16. In a quasi-experiment, the experimenter manipulates the _____ but does not _____.

    a. dependent variable; manipulate the independent variable

    b. independent variable; randomly assign the subjects

    c. control group; manipulate the experimental group

17. In a correlational study, the experimenter _____.

    a. does not manipulate the independent variable or randomly assign the subjects

    b. does manipulate the independent variable and does randomly assign the subjects

    c. never makes a Type I error

    d. never makes a Type II error

18. In a true experiment, the researcher _____.

    a. manipulates the independent variable

    b. randomly assigns the subjects

    c. always rejects the null hypothesis

    d. both "a" and "b," but not "c"

19. Assuming no other aspect of the experiment changes, if the probability of Type I error is decreased from .05 to .01, the probability of Type II error will _____.

    a. decrease

    b. stay the same

    c. increase

20. The strongest statement concerning the relationship of two variables can be made by a researcher following a _____.

    a. true experiment

    b. quasi-experiment

    c. correlational study

    d. all lead to statements of equivalent strength

SPSS Problem: Chapter 6

1. Twenty subjects report how many siblings they have:

0	2	3	1
1	0	2	5
4	3	2	2
4	5	3	2
0	2	3	1

Enter these data in SPSS and then find the frequencies and make a bar graph.

7

FINDING DIFFERENCES WITH NOMINAL DATA—I

The Goodness-of-Fit Chi-Square

Statistics may be defined as "a body of methods for making wise decisions in the face of uncertainty."

—W. A. Wallis

We begin our exploration of inferential statistical procedures with an examination of relationships using the simplest type of data. Recall that nominal data consist only of frequencies. An example of nominal data would be if you were to determine how many members of a group consider themselves to be Republicans, how many consider themselves to be Democrats, how many have some other party affiliation, and how many have no affiliation at all. You would simply determine the frequency in each category.

In this chapter and in Chapter 8, we will be utilizing procedures that do not make assumptions about a population's parameters, such as its variability, and do not assume that the population is normally distributed. They are, thus, nonparametric as well as distribution free, but we will follow convention and simply refer to them as nonparametric procedures. Later, when we are dealing with interval or ratio data, we will study tests that do make assumptions about population parameters and distributions. Those are called parametric procedures. In this chapter, we will begin our discussion of the nonparametric inferential procedures with the goodness-of-fit chi-square test. This test is underlined in Table 7.1.

Table 7.1	Overview Table of Inferential Statistical Procedures for Finding if There Is a Difference

	Type of Data			
	Nominal (Frequency)		**Ordinal** (Ranked)	**Interval/Ratio** (Continuous Measure)

Inferential Statistics (Finding Relationships)

Statistical procedures for difference and interaction designs

	Nominal		Ordinal	Interval/Ratio
One variable with at least two outcomes	Goodness-of-fit chi-square	**One IV with one sample—one DV**		One-sample z score or one-sample t test
		One IV with two or more independent samples—one DV	*Kruskal–Wallis H* [a]	One-way between-subjects ANOVA (only two independent samples—independent samples t test)
		One IV with one sample having two or more repeated measures—one DV		One-way within-subjects ANOVA (only two repeated measures—dependent samples t test)
Two variables, each with at least two outcomes	Chi-square test of independence	**Two IV each with two or more independent samples—one DV**		Two-way between-subjects ANOVA

Statistical procedures for association designs

Correlation	Phi		*Spearman r* [b]	Pearson r
Regression				Linear regression *Multiple regression* [c]

Notes. IV, independent variable; DV, dependent variable; ANOVA, analysis of variance. Research designs are shown in boldface. The italicized item is reviewed in Appendix A.

GOODNESS-OF-FIT CHI-SQUARE

Assume that you have a coin and you want to know if it is "fair." Of course, a fair coin should land heads 50% of the time and tails 50% of the time. However, some deviation from the expected 50/50 split would not be surprising. After all, if you tossed a coin a 100 times and found that there were 49 heads and 51 tails, most observers would say that this is close enough to the expected 50/50 proportion. But this raises the question of how far from 50/50 you would have to be in order to reject the view that the coin is fair and accept the alternative that the coin is biased. Hopefully, you have noticed that we have just stated a null and an alternative hypothesis. In Chapter 6, we learned that the null hypothesis is a statement of how the world is assumed to be. In our current case, we assume that the coin is fair and will thus land with a 50/50 split in a long series of tosses. The alternative hypothesis is that the coin is not fair and that the proportion of heads to tails will deviate from the expected 50/50 ratio. The question for us is how great the deviation must be for us to reject the null hypothesis and accept the alternative hypothesis. In science, we want a process that will lead to a consistent decision regardless of who the decision maker is. In other words, we cannot just leave it up to each individual to decide whether a particular outcome is plausible.

This may all seem unnecessary, even unimportant, but it is not. Decisions matter and the process by which they are derived is critical. In everyday life, we are used to being rather "sloppy" in our decision making. We are all affected by our emotions, and on occasion, we make decisions based on too little information. As a result, we make mistakes. Several approaches have been developed to reduce the likelihood of coming to erroneous decisions. In philosophy, this includes the study of logic. In science, there are a set of procedures known collectively as the scientific method. A critical component of the scientific process is that we base our decisions on the evidence that we have collected. We then employ accepted statistical procedures to arrive at a decision.

An advantage of the scientific approach is that it assures an outcome that is more than just someone's opinion. By utilizing the statistical procedures given in this book, you will be able to reach the same decisions as everyone else, anywhere. In other words, no more personal opinion.

For example, let's assume that your kind, thoughtful professor meets you in the hall one day before class. As both of you have come to class early, there is time to engage in stimulating intellectual conversation. Instead, and hopefully unrealistically, your professor suggests that you pass the time by wagering on the outcome of coin tosses, and he or she just happens to have a favorite coin to use. You, of course, cannot imagine that your professor would be anything less than scrupulously honest, so you accept the offer to bet your hard-earned lunch money. Your professor indicates that he or she is rather partial to heads. You do not mind. Why should you? After all, tails should come up as often as heads, assuming of course that the coin is fair.

At the end of 10 tosses, you note that while you have won 3 times, your professor has won 7 times. What should you think? While hopefully not a likely situation, the implications of your decision should be clear. If you retain the null hypothesis, which in this case would be that the coin is fair, then you might continue to play the game, and there would be no reason to accuse your professor of engaging in dishonest behavior. However, if you accept the alternative hypothesis that the coin is not fair, then you might conclude that your professor has knowingly engaged in dishonest behavior. It would be very awkward for you to accuse your professor of dishonesty based simply on your personal opinion. You would want to be on firmer footing, just in case the department chair or the dean happened to get involved. The issue is straightforward. Quite simply, is a 7:3 ratio different enough from the expected 5:5 ratio to warrant the conclusion that your professor is using a biased coin?

To answer this question, we must employ an inferential statistical procedure appropriate for finding if there is a difference. As Table 7.1 indicates, there are a number of procedures to choose from.

Fortunately, the process for choosing the correct procedure is straightforward. We first note that we have nominal data and there is only one variable of interest (the outcome of flipping the coin). Furthermore, this variable has two possible outcomes, either heads or tails. Thus, referring to Table 7.1, we find that the goodness-of-fit chi-square test (which has the symbol χ^2) would be appropriate. More specifically, this test uses frequency data from one variable, in this case the outcome of flipping a single coin, to determine whether the proportion that has been obtained matches the proportion that would be expected if the null hypothesis were correct. In our case, the data can be summarized using a bar graph (Figure 7.1).

Independent: two events, samples, or variables are independent if knowing the outcome of one does not enhance our prediction of the other.

Observed frequencies: with nominal data, the actual data that were collected.

Remember, the null hypothesis is that the coin is fair. In other words, we expect there to be 5 heads and 5 tails in 10 tosses of a fair coin. Furthermore, the chi-square test assumes that no observed event influences another, in other words, that the outcome of one flip of the coin does not affect the outcome of any other flip. In statistical terms, we would say that the outcomes are **independent**. (This concept will be discussed in more detail in Chapter 8.)

The goodness-of-fit chi-square compares the **observed frequencies** with what the **expected frequencies** would be, assuming that the null hypothesis is true. If the null

---

Figure 7.1 Bar Graph of Coin Tosses

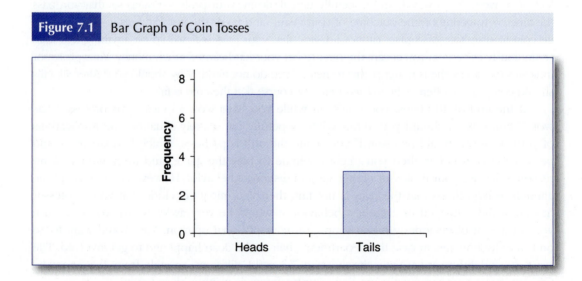

hypothesis is correct, then there should be a close correspondence between these two sets of frequencies. In our example of the coin toss, we should get a proportion close to 50/50 if the coin is fair. Of course, some discrepancy is likely. The

Expected frequencies: with nominal data, the outcome that would be expected if the null hypothesis were true.

issue is whether our result of 7 heads and 3 tails is so unlikely to have happened by chance that we should reject the null and accept the alternative hypothesis.

The calculation of the goodness-of-fit chi-square is straightforward, though it may not appear to be at first glance:

$$\chi^2 = \Sigma \frac{(f_o - f_e)^2}{f_e},$$

where f_o is the observed frequency and f_e is the expected frequency.

Though this equation may look intimidating, it is simply a mathematical statement that specifies what arithmetic operations are to be undertaken and in what order. I assure you that this is not difficult. You just need to proceed through the steps in the correct order.

Step 1: We must determine what the expected frequencies are, which we have already done. They are 5 heads and 5 tails.

Step 2: The equation indicates that you are to find the difference between an observed frequency and the corresponding expected frequency $(f_o - f_e)$. In our case, there are two observed frequencies, 7 heads and 3 tails. The expected frequency for each is 5. You, therefore, calculate the first difference, which is 7 − 5. This equals 2.

Step 3: You square the difference that you have obtained $(f_o - f_e)^2$. In our case, this would be 2 squared which equals 4.

Step 4: You divide the squared difference that you have just calculated by its frequency expected $[(f_o - f_e)^2/f_e]$, which in this case is 5. The result would be 4/5, which equals 0.8.

Step 5: You repeat Steps 1 through 4 for each of your categories. In our example, there is only one additional category, tails. We, therefore, go back to Step 1 and confirm that the expected frequency for tails is 5. Next, we calculate 3 − 5 (the number of tails we observed minus the expected number of tails, if the null hypothesis is correct), which equals −2. Then, as indicated in Step 3, we square −2 to obtain 4. Next, as Step 4 indicates, we divide our outcome of 4 by the expected frequency of 5 and obtain 0.8. Table 7.2 summarizes these steps.

As a check on our work, the sum of the differences between the observed and expected frequencies should equal 0. In our example, we have differences of +2 and −2. Their sum, as expected, is 0.

Step 6: We sum the values that we have calculated. In this case, there are two categories, heads and tails, so we sum two numbers, 0.8 + 0.8, to obtain 1.6.

Congratulations! You have just calculated your first goodness-of-fit chi-square. Please note that while there are a number of steps, each step is simple. Furthermore, remember that it is critical that you conduct the steps in the correct sequence. Now you are ready to make your

Table 7.2	Steps in Calculating a Goodness-of-Fit Chi-Square

Values	f_o	f_e	$f_o - f_e$	$(f_o - f_e)^2$	$\dfrac{(f_o - f_e)^2}{f_e}$
Heads	7	5	2	4	0.8
Tails	3	5	−2	4	0.8
			$\Sigma = 0$		$\Sigma = 1.6$

first statistical decision—to decide whether there is evidence for a difference. To complete the process, we must interpret what our chi-square value of 1.6 indicates. After all, 1.6 light years is a great many miles, but 1.6 inches is only a small distance. How do we interpret a chi-square of 1.6? To answer this, we will need to consult the appropriate statistical table, one of many in this book. Before doing so, however, let's reexamine the steps that we have just completed and see what they indicate.

In Step 1, we find the expected frequencies. These are derived from our null hypothesis. In Step 2, the difference between each observed frequency and its expected frequency is calculated. Clearly, the closer our data match what is predicted from the null hypothesis, the smaller this difference will be. For instance, if we had obtained 5 heads and 5 tails in the 10 tosses, then the observed frequencies would have perfectly matched the expected frequencies, and the differences would have each been zero. Alternatively, if our outcome had been 9 heads and only 1 tail, then the differences calculated in Step 2 would have been considerably more than those that we generated.

In Step 3, we square the differences we calculated in Step 2. As a result, the outcome has a positive sign, regardless of the sign of the difference that was obtained from Step 2. This was evident when we looked at our outcome of 3 tails, and from Step 2 calculated a difference of −2. This was then squared to give 4, not −4. Therefore, all of the numbers generated in Step 3 will be positive. Furthermore, a large outcome indicates that there is a large discrepancy between our observed and our expected frequencies, while a small outcome indicates that there is only a small discrepancy.

In Step 4, we divide each category's squared difference by the expected frequency for that category. With this division, we put each of the squared differences that we calculate into perspective. Fundamentally, the numerator of the chi-square equation provides a measure of how big the discrepancy is between our observed and expected frequencies. The denominator provides a standard against which to measure this deviation. For instance, in Step 2, we found a deviation of either +2 or −2. Each of these outcomes was squared in Step 3, and each of these squared deviations was related to an expected frequency of 5 in Step 4. Any particular deviation is more impressive when compared against a small rather than a large standard. For instance, to miss an expected outcome of 50 by only 4 is not nearly as evident as to miss an expected outcome of 5 by 4. Put another way, if you lose 10 pounds, this is more noticeable if your starting weight is 120 pounds than if it is 320 pounds.

We now understand that the outcome of Step 6, 1.6, is necessarily positive, and we have some intuitive feel for its size. But we are still unable to conclude whether the coin the professor tossed was fair. To do that we need to consult the appropriate table, in this case the chi-square table (Table J.2 in Appendix J). A cursory inspection of the chi-square table reveals a surprisingly large number of entries. A closer inspection shows that the table is arranged into rows and columns. The meaning of the columns with headings indicating a proportion is no mystery. From previous chapters, you are familiar with the concept that regions of a distribution can be associated with specific areas or proportions. Furthermore, you will recall the distinction between Type I and Type II errors and how, as a compromise, scientists commonly set alpha at .05. In our case, we will follow this convention; thus, we will be dealing with the column headed by .05.

We are still left with the issue of why there are so many rows of numbers in the table, and why each row is preceded by a number associated with the two letters, *df*. The answer is that if there was only one chi-square distribution, then there would only be a need for one row of critical values in the table. As there are many rows of values in the chi-square table, this implies that there is a series of chi-square distributions. Now we will explain why this is the case.

To calculate a chi-square value, there must be at least two possible outcomes to whatever we are examining. In our example, these were heads and tails for the tosses of a coin. Clearly, if only one outcome were possible, as with a coin with two heads, then the observed frequency and the expected frequency would have to match perfectly. No matter how many times you tossed this special coin, the outcome would always be heads. But in our case of a coin with heads and tails, there are two possible outcomes. So the difference between the frequency observed and the frequency expected can be found and a chi-square statistic can be calculated. But how many of these outcomes can vary? You might be inclined to say that as there are two outcomes that are possible, the number of heads and the number of tails, then each could vary. However, after the data are all collected, there is actually only one outcome that is free to vary.

On any single toss of a coin, you can obtain either a head or a tail. In our example, there were 10 tosses. Once you know that 7 of these were heads, then you also know that the number of tails has to be 3. It cannot be any other number. The number of tails is not free to vary. Thus, in a study with two possible outcomes, there is actually only one outcome that is free to vary. Stated in a more general way, for the goodness-of-fit chi-square, the **degrees of freedom** (**df**; the number of outcomes that can vary) is equal to the number of categories of outcomes minus one.

For the goodness-of-fit chi-square test, the equation for the degrees of freedom, abbreviated as *df*, is

> *Degrees of freedom (df): the number of observations out of the total that are free to vary.*

$df = c - 1$, where "c" is the number of categories. For our example, the $df = 1$. This is because there were two categories of outcome (heads or tails), from which we subtract one. This is the smallest number of degrees of freedom that is possible. However, higher numbers of degrees of freedom are possible. For instance, in tossing a die (singular of dice), there are six possible outcomes, and thus, there are 5 df. Once you know the number of total tosses and the number of times that five of the six sides came up, then you also know the value of the last side. If there were a total of 10 tosses, and the Numbers 1 through 5 came up eight times, then you would know that the Number 6 came up two times. In other words, there are six possible outcomes, but only 5 df. Once five of the frequencies are specified, the sixth is determined.

The reason degrees of freedom matter is that the shape of the chi-square distribution varies depending on the number of degrees of freedom. This is a consequence of the mathematical equation for chi-square. In this book, we will simply accept that there in not a single chi-square distribution, but rather a family of distributions, with the shape of each dependent on the number of categories of data or, more precisely, on the number of degrees of freedom. The shapes of representative chi-square distributions are illustrated in Figure 7.2.

Since in our example of 7 heads and 3 tails there is only 1 df, we will, for now, concentrate on the chi-square distribution that corresponds to 1 df, as is shown in Figure 7.3. The distribution illustrates the chi-square values that would be expected if the null hypothesis were in fact true. This is a theoretical distribution. It is a plot assuming that we have calculated an infinite number of chi-square values. On the X-axis are the chi-square values, on the Y-axis are the corresponding relative frequencies. What we have is a distribution in which the highest frequencies are associated with small values of chi-square, and low frequencies are associated with large values of chi-square.

As was just stated, Figure 7.3 is an example of a theoretical distribution. No one actually collected an infinite number of chi-square outcomes. However, through a set of mathematical procedures collectively known as calculus, the areas associated with different regions of this

| **Figure 7.2** | Shapes of Representative Chi-Square Distributions |

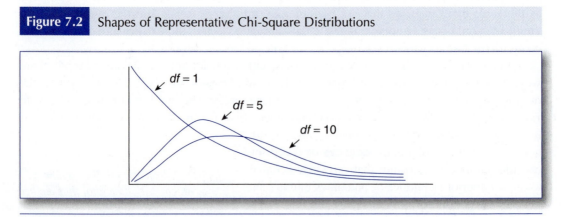

Note. df, degrees of freedom.

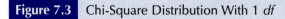

| **Figure 7.3** | Chi-Square Distribution With 1 *df* |

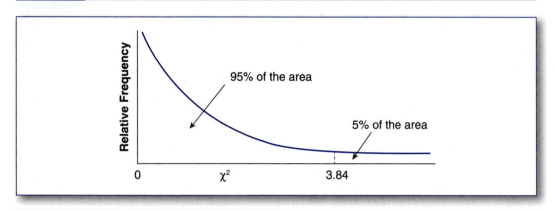

Note. df, degrees of freedom; χ^2, chi-square.

distribution have been obtained. Happily, you do not need to know any calculus to understand what is to follow. We are just going to benefit from the efforts of those who do. Thus, the situation is analogous to using a computer or a car. Most of us really do not understand how a computer or a car works, but that does not in any way preclude us from using computers and cars.

The vertical distance between a point on the *X*-axis and the chi-square curve indicates the relative likelihood of a particular chi-square value occurring. And, the total area enclosed between the *X*-axis and the chi-square curve corresponds to the likelihood of all of the possible outcomes, which is 100%. Furthermore, through calculus, it has been determined that 95% of the area of the chi-square distribution with 1 *df* falls to the left of, or below, a chi-square value of 3.84. This means that 5% of the area falls to the right of, or above, a chi-square value of 3.84 (Figure 7.3). This concept is so critically important that this area is given two names, the **critical region** and the **area of rejection**. In other words, if the null hypothesis is correct, then only 5% of the time will we obtain a value of chi-square by chance that is greater than 3.84, and thus so extreme that it falls in the critical region or area of rejection. The remaining 95% of the time, we will obtain a value less than 3.84. Put differently, if we set alpha equal to .05, as we agreed to do previously, then we will reject the null hypothesis if the obtained chi-square value with 1 *df* is greater than 3.84, for 5% of the area of the distribution is above this point. Thus, 3.84 is an example of the concept of a critical value. By using this critical value, we can be confident that when we reject the null hypothesis and accept the alternative

Critical region: area of the distribution equal to the alpha level. It is also called the area of rejection.

Area of rejection: area of the distribution equal to the alpha level. It is also called the critical region.

hypothesis, we will have made a Type I error only 5% of the time. In other words, in only 5% of the cases will we reject the null hypothesis when it is in fact correct.

Now, going back to our example of 10 coin tosses with an outcome of 7 heads and 3 tails, you will recall that we obtained a chi-square value of 1.6. This value is less than the critical value that we have determined for 1 *df*, which is 3.84. Therefore, the outcome of 10 tosses with 7 heads and 3 tails does not deviate enough from what was expected to justify the rejection of the null hypothesis that the coin is fair. Or, put another way, we do not conclude from the evidence that the professor is using a biased coin. Instead, we conclude that the outcome is simply the result of chance.

Another Example

To be certain that you understand the material that has just been covered, we will now do another example. In this case, let us assume that the outcome of the 10 coin tosses had been 9 heads and 1 tail. This outcome is illustrated with a bar graph in Figure 7.4. What would you now conclude if alpha is set equal to .05? Each of the steps is shown below and summarized in Table 7.3.

We start by stating the null and alternative hypotheses. Remember, the null hypothesis is signified by H_0 and the alternative hypothesis by H_1. For our example, we note the following:

H_0: The coin is fair.

H_1: The coin is not fair; in other words, the observed frequencies are predicted to differ significantly from those expected if the coin were fair.

Figure 7.4	Bar Graph of Coin Tosses

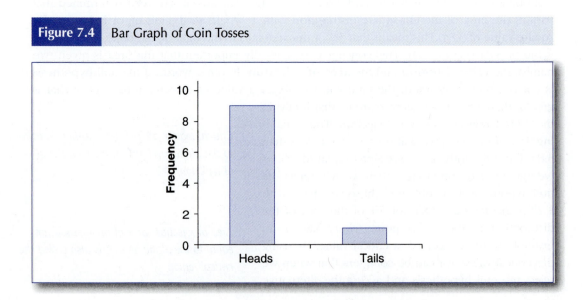

Table 7.3	Steps in Calculating a Goodness-of-Fit Chi-Square

Values	f_o	f_e	$f_o - f_e$	$(f_o - f_e)^2$	$\dfrac{(f_o - f_e)^2}{f_e}$
Heads	9	5	4	16	3.2
Tails	1	5	−4	16	3.2
			$\Sigma = 0$		$\Sigma = 6.4$

Using the equation given previously, the first step in calculating the goodness-of-fit chi-square is to determine the expected frequencies. As before, assuming that the coin is fair, the expected frequencies are 5 heads and 5 tails in 10 tosses. Next, we determine the difference between an observed frequency and the expected frequency. The difference for the first category, heads, is $9 - 5 = 4$. In Step 3, this outcome is squared, giving us $4^2 = 16$. Then, in Step 4, this value is divided by the expected frequency of 5, giving us $16/5 = 3.2$. We then repeat the steps for the second category, tails. For Step 1, the expected frequency would be 5. For Step 2, we would have $1 - 5 = -4$. In Step 3, this outcome is squared, giving us 16. As before, in the Step 4, this value is divided by the expected frequency of 5, giving us $16/5 = 3.2$. We then add our results from Step 4 to obtain $3.2 + 3.2 = 6.4$. As a check on our work, we find that the sum of the differences between observed and expected frequencies, in this case +4 and −4, is 0. Once again, we have 1 *df*, for there are two categories and $df = c - 1$. Finally, we compare our obtained outcome of 6.4 with the critical value of chi-square with 1 *df*, which is 3.84, as before. As our outcome falls to the right of the critical value (Figure 7.3) and thus represents a highly unlikely outcome, we reject the null hypothesis and accept the alternative hypothesis. In other words, our outcome has fallen in the area of rejection, so we have sufficient grounds to conclude that it is unlikely that the coin is fair.

Congratulations again! You have calculated another goodness-of-fit chi-square and have come to another decision concerning a relationship, but be careful interpreting the outcome. You can now be *reasonably confident* that the coin is biased, but you have *not proven* that it is biased. Remember that it is possible that you have made a Type I error and have rejected the null hypothesis when in fact it is true. We indicate this by stating that we have found a statistically significant outcome.

The term **significant** has a very precise meaning in statistics. It simply indicates that an outcome was unlikely to have occurred by chance. In the example that we have just completed, we know how unlikely, for alpha was set at .05. Thus, the probability is only 1 in 20 that by chance alone we could have obtained results this divergent from what was expected. We conclude, therefore, that this outcome is so unlikely to have been due solely to chance that we reject the null hypothesis

Significant: in statistics, a measure of how unlikely it is that an event occurred by chance.

that the coin is fair and, instead, accept the alternative hypothesis that the coin is not fair. This is all that statistical significance indicates.

Thus, statistical significance refers to a probability. It is dealing solely with the likelihood of an outcome. It is important to note that this is not what the term *significance* implies in our everyday conversations. When we use the term *significant* in a conversation, we are generally interested in how meaningful or important an outcome is, not how likely or unlikely it is. No statistical procedure can completely capture how meaningful or important an outcome is, for these judgments are subjective and relative. However, later in this text, we will see that there are statistical procedures that will assist you in coming to a conclusion concerning these qualities.

It is important to remember that the statistical procedures that you are learning in this course do not ensure that you will always make the correct decisions. What they do instead is provide you with an accepted system for making decisions, and with this system, you will know the probability of making certain types of errors. In our examples, we have set alpha equal to .05, and thus, there is only a 5% chance that we will make a Type I error and reject the null hypothesis, when in fact it is correct.

PROGRESS CHECK

Assume you toss a coin 10 times and obtain 8 heads and 2 tails.

1. What would the value of the chi-square be?

2. How many degrees of freedom are there?

3. Would you conclude that the coin is biased if alpha is set at .05?

Answers: 1. 3.6.   2. One.   3. No.

Our examples to this point have utilized 1 *df*. However, as was noted previously, there are actually a series of chi-square distributions, each associated with its unique degree of freedom. Returning to Figure 7.2, you will note that the chi-square distributions shown are all positively skewed. However, the specific shape depends on the number of degrees of freedom.

This turns out to be critically important. For instance, Figure 7.5 indicates that with 1 *df*, 5% of the area of the distribution is located to the right of a chi-square value of 3.84. Thus, in only 5% of the cases would you expect to obtain a chi-square value greater than 3.84 with 1 *df*, if the null hypothesis is in fact true. Put another way, the odds of obtaining a chi-square value greater than 3.84 with 1 *df* is one chance in 20, if the null hypothesis is in fact true. This also means that in 95% of the cases, we would expect to obtain a chi-square value of less than 3.84, with 1 *df*, if the null hypothesis is true. This is indicated by the area to the left of the value of 3.84. The logic is exactly the same for other degrees of freedom, but the critical value associated with the 5% area becomes larger as the degrees of freedom increase. This is evident from an inspection of Figure 7.5. It is also evident from an inspection of the chi-square table (Table J.2 in Appendix J). Proceeding down the column headed by the value of .05, for 1 *df*, the critical value is 3.84; for 5 *df*, it is 11.07; and for 10 *df*, it is 18.31.

To illustrate, if we return to our initial example where we determined that with 10 tosses there were 7 heads but only 3 tails, you will remember that we calculated a chi-square value of 1.6. By turning to the chi-square table (Table J.2 in Appendix J) and using the row labeled 1 *df* and the column labeled .05, we find the value of 3.84. Our outcome of 1.6 is less than 3.84. By referring to Figure 7.3 or 7.5, we can see that our outcome is to the left of the value of 3.84 and does not fall in the region of rejection. Thus, it represents an outcome that is expected to occur more frequently than 5% of the time. In other words, we do not have sufficient evidence to warrant the rejection of the null hypothesis. Accordingly, based on these data, we tentatively accept that the coin is fair and conclude that we have just had a string of bad luck.

A Final Example of the Goodness-of-Fit Chi-Square

You are now able to deal with larger problems. For instance, let us assume that you want to know if a die is fair. Your null hypothesis is that the die is fair. The alternative hypothesis is that it is not fair.

H_0: The die is fair.

H_1: The die is not fair. In other words, it is biased in some way.

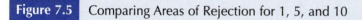

Figure 7.5   Comparing Areas of Rejection for 1, 5, and 10

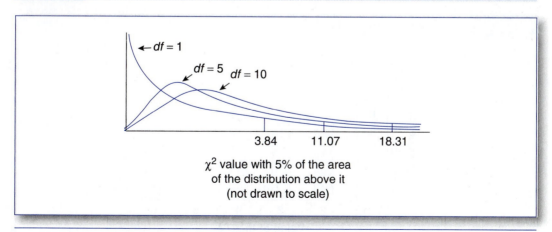

Note. df, degrees of freedom.

As is usual, you set alpha at .05. You then toss the die 100 times and obtain the observed frequencies illustrated with a bar graph in Figure 7.6. To calculate the goodness-of-fit chi-square, we use the same steps we used previously. In Step 1, we calculate the expected frequencies. Assuming that the die is fair, we simply divide 100, the total number of tosses, by the number of possible outcomes. This would be 100/6 = 16.67. Of course, this is not an expected frequency that could actually happen, but for the purposes of calculating the chi-square, it is the expected frequency that we would use. In Step 2, we find the difference between the observed frequencies and the expected frequencies. In Step 3, we square the differences that were just obtained. In Step 4, we divide each squared difference by its expected frequency. The results of these steps are illustrated in Table 7.4. In Step 5, as a check on our work, we find that the sum of the differences between observed and expected frequencies, except for minor rounding error, is 0. In Step 6, we add up the six values that were just obtained and find that 0.67 + 0.43 + 0.17 + 0.11 + 1.31 + 1.12 = 3.81. Our degrees of freedom equal the number of categories minus one ($df = c - 1$). In this case, df would equal $6 - 1 = 5$. Referring to the chi-square table (Table J.2 in Appendix J) and looking across the row for 5 df and down the column labeled .05, we find that the critical value is 11.07. Our chi-square value is 3.81, which is less than 11.07, and thus, we retain the null hypothesis that the die is fair.

If the outcome had been large enough to warrant rejecting the null, we would then examine the actual frequencies that were obtained to determine in what manner the die was biased.

Reporting the Results of the Goodness-of-Fit Chi-Square

If you were to report the results of the chi-square test that was just completed, it would be important for the reader to be given sufficient information to fully understand the outcome. While there

| **Figure 7.6** | Bar Graph of Tosses of a Die |

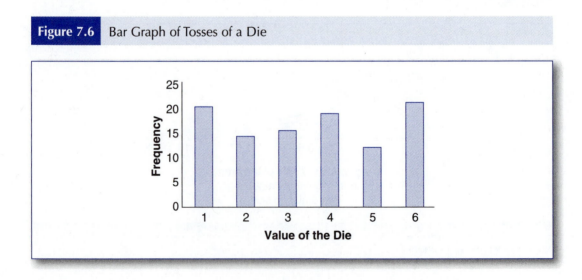

Table 7.4   Steps in Calculating a Goodness-of-Fit Chi-Square

Values	f_o	f_e	$f_o - f_e$	$(f_o - f_e)^2$	$\dfrac{(f_o - f_e)^2}{f_e}$
1	20	16.67	3.33	11.09	0.67
2	14	16.67	−2.67	7.13	0.43
3	15	16.67	1.67	2.79	0.17
4	18	16.67	1.33	1.77	0.11
5	12	16.67	−4.67	21.81	1.31
6	21	16.67	4.33	18.75	1.12
			$\Sigma = 0$		$\Sigma = 3.81$

are a number of conventions in use, fortunately they are quite similar. In this text, we will utilize the style of the American Psychological Association. For our results, you would want to state something to the effect of "the results of the testing of the die did not provide sufficient evidence to reject the null hypothesis that the die was fair $(\chi^2(5, n = 100) = 3.81, p > .05)$." The degrees of freedom are indicated by the value 5. The n is the number of tosses, in this case 100. The value of the obtained chi-square is 3.81 and the $p > .05$ indicates that the *probability* of this outcome is *greater* than the alpha level of 5%. Be careful. Our obtained chi-square value was *less* than the critical value listed in the chi-square table (Table J.2 in Appendix J). Thus, the probability of our obtained outcome is *greater* than our alpha, which was set equal to .05.

Purpose and Limitations of Using the Goodness-of-Fit Chi-Square Test

1. *Compares observed and expected frequencies:* The goodness-of-fit chi-square is testing whether the observed frequencies differ from the frequencies that are expected if the null hypothesis is correct.

2. *Overall test of significance:* The chi-square test indicates whether a difference in the relative frequencies exists. In designs with more than 1 *df*, a goodness-of-fit chi-square test with a statistically significant outcome does not indicate where the difference(s) is (are). Generally, inspection of the observed frequencies is all that is needed to indicate where the difference(s) is (are) located.

3. *No measure of effect size:* The chi-square is a test of significance. It indicates whether or not a difference in proportions is likely to have occurred by chance if the null

hypothesis is correct. With the goodness-of-fit chi-square, no measure of effect size is calculated. This concept will be explained later in the book.

4. *Expected frequencies cannot be too small:* For the goodness-of-fit chi-square, the minimum acceptable size of any expected frequency is 5.

Assumptions of the Chi-Square Test

1. *Nominal data:* The data are in the form of frequencies or can be converted to frequencies.

2. *Observations are independent:* In other words, a subject or event is only counted once and is not matched with another subject or event.

CONCLUSION

The goodness-of-fit chi-square is used when you have nominal data and one variable. More specifically, this procedure is used when you want to determine whether the observed frequencies differ from expected frequencies. As the chi-square test is using nominal data, or data that have been converted into nominal data, it is a nonparametric procedure. No assumptions are being made about the shape of a population distribution or the values of any population parameter, such as the mean or variability. In fact, as you know, neither a mean nor a measure of variability is calculated with nominal data.

As we have seen, the procedure to calculate the chi-square value is straightforward, though there are a number of steps. It is important, however, to remember that the critical value necessary to decide whether to reject the null hypothesis varies depending on the degrees of freedom of the study. As the course progresses, you will see that this characteristic is shared with most other statistical procedures.

Chapter Resources

GLOSSARY OF TERMS

Area of rejection: area of the distribution equal to the alpha level. It is also called the critical region.

Critical region: area of the distribution equal to the alpha level. It is also called the area of rejection.

Degrees of freedom (df): the number of observations out of the total that are free to vary.

Expected frequencies: with nominal data, the outcome that would be expected if the null hypothesis were true.

Independent: two events, samples, or variables are independent if knowing the outcome of one does not enhance our prediction of the other.

Observed frequencies: with nominal data, the actual data that were collected.

Significant: in statistics, a measure of how unlikely it is that an event occurred by chance.

Questions: Chapter 7

(Answers to odd-numbered items are provided in Appendix I.)

1. Rejecting the null hypothesis when in fact it is true is an example of _____.
   a. Type I error
   b. Type II error
   c. Type III error

2. The chi-square test deals with _____ data.
   a. nominal
   b. ordinal
   c. interval
   d. ratio

3. The data in a one-sample chi-square test consist of _____.
   a. observed frequencies
   b. expected frequencies
   c. degrees of freedom
   d. none of the above

4. In the statistical statement, $\chi^2(5, n = 100) = 3.81, p > .05$, the degrees of freedom are equal to _____.
   a. 5
   b. 99
   c. 100
   d. 3.81

5. With a one-sample chi-square test, the degrees of freedom are equal to the _____.
   a. number of categories
   b. number of subjects
   c. number of categories minus one
   d. highest frequency minus two

6. If it is reported that a one-sample chi-square test has a $p > .05$. This indicates that the results are _____.

    a. not possible

    b. not statistically significant

    c. statistically significant

    d. not of interest

7. Practically speaking, degrees of freedom are important because they are _____.

    a. used in calculating the chi-square value

    b. used in collecting the chi-square data

    c. used in interpreting the chi-square value

    d. none of the above

8. The critical region is _____.

    a. equal to the alpha level

    b. equal to the size of beta

    c. the same as the region of rejection

    d. both "a" and "c"

9. If knowing that the Buffalo Bills won a football game last weekend does not aid in predicting whether they will win next weekend, statisticians would say the two events are _____.

    a. free

    b. independent

    c. expected

    d. critical

For Questions 10 to 16 use the following information: Suppose you toss a coin 100 times and observe 40 heads and 60 tails.

10. What is the null hypothesis?

    a. The coin is fair.

    b. The coin is not fair.

    c. The observed 40:60 frequencies are *not* statistically different from the expected 50:50 ratio.

    d. The observed 40:60 frequencies are statistically different from the expected 50:50 ratio.

    e. Both "a" and "c" are correct.

11. What is the calculated value of chi-square?

    a. 1

    b. 2

    c. 3

    d. 4

    e. 5

12. How many degrees of freedom are there?

    a. 1

    b. 2

    c. 3

    d. 4

    e. 5

13. Assuming alpha is equal to .05, what is the critical value?

    a. 2.68

    b. 3.84

    c. 4.00

    d. 4.32

    e. 6.63

14. What is your decision?

    a. Accept the null hypothesis.

    b. Reject the null hypothesis.

    c. Neither accept nor reject the null hypothesis as there is insufficient data to come to a decision.

15. What is the probability of having made a Type I error?

    a. 50%

    b. 10%

    c. 5%

    d. 1%

    e. The probability of Type I error is not known.

16. What is the probability of having made a Type II error?

    a. 50%

    b. 10%

c. 5%

d. 1%

e. The probability of Type II error is not known.

For Questions 17 to 23, use the following information: Suppose we toss a die 144 times, and all we observe is that the Number 1 occurs 36 times. (*Hint:* We also now know that the other category consisting of outcomes 2 to 6 occurred 108 times.)

17. What is the null hypothesis?

a. The die is fair.

b. The die is not fair.

c. The observed 36:144 frequencies are *not* statistically different from the expected 1:6 ratio.

d. The observed 36:144 frequencies are statistically different from the expected 1:6 ratio.

e. Both "a" and "c" are correct.

18. What is the calculated value of chi-square? (*Hint:* You only have two categories.)

a. 1

b. 4.2

c. 5.7

d. 7.2

e. 9.1

19. How many degrees of freedom are there? (*Hint:* You only have two categories.)

a. 1

b. 2

c. 3

d. 4

e. 5

20. Assuming alpha is equal to .01, what is the critical value?

a. 2.68

b. 3.84

c. 4.00

d. 4.32

e. 6.64

21. What is your decision?

    a. Accept the null hypothesis.

    b. Reject the null hypothesis.

    c. Neither accept nor reject the null hypothesis as there is insufficient data to come to a decision.

22. What is the probability of having made a Type I error?

    a. 50%

    b. 10%

    c. 5%

    d. 1%

    e. The probability of Type I error is not known.

23. What is the probability of having made a Type II error?

    a. 50%

    b. 10%

    c. 5%

    d. 1%

    e. The probability of Type II error is not known.

Use the following information in Questions 24 to 30. Riniolo, Koledin, Drakulic, and Payne (2003) reported that 15 of 20 eyewitnesses to the sinking of the *Titanic* reported that the ship was breaking apart before it actually sank.

24. What is the null hypothesis?

    a. The observed frequencies are *not* statistically different from the expected 50:50 ratio.

    b. The observed frequencies are statistically different from the expected 50:50 ratio.

25. What is the calculated value of chi-square?

    a. 1

    b. 3.2

    c. 5

    d. 7.2

26. How many degrees of freedom are there?

    a. 1

    b. 2

    c. 3

    d. 4

    e. 5

27. Assuming alpha is equal to .05, what is the critical value?

    a. 2.68

    b. 3.84

    c. 4.00

    d. 4.32

    e. 6.64

28. What is your decision?

    a. Accept the null hypothesis.

    b. Reject the null hypothesis.

    c. Neither accept nor reject the null hypothesis as there is insufficient data to come to a decision.

29. What is the probability of having made a Type I error?

    a. 50%

    b. 10%

    c. 5%

    d. 1%

    e. The probability of Type I error is not known.

30. What is the probability of having made a Type II error?

    a. 50%

    b. 10%

    c. 5%

    d. 1%

    e. The probability of Type II error is not known.

    Problems 31 to 34 utilize SPSS.

SPSS

USING SPSS WITH THE GOODNESS-OF-FIT CHI-SQUARE

To Begin SPSS

Step 1: To activate the program. You can accomplish this by double clicking on the SPSS icon on the computer's desktop or, if this icon is not evident, by clicking on "Program" and then on SPSS. If you have the PASW version of SPSS, you will then see the window displayed in Figure 7.7. (Other versions of SPSS will have a very similar window.)

Figure 7.7 The Initial SPSS (PASW) Window

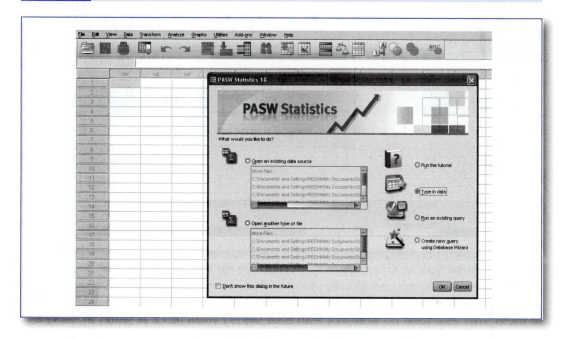

Step 2: Click on "Type in data" and then click on "OK." At the bottom left of this current window are two "switches," one labeled "Data View," which is highlighted in yellow, and the other "Variable View."

Step 3: Click on "Variable View." Near the top of this page is a row of column headings, beginning with "Name," then "Type," and proceeding to "Role." For the present, we will only be dealing with the columns headed by "Name," "Label," "Values," and "Measure."

Step 4: Click within the upper left "cell," and it will turn yellow. You now type the name of the first variable for which you have data. We are going to utilize the same data and labels as were previously employed in Figure 7.1. These data dealt with the results of tossing a coin. We have called this variable "headstails."

Step 5: Click twice on the first empty "cell" under the column heading "Label." In this cell, you can type a more extensive description of your variable. In our case, type "Heads and Tails."

Step 6: Click on the first empty "cell" under the column heading "Values." Then, click on the small blue square. A box will appear as in Figure 7.8. In the blank space to the right of "Value," type the number "1." Then, type a brief description of this value of the variable in the blank space to the right of "Label." In our case, type "heads." Finally, click on "Add." Your label for a value of 1 will appear in the large white region in the center of the window. Now repeat the above steps in this section for the value "2," which is given the label "tails." Figure 7.8 illustrates what you will see immediately before clicking on "Add" after defining the second label. Then click on "OK."

Figure 7.8   The Value Labels Window

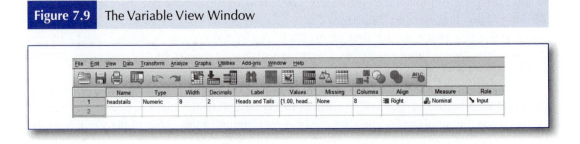

Step 7: Click on the first empty "cell" under the column heading "Measure." As we are dealing with nominal data, select "Nominal" as is shown in Figure 7.9. We have now completed the SPSS "Variable View" window.

Figure 7.9   The Variable View Window

To Enter Data in SPSS

Step 8: Click on the "Data View" option at the lower left corner of the window. The variable "headstails" will be present in the Data View window.

Step 9: In the column under "headstails" enter the value "1" for each "head" and the value "2" for each "tail." I have entered the seven heads followed by the three tails, but the order does not matter (Figure 7.10). (As our data consist of the results of only 10 coin tosses, we are entering the result of each toss. This can quickly become tedious with large data sets. The next example will show an alternative way to enter your data.)

| Figure 7.10 | Entering Data |

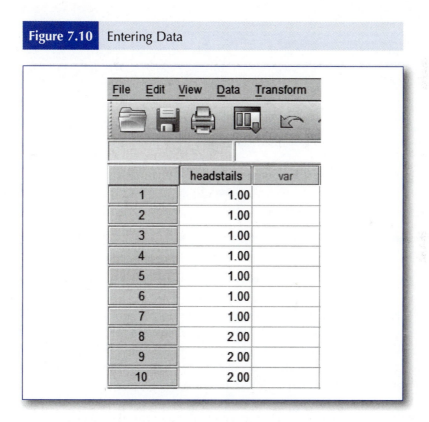

To Conduct a Goodness-of-Fit Chi-Square With SPSS

Step 10: Click the cursor on "Analyze" along the row of SPSS commands above the data you entered, then move to "Nonparametric Tests." A new box appears. Click on "One Sample . . ."

Step 11: A new window will appear, as is shown in Figure 7.11. There are three tabs at the top left. Click on "Fields." A new window will appear.

Figure 7.11   Defining the Chi-Square

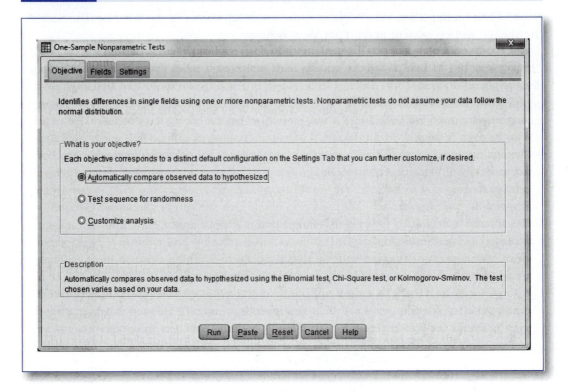

Step 12: Click on the central arrow to move "Heads and Tails" to the right side, labeled "Test Fields," as is shown in Figure 7.12.

Step 13: Now click on the tab "Settings" in the upper left-hand corner. Then click on "Choose Tests" and "Customize tests," and then click on the second box. The new window will appear as shown in Figure 7.13.

Step 14: Click "Run." SPSS then calculates the desired chi-square and the results are shown in Figure 7.14. This output indicates the null hypothesis that is being tested, the statistical test employed (in this case, a one-sample chi-square test), and the significance level, and SPSS even provides a statement of the decision (in this case, that you are to retain the null hypothesis).

Step 15: Double click anywhere inside the "Hypothesis Test Summary" (Figure 7.14), and you will be given additional information (Figure 7.15). In this figure, the output of Figure 7.14 is repeated, and a bar graph of the obtained as well as expected heads and tails is provided (note that there were three tails and due to the range of values on the *Y*-axis, there is no column for this value). In addition, the total sample size, the actual

Figure 7.12   Continuing to Define the Chi-Square

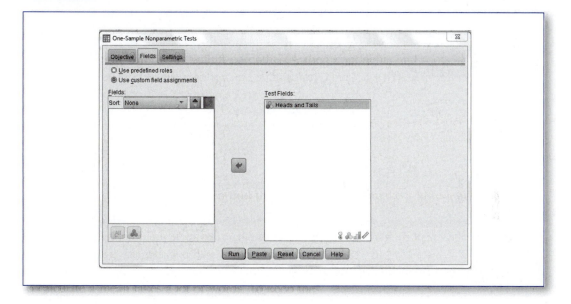

Figure 7.13   Continuing to Define the Chi-Square

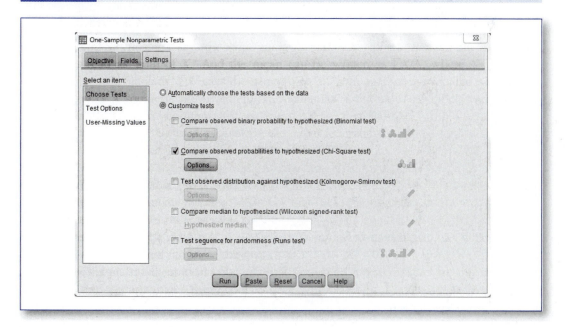

value of the chi-square, its degrees of freedom, and the probability of this outcome are provided. You should confirm that this is the same result as was found earlier in this chapter.

Figure 7.14   The Chi-Square Output in SPSS

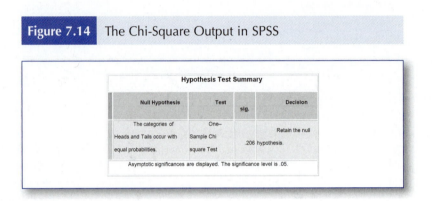

Figure 7.15   The Chi-Square Output in SPSS

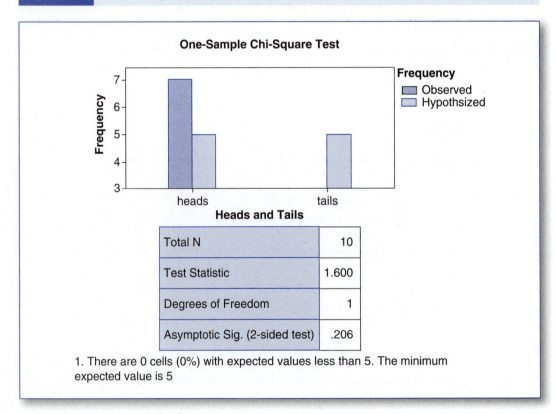

OUR SECOND EXAMPLE USING SPSS WITH THE GOODNESS-OF-FIT CHI-SQUARE

To Begin SPSS

Steps 1, 2, and 3: The first three steps remain the same.

Step 4: As before, you now identify your variable. We are going to utilize the same data and label as were previously employed in Figure 7.6 and Table 7.4. These data dealt with the results of rolling a die. In the first cell under "Names," type "values."

Step 5: Click on the first empty "cell" under the column heading "Label." In this cell, you can type a more extensive description of your variable. In our case, type "Number showing on the die." Note that to see the entire label, you may need to expand the size of this cell by placing your cursor on the right border of the "Label" heading and moving to the right.

Step 6: Click on the first empty "cell" under the column heading "Values." Then click on the small blue square. A box will appear as shown in Figure 7.16. In the blank space to the right of "Value," type the number "1." Then type a brief description of this value of the variable in the blank space to the right of "Label." In our case, type "1" as this is a clear indication of the value of the die. Finally, click on "Add." Your label for a value of 1 will appear in the large white region in the center of the window. Now repeat the above steps in this section for the value "2," which is given the label "2," etc. Figure 7.16 illustrates what you will see immediately before clicking on "Add" after defining the last label. Then click on "OK."

Figure 7.16   The Value Labels Window

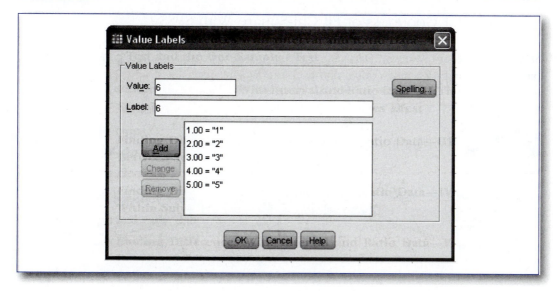

Step 7: Click on the first empty "cell" under the column heading "Measure." As we are dealing with nominal data, select "Nominal" as is shown in Figure 7.17. You could shift to the data window and sequentially enter the result of each roll of the die. However, this would quickly become tedious. Instead, we will use SPSS's ability to construct a chi-square table of results. To do so, we need to create another variable so that SPSS can be instructed that the numbers we will be entering are the frequencies that occurred for each of the six possible outcomes of tossing a die.

Step 8: In the first empty "cell" under "Name," we type the name of this new variable. I have chosen "Frequency."

Step 9: Move across the row and click on the empty "cell" under the column heading "Label." In this cell, you can type a more extensive description of your variable. In our case, we type "Frequency of each number."

Step 10: Continue to move across the row and click on the empty "cell" under the column heading "Measure." As we are dealing with frequencies, select "Nominal," which is the SPSS designation for nominal data. This is shown in Figure 7.17. We have now completed the SPSS "Variable View" window.

To Enter Data in SPSS

Step 11: Click on the "Data View" option at the lower left-hand corner of the window. The variables "Values" and "Frequency" will be present in the Data View window.

Step 12: Type in the values of "1" through "6" for "values" and the corresponding frequencies as is shown in Figure 7.18.

To Conduct a Goodness-of-Fit Chi-Square With SPSS

Step 13: Click your cursor on "Data" along the row of SPSS commands above the numbers you have entered and then move down and click on "Weight cases."

Figure 7.17   The Variable View Window

	Name	Type	Width	Decimals	Label	Values	Missing	Columns	Align	Measure	Role
1	Values	Numeric	8	2	Number showing on the die	{1.00, 1}...	None	8	Right	Nominal	Input
2	Frequency	Numeric	8	2	Frequency of each number	None	None	8	Right	Nominal	Input
3											

Figure 7.18 Entering Data

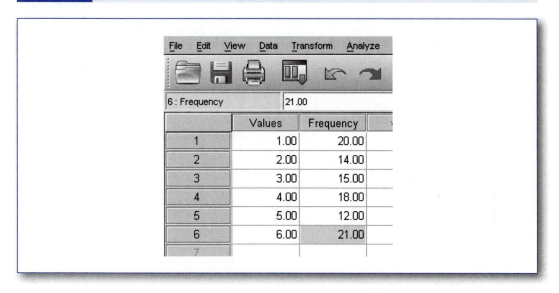

Step 14: In the new window, click on the small circle just to the left of "Weight cases by" and then highlight "Frequency of each number" and click on the arrow in the center of the window (Figure 7.19). The result is shown in Figure 7.20. Then click on "OK." You have just indicated to SPSS that the numbers in the variable "Frequencies" are not scores but rather are frequencies. This is indicated by the statement "WEIGHT BY Frequency."

Step 15: Return to the "Data View" window by clicking on the X in the red box in the upper right-hand corner. A new window will appear. There is no need to save this output, so click on the "NO" option.

Step 16: Click the cursor on "Analyze" along the row of SPSS commands above the data you entered, then move to "Nonparametric Tests." A new box appears. Click on "One Sample . . ."

Step 17: A new window will appear, as is shown in Figure 7.21. There are three tabs at the top left. Click on "Fields." A new window will appear.

Step 18: Click on "Number showing on the die" and then click on the central arrow to move "Number showing on the die" to the right side, labeled Test Fields, as is shown in Figure 7.22.

Step 19: Now click on the tab "Settings" in the upper left-hand corner. Then click on "Choose Tests" and "Customize tests," and then click on the second box. The new window will appear as in Figure 7.23.

Step 20: Click "Run." SPSS then calculates the desired chi-square and the results are shown in Figure 7.24. This output indicates the null hypothesis that is being tested, the statistical test employed (in this case, a one-sample chi-square test) the significance level and SPSS provides a statement of the decision (in this case, that you are to retain the null hypothesis).

Figure 7.19 The Weight Cases Window

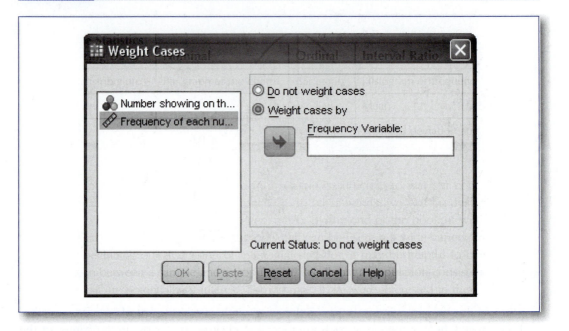

Figure 7.20 The Completed Weight Cases Window

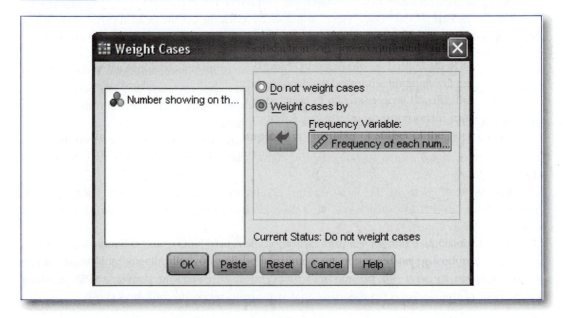

Figure 7.21 Defining the Chi-Square

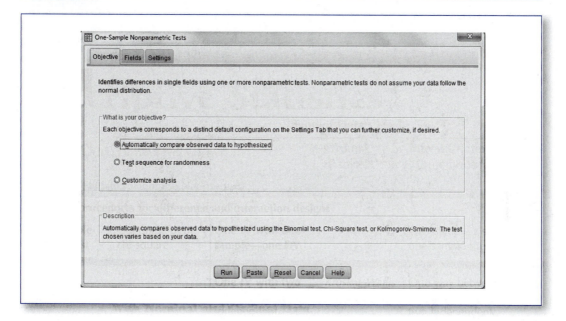

Figure 7.22 Continuing to Define the Chi-Square

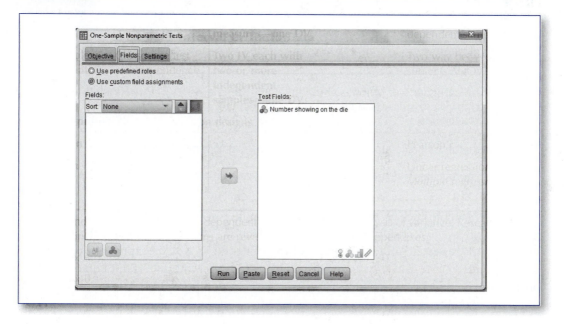

Figure 7.23   Continuing to Define the Chi-Square

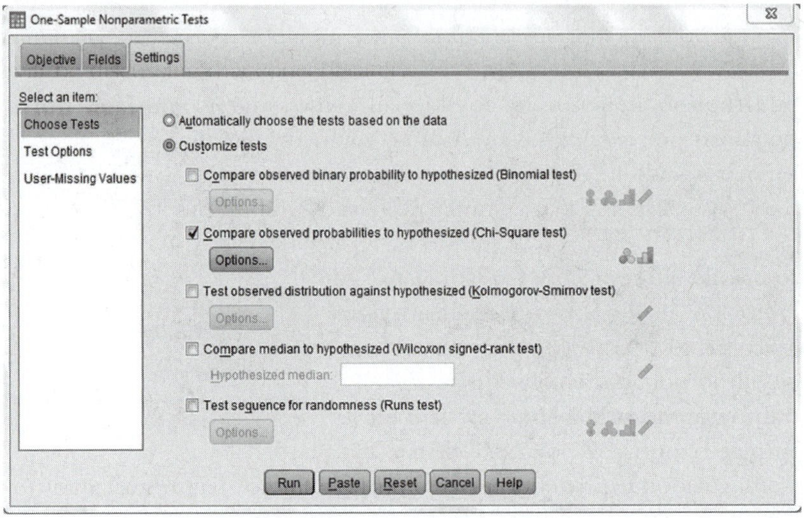

Figure 7.24   The Chi-Square Output in SPSS

Hypothesis Test Summary

	Null Hypothesis	Test	Sig.	Decision
1	The categories of Number showing on the die occur with equal probabilities.	One-Sample Chi-Square Test	.579	Retain the null hypothesis.

Asymptotic significances are displayed. The significance level is .05.

Step 21: Double click anywhere inside the "Hypothesis Test Summary" box (Figure 7.24), and you will be given additional information (Figure 7.25). In this figure, the output of Figure 7.24 is repeated, and a bar graph of the obtained as well as expected tosses of the die is provided (note that the number 5 occurred 12 times, but due to the range of values on the *Y*-axis, there is no column for this value). In addition, the total sample size, the

Figure 7.25	The Chi-Square Output in SPSS

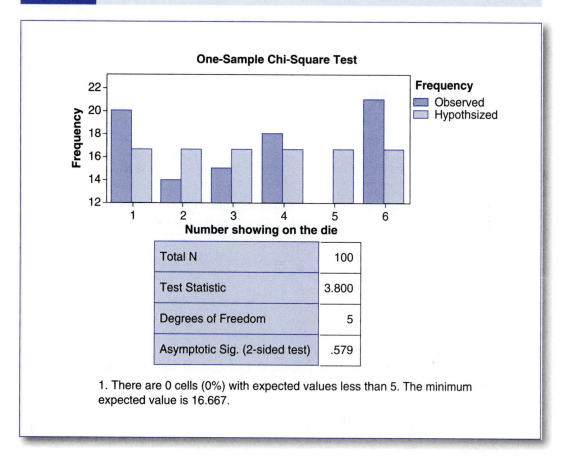

1. There are 0 cells (0%) with expected values less than 5. The minimum expected value is 16.667.

actual value of the chi-square, its degrees of freedom, and the probability of this outcome are provided. You should confirm that this is the same result, except for rounding error, as was found earlier in this chapter.

To check that you understand how to conduct the chi-square test with SPSS, use the coin toss data in Figure 7.4 and confirm that you obtain the same outcome when using SPSS.

SPSS Problems: Chapter 7

The following four problems are based on the example of tossing a die that was illustrated in Figure 7.6, but this time, double each of the obtained frequencies. This will result in a total of 200 tosses.

31. What is the value of this chi-square?

    a. 1.9

    b. 3.8

    c. 7.6

    d. 11.4

32. How many degrees of freedom are there?

    a. 1

    b. 5

    c. 10

    d. 15

33. Thus, doubling each of the obtained frequencies causes the chi-square to _____. (Compare the chi-square value obtained in Question 31 with the value calculated in the text for the original data.)

    a. halve

    b. remain unchanged

    c. double

    d. triple

34. Doubling each of the obtained frequencies causes the degrees of freedom to _____. (Compare the degrees of freedom obtained in Question 32 with the value calculated in the text for the original data.)

    a. become 1

    b. remain unchanged

    c. double

    d. triple

8

FINDING DIFFERENCES WITH NOMINAL DATA—II

The Chi-Square Test of Independence

Science is not a collection of facts but a way of interrogating the world.

—Sharon Begley

The chi-square statistic is not limited to analyzing frequencies obtained with a single variable, as was the case in Chapter 7. Another form of the chi-square statistic, the *chi-square test of independence*, is used when we have a design that involves nominal data and two variables. This test is underlined in Table 8.1.

ANALYZING A DIFFERENCE DESIGN WITH TWO VARIABLES, EACH WITH AT LEAST TWO OUTCOMES

In Chapter 7, we noted that in the field of statistics, "independent" has a very specific meaning, for it signifies that two events, samples, or variables are *not* related in a predicable fashion. The term **dependent** is used if there is a predictable relationship. For instance, if a coin is fair, then the outcome of tosses will be independent. Thus, whether or not a head or tail was just tossed does not affect the outcome of the next flip. And, if a coin is fair, then the likelihood of

> *Dependent: two events, samples or variables are dependent if knowing the outcome of one enhances our prediction of the other.*

Table 8.1	Overview Table of Inferential Statistical Procedures for Finding if There Is a Difference

| | **Type of Data** | | |
	Nominal (Frequency)	**Ordinal** (Ranked)	**Interval/Ratio** (Continuous Measure)
<u>**Inferential Statistics**</u> (Finding Relationships)			
Statistical procedures for difference and interaction designs			
One variable with at least two outcomes	Goodness-of-fit chi-square	**One IV with one sample—one DV**	One-sample z score or one-sample t test
		One IV with two or more independent samples—one DV	*Kruskal–Wallis H*
			One-way between-subjects ANOVA (only two independent samples—independent samples t test)
		One IV with one sample having two or more repeated measures—one DV	One-way within-subjects ANOVA (only two repeated measures—dependent samples t test)
Two variables, each with at least two outcomes	<u>Chi-square test of independence</u>	**Two IV each with two or more independent samples—one DV**	Two-way between-subjects ANOVA

Notes. IV, independent variable; DV, dependent variable; ANOVA, analysis of variance. Research designs are shown in boldface. The italicized item is reviewed in Appendix A.

observing a head or tail on any one toss is 50%, regardless of what the outcomes of the previous tosses were. Unfortunately, many individuals do not understand the concept of statistical independence and instead assume that if tails has come up a number of times in a row, then it is more likely that the next toss will be a head. This is known as the "**gambler's fallacy**"; it has undoubtedly been responsible for the loss of a great deal of money.

In the scientific literature, there are numerous reports of studies with nominal data using two or

Gambler's fallacy: the incorrect assumption that if an event has not occurred recently, then the probability of it occurring in the future increases.

more variables. For example, Sandson, Bachna, and Morin (2000) examined the relationship between attention-deficit/hyperactivity disorder (ADHD) and omission errors in vision. More specifically, they examined on which side, the left or right, a person is less likely to see a stimulus. Neglecting to see a stimulus is known as an omission error. The null and alternative hypotheses were as follows:

H_0: *There is no difference* in the distribution of omission errors between the subjects diagnosed with ADHD or without ADHD.

H_1: *There is a difference* in the distribution of omission errors between the subjects diagnosed with ADHD or without ADHD.

In this study, each subject was assigned to either the ADHD or the no ADHD condition depending on whether one had previously been diagnosed with ADHD. Note that the assignment for a subject is independent of the assignment of any other subject. The likelihood of each subject making omission errors was then assessed, and as no subject's outcome affects any other's, these data are also independent.

It is important to understand that each of the 87 subjects provided only a single datum (this is the singular of data, which is plural). The data, therefore, consist of joint frequencies. For instance, 36 subjects had been diagnosed with ADHD *and* exhibited more omissions on the right side. As is usually the case, in this study alpha was set at .05.

The data for this study are presented in Table 8.2.

As we have nominal data and there are two variables (ADHD diagnosis and omission side), each with two outcomes, Table 8.1 indicates that a chi-square test of independence should be employed. With two possible outcomes for each variable, there are two columns and two rows of data in Table 8.2, and this is called a 2 × 2 chi-square test of independence.

The name of this chi-square test may come as a surprise. After all, we already know that each subject's data are independent. Why, then, is the test called a test for independence? What independence is there to test for?

Table 8.2 Summary of the Data for the First Example

		Was the Subject Diagnosed With ADHD?	
		Yes	No
Side with more omission errors	**Right**	36	25
	Left	22	4

Note. ADHD, attention-deficit/hyperactivity disorder.

The chi-square test of independence examines whether the variables in a study are independent. More specifically, in this example, it is testing whether there is an **interaction** between two variables. The interaction referred to in the context of our 2 × 2 chi-square test is whether the proportions observed for each sample differ. In other words, do subjects diagnosed with ADHD show a different pattern of omission errors than do subjects without the diagnosis? If the relative frequencies are similar, the outcome of the chi-square test *will not be* statistically significant. However, if the relative frequencies differ enough, the outcome of the chi-square test *will be* statistically significant. As was the case previously, we cannot leave the decision of how much the relative frequencies must differ to individual opinion. Instead, we employ an agreed-on statistical procedure to come to a decision concerning the relationship among the populations.

The equation for the chi-square test of independence is the same as the equation we used in Chapter 7 for the goodness-of-fit chi-square. And, as before, we compare our outcome with the critical value listed in the chi-square table (Table J.2 in Appendix J). In the present case, though, there are a few more calculations involved; however, none are challenging.

Step 1, as before, is to determine the expected frequencies. In the goodness-of-fit chi-square, which was discussed in the Chapter 7, the expected frequencies were a direct consequence of the definition of the null hypothesis. For instance, if the null hypothesis was that a coin was fair, then it followed that heads and tails would be expected to occur in equal numbers in a series of tosses. The situation is somewhat more complex with the chi-square test of independence.

The expected frequencies for a chi-square test of independence again reflect the null hypothesis but must be calculated using the following equation:

$$\text{Expected frequency of a cell} = \frac{(\text{Frequency of its row})(\text{Frequency of its column})}{\text{Total } n}.$$

The first issue is to understand the concept of a "cell." In a 2 × 2 chi-square, there are four frequencies. Thus, the 2 × 2 chi-square can be thought of as having four places, or cells, for data. The chi-square test will determine whether the pattern of frequencies in the four cells differ significantly from what would be expected by chance. As is clear from the above equation, before calculating the expected frequency for a cell, it is first necessary to calculate the row totals, the column totals, and the total number of subjects. These are called marginal totals. Thus, the marginal total for the first row of our example is 36 + 25, which equals 61. Similarly, the marginal total for the first column is 36 + 22, which equals 58. For our 2 × 2 study, all of the marginal totals, as well as the total number of subjects, are shown in Table 8.3.

Table 8.3	Original Data With Marginal Totals for the First Example

		Diagnosed With ADHD		Marginal Total
		Yes	No	
Side with more omission errors	Right	36	25	61
	Left	22	4	26
	Marginal total	58	29	87

Note. ADHD, attention-deficit/hyperactivity disorder.

We now must calculate the expected frequency for each cell. The order in which these expected frequencies are calculated is irrelevant. However, some logical pattern should be followed so that no cell is omitted or counted twice. We will begin with the upper left cell. This cell has a row total of 61 and a column total of 58. The total number of subjects in the study is 87. Therefore, using the above equation, the expected frequency for this cell is (61)(58)/87, which equals 40.67. We now calculate the expected frequency of the next cell in the row. For this cell, we would have a row total of 61 and a column total of 29. We substitute these values into the equation given above and divide by the total number of subjects in the study to obtain the expected frequency of 20.33. We then proceed with the two cells of the second row. The results are shown in Table 8.4.

Table 8.4	Expected Frequencies for the First Example

		Diagnosed With ADHD	
		Yes	No
Side with more omission errors	Right	40.67	20.33
	Left	17.33	8.67

Note. ADHD, attention-deficit/hyperactivity disorder.

We could then proceed by constructing a table as we did in Chapter 7, when we determined the value of the goodness-of-fit chi-square (Table 8.5).

| Table 8.5 | Steps in Calculating a Chi-Square for the First Example |

Cells	f_o	f_e	$f_o - f_e$	$(f_o - f_e)^2$	$\dfrac{(f_o - f_e)^2}{f_e}$
1	36	40.67	−4.67	21.81	0.54
2	25	20.33	4.67	21.81	1.07
3	22	17.33	4.67	21.81	1.26
4	4	8.67	−4.67	21.81	2.52
			$\Sigma = 0$		$\Sigma = 5.39$

However, you may find that it is more efficient to directly calculate our chi-square:

$$\chi^2 = \Sigma \frac{(\text{Frequency observed} - \text{Frequency expected})^2}{\text{Frequency expected}}.$$

This can be written as

$$\chi^2 = \Sigma \frac{(f_o - f_e)^2}{f_e}.$$

For our example,

$$\chi^2 = \frac{(36 - 40.67)^2}{40.67} + \frac{(25 - 20.33)^2}{20.33} + \frac{(22 - 17.33)^2}{17.33} + \frac{(4 - 8.67)^2}{8.67}$$

$$= 0.54 + 1.07 + 1.26 + 2.52$$

$$= 5.39.$$

As with the goodness-of-fit chi-square, we must now consult the chi-square table (Table J.2 in Appendix J) to compare our outcome with the critical value. To do so, we must first determine our degrees of freedom (df). For the chi-square test of independence,

Degrees of freedom = (Number of rows − 1) (Number of columns − 1).

For our example, since we have 2 rows and 2 columns, we have degrees of freedom = (2 − 1) (2 − 1), which equals 1 × 1 or 1. With alpha equal to .05, the critical value, found in the chi-square table (Table J.2 in Appendix J), is 3.84. As our obtained chi-square, 5.39, is larger than the critical value, we reject the null hypothesis that the two samples came from populations with equal proportions for side of omission and accept the alternative hypothesis that the samples came from populations with proportions that differed for side of omission. Put another way, we found that there was an interaction between the two variables, ADHD diagnosis and the side on which stimuli are missed. Specifically, inspection of Table 8.2 indicates that individuals without the ADHD diagnosis were less likely to omit stimuli presented to the left side than were those individuals with the ADHD diagnosis.

It may be helpful to review what we have just accomplished. We began with two samples and utilized a chi-square statistic to come to a decision concerning the populations from which they were drawn. The procedure we used has several advantages over simply looking at the data and jumping to a conclusion. First, the steps are agreed on, and thus, others will proceed as we did and will come to the same decision. Personal opinion is *not* the basis for our conclusion. Second, by setting alpha at a particular value, in this case .05, we have defined the magnitude of our Type I error rate. Remember, there is no guarantee that we made the correct decision when we rejected the null hypothesis. It is possible that, by chance, we obtained two very unlikely samples. At least we know, though, that the probability of having rejected the null hypothesis when in fact it was true is only .05 or 5%.

We would report our finding in a journal article in the same way that we would report a goodness-of-fit chi-square, giving the degrees of freedom, the number of subjects, the calculated chi-square value, and the alpha level. We would, therefore, report $\chi^2(1, n = 87) = 5.39, p < .05$.

Another Example

To be certain that you understand the steps that we have just taken, another example may be helpful. It has been reported that men are generally more distressed by the sexual infidelity than the emotional infidelity of their partners, whereas women are more distressed by the emotional infidelity than the sexual infidelity of their partners. Mathes (2003) reexamined this issue. His results are summarized in Table 8.6. What would the null and alternative hypotheses be, and with an alpha of .05, what would your conclusion be?

Each of the steps will be shown below, but it is strongly suggested that you try this example on your own and use the text as a check on the accuracy of your work. At the end of this example, we will discuss what statistical significance indicates as well as what it does not indicate.

Table 8.6 Summary of the Data for the Second Example

	Women	Men
More distressed by emotional infidelity	42	12
More distressed by sexual infidelity	17	48

We begin by stating the null and alternative hypotheses. From the Mathes (2003) study, the hypotheses would be as follows:

H_0: *There is no difference* in the distribution of answers for women and men.

H_1: *There is a difference* in the distribution of answers for women and men.

The next step, as before, is to determine the expected frequencies. They are found by using the equation that was utilized in the previous example:

$$\text{Expected frequency of a cell} = \frac{(\text{Frequency of its row})(\text{Frequency of its column})}{\text{Total } n}.$$

Before we can calculate the expected frequency for each cell, it is first necessary to calculate the row totals, the column totals, and the total number of subjects. For our 2 × 2 study, these totals are indicated in Table 8.7.

Table 8.7   Original Data With Marginal Totals for the Second Example

	Women	Men	Marginal Total
More distressed by emotional infidelity	42	12	54
More distressed by sexual infidelity	17	48	65
Marginal total	59	60	119

We now can calculate the expected frequency for each cell, which is given by (Row total) (Column total)/Total n. Thus, for the upper left cell, the expected frequency would be (54) (59)/119, which equals 26.77. The same procedure would be followed to find the remaining three expected frequencies. The result of these calculations is shown in Table 8.8.

Table 8.8   Expected Frequencies for the Second Example

	Women	Men
More distressed by emotional infidelity	26.77	27.23
More distressed by sexual infidelity	32.23	32.77

We can now calculate the chi-square, first calculating [(Frequency observed − Frequency expected)^2/Frequency expected] for each of the four cells, and then adding the results together:

$$\chi^2 = \Sigma \frac{(f_o - f_e)^2}{f_e}$$

$$= \frac{(42 - 26.77)^2}{26.77} + \frac{(12 - 27.23)^2}{27.23} + \frac{(17 - 32.23)^2}{32.23} + \frac{(48 - 32.77)^2}{32.77}$$

$$= 8.66 + 8.52 + 7.20 + 7.08$$

$$= 31.46.$$

Next, we must find our degrees of freedom. For a 2 × 2 chi-square, the degrees of freedom would equal (2 − 1)(2 − 1), or 1 × 1 = 1. Referring to the chi-square table (Table J.2 in Appendix J), we find that the critical value for 1 *df* with alpha set at .05 is 3.84. As our obtained chi-square of 31.46 is greater than this critical value, we reject the null and accept the alternative hypothesis. In fact, a chi-square of 31.46 has a likelihood of happening, by chance, of less than .001, or 1 chance in 1,000. We recognize, of course, that we may have made a Type I error, and thus have not proven that there is a relationship between the two populations. Most researchers would indicate that the calculated chi-square was substantially greater than the critical value of 3.84 by showing that the probability was considerably less than .05. In a journal, the outcome would be reported as $\chi^2 = (1, n = 119) = 31.46, p < .001$.

We have just completed our second chi-square test of independence. Hopefully, by this point, you agree that there is nothing particularly challenging about analyzing data with this statistical test. It is, of course, important to proceed through each step in a careful manner, but no step is mathematically or conceptually difficult.

PROGRESS CHECK

1. With the goodness-of-fit chi-square, the expected frequencies are _____, whereas with a chi-square test of independence, they must be _____.

2. With the chi-square test of independence, if the relative frequencies are similar, the outcome will _____ statistically significant.

3. The equation for the chi-square test of independence is _____ as the equation for the goodness-of-fit chi-square.

Answers: 1. known; calculated. 2. not be. 3. the same.

This is a good time to examine in more detail what we have and have not found. In our just completed chi-square test of independence, our calculated outcome was greater than the critical value that we obtained from the chi-square table (Table J.2 in Appendix J). Thus, we concluded that there was a statistically significant difference between the genders for what causes distress within a relationship. This indicates that the discrepancy that was noted in the obtained proportions was unlikely to have occurred by chance. However, it is important to understand how statistical significance in a chi-square is dependent on two characteristics of the data: (1) the magnitude of the differences in the proportions and (2) the sample size.

To see how sample size affects the chi-square, we will, for illustration purposes, simply double each of the numbers in Table 8.6, which also doubles the marginal totals. This is illustrated in Table 8.9. By doing so, we have not changed the relative proportions; we have simply doubled the size of the study. Please check that the new value of the chi-square would be 62.87. Note that while the proportions within the chi-square tables (Tables 8.6 and 8.9) have stayed the same, as have the degrees of freedom, the magnitude of the calculated chi-square has doubled! (If you do the calculations, you will notice that there is a very minor discrepancy due to rounding error.) This means that we now have an even less likely outcome than was previously found. Why would this be the case? Actually, a moment's thought will confirm that this is exactly what one would expect to happen. The chi-square test of independence indicates the likelihood that an outcome would occur *by chance* if the null hypothesis were true. Though the obtained proportions have remained the same, the new outcome is less likely because it is now based on twice the data. You would be more confident that you are a good student if you have obtained four As instead of just two. The chi-square is influenced in the same manner—we are more confident of an effect if it is based on more data.

If you have followed the logic of the argument, then it should be clear that this raises a problem for how we interpret a significant statistical outcome. We have found that the size of the calculated chi-square is affected by the size of the set of data in the study. It follows, then, that while a significant outcome could occur from having a large effect with a relatively large data set, as in our example, it could also occur by either having a very large effect in a small data set, or having only a small effect in a very large data set. Therefore, a statistically significant chi-square based on a small data set may actually be more impressive than a significant chi-square that is based on a much larger sample! This is true because to have a statistically

Table 8.9 Illustration of the Data in the Second Example Being Doubled

	Women	Men	Marginal Total
More distressed by emotional infidelity	84	24	108
More distressed by sexual infidelity	34	96	130
Marginal total	118	120	238

significant outcome with only a modest sample size means that your variable must have had a large effect, and having a large effect is closer to what we generally mean by the word "significance" in our everyday conversations. Fortunately, there is a statistical measure of **effect size** for use with a 2 × 2 chi-square test; it is the phi coefficient (pronounced fie). Phi is the Greek letter represented by the symbol ϕ. A measure of effect size is usually only calculated after a statistically significant outcome has been found. Assuming that

Effect size: a measure of how strong a statistically significant outcome is.

your study had sufficient power (reviewed in Appendix D), in most cases, it would not make sense to find a measure for how strong an effect is unless you first found evidence that the effect existed. Fortunately, the phi coefficient can easily be obtained once a statistically significant 2 × 2 chi-square has been calculated, as is evident with the following equation:

$$\phi = \sqrt{\frac{\chi^2}{n}}.$$

A value of phi greater than .5 is considered to be indicative of a large effect, values between .3 and .5 are considered to be indicative of medium-sized effects, and those below .3 are indicative of small effects.

One of the advantages of the phi coefficient is that, unlike the chi-square, it is not affected by the sample size. You can confirm this by calculating phi based on the data presented in Table 8.6 and calculating phi again for the doubling of these data, which are illustrated in Table 8.9. As the following calculations show, the two phi coefficients are identical:

$$\phi = \sqrt{\frac{31.46}{119}}$$

$$= .51.$$

$$\phi = \sqrt{\frac{62.87}{238}}$$

$$= .51.$$

The relative proportions, which are indicative of the effect sizes, remained the same within the two tables, and thus, the phi coefficients remained the same. Our calculated phi coefficient of .51 indicates a large-sized effect.

Reporting the Results of a 2 × 2 Chi-Square Test of Independence

Previously, you were shown how to report the outcome of a chi-square test in the scientific literature. Increasingly, journals are also requiring that some measure of effect size be reported. For the data in Table 8.6, we would therefore report $\chi^2 = (1, n = 119) = 31.46$, $p < .001$, $\phi = .51$.

We have just concluded a section dealing with the 2 × 2 chi-square test of independence. Before proceeding with a more complex design using the chi-square test of independence, it might be good to pause and review what we have covered. We have been exploring what is known as statistics for difference designs. Difference designs are examples of inferential statistics because they are used to make decisions concerning populations based on data derived from samples.

We have begun our exploration of the statistics for difference designs with the procedures that use nominal data. These are listed in Table 8.1. As you may recall, with nominal data, we are dealing with the frequencies with which outcomes occur. Thus far, we have studied the chi-square test and have learned how it can be used to analyze data from one (goodness-of-fit chi-square) or two (chi-square test of independence) variables. We have also learned about degrees of freedom, how to determine a critical value from a statistical table, and why it is important to also report the effect size, as measured by the phi coefficient. The same general approach applies to the statistical tests utilized with ordinal as well as interval or ratio data. For now, we will continue our exploration of the chi-square test by turning to a more complex example. While this more complex example will involve some additional calculation, you will see that much of what you have learned will carry over. This is a pattern that will repeat in later chapters. You will see similar issues raised repeatedly. And by mastering how to analyze nominal data, you are well on your way to mastering how statistical procedures are used for any form of data.

We conclude our discussion of the chi-square test of independence with a review of a study by Perfect (2003). He examined factors that might influence the accuracy of witness identification of suspects in a police lineup. Previous work had found, surprisingly, that if an eyewitness described a perpetrator, he or she was *less* accurate in picking the perpetrator out of a subsequent lineup. The study by Perfect (2003) tested undergraduates to determine how different types of intervening activity would affect their subsequent success with a lineup. For the control group, the intervening activity was simply reading a magazine article for 10 minutes. One experimental group was presented a series of stimuli, and they engaged in a task that required concentration on the details. A second experimental group engaged in a task that required concentration on more global aspects of stimuli. The null and alternative hypotheses were as follows:

H_0: *Type of task does not affect* eyewitness success.

H_1: *Type of task does affect* eyewitness success.

Note that each sample was independent; no subject was in more than one sample, nor were the subjects in one sample matched in any way with the subjects in the other two samples. Furthermore, note that the data are nominal; each subject was either successful or not successful with the lineup identification. In this study, alpha was set at .05.

As with all chi-square procedures, the data can be represented simply, as is shown in Table 8.10.

Table 8.10	Summary of the Data for the Third Example

	Subject Group		
	Control	**Detail**	**Global**
Successful identification	21	24	13
Not successful identification	9	6	17

As there are 3 columns of nominal data (the undergraduates were each assigned to one of three conditions) and 2 rows (each undergraduate was either successful or not successful with their identification), this is a 3 × 2 design. More specifically, this is a 3 × 2 chi-square test of independence.

Step 1, as before, is to determine the expected frequencies. They are found by using the same equation as for a 2 × 2 chi-square:

$$\text{Expected frequency of a cell} = \frac{(\text{Frequency of its row})(\text{Frequency of its column})}{\text{Total } n}.$$

Once again, before calculating the expected frequency for a cell, it is first necessary to calculate the row totals, the column totals, and the total number of subjects. For our 3 × 2 study, these totals are indicated in Table 8.11.

We now must calculate the expected frequency for each cell. Beginning with the upper left cell, we have a row total of 58 and a column total of 30. The total number of subjects in the study is 90. Therefore, using the above equation, the expected frequency for this cell is (58)(30)/90, which equals 19.33. We now calculate the expected frequency of each of the

Table 8.11	Original Data With Marginal Totals for the Third Example

	Control	**Detail**	**Global**	**Marginal Total**
Successful identification	21	24	13	58
Not successful identification	9	6	17	32
Marginal total	30	30	30	90

other cells in the row. When this has been completed, we proceed with the cells of the second row. The results are shown in Table 8.12.

| Table 8.12 | Expected Frequencies for the Third Example |

	Control	Detail	Global
Successful identification	19.33	19.33	19.33
Not successful identification	10.67	10.67	10.67

We can now directly calculate our chi-square,

$$\chi^2 = \Sigma \frac{(f_o - f_e)^2}{f_e}$$

$$= \frac{(21-19.33)^2}{19.33} + \frac{(24-19.33)^2}{19.33} + \frac{(13-19.33)^2}{19.33} +$$

$$\frac{(9-10.67)^2}{10.67} + \frac{(6-10.67)^2}{10.67} + \frac{(17-10.67)^2}{10.67}$$

$$= 0.14 + 1.13 + 2.07 + 0.26 + 2.04 + 3.76$$

$$= 9.40.$$

As always, we now consult the chi-square table (Table J.2 in Appendix J) to compare our outcome with the critical value. To do so, we must determine our degrees of freedom. For the chi-square test of independence,

Degrees of freedom = (Number of rows − 1) (Number of columns − 1).

For our example, since we have 2 rows and 3 columns, we have $df = (2 - 1)(3 - 1)$, which equals 1×2, or 2. With alpha equal to .05, the critical value, found in the chi-square table (Table J.2 in Appendix J), is 5.99. As our obtained chi-square, 9.40, is greater than the critical value, we reject the null hypothesis that the type of task does not affect eyewitness success and accept the alternative hypothesis that the type of task does affect eyewitness success. Alternatively, we could state that the samples came from populations with different proportions. Thus, we have found that there is an interaction or relationship between the variables. Specifically, success rate depends on the type of intervening activity engaged in by the eyewitness.

We are still faced with two issues. First, we have not yet calculated a measure for effect size. The phi coefficient is not appropriate, for it is limited to 2 × 2 chi-squares. Second, the chi-square procedure provides an overall test of significance for the entire study, but it does not indicate where the significant difference(s) is (are). With a 2 × 2 chi-square, this is not an issue, for there are only two samples, and thus, if there is a significant outcome, the difference has to be between the two samples. With three or more samples, the issue is not so clear. For instance, in our case, there are three samples. The significant difference(s) in the obtained proportions could be between a pair of samples (between Sample 1 and Sample 2, between Sample 1 and Sample 3, or between Sample 2 and Sample 3), any two of these comparisons, or all three of these comparisons. In addition, more complex comparisons could be involved, such as Sample 1 versus a combination of Samples 2 and 3, or Sample 2 versus a combination of Samples 1 and 3, or Sample 3 versus a combination of Samples 1 and 2. In this book, we will deal only with what are called pairwise comparisons, the comparisons involving the initial samples, not any of the more complex combinations. The chi-square test that we have just completed does not specify which of these outcomes is significant. It simply indicates that there is at least one comparison within the data that is significant. We will examine the issue of effect size first and then describe a procedure for specifying where a difference within a significant chi-square is located.

With a 2 × 2 chi-square, the phi coefficient provides a measure of effect size. Fortunately, only a minor modification is required to provide a measure of effect size for any size chi-square. The appropriate measure is Cramer's V. The formula is as follows:

$$\text{Cramer's } V = \sqrt{\frac{\chi^2}{n(df)}},$$

where df = the *smaller* of $(r - 1)$ and $(c - 1)$.

Note that the equation is very similar to the equation provided earlier for the phi coefficient. In fact, the only difference is the inclusion of the degrees of freedom (be aware that the definition of df has changed, it is *not* the same as the df from the overall chi-square). Also, note that in the situation where there is 1 df, the phi coefficient and Cramer's V are identical. In our case, df for Cramer's V = 1, as the smaller of the rows − 1 or columns − 1 is equal to 2 − 1 = 1.

We calculate Cramer's V as follows:

$$\text{Cramer's } V = \sqrt{\frac{9.4}{(90)(1)}}$$

$$= \sqrt{\frac{9.4}{90}}$$

$$= .32.$$

The interpretation of Cramer's V is slightly more complex than the interpretation was for the phi coefficient. As Table 8.13 indicates, the interpretation of the effect size will vary depending on the df used in the calculation of Cramer's V (Cohen, 1988).

By checking Table 8.13, you will see that, with 1 df, the interpretations of Cramer's V is the same as was previously given for the phi coefficient. This is what one would expect, for they provide the same outcome when there is 1 df. In our case, we obtained a Cramer's V of .32 with 1 df, which would be a medium-sized effect.

We now turn to our second question: How do we identify the specific samples that differ when a chi-square with more than 1 df has been found to be statistically significant? What we are dealing with here are called post hoc comparisons. **Post hoc comparisons** are employed when overall tests of significance involve more than two samples. From Table 8.1 (or Appendix K), you will see that studies with more than two samples can occur not only with chi-square designs but also following a significant Kruskal–Wallis H test when there are ordinal data (reviewed in Appendix A), and with analyses of variance when there are interval or ratio data.

Post hoc comparisons: statistical procedures utilized following an initial, overall test of significance to identify the specific samples that differ.

In our current example, we have a significant 3×2 chi-square. If it were not significant, we would not conduct any post hoc test. However, since it is significant, and we want to know where the difference(s) is (are), we would conduct every pairwise comparison. With three groups (2 df), there are three possible pairwise comparisons, as we noted previously—between Sample 1 and Sample 2, between Sample 1 and Sample 3, and between Sample 2 and Sample 3. Therefore, we would compute three additional 2×2 chi-square statistics, each testing one of the above comparisons. Thus, one 2×2 chi-square would compare the proportions obtained from the control group with the proportions obtained from the "Detail" experimental group. Another would compare the proportions obtained from the control group with the proportions obtained from the "Global" experimental group. The final would compare the proportions obtained from the "Detail" group with the proportions obtained from the "Global" experimental group.

There is a potential problem, however, when you conduct multiple comparisons. If you keep alpha equal to .05 for each comparison, then when you conduct a large number of

| Table 8.13 | Interpretation of Cramer's V |

	Small Effect	**Medium Effect**	**Large Effect**
$df = 1$	Between .10 and .30	Between .30 and .50	Greater than .50
$df = 2$	Between .07 and .21	Between .21 and .35	Greater than .35
$df = 3$	Between .06 and .17	Between .17 and .29	Greater than .29

comparisons, you may find statistical significance when there is no relationship in the populations. Here is why. With alpha set at .05 for a comparison, you know there is a 5% chance of making a Type I error. In other words, there is 1 chance in 20 that you will reject the null hypothesis when in fact it is correct. But what happens if you conduct a series of statistical tests, each with their alpha set at .05? Clearly, since each comparison has 1 chance in 20 of leading to a Type I error, if you conduct numerous comparisons, it will become very likely that you will commit at least one Type I error. The problem is that alpha is being set per comparison. Earlier we found that studies with very large sample sizes may lead to statistically significant but meaningless outcomes; and you learned that the phi coefficient or Cramer's *V* provides a solution to the problem of interpreting effect size. As you might expect, there is also a solution for the problem of error rate that arises from conducting a large number of post hoc comparisons.

Once we obtain a significant chi-square test of independence based on more than 1 *df*, the next step is to conduct a series of additional 2 × 2 chi-squares to identify the specific samples that differ. These post hoc comparisons are conducted in exactly the same way as we learned previously. However, we also employ an additional step to control for the increased likelihood of Type I error that would result from conducting a series of post hoc comparisons. One of the easiest methods is to divide the overall alpha rate that you want to maintain by the number of post hoc comparisons you make. In our case, as usual, we would set our overall alpha at .05. We would then divide .05 by the number of post hoc chi-square tests that we conduct and use this more stringent requirement when determining our critical values. By doing so, we maintain the overall, or experiment-wise, error rate at .05. This is known as the **Bonferroni method** of controlling the error rate.

> *Bonferroni method: a procedure to control the Type I error rate when making numerous comparisons. In this procedure, the alpha level that the experimenter sets is divided by the number of comparisons.*

In the current example, we would conduct all three of the possible pairwise comparisons, as shown below. Using the Bonferroni method, we would divide our initial alpha of .05 by 3, since we made three comparisons. Thus, when determining the critical value, we would look in a table for alpha equal to .05/3 = .0167. Since, the chi-square table (Table J.2 in Appendix J) that we have used previously does not include this particular alpha, we would need to turn to a table that includes a series of chi-square values for 1 *df* and numerous alpha levels or utilize a computer program. For an alpha of .0167 with 1 *df*, the critical value is 5.73. If the Bonferroni method had not been utilized, our critical value, with 1 *df*, would have been 3.84. Let us see what difference this makes.

The data and marginal totals for the comparison between the "Control" and "Detail" groups are shown in Table 8.14.

The expected frequencies are shown in Table 8.15.

You should confirm that the chi-square value for this comparison is 0.8.

The data and marginal totals for the comparison between the "Control" and "Global" groups are shown in Table 8.16.

Table 8.14	Post Hoc Comparison for the Control and Detail Groups: Original Data With Marginal Totals

	Control	Detail	Marginal Total
Successful identification	21	24	45
Not successful identification	9	6	15
Marginal total	30	30	60

Table 8.15	Expected Frequencies for the Post Hoc Comparison

	Control	Detail
Successful identification	22.5	22.5
Not successful identification	7.5	7.5

Table 8.16	Post Hoc Comparison for the Control and Global Groups: Original Data With Marginal Totals

	Control	Global	Marginal Total
Successful identification	21	13	34
Not successful identification	9	17	26
Marginal total	30	30	60

The expected frequencies are shown in Table 8.17.

Table 8.17	Expected Frequencies for the Post Hoc Comparison

	Control	Global
Successful identification	17	17
Not successful identification	13	13

You should confirm that the chi-square value for this comparison is 4.34.

Finally, the data and marginal totals for the comparison between the "Detail" and "Global" groups are shown in Table 8.18.

The expected frequencies are shown in Table 8.19.

You should confirm that the chi-square value for this comparison is 8.54.

Note that each of these three 2×2 chi-square tests has 1 *df*. Therefore, two of these three post hoc comparisons would be statistically significant at the .05 level, *if the Bonferroni method were not used*, as two of the outcomes are greater than the critical value of 3.84. However, note that only one of our three post hoc tests met the more conservative criterion of 5.73 set by the Bonferroni method. When reporting our finding, we use the 5.73 criterion, but report $p < .05$ since, with the Bonferroni method, this is what we set as the "Experiment-wise" Type I error rate.

Reporting the Results of a Chi-Square Test of Independence Larger Than 2×2

For the data in the overall 3×2 chi-square in Table 8.10, we would report in the literature that $\chi^2(2, n = 90) = 9.40, p < .01$, Cramer's $V = .32$. This would be followed by a statement indicating that three post hoc pairwise comparisons, using the Bonferroni method, were then conducted, and only the comparison of the "Detail" group with the "Global" group

Table 8.18	Post Hoc Comparison for the Detail and Global Groups: Original Data With Marginal Totals

	Detail	Global	Marginal Total
Successful identification	24	13	37
Not successful identification	6	17	23
Marginal total	30	30	60

Table 8.19	Expected Frequencies for the Post Hoc Comparison

	Detail	Global
Successful identification	18.5	18.5
Not successful identification	11.5	11.5

was found to be significant ($\chi^2(1, n = 60) = 8.54, p < .05$). With these statements, we have provided the reader with a great deal of information. We indicated that we conducted an overall chi-square test for an independent samples experiment; we told the reader the number of degrees of freedom in the design, as well as the number of participants in the study; and we indicated the size of the chi-square and noted that it was statistically significant. Furthermore, we provided a measure of effect size so that the readers can judge the strength of the relationship. The readers are thus in a position to make an informed decision about how meaningful the outcome is. Finally, we indicated where, within the study, this significant effect occurred. All of this was communicated efficiently, using a minimum number of words.

A Final Observation

The chi-square test of independence has been discussed as a procedure for finding if there is a difference. Thus, it is used with true experiments as well as quasi-experimental designs. It is important to note that the chi-square test is also often used with studies that are examining whether there is an association between variables rather than a difference. For instance, the author of this text enjoys watching football. It was recently reported in the *Buffalo News* that if the Buffalo Bills quarterback threw two or more interceptions in a game, the win–loss ratio was a disappointing 1:13. However, in those games in which he threw none or only one interception, the win–loss ratio improved to 8:8. These data can be analyzed with a chi-square test. However, it should be recognized that this is a correlational design, and thus, we need to be cautious in making any claims concerning the nature of this association. Finally, while the chi-square test is often employed with correlational studies that have nominal data, there are alternative procedures. One of these, phi correlation (this is a different procedure from the chi coefficient discussed previously as a measure of effect size), will be discussed in Chapter 14.

PURPOSE AND LIMITATIONS OF THE CHI-SQUARE TEST OF INDEPENDENCE

It is a test for interaction or difference in proportions: The null hypothesis is that the observed frequencies are distributed in similar proportions within each of the groups. In other words, the relative frequencies are the same for each of the groups, and thus, any difference in the proportions is due to chance.

It provides an overall test of significance: In designs that are larger than 2 × 2, a statistically significant outcome indicates that a difference in the relative frequencies exists between the groups, but the overall chi-square test does not indicate where the difference(s) is (are). Subsequent post hoc chi-square tests are conducted to identify the specific groups that differ.

The test does not provide a measure of effect size: The chi-square is a test of significance. It indicates whether or not an outcome is likely to have occurred by chance if the null hypothesis is correct. If the chi-square statistic is significant, a measure of effect size, phi or Cramer's *V*, is then calculated.

The expected frequencies cannot be too small: For the 2 × 2 chi-square, in other words, when *df* = 1, the minimum acceptable expected frequency for any cell is 5. When *df* > 1, no more than 20% of the cells can have an expected frequency that is less than 5, and no cell can have an expected frequency of 0. If the data do not meet these requirements, more data should be collected or an alternative statistical procedure could be used. Alternatively, in the case of larger chi-square designs, rows or columns could be combined in a meaningful manner so that the expected frequencies are increased.

CONCLUSION

We have now completed the section of the book dealing with the chi-square statistic. Before continuing with the study of additional statistical procedures, it may be helpful to take a few moments to review what we have accomplished and to put it into perspective. By referring to Table 8.1 (or Appendix K), you will see that we have been progressing down the column for nominal data. Specifically, we have learned how to analyze nominal data in designs with one or two variables. We will not be discussing situations that involve nominal data with other designs as these are less commonly encountered.

Before proceeding, please take a moment to review Table 8.1 (or Appendix K) in order to once again see the relationships among the statistical procedures. We have dealt with nominal data in this chapter and in Chapter 7. In Chapter 9, we will begin to review the procedures for interval or ratio data. Procedures for ordinal data are less commonly used, though for each difference design that we will discuss for interval or ratio data, there is a parallel situation for ordinal data (the Kruskal–Wallis *H* test is included in Appendix A). Fortunately, much that you have learned thus far will carry over to these procedures. For instance, degrees of freedom, critical values, the distinction between statistical significance and effect size, and the issue of post hoc tests will all be seen again when we review the procedures used with interval or ratio data. Accordingly, this chapter had a dual purpose. First, it presented you with an overview of the statistics that are employed to find differences when utilizing nominal data. Second, it introduced you to the organization of inferential statistical procedures. This double purpose will continue for the remainder of the text. It is important, as you master the use of specific statistical procedures, that you learn how each new test is related to the others. It is only when you have gained this perspective that you will truly be knowledgeable about statistics.

Chapter Resources

GLOSSARY OF TERMS

Bonferroni method: a procedure to control the Type I error rate when making numerous comparisons. In this procedure, the alpha level that the experimenter sets is divided by the number of comparisons.

Dependent: two events, samples or variables are dependent if knowing the outcome of one enhances our prediction of the other.

Effect size: a measure of how strong a statistically significant outcome is.

Gambler's fallacy: the incorrect assumption that if an event has not occurred recently, then the probability of it occurring in the future increases.

Interaction: a statistical term indicating that the effects of two or more variables are not independent.

Post hoc comparisons: statistical procedures utilized following an initial, overall test of significance to identify the specific samples that differ.

Questions: Chapter 8

(Answers to odd-numbered items are provided in Appendix I.)

1. When an experimenter concludes that the results of a statistical test are significant, this indicates that _____.

   a. the outcome is especially important

   b. the outcome is unlikely to have occurred by chance

   c. the experimenter has made an error

2. With a 2 × 2 chi-square, the minimum expected frequency that can occur in any cell is _____.

   a. 1

   b. 3

   c. 5

   d. 7

3. If a chi-square test is found to be significant, what measure of effect size should then be utilized?

   a. Phi

   b. Bonferroni

   c. Cramer's V

   d. Both "a" and "b" would always be appropriate.

   e. Either "a" or "b" would be correct depending on the specific chi-square.

4. The chi-square test of independence is a test for _____.

   a. interaction

   b. effect size

   c. importance

   d. none of the above

5. If there is no interaction, then a 2 × 2 chi-square will _____.

   a. be statistically significant

   b. not be statistically significant

   c. not have to have to meet the assumptions of the test in order to be used

   d. be more difficult to calculate

6. George, a particularly poor statistics student, notes that the last three times a coin has been tossed, it has come up heads. He therefore concludes that it is time for it to come up tails. This is an example of the _____.

   a. gambler's fallacy

   b. Bonferroni method

   c. statistical significance

   d. none of the above

7. Following a significant 2 × 5 chi-square, the researcher would _____.

   a. utilize the Bonferroni method

   b. employ phi

   c. check that all of the cells have a sample size of at least 25

   d. conduct Cramer's *V*

   e. both "a" and "d"

8. If the frequency within each cell in a 2 × 2 chi-square is tripled, what happens to the size of the chi-square outcome?

   a. It stays the same.

   b. It doubles.

   c. It triples.

   d. It cannot be determined.

9. If the frequency within each cell in a 2 × 2 chi-square is tripled, what happens to the size of the subsequent phi?

   a. It stays the same.

   b. It doubles.

   c. It triples.

   d. It cannot be determined.

10. The Bonferroni method would be utilized _____.

   a. following a statistically significant 2 × 2 chi-square

   b. following a statistically significant 2 × 3 chi-square

   c. following a statistically significant phi

   d. all of the above

11. With a 2 × 2 chi-square, _____ provides a measure of effect size.

   a. Bonferroni

   b. the interaction

   c. the phi coefficient

   d. none of the above

Assume that an NFL (National Football League) team has a new coach. In his first two seasons, the team has the following record.

	Season	
	1	**2**
Win	2	6
Loss	14	10

12. How many degrees of freedom do you have?

   a. 1

   b. 2

   c. 3

   d. 4

13. What is the value of the chi-square?

   a. 2.667

   b. 1.456

   c. 2.441

   d. 3.048

14. Has the team's record significantly changed, assuming an alpha of .05?

   a. Yes

   b. No

Now assume that the coach has led the team for an additional year and he has the following record:

	Season		
	1	**2**	**3**
Win	2	6	9
Loss	14	10	7

15. How many degrees of freedom do you have?

    a. 1

    b. 2

    c. 3

    d. 4

16. What is the value of the chi-square?

    a. 3.114

    b. 5.423

    c. 6.740

    d. 9.003

17. Which of the groups differs?

    a. 1 versus 2

    b. 1 versus 3

    c. 2 versus 3

    d. Both 1 versus 3 and 2 versus 3

Problems 18 to 23 utilize SPSS.

SPSS

OUR FIRST EXAMPLE USING SPSS WITH THE CHI-SQUARE TEST OF INDEPENDENCE

To Begin SPSS

Step 1: Activate the program. If you have the PASW version of SPSS, you will then see the window displayed in Figure 8.1. (Other versions of SPSS will have a very similar window.)

Figure 8.1   The Initial SPSS (PASW) Window

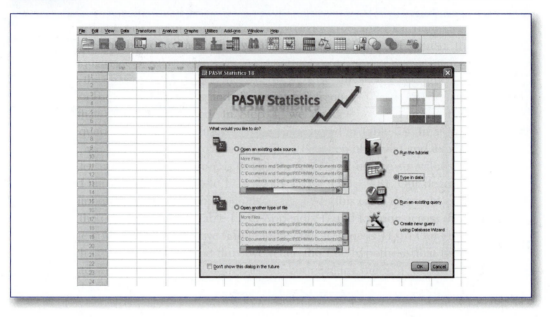

Step 2: Click on "Type in data," and then click on "OK."

Step 3: Click on "Variable View" at the lower left corner of the window. Near the top of the new page is a row of column headings, beginning with "Name," then "Type," and proceeding to "Role." For the present, we will only be dealing with the columns headed by "Name," "Label," "Values," and "Measure."

Step 4: Click on the first empty rectangle (called a "cell") under the column heading "Name." You now type the name of the first variable for which you have data. We are going to utilize the same data and labels as were previously employed in Table 8.2. These data dealt with the question of whether there is an association between whether an individual had been diagnosed with ADHD and the side of omission errors. We have called these variables "ADHD" and "omission." Therefore, type "ADHD" in the first empty cell under "Name."

Step 5: Click twice on the first empty cell under the column heading "Label." In this cell, you can type a more extensive description of your variable. In our case, type "Diagnosed with ADHD?" Note that to see the entire label, you may need to expand the size of this cell by placing your cursor on the right border of the Label heading and moving to the right.

Step 6: Click on the first empty cell under the column heading "Values." Then click on the small blue square. A box will appear. In the blank space to the right of "Value," type the number "1." Then, type a brief description of this value of the variable in the blank space to the right of "Label." In our case, type "yes." Finally, click on "Add." Your label for a value of 1 will appear in the large white region in the center of the window. Now repeat the above steps in this section for the value "2," which is given the label "no" (Figure 8.2). Then click on "OK."

Figure 8.2   The Value Labels Window

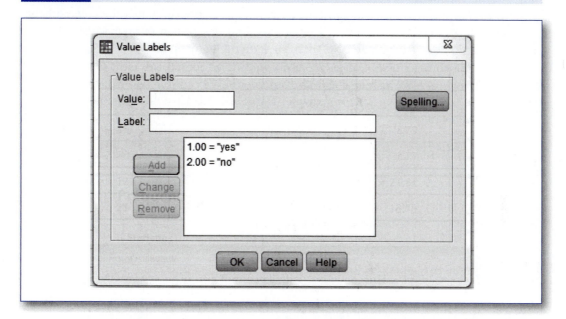

Step 7: Click on the first empty cell under the column heading "Measure." As we are dealing with nominal data, select "Nominal" as is shown in Figure 8.3.

Step 8: Repeat Steps 4 to 7, except that you type "omission" in the first empty cell under "Name." Then type "Side with more omission errors" for the "Label," and the value labels are now "right" and "left" instead of "yes" and "no." As before, select "Nominal" in the column under the column heading "Measure." The result is shown in Figure 8.3. You could now shift to the data window and sequentially enter the data for each subject. However, this can quickly become tedious. SPSS permits the rapid construction of the chi-square table of results. To do so, we need to create another variable so that SPSS can be instructed that the numbers stand for the frequencies that occurred.

Figure 8.3   The Variable View Window

	Name	Type	Width	Decimals	Label	Values	Missing	Columns	Align	Measure	Role
1	ADHD	Numeric	8	2	Diagnosed with ADHD?	{1.00, yes}...	None	8	Right	Nominal	Input
2	omission	Numeric	8	2	Side with more omission errors	{1.00, right}...	None	8	Right	Nominal	Input

Step 9: In the empty cell directly under "omission," type the name of this new variable. I have chosen "Frequency."

Step 10: Move across the row, and click twice on the empty cell under the column heading "Label." In this cell, you can type a more extensive description of your variable. In our case, there is no need for an extensive label, so we type "Frequency."

Step 11: Continue to move across the row, and click on the empty cell under the column heading "Measure." As we are dealing with frequencies, select "Nominal," which is the SPSS designation for nominal data. This is shown in Figure 8.4. We have now completed the SPSS "Variable View" window.

To Enter Data in SPSS

Step 12: Click on the "Data View" option at the lower left corner of the window. The variables "ADHD," "omission" and "Frequency" will be present.

Figure 8.4 The Variable View Window

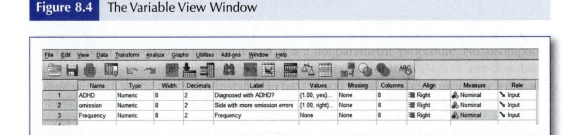

Step 13: Type in the Values of "1" and "2" for "ADHD" and "omission" as shown in Figure 8.5. Each combination of these numbers specifies a chi-square cell for which data in the form of a frequency is now entered in the third column. It is important that the correct frequencies are associated with each chi-square cell as is shown in Figure 8.5.

To Conduct a Chi-Square Test of Independence

Step 14: Click your cursor on "Data" along the row of SPSS commands above the numbers you have entered, and then move down and click on "Weight Cases."

Step 15: In the new window, click on the small circle just to the left of "Weight cases by" and then highlight "Frequency" (Figure 8.6). Now click on the arrow in the center of the window. The result will look like Figure 8.7. Then click on "OK." (You have just indicated to SPSS that the numbers in the variable "Frequencies" are not scores but rather are frequencies.)

Figure 8.5 Entering Data

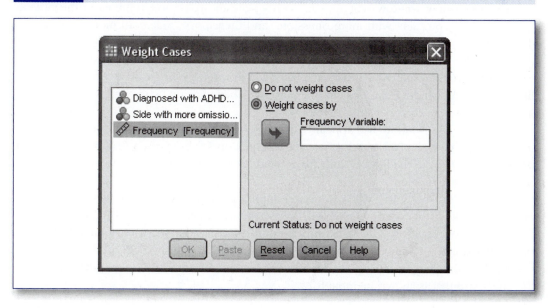

Exit the window with the statement "WEIGHT BY Frequency." Do not save this output.

Figure 8.6 The Weight Cases Window

| Figure 8.7 | The Weight Cases Window |

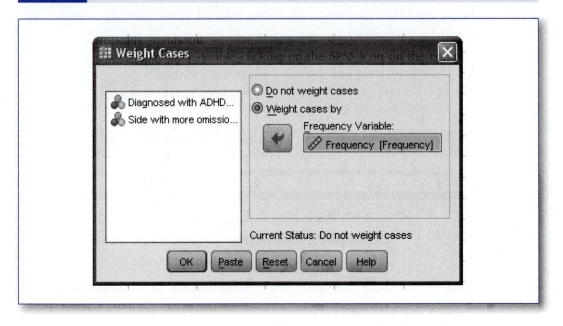

Step 16: Click the cursor on "Analyze" along the row of SPSS commands above the data you entered, then move to "Descriptive Statistics," then click on "Crosstabs." (You do not use the nonparametric statistics command with a chi-square test of independence.)

Step 17: A new window will appear. To re-create the rows and columns in the original data table, click on "Side with more omission," and then move "Side with more omission" to the box under "Row(s)" by clicking on the top arrow. Now move "Diagnosed with ADHD?" to the box under "Column(s)" by clicking on "Diagnosed with ADHD?" and then clicking on the second arrow. The result will be that each label will move to the appropriate box on the right-hand side of the window, as is shown in Figure 8.8. Then click on "Statistics," which is located in the top, right-hand corner of the window.

Step 18: A new window will appear. This window provides a number of statistical options that are available with SPSS. In this book, we will limit ourselves to just a few of these, so click on the small boxes to the left of "Chi-square," and "Phi and Cramer's *V*" as is shown in Figure 8.9. Then click "Continue."

Step 19: Click on "Cells" which is located in the top, right corner of the window shown in Figure 8.8. Within this window, click on "Expected" as shown in Figure 8.10. Then click on "Continue." Now click on "OK." SPSS provides an extensive output. We are interested in the obtained, expected, and marginal frequencies (Table 8.20); the desired chi-square (Table 8.21) (SPSS calls it the Pearson chi-square, we can ignore the other rows of the output); and finally, the effect size that is shown in Table 8.22.

Figure 8.8 Defining Crosstabs

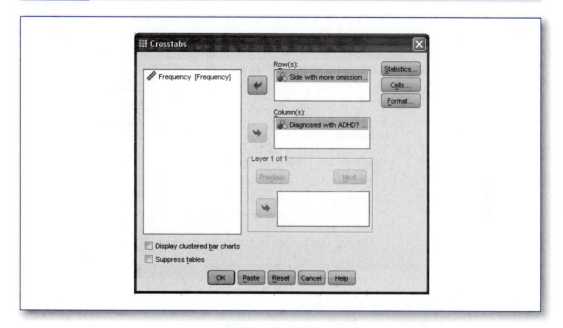

Figure 8.9 Defining Crosstabs

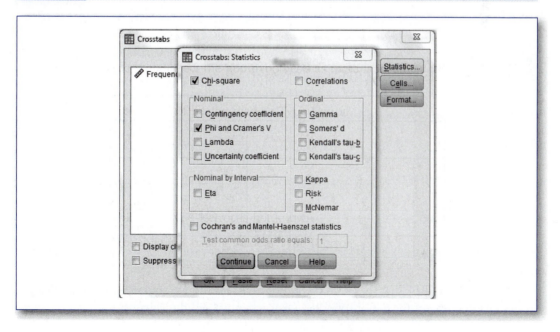

Figure 8.10   Continuing to Define Crosstabs

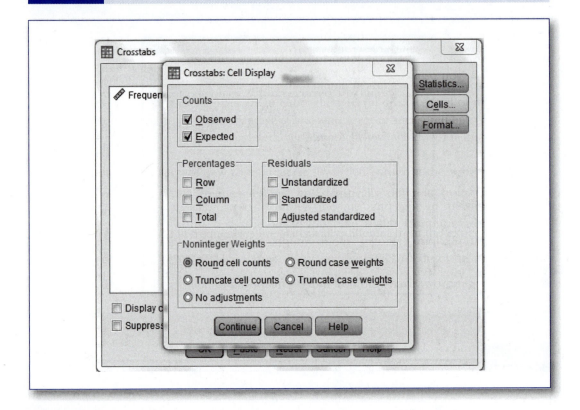

Table 8.20   The Crosstabs Output: Obtained, Expected, and Marginal Frequencies

Side with more omission errors * Diagnosed with ADHD? Crosstabulation

			Diagnosed with ADHD?		Total
			yes	no	
Side with more omission errors	right	Count	36	25	61
		Expected Count	40.7	20.3	61.0
	left	Count	22	4	26
		Expected Count	17.3	8.7	26.0
Total		Count	58	29	87
		Expected Count	58.0	29.0	87.0

You should confirm that these are the same results for the chi-square as was found earlier in this chapter, except for minor rounding error when we did the calculations.

Table 8.21	The Crosstabs Output: Summary Chi-Square Table

Chi square Tests

	Value	df	Asymp. Sig. (2–sided)	Exact Sig. (2–sided)	Exact Sig. (1–sided)
Pearson Chi square	5.376[a]	1	.020		
Continuity Correction[b]	4.286	1	.038		
Likelihood Ratio	5.859	1	.015		
Fisher's Exact Test				.025	.017
Linear–by–Linear Association	5.314	1	.021		
N of Valid Cases	87				

a. 0 cells (.0%) have expected count less than 5. The minimum expected count is 8.67.
b. Computed only for a 2x2 table

Table 8.22	The Crosstabs Output: Effect Size

Symmetric Measures

		Value	Approx. Sig.
Nominal by Nominal	Phi	–.249	.020
	Cramer's V	.249	.020
N of Valid Cases		87	

OUR SECOND EXAMPLE USING SPSS WITH THE CHI-SQUARE TEST OF INDEPENDENCE

To Begin SPSS

Steps 1, 2, and 3: These are the same as for the previous example.

Step 4: Click on the first empty rectangle (called a "cell") under the column heading "Name." You now type the name of the first variable for which you have data. We are going to utilize the same data and labels as were previously employed in Table 8.10. These data dealt with the question of whether there is an association between the experimental condition an individual had been assigned to and their success at making a correct identification. We have called these variables "subgroup" and "ID." Therefore, type "subgroup" in the first empty cell under "Name."

Step 5: Click twice on the first empty cell under the column heading "Label." In this cell, you can type a more extensive description of your variable. In our case, type "Subject Group."

Step 6: Click on the first empty cell under the column heading "Values." Then click on the small blue square. A box will appear. In the blank space to the right of "Value," type the number "1." Then, type a brief description of this value of the variable in the blank space to the right of "Label." In our case, type "control." Finally, click on "Add." Your label for a value of 1 will appear in the large white region in the center of the window. Now repeat the above steps in this section for the value "2," which is given the label "detail," and for the value "3," which is given the label "global" (Figure 8.11). Then click on "OK."

Figure 8.11	The Value Labels Window

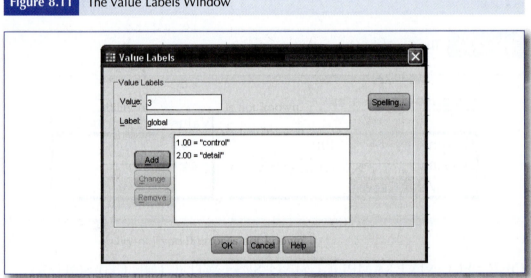

Step 7: Click on the first empty cell under the column heading "Measure." As we are dealing with nominal data, select "Nominal."

Step 8: Repeat Steps 4 to 7, except that you type "ID" in the first empty cell under "Name," type "Eyewitness Success" for the "Label," and you now have two value labels, "successful" and "not successful," instead of "control," "detail," and "global" (Figure 8.12). As before, select "Nominal" in the column under the column heading "Measure." You could now shift to the data window and sequentially enter the data for each subject. However, as always, this can quickly become tedious. Instead, we need to create another variable so that SPSS can be instructed that the numbers stand for the frequencies that occurred.

Figure 8.12 The Value Labels Window

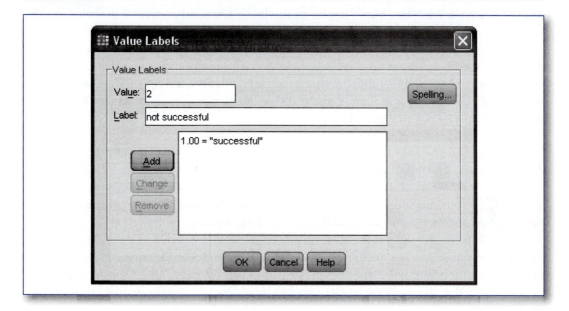

Step 9: In the empty cell directly under "ID," type the name of this new variable. Once again, I chose "frequency."

Step 10: Move across the row, and click twice on the empty cell under the column heading "Label." In this cell, you can type a more extensive description of your variable. In our case, there is no need for an extensive label, so we type "Frequency."

Step 11: Continue to move across the row and click on the empty cell under the column heading "Measure." As we are dealing with frequencies, select "Nominal," which is the SPSS designation for nominal data. This is shown in Figure 8.13. We have now completed the SPSS "Variable View" window.

Figure 8.13 The Variable View Window

	Name	Type	Width	Decimals	Label	Values	Missing	Columns	Align	Measure	Role
1	subgroup	Numeric	8	2	Subject Group	{1.00, contr...	None	8	Right	Nominal	Input
2	ID	Numeric	8	2	Eyewitness Success	{1.00, succ...	None	8	Right	Nominal	Input
3	frequency	Numeric	8	2	Frequency	None	None	8	Right	Nominal	Input

To Enter Data in SPSS

Step 12: Click on the "Data View" option at the lower left-hand corner of the window. The variables "subgroup," "ID," and "frequency" will be present.

Step 13: Type in the values of "1," "2," and "3" for "subgroup" and the values "1" and "2" for "ID" as shown in Figure 8.14. Each combination of these numbers specifies a chi-square cell (there are 6 cells in this study) for which data in the form of a frequency are now entered in the third column. It is important that the correct frequencies are associated with each chi-square cell as is shown in Figure 8.14.

To Conduct a Chi-Square Test of Independence

Step 14: Click your cursor on "Data" along the row of SPSS commands above the numbers you have entered and then move down and click on "Weight cases."

Step 15: In the new window, click on the small circle just to the left of "Weight cases by," and then highlight "Frequency" (Figure 8.15). Now click on the arrow in the center of the window. The result will look like Figure 8.16. Then click on "OK" (You have just indicated to SPSS that the numbers in the variable "Frequencies" are not scores but rather are frequencies.)

Exit the window with the statement "WEIGHT BY Frequency." Do not save this output.

Figure 8.14   Entering Data

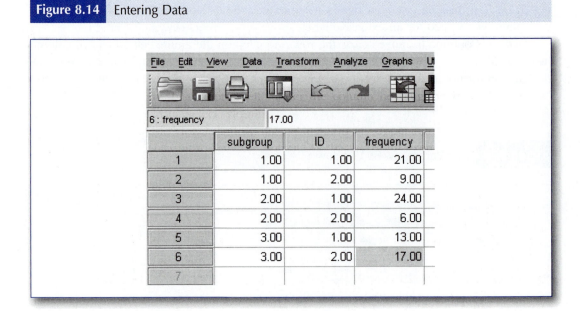

Figure 8.15   The Weight Cases Window

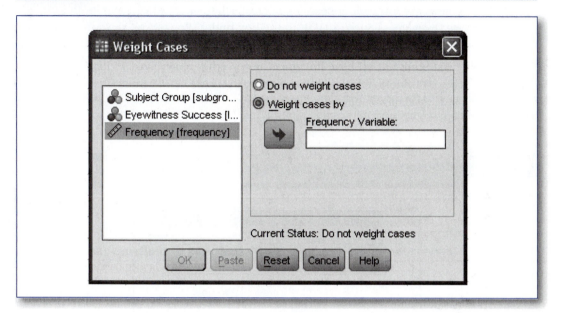

Figure 8.16   The Weight Cases Window

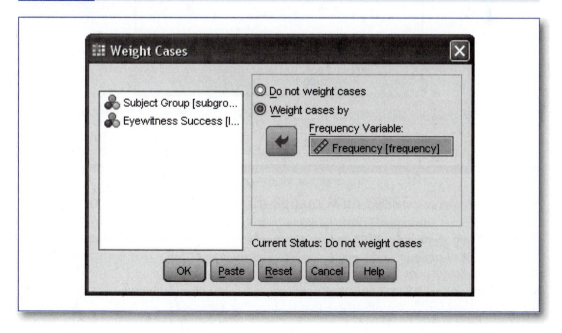

Step 16: Click the cursor on "Analyze" along the row of SPSS commands above the data you entered, then move to "Descriptive Statistics," then click on "Crosstabs."

Step 17: A new window will appear. To re-create the rows and columns in the original data table, move "Eyewitness Success (ID)" to the box under "Row(s)" by clicking on "Eyewitness Success (ID)" and then clicking on the top arrow. Next, move "Subject Group (subgroup)" to the box under "Column(s)" by clicking on "Subject Group (subgroup)" and then clicking on the second arrow. The result will be that each label will move to the appropriate box on the right-hand side of the window, as is shown in Figure 8.17. Then click on "Statistics," which is located in the top, right-hand corner of the window.

Figure 8.17   Defining Crosstabs

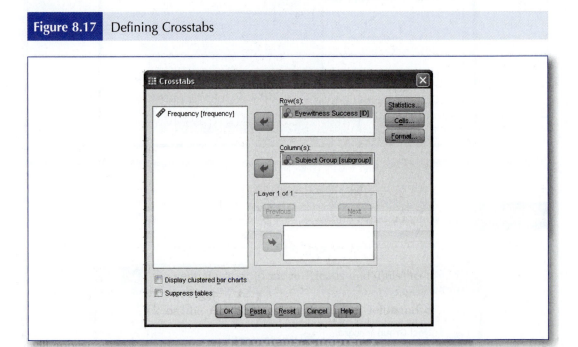

Step 18: A new window will appear. This window provides a number of statistical options that are available with SPSS. In this book, we will limit ourselves to just a few of these, so click on the small boxes to the left of "Chi-square" and "Phi and Cramer's V" as is shown in Figure 8.18. Then click on "Continue."

Step 19: Click on "Cells," which is located in the top, right-hand corner of the window shown in Figure 8.18. Within the new window, click on "Expected" as shown in Figure 8.19. Then click on "Continue." Now click on "OK." SPSS provides an extensive output. We are interested in the obtained, expected, and marginal frequencies (Table 8.23); the desired chi-square (Table 8.24) (it is called Pearson chi-square in SPSS, we can ignore the other rows of the output); and finally, the effect size that is shown in Table 8.25.

Figure 8.18 Defining Crosstabs

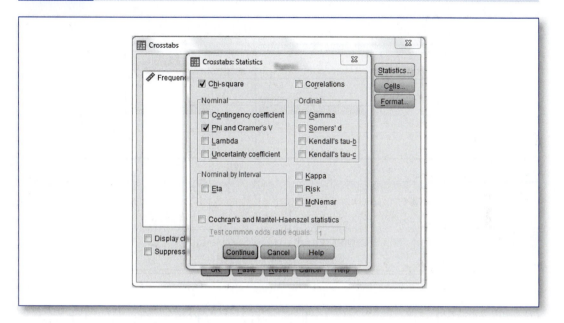

Figure 8.19 Continuing to Define Crosstabs

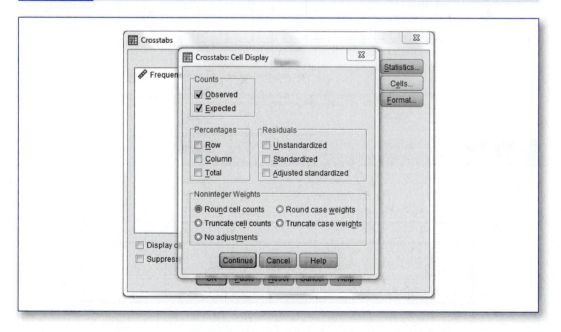

Table 8.23   The Crosstabs Output: Obtained, Expected, and Marginal Frequencies

Eyewitness Success * Subject Group Crosstabulation

			Subject Group			Total
			control	detail	global	
Eyewitness Success	successful	Count	21	24	13	58
		Expected Count	19.3	19.3	19.3	58.0
	not successful	Count	9	6	17	32
		Expected Count	10.7	10.7	10.7	32.0
Total		Count	30	30	30	90
		Expected Count	30.0	30.0	30.0	90.0

Table 8.24   The Crosstabs Output: Summary Chi-Square Table

Chi square Tests

	Value	df	Asymp. Sig. (2–sided)
Pearson Chi square	9.407[a]	2	.009
Likelihood Ratio	9.417	2	.009
Linear–by–Linear Association	4.603	1	.032
N of Valid Cases	90		

a. 0 cells (.0%) have expected count less than 5. The minimum expected count is 10.67.

Table 8.25   The Crosstabs Output: Effect Size

Symmetric Measures

		Value	Approx. Sig.
Nominal by Nominal	Phi	.323	.009
	Cramer's V	.323	.009
N of Valid Cases		90	

Once again, you should confirm that this is the same result for the chi-square as was found earlier in this chapter, except for minor rounding error when we did the calculations.

To confirm that you understand how to use SPSS, redo the chi-squares that were calculated in the text for the data in Tables 8.6 and 8.9, but this time using SPSS.

SPSS Problems: Chapter 8

Problems 18 to 23 are based on a study by Chou, Ho, and Chi (2006), which reported the frequency of depressive symptoms for Chinese older adults who were living alone or not living alone.

18. For the 90 men who lived alone, 23 reported depressive symptoms. For the 851 men who did not live alone, 152 reported depressive symptoms. We are interested in whether there is a difference in the rate of symptoms for these two groups of men. What is the value of the 2×2 chi-square?

   a. 3.183

   b. 4.791

   c. 5.482

   d. 9.236

19. How many degrees of freedom are there?

   a. 1

   b. 2

   c. 3

   d. 4

20. Is the result statistically significant if we are using a 5% region of rejection?

   a. Yes

   b. No

21. For the 91 women who lived alone, 29 reported depressive symptoms. For the 971 women who did not live alone, 206 reported depressive symptoms. We are interested in whether there is a difference in the rate of symptoms for these two groups of women. What is the value of the 2×2 chi-square?

   a. 3.183

   b. 4.791

   c. 5.482

   d. 9.236

22. How many degrees of freedom are there?

    a. 1

    b. 2

    c. 3

    d. 4

23. Is the result statistically significant if we are using a 5% region of rejection?

    a. Yes

    b. No

9

FINDING DIFFERENCES WITH INTERVAL AND RATIO DATA—I

The One-Sample z Test and the One-Sample t Test

Maturity is the capacity to endure uncertainty.

—John Finley

In Chapter 6, we began a description of the scientific method. In Chapters 7 and 8, we introduced our discussion of inferential statistical procedures with the chi-square test, which utilizes nominal data. In the current chapter, we begin the examination of the inferential statistical procedures used with interval and ratio data (the discussion of two inferential statistical procedures used with ordinal data is given in Appendixes A and B). Our review of the inferential statistical procedures for interval and ratio data will be proceeding down the final column of Table 9.1. With interval and ratio (as well as ordinal) data, you are more likely to encounter designs where there is a clear distinction between independent and dependent variables than you are when using nominal data. This difference is indicated in Table 9.1 by the separation between the columns for nominal versus ordinal and interval or ratio data and by the bolded descriptions of their research designs.

We begin with the difference design that has one independent variable and only one sample of subjects. With interval or ratio data, this design employs two very similar procedures, either the one-sample *z* test or the one-sample *t* test. These tests are underlined in

| Table 9.1 | Overview of Inferential Statistical Procedures for Difference and Interaction Designs |

Type of Data

	Nominal (Frequency)	Ordinal (Ranked)	Interval/Ratio (Continuous Measure)
<u>**Inferential Statistics**</u> (Finding Relationships)			
Statistical procedures for difference and interaction designs			
One variable with at least two outcomes	Goodness-of-fit chi-square	**One IV with one sample—one DV**	<u>One-sample z score or one-sample t test</u>
		One IV with two or more independent samples—one DV	*Kruskal–Wallis H* One-way between-subjects ANOVA (only two independent samples—independent samples t test)
		One IV with one sample having two or more repeated measures—one DV	One-way within-subjects ANOVA (only two repeated measures—dependent samples t test)
Two variables, each with at least two outcomes	Chi-square test of independence	**Two IV each with two or more independent samples—one DV**	Two-way between-subjects ANOVA

Notes. IV, independent variable; DV, dependent variable; ANOVA, analysis of variance. Research designs are shown in boldface. The italicized item is reviewed in Appendix A.

Table 9.1. These two procedures examine the same question: Do the data collected from a single sample match what would be expected from a known or hypothesized population? Later chapters will examine designs that involve interval or ratio data and comparisons between experimental and control groups.

The first procedure that we will review is the one-sample z test. Then, we will cover the one-sample t test.

ONE-SAMPLE z TEST

You are already familiar from Chapters 3 and 4 with the use of a z score as a descriptive statistic, and much of what you learned will be applicable here. As you recall, a z score is simply the number of standard deviations (*SD*s) a datum is from its mean. Furthermore, if the distribution of scores is normal, then the probability of outcomes can be determined. For example, intelligence quotient (IQ) is normally distributed, and the most commonly used IQ tests have a μ of 100 and a σ of 15. An IQ score of 145 is thus 3 *SD*s greater than the mean, and the *z* score corresponding to an IQ of 145 is 3 [remember, $z = (X - μ)/σ$]. Use of the *z* table enables you to determine that 99.87% of individuals will have an IQ less than 145. Thus, only 13 out of 10,000 people would be expected to have an IQ score greater than 145.

The one-sample *z* test is an inferential procedure. It requires that a sample is drawn randomly from a normally distributed population, and then we examine whether the obtained sample mean differs from a known or hypothetical value. For instance, let us assume that we are interested in whether engaging in a series of mental exercises will change IQ scores. The null hypothesis would be that the mean of the sample would *not* differ significantly from the population mean, which is 100. The alternative hypothesis would be that there is a difference between the sample mean and the population mean.

This may appear to be just another example of the procedures that you learned for calculating a *z* score in Chapters 3 and 4, combined with some hypothesis-testing concepts from Chapter 6. To a certain extent, this is correct. However, our current use of the *z* test differs from our previous use of the *z* score in a critical way, though at first it may seem minor. The critical difference is that in our current example, we are dealing with the *mean of a sample*, whereas Chapters 3 and 4 dealt with converting a *single score or a group of scores* into standard deviations.

In our current example, we began by randomly selecting a sample. We would not be surprised if the mean IQ score of our sample differed slightly from the population mean of 100. Though the sample was randomly selected, some variation would be expected. Since we would not be surprised if one sample's mean differed from the population mean, it follows that if we selected a very large number of samples, all of the same size and from the same population, we would also expect to find variability in their means. But how much variability? While small variations would be expected, large variations would not be. The reason for this is that to get a large variation, a sample would have to have a preponderance of subjects with either very low or very high IQs. Since the samples are being selected randomly, this is not likely to occur. If we graphed the means of a large number of samples, all of the same size, we would obtain a distribution such as shown in Figure 9.1. This distribution is called the **sampling distribution of the mean**.

Sampling distribution of the mean: a theoretical probability distribution of sample means. The samples are all of the same size and are randomly selected from the same population.

Notice again that the sampling distribution of the mean is dealing with sample *means* (*M*). Thus, each point in the distribution is an *M*. If we wanted to find the "average" of the sample means, we could, of course, find the mean of these sample means. This probably sounds a bit strange, but the mean of these sample means, or the grand mean, which is represented by the symbol M_G, provides an excellent estimate of the population mean which, you recall, has the symbol μ. Furthermore, it can be shown

Figure 9.1   The Sampling Distribution of the Mean

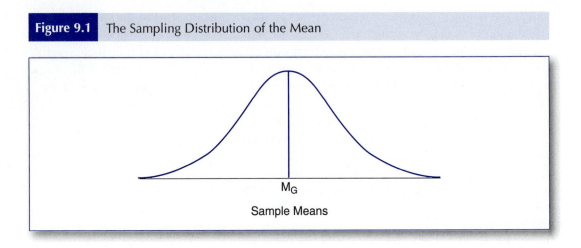

M_G

Sample Means

mathematically that if the samples are being selected from a normally distributed population, such as IQ, then the sampling distribution of the mean is also normally distributed. Thus, it is symmetrical, and most of the sample means are grouped near the middle of the distribution.

The question remains, how discrepant do the sample and population means have to be in order to reject the null hypothesis that an observed difference is due to chance variation? In other words, how large a difference must be observed to conclude that the mental exercises had an effect on the IQ scores? There is no absolute answer to this question. Statisticians provide an answer based on the likelihood or probability of the null hypothesis being true. As was pointed out earlier, if the difference between the sample and population means is due to chance, then it is expected that in most cases this difference will be small. In only a few cases would a large discrepancy be expected by chance. Thus, the larger the difference between the two means, the less likely this difference is due to chance.

As was noted in Chapter 6, in most fields, it has come to be accepted that if an outcome would be expected to occur, by chance, less than 1 time in 20, we reject the null hypothesis and accept the alternative hypothesis. One time in 20 is equivalent to .05 or 5%. It was also pointed out that there is nothing magical about .05. A different criterion such as .01 can be, and sometimes is, chosen. If a criterion of .01 is chosen, then, we retain the null hypothesis unless an outcome is so unlikely that it would be expected to occur in less than 1 out of 100 cases by chance. The criterion chosen is, of course, the alpha level and its symbol is the Greek letter, α. Recall from Chapter 7 that the critical region encompasses the most extreme possible outcomes. In the current example, the critical region is divided into two portions of the sampling distribution of the mean. This is because our null hypothesis does not state whether the treatment will increase or decrease the IQ scores of the sample. Consequently, as our total area of rejection is equal to α, the probabilities of each of the two critical regions is equal to $\alpha/2$ (Figure 9.2).

In the current example, the null hypothesis was that the treatment would not have an effect. The alternative hypothesis was that the treatment would have an effect. The null

Figure 9.2 Two-Tailed Test: The Area of Rejection Is Split Between the Two Tails

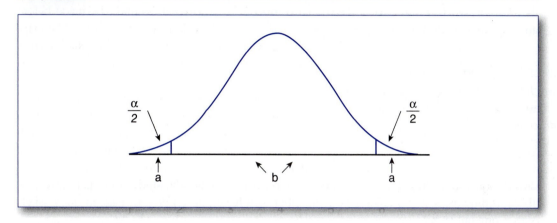

hypothesis could be rejected, therefore, if the sample's mean IQ was either much smaller or much larger than the population's mean IQ. Because an extreme outcome in either direction would result in the rejection of the null hypothesis, this is an example of what is called a **two-tailed or nondirectional test**. In a few moments, we will see that a directional, or one-tailed test, is also possible. For now, it is important that you understand that if the mean of the sample is so different from the population mean that it falls in the region of rejection on the sampling distribution of the mean, indicated by the letter "a" in each tail of Figure 9.2, the null hypothesis will be rejected. If we reject the null hypothesis, the alternative hypothesis will be accepted. However, if the mean of the sample is not so different from the mean of the popu-lation that it falls in the extreme tails represented by the letter "a" (the region of rejection), then the null hypothesis will be retained. This situation is indi-cated by the letter "b" in Figure 9.2.

Two-tailed or nondirectional test: an analysis in which the null hypothesis will be rejected if an extreme outcome occurs in either direction. In such a test, the alpha level is divided into two equal parts.

If the alternative hypothesis in our IQ study had been that the mental exercises would *increase* the mean IQ of the sample, it would be a directional pre-diction. In this case, the entire region of rejection would be put in the upper tail of the sampling distribution of the mean. This is illustrated in Figure 9.3. Similarly, if the original alternative hypothesis had been that the mental exercises would *decrease* the mean IQ of the sample, this would also be a directional prediction. In this case, how-ever, the entire region of rejection would be put in the lower tail of the distribution, as is illustrated in Figure 9.4. As will be shown shortly, putting the entire region of rejection in one tail has the advantage that a difference between the two means does not have to be as large to reject the null hypothesis. However, to reject the null hypothesis, the result must be in the predicted direction. With a directional prediction, no matter how large the observed difference, if it is in the direction opposite to what was predicted, the null hypothesis is retained. In other words, if you use a

one-tailed or directional test you are "putting all of your eggs in one basket." For this reason, one-tailed tests are *much less commonly used* than two-tailed tests. It is also important to note that the decision whether you have a directional or nondirectional hypothesis must be made before any data are collected. The decision is based on the results of previous research. It would be inappropriate to collect your data, determine the direction of the difference, and then decide to use a one-tailed test.

One-tailed or directional test: an analysis in which the null hypothesis will be rejected if an extreme outcome occurs in only one direction. In such a test, the single area of rejection is equal to alpha.

If you have enough information from previous research to choose a one-tailed test, this will make it easier to reject the null hypothesis and, thus, will increase the statistical power. Of course, this assumes that your results actually turn out to be in the predicted direction. If they don't, your only recourse is to conduct the study over again, presumably this time using a two-tailed test. Remember, you have put "all of your eggs in one basket" with a one-tailed test.

Summarizing to this point, when conducting an experiment, we tentatively accept that the null hypothesis is true unless there is sufficient evidence from the experiment to indicate that this is unlikely. The criterion for deciding how unlikely the outcome must be to reject the null

Figure 9.3   One-Tailed Test With the Area of Rejection in the Upper Tail

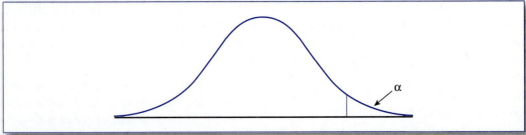

Figure 9.4   One-Tailed Test With the Area of Rejection in the Lower Tail

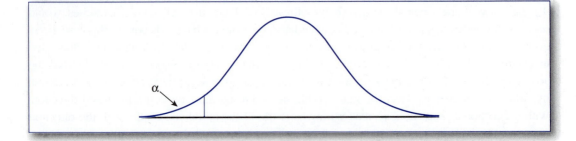

hypothesis is set by the experimenter when the alpha level is chosen. If the null hypothesis is rejected, we then tentatively accept that the alternative hypothesis is correct. Remember, with statistics we do not "prove" that a difference exists. Instead, we are making informed decisions, and we can make errors. However, the use of the statistical procedures outlined in this text will reduce the likelihood of making an error.

To determine whether there is sufficient evidence to reject the null hypothesis, we need to locate the position of our sample's mean on the theoretical frequency distribution of all possible sample means which, you may recall, is called the sampling distribution of the mean. This requires that we have a measure of the variability of this distribution.

It should be obvious that the sample means will differ from each other less than the individual scores will differ in the population from which these samples are drawn. For instance, it is possible that a single score randomly selected from a population will be extreme, and thus differ substantially from the population mean; but it is unlikely that even a relatively small sample would consist entirely of extreme scores and all of them in the same direction. As a result, the means of samples should be grouped more closely to the population mean than the original scores were. Furthermore, the larger the sample, the less likely it would be that an extreme group of subjects would be randomly selected. Thus, the larger the randomly selected samples, the closer their means should be to the population mean. This is an example of what is known in the field of statistics as the **law of large numbers**. It states that the larger the size of the random sample, the better the estimate of population parameters such as the mean. How much the variability is reduced is determined with the following equation:

> *Law of large numbers: the larger the sample size, the better the estimate of population parameters such as μ.*

$$\sigma_M = \frac{\sigma}{\sqrt{n}}.$$

We have a new symbol, σ_M, in this equation. It is the standard deviation of sample means or, alternatively, it is defined as the standard deviation of the sampling distribution of means. It is a measure of how much sample *means* are expected to vary and is encountered so frequently that it has its own name, the **standard error** or, more precisely, the standard error of the mean. The equation states that σ_M is equal to σ, the population standard deviation, divided by $\sqrt{n}$, the square root of the sample size. Thus, as the sample size increases, σ_M will decrease, just as we suspected. This equation may be clearer if we substitute σ_X for σ in the previous equation

> *Standard error: the standard deviation of the sampling distribution of a statistic. For example, the standard error of the mean is the standard deviation of the sampling distribution of means.*

$$\sigma_M = \frac{\sigma_X}{\sqrt{n}}.$$

Note that the symbols σ_X and σ are two ways of identifying the same concept, the standard deviation of population *scores*. You may find it easier to substitute the symbol σ_X for σ to assist you in remembering what is varying. With σ_X, we have a measure of the variability of *scores*. With σ_M, we have a measure of the variability of *sample means*.

The equation $\sigma_M = \sigma_X / \sqrt{n}$ indicates that there is a relationship between the variability of sample means (σ_M), the variability of the population of scores (σ_X), and the sample size (n). Specifically, the variability of sample means, also called the standard error (σ_M), will *increase* as the variability of the population of scores (σ_X) *increases* and the sample size (n) *decreases*. Alternatively, the variability of sample means (σ_M) will *decrease* as the variability of the population of scores (σ_X) *decreases* and the sample size (n) *increases*. These relationships will be clearer with some examples. We will begin by changing the sample size, n.

Let us assume that our sample consisted of 9 subjects. How will σ_M and σ_X be related?

$$\sigma_M = \frac{\sigma_X}{\sqrt{n}}$$

$$= \frac{\sigma_X}{\sqrt{9}}$$

$$= \frac{\sigma_X}{3}.$$

Thus, if the sample size is 9, σ_M (the variability of sample means) will be equal to only 1/3 of σ_X (the variability of scores). Put another way, if the sample size is 9, the means of these samples are expected to vary only 1/3 as much as the scores vary.

What if the sample size was increased to 81?

$$\sigma_M = \frac{\sigma_X}{\sqrt{n}}$$

$$= \frac{\sigma_X}{\sqrt{81}}$$

$$= \frac{\sigma_X}{9}.$$

Thus, if the sample size is 81, σ_M will be reduced to only 1/9 of σ_X.

What if the sample size had been only 1?

$$\sigma_M = \frac{\sigma_X}{\sqrt{n}}$$

$$= \frac{\sigma_X}{\sqrt{1}}$$

$$= \frac{\sigma_X}{1}$$

$$= \sigma_X.$$

Thus, if the sample size is 1, σ_M will be equal to σ_X. This makes sense, for in this case, each score is also being treated as a sample mean.

Now we will explore what happens when the variability of the scores, in other words, the size of σ_X, is increased. Specifically, if the size of σ_X is doubled from 15 to 30 while the sample size remains constant with an n of 9, how does σ_M change?

$$\sigma_M = \frac{\sigma_X}{\sqrt{n}}$$

$$= \frac{15}{\sqrt{9}}$$

$$= \frac{15}{3}$$

$$= 5,$$

and

$$\sigma_M = \frac{\sigma_X}{\sqrt{n}}$$

$$= \frac{30}{\sqrt{9}}$$

$$= \frac{30}{3}$$

$$= 10.$$

Thus, as the variability of the scores doubles, in other words, as the size of σ_X doubles, so does the size of σ_M. Put another way, samples drawn from more variable populations are expected to vary more than samples drawn from less variable populations.

As was just reviewed, it can be proven mathematically that if you randomly select a large number of samples, all of the same size, from a normally distributed population, the distribution of these sample means (the sampling distribution of means) will also be normally distributed. It is unlikely that you would ever do this, but the conclusion is important. Furthermore, you have learned that the mean of these sample means (M_G) would be an excellent predictor of the population mean, μ. And the standard deviation of the sampling distribution of means (the standard error) would equal the standard deviation of the population divided by the square root of the sample size.

One implication of the above paragraph is that we could, theoretically, construct a series of normal curves. Each of these sampling distributions of the mean would be based on samples of a different size. Furthermore, the variability of each of these sampling distributions would be equal to its standard error, which would decrease as the sample size increased (Figure 9.5).

Figure 9.5   Effect of Sample Size on the Shape of the Sampling Distribution

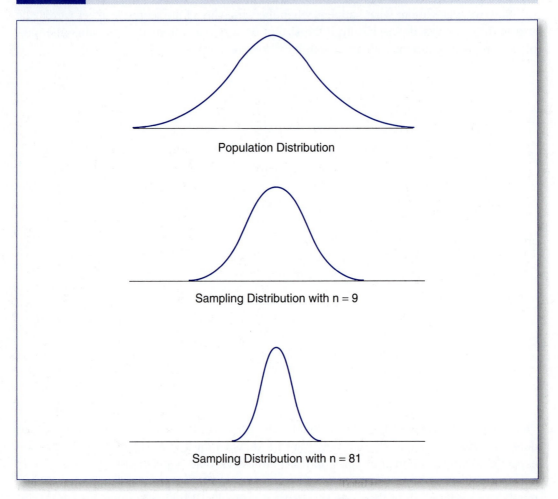

The discussion to this point has been quite theoretical. Obviously, no one is going to actually create sampling distributions of the mean for every different sample size. It would require the collection of large numbers of samples, which would be very time-consuming. However, since we know what the shape (normal) and variability ($\sigma_x / \sqrt{n}$) of the sampling distribution of the mean would be, you will see that we can then use the z test to differentiate between the null and alternative hypotheses.

In Chapters 3 and 4, you learned that a raw score can be converted into a z score with the following equation:

$$z = \frac{X - \mu}{\sigma}.$$

What this equation accomplishes is to take the difference between a score and its population mean and divide this difference by the population standard deviation. The result is that a deviation in the original units of measurement is converted into a deviation in standard deviation units. This, in turn, permits us to determine probabilities using the z table (Appendix J, Table J.1), assuming, of course, that the original population was normally distributed.

The equation may be clearer if it is rewritten as follows:

$$z = \frac{X - \mu}{\sigma_X}.$$

Since σ_X is equivalent to σ, nothing has actually changed, but with this form of the equation, it is evident that σ_X is referring to the variability of scores.

In our example of the sample of subjects who have engaged in mental exercises, we are not dealing with a single score. Instead, we are dealing with a sample of scores. However, the logic of converting a deviation in original units of measurement into a deviation in standard deviation units, and then referring to the z table, remains the same. The equation is simply modified to reflect that we are comparing a sample mean, instead of a single score, to the population mean. This requires, in turn, that we divide by a measure of how much sample means are expected to vary. The result is as follows:

$$z = \frac{M - \mu}{\sigma_M}.$$

It is important that you recognize the parallel between obtaining a z score, which was described in Chapters 3 and 4, and conducting a z test

To Find a z Score	To Conduct a z Test
$z = \dfrac{X - \mu}{\sigma_X}$	$z = \dfrac{M - \mu}{\sigma_M}$

In each case, we are converting a deviation, either $(X - \mu)$ or $(M - \mu)$, into standard deviation units. This requires that we divide the obtained deviation by the appropriate measure for the standard deviation. In the case of $X - \mu$, we are dealing with how much a *score* deviates from its population mean, and so we divide by the standard deviation of scores (σ_X). In the case of $M - \mu$, we are dealing with how much a *sample mean* deviates from its population mean, and so we divide by the standard deviation of sample means, which is also called the standard error (σ_M). In either case, we then refer to the z table.

Returning to our mental exercises example, let us assume that, based on a sample size of 25, the mean of the sample of IQ scores was 105. Recall that the mean of the population of

IQ scores is known to be 100, and the standard deviation is 15. The null hypothesis would state that any difference between the sample and population means is due to chance. The alternative hypothesis is that there is a true difference between the two means. The z test can be used to decide between these two hypotheses. As is common, we set $\alpha = .05$. Since this is a two-tailed test, one half of the area of rejection will be located in each tail of the theoretical frequency distribution. In other words, the area of rejection will consist of .05/2, which equals .025, in each tail (Figure 9.6). From the z table, we ascertain that an area of .025 in the tail of the distribution is equivalent to a z of 1.96.

We can now conduct our z test:

$$z = \frac{M - \mu}{\sigma_M}.$$

M and μ are known and can be substituted directly into the equation:

$$z = \frac{105 - 100}{\sigma_M}.$$

However, σ_M needs to be calculated from the equation

$$\sigma_M = \frac{\sigma_X}{\sqrt{n}}$$

$$= \frac{15}{\sqrt{25}}$$

$$= \frac{15}{5}$$

$$= 3.$$

Figure 9.6   Two-Tailed Test With Alpha Equal to .05

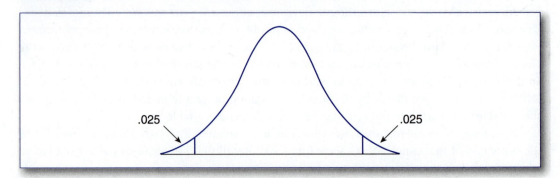

.025   .025

We can now substitute this value into our equation for z:

$$z = \frac{105 - 100}{\sigma_M}$$

$$= \frac{105 - 100}{3}$$

$$= \frac{5}{3}$$

$$= 1.67.$$

Recall that we previously determined that an area of .025 in the tail of the distribution is equivalent to a critical value of 1.96. As this is a two-tailed test, the number from the z table should be thought of as an absolute value. Thus, an obtained z beyond ±1.96 leads us to reject the null hypothesis. With an obtained value within ±1.96, we do not reject the null hypothesis. In our example, the obtained z of 1.67 is less than the critical value of 1.96, so we retain the null hypothesis. We could report this finding in an article by saying, "There was not sufficient evidence that the IQ scores of subjects who have engaged in mental exercise ($M = 105$) differed from the expected population mean ($z = 1.67$, $p > .05$)."

It is instructive to reexamine the previous example assuming that a one-tailed test had been appropriate. Remember, the option of a one-tailed test would need to have been chosen before the data were collected, but for illustration purposes, let us assume that prior data had suggested that mental exercises would have increased IQ scores. If so, we would have been justified to utilize a one-tailed test with all of the rejection area in the high end of the curve. The critical value of z, obtained from the z table with $\alpha = .05$, would now be 1.64 or 1.65. As this is a one-tailed test, the direction of the outcome is important. The null hypothesis is now that mental exercises will increase IQ, and thus, we will reject the null only if the obtained value of z is greater than the critical value. As our obtained z of 1.67 is greater than the critical value and is in the predicted direction, it would be interpreted as indicating a statistically significant difference.

To be certain that you understand the use of the z test, we will review another example. Let us assume that we are interested in ascertaining whether high school students with low grade point averages have the same SAT scores as other students. The null hypothesis would be that the mean SAT of these students is the same as the mean SAT for the general population, which is 500. The alternative hypothesis would be that the mean SAT score of these students differs from what is found with the general population. As no direction was specified for an outcome, this is a two-tailed test and, as usual, we set $\alpha = .05$. To differentiate between the null and alternative hypotheses, we collect SAT scores from a random sample of 49 high school students who have low grade point averages. We find that the mean SAT of this sample is 467. As it is known that the standard deviation of the SAT test is 100, we can now conduct our z test:

$$z = \frac{M - \mu}{\sigma_M}.$$

M and μ are known and can be substituted directly into the equation:

$$z = \frac{467 - 500}{\sigma_M}.$$

As before, σ_M needs to be calculated from the equation:

$$\sigma_M = \frac{\sigma_X}{\sqrt{n}}$$

$$= \frac{100}{\sqrt{49}}$$

$$= \frac{100}{7}$$

$$= 14.29.$$

We can now substitute this value for the standard error into our equation for z:

$$z = \frac{467 - 500}{\sigma_M}$$

$$= \frac{467 - 500}{14.29}$$

$$= \frac{-33}{14.29}$$

$$= -2.31.$$

Referring to the z table, for a two-tailed test with an $\alpha = .05$, the critical value is 1.96. Recall that as this is a two-tailed test, the critical value from the z table is interpreted as being an absolute value. As our obtained z of −2.31 has a greater absolute value than the critical value, we reject the null hypothesis that there is no difference between the SAT scores of high school students with low grade point averages and the SAT scores of the general population, and we accept the alternative hypothesis that there is a difference.

Reporting the Results of the One-Sample z Test

In an article, we could say, "There was evidence that high school students who had low grade point averages had lower SAT scores ($M = 467$) than the general population ($z = -2.31$, $p < .05$)."

Confidence Interval for *z*

We can also, in a sense, solve a *z* test problem in reverse to find what is called a confidence interval. A **confidence interval** is a range of values that has a known probability of including the population parameter. For instance, let us assume that a sample of 9 students taking statistics has a mean IQ of 120. We could now use this information to estimate the value of the population mean. For instance, we could ask what range of values has a 60% likelihood of including the population mean.

We begin with a figure, so we can visualize what we are seeking (Figure 9.7). Note that the area of the distribution corresponding to 60% has been divided into two equal regions around μ, each of 30%.

> *Confidence interval: the range of values that has a known probability of including the population parameter, usually the mean.*

| Figure 9.7 | Illustration of a 60% Confidence Interval |

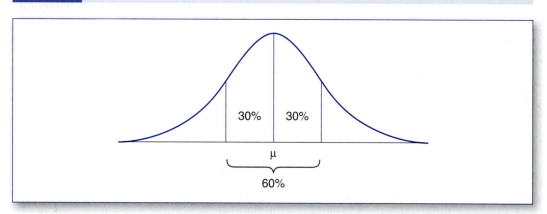

| Figure 9.8 | Identification of the Equivalent z Scores for a 60% Confidence Interval |

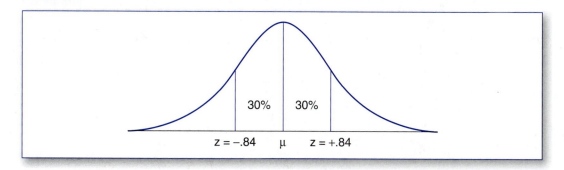

Figure 9.9	Equations Utilized to Determine the Lower and Upper Confidence Interval Limits

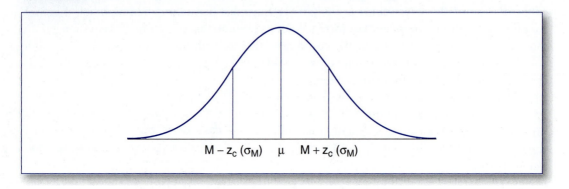

$$M - z_c\ (\sigma_M) \qquad \mu \qquad M + z_c\ (\sigma_M)$$

Next, we turn to the z table to ascertain the z value that will include 30% of the distribution between the mean and itself. This is approximately 0.84. Since we will be finding an interval that extends above and below the population mean, we are looking for an interval that extends from −0.84 to +0.84 standard errors from the population mean. This is shown in Figure 9.8.

But we were not asked to find the z values, we were asked to find the equivalent mean IQ scores based on samples of size 9. To convert our two z scores (−0.84 and +0.84) into equivalent mean IQ scores, we calculate the following intervals:

$$M - z_c\ (\sigma_M) \leq \mu \leq M + z_c\ (\sigma_M),$$

where z_c is the critical value for z obtained from the z table. The lower limit of the confidence interval is $M - z_c\ (\sigma_M)$, and the upper limit is $M + z_c\ (\sigma_M)$. This is shown in Figure 9.9.

In our example, the values of M and z_c are known and can be substituted directly into the equation. However, σ_M needs to be calculated from the equation:

$$\sigma_M = \frac{\sigma_X}{\sqrt{n}}.$$

The standard deviation of the IQ test is 15, and our sample size is 9, therefore,

$$\sigma_M = \frac{15}{\sqrt{9}}$$

$$= \frac{15}{3}$$

$$= 5.$$

Substituting, we obtain

$$120 - 0.84(5) \leq \mu \leq 120 + 0.84(5)$$
$$120 - 4.2 \leq \mu \leq 120 + 4.2$$
$$115.8 \leq \mu \leq 124.2.$$

Based on our sample of size 9 with a mean of 120 and a standard error of 5, we are, therefore, 60% confident that the population mean IQ of the statistics students will fall within a range of 115.8 to 124.2. This interval is illustrated in Figure 9.10.

What is the effect if you kept all other values the same but changed from a 60% confidence interval to a 95% confidence interval? You would begin, as before, by dividing .95 by 2 to obtain .475. This is the proportion of the curve desired on each side of the population mean. By referring to the z table, we determine that a proportion of .475 is equivalent to a z score of 1.96. Therefore, we would be looking for an interval that extends from 1.96 *SD* units below the mean to 1.96 *SD* units above the mean. This is illustrated in Figure 9.11.

The confidence interval would again be calculated as follows:

$$M - z_c (\sigma_M) \leq \mu \leq M + z_c (\sigma_M)$$
$$120 - 1.96(5) \leq \mu \leq 120 + 1.96(5)$$
$$120 - 9.8 \leq \mu \leq 120 + 9.8$$
$$110.2 \leq \mu \leq 129.8.$$

This confidence interval is illustrated in Figure 9.12. As you would expect, the 95% confidence interval is considerably larger than the 60% confidence interval we calculated previously.

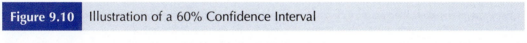

Figure 9.10 Illustration of a 60% Confidence Interval

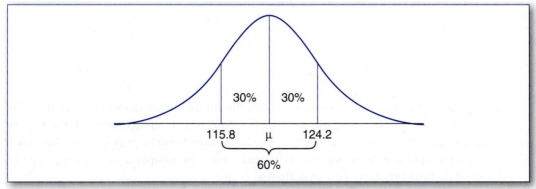

| Figure 9.11 | Determining a 95% Confidence Interval |

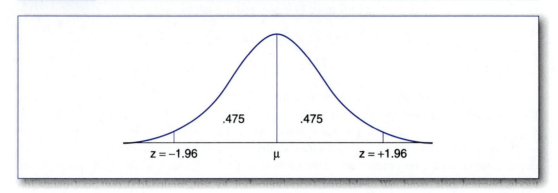

| Figure 9.12 | Illustration of a 95% Confidence Interval |

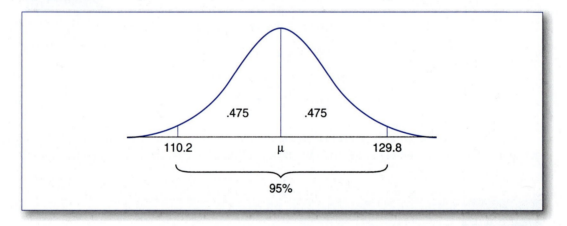

WRAP UP

Purpose of Using the One-Sample z Test

Test for difference: The null hypothesis is that the sample mean does not differ from the hypothesized or known population mean. Therefore, any difference between the sample and population means is due to chance. The alternative hypothesis is that the difference between the two means is not due to chance. The one-sample z test is employed to differentiate between these two hypotheses.

Assumptions of the One-Sample *z* Test

1. *Interval or ratio data.* The data are on an interval or ratio scale of measurement.

2. *Random sample.* The sample is drawn at random from the population.

3. *Normally distributed population.* The population from which the sample is drawn has a normal distribution of scores.

4. *The population standard deviation is known.*

Summary of the One-Sample *z* Test

The one-sample *z* test is an inferential statistical procedure used to differentiate between null and alternative hypotheses. To use the one-sample *z* test, it is necessary that the population from which the sample is drawn be normally distributed and that its standard deviation be known. If these conditions are met, it is then the case that the sampling distribution of the mean will also be normally distributed and will have a standard error of $\sigma_X/\sqrt{n}$. The *z* test can then be conducted and the *z* table consulted to determine whether to accept the null hypothesis or, instead, to reject the null and accept the alternative hypothesis. Alternatively, a confidence interval can be created.

PROGRESS CHECK

Assume we are interested in whether a SAT review course actually increases SAT scores. To determine this, we randomly select 100 individuals from the general population who then take the SAT review course. At the conclusion of the course, they take the SAT exam. Their mean SAT score is 517. (Recall that the mean SAT score for the general population is 500 and the standard deviation is 100.)

1. Is this a one- or two-tailed test?

2. What is the obtained value for *z*?

3. What is your decision?

Answers: 1. One-tailed. 2. 1.7. 3. Reject the null hypothesis.

THE ONE-SAMPLE *t* TEST

Although the *z* test can be very useful, it is limited in that it cannot be used unless the value of the population standard deviation is known. As a consequence, in many situations, it is not possible to calculate a z statistic. However, when we do not know the value of the population standard deviation, we can estimate it from the sample data. Then, we can use a very similar statistical procedure to the z test that is called the t test.

In Chapter 4, you learned how to calculate the sample standard deviation. We will see shortly that with a slight modification, the sample standard deviation can serve as the basis for estimating σ_X. The symbol for the sample standard deviation used in Chapter 4 was s. However, just as we added the subscript x to the symbol σ to clarify that we are referring to the standard deviation of scores, we will now use s_X in the place of s.

To reacquaint you with the definitions and calculations that you previously learned, the symbols describing population parameters and sample statistics are presented in Table 9.2, and the equations that were covered in Chapter 4 are shown in Table 9.3.

An initial guess for how to estimate the population standard deviation, σ_X, would be to use the sample standard deviation, s_X. However, it turns out that s_X is a **biased estimator** of σ_X. A biased estimator does not accurately predict what it is intended to because of systematic

Table 9.2   Symbols Used When Describing Population Parameters and Sample Statistics

	Population Parameter	Sample Statistic
Size of data set	N	n
Mean	μ	M
Variance	σ_X^2	s_X^2
Standard deviation	σ_X	s_X

Table 9.3   Equations for Population and Sample Standard Deviations

Population	Sample
$\sigma_X = \sqrt{\dfrac{\sum (X-\mu)^2}{N}}$	$s_X = \sqrt{\dfrac{\sum (X-M)^2}{n}}$
$\sigma_X = \sqrt{\dfrac{SS}{N}}$	$s_X = \sqrt{\dfrac{SS}{n}}$
$\sigma_X = \sqrt{\dfrac{\sum x^2}{N}}$	$s_X = \sqrt{\dfrac{\sum x^2}{n}}$

error. In our case, though s_X provides an accurate measure of sample variability, it consistently underestimates the value of σ_X. This is because a sample consists of a subset of a population and is likely, therefore, not to include the low frequency scores that tend to be more diverse. This becomes more of an issue as the sample size gets smaller. Fortunately, there is a simple solution. Instead of dividing the sum of the squared deviations from the sample mean by the sample size, n, we divide by $n - 1$. When we do this, the systematic error is eliminated. In other words, we can compute two different measures of the standard deviation from any sample. One uses n in the denominator and is appropriate if we are interested in the variability of the sample. The other uses $n - 1$ in the denominator and is appropriate if we are interested in using the sample to estimate the variability of the population from which it was chosen. To prevent confusion, in this text, I will add the subscript letter "P" whenever we are using sample data to estimate the population variability. The two sets of equations, along with the population standard deviation (σ_X) being estimated, are illustrated in Table 9.4. Fortunately, the mean is an unbiased estimator, and thus, we do not need to make any correction to its calculation.

> Biased estimator: an estimator that does not accurately predict what it is intended to because of systematic error.

We now have an unbiased estimator of σ_X. However, when we use s_{XP} to estimate σ_X, we no longer use the z test. Instead, we use what is called the t test. As the following equations indicate, the z and the t tests are very closely related:

$$z = \frac{M - \mu}{\sigma_M},$$

where the standard error, $\sigma_M = \sigma_X / \sqrt{n}$.

Table 9.4	Equations for the Standard Deviation

Population	When Describing a Sample	When Estimating a Population
σ_X	$s_X = \sqrt{\dfrac{\sum(X - M)^2}{n}}$	$s_{XP} = \sqrt{\dfrac{\sum(X - M)^2}{n-1}}$
σ_X	$s_X = \sqrt{\dfrac{SS}{n}}$	$s_{XP} = \sqrt{\dfrac{SS}{n-1}}$
σ_X	$s_X = \sqrt{\dfrac{\sum x^2}{n}}$	$s_{XP} = \sqrt{\dfrac{\sum x^2}{n-1}}$

And

$$t = \frac{M - \mu}{s_M},$$

where the standard error, $s_M = s_{XP} / \sqrt{n}$.

Clearly, the only difference between the equations is that with the t test we use an estimate of the standard error derived from the sample (s_M), whereas for the z test we use the standard error of the population (σ_M).

It would be reasonable, but unfortunately incorrect, to assume that if we had the required data we could calculate the t statistic and enter the z table to find the appropriate proportions. The problem is that while s_{XP} is an *unbiased* estimator for σ_X, it is not always an *accurate* estimator. In other words, there is still error, and the smaller the sample, the greater the error. This, in turn, affects the interpretation of sample data. Specifically, the probabilities found using the normal distribution to interpret $M - \mu$ differences are inaccurate, slightly for moderately sized samples, more dramatically for small samples. Accordingly, to accurately interpret the $M - \mu$ differences, it is necessary to take into account that s_M is more divergent from σ_M, when sample sizes are small. As a result, there is no single distribution for use with the t test; there is a series or family of distributions, one for each sample size. When the sample size is small, the difference between the t distribution and the normal distribution (used with z) is substantial. As the sample size increases, the difference between the two distributions becomes smaller. With an infinite sample size, the t distribution is equal to the normal distribution. Practically speaking, with samples larger than 30, there is little difference between the distributions. The relationship of the family of t distributions to the normal or z distribution is illustrated in Figure 9.13.

From an inspection of Figure 9.13, it is evident that with small sample sizes the t distributions have a greater proportion of their areas located in the extreme tails than occurs with the normal distribution. This means that to include a particular percentage of the curve, such as

Figure 9.13　Relationship Between Sample Size and the t Distribution

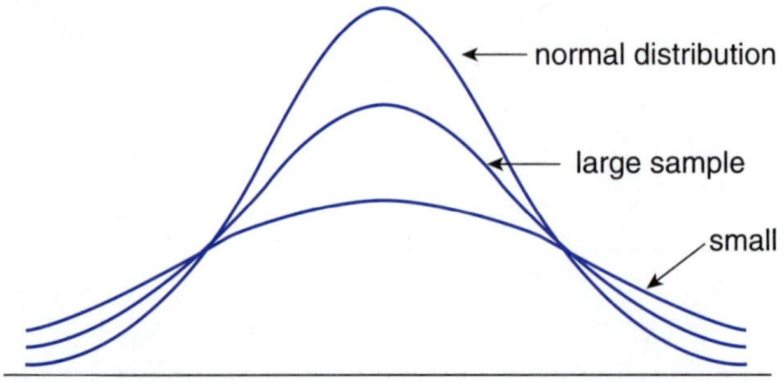

95%, we will have to move farther out into the tails. In other words, while we have found from the z table that ±1.96 *SD* from the mean will include 95% of the area of the normal curve, it will be necessary to move farther from the mean to include 95% when we are using a t distribution. How much farther will depend on the specific sample size or, more precisely, the degrees of freedom (*df*). In other words, just as with the chi-square table, there will be a different value for each different degrees of freedom. In the case of the t distribution, $df = n - 1$, where n is the sample size.

Turning to the t table (note the change from z to t tables; Appendix J, Table J.3), we begin by assuming we have a two-tailed test with alpha set at .05. Proceeding to the bottom of the column headed by .05, we find 1.96. This is the same value as in the z table and indicates that if the sample size were infinite the t distribution would be normal, and thus, the critical value would be the same as with the z distribution. As you go up this column, in other words, as the sample size and number of degrees of freedom decreases, the critical value of t increases. With 60 *df*, the value of t is 2.000. This is only slightly larger than 1.96. However, with 10 *df*, the critical value of t is up to 2.228, and with 1 *df*, it has increased dramatically to 12.706. The increase in the size of the critical value for t as degrees of freedom decreases is the consequence of the shapes of the family of t distributions illustrated in Figure 9.13.

The effect of degrees of freedom on the critical value of the t distribution can be illustrated with an example. Let us assume that we have a sample of 6 subjects randomly selected from a normally distributed population with a mean of 10. Following a treatment, these subjects have been found to have an M of 14.4 and a standard error, s_M, of 2. The null hypothesis is that the treatment did not have an effect. The alternative hypothesis is that the treatment did have an effect. This is a nondirectional, two-tailed test, and we set $\alpha = .05$. The value of t would be

$$t = \frac{M - \mu}{s_M},$$

Substituting, we have

$$t = \frac{14.4 - 10}{2}$$

$$= \frac{4.4}{2}$$

$$= 2.2,$$

and

$$df = n - 1$$

$$= 6 - 1$$

$$= 5.$$

Referring to the *t* table, we find that the critical value for *t* for a two-tailed test with $\alpha = .05$ and with 5 *df* is 2.571. As this value is greater than the obtained *t* of 2.2, we retain the null hypothesis. This outcome is illustrated in Figure 9.14.

Reporting the Results of a One-Sample *t* Test

In an article, we would say, "There was insufficient evidence to reject the hypothesis that the sample ($M = 14.4$, $SD = 2$) was drawn from a population with a mean of 10 ($t(5) = 2.2$, $p > .05$)."

It is important to realize that if we had had 12 or more degrees of freedom, then an outcome this large would have been statistically significant. Thus, the disadvantage with a small sample size is that you will need a larger experimental effect to find a statistically significant difference. In other words, with a small sample size, the power of the statistical test is low, and, as you are more likely to retain the null when in fact it is false, you are more likely to make a Type II error. This issue is discussed in more detail in Appendix D.

Assuming everything stayed the same except that we had 12 *df*, the significant, one-sample *t* test would indicate that the outcome was unlikely to be due to chance. However, it would not indicate the effect size (the percent of variance explained by the treatment). This can be found by calculating eta squared (η^2):

$$\eta^2 = \frac{t^2}{t^2 + df}.$$

Figure 9.14 Comparison of Obtained and Critical Values for *t*

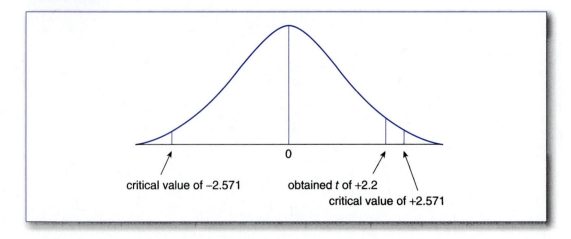

For our example with 12 *df*, this would be

$$\eta^2 = \frac{2.2^2}{2.2^2 + 12}$$

$$= \frac{4.84}{4.84 + 12}$$

$$= \frac{4.84}{16.84}$$

$$= .287 \text{ or } 28.7\%.$$

Thus, in this example, the treatment would have accounted for 28.7% of the total variance. In an article, after reporting the significant *t*, we would say, "η^2 equals .287."

Confidence Interval for *t*

Just as with *z*, we can also, in a sense, solve a *t* test problem in reverse to find a confidence interval.

The procedure for finding the confidence interval for a one-sample *t* statistic is straightforward:

$$M - t_c (s_M) \leq \mu \leq M + t_c (s_M).$$

In this equation, M is the sample mean, t_c is the critical value of *t* found in the *t* table, and s_M is the estimate of the standard error from the sample.

For our example with a sample size of 6, we would have

$$14.4 - (2.571)(2) \leq \mu \leq 14.4 + (2.571)(2).$$

This equals

$$14.4 - 5.142 \leq \mu \leq 14.4 + 5.142$$

or

$$9.26 \leq \mu \leq 19.54.$$

In other words, with a sample size of 6 (and thus 5 *df*), we are 95% confident that the population mean will fall between 9.26 and 19.54. It is important to note that this interval includes the hypothetical population mean of 10, which indicates that our *t* test was not statistically significant. However, if we had used a larger sample, the confidence interval would be smaller. If you recalculate the confidence interval, except this time assuming a larger sample size of 13 (and thus 12 *df*), you will see that the population mean of 10 is no longer included within the confidence interval.

To summarize to this point, the one-sample *t* statistic is much like the one-sample *z* that was covered previously in this chapter. Both assume that the sample is drawn from a normally distributed population. Each can be used to test a hypothesis or to construct a confidence interval. However, whereas the *z* statistic requires that we know the population standard deviation, σ_X, to calculate the standard error, σ_M, the *t* statistic is more flexible because it uses an estimate of σ_X derived from the sample, s_{XP}. However, particularly with small samples, there is error when using this estimate. As a result of this error, the *t* distribution for small degrees of freedom differs substantially from the normal distribution. To account for this discrepancy, there is a family of *t* distributions.

Central Limit Theorem

The *t* test assumes that the sample is drawn from a normally distributed population. If the population is normally distributed, then the sampling distributions that are derived from it are also normal. This has permitted statisticians to specify the probabilities that we find in the tables. It may have occurred to you that this raises a problem, for how would a researcher possibly know if the population has a normal distribution unless, as with the IQ test and SAT, this has been previously determined? Fortunately, it can be shown mathematically that for randomly drawn samples with 30 or more subjects, this is not an issue.

As the sample size increases, the shape of the distribution of sample means (sampling distribution of the mean) rapidly approximates the normal distribution *irrespective of the shape of the population from which it is drawn*. This is summarized in what statisticians call the **central limit theorem**. If the original population is normally distributed, then the shape of the distribution of sample means will be normal regardless of the sample size. Furthermore, if the original distribution is approximately normal, then even with a small sample size the shape of the distribution of sample means will be close to normal. However, if the original distribution is markedly nonnormal, then the sample

> *Central limit theorem:*
>
> *—with increasing sample sizes, the shape of the distribution of sample means (sampling distribution of the mean) rapidly approximates the normal distribution irrespective of the shape of the population from which it is drawn.*
>
> *—the mean of the distribution of sample means is an unbiased estimator of the population mean.*
>
> *—and the standard deviation of the distribution of sample means*
> $(\sigma_M) = \sigma_X / \sqrt{n}$.

size will have to be larger before the shape of the distribution of sample means will approach being normal. Unfortunately, since we usually don't know what the shape of the original population is, we don't know precisely how large a sample needs to be to have a sampling distribution that is approximately normally distributed. As a general rule of thumb, so long as the sample has 30 or more subjects, you can safely use the critical values obtained from the *t* table.

The implications of the central limit theorem are critically important for using statistics. Though the *t* test is based on the assumption that the underlying population is normally distributed, so long as the sample has at least 30 subjects, we don't have to be concerned about this assumption. With 30 or more subjects, the central limit theorem indicates that the sampling distribution of the mean will approach normal, and thus, we can use the table developed for *t* to ascertain needed probabilities. However, there is a limit to how small the sample can be. If the sample is less than 30, then the conservative approach would be to not use the *t* test unless it was known that the underlying population distribution was approximately normal.

We have now nearly finished our introduction to the one-sample *t* test. In closing, we will list the purpose and limitations, and then the assumptions, of the one-sample *t* test, followed by a brief conclusion.

Purpose and Limitations of Using the One-Sample *t* Test

1. *Test for difference:* With a two-tailed test, the null hypothesis is that the treatment does not have an effect. Therefore, any difference between the sample mean and hypothesized population mean is due to chance. The alternative hypothesis is that the treatment does have an effect and, therefore, the two means are significantly different. The one-sample *t* test is employed to differentiate between these two hypotheses.

2. *Does not provide a measure of effect size:* The one-sample *t* test is a test of significance. It indicates whether or not an outcome is likely to have occurred by chance if the null hypothesis is correct. If the *t* test is significant, a measure of effect size such as eta squared (η^2) should then be calculated.

3. *Sample size is important:* For the one-sample *t* test, if the sample size is 30 or greater, the assumption that the population is normal can be safely ignored. If the sample size is less than 30, then the underlying population must be at least approximately normally distributed. If you cannot collect a larger sample and do not know if the assumption of normality has been met, it is best to turn to an alternative test on the same row of Table 9.1.

Assumptions of the One-Sample *t* Test

1. *Interval or ratio data:* The data are on an interval or ratio scale of measurement.

2. *Random sample:* The sample is drawn at random from the population.

3. *Normally distributed population:* The population has a normal distribution of scores.

CONCLUSION

We have now completed the section of the book dealing with the one-sample z and t tests. Before continuing with the study of additional statistical procedures, it may be helpful to take a few moments to review what we have accomplished and to put it into perspective. By referring to Table 9.1 (or Appendix K), you will see that we have begun our review of difference designs for use with interval or ratio data. Specifically, we have learned how to analyze data from a design that uses only one sample. We will soon be discussing more complex designs for use with independent samples as well as designs that use repeated measures. Before doing so, please review Table 9.1 (or Appendix K) to once again see the relationships among the statistical procedures.

Chapter Resources

GLOSSARY OF TERMS

Biased estimator: an estimator that does not accurately predict what it is intended to because of systematic error.

Central limit theorem:

—with increasing sample sizes, the shape of the distribution of sample means (sampling distribution of the mean) rapidly approximates the normal distribution irrespective of the shape of the population from which it is drawn.

—the mean of the distribution of sample means is an unbiased estimator of the population mean.

—and the standard deviation of the distribution of sample means $(\sigma_M) = \sigma_X/\sqrt{n}$.

Confidence interval: the range of values that has a known probability of including the population parameter, usually the mean.

Law of large numbers: the larger the sample size, the better the estimate of population parameters such as μ.

One-tailed or directional test: an analysis in which the null hypothesis will be rejected if an extreme outcome occurs in only one direction. In such a test, the single area of rejection is equal to alpha.

Sampling distribution of the mean: a theoretical probability distribution of sample means. The samples are all of the same size and are randomly selected from the same population.

Standard error: the standard deviation of the sampling distribution of a statistic. Thus the standard error of the mean is the standard deviation of the sampling distribution of means.

Two-tailed or nondirectional test: an analysis in which the null hypothesis will be rejected if an extreme outcome occurs in either direction. In such a test, the alpha level is divided into two equal parts.

Questions: Chapter 9

(Answers to odd-numbered items are provided in Appendix I.)

1. Which of the following is *not* true of the sampling distribution of the mean?

   a. Distribution is symmetrical.

   b. Distribution is normal.

   c. Distribution is unimodal.

   d. All of the above are true.

2. In a _____ all of the region of rejection is placed in one end of the distribution.

   a. two-tailed test

   b. one-tailed test

   c. nondirectional test

   d. none of the above

3. An experimenter wants to test whether a particular intervention will change students' grades. This is an example of a _____ test.

   a. one-tailed

   b. two-tailed

   c. three-tailed

4. In a one-tailed test, the area of rejection is _____.

   a. placed in one tail, but it does not matter which tail

   b. divided equally in the two tails

   c. placed in one tail based on the previous literature

   d. always less than in a two-tailed test

5. The one-sample *t* test is used instead of the one-sample *z* test when _____ is *not* known.

   a. the population mean

   b. the population size

   c. the population standard deviation

6. The outcome of the one-sample z test is a number measured in _____.

   a. the units of the original data, such as meters or pounds

   b. standard error units

   c. units that vary with each problem

   d. none of the above

7. With a t test, the _____ must be estimated.

   a. population mean

   b. population size

   c. population standard deviation

8. Degrees of freedom are used with _____.

   a. one-sample z test

   b. one-sample t test

   c. both the one-sample z and t tests

9. If we compare the z and t tables, assuming the criterion remains .05, the critical value for z will be _____ the critical value of t.

   a. smaller than

   b. larger than

   c. the same as

10. The statement that "the shape of the distribution of sample means (sampling distribution of the mean) rapidly approximates the normal distribution irrespective of the shape of the population from which it is drawn" is a part of the definition of _____.

    a. a confidence interval

    b. degrees of freedom

    c. the central limit theorem

    d. the law of large numbers

11. The mean of a large sample provides a better estimate of the population mean than the mean of a small sample. This is an example of _____.

    a. a confidence interval

    b. degrees of freedom

    c. the central limit theorem

    d. the law of large numbers

12. Another name for the standard deviation of the sampling distribution of means is the _____.

    a. ultimate standard deviation

    b. positive standard deviation

    c. standard error

    d. maximum standard error

13. The confidence interval has a known probability of including the _____.

    a. population parameter

    b. sample statistic

    c. either the population parameter or the sample statistic

For Questions 14 to 19, use the following information: A researcher is interested in whether drinking orange juice will have an effect on IQ. Accordingly, 25 randomly selected subjects drink orange juice and the group is subsequently found to have a mean IQ of 102. Is this a sufficient difference to conclude that drinking orange juice affects IQ? Set $\alpha = .05$. (Remember, the mean of the commonly used IQ tests is 100 and the standard deviation is 15.)

14. What is the null hypothesis?

    a. Orange juice affects IQ.

    b. Orange juice does not affect IQ.

15. What is the standard error?

    a. 15

    b. 3

    c. 9

    d. 1

16. What is the value of z for these data?

    a. .67

    b. 1.0

    c. 1.8

    d. 3.0

17. Is this a one- or two-tailed test?

    a. one-tailed test

    b. two-tailed test

18. What is the critical value from the z table?

    a. 1.96

    b. 2.58

    c. 1.64 or 1.65

    d. 1.00

19. What conclusion do you make?

    a. Retain the null hypothesis—there is not sufficient evidence to conclude that orange juice affects IQ

    b. Reject the null hypothesis—there is sufficient evidence to conclude that orange juice affects IQ

    c. There is not sufficient evidence to come to any decision

For Questions 20 to 25, use the following information: A researcher is interested in whether giving rats a particular diet will have an effect on how fast they run a maze. Accordingly, 20 randomly selected subjects are given the experimental diet, and this group is subsequently found to have a mean run time of 130 seconds. Is there a sufficient difference to conclude that the diet has had an effect on running speed if it is known that the mean of the population of rats without the special diet is 125 seconds and the standard deviation of the population is 10.5 seconds? Use $\alpha = .05$.

20. What is the null hypothesis?

    a. The experimental diet affects running speed.

    b. The experimental diet does not affect running speed.

21. What is the standard error?

    a. 10.5

    b. 20

    c. 4.47

    d. 2.35

22. What is the value of z for these data?

    a. 5

    b. 1.96

    c. 2.13

    d. 3.0

23. Is this a one- or two-tailed test?

    a. One-tailed test

    b. Two-tailed test

24. What is the critical value from the z table?

    a. 1.96

    b. 2.58

    c. 1.64 or 1.65

    d. 1.00

25. What conclusion do you make?

    a. Retain the null hypothesis—there is not sufficient evidence to conclude that the diet affects running speed.

    b. Reject the null hypothesis—there is sufficient evidence to conclude that the diet affects running speed.

    c. There is not sufficient evidence to come to any decision.

For Questions 26 to 33, use the following information: A researcher is interested in whether giving a particular fertilizer will have an effect on crop production. Accordingly, 20 randomly selected plants are given the experimental fertilizer, and this group is subsequently found to produce a mean of 30 pounds of fruit. Is there a sufficient difference to conclude that the fertilizer has had an effect if it is hypothesized that the mean production without the fertilizer is 25 pounds and the estimate of the population standard error, derived from the sample, is 2.13 pounds? Use $\alpha = .05$.

26. What is the null hypothesis?

    a. The experimental fertilizer affects crop production.

    b. The experimental fertilizer does not affect crop production.

27. Would you employ a z or a t test for these data?

    a. z test

    b. t test

28. What is the value of the statistical test for these data?

    a. 2.35

    b. 1.96

    c. 2.19

    d. 3.06

29. Is this a one- or a two-tailed test?

    a. One-tailed test

    b. Two-tailed test

30. How many degrees of freedom are there?

    a. 18

    b. 19

    c. 20

    d. 21

    e. It is not possible to determine the degrees of freedom for these data

31. What is the critical value from the appropriate table, assuming alpha is set at .05?

    a. 1.96

    b. 2.58

    c. 2.093

    d. 3.441

32. What conclusion do you make?

    a. Retain the null hypothesis—there is not sufficient evidence to conclude that the fertilizer affects crop production.

    b. Reject the null hypothesis—there is sufficient evidence to conclude that the fertilizer affects crop production.

    c. There is not sufficient evidence to come to any decision.

33. What is the confidence interval that has a 95% probability of including the population mean?

    a. $24.77 \leq \mu \leq 35.23$

    b. $28.52 \leq \mu \leq 31.48$

    c. $26.54 \leq \mu \leq 33.46$

    d. $20.15 \leq \mu \leq 39.85$

    e. $25.54 \leq \mu \leq 34.46$

For Questions 34 to 36 assume that a sample of 16 students taking statistics has a mean IQ of 108. What range of sample means has a 95% probability of including the population mean?

34. What is the standard error?

    a. 3.75

    b. 15

    c. 4

    d. 16

35. What is the critical value from the z table?

    a. 1.96

    b. 2.58

    c. 1.64 or 1.65

    d. .67

36. What is the confidence interval that has a 95% probability of including the population mean?

    a. $105.49 \leq \mu \leq 110.51$

    b. $103.5 \leq \mu \leq 112.5$

    c. $100.65 \leq \mu \leq 115.35$

    d. $100 \leq \mu \leq 116$

For Questions 37 to 39, use the same information as in the previous questions except answer what range of sample means has a 50% probability of including the population mean.

37. What is the standard error?

    a. 3.75

    b. 15

    c. 4

    d. 16

38. What is the critical value from the z table?

    a. 1.96

    b. 2.58

    c. 1.64 or 1.65

    d. .67

39. What is the confidence interval that has a 50% probability of including the population mean?

    a. $105.49 \leq \mu \leq 110.51$

    b. $103.5 \leq \mu \leq 112.5$

    c. $100.65 \leq \mu \leq 115.35$

    d. $100 \leq \mu \leq 116$

SPSS procedures are rarely used for the statistical tests described in this chapter.

FINDING DIFFERENCES WITH INTERVAL AND RATIO DATA—II

The Independent Samples t *Test and the Dependent Samples* t *Test*

Science is simply common sense at its best, that is, rigidly accurate in observation, and merciless to fallacy in logic.

—Thomas Huxley

This chapter will cover two of the most commonly employed statistical tests. Both are conceptually similar and, as you will see, each is closely related to the one-sample t test that was reviewed in Chapter 9. The first of these tests is called the independent samples t test. After discussing this procedure, we will turn to the dependent samples t test. These tests are underlined in Table 10.1.

INDEPENDENT SAMPLES *t* TEST

We often see studies that compare one group of subjects that receives a treatment with another group that serves as a control and does not receive the treatment. For instance, we could study the effect of background noise on learning and memory by randomly assigning subjects to

Table 10.1	Overview of Inferential Statistical Procedures Difference and Interaction Designs

Type of Data

	Nominal (Frequency)		Ordinal (Ranked)	Interval/Ratio (Continuous Measure)
<u>**Inferential Statistics**</u> (Finding Relationships)				
Statistical procedures for difference and interaction designs				
One variable with at least two outcomes	Goodness-of-fit chi-square	**One IV with one sample—one DV**		One-sample z score or one-sample t test
		One IV with two or more independent samples—one DV	*Kruskal–Wallis H*	One-way between-subjects ANOVA (only two independent samples—<u>independent samples t test</u>)
		One IV with one sample having two or more repeated measures—one DV		One-way within-subjects ANOVA (only two repeated measures—<u>dependent samples t test</u>)
Two variables, each with at least two outcomes	Chi-square test of independence	**Two IV each with two or more independent samples—one DV**		Two-way between-subjects ANOVA

Notes. IV, independent variable; DV, dependent variable; ANOVA, analysis of variance. Research designs are shown in boldface. The italicized item is reviewed in Appendix A.

either read a passage in a quiet classroom or while listening to loud music. Subsequently, we could compare their retention of the passage's information. Alternatively, two preexisting groups, such as men and women, might be compared on some measure, such as their reaction to bright light. These are both examples of the two independent samples design. Studies that compare two independent groups are very popular and, if the data are interval or ratio, can be analyzed with a form of the t test that is called the independent samples t test, the t test for independent samples, or just the independent t test.

Table 10.1 indicates that with this experimental design and ordinal data, we would use the Kruskal–Wallis H test (reviewed in Appendix A). With interval or ratio data, either the independent samples t test or the one-way between-subjects ANOVA (analysis of variance;

reviewed in Chapter 11) is appropriate. The advantage of the independent samples *t* test compared with the ANOVA is that it is easier to calculate. However, the one-way between-subjects ANOVA is more flexible as it can be used with designs that have more than two samples.

As was just noted, the *t* test for two independent samples (independent samples *t* test) is conceptually very similar to the *t* test for one sample of subjects, which was reviewed in Chapter 9. When there is only one sample, the *t* test examines whether a deviation between the sample mean (*M*) and the population mean (μ) is likely to have happened by chance. This is accomplished by converting this difference into standard deviation units. As you recall, what distinguishes the one-sample *t* test from the one-sample *z* test is that with the *t* test we do not need to know the value of the population standard deviation. Instead, we substitute an estimate of the standard deviation derived from the sample. This estimated standard deviation in a one-sample *t* test is called the standard error of the mean (s_M). Dividing the difference between the sample mean and the population mean by s_M converts the outcome into standard deviation units. Specifically, for a one-sample study

$$t = \frac{M - \mu}{s_M},$$

where the standard error, $s_M = \dfrac{s_{XP}}{\sqrt{n}}$.

As there are a series of *t* distributions, the degrees of freedom (*df*), which for the one-sample *t* test are equal to $n - 1$, must then be calculated. Finally, the value calculated for *t* is compared with the critical value obtained from the *t* table (Appendix J, Table J.3).

With the independent samples *t* test, the logic is essentially the same. However, as we are now dealing with two sample means, not one, we are no longer examining whether a deviation between a single sample mean and a population mean ($M - \mu$) is likely to have happened by chance. Instead, we are comparing the difference of a pair of sample means ($M_1 - M_2$) to the proposed difference between a pair of population means ($\mu_1 - \mu_2$). More specifically, we are examining whether this difference [$(M_1 - M_2) - (\mu_1 - \mu_2)$] is likely to have happened by chance. To do so, we substitute a *difference between means* for each *mean* in the above one-sample *t* equation.

> Standard error of the difference between sample means $\left(s_{(M_1-M_2)}\right)$: the standard deviation of the sampling distribution of the difference between sample means.

Thus, instead of a single sample mean (*M*), we substitute the difference between sample means ($M_1 - M_2$). And instead of a single population mean (μ), we substitute the difference between population means ($\mu_1 - \mu_2$). Finally, instead of dividing by a standard error *of the mean* (s_M), we substitute the **standard error of the difference between sample means** ($\boldsymbol{S_{(M_1-M_2)}}$) (Note that $s_{(M_1-M_2)}$ is a single number.) The resulting *t* equation is as follows:

$$t = \frac{\left(M_1 - M_2\right) - (\mu_1 - \mu_2)}{s_{(M_1-M_2)}}.$$

The parallels between the one-sample t test and the independent samples t test may become clearer by referring to Table 10.2.

As you will see, the equation for the independent samples t test is easy to use. However, before turning to an example, we will first review what this equation is accomplishing and then turn to an explanation of the logic underlying this form of the t test.

The numerator of the independent samples t test indicates that we are to find the difference between our sample means and from this subtract the proposed difference between the population means. Finding sample means is not difficult and, clearly, neither is finding their difference.

The proposed difference between the population means is a reflection of the null hypothesis. For instance, if the null hypothesis is that the treatment will not have an effect, then the control and experimental population means are assumed to be equal, and thus, $\mu_1 - \mu_2$ is predicted to be zero. In this case, which is quite common, the numerator of the equation for t reduces to simply the difference between the sample means. On the other hand, the null hypothesis might state that $\mu_1 - \mu_2$ is not zero. For instance, previous research may suggest that there is a preexisting difference between two groups. An example would be that men are generally a few inches taller than women, and thus, the hypothesized difference between the heights of men and women would not be zero.

The difference between the sample means and the population means is then divided by the appropriate standard deviation measure. In the case of the independent samples t test, this is the standard error of difference between sample means $\left(s_{(M_1 - M_2)} \right)$. This will convert the difference found in the numerator into standard deviation units. Then, the outcome is interpreted by referring to the t table.

The Logic of the Independent Samples t Test

Before turning to an example, it is important to understand the justification for utilizing the t table with the independent samples t test. We will begin with a review of the logic of the z score and then turn to the one-sample z and one-sample t tests as these form the basis for

Table 10.2   Parallels Between the One-Sample t Test and the Independent Samples t Test

One-Sample t Test		Independent Samples t Test	
Sample mean	M	Difference between sample means	$M_1 - M_2$
Population mean	μ	Proposed difference between population means	$\mu_1 - \mu_2$
Standard error of the mean	s_M	Standard error of the difference between sample means	$s_{(M_1 - M_2)}$

the independent samples t test. This discussion is somewhat theoretical, but it is useful in understanding the logic of these statistical tests.

In Chapter 4, it was noted that to convert a score (X) into a z score, we use the equation $z = (X - \mu)/\sigma_X$. In this equation, we are dividing the difference ($X - \mu$) by a standard deviation (σ_X) to convert the difference into standard deviation units. If the distribution of the population of scores (X) is normal, we can then use the z table to determine the probabilities associated with this score.

The logic for the one-sample z test is the same: We take a difference, this time ($M - \mu$), and divide by a standard deviation. However, as we are now dealing with a sample mean (M) rather than a score (X), we need to divide by a measure of the variability of sample means. This measure of variability is called the standard error of the mean and has the symbol σ_M. Thus, the equation for a z test becomes $z = (M - \mu)/\sigma_M$. To be able to then refer to the z table (Appendix J, Table J.1), we need to know that the theoretical distribution of sample means, which is called the sampling distribution of the mean, is normal. Fortunately, if the population of scores from which the sample was drawn was normal, then, it can be shown that the sampling distribution of the mean is also normally distributed. We can, therefore, conduct a z test and compare the outcome to the critical value obtained from the z table.

Recall that to conduct a z test, we need to know the standard deviation of the population (σ_X) from which the sample was drawn. We can then calculate the standard error of the mean, for $\sigma_M = \sigma_X/\sqrt{n}$. Unfortunately, in most cases, we do not know σ_X. However, in Chapter 9, you learned that it can be estimated from the variability in the sample. We have given this estimate of σ_X derived from the sample the symbol s_{XP}. And just as with the z test, we can then calculate an estimate of the standard error of the mean, for $s_M = s_{XP}/\sqrt{n}$. The equation for the one-sample t test then becomes $t = (M - \mu)/s_M$, which is identical to the equation for the one-sample z test except that we are using s_M as an estimate of σ_M. To then be able to use the z table, we would need to know that s_{XP} provides an unbiased and accurate estimate of σ_X. Unfortunately, while s_{XP} is an unbiased estimator of σ_X, it is not always accurate, and the smaller the sample size, the less accurate it is. As a consequence, we do not use the z table with a t test but, instead, turn to the t table and take the sample size into account by calculating the degrees of freedom.

The logic for the independent samples t test (two independent samples t test) parallels what was just said for the one-sample t test. Once again, we have a difference being converted into standard deviation units. And once again, we must use the appropriate estimate of the variability to do so. Finally, we must utilize the t table rather than the z table and take into account the degrees of freedom. What is new is that we are now comparing the difference of two sample means ($M_1 - M_2$) against the predicted difference of the means of the populations from which these samples were drawn ($\mu_1 - \mu_2$). And to convert this difference of sample and population means into standard deviation units, we must divide by an appropriate measure of variability, in this case the standard error of the difference between sample means $\left(s_{(M_1 - M_2)}\right)$. The result, as was noted previously, is that the equation for the independent samples t test closely parallels the form of the one-sample t test.

And it was noted previously in the discussion of the logic of the z test that if the population of scores from which the sample was drawn was normally distributed, then the sampling distribution of the mean would also be normally distributed. Similarly, it can be shown that the sampling distribution of the difference between sample means is normally distributed if the populations from which the samples are drawn are normally distributed. However, because we are utilizing an estimate of the population standard deviation of the difference between means which is derived from the samples, we must once again use the t table rather than the z table. Thus, the logic of the independent samples t test directly parallels the logic of the one-sample t test.

An example illustrating the calculation of an independent samples t test will assist you in seeing the parallel between this statistical procedure and the one-sample t test, which was covered in Chapter 9.

An Example of an Independent Samples t Test

An example of a two independent samples design would be a fictitious comparison of the effectiveness of two methods for teaching statistics. To conduct the study, each subject would be randomly assigned to either the standard procedure or an alternative procedure (the sample sizes do not have to be equal). The standard procedure could be considered the control condition, and the alternative procedure would be the experimental condition. As is often the case, the null hypothesis is that there is no difference between the conditions. The alternative hypothesis is that there is a difference. After exposure to either the standard or alternative teaching procedure, the subjects would be tested to determine their mastery of statistics. This is a two-tailed test and assuming that alpha was set to .05, what should the researcher decide about the effectiveness of the teaching procedures if the following scores were obtained on a quiz (Table 10.3)?

Recall that the equation for t with two independent samples was given previously as follows:

$$t = \frac{(M_1 - M_2) - (\mu_1 - \mu_2)}{s_{(M_1 - M_2)}},$$

where $s_{(M_1 - M_2)}$ is the standard error of the difference between sample means. Inspection of Table 10.3 will indicate that the sample means (M_1 and M_2) as well as the deviations of each score from their sample mean (columns $X_1 - M_1$ and $X_2 - M_2$) have been calculated. And, as expected, the sum of the deviations for each group, which can be symbolized as Σx_1 and Σx_2 respectively, are each equal to 0. In addition to the sample means, we will also need values for the sum of squared deviations from the mean. The sum of the squared deviations from the mean for the control group, which can be symbolized as $\Sigma(X_1 - M_1)^2$ or as Σx_1^2, is found to equal 20. The sum of the squared deviations from the mean for the experimental group, which can be symbolized as $\Sigma(X_2 - M_2)^2$ or as Σx_2^2, is equal to 28.

| Table 10.3 | Example 1: Two Samples of Ratio Data and the Initial Calculations |

Control Condition			Experimental Condition		
X_1	$X_1 - M_1$	$(X_1 - M_1)^2$	X_2	$X_2 - M_2$	$(X_2 - M_2)^2$
8	2	4	13	3	9
7	1	1	12	2	4
7	1	1	11	1	1
7	1	1	9	−1	1
4	−2	4	8	−2	4
3	−3	9	7	−3	9
$\sum X_1 = 36$	$\sum x_1 = 0$	$\sum x_1^2 = 20$	$\sum X_2 = 60$	$\sum x_2 = 0$	$\sum x_2^2 = 28$
$n_1 = 6$			$n_2 = 6$		
$M_1 = 36/6$			$M_2 = 60/6$		
$= 6$			$= 10$		

As the difference between the population means $(\mu_1 - \mu_2)$ was hypothesized to be zero, the equation for t becomes

$$t = \frac{(M_1 - M_2) - 0}{s_{(M_1 - M_2)}}$$

$$= \frac{(6 - 10) - 0}{s_{(M_1 - M_2)}}$$

$$= \frac{-4}{s_{(M_1 - M_2)}}.$$

To find the value of the denominator of this equation, $s_{(M_1 - M_2)}$, we must first find the values of $s_{XP_1}^2$ and $s_{XP_2}^2$.

The estimate of the population variance for the control group (Condition 1) is as follows:

$$s_{XP_1}^2 = \frac{\sum (X_1 - M_1)^2}{(n_1 - 1)}$$

$$= \frac{\sum x_1^2}{(n_1 - 1)}$$

$$= \frac{20}{6-1}$$

$$= \frac{20}{5}$$

$$= 4.$$

For the experimental group (Condition 2), the estimate of the population variance is as follows:

$$s^2_{XP_2} = \frac{\Sigma(X_2 - M_2)^2}{(n_2 - 1)}$$

$$= \frac{\Sigma x^2_2}{(n_2 - 1)}$$

$$= \frac{28}{(6-1)}$$

$$= \frac{28}{5}$$

$$= 5.6.$$

The value of the standard error of the difference between sample means is found with the following particularly impressive looking equation. Fortunately, as you will see, it is easy to use.

$$s_{(M_1 - M_2)} = \sqrt{\frac{(n_1 - 1)s^2_{XP_1} + (n_2 - 1)s^2_{XP_2}}{n_1 + n_2 - 2}\left(\frac{1}{n_1} + \frac{1}{n_2}\right)}$$

$$= \sqrt{\frac{(6-1)(4) + (6-1)(5.6)}{6 + 6 - 2}\left(\frac{1}{6} + \frac{1}{6}\right)}$$

$$= \sqrt{\frac{(5)(4) + (5)(5.6)}{10}\left(\frac{2}{6}\right)}$$

$$= \sqrt{\frac{20 + 28}{10}\left(\frac{1}{3}\right)}$$

$$= \sqrt{\frac{48}{10}\left(\frac{1}{3}\right)}$$

$$= \sqrt{4.8\left(\frac{1}{3}\right)}$$

$$= \sqrt{1.6}$$

$$= 1.265.$$

The value for t is therefore

$$t = \frac{-4}{s_{(M_1 - M_2)}}$$

$$= \frac{-4}{1.265}$$

$$= -3.162,$$

where

$$df = n_1 + n_2 - 2$$

$$= 6 + 6 - 2$$

$$= 12 - 2$$

$$= 10.$$

The critical value of t obtained from the t table for a two-tailed test with $\alpha = .05$ and 10 df is found to be 2.228. Our value of -3.162 is more standard deviation units from the mean than is the critical value, and thus, we reject the null hypothesis that the control and experimental groups come from populations with equal means and accept the alternative hypothesis that the sample means are different. In other words, we conclude that the treatment had an effect. More specifically, we note that as the mean score for the experimental condition is greater than the mean score for the control condition, there is evidence that the alternate teaching procedure increased students' scores. (It is important to understand that our negative value for t indicates that student scores went up in the experimental condition.)

However, we do not know how large the effect was. To ascertain the percentage of variance explained by the treatment, we calculate eta squared (η^2). For the independent samples t, eta squared is found with the same equation as is used with the one-sample t test, which is as follows:

$$\eta^2 = \frac{t^2}{t^2 + df}.$$

For our example with 10 *df*, this would be

$$\eta^2 = \frac{-3.162^2}{-3.162^2 + 10}$$

$$= \frac{9.998}{9.998 + 10}$$

$$= \frac{9.998}{19.998}$$

$$= 0.50 \text{ or } 50\%.$$

Thus, in this example, the treatment accounted for 50% of the total variance.

Reporting the Results of an Independent Samples *t* Test

In an article, we would report, "There was sufficient evidence to reject the null hypothesis that the teaching techniques were equivalent ($t(10) = -3.162$, $p < .05$)." After reporting the significant *t*, we would say, "η^2 was equal to .50."

Confidence Interval for Independent Samples *t* Test

The procedure for finding the confidence interval for a two-sample *t* test (independent samples *t*) statistic is similar to what was used with a one-sample *t* test:

For one-sample *t* test,

$$M - t_c(s_M) \leq \mu \leq M + t_c(s_M).$$

For two-sample *t* test (independent samples *t* test),

$$\left[(M_1 - M_2) - t_c\left(s_{(M_1-M_2)}\right)\right] \leq (\mu_1 - \mu_2) \leq \left[(M_1 - M_2) + t_c\left(s_{(M_1-M_2)}\right)\right].$$

Note that in both cases the critical *t* value (t_c) from the table is found by using the two-tailed entry, even if the original *t* was found to be significant with a one-tailed test.

For our example, we would have the following:

$$[(6 - 10) - (2.228)(1.265)] \leq (\mu_1 - \mu_2) \leq [(6 - 10) + (2.228)(1.265)].$$

This equals

$$-4 - 2.82 \leq (\mu_1 - \mu_2) \leq -4 + 2.82,$$

or

$$-6.82 \leq (\mu_1 - \mu_2) \leq -1.18.$$

In other words, with 10 *df*, we are 95% confident that the experimental population mean will be between 1.18 and 6.82 points greater than (be careful with the sign of the difference) the control population mean.

To summarize to this point, the two-sample *t* test (independent samples *t*) statistic is much like the one-sample *t* test. Both assume that the sample(s) is (are) drawn from a normally distributed population(s). Each can be used to test a hypothesis or to construct a confidence interval. Finally, each *t* statistic is flexible because, unlike the *z* test, it uses an estimate derived from the sample(s) to determine the necessary standard error.

A Second Example of an Independent Samples *t* Test

In the previous example of the *t* test, each subject was randomly assigned to either the control or the experimental group. The *t* test is also commonly used when the subjects cannot be randomly assigned. For instance, a researcher might want to study why there are fewer women than men in fields of engineering. One way to examine this question is to determine how attractive engineering fields are to men and women. Let us assume that an initial study found that men rated engineering fields as being 10 points more attractive on some measure than women did. The researcher might then want to determine the effect of an intervention designed to increase women's interest in engineering. In this study, there would be two groups, men and women. Obviously, however, a subject cannot be randomly assigned to be either a man or a woman. A subject comes to the experiment already being a man or a woman. Nevertheless, a *t* test can be used to analyze the results.

Specifically, in this example, let us assume that the researcher wanted to test the effectiveness of an intervention consisting of a talk, several readings, and a meeting with a successful woman engineer. The null hypothesis is that the intervention would not decrease the difference between men and women, and therefore, the women would continue to rate engineering fields as being 10 points less attractive than men do. The alternative hypothesis is that the intervention would decrease the difference in the rating of interest in engineering. This is a one-tailed hypothesis as a directional prediction is being made. The researcher planned to include equal numbers of men and women but, as is often the case, several subjects dropped out of the study for various reasons. As a result, at the end of the study, there were only seven women and five men. Their hypothetical ratings of the attractiveness of engineering, along with additional calculations, are listed in Table 10.4.

| Table 10.4 | Example 2: Using the t Test With Nonrandom Assignment of Subjects |

Men			Women		
X_1	$X - M_1$	$(X_1 - M_1)^2$	X_2	$X_2 - M_2$	$(X_2 - M_2)^2$
90	13.4	179.56	87	14.7	216.09
82	5.4	29.16	80	7.7	59.29
76	−0.6	0.36	76	3.7	13.69
72	−4.6	21.16	74	1.7	2.89
63	−13.6	184.96	70	−2.3	5.29
			65	−7.3	53.29
			54	−18.3	334.89
$\sum X_1 = 383$	$\sum x_1 = 0$	$\sum x_1^2 = 415.2$	$\sum X_2 = 506$	$\sum x_2 = 0$	$\sum x_2^2 = 685.43$
$n_1 = 5$ $M_1 = 383/5$ $= 76.6$			$n_2 = 7$ $M_2 = 506/7$ $= 72.3$		

Recall that the equation for the independent samples t test is

$$t = \frac{(M_1 - M_2) - (\mu_1 - \mu_2)}{s_{(M_1 - M_2)}},$$

where $s_{(M_1 - M_2)}$ is the standard error of the difference between sample means.

As the difference between the population means was hypothesized to be 10 points, this equation becomes

$$t = \frac{(M_1 - M_2) - 10}{s_{(M_1 - M_2)}}$$

$$= \frac{(76.6 - 72.3) - 10}{s_{(M_1 - M_2)}}$$

$$= \frac{4.3 - 10}{s_{(M_1 - M_2)}}$$

$$= \frac{-5.7}{s_{(M_1 - M_2)}}.$$

To find the value of the standard error, $s_{(M_1-M_2)}$, we must first find $s^2_{XP_1}$ and $s^2_{XP_2}$. The estimate of the population variance for the men (Group 1) is as follows:

$$s^2_{XP_1} = \frac{\Sigma x_1^2}{(n_1 - 1)}$$

$$= \frac{415.2}{5-1}$$

$$= \frac{415.2}{4}$$

$$= 103.8.$$

For the women (Group 2), the estimate of the population variance is as follows:

$$s^2_{XP_2} = \frac{\Sigma x_2^2}{(n_2 - 1)}$$

$$= \frac{685.43}{(7-1)}$$

$$= \frac{685.43}{(6)}$$

$$= 114.24.$$

We can now find

$$s_{(M_1-M_2)} = \sqrt{\frac{(n_1 - 1)s^2_{XP_1} + (n_2 - 1)s^2_{XP_2}}{n_1 + n_2 - 2}\left(\frac{1}{n_1} + \frac{1}{n_2}\right)}$$

$$= \sqrt{\frac{(5-1)(103.8) + (7-1)(114.24)}{5+7-2}\left(\frac{1}{5} + \frac{1}{7}\right)}$$

$$= \sqrt{\frac{(4)(103.8) + (6)(114.24)}{10}(0.2 + 0.143)}$$

$$= \sqrt{\frac{415.2 + 685.44}{10}(0.343)}$$

$$= \sqrt{(110.064)(0.343)}$$

$$= \sqrt{37.75}$$

$$= 6.14.$$

The value for t is therefore

$$t = \frac{-5.7}{6.14}$$

$$= -0.928,$$

where

$$df = n_1 + n_2 - 2,$$

$$= 5 + 7 - 2$$

$$= 12 - 2$$

$$= 10.$$

From the t table, the critical value of a one-tailed t with $\alpha = .05$ and 10 df is found to be 1.812. As our value of -0.928 is fewer standard deviation units from the mean than is the critical value, we do not reject the null hypothesis. We conclude that there is not sufficient evidence that the intervention affected the women's interest in engineering relative to the men's interest. However, the researcher should recognize that the outcome is in the predicted direction (be careful of the meaning of the obtained t) and that the samples are much too small. Finally, eta squared is not calculated because a significant outcome was not obtained.

Purpose and Limitations of Using the Independent Samples t Test

1. *Test for difference:* The null hypothesis is usually that the treatment does not have an effect. Therefore, if the null hypothesis is retained, any difference between the sample means is assumed to be due to chance. The alternative hypothesis is that the treatment does have an effect and, therefore, that the two samples are drawn from populations with different means. The independent samples t test is employed to differentiate between these two hypotheses.

2. *Does not provide a measure of effect size:* The independent samples t test is a test of significance. It indicates whether or not an outcome is likely to have occurred by chance if the null hypothesis is correct. If the t test is significant, a measure of effect size, such as eta squared, should then be calculated.

3. *Sample size is important:* For the independent samples *t* test, if each sample size is 30 or greater then the assumption that the population is normal can be safely ignored. If the sample size is less than 30, then it is important that the underlying populations be normally distributed. If you cannot collect a larger sample and do not know if the assumption of normality has been met, it may be best to turn to an alternative test on the same row of Table 10.1.

4. *Compares two sample means:* The independent samples *t* test is limited to comparing two sample means.

Assumptions of the Independent Samples *t* Test

1. *Interval or ratio data:* The data are on an interval scale of measurement or a ratio scale of measurement.

2. *Random samples:* Each sample is drawn at random from a population.

3. *Normally distributed populations:* Each population from which a sample is drawn has a normal distribution of scores.

4. *Population variances are equal:* The two populations from which samples are drawn have equal variances.

Effect of Violating the Assumptions

The *t* test has been found to be robust. This means that it leads to accurate decisions even when some assumptions are violated. However, if the sample sizes are dramatically unequal, the sample distributions have obviously different shapes or the sample variances are clearly not equal, you should not use the *t* test. Instead, you might consider converting your interval or ratio data into ordinal data and then turn to an appropriate test for the same experimental design in Table 10.1.

Conclusion

The independent samples *t* test is a commonly used statistical procedure. It compares two sample means and is easy to calculate. As you will see in Chapter 11, the independent samples *t* test is a special case of the one-way between-subjects ANOVA, and any time you used the two-tailed independent samples *t* test, you could have used the more flexible one-way between-subjects ANOVA. However, the calculations for the one-way between-subjects ANOVA are more involved.

PROGRESS CHECK

In a hypothetical study, a researcher is interested in whether taking a motorcycle driving safety course decreases the subsequent number of accidents experienced by motorcycle drivers. To determine this, the researcher checks the driving statistics for a 10-year period for motorcycle drivers who either did, or did not, attend a safety course. The mean number of accidents reported for the drivers who took the course was 1.24. The mean number of accidents reported for the drivers who did not take the course was 1.62. And the standard error of the difference between sample means was .30. There were 22 *df* and the alpha was set at .05.

1. Is this a one- or two-tailed test?

2. What is the value of *t*?

3. What is your decision?

Answers: 1. One-tailed.   2. $\mp$ 1.27 (The sign depends on the order the sample means are entered into the equation.)   3. Accept the null hypothesis.

DEPENDENT SAMPLES *t* TEST

You have just learned that the independent samples *t* test is appropriate for experimental designs that have one independent variable with two samples, and it was shown that the independent samples *t* test was closely related to the one-sample *t* test that was covered in Chapter 9.

The fundamental difference when using the dependent samples *t* test is that we no longer have independent samples. Instead, the subjects assigned to each value of the treatment are related in some manner. Most commonly, there are repeated measures on the same subjects. The dependent samples *t* test is underlined in Table 10.1.

The dependent samples *t* test is also closely related to the one-sample *t* test. As you recall, when there is one sample, the *t* test converts a deviation between the sample mean (*M*) and the hypothetical population mean (μ) into standard deviation units by dividing the difference between these means by the estimate of the standard deviation of sample means. This estimated standard deviation is called the standard error of the mean (s_M). Specifically, for a one-sample study,

$$t = \frac{M - \mu}{s_M},$$

where the standard error, $s_M = s_{XP} / \sqrt{n}$.

The essential difference when employing the dependent samples t test is that instead of considering a mean of scores (M), we are now dealing with the mean of a set of difference scores (M_D). Each of these difference scores consists of either two scores from the same individual (repeated measures design) or two scores from pairs of matched subjects (matched samples design). The mean of these difference scores is then compared with the expected value of this mean (μ_D). The result is that the numerator of the dependent t test ($M_D - \mu_D$) looks quite similar to the numerator of the one-sample t test ($M - \mu$).

In the one-sample t test, the value obtained in the numerator is then divided by an estimate of the variability of sample means (s_M). Similarly, with the dependent samples t test, the value obtained in the numerator is then divided by an estimate of the variability of the means of difference scores. This is called the **standard error of the mean difference** (s_{M_D}). And as we are employing an estimate of this measure of variability derived from the data, we must use the t table rather than the z table. Finally, we must also account for the degrees of freedom.

> *Standard error of the mean difference (s_{M_D}): the standard deviation of the sampling distribution of the mean difference between measures.*

Of course, the use of the t table with the dependent t test assumes that the theoretical frequency distribution of the means of difference scores is normally distributed, just as with the one-sample t test it was assumed that the theoretical frequency distribution of sample means was normally distributed. Fortunately, it has been shown that so long as the distributions of the original scores are normal, the distribution of the means of their differences will also be normal. The logic for the dependent t test therefore closely parallels the logic of the one-sample t test. And, not surprisingly, the equation for the dependent samples t test will also look very much like the one-sample t test that was reviewed in Chapter 9. Specifically, for a one-sample t test,

$$t = \frac{M - \mu}{s_M},$$

where the standard error of the mean, $s_M = s_{XP}/\sqrt{n}$, n is equal to the number of scores, and the df is equal to $n - 1$.

For a dependent samples t test,

$$t = \frac{M_D - \mu_D}{s_{M_D}},$$

where the standard error of the mean difference, $s_{M_D} = s_{DP}/\sqrt{n}$, n is equal to the number of *pairs* of scores, and the df is equal to $n - 1$.

In most cases, the null hypothesis is that the difference between population means (μ_D) is zero. The equation for the dependent t test then becomes

$$t = \frac{M_D}{s_{M_D}}.$$

The parallels between the one-sample t test and the dependent samples t test may become clearer by referring to Table 10.5.

Table 10.5   Parallels Between the One-Sample t Test and the Dependent Samples t Test

	One-Sample t Test	**Dependent Samples t Test**
Sample mean	M (could be written as M_X)	M_D
Population mean	μ (could be written as μ_X)	μ_D
Standard error	s_M (could be written as s_{M_X})	s_{M_D}
Relationship of standard error and standard deviation	$s_M = \dfrac{s_{XP}}{\sqrt{n}}$	$s_{M_D} = \dfrac{s_{DP}}{\sqrt{n}}$

To summarize to this point, in both the one-sample t test and the dependent samples t test, the result of a comparison is then divided by the appropriate measure of variability. This converts our difference (found in the numerator) into standard deviation units. Thus, the logic of the dependent samples t test directly parallels the logic of the one-sample t test. Fundamentally, a measure of difference found in the numerator is being converted into standard deviation units by dividing by a standard error. Then the outcome is interpreted by referring to the t table.

The dependent samples t test can also be related to the independent samples t test. Recall that in the independent samples t test, we are comparing two sample means. The difference obtained in the numerator is then divided by the appropriate measure of variability. The magnitude of the numerator of the independent samples t test reflects the effect of the independent variable. If the independent variable does not cause a change in the dependent variable, the sample means will not be affected and the numerator is expected to be approximately zero. How large the change in the numerator must be in order to be statistically significant depends on how large the denominator of the t test is. If the denominator is very small, then even a relatively small difference in the numerator will be found to be statistically significant. However, if the denominator is very large, then even a relatively large difference in the numerator may not be found to be statistically significant.

The denominator of the independent samples t test is a standard error. The equation for the standard error of the difference between sample means is as follows:

$$s_{(M_1 - M_2)} = \sqrt{\frac{(n_1 - 1)s_{XP_1}^2 + (n_2 - 1)s_{XP_2}^2}{n_1 + n_2 - 2}\left(\frac{1}{n_1} + \frac{1}{n_2}\right)}.$$

This is a complex equation. Inspection indicates that the magnitude of this standard error is dependent on the estimates of the population variances derived from the two samples and from the sample sizes. Perhaps the simplest way to think of *decreasing* this standard error, which would *increase* the obtained value of the independent samples *t* test, would be to increase the sample sizes. This, however, would require additional time as well as resources and, consequently, may not be possible. Alternatively, since each estimate of population variance is a reflection of how much variability there is within a sample, this standard error could be decreased by reducing the variability of the samples. If there is very little variability within the samples, then the standard error will be small and then even a small difference between sample means will be found to be significant. If, on the other hand, there is substantial variability within the samples, there will need to be a much larger difference in the numerator before we can conclude there was a significant outcome.

With a dependent samples *t* test, the subjects are not independent. Instead, they are related in some way. Most commonly, the same subjects are used in both treatment conditions. This is what is called a repeated measures design since each subject is being repeatedly tested. Alternatively, pairs of similar subjects could be chosen. Then, one member of each pair would be randomly assigned to each condition. This is called a matched samples design. With either the repeated measures or matched samples designs, the subjects of the two samples are likely to be much more similar than would have been the case if two independent samples were chosen at random. As a result, variability in the denominator of the *t* equation is being reduced and, consequently, the calculated value of *t* is likely to increase.

Calculation of the Dependent Samples *t* Test

For an example of a repeated measures study, let us assume that you are interested in testing whether a fuel additive will change a car's gas mileage as claimed in an advertisement. You could randomly assign each vehicle to either the control (no additive) or experimental (additive) condition, and subsequently, use an independent samples *t* test to compare their mileages. Alternatively, you could compare the mileage of the same vehicles with and without the additive. In this case, there would be two measures for each vehicle. If the null hypothesis was that the additive would have no effect, then the population mean mileage without the additive (μ_{wo}) would equal the population mean mileage with the additive (μ_w). Thus, the null hypothesis would state that $\mu_{wo} - \mu_w = 0$. The alternative hypothesis would be that $\mu_{wo} - \mu_w \neq 0$. This is a two-tailed test and, as usual, we set $\alpha = .05$. The hypothetical data and initial computations are shown in Table 10.6.

It is important to note that while there are two sets of mileage data, there is only one sample of vehicles, and thus, only one set of difference scores.

Table 10.6   Example 1: Repeated Measures Data and Initial Calculations

Vehicle	Mileage Without Additive	Mileage With Additive	Difference D	$D - M_D$	$(D - M_D)^2$
1	12	13	−1	−0.5	0.25
2	13	15	−2	−1.5	2.25
3	15	14	1	1.5	2.25
4	17	17	0	0.5	0.25
5	20	24	−4	−3.5	12.25
6	25	22	3	3.5	12.25
			$\Sigma D = -3$	$\Sigma(D - M_D) = 0$	$\Sigma(D - M_D)^2 = 29.5$

$$M_D = \frac{\Sigma D}{n}$$
$$= -3/6$$
$$= -0.5$$

where n = the number of *pairs* of scores.

In our example, the null hypothesis is that the fuel additive does not have an effect. In other words, the null hypothesis is that there is no difference between the population means, and thus, $\mu_D = 0$. We can, therefore, use the following equation to determine t:

$$t = \frac{M_D}{s_{M_D}}.$$

The numerator of this equation, M_D, is simply $\Sigma D/n$, where n is equal to the number of *pairs* of scores. As is indicated in Table 10.6, this is −3/6 or −.5. It is important to recognize that this negative value indicates that mileage is *higher* with an additive, not lower, for the sign, + or −, is determined by the order in which the subtraction occurs. The question we now need to address is whether this change of −.5 is statistically significant.

To find the standard error, s_{M_D}, we note that $s_{M_D} = s_{DP}/\sqrt{n}$. And, just as the standard deviation of scores when estimating the population standard deviation, s_{XP}, is equal to

$$s_{XP} = \sqrt{\frac{\Sigma(X - M)^2}{n - 1}}.$$

s_{DP}, the estimate of the population standard deviation of the differences between scores, is equal to

$$s_{DP} = \sqrt{\frac{\Sigma(D - M_D)^2}{n-1}}.$$

Substituting from Table 10.6, we have

$$s_{DP} = \sqrt{\frac{29.5}{6-1}}$$

$$= \sqrt{\frac{29.5}{5}}$$

$$= \sqrt{5.9}$$

$$= 2.429.$$

We can now determine the standard error, s_{M_D}, by noting that

$$s_{M_D} = \frac{s_{DP}}{\sqrt{n}}$$

$$= \frac{2.429}{\sqrt{6}}$$

$$= \frac{2.429}{2.449}$$

$$= 0.992.$$

This is the denominator that we were seeking.

The equation for t therefore becomes

$$t = \frac{M_D}{s_{M_D}}$$

$$= \frac{-0.5}{0.992}$$

$$= -0.50.$$

The *df* are $n - 1$, where n is the number of pairs of scores. We therefore have $6 - 1$ or 5 *df*.

The critical value for a two-tailed t test with α equal to .05 and 5 *df* is 2.571. (Recall that as this is a two-tailed test, this critical value can be either +2.571 or −2.571.) As our obtained value for t is equal to −0.50, which is fewer standard deviation units from the mean than −2.571, we retain the null hypothesis and conclude that there is not enough evidence to support the view that the fuel additive changed the gas mileage of the vehicles tested. If the null hypothesis had been rejected, we would have then calculated eta squared to indicate the effect size, where $\eta^2 = t^2/(t^2 + df)$.

A Second Example of a Dependent Samples t Test

It was stated earlier in this chapter that while repeated measures is the most commonly used design with the dependent samples t test, you can also use the matched samples design as well. For instance, let us assume that you continued to be interested in achieving better fuel economy. This time, instead of trying a fuel additive, you decide to test what effect appropriate vehicle maintenance would have. Your null hypothesis, based on claims of advertisements, is that recommended maintenance increases fuel economy by 1 mile/gallon. Your alternative hypothesis is that it does not increase the gas mileage by this amount.

It is important to note that you need to be careful with this null hypothesis. As it includes the word "increases," you might assume that this is a one-tailed test. However, this is not the case. The word "increases" refers to a specific standard, 1 mile/gallon, that the outcome will be compared against. The null hypothesis would be rejected if either the outcome is significantly higher or lower than this standard. Therefore, this is still a two-tailed test.

We begin by selecting pairs of different types of vehicles (SUVs [sports utility vehicles], large sedans, small sedans, minivans, sports cars, etc.), all of the same approximate age and mileage. A member of each pair of vehicles is then randomly assigned to each of two groups. One group of vehicles serves as the control group. Each vehicle of the other group, the experimental vehicles, receives a tune-up. Then, the gas mileage of each vehicle is determined, as is shown in Table 10.7. As usual, we will set $\alpha = .05$.

As with the repeated measures design, with the matched samples design, we begin with two sets of data but end with one set of difference scores. To test whether the null hypothesis should be rejected, we once again conduct the dependent samples t test. The current null hypothesis is that the vehicles with a tune-up will have a 1 mile/gallon greater fuel economy than the vehicles without a tune-up, and thus μ_D, which reflects the hypothesized effect of the experimental treatment, is equal to +1. Since μ_D is not equal to 0, we must use the longer version of the dependent t test equation:

$$t = \frac{M_D - \mu_D}{s_{M_D}},$$

where the standard error, $s_{M_D} = s_{DP} / \sqrt{n}$.

There are two terms in the numerator of the t equation, and since we have a value for each, you might reasonably assume that all we now have to do is to substitute them into the numerator. However, using a dependent t test requires understanding as well as the ability to calculate. We have indicated that as the null hypothesis is that fuel economy will increase by 1 mile/gallon, $\mu_D = +1$. In other words, increased fuel economy is associated with an increase in scores. However, inspection of Table 10.7 will indicate that an increase in fuel economy in the experimental vehicles is associated with negative values for D. This is simply due to the order in which the treatment conditions were listed in the table. However, as the mean of the difference scores (M_D) is equal to $\Sigma D/n$, an overall increase in fuel

Table 10.7	Example 2: Matched Samples and Initial Calculations

Vehicle Pair	Mileage of Control Vehicles	Mileage of Experimental Vehicles	D	$D - M_D$	$(D - M_D)^2$
1	12	16	−4	−2	4
2	13	15	−2	0	0
3	15	14	1	3	9
4	17	19	−2	0	0
5	20	24	−4	−2	4
6	25	25	0	2	4
7	26	27	−1	1	1
8	28	30	−2	0	0
9	29	33	−4	−2	4
			$\Sigma D = -18$	$\Sigma(D - M_D) = 0$	$\Sigma(D - M_D)^2 = 26$

$$M_D = \frac{\Sigma D}{n}$$
$$= \frac{-18}{9}$$
$$= -2$$

where n = the number of *pairs* of scores.

economy for the experimental vehicles will lead to a negative value for M_D. Clearly, an increase in fuel economy cannot simultaneously result in a positive change in one situation (our statement of the null hypothesis) and a negative change in another (the result of our calculations in the table). We need to be consistent. Therefore, recognizing that the order in which we subtracted in the table is arbitrary, we understand that M_D should reflect that there is an improvement in mileage, not a decrease. Therefore, M_D is entered into the equation for t as 2, not −2. The numerator is, therefore, 2 − 1, which is equal to 1.

The denominator, s_{M_D}, is equal to $s_{DP} / \sqrt{n}$. To determine s_{DP}, we once again utilize the following equation:

$$s_{DP} = \sqrt{\frac{\Sigma(D - M_D)^2}{n - 1}},$$

where n is equal to the number of *pairs* of scores.

Substituting from Table 10.7, we have

$$s_{DP} = \sqrt{\frac{26}{9-1}}$$

$$= \sqrt{\frac{26}{8}}$$

$$= \sqrt{3.25}$$

$$= 1.803.$$

We can now determine the standard error of the differences, s_{M_D}, by noting that

$$s_{M_D} = \frac{s_{DP}}{\sqrt{n}}$$

$$= \frac{1.803}{\sqrt{9}}$$

$$= \frac{1.803}{3}$$

$$= 0.601.$$

This is the denominator of the equation for t.
    The calculation of t therefore becomes

$$t = \frac{M_D - \mu_D}{s_{M_D}}$$

$$= \frac{1}{0.601}$$

$$= 1.67.$$

The df are $n - 1$, where n is the number of pairs of scores. We therefore have $9 - 1$ or 8 df.
    The critical value for a two-tailed t test with $\alpha = .05$ and 8 df is 2.306. As our obtained $t = 1.67$, which is less than 2.306, we retain the null hypothesis and conclude that there is not enough evidence to support the claim that the maintenance changed the gas mileage of the vehicles tested by other than 1 mile/gallon. However, we would recognize that the sample size is very small.
    To illustrate how the specification of the null hypothesis can affect the outcome of a study, let us assume that the original null hypothesis had been that vehicle maintenance does not affect fuel economy. (*Note that this example is solely for illustration purposes. In a research situation you cannot restate your null hypothesis once you have started to collect data. To do so would be highly unethical.*)

In this case, the hypothesized difference between the population means for the vehicle fuel economies would have been zero. We could, therefore, use the shorter version of the dependent t equation, or simply substitute 0 for μ_D in the numerator of the longer version:

$$t = \frac{M_D - \mu_D}{s_{M_D}}.$$

The numerator now becomes 2 − 0, which is equal to 2. (Remember, we are using a positive number to indicate an increase in fuel economy.) As none of the scores have changed, the denominator remains unchanged. The t equation thus becomes

$$t = \frac{2}{0.601}$$

$$= 3.33.$$

The df remain $n - 1$, where n is the number of pairs of scores. We therefore have 9 − 1 or 8 df.

We found previously that the critical value for a two-tailed test with α equal to .05 and 8 df is 2.306. As our obtained $t = 3.33$, which is greater than 2.306, we would now reject the null hypothesis that maintenance does not affect mileage and conclude that the maintenance changed the gas mileage of the vehicles tested. Clearly, how the null hypothesis is defined matters!

If this had been our original null hypothesis, we would proceed by calculating eta squared to indicate the effect size:

$$\eta^2 = \frac{t^2}{t^2 + df},$$

where η^2 is the percentage of variance explained by the treatment.

For our example with 8 df, this would be

$$\eta^2 = \frac{3.33^2}{3.33^2 + 8}$$

$$= \frac{11.09}{11.09 + 8}$$

$$= \frac{11.09}{19.09}$$

$$= 0.581 \text{ or } 58.1\%.$$

Thus, in this example, the treatment would have accounted for 58.1% of the total variance.

Reporting the Results of a Dependent Samples *t* Test

In an article, we would report, "There was sufficient evidence to reject the null hypothesis that performing maintenance on a vehicle has no effect on the gas mileage ($t(8) = 3.33$, $p < .05$). η^2 is equal to 58.1%."

Confidence Interval for Dependent Samples *t* Test

The procedure for finding a confidence interval for a dependent samples *t* test statistic is almost identical to what was used with a one-sample *t* test:

For the one-sample *t* test,

$$M - t_c\,(s_M) \leq \mu \leq M + t_c\,(s_M).$$

For the dependent samples *t* test,

$$M_D - t_c(s_{M_D}) \leq \mu_D \leq M_D + t_c(s_{M_D}).$$

For our just completed example, we would have

$$2 - (2.306)(.601) \leq \mu_D \leq 2 + (2.306)(.601).$$

This equals

$$2 - 1.386 \leq \mu_D \leq 2 + 1.386,$$

or

$$0.61 \leq \mu_D \leq 3.39.$$

In other words, with 8 *df*, we are 95% confident that the experimental population mean for the difference in fuel economy will be between 0.61 and 3.39 miles/gallon.

Thus, the dependent samples *t* test statistic is much like the one-sample *t* test. Both assume that the samples are drawn from normally distributed populations, and each can be used to test a hypothesis or to construct a confidence interval. Finally, the steps involved in calculating both *t* test statistics are very similar.

Purpose and Limitations of Using the Dependent Samples *t* Test

1. *Test for difference:* The null hypothesis is usually that the treatment does not have an effect. If the null is correct, any difference between the treatment condition means is due to chance. The alternative hypothesis is that the treatment does have an effect and the difference is not due to chance. The dependent samples *t* test is employed to differentiate between these two hypotheses.

2. *Does not provide a measure of effect size:* The dependent samples *t* test is a test of significance. It indicates whether or not an outcome is likely to have occurred by chance if the null hypothesis is correct. If the *t* test is significant, a measure of effect size, such as eta squared, should then be calculated.

3. *Sample size is important:* For the dependent samples *t* test, if the sample size is 30 or greater, then the assumption that the underlying population is normal can be safely ignored. If the sample size is less than 30, then it is important that the underlying population be normally distributed. If you cannot collect a larger sample and do not know if the assumption of normality has been met, it may be best to turn to an alternative test.

4. *Compares a difference mean to a hypothetical difference:* With the repeated measures design, the difference is obtained from two measures from the same subject. With the matched samples design, the difference is obtained from two subjects paired on some important variable. The *t* test compares this obtained difference with the difference specified in the null hypothesis.

5. *Carryover effects are a concern:* A repeated measures design is a type of **longitudinal study**. In a longitudinal study, subjects are measured repeatedly across time. A concern with any longitudinal study is that the effect of a treatment or intervention at one point in time may affect or carry over to another point in time. For instance, for most of us running 5 miles in the morning is likely to affect how quickly we can ride a bicycle 15 miles in the afternoon. One solution to control for **carryover effects** is to employ **counterbalancing**. In counterbalancing, one half of the subjects are exposed to Condition A first, and then later to Condition B. The other half of the subjects are first exposed to Condition B, and subsequently to Condition A. With our example, one half of us would

Longitudinal study: a study in which subjects are measured repeatedly across time. A repeated measures design is a type of longitudinal study.

Carryover effect: a treatment or intervention at one point in time may affect or carryover to another point in time.

Counterbalancing: a method used to control for carryover effects. In counterbalancing, the order of the treatments or interventions is balanced so that an equal number of subjects will experience each order of presentation.

run in the morning and ride the bicycle in the afternoon. The other half would ride in the morning and run in the afternoon. You should note that counterbalancing will not always be effective. An improvement in this case would be not only to use counterbalancing but also to have a more lengthy rest period between the running and the cycling.

Assumptions of the Dependent Samples *t* Test

1. *Interval or ratio data:* The data are on either an interval or a ratio scale of measurement.

2. *Random samples:* The sample in a repeated measures design is drawn at random from a population. The samples in a matched samples design are determined by randomly assigning a member of each pair to each of the two conditions.

3. *Normally distributed populations:* The population from which a sample is drawn has a normal distribution of scores.

Effect of Violating the Assumptions

The assumption that is most likely to be violated is that the underlying population is normally distributed, and the *t* test is robust with regard to this assumption. To be robust, a statistical test leads to accurate decisions even when an assumption is violated. However, if the sample size is very small and the population is likely to differ dramatically from normal, you should not use the dependent samples *t* test. Instead, you should consider converting your interval or ratio data into an ordinal measurement and then turn to an appropriate test for the same experimental design.

Conclusion

The dependent samples *t* test is useful and easy to calculate. It has the benefit over the independent samples *t* that by utilizing repeated measures or matched samples the resulting *t* statistic is likely to be larger. However, degrees of freedom are lost. And, as you will see in Chapter 12, compared with the one-way within-subjects ANOVA, the dependent samples *t* test is easier to calculate, but it is more limited.

COMPARISON OF THE DEPENDENT SAMPLES *t* TEST AND THE INDEPENDENT SAMPLES *t* TEST

The beginning of this chapter described the independent samples *t* test. This was followed with a review of the dependent samples *t* test. While the independent samples *t* test is used more frequently, there are definite advantages to repeated measures or matched samples designs. And there are disadvantages.

There are fundamentally three disadvantages to the repeated measures and matched samples designs. First, these studies frequently entail more work to conduct. With matched samples studies, for instance, you need to identify the variable on which to match (e.g., intelligence quotient, height, personality, age, etc.), measure each subject on this variable, form pairs of similar subjects, and then randomly assign a member of each pair to each of the two groups. These steps can be time consuming.

Second, there is an increased risk of losing subjects. With repeated measures studies, you may need to convince subjects to return for a second test and thus may lose subjects. With matched samples designs, if one member of a pair drops out of the study, you lose both.

Third, in a sense you lose half of your degrees of freedom compared with an independent samples design. For a dependent samples t test, the degrees of freedom are determined by $n - 1$, where n is equal to the *number of pairs of scores*. Thus, you have one degree of freedom for every two scores that you collect because it takes a pair of scores to obtain one difference measure. With the independent samples t test, the degrees of freedom are also determined by $n - 1$, but in this case, n is equal to the *number of scores*. Inspection of the t table will indicate that a reduction in the number of degrees of freedom will translate into a larger critical value for t, and thus with a dependent samples t test, a larger difference is required for the null hypothesis to be rejected.

Considering these drawbacks, it may seem surprising that the dependent samples t test is ever used. However, there are substantial advantages to offset the disadvantages just listed. One of the major advantages of the repeated measures design is that you get more information from each subject than you would with an independent samples design. This becomes critical if you are dealing with hard-to-obtain subjects. For instance, if you were interested in the efficacy of an intervention with males between 13 and 16 years of age who are undergoing a specific form of therapy for a particular condition, your subject pool is likely to be severely limited. It makes sense, therefore, to obtain as much data as possible from each subject.

Another reason to employ a repeated measures or matched subjects design is to reduce the amount of variability in the denominator of the t equation. If the standard error (the denominator) is reduced, the value of the obtained t will increase (assuming the numerator stayed the same). Both repeated measures, which in a sense use a subject as their own control, and matched samples, where a subject is paired with someone who is similar on some measure, are techniques that are likely to reduce the size of the standard error.

In effect, therefore, use of the dependent samples t test is a balancing act. The researcher gains by increasing the amount of information obtained from each subject and by the potential to reduce the standard error, which will increase the size of the t ratio. But the researcher pays a price in added work, greater risk of losing subjects, and the loss of degrees of freedom.

Chapter Resources

GLOSSARY OF TERMS

Carryover effect: a treatment or intervention at one point in time may affect or carryover to another point in time.

Counterbalancing: a method used to control for carryover effects. In counterbalancing, the order of the treatments or interventions is balanced so that an equal number of subjects will experience each order of presentation.

Longitudinal study: a study in which subjects are measured repeatedly across time. A repeated measures design is a type of longitudinal study.

Standard error of the difference between sample means ($S_{(M_1-M_2)}$): the standard deviation of the sampling distribution of the difference between sample means.

Standard error of the mean difference (S_{M_D}): the standard deviation of the sampling distribution of the mean difference between measures.

Questions: Chapter 10—Independent Samples *t* Test

(Answers to odd-numbered items are provided in Appendix I.)

1. The independent samples *t* test compares _____ groups of _____ data.

   a. two; nominal

   b. two or more; interval/ratio

   c. two; interval/ratio

   d. two or more; ordinal

2. The advantage of the independent samples *t* test is that it is relatively easy to calculate. However, the one-way between-subjects ANOVA is _____.

   a. even easier to calculate

   b. more flexible

   c. able to deal with ordinal data

   d. none of the above

3. The logic of the independent samples *t* test directly parallels the logic of the one-sample *t* test, for a measure of difference found in the numerator is converted into _____ by dividing by a standard error.

   a. standard deviation units

   b. an *F* ratio

    c. a correlation

    d. a measure of effect size

4. Following a significant *t* test, we would calculate _____.

    a. post hoc tests

    b. eta squared (η^2)

    c. a linear regression

    d. we don't calculate anything, we're finished

5. All else being equal, the means of larger samples would be expected to vary _____ the means of smaller samples.

    a. more than

    b. the same as

    c. less than

For Questions 6 to 19, use the following: An experimenter is interested in whether drinking warm milk before going to bed will help people sleep. The experimenter randomly assigns subjects to two groups. The data consist of subjects' ratings of how well they slept, with higher ratings indicating better sleep:

Control group: 3, 4, 6, 5, 2

Experimental group: 5, 9, 6, 8

6. What is the null hypothesis?

    a. Drinking warm milk will help people sleep better.

    b. Drinking warm milk will not help people sleep better.

7. What is the alternative hypothesis?

    a. Drinking warm milk will help people sleep better.

    b. Drinking warm milk will not help people sleep better.

8. Is this a one- or two-tailed *t* test?

    a. One-tailed

    b. Two-tailed

9. What is the mean of the control group?

    a. 2

    b. 3.5

    c. 4

    d. 6.67

10. What is the mean of the experimental group?

   a. 3.6

   b. 7.0

   c. 8

   d. 8.2

11. What is the variance of the control group?

   a. 1.13

   b. 2.50

   c. 3.33

   d. 4.67

12. What is the variance of the experimental group?

   a. 1.13

   b. 2.50

   c. 3.33

   d. 4.67

13. What is the standard error of the difference between means?

   a. 1.13

   b. 2.50

   c. 3.33

   d. 4.67

14. What is the value of t?

   a. −2.65

   b. +2.65

   c. −3.14

   d. +3.14

15. How many degrees of freedom are there?

   a. 9

   b. 7

   c. 5

   d. 3

16. What is the critical value of t from the table with alpha set to .05?

   a. 3.679

   b. 1.462

   c. 1.997

   d. 1.895

17. The outcome is _____.

    a. statistically significant

    b. not statistically significant

18. The value of eta squared (η^2) is _____.

    a. 0

    b. .23

    c. .36

    d. .50

19. The 95% confidence interval would be from _____ to _____.

    a. 4; 7

    b. 2.5; 3.33

    c. −5.67; −.33

    d. −2.65; 1.13

Questions: Chapter 10—Dependent Samples *t* Test

20. The dependent samples *t* test is a procedure that a researcher can use to increase the magnitude of *t* by reducing the variability, thereby reducing the size of the _____.

    a. numerator

    b. denominator

    c. difference between means

21. If pairs of similar subjects are chosen, and then one member of each pair is randomly assigned to each condition, this is called a (an) _____ design.

    a. repeated measures

    b. independent samples

    c. matched samples

    d. inappropriate

22. Compared with an independent samples *t* test, with repeated measures, you are gathering _____ information from each subject.

    a. more

    b. less

    c. exactly the same amount of

    d. approximately the same amount of

23. If the dependent samples t test is found to be significant, we then _____.

    a. conduct Tukey HSD tests

    b. calculate eta squared (η^2) to indicate the effect size

    c. use a chi-square test to determine where the significance is

    d. stop—we are finished

24. There are disadvantages to the repeated measures and matched samples designs. Which of the following is *not* a disadvantage?

    a. They frequently entail more work.

    b. They can be time consuming.

    c. There is an increased risk of losing subjects.

    d. You lose degrees of freedom.

    e. All of the above are disadvantages.

25. A concern(s) with any longitudinal study is (are) _____.

    a. that the study will take years to complete

    b. carryover effects

    c. need to employ additional experimenters

    d. all of the above

A faculty member wishes to determine whether exercise will influence the number of classes statistics students miss. He takes four students and in the first condition (control), they do not exercise, while in the second condition (experimental), they do exercise. The following data are obtained:

Subject	Control Condition	Experimental Condition
1	6	5
2	4	3
3	2	4
4	7	8

26. What is the null hypothesis?

    a. Exercise has no effect.

    b. Exercise has an effect.

27. What is the alternative hypothesis?

    a. Exercise has no effect.

    b. Exercise has an effect.

28. Is this a one- or two-tailed t test?

    a. One-tailed

    b. Two-tailed

29. What is the mean of the difference scores?

    a. −2.1

    b. −.25

    c. −2.7

    d. 3

30. What is the value of s_{Dp}?

    a. 2.25

    b. 0.75

    c. 1.50

    d. −0.333

31. What is the value of s_{M_D}?

    a. 2.25

    b. 0.75

    c. 1.50

    d. −.333

32. What is the value of t?

    a. 2.25

    b. 0.75

    c. 1.50

    d. −.333

33. How many degrees of freedom are there?

    a. 4

    b. 3

    c. 2

    d. 1

34. What is the critical value of t from the table with alpha set to .05?

    a. 1.895

    b. 2.336

    c. 3.182

    d. 4.412

35. Is the outcome statistically significant?

    a. Yes

    b. No

Problems 36 to 41 utilize SPSS.

SPSS

USING SPSS WITH THE INDEPENDENT SAMPLES T TEST

To Begin SPSS

Step 1: The first step, as before, is to activate the program.

Step 2: Click on "Type in data" and then click on "OK."

Step 3: Click on "Variable View." For the present, we will only be dealing with the columns headed by "Name," "Label," "Values," and "Measure."

Step 4: Click on the first empty rectangle (called a "cell") under the column heading "Name" and type the name of the first variable for which you have data. We are going to utilize the same data and labels as were previously employed in Table 10.3. These data dealt with a fictitious comparison of the effectiveness of two methods for teaching statistics. We have called these procedures "Control" and "Experimental." Therefore, type "Procedure" in the first empty cell under "Name."

Step 5: Click on the first empty cell under the column heading "Label" and type "Procedure of the Study." Note that to see the entire label, you may need to expand the size of this cell by placing your cursor on the right border of the Label heading and moving to the right.

Step 6: Click on the first empty cell under the column heading "Values." Then click on the small blue square. A box will appear. In the blank space to the right of "Value," type the number "1." Then, type a brief description of this value of the variable in the blank space to the right of "Label." In our case, type "Control." Finally, click on "Add." Your label for a value of 1 will appear in the large white region in the center of the window. Now repeat the above steps in this section for the value "2," which is given the label "Experimental" (Figure 10.1). Then click on "OK."

Step 7: Click on the first empty cell under the column heading "Measure." As we are dealing with labels for groups, select "Nominal."

Step 8: Repeat Steps 4 to 7 except that you type "Data" in the first empty cell under "Name" and for the label. Finally, select "Scale" in the column under the column heading "Measure" as we have interval or ratio data. The result is shown in Figure 10.2. We must now shift to the data window and sequentially enter the data for each subject.

Figure 10.1 The Value Labels Window

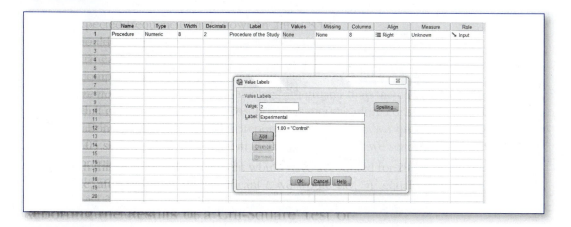

Figure 10.2 The Variable View Window

	Name	Type	Width	Decimals	Label	Values	Missing	Columns	Align	Measure	Role
1	Procedure	Numeric	8	2	Procedure of the Study	(1.00, Contr...	None	8	≡ Right	⬥ Nominal	↘ Input
2	Data	Numeric	8	2	Data	None	None	8	≡ Right	⬥ Scale	↘ Input
3											

To Enter Data in SPSS

Step 9: Click on the "Data View" option at the lower left-hand corner of the variable view window.

Step 10: For each subject in the control condition, type the value "1" in the column "Procedure" and their test score in the column "Data." Continue by entering "2" for each subject in the experimental condition with their data (Figure 10.3).

To Conduct an Independent Samples *t* Test

Step 11: Click the cursor on "Analyze" along the row of SPSS commands above the data you entered, then move to "Compare Means." Then click on "Independent-Samples T Test."

Step 12: A new window will appear. The test variable and the grouping variable need to be identified. In our case, "Procedure" is the label of the grouping variable. This is indicated by moving "Procedure" to the box under "Grouping Variable" by clicking on the word Procedure and then on the bottom arrow. The result is shown in Figure 10.4.

Figure 10.3 Completed Data Entry

	Procedure	Data	var
1	1.00	8.00	
2	1.00	7.00	
3	1.00	7.00	
4	1.00	7.00	
5	1.00	4.00	
6	1.00	3.00	
7	2.00	13.00	
8	2.00	12.00	
9	2.00	11.00	
10	2.00	9.00	
11	2.00	8.00	
12	2.00	7.00	
13			

Figure 10.4 The Independent Samples *t* Test Window

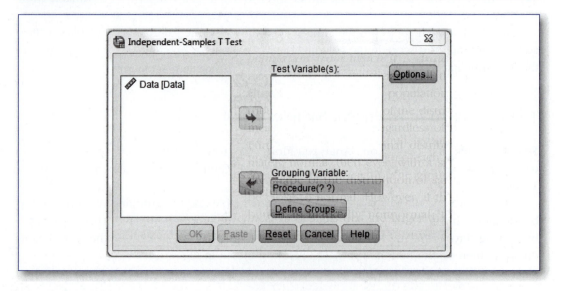

Notice that there are now two question marks following the name of our grouping variable. Click on "Define Groups" and identify the numbers associated with our control and experimental conditions, in this case 1 and 2 (Figure 10.5). Then click "Continue."

Figure 10.5 The Defining Groups Window

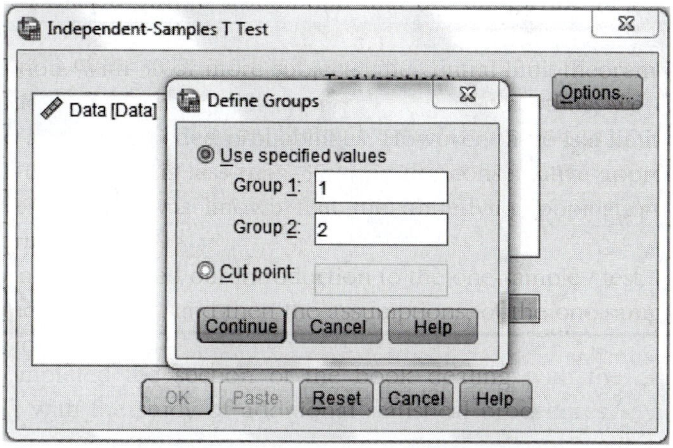

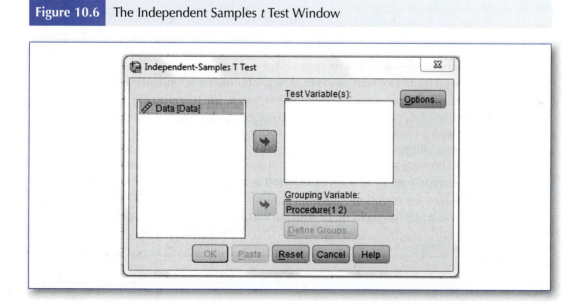

You will now be returned to the previous window (Figure 10.6).

Figure 10.6 The Independent Samples *t* Test Window

The word "Data" will be highlighted. Click on the top arrow in the middle of the window. The result is shown in Figure 10.7. Now click "OK," and SPSS will conduct the independent samples *t* test.

Figure 10.7   Completed Independent Samples *t* Test Window

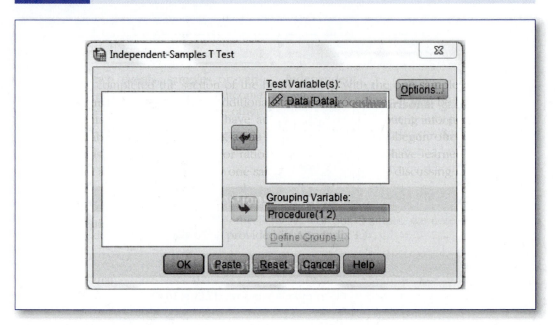

The summary of the descriptive statistics are shown in Table 10.8. The values for the control and experimental means are the same as we calculated previously. We did not calculate standard deviations. However, we did calculate variances, and the standard deviations given in Table 10.8 are equal to the square root of the variances we previously calculated.

Table 10.8   The Independent Samples *t* Test Output: Descriptives

Group Statistics					
	Procedure of the Study	N	Mean	Std. Deviation	Std. Error Mean
Data	Control	6	6.0000	2.00000	.81650
	Experimental	6	10.0000	2.36643	.96609

The summary of the inferential statistics are shown in Table 10.9.

| Table 10.9 | The Independent Samples *t* Test Output: Summary Table |

Independent Samples Test

		Levene's Test for Equality of Variances		t-test for Equality of Means					95% Confidence Interval of the Difference	
		F	Sig.	t	df	Sig. (2-tailed)	Mean Difference	Std. Error Difference	Lower	Upper
Data	Equal variances assumed	.455	.515	-3.162	10	.010	-4.00000	1.26491	-6.81840	-1.18160
	Equal variances not assumed			-3.162	9.730	.010	-4.00000	1.26491	-6.82905	-1.17095

There are two rows to this printout. If you refer to the row "Equal variances assumed," you will find the same value for *t* and *df* that we calculated previously, as well as a value of .01 for the two-tailed significance that agrees with our decision to reject the null hypothesis.

A Limitation Using SPSS With the Independent Samples *t* Test

In the just completed example, the null hypothesis was that there was no difference between the population means from which the samples were drawn. In the second example of the independent samples *t* test that was described previously in the chapter, the null hypothesis was that the difference between the population means was 10 (data are given in Table 10.4). The SPSS procedure that we have just reviewed cannot account for a situation where the null hypothesis is not 0. Fortunately, in the vast majority of cases, the null hypothesis for an independent *t* test is that the difference between the population means is 0, so this is not a serious limitation.

USING SPSS WITH THE DEPENDENT SAMPLES *t* TEST

(Note That SPSS Calls This the Paired Samples *t* Test.)

To Begin SPSS

Step 1 and Step 2: The initial steps are the same as with the independent samples *t* test.

Step 3: Click on "Variable View." For the present, we will only be dealing with the columns headed by "Name," "Label," and "Measure."

Step 4: We are going to utilize the same data as we previously employed in Table 10.6. These data dealt with a fictitious comparison of the effectiveness of a fuel additive. Click on the first empty cell under the column heading "Name." You now type a descriptive name of the first measure for vehicle number 1. Remember that SPSS limits variable names. I have chosen "woadditive" for the mileage of a vehicle without an additive.

Step 5: Click on the first empty cell under the column heading "Label." In this cell, I typed a more extensive description of the variable, "Mileage without additive." Note that to see the entire label, you may need to expand the size of this cell by placing your cursor on the right border of the Label heading and moving to the right.

Step 6: Click on the first empty cell under the column heading "Measure." As we are dealing with mileages, which are examples of ratio data, select "Scale."

Step 7: Repeat Steps 4 to 6 except that you type "wadditive" in the first empty cell under "Name" and for the label type "Mileage with additive." Finally, select "Scale" in the column under the column heading "Measure" as we have ratio data. The result is shown in Figure 10.8. We must now shift to the data window and sequentially enter the data for each subject.

Figure 10.8	The Variable View Window

	Name	Type	Width	Decimals	Label	Values	Missing	Columns	Align	Measure	Role
1	woadditive	Numeric	8	2	Mileage without additive	None	None	8	Right	Scale	Input
2	wadditive	Numeric	8	2	Mileage with additive	None	None	8	Right	Scale	Input
3											

To Enter Data in SPSS

Step 8: Click on the "Data View" option at the lower left-hand corner of the variable view window.

Step 9: For each vehicle, type the mileage without and with an additive in the appropriate column (Figure 10.9).

To Conduct a Dependent Samples *t* Test

Step 10: Click the cursor on "Analyze" along the row of SPSS commands above the data you entered, then move to "Compare Means." Finally, click on "Paired-Samples T Test."

Step 11: A new window will appear (Figure 10.10).

We have only two measures for each vehicle. The first one selected will be moved to the right side of the figure under Variable 1. The second measure selected will be positioned under Variable 2. Our measure "Mileage without add . . ." is highlighted and clicking

Figure 10.9 Completed Data Entry

	woadditive	wadditive	var
1	12.00	13.00	
2	13.00	15.00	
3	15.00	14.00	
4	17.00	17.00	
5	20.00	24.00	
6	25.00	22.00	
7			

Figure 10.10 Paired Samples *t* Test Window

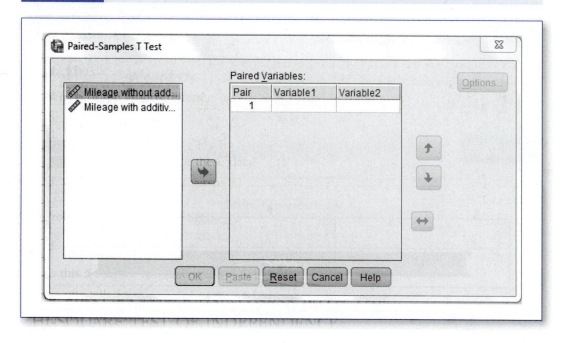

on the arrow will copy it to the right under Variable 1. Our second measure, "Mileage with additive . . ." is now highlighted and clicking on the arrow will copy it to the right under Variable 2. This is shown in Figure 10.11. Now click "OK," and SPSS will conduct a dependent samples *t* test.

Figure 10.11 Completed Paired Samples *t* Test Window

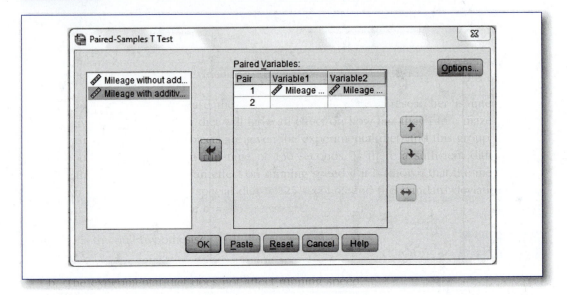

The summary of the descriptive statistics are shown in Table 10.10. We did not previously calculate the mean and standard deviations, but these are easy to check if you would like to do so.

Table 10.10 The Dependent Samples *t* Test Output: Descriptives

Paired Samples Statistics

		Mean	N	Std. Deviation	Std. Error Mean
Pair 1	Mileage without additive	17.0000	6	4.85798	1.98326
	Mileage with additive	17.5000	6	4.50555	1.83938

The next portion of the output provides information about the degree to which the two measures of mileage for each vehicle are related to each other (Table 10.11). In other words, if a particular vehicle gets a high mileage without an additive does it also tend to have a high mileage when it has an additive? This topic will be covered in detail in Chapter 14 when we review correlations.

| Table 10.11 | Relationship Between the Measures of Mileage |

Paired Samples Correlations

		N	Correlation	Sig.
Pair 1	Mileage without additive & Mileage with additive	6	.868	.025

The remainder of the analyses is shown in Table 10.12.

| Table 10.12 | The Dependent Samples *t* Test Output: Summary Table |

Paired Samples Test

		Paired Differences							
					95% Confidence Interval of the Difference				
		Mean	Std. Deviation	Std. Error Mean	Lower	Upper	t	df	Sig. (2-tailed)
Pair 1	Mileage without additive - Mileage with additive	-.50000	2.42899	.99163	-3.04907	2.04907	-.504	5	.636

There is a great deal of information given in Table 10.12. The mean difference between the mileage without and with an additive is −0.5 miles/gallon. Then the standard deviation of the difference in mileage is given. We calculated this value to be 2.429, which is the same as in Table 10.12 except for minor rounding error. Furthermore, our calculated value for the standard error was 0.992, which is essentially the same as provided in the table. SPSS then provides the lower and upper limits of the 95% confidence interval and the value of *t* with its *df*. These later values agree with what we calculated, as does the significance (two-tailed), which corresponds with our decision to not reject the null hypothesis.

SPSS Problems: Chapter 10

An example of an independent samples t test

Questions 36 to 38 are based on the following hypothetical study:

A physics professor is disturbed to learn that many students apparently do not have a good understanding of facts related to motion. For instance, many do not understand that on a moving carousel the riders on the inside are traveling more slowly than those nearer the outside edge. The professor decides to examine whether passing a college-level physics class improves students' understanding of motion. Specifically, the professor compares two groups, one consisting of students who have passed an introductory physics course and the other consisting of students who have not taken such a course. (Note that this is a quasi-experimental design.) The professor measures knowledge of motion on a 50-point scale, with higher numbers indicating better knowledge of motion. Is there significant evidence that the physics course has had an impact on student understanding? (Use a two-tailed test with alpha equal to .05.)

Scores for Students Who Have Passed a Physics Course	Scores for Students Who Have Not Taken a Physics Course
45	40
47	38
41	36
38	35
46	38
44	42
42	45
42	31
	35
	47

36. What is the value of t?

    a. 1.445

    b. 2.242

    c. 3.739

    d. 4.127

37. What are the df?

    a. 12

    b. 14

    c. 16

    d. 18

38. Is the outcome statistically significant?

    a. Yes

    b. No

An example of a dependent samples t *test*

Questions 39 to 41 are based on the following hypothetical study:
A number of studies have indicated that conservatives are more anxious than liberals. In order to test whether an increase in anxiety changes views of conservatism/liberalism, a faculty member measures the political views of students early in a semester and again just before they take an important, cumulative final exam in a required course with a reputation for being difficult. The scale goes from 0 (very liberal) to 10 (very conservative). Assuming that the following results are obtained, is there a significant shift in political views? (Use a two-tailed test with alpha equal to .05.)

Student	Assessment 1	Assessment 2
1	6	6
2	6	7
3	4	5
4	3	4
5	5	6
6	5	7
7	9	8
8	9	10
9	6	5
10	7	6

39. What is the value of t?
    a. −1.177
    b. −2.361
    c. −3.904
    d. −4.846

40. What are the *df*?
    a. 6
    b. 7
    c. 8
    d. 9

41. Is the outcome statistically significant?
    a. Yes
    b. No

FINDING DIFFERENCES WITH INTERVAL AND RATIO DATA—III

The One-Way Between-Subjects ANOVA

> *Enter to grow in wisdom.*
>
> —Inscription on the outside of the 1890
> gate to Harvard Yard

As Table 11.1 indicates, when testing for a difference with interval or ratio data, a commonly used procedure is the analysis of variance (abbreviated ANOVA). It is best to think of ANOVA as a general approach to analyzing data rather than as a specific procedure, for ANOVAs can be used with a wide variety of experimental designs.

Recall that in an experiment, the researcher is in control or manipulates something, such as how much sleep subjects get. The researcher then looks at the consequence. Thus, two things vary in a simple experiment. One variable is controlled or manipulated by the experimenter and is called the independent variable (IV). The experimenter wishes to determine whether the magnitude of the other variable is dependent on the value of the IV that the subject receives. For instance, if an experimenter manipulates how much sleep subjects receive, this is the IV. If the experimenter is interested in how sleep deprivation affects math performance, then math performance is the dependent variable (DV). ANOVAs are particularly useful because they can deal simultaneously with more than one IV. In fact, the ANOVAs are

287

Table 11.1	Overview of Inferential Statistical Procedures for Difference and Interaction Designs

Type of Data

	Nominal (Frequency)		Ordinal (Ranked)	Interval/Ratio (Continuous Measure)
Inferential Statistics (Finding Relationships)				
Statistical procedures for difference and interaction designs				
One variable with at least two outcomes	Goodness-of-fit chi-square	**One IV with one sample—one DV**		One-sample z score or one-sample t test
		One IV with two or more independent samples—one DV	*Kruskal–Wallis H*	<u>One-way between-subjects ANOVA</u> (only two independent samples—independent samples t test)
		One IV with one sample having two or more repeated measures—one DV		One-way within-subjects ANOVA (only two repeated measures—dependent samples t test)
Two variables, each with at least two outcomes	Chi-square test of independence	**Two IV each with two or more independent samples—one DV**		Two-way between-subjects ANOVA

Notes. IV, independent variable; DV, dependent variable; ANOVA, analysis of variance. Research designs are shown in boldface. The italicized item is reviewed in Appendix A.

such a popular approach that a specific vocabulary is associated with them. When using an ANOVA, an IV is called a **factor**. When the design includes more than one factor, the analysis is called a **factorial ANOVA**. In this chapter, we are only dealing with one IV. Thus, we are reviewing what could be described more completely as the single-factor between-subjects ANOVA. Instead of single-factor, often the phrase "one-way" is used. It follows that the single-factor between-subjects ANOVA is also called the one-way between-subjects ANOVA (this is underlined in Table 11.1).

> **Factor:** with an ANOVA, the term Factor is used instead of independent variable.

> **Factorial ANOVA:** an ANOVA with more than one factor.

ANOVA is not the only procedure that can be used when looking for a difference between subjects with interval or ratio data. In Chapter 10, you learned that the independent samples t test is also commonly employed, but it can only be used with designs that have two samples of subjects. One of the strengths of the between-subjects ANOVA is that it can simultaneously analyze the data from studies with two or more values of an IV. For instance, instead of just having a control group and an experimental group, as is the case with the independent samples *t* test, we could now have a control group and a number of experimental groups. Thus, while the independent samples *t* test examines the difference between two sample means, the ANOVA provides an overall test of the significance of the difference between all of the sample means. In doing so, the ANOVA controls for the **experiment-wise error** rate. In other words, if α is set at .05, with an ANOVA, there is only one chance in 20 of making a Type I error for the entire set of comparisons.

It is critical to understand what the last sentence means. When a single statistical test is calculated to determine if a difference exits between two groups, with α set to .05, there is a 5% chance of rejecting the null hypothesis when, in fact, it is correct. This

> **Experiment-wise error:** *the likelihood of making at least one Type I error with any of the experiment's comparisons.*

is a Type I error. As the number of comparisons is increased, with a procedure such as the independent samples *t* test, the probability of making a Type I error *for each comparison* remains at .05. This is the **pairwise error rate**. However, the likelihood of making a Type I error *across all the comparisons* increases rapidly. Put another way, the probability of making a Type I error remains .05 for each **pairwise comparison**, but the experiment-wise error rate increases dramatically as the number of pairwise comparisons increases. (We encountered a similar situation when utilizing the chi-square test of independence.) The likelihood of making at least one Type I error is given by the following equation:

$$\text{Likelihood of at least one Type I error} = 1 - (1 - \alpha)^c,$$

where α is the alpha level and *c* is the number of pairwise comparisons.

$$\text{The number of pairwise comparisons} = \frac{k(k-1)}{2},$$

where *k* is the number of samples or groups.

If the experiment consists of only two groups, there can only be one pairwise comparison. In this case, with α equal to .05, the likelihood of making a Type I error becomes $1 - (1 - .05)^1$. This is equal to .05. Additional outcomes are recorded in Table 11.2.

> **Pairwise error rate:** *the likelihood of making a Type I error for a single comparison between-sample means. This is equal to α, which is usually .05 or .01.*

As Table 11.2 indicates, as the number of groups or samples rises, the number of pairwise comparisons increases rapidly. With two groups, there is only one pairwise comparison. However, with 12 samples, there would be 66 pairwise comparisons. This raises two concerns. First, while

> **Pairwise comparison:** *comparison between two sample means.*

calculating a single independent samples *t* test is not difficult, calculation of 66 *t* tests is a chore. Second, and more important, the likelihood of making a Type I error increases

Table 11.2	Likelihood of Making at Least One Type I Error		
Number of Groups or Samples	Number of Pairwise Comparisons	Pairwise Error Rate	Likelihood of At Least One Type I Error
2	1	.05	.05
6	15	.05	.54
12	66	.05	.97

dramatically when numerous t tests are calculated. It follows that the null hypothesis, according to which all of the sample means are equal, will almost certainly be rejected if a large series of t tests is conducted. Clearly, what is needed is a method to control the experiment-wise error rate as the number of pairwise comparisons increases, and the ANOVA accomplishes this elegantly.

To discuss the ANOVAs, we need to master some additional vocabulary. When using ANOVAs, each value of an IV is called a **level**. If we are studying the effect of hours of sleep, then each different amount of sleep to which subjects are assigned is a level. Furthermore, when each subject is randomly assigned to only one of the levels, it is a **between-subjects design**. Thus, the name one-way between-subjects ANOVA conveys a great deal of information to a statistician. First, the phrase one-way identifies that we are dealing with a research design that has only one IV. Second, the phrase between subjects clarifies that each subject is randomly assigned to one of the groups, and each group of subjects receives a different value of the IV. Finally, as you have learned, ANOVA indicates that there can be more than two groups of subjects.

Level: with an ANOVA, the number of values of the independent variable.

Between-subjects design: with an ANOVA, those designs in which each subject receives a single level of a factor.

This has all been rather theoretical. Fortunately, the logic becomes easier once you see how an ANOVA is used.

As the name analysis of variance implies, the ANOVA is based on a comparison of variances. It may at first seem peculiar to test differences between means by examining variances, but this has turned out to be a very valuable approach. Fortunately, the logic of the ANOVA is straightforward.

The word "analysis" can be defined as the examination of the parts that make up some whole. In an ANOVA, it is the variance that will be analyzed. An ANOVA starts with the assumption that the variances of the populations from which the samples are selected are equal. The essence of the between-subjects ANOVA is that it estimates the variances of these populations in two different ways. Fortunately, you are familiar with both approaches.

We learned in Chapter 9 that if we randomly select a sample from a population, the standard deviation of the sample, s_{XP}, can be used to estimate the population standard deviation, σ_X, where

$$s_{XP} = \sqrt{\frac{\Sigma(X - M)^2}{n - 1}}.$$

It follows that the variance estimate derived from the sample, s_{XP}^2, is an unbiased estimator of the population variance, σ_X^2, where

$$s_{XP}^2 = \frac{\Sigma(X - M)^2}{n - 1}.$$

If we continue to randomly select samples from this population, we can combine or pool the variance estimates to find an even more precise estimate of σ_X^2. Assuming equal sample sizes, the combined or pooled estimate of the population variance becomes

$$s_{XP}^2 \text{ pooled } = \frac{s_{XP_1}^2 + s_{XP_2}^2 + \cdots + s_{XP_k}^2}{k},$$

where k is the number of samples.

When dealing with ANOVAs, this term is called the **mean square within (MS_w)**. This is an appropriate term, for it can be thought of as an *average of the sums of squares obtained by looking at the variability within each of the samples.*

Alternatively, we could estimate σ_X^2 by examining how much the sample means vary from each other. If the sample means do not vary substantially,

> **Mean square within (MS$_w$):** *the estimate of σ_X^2 obtained by pooling the variances of the scores from their sample means. It is thus based on the variability within each of the samples.*

it suggests that σ_X^2 is small (you would also have to account for the size of the sample). However, if the sample means do vary substantially, it suggests that σ_X^2 is large.

A more precise account would begin by noting that a single sample's mean, M, is an unbiased estimator of the population mean, μ. This estimate can be improved by calculating a series of sample means from samples of the same size, and then calculating the mean of these sample means, which we have called the grand mean, M_G. The standard deviation of these sample means from M_G is known as the standard error of the mean. The variance of these means, calculated to estimate the population parameter, is as follows:

$$s_M^2 = \frac{\Sigma(M - M_G)^2}{k - 1},$$

where k is the number of samples.

Do not be concerned by the appearance of this equation. It is actually the same equation that was just given for s_{XP}^2 except that means (M) are substituted for scores (X), the mean of sample means (M_G) is substituted for the sample mean (M), and the number of samples (k) is substituted for the number of subjects (n). Just as s_{XP}^2 provides an unbiased estimator of σ_X^2, an unbiased estimate of σ_M^2 is provided by s_M^2. But with the between-subjects ANOVA, we are interested in estimating σ_X^2, not σ_M^2. However, we learned previously in Chapter 9 that $s_M = s_{XP} / \sqrt{n}$, where n is the sample size. Squaring each side gives $s_M^2 = s_{XP}^2 / n$. As s_{XP}^2 is an unbiased estimator of σ_X^2, we can, therefore, estimate σ_X^2 from s_M^2. This estimate of σ_X^2 is called the **mean square between (MS_{Bet})**. Please note that we are not calling this MS_B. The term MS_B is used in more complex ANOVAs and is not defined the same way as MS_{Bet}.

Mean square between (MS_{Bet}): the estimate of σ_X^2 obtained from the deviations of the sample means from M_G. It is thus based on the variability between the samples.

What is essential to note is that we now have two methods for estimating σ_X^2. We can find s_{XP}^2 by pooling the measure of the *variability within each sample*, or we can find s_M^2 by measuring the *variability of sample means*, and from it find s_{XP}^2. These two estimates of σ_X^2 may or may not be similar.

The key to understanding ANOVA is that if the samples are all drawn from the same population, or populations with the same mean, these two estimates of σ_X^2 will be approximately the same. However, if the samples are drawn from populations with different means, the two estimates of σ_X^2 may differ substantially. An example will clarify the reasoning.

Let us assume that from a population we randomly select a sample of 41 subjects and obtain an M of 5 and an s_{XP}^2 of 2.5. If we were to continue to draw samples of size 41 from the same population, we would expect the means of these samples to be approximately 5 and their variances to be approximately 2.5. This would be similar to the situation where there is no treatment effect. An excellent estimate of the population variance, σ_X^2, would be determined by calculating the pooled s_{XP}^2 based on all of these samples. As we just reviewed, this is called the mean square within (MS_W). However, the population variance, σ_X^2, could also be estimated by calculating s_M^2, which is a measure of how much the sample means vary from each other. Since $s_M^2 = s_{XP}^2 / n$, we can once again determine an s_{XP}^2 to be used as an unbiased estimator of σ_X^2. This estimate of σ_X^2 leads to what is called the mean square between (MS_{Bet}). It can be shown mathematically that if there is no treatment effect, these two estimates of σ_X^2 will be approximately equal. In other words, *if there is no treatment effect, the mean square within (MS_W) estimate of σ_X^2 will approximately equal the mean square between (MS_{Bet}) estimate*. Put another way, the ratio of $(MS_{Bet})/(MS_W)$ should be approximately 1 if there is no treatment effect.

Now let us assume that there is a treatment effect of three points. In this case, the control group has an M of 5 and a s_{XP}^2 of 2.5, but the treatment group has an M of 8. Since adding a constant to every score does not change the standard deviation or variance of a sample (this was discussed in Chapter 3), the s_{XP}^2 of the treatment group would still be 2.5. In other words, the addition of a treatment effect does not affect the variability within each of the groups, and thus, *the mean square within (MS_W) estimate of variability does not change*. However, the addition of a treatment effect does cause the sample means to be more different, and thus, the *mean square between (MS_{Bet}) estimate of variability is expected to be larger*. Put another way, the ratio of $(MS_{Bet})/(MS_W)$ should be greater than 1 if there is a treatment effect.

The ratio of $(MS_{Bet})/(MS_W)$ is given a name in statistics. It is called the *F* ratio in honor of Sir Ronald Fisher who made major contributions to the development of the ANOVA. It is the ratio of two estimates of the population variance:

$$F = \frac{MS_{Bet}}{MS_W} = \frac{\text{Between groups estimate of } \sigma_X^2}{\text{Within groups estimate of } \sigma_X^2}.$$

As you just learned, if there is no treatment effect, this ratio should be approximately 1. If there is a treatment effect, the *F* ratio should be greater than 1. Therefore, to determine if there is a treatment effect, we have to calculate the *F* ratio and refer to the appropriate table to determine if the outcome is greater than would be expected by chance. That is all there is to calculating a one-way between-subjects ANOVA. Fortunately, while more complex ANOVAs involve more calculations, the logic remains the same.

A FIRST EXAMPLE

We will begin with a very simple example of a between-subjects ANOVA. While this statistical procedure can deal with more than two groups, we will start with just two to keep the computations simple. The data we will be dealing with are indicated in Table 11.3 along with the calculation of the sample means and sum of the squared deviations from the mean. Note that for the entries in the experimental condition, a value of 3 has been added to each score in the control condition. As expected, this increases the value of the sample mean by 3 but does not affect the variability of the sample.

It is critical when using ANOVAs that you know what you are calculating and that you keep your calculations clearly defined. We begin with a table showing what it is that must be calculated (Table 11.4).

It is important to note that a value must be calculated for every entry that is underlined in Table 11.4. We will begin by entering the three values for *SS*, then calculate three values for degrees of freedom (*df*), two values for *MS*, and finally one *F* ratio. As you will see, no step is difficult. It is essential, however, that you clearly identify each item you are calculating so that you do not become confused.

The first values in Table 11.4 that must be filled in are the sums of squares (*SS*). It can be shown mathematically that the total *SS* is equal to the between-groups *SS* plus the within-groups *SS*. In other words

$$SS_T = SS_{Bet} + SS_W.$$

Table 11.3   Simple Example and Initial Calculations

Control Condition			Experimental Condition		
X_1	$X_1 - M_1$	$(X_1 - M_1)^2$	X_2	$X_2 - M_2$	$(X_2 - M_2)^2$
7	2	4	10	2	4
6	1	1	9	1	1
5	0	0	8	0	0
4	−1	1	7	−1	1
3	−2	4	6	−2	4
$\sum X_1 = 25$	$\sum x_1 = 0$	$\sum x_1^2 = 10$	$\sum X_2 = 40$	$\sum x_2 = 0$	$\sum x_2^2 = 10$
$n = 5$			$n = 5$		
$M_1 = 25/5$			$M_2 = 40/5$		
$= 5$			$= 8$		

Table 11.4   Summary Table for the One-Way Between-Subjects ANOVA

Source of Variation	SS	df	MS	F
Between groups	SS_{Bet}	df_{Bet}	MS_{Bet}	F ratio
Within groups	SS_W	df_W	MS_W	
Total	SS_T	df_T		

Note. ANOVA, analysis of variance; *SS*, sum of squares; *df*, degrees of freedom; *MS*, mean square; SS_{Bet}, sum of squares between; df_{Bet}, degrees of freedom between; MS_{Bet}, mean square between; SS_W, sum of squares within; df_W, degrees of freedom within; MS_W, mean square within.

The calculations are easiest if we begin by calculating SS_T before finding SS_{Bet} and SS_W. SS_T can be found by first calculating the mean of all of our scores (to keep the computations brief, in this example, there are only 10), which is known as the **grand mean**, and then determining the sum of the squared deviations of each score from this grand mean. This can be represented as follows:

$$SS_T = \Sigma(X - M_G)^2,$$

where M_G is the mean of all of the scores, in other words the grand mean. It is found using the following equation:

$$M_G = \frac{\Sigma X}{N},$$

where N is the total number of subjects.

For our example with 10 scores (ignoring that they come from two groups), this calculation is shown in Table 11.5.

Grand mean (M_G): *the mean of all of the scores.*

This value of SS_T is then entered in our table.

The SS_{Bet} can be found by determining the square of the deviations of each sample mean from the grand mean and then multiplying by the *sample* size.

Table 11.5   Calculation of the Sums of Squares Total

X	X − M$_G$	(X − M$_G$)²
7	0.5	0.25
6	−0.5	0.25
5	−1.5	2.25
4	−2.5	6.25
3	−3.5	12.25
10	3.5	12.25
9	2.5	6.25
8	1.5	2.25
7	0.5	0.25
6	−0.5	0.25
$\Sigma X = 65$	$\Sigma(X - M_G) = 0$	$\Sigma(X - M_G)^2 = 42.5 = SS_T$
$N = 10$		
$M_G = 65/10$		
$\quad = 6.5$		

Note. M_G, grand mean; SS_T, sum of squares total.

Thus, conceptually,

$$SS_{Bet} = \Sigma[(M - M_G)^2 n],$$

where n is the sample size.

For our example,

$$SS_{Bet} = (5 - 6.5)^2(5) + (8 - 6.5)^2(5)$$

$$= (-1.5)^2(5) + (1.5)^2(5)$$

$$= (2.25)(5) + (2.25)(5)$$

$$= 11.25 + 11.25$$

$$= 22.5.$$

This value is then entered in our table.

The SS_W can be found by subtracting each score from its sample mean and squaring this deviation. The sum of these squared deviations for all of the scores in each of the groups would be SS_W. Thus, conceptually,

$$SS_W = \Sigma[\Sigma(X - M)^2],$$

where M is the mean of a group.

In other words, with only two groups

$$SS_W = \Sigma x_1^2 + \Sigma x_2^2 \, .$$

Fortunately, we have already calculated these values in Table 11.3.

$$SS_W = 10 + 10$$

$$= 20.$$

This value is then entered into our ANOVA table.

To check our calculations, we make use of the fact that

$$SS_T = SS_{Bet} + SS_W$$

$$42.5 = 22.5 + 20$$

$$42.5 = 42.5.$$

We now must calculate the df for between groups, within groups, and total. The degrees of freedom for between groups is equal to the number of groups -1. Thus,

$$df_{\text{Bet}} = k - 1,$$

where k is the number of levels of the IV. In our example,

$$df_{\text{Bet}} = 2 - 1$$
$$= 1.$$

This value is then entered in our table.

To find the degrees of freedom for within groups, we first subtract 1 from the total number of subjects in each group and then sum the resulting values across all of the groups. Thus,

$$df_{\text{w}} = \Sigma(n - 1),$$

where n is the number of subjects in each group or sample. In our example,

$$df_{\text{w}} = (5 - 1) + (5 - 1)$$
$$= 4 + 4$$
$$= 8.$$

Alternatively, the following equation can be used to calculate df_{w}:

$$df_{\text{w}} = N - k,$$

where N is the total number of subjects in all the groups or samples and k is the number of groups or samples.

$$df_{\text{w}} = 10 - 2$$
$$= 8.$$

This value is then entered in our table.

To find the degrees of freedom total, we subtract 1 from the total number of subjects. Thus,

$$df_{\text{T}} = N - 1,$$

where N is the total number of subjects in all the groups or samples.

In our example,

$$df_{\text{T}} = 10 - 1$$
$$= 9.$$

This value is then entered in our table.

As a check on our calculations,

$$df_T = df_{Bet} + df_w$$

$$9 = 1 + 8$$

$$9 = 9.$$

The *MS* between groups and the *MS* within groups are found by dividing the appropriate *SS* by its *df*. Thus,

$$MS_{Bet} = \frac{SS_{Bet}}{df_{Bet}}$$

$$= \frac{22.5}{1}$$

$$= 22.5.$$

And

$$MS_w = \frac{SS_w}{df_w}$$

$$= \frac{20}{8}$$

$$= 2.5.$$

These values are then entered in our table.

Finally, we calculate our *F* ratio:

$$F = \frac{MS_{Bet}}{MS_w}$$

$$= \frac{22.5}{2.5}$$

$$= 9.$$

This value is then entered in our table, and the table is complete (Table 11.6).

To determine whether this *F* ratio of 9 is significantly different from a value of 1, which you will recall is what would be expected if the IV had no effect, we must enter the *F* table (Appendix J, Table J.4). The *F* ratio is based on two *MS* estimates, each with its *df*. To find the critical value of *F*, we locate the column corresponding to the degrees of freedom of our numerator and the row corresponding to the degrees of freedom of our denominator. For our

| Table 11.6 | Completed Summary Table for the One-Way Between-Subjects ANOVA |

Source of Variation	SS	df	MS	F
Between groups	22.5	1	22.5	9
Within groups	20	8	2.5	
Total	42.5	9		

Note. ANOVA, analysis of variance; *SS*, sum of squares; *df*, degrees of freedom; *MS*, mean square.

F, this would be 1 and 8 *df*, respectively. At the intersection of this column and row, there are two values. One is the critical value for an α of .05, the other is the critical value for an α of .01. Continuing with the α of .05 that we commonly use, the critical value of *F* is 5.32. As our obtained *F* of 9 is larger than the critical value, we reject the null hypothesis that the samples came from populations with equal means and accept the alternative hypothesis that the population means differ. Put differently, we conclude that our IV had an effect.

While a significant *F* indicates that the IV had an effect, it does not specify how large the effect was. To ascertain the percentage of variance explained by the treatment (i.e., the effect size), we can once again calculate eta squared (η^2). With a one-way between-subjects ANOVA,

$$\eta^2 = \frac{SS_{Bet}}{SS_T},$$

where η^2 is the proportion of variance explained by the treatment.
    In our example,

$$\eta^2 = \frac{22.5}{42.5}$$

$$= 0.529 \text{ or } 52.9\%.$$

Reporting the Results of a One-Way Between-Subjects ANOVA

In a paper, we would report the *F* ratio that was obtained as well as the degrees of freedom used and the measure of effect size. Specifically, we would report that "the sample means were found to differ significantly ($F(1, 8) = 9, p < .05$), with η^2 equal to .529."

PROGRESS CHECK

1. If there is a statistically significant treatment effect, the mean square between (MS_{Bet}) estimate of σ_X^2 will be ___ than the mean square within (MS_W) estimate, and the F ratio will be greater than ___.

2. The numerator of the F ratio is the ___ while the denominator of the F ratio is the ___.

3. The measure of effect size for a one-way between-subjects ANOVA is ___.

Answers: 1. greater; 1. 2. (MS_{Bet}); (MS_W); 3. eta squared

A SECOND EXAMPLE

Let us assume that a group of researchers want to study weight loss in dieters who receive information about the benefits of exercise. The researchers choose a design that consists of a control group and two experimental groups. The control group does not receive any special intervention. Subjects in the first experimental group attend a 30-minute informational meeting that details the benefits of engaging in an exercise program. The second experimental group is treated similarly to the first experimental group except that for the second experimental group, the informational meeting extends for half a day. The null hypothesis is that the populations from which these three samples are drawn have equal means. We will set the experiment-wise α at .05. The number of pounds lost during the following 6 months, the dependent measure, is recorded in Table 11.7, along with the deviation from the appropriate sample mean, and the squared deviation from the sample mean. Note that the sample sizes do not have to be equal.

Table 11.7   ANOVA Data and Initial Calculations

Control Group			Experimental Group I			Experimental Group II		
X_1	$X_1 - M_1$	$(X_1 - M_1)^2$	X_2	$X_2 - M_2$	$(X_2 - M_2)^2$	X_3	$X_3 - M_3$	$(X_3 - M_3)^2$
7	−5.6	31.36	10	−5.2	27.04	19	−3	9
11	−1.6	2.56	14	−1.2	1.44	20	−2	4
11	− 1.6	2.56	15	−0.2	0.04	24	2	4
16	3.4	11.56	18	2.8	7.84	25	3	9
18	5.4	29.16	19	3.8	14.44			

Control Group			Experimental Group I			Experimental Group II		
X_1	$X_1 - M_1$	$(X_1 - M_1)^2$	X_2	$X_2 - M_2$	$(X_2 - M_2)^2$	X_3	$X_3 - M_3$	$(X_3 - M_3)^2$
$\Sigma X_1 = 63$	$\Sigma x_1 = 0$	$\Sigma x_1^2 = 77.2$	$\Sigma X_2 = 76$	$\Sigma x_2 = 0$	$\Sigma x_2^2 = 50.8$	$\Sigma x_3 = 88$	$\Sigma x_3 = 0$	$\Sigma x_3^2 = 26$
$n = 5$			$n = 5$			$n = 4$		
$M_1 = 63/5$			$M_2 = 76/5$			$M_3 = 88/4$		
$=12.6$			$= 15.2$			$= 22$		

The next step is to create a table showing what must be calculated (Table 11.4).

As each value is determined, it is entered into the table. We will begin by finding the values for SS.

To find the SS, we start with the following equation:

$$SS_T = SS_{Bet} + SS_W,$$

where $SS_T = \Sigma(X - M_G)^2$. Note that M_G is the mean of all of the scores, in other words, the grand mean. It is found using the following equation:

$$M_G = \frac{\Sigma X}{N}.$$

For our example with a total of 14 scores, this calculation is shown in Table 11.8.

The SS_{Bet} can be found by determining the square of the deviations of each sample mean from the grand mean and then multiplying by the sample size.

Conceptually,

$$SS_{Bet} = \Sigma[(M - M_G)^2 n],$$

where n is the sample size.

For our example,

$$SS_{Bet} = (12.6 - 16.214)^2(5) + (15.2 - 16.214)^2(5) + (22 - 16.214)^2(4)$$

$$= (-3.614)^2(5) + (1.014)^2(5) + (5.786)^2(4)$$

$$= (13.061)(5) + (1.028)(5) + (33.478)(4)$$

$$= 65.305 + 5.140 + 133.912$$

$$= 204.357.$$

Table 11.8	Calculation of the Sums of Squares Total	

X	$X - M_G$	$(X - M_G)^2$
7	−9.214	84.898
11	−5.214	27.186
11	−5.214	27.186
16	−0.214	0.046
18	1.786	3.190
10	−6.214	38.614
14	−2.214	4.902
15	−1.214	1.474
18	1.786	3.190
19	2.786	7.762
19	2.786	7.762
20	3.786	14.334
24	7.786	60.623
25	8.786	77.194
$\Sigma X = 227$	$\Sigma(X - M_G) = 0$	$\Sigma(X - M_G)^2 = 358.36 = SS_T$

$N = 14$

$M_G = 227/14$

$\quad = 16.214$

Note. M_G, grand mean; SS_T, sum of squares total.

The SS_W can be found by subtracting each score from its sample mean and squaring this deviation. The sum of these squared deviations for all of the scores in each of the groups would be SS_W. Thus, conceptually,

$$SS_W = \Sigma[\Sigma(X - M)^2],$$

where M is the mean of a group.

In other words, with three groups

$$SS_W = \sum x_1^2 + \sum x_2^2 + \sum x_3^2.$$

Fortunately, we have already calculated these values in Table 11.7.

$$SS_W = 77.2 + 50.8 + 26$$

$$= 154.$$

To check our calculations, we make use of the fact that

$$SS_T = SS_{Bet} + SS_W$$

$$358.36 = 204.36 + 154$$

$$358.36 = 358.36.$$

We now must calculate the *df* for between groups, within groups, and total. The degrees of freedom for between groups is equal to the number of groups minus 1. Thus,

$$df_{Bet} = k - 1,$$

where *k* is the number of levels of the IV.

In our example,

$$df_{Bet} = 3 - 1$$

$$= 2.$$

To find the degrees of freedom for within groups, we first subtract 1 from the total number of subjects in a group and then sum across all of the groups. Thus,

$$df_W = \Sigma(n - 1),$$

where *n* is the number of subjects in each group or sample.

In our example,

$$df_W = (5 - 1) + (5 - 1) + (4 - 1)$$

$$= 4 + 4 + 3$$

$$= 11.$$

Alternatively, we could find df_W by subtracting the number of groups from the total number of subjects:

$$df_W = N - k$$

$$= 14 - 3$$

$$= 11.$$

To find the degrees of freedom total, we subtract 1 from the total number of subjects. Thus,

$$df_T = N - 1,$$

where N is the total number of subjects in all the groups or samples.

In our example,

$$df_T = 14 - 1$$

$$= 13.$$

As a check on our calculations,

$$df_T = df_{Bet} + df_W$$

$$13 = 2 + 11$$

$$13 = 13.$$

The MS between groups and the MS within groups are found by dividing the appropriate SS by its df. Thus,

$$MS_{Bet} = \frac{SS_{Bet}}{df_{Bet}}$$

$$= \frac{204.36}{2}$$

$$= 102.18.$$

Similarly,

$$MS_W = \frac{SS_W}{df_W}$$

$$= \frac{154}{11}$$

$$= 14.$$

Finally,

$$F = \frac{MS_{\text{Bet}}}{MS_{\text{W}}}$$

$$= \frac{102.18}{14}$$

$$= 7.30.$$

The table is now complete (Table 11.9).

To determine whether this *F* ratio of 7.30 is significantly different from a value of 1, which you will recall is what would be expected if the IV had no effect, we must enter the *F* table. Remember, the *F* ratio is based on two *MS* estimates, each with its degrees of freedom. To find the critical value of *F*, we locate the column corresponding to the degrees of freedom of our numerator and the row corresponding to the degrees of freedom of our denominator. For our *F*, this would be 2 and 11 degrees of freedom, respectively. At the intersection of this column and row, there are two values. One is the critical value for an α of .05, the other is the critical value for an α of .01. The critical value of *F* with the α of .05 is 3.98. As our obtained *F* of 7.30 is larger than the critical value, we reject the null hypothesis that the samples came from populations with equal means and accept the alternative hypothesis that the population means differ. Put differently, we conclude that our IV had an effect on our DV.

While a significant *F* indicates that the IV had an effect, with three or more treatment levels, it does not specify which means differ. It was noted previously that the number of pairwise comparisons in an experiment is given by the equation:

$$\text{Number of pairwise comparisons} = \frac{k(k-1)}{2},$$

where *k* is the number of samples, groups, or treatment levels.

Table 11.9 Completed Summary Table for the One-Way Between-Subjects ANOVA

Source of Variation	SS	df	MS	F
Between groups	204.36	2	102.18	7.30
Within groups	154	11	14	
Total	358.36	13		

Note. ANOVA, analysis of variance; *SS*, sum of squares; *df*, degrees of freedom; *MS*, mean square.

In our case, as $k = 3$, there are $[3(3 − 1)]/2$, which equals 3, pairwise comparisons. Specifically, the 3 pairwise comparisons are between the mean of Group I and the mean of Group II, the mean of Group II and the mean of Group III, and the mean of Group I and the mean of Group III. With a significant F, any one, any two, or all three of these comparisons may be significant. The significant F simply indicates that at least one of the group means differs from another. To specify which means differ, we need to conduct what are called post hoc tests. You are familiar with the concept of post hoc tests, for we used them following a significant chi-square test in Chapter 8, when the chi-square design was larger than a 2 × 2.

A number of post hoc tests have been proposed for use after a significant F ratio is found. One of the most popular and easiest to calculate is Tukey's honestly significant difference (HSD) test. Calculation of Tukey's HSD leads to a critical value that is compared with the difference of each of the post hoc pairwise comparisons of means in the study. Specifically,

$$\text{Critical value} = q\sqrt{\frac{MS_{\text{w}}}{n}},$$

where q is found from the q table and where n = the number of subjects in *each* sample, if this number is the same for all of the samples.

Or

$$n = \frac{\text{Number of means}}{\sum \dfrac{1}{\text{Number of subjects in each sample}}},$$

if the sample size is not the same for all of the samples.

In our example, we do not have an equal number of subjects in each sample. We therefore calculate the n for use in finding the critical value as follows:

$$n = \frac{3}{\dfrac{1}{5} + \dfrac{1}{5} + \dfrac{1}{4}}$$

$$= \frac{3}{0.2 + 0.2 + 0.25}$$

$$= \frac{3}{0.65}$$

$$= 4.62.$$

To find the critical value, we now substitute into the equation

$$\text{Critical value} = q\sqrt{\frac{MS_{\text{w}}}{n}}.$$

MS_W comes from the ANOVA table we just completed for the problem, and n has just been calculated. The value for q is found in the q table (Appendix J, Table J.5). The column to use is determined by the number of means being compared, in our case 3. The row is determined by the degrees of freedom of the MS_W, in our case 11. With α equal to .05, q is equal to 3.82. We can now find the critical value

$$\text{Critical value} = 3.82\sqrt{\frac{14}{4.62}}$$

$$= 3.82\sqrt{3.03}$$

$$= (3.82)(1.74)$$

$$= 6.65.$$

The difference between means for a pairwise comparison must be *as great or greater* than the critical value from Tukey's HSD to be considered significantly different. With ANOVAs with a large number of levels, it is wise to construct a table with all of the pairwise comparisons in a logical order to ensure that none is overlooked. As we are only making three pairwise comparisons, we can dispense with the table and simply list them:

Difference between the means of Group I and Group II = 12.6 − 15.2 = −2.6.

Difference between the means of Group I and Group III = 12.6 − 22 = −9.4.

Difference between the means of Group II and Group III = 15.2 − 22 = −6.8.

It is important to note that when comparing the differences between group means (in our case, −2.6, −9.4, and −6.8) to the critical value, we ignore the sign, as this simply indicates the order in which the sample means were subtracted. Our critical value is 6.65. Therefore, the difference between the means of Group I and Group II, which is 2.6, is not significant. The difference between the means of Group I and Group III, which is 9.4, and the difference between the means of Group II and Group III, which is 6.8, are significant.

To ascertain the percentage of variance explained by the treatment, we calculate eta squared (η^2). With a one-way between-subjects ANOVA,

$$\eta^2 = \frac{SS_{Bet}}{SS_T},$$

where η^2 is the proportion of variance explained by the treatment.

In our example,

$$\eta^2 = \frac{204.36}{358.36}$$

$$= 0.570 \text{ or } 57.0\%.$$

Reporting the Results of a One-Way Between-Subjects ANOVA

In a paper, we would report the F ratio that was obtained as well as the df of its numerator and denominator, which pairwise comparisons were significantly different, and the measure of effect size. Specifically, we would report,

> The sample means were found to differ significantly ($F(2, 11) = 7.30, p < .05$). Tukey's HSD test indicated that the control group differed from the second experimental group, but not the first, and the two experimental groups differed from each other. A measure of effect size, η^2, was .570.

Purpose and Limitations of Using the One-Way Between-Subjects ANOVA

1. *Test for difference:* The null hypothesis is that the treatment does not have an effect. Therefore, if the null is correct, any difference between the sample means is due to chance. The alternative hypothesis is that the treatment does have an effect, and therefore, the samples are drawn from populations with different means. The one-way between-subjects ANOVA is employed to differentiate between these two hypotheses.

2. *Does not provide a measure of effect size:* The one-way between-subjects ANOVA is a test of significance. It indicates whether or not an outcome is likely to have occurred by chance if the null hypothesis is correct. If the F test is significant, a measure of effect size, such as eta squared (η^2), should then be calculated.

3. *Sample size is important:* For the one-way between-subjects ANOVA, if each sample size is 30 or greater, then the assumption that the population from which it is drawn is normal can be safely ignored. If the sample size is less than 30, then it is important that the underlying population be normally distributed. If you cannot collect a larger sample and do not know if the assumption of normality has been met, it may be best to turn to an alternative test on the same row of Table 11.1.

4. *Compares two or more sample means:* The one-way between-subjects ANOVA is appropriate to use when each subject is randomly assigned to one level of the IV.

5. *Does not indicate where the effect is:* With designs with more than two levels to the IV, a significant F should be followed by a post hoc procedure such as Tukey's HSD test to specify the location of the effect.

Assumptions of the One-Way Between-Subjects ANOVA

Interval or ratio data: The data are on an interval or ratio scale of measurement.

Random samples: Each sample is drawn at random from a population.

Independence within treatment levels: The data within each treatment level are independent.

Normally distributed populations: Each population from which a sample is drawn has a normal distribution of scores.

Population variances are equal: The populations from which samples are drawn have equal variances.

Effect of Violating the Assumptions

The F test has been found to be robust. This means that the F test leads to accurate decisions even when some assumptions are violated so long as each sample size is at least 30 (refer to the discussion of the central limit theorem in Chapter 9). However, if the sample sizes are dramatically unequal or if any sample is substantially less than 30, the sample distributions have obviously different shapes, or the sample variances are clearly not equal, you should not use the F test. Instead, you should consider converting your interval or ratio data to an ordinal measurement and then turn to the Kruskal–Wallis H test, which is reviewed in Appendix A. Also, if samples are not randomly drawn, then you have a quasi-experiment and thus less confidence in the interpretation of a significant outcome.

CONCLUSION

The one-way between-subjects ANOVA is a very flexible test and serves as an introduction to the more complex ANOVAs that will be covered in subsequent chapters. The major advantage of the ANOVA is that it controls the experiment-wise error rate while simultaneously comparing two or more sample means.

FINAL THOUGHTS: THE RELATIONSHIP BETWEEN THE *t* TEST AND THE *F* TEST

Though the calculations for the independent samples t test (reviewed in Chapter 10) and the one-way between-subjects ANOVA with two groups appear to be quite different, these tests are closely related. In fact, the independent samples t test is a special case of the one-way between-subjects ANOVA. It is possible, for instance, to convert the outcome obtained with one test into the value of the other using the following equation:

$$t^2 = F.$$

Substituting the value of $F = 9$ that was found using the one-way between-subjects ANOVA in Table 11.6, we have

$$t^2 = 9.$$

Therefore, $t = 3$. You are encouraged to verify that this is indeed the case by redoing the example as a t test.

Since the values obtained with the t and F tests can be converted into each other, it should not be a surprise that these tests will always lead to the same decision as to whether the null hypothesis should be retained or rejected.

Similarly, the estimate of the effect size will be the same regardless of whether you calculate an independent samples t test or the one-way between-subjects ANOVA with two groups. You are encouraged to verify that this is the case for our examples.

Chapter Resources

GLOSSARY OF TERMS

Between-subjects design: with an ANOVA, those designs in which each subject receives a single level of a factor.

Experiment-wise error: the likelihood of making at least one Type I error with any of the experiment's comparisons.

Factor: with an ANOVA, the term *factor* is used instead of independent variable.

Factorial ANOVA: an ANOVA with more than one factor.

Grand mean (M_G): the mean of all of the scores.

Level: with an ANOVA, the number of values of the independent variable.

Mean square between (MS_{Bet}): the estimate of σ_X^2 obtained from the deviations of the sample means from M_G. It is thus based on the variability between the samples.

Mean square within (MS_W): the estimate of σ_X^2 obtained by pooling the variances of the scores from their sample means. It is thus based on the variability within each of the samples.

Pairwise comparison: comparison between two sample means.

Pairwise error rate: the likelihood of making a Type I error for a single comparison between sample means. This is equal to α, which is usually .05 or .01.

Questions: Chapter 11

(Answers to odd-numbered items are provided in Appendix I.)

1. The sum of squares total in a one-way between-subjects ANOVA is equal to _____.
   a. the sum of all of the squared scores
   b. the sum of all the scores, squared

  c. the sum of the squared deviations of all of the scores from their grand mean

  d. the square root of the sum of the squared deviations of all of the scores from their mean

2. In a one-way between-subjects ANOVA, SS_T is equal to _____.

  a. SS_W

  b. SS_{Bet}

  c. $SS_{Bet} + SS_W$

  d. $SS_{Bet} - SS_W$

  e. $SS_{Bet} \times SS_W$

3. "Within variability" provides an estimate of _____ by looking at _____.

  a. control group variability; how much sample means vary

  b. population variability; how much scores vary from their sample means

  c. experimental group(s) variability; how much sample means vary

  d. how much sample means vary; population variability

4. Another term for "mean square" is _____.

  a. variance

  b. standard deviation

  c. range

  d. square of the sum of all of the sample means

5. If there is no treatment effect, the *F* ratio is expected to approximately equal _____.

  a. 0

  b. 1

  c. 2

  d. twice the number of experimental conditions

  e. would vary depending on the experimental design

6. If the *F* ratio from a one-way between-subjects ANOVA with two levels is found to be statistically significant, the researcher should _____.

  a. announce that the finding is important

  b. conduct a post hoc test to determine which groups differ

  c. calculate eta squared

  d. none of the above, there is nothing further to do

7. The *F* ratio can only be significant if it is _____.

  a. less than 1

  b. equal to 1

c. greater than 1

d. an F ratio can never be significant

8. If the *F* ratio from a one-way between-subjects ANOVA with more than two levels is found to be statistically significant, the researcher should _____.

a. announce that the finding is important

b. conduct a post hoc test to determine which groups differ

c. recalculate as it is obvious that an error has occurred

d. none of the above, there is nothing further to do

9. In a one-way between-subjects ANOVA, there are how many independent variables and how many dependent variables?

a. 1; 1

b. 1; 2

c. 2; 1

d. 2; 2

e. You cannot be certain as they vary

Questions 10 to 14 are based on the following table:

Source of Variation	SS	df	MS	F
Between groups	___	2	___	___
Within groups	100	___	___	
Total	400	12		

10. What is the *SS* for between groups?

a. 300

b. 500

c. 40,000

d. 100

11. What is the value of *df* for within groups?

a. 14

b. 10

c. 33

d. 26

12. What is *MS* for between groups?

    a. 150

    b. 600

    c. 298

    d. 502

13. What is *MS* for within groups?

    a. 1,000

    b. 50

    c. 25

    d. 10

14. What is the value of the *F* ratio?

    a. 60

    b. 15

    c. 2.5

    d. 1

Questions 15 to 19 are based on the following information:

A group of 18 students take their final exam in statistics. Each student is randomly assigned to one of three rooms—quiet, moderately noisy, and noisy. The number of errors for each student is shown in the following table.

Level of Background Noise		
Quiet	**Moderate**	**Noisy**
9	7	6
10	9	8
8	8	10
13	13	7
12	11	11
14	12	12

15. What is the df_{Bet}?

    a. 1

    b. 2

    c. 3

    d. 4

16. What is the SS_w?

    a. 12

    b. 36

    c. 84

    d. 96

17. What is the MS_{Bet}?

    a. 6

    b. 12

    c. 36

    d. 146

18. What is the value of the F ratio?

    a. 0

    b. 26.071

    c. 0.915

    d. 1.071

19. Is the outcome statistically significant with alpha equal to .05?

    a. Yes

    b. No

Questions 20 and 21 deal with the relationship of F and t.

20. It is possible to convert the outcome obtained with a t test into the value of a between-subjects ANOVA using the equation _____.

    a. $F = 2t$

    b. $t^2 = F$

    c. $t/6 = 10F$

    d. $t = F$

21. The t and F tests will _____ lead to the same decision as to whether the null hypothesis should be retained or rejected.

    a. always

    b. sometimes

    c. never

Problems 22 to 26 utilize SPSS.

SPSS

USING SPSS WITH THE ONE-WAY BETWEEN-SUBJECTS ANOVA

To Begin SPSS

Step 1: The first step is to activate the program.

Step 2: Click on "Type in data" and then click on "OK."

Step 3: Click on "Variable View." For the present, we will only be dealing with the columns headed by "Name," "Label," "Values," and "Measure."

Step 4: Click on the first empty rectangle (called a "cell") under the column heading "Name." You now type the name of the first variable for which you have data. We are going to utilize the same data and labels as were previously employed in Table 11.7. These data dealt with the question of whether receiving information about the benefits of exercise would affect weight loss. We have called these variables "Condition" and "Data." Therefore, type "Condition" in the first empty cell under "Name."

Step 5: Click on the first empty cell under the column heading "Label," and type "Experimental Group."

Step 6: Click on the first empty cell under the column heading "Values." Then click on the small blue square. A box will appear. In the blank space to the right of "Value," type the Number "1." Then type a brief description of this value of the variable in the blank space to the right of "Label." In our case, type "Control." Finally, click on "Add." Your label for a Value 1 will appear in the large white region in the center of the window. Now repeat the above steps in this section for the Value "2," which is given the label "Exp 1," and for the Value "3," which is given the label "Exp 2" (Figure 11.1). Then click on "OK."

Figure 11.1 The Value Labels Window

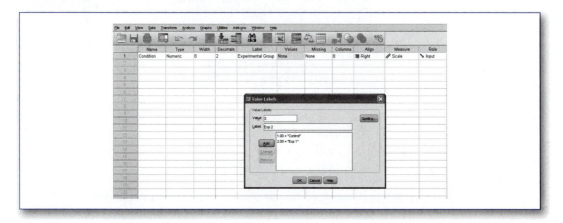

Step 7: Click on the first empty cell under the column heading "Measure." As we are dealing with labels for groups, select "Nominal."

Step 8: Repeat Steps 4 to 7 except that you type "Data" in the first empty cell under "Name" and for the "Label." Finally, select "Scale" in the column under the column heading "Measure" as we have interval or ratio data. The result is shown in Figure 11.2.

Figure 11.2	The Variable View Window

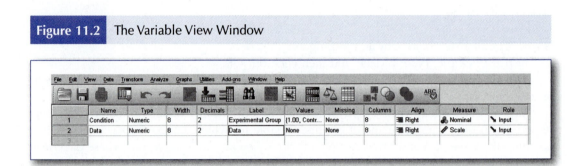

To Enter Data in SPSS

Step 9: Click on the "Data View" option at the lower left corner of the window. The variables "Condition" and "Data" will be present.

Step 10: For each subject in the control condition, type the Value "1" in the column "Condition," and their weight loss in the column "Data" (Figure 11.3). Continue by entering "2" for each subject in Group 2 with their data, and finally "3" for each subject in Group 3 with their data (Figure 11.4).

Figure 11.3	Entering the Data for the First Condition

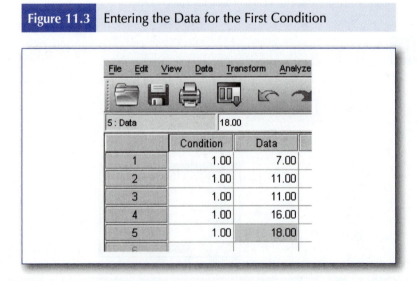

Figure 11.4	Completed Data Entry

To Conduct a One-Way Between-Subjects ANOVA

Step 11: Click the cursor on "Analyze" along the row of SPSS commands above the data you entered, then move to "Compare Means," then click on "one-way ANOVA."

Step 12: A new window will appear. This asks for the DV and the IV (called a Factor) to be identified. In our case, Data is the label of the DV. This is indicated by moving "Data" to the box under "Dependent list" by clicking on the top arrow, as is shown in Figure 11.5. Then move "Experimental Group" to the box under "Factor" by clicking on the second arrow. The result will be that each label will move to the appropriate box on the right-hand side of the window, as is shown in Figure 11.6. Then click on "Post Hoc." which is located in the top, right corner of the window.

Step 13: A new window will appear. This window provides a number of statistical options that are available with SPSS. In this book, we will limit ourselves to just Tukey's HSD test as is shown in Figure 11.7. Then click on "Continue."

Step 14: Now click on "Options." A new window will appear. If you click on the box in front of "Descriptive" (Figure 11.8), SPSS will generate a useful summary of the data. Click on "Continue."

Figure 11.5 The One-Way ANOVA Window

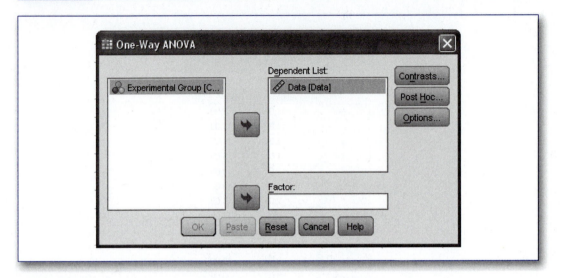

Figure 11.6 The One-Way ANOVA Window (Continued)

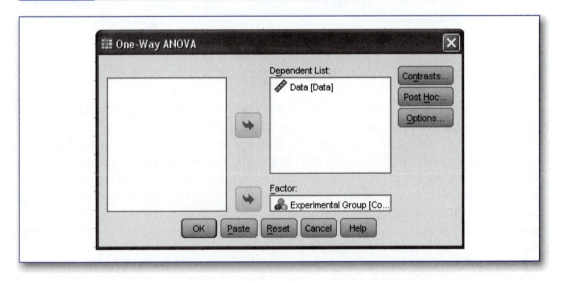

Step 15: Now click on "OK." SPSS calculates the desired one-way ANOVA with descriptive statistics and Tukey's HSD post hoc test as is shown in Tables 11.10 to 11.13. The first section of the analysis is a table of descriptive statistics (Table 11.10). You should compare the means of the samples that we calculated in Table 11.7 with the means calculated by SPSS. In addition,

Figure 11.7	Identifying the Post Hoc Test

Figure 11.8	Specifying Descriptives

standard deviations and additional information that might be of interest are included. Next is the summary ANOVA table (Table 11.1), which is the same as we found earlier with hand calculation (Table 11.9) except that we rounded off our calculations. Table 11.12 shows the results of Tukey's HSD post hoc test. In the first two rows of the analysis, Group 1 is compared

| Table 11.10 | The One-Way ANOVA Output: Descriptives |

Descriptives
Data

	N	Mean	Std. Deviation	Std. Error	95% Confidence Interval for Mean		Minimum	Maximum
					Lower Bound	Upper Bound		
Control	5	12.6000	4.39318	1.96469	7.1452	18.0548	7.00	18.00
Exp 1	5	15.2000	3.56371	1.59374	10.7751	19.6249	10.00	19.00
Exp 2	4	22.0000	2.94392	1.47196	17.3156	26.6844	19.00	25.00
Total	14	16.2143	5.25033	1.40321	13.1828	19.2457	7.00	25.00

| Table 11.11 | The One-Way ANOVA Output: Summary Table |

ANOVA
Data

	Sum of Squares	df	Mean Square	F	Sig.
Between Groups	204.357	2	102.179	7.298	.010
Within Groups	154.000	11	14.000		
Total	358.357	13			

with the other two groups and the difference with Group 3 is found to be statistically significant (this is indicated with an *) as well as by a significance level less than .05 (in this case .008). In addition, 95% confidence intervals are provided. The next two pairs of rows provide the comparisons for Group 2 and Group 3. Table 11.13 provides additional information concerning Tukey's HSD post hoc test.

To confirm that you understand how to use SPSS, redo the between-subjects ANOVA that was calculated in the text for the data in Table 11.3, but this time using SPSS. Then redo the ANOVA dealing with level of background noise (Questions 15–19) to check your answers.

Table 11.12 The One-Way ANOVA Output: Tukey Multiple Comparisons

Multiple Comparisons
Data
Tukey HSD

(I) Experimental Group	(J) Experimental Group	Mean Difference (I–J)	Std. Error	Sig.	95% Confidence Interval	
					Lower Bound	Upper Bound
Control	Exp 1	-2.60000	2.36643	.534	-8.9914	3.7914
	Exp 2	-9.40000*	2.50998	.008	-16.1791	-2.6209
Exp 1	Control	2.60000	2.36643	.534	-3.7914	8.9914
	Exp 2	-6.80000*	2.50998	.049	-13.5791	-.0209
Exp 2	Control	9.40000*	2.50998	.008	2.6209	16.1791
	Exp 1	6.80000*	2.50998	.049	.0209	13.5791

*. The mean difference is significant at the .05 level.

Table 11.13 The One-Way ANOVA Output: Tukey Post Hoc Summary

Data
Tukey HSD[a,b]

Experimental Group	N	Subset for alpha = 0.05	
		1	2
Control	5	12.6000	
Exp 1	5	15.2000	
Exp 2	4		22.0000
Sig.		.559	1.000

Means for groups in homogeneous subsets are displayed.
a. Uses Harmonic Mean Sample Size = 4.615.
b. The group sizes are unequal. The harmonic mean of the group sizes is used. Type I error levels are not guaranteed.

SPSS Problems: Chapter 11

For Questions 22 to 26, we examine the effect of adding a constant (in this case 10) to every score in the noisy condition of the data used for Questions 15 to 19. (Compare your answers for these data to your previous answers.)

Level of Background Noise		
Quiet	Moderate	Noisy
9	7	16
10	9	18
8	8	20
13	13	17
12	11	21
14	12	22

22. What is the df_{Bet}?

    a. 1

    b. 2

    c. 3

    d. 4

23. What is the SS_{w}?

    a. 12

    b. 36

    c. 84

    d. 96

24. What is the MS_{Bet}?

    a. 6

    b. 12

    c. 36

    d. 146

25. What is the value of the F ratio?

    a. 0

    b. 26.071

    c. .915

    d. 1.071

26. Is the outcome statistically significant with alpha equal to .05?

    a. Yes

    b. No

12

FINDING DIFFERENCES WITH INTERVAL AND RATIO DATA—IV

The One-Way Within-Subjects ANOVA

The null hypothesis is never proved or established, but is possibly disproved, in the course of experimentation.

—R. A. Fisher

The logic of the one-way *within-subjects* analysis of variance (ANOVA) is very similar to what we already learned for the one-way *between-subjects* ANOVA. Both include one independent variable (IV) with two or more levels and culminate in the calculation of an F ratio. To review, the F is the ratio of two estimates of the population variance, σ_X^2. With the one-way *between-subjects* ANOVA, the estimate in the *numerator* is based on the variability of the *sample means*. This estimate of σ_X^2 is called the mean square between (MS_{Bet}). It includes the effect of our treatment as well as expected sample variation if there were no treatment effect (also called error).

With the one-way *between-subjects* ANOVA, the estimate of the population variance, σ_X^2, in the *denominator* of the F ratio is obtained by noting how much each *score* varies from its sample mean. The combined estimate of σ_X^2 from all of the samples, s_{XP}^2 pooled, is more accurate than the estimate derived from a single sample. If the samples sizes are all equal, the combined or pooled estimate from all of the samples becomes

$$s^2_{XP} \, \text{pooled} = \frac{s^2_{XP_1} + s^2_{XP_2} + \cdots + s^2_{XP_k}}{k},$$

where $s^2_{XP_k}$ is a sample variance and k is the number of samples.

This term is called the mean square within (MS_W). As it is determined by looking within each sample and is based on how much each score varies from its sample mean, it does not reflect the effect of the treatment and, thus, is solely a measure of variability within samples, or error.

For the one-way *between-subjects* ANOVA, the F ratio is

$$F = \frac{MS_{Bet}}{MS_W}$$

$$= \frac{\text{Estimate of } \sigma^2_X \text{ based on treatment} + \text{Error}}{\text{Estimate of } \sigma^2_X \text{ based only on error}}.$$

If there is no treatment effect, then F will be the ratio of two estimates of error, which should be approximately equal, and thus, the ratio would be about one. If, on the other hand, the treatment effect is large relative to the size of the error, then the F ratio will be substantially greater than one.

To increase the size of the F ratio, and thereby increase the likelihood of rejecting the null hypothesis, we could try to increase the size of the numerator or decrease the size of the denominator. To increase the numerator, we would increase the variability due to the treatment, which would reflect a greater effect of the independent variable. Alternatively, we could increase the size of the F ratio by decreasing the magnitude of the denominator, which can be achieved by reducing the variability due to error. The one-way *within-subjects* ANOVA is a procedure that is designed to decrease the magnitude of the denominator by reducing the size of the variability due to error.

As was just reviewed, the size of the variability due to error reflects how much the scores in a sample vary from their sample mean. Since all the individuals in a sample receive the same level of the independent variable, or treatment, these deviations from the sample mean are not due to the treatment. So why do subjects within a sample differ from the sample mean and thus from each other as well? There are two reasons. First, the subjects within a sample differ because the sample reflects the variability of the population from which it was chosen. If there is a great deal of variability in the population, then we expect that there will be more variability in the sample than if there was little variability in the population. For instance, people's IQ (intelligence quotient) scores differ. If we randomly assign individuals to a sample, we expect the IQ scores of these individuals also to differ. Second, events occur over which the experimenter does not have control, and these events can affect subjects' behavior. For instance, if a subject has a car accident on the way to the experiment, it would not be surprising if it affected their performance. This error is independent of the level of the independent variable. The subject's performance might have been affected no matter what treatment level was assigned.

In other words, the outcome of a study may be affected by three sources of variability. One source of variability is the level of the treatment that the subject receives. If the treatment has an effect, then it should affect the behavior of the subjects and thus cause samples to differ. This is what the experimenter is interested in determining. Unfortunately, there are two other sources of variability, collectively known as error, which can make this determination difficult. One source of error reflects the variability of the population(s) from which the subjects are selected. We will call this **preexisting subject differences**. The other source of error is due to unsystematic events (e.g., changes in the temperature, whether a car accident occurred, or if a subject was just accepted into graduate school) that coincide with the testing. We will call this unsystematic error **residual error**. Good, general experimental procedures can reduce, but not eliminate, residual error, the error due to unsystematic events. The one-way *within-subjects* ANOVA is a specific procedure that can be very effective in eliminating the other source of error, the preexisting subject differences. The one-way within-subjects ANOVA is underlined in Table 12.1.

> *Preexisting subject differences: relatively stable subject characteristics. These differences between subjects are a form of error in an ANOVA.*

Let us assume that we randomly select three samples of the same size from a population that has a great deal of variability. The subject differences, or variability within the samples, would presumably be quite large, as would be the MS_W. This is because MS_W is an estimate of the population variance based

> *Residual error: changeable subject characteristics. These differences between subjects are a form of error in an ANOVA.*

on the variability within samples. It reflects preexisting subject differences and residual error, but not treatment.

How could we reduce the error due to preexisting subject differences? One solution would be to use matched samples. We could pretest the members of the population on some characteristic important to the research, perhaps age, IQ, or medical history depending on the study, and then we could match the subjects in each sample on this variable. We could then statistically remove the variability due to this characteristic. This design is called a one-way *matched-subjects* ANOVA.

An even more effective way to reduce the error due to subject differences is to use repeated measures on the same subjects. In a sense, the repeated measures design is the ultimate example of matching. However, instead of having to pretest and then match on one or a few variables that we have reason to believe are important, each subject is matched to himself or herself. In other words, it is as if there is a match on all variables that occurred before the introduction of the independent variable. Because of this level of matching, each subject in a repeated measures design is sometimes said to be serving as his or her own control. Since

Table 12.1	Overview of Inferential Statistical Procedures for Difference and Interaction Designs

Type of Data

	Nominal (Frequency)		Ordinal (Ranked)	Interval/Ratio (Continuous Measure)

Inferential Statistics (Finding Relationships)

Statistical procedures for difference and interaction designs

	Nominal (Frequency)		Ordinal (Ranked)	Interval/Ratio (Continuous Measure)
One variable with at least two outcomes	Goodness-of-fit chi-square	**One IV with one sample—one DV**		One-sample z score or one-sample t test
		One IV with two or more independent samples—one DV	Kruskal–Wallis H	One-way between-subjects ANOVA (only two independent samples—independent samples t test)
		One IV with one sample having two or more repeated measures—one DV		One-way within-subjects ANOVA (only two repeated measures—dependent samples t test)
Two variables, each with at least two outcomes	Chi-square test of independence	**Two IV each with two or more independent samples—one DV**		Two-way between-subjects ANOVA

Notes. IV, independent variable; DV, dependent variable; ANOVA, analysis of variance. Research designs are shown in boldface. The italicized item is reviewed in Appendix A.

the same subjects are now in each "sample," the sample means should be identical except for the effects of the treatment and residual error. Thus, a repeated measures design eliminates preexisting subject differences as a source of error.

We previously noted that for the one-way *between-subjects* ANOVA, the F ratio is

$$F = \frac{MS_{\text{Bet}}}{MS_{\text{W}}}$$

$$= \frac{\text{Estimate of } \sigma_X^2 \text{ based on treatment} + \text{Error}}{\text{Estimate of } \sigma_X^2 \text{ based only on error}}.$$

We have now found that there are two types of error, what we are calling preexisting subject differences and residual error. Therefore, the F ratio can be rewritten as follows:

$$F = \frac{\text{Estimate of } \sigma_X^2 \text{ based on treatment} + \text{Preexisting subject differences} + \text{Residual error}}{\text{Estimate of } \sigma_X^2 \text{ based only on preexisting subject differences} + \text{Residual error}}.$$

With the one-way *within-subjects* ANOVA (also known as the single-factor within-subjects ANOVA, the single-factor repeated measures ANOVA or the one-way repeated measures ANOVA), the preexisting subject differences are eliminated as a source of error from both the numerator and the denominator of the F ratio. As a result, the F ratio becomes

$$F = \frac{\text{Estimate of } \sigma_X^2 \text{ based on treatment} + \text{Residual error}}{\text{Estimate of } \sigma_X^2 \text{ based only on residual error}}.$$

Eliminating the preexisting subject differences from both the numerator and the denominator of the F ratio can have a dramatic effect on the F ratio. For instance, with a one-way *between-subjects* ANOVA, if the treatment estimate of variance is 20, the preexisting subject differences estimate is 10, and the residual error estimate is 5, the F ratio is as follows:

$$F = \frac{\text{Estimate of } \sigma_X^2 \text{ based on treatment} + \text{Preexisting subject differences} + \text{Residual error}}{\text{Estimate of } \sigma_X^2 \text{ based only on preexisting subject differences} + \text{Residual error}}$$

$$= \frac{20 + 10 + 5}{10 + 5}$$

$$= \frac{35}{15}$$

$$= 2.33.$$

However, with a one-way *within-subjects* ANOVA, the variability due to the preexisting subject differences would be eliminated from both the numerator and the denominator, and the F ratio would become

$$F = \frac{\text{Estimate of } \sigma_X^2 \text{ based on treatment} + \text{Residual error}}{\text{Estimate of } \sigma_X^2 \text{ based only on residual error}}$$

$$= \frac{20 + 5}{5}$$

$$= \frac{25}{5}$$

$$= 5.$$

Clearly, use of the one-way *within-subjects* ANOVA design can dramatically increase the size of the F ratio and, therefore, assist a researcher in detecting whether an independent variable has had an effect.

A FIRST EXAMPLE

The one-way *within-subjects* ANOVA can be used to analyze interval or ratio data from designs with two or more repeated measures. For our first example, we will examine whether a fuel additive changes car mileage (this problem was also analyzed with the dependent samples t test in Chapter 10). The data and the steps leading to the calculation of the sums of the squared deviations from the mean as well as the subject totals are reproduced in Table 12.2. (We will be referring to these calculations shortly.) The null hypothesis is that the fuel additive does not affect mileage. The alternative hypothesis is that it does. The alpha level is set at .05.

It is critical when using ANOVAs that you know what you are calculating and that you keep your calculations clearly defined. It is thus important that we begin with a table showing what it is that must be calculated (Table 12.3). You will recognize that the table for the one-way within-subjects ANOVA is similar, but not identical, to the table that we used with the one-way between-subjects ANOVA.

Table 12.2   First Example

Vehicle (Subject)	Mileage Without Additive			Mileage With Additive			Subject Totals
	X_1	X_1-M_1	$(X_1-M_1)^2$	X_2	X_2-M_2	$(X_2-M_2)^2$	$(\Sigma X_{Subject})$
1	12	−5	25	13	−4.5	20.25	25
2	13	−4	16	15	−2.5	6.25	28
3	15	−2	4	14	−3.5	12.25	29
4	17	0	0	17	−0.5	0.25	34
5	20	3	9	24	6.5	42.25	44
6	25	8	64	22	4.5	20.25	47
	$\Sigma X_1 = 102$	$\Sigma x_1 = 0$	$\Sigma x_1^2 = 118$	$\Sigma X_2 = 105$	$\Sigma x_2 = 0$	$\Sigma x_2^2 = 101.5$	$\Sigma\left(\Sigma X_{Subject}\right) = 207$
	$n = 6$			$n = 6$			
	$M_1 = 102/6$			$M_2 = 105/6$			
	$= 17$			$= 17.5$			

Table 12.3	Summary Table for the One-Way Within-Subjects ANOVA			
Source of Variation	**SS**	**df**	**MS**	**F**
Between levels	$\underline{SS}_{Bet}$	$\underline{df}_{Bet}$	$\underline{MS}_{Bet}$	$\underline{F}$ ratio
Subjects	$\underline{SS}_{Subjects}$	$\underline{df}_{Subjects}$		
Within residual	$\underline{SS}_{Residual}$	$\underline{df}_{Residual}$	$\underline{MS}_{Residual}$	
Total	$\underline{SS}_{T}$	$\underline{df}_{T}$		

Note. ANOVA, analysis of variance; *SS*, sum of squares; *df*, degrees of freedom; *MS*, mean square.

It is important to note that a value must be recorded for every entry underlined in Table 12.3. Thus, we will begin by finding four values for *SS* and then calculate four values for *df*, two values for *MS*, and one *F* ratio. You will see that this involves a substantial amount of calculation, but just as with the one-way between-subjects ANOVA, the advantage of the current ANOVA is that it can be used with more than two levels of the independent variable. And no step is difficult. It is critical, however, that you clearly identify each item you are calculating so that you do not become confused.

Our first step, as with the one-way between-subjects ANOVA, is to find each of the sum of squares (*SS*). Specifically, it was noted in Chapter 11 that

$$SS_T = SS_{Bet} + SS_W.$$

In the one-way within-subjects ANOVA, the SS_W is partitioned into $SS_{Subjects}$ and $SS_{Residual}$. Thus, in a one-way within-subjects ANOVA,

$$SS_T = SS_{Bet} + SS_{Subjects} + SS_{Residual}.$$

We begin our calculations by finding SS_T in the same way as with a one-way between-subjects ANOVA:

$$SS_T = \sum(X - M_G)^2,$$

where M_G, the grand mean, is the mean, of all of the scores.

The grand mean, M_G, is found using the following equation:

$$M_G = \frac{\sum X}{N},$$

where N is the total number of data points or scores.

For our example with a total of 12 scores from 6 subjects, this calculation is shown in Table 12.4.

The SS_{Bet} for a one-way within-subjects ANOVA is found, as in a one-way between-subjects ANOVA, by determining the square of the deviations of each sample mean from the grand mean and then multiplying by the number of subjects in the sample. It is important to note that while the equation and thus the computations used to determine the SS_{Bet} are the same for the between-subjects and within-subjects ANOVAs, this term is interpreted somewhat differently depending on which ANOVA is being utilized. The SS_{Bet} for a between-subjects ANOVA is affected by preexisting subject differences such as IQ, gender, and height due to each group being composed of different subjects. However, in a within-subjects design, differences between the treatment means cannot be due to pre-existing subject differences since the same subjects receive each of the treatment levels. Thus, while the MS_{Bet} for a one-way *between-subjects* ANOVA (the numerator of the *F*

Table 12.4 Calculation of M_G and SS_T for the First Example

X	$X - M_G$	$(X - M_G)^2$
12	−5.25	27.5625
13	−4.25	18.0625
15	−2.25	5.0625
17	−0.25	0.0625
20	2.75	7.5625
25	7.75	60.0625
13	−4.25	18.0625
15	−2.25	5.0625
14	−3.25	10.5625
17	−0.25	0.0625
24	6.75	45.5625
22	4.75	22.5625
$\Sigma X = 207$ $N = 12$ $M_G = 207/12$ $= 17.25$	$\Sigma(X - M_G) = 0$	$\Sigma(X - M_G)^2 = 220.25 = SS_T$

ratio) consists of an estimate of the population variance based on treatment plus preexisting subject differences plus residual error, the MS_{Bet} for a one-way *within-subjects* ANOVA does not include preexisting subject differences and thus consists only of an estimate of the population variance based on treatment plus residual error. Conceptually,

$$SS_{Bet} = \Sigma[(M - M_G)^2 n],$$

where n is the number of subjects in the study.

Based on the calculations in Tables 12.2 and 12.4,

$$SS_{Bet} = (17 - 17.25)^2(6) + (17.5 - 17.25)^2(6)$$
$$= (-0.25)^2(6) + (0.25)^2(6)$$
$$= (0.0625)(6) + (0.0625)(6)$$
$$= 0.375 + 0.375$$
$$= 0.75.$$

As $SS_T = SS_{Bet} + SS_W$, it is now easy to calculate the SS_W:

$$220.25 = 0.75 + SS_W$$
$$219.50 = SS_W.$$

Alternatively, in a one-way between-subjects ANOVA and in a one-way within-subjects ANOVA, the SS_W can be found by subtracting each score from its sample mean and squaring this deviation. The sum of these squared deviations for all of the scores in each of the groups would be SS_W. Thus, conceptually,

$$SS_W = \Sigma[\Sigma(X - M)^2],$$

where M is the mean of a group.

In other words, with two groups,

$$SS_W = \Sigma x_1^2 + \Sigma x_2^2.$$

Fortunately, we have already calculated these values in Table 12.2:

$$SS_W = 118 + 101.5$$
$$= 219.5.$$

As expected, this is the same value we obtained earlier.

This value is *not* entered into our ANOVA table, for in a within-subjects ANOVA, it must be partitioned into SS_{Subjects} and SS_{Residual}. However, we can check our calculations to this point, as

$$SS_T = SS_{\text{Bet}} + SS_W$$

$$220.25 = 0.75 + 219.5$$

$$220.25 = 220.25.$$

The SS_{Subjects}, which is the part of SS_W that is due to preexisting subject differences, is found by determining the square of the deviations of the mean of each subject's total from the grand mean and then multiplying by the number of treatment levels. Conceptually,

$$SS_{\text{Subjects}} = \left[\Sigma \left(\frac{\Sigma X_{\text{Subject}}}{k} - M_G \right)^2 \right] k,$$

where the subject's total, $\Sigma X_{\text{Subject}}$, is obtained from Table 12.2, the grand mean, M_G, is obtained from Table 12.4, and k is the number of treatment levels, in this case 2.

This calculation is shown in Table 12.5.

Table 12.5   Calculation of SS_{Subjects} for the First Example

Subject	$\Sigma X_{\text{Subject}}$	$\dfrac{\Sigma X_{\text{Subject}}}{k}$	$\dfrac{\Sigma X_{\text{Subject}}}{k} - M_G$	$\left(\dfrac{\Sigma X_{\text{Subject}}}{k} - M_G \right)^2$
1	25	12.5	−4.75	22.5625
2	28	14.0	−3.25	10.5625
3	29	14.5	−2.75	7.5625
4	34	17.0	−0.25	0.0625
5	44	22.0	4.75	22.5625
6	47	23.5	6.25	39.0625
			$\Sigma \left(\dfrac{\Sigma X_{\text{Subject}}}{k} - M_G \right) = 0$	$\Sigma \left(\dfrac{\Sigma X_{\text{Subject}}}{k} - M_G \right)^2 = 102.375$

$$SS_{\text{Subjects}} = \left[\Sigma \left(\frac{\Sigma X_{\text{Subject}}}{k} - M_G \right)^2 \right] k = (102.375)(2)$$

$$= 204.75$$

Remember that SS_W is being partitioned into $SS_{Subjects}$ and $SS_{Residual}$. The $SS_{Subjects}$ is the reduction to the denominator of the F ratio achieved by using a within-subjects design. The value for $SS_{Subjects}$ is then entered in our table.

As was noted previously, in a within-subjects ANOVA,

$$SS_T = SS_{Bet} + SS_{Subjects} + SS_{Residual},$$

where $SS_{Subjects} + SS_{Residual} = SS_W$.

To determine the value of $SS_{Residual}$, we must subtract the value of $SS_{Subjects}$ from SS_W. In our example, this would be $219.5 - 204.75 = 14.75$. This is the value for $SS_{Residual}$ that is entered in the within-subjects ANOVA table. Once again, it is important to note how the measure of error that will be used in the denominator of the F ratio has been reduced through the use of a within-subjects design.

We now must calculate the degrees of freedom (df) for between levels, subjects, residual, and total. Fortunately, these numbers are easy to obtain.

The degrees of freedom for between levels is equal to the number of levels minus 1. Thus,

$$df_{Bet} = k - 1,$$

where k is the number of treatment levels. In our example,

$$df_{Bet} = 2 - 1$$

$$= 1.$$

In a one-way between-subjects ANOVA, we would now determine the df_W. In a one-way within-subjects ANOVA, df_W is partitioned into $df_{Subjects}$ and $df_{Residual}$ just as SS_W was partitioned into $SS_{Subjects}$ and $SS_{Residual}$. The degrees of freedom for subjects is equal to the *number of subjects* minus 1. (Note that the data consist of 12 mileages, but there are only 6 subjects, in this case cars.) Thus,

$$df_{Subjects} = n - 1,$$

where n is the number of subjects,

$$df_{Subjects} = 6 - 1$$

$$= 5.$$

The $df_{Subjects}$ is the number of degrees of freedom by which the denominator of the F ratio is reduced due to using a within-subjects design.

To find the degrees of freedom for residual, we subtract 1 from the total number of subjects and multiply this by the number of levels minus 1. Thus,

$$df_{Residual} = (n - 1)(k - 1),$$

where n is the number of subjects and k is the number of levels. In our example,

$$df_{\text{Residual}} = (6 - 1)(2 - 1)$$
$$= 5 \times 1$$
$$= 5.$$

To find the degrees of freedom for total, we subtract 1 from the total number of data points. Thus,

$$df_{\text{T}} = N - 1,$$

where N is the total number of data points. In our example,

$$df_{\text{T}} = 12 - 1$$
$$= 11.$$

These values for df are entered in our summary table.

As a check on our calculations,

$$df_{\text{T}} = df_{\text{Bet}} + df_{\text{Subjects}} + df_{\text{Residual}}$$
$$11 = 1 + 5 + 5$$
$$11 = 11.$$

You will recall that in a one-way between-subjects ANOVA (reviewed in Chapter 11), the value of the F ratio is obtained by dividing the estimate of the population variance derived from the comparison of group means (MS_{Bet}) by the estimate of the population variance derived from within groups (MS_{W}). In a one-way within-subjects ANOVA, we also calculate an F ratio. However, the calculation of the MS_{Bet} takes into account that each subject experiences every treatment level. As a result, the variability due to preexisting subject differences is not included in the calculation of the MS_{Bet} and thus is not included in the numerator of the F ratio. In addition, as the SS_{Subjects} has been partitioned out of the SS_{W} in a within-subjects ANOVA, leaving only SS_{Residual}, the denominator of the F ratio is also reduced by eliminating the variability due to preexisting subject differences. As in a one-way between-subjects ANOVA, the F ratio for a one-way within-subjects ANOVA is the ratio of two estimates of population variability. However, in the within-subjects ANOVA, it is MS_{Bet} divided by MS_{Residual}. Each is found by dividing the appropriate SS by its df. Thus,

$$MS_{\text{Bet}} = \frac{SS_{\text{Bet}}}{df_{\text{Bet}}}$$

$$= \frac{0.75}{1}$$

$$= 0.75.$$

And

$$MS_{Residual} = \frac{SS_{Residual}}{df_{Residual}}$$

$$= \frac{14.75}{5}$$

$$= 2.95.$$

The final calculation is to determine the value of the F ratio. The equation for the F ratio for a one-way within-subjects ANOVA is as follows:

$$F = \frac{MS_{Bet}}{MS_{Residual}}$$

$$= \frac{0.75}{2.95}$$

$$= 0.25.$$

The table is now complete (Table 12.6).

Recall that if the independent variable had no effect, we would expect the value of the F ratio to equal 1. As our value is less than 1, we know without entering the F table that this outcome is not statistically significant. Nevertheless, if you wanted to use the F table to find the critical value of F, you would locate the column corresponding to the degrees of freedom of our numerator and the row corresponding to the degrees of freedom of our denominator. From Table 12.6, we see that for our F this would be 1 and 5 *df*, respectively. We chose an α of .05. At the intersection of our column and row in the F table, we find the critical value of 6.61. As our obtained F of 0.25 is less than the critical value, we retain the null hypothesis that the fuel additive did not affect the gas mileage.

Table 12.6	First Example: Completed Summary Table for the One-Way Within-Subjects ANOVA

Source of Variation	SS	df	MS	F
Between levels	0.75	1	0.75	0.25
Subjects	204.75	5		
Within residual	14.75	5	2.95	
Total	220.25	11		

Note. ANOVA, analysis of variance; *SS*, sum of squares; *df*, degrees of freedom; *MS*, mean square.

Since the F was not significant, we do not calculate the effect size, eta squared (η^2), which would give the percentage of variance explained by the treatment. And even if the F was significant, we would not conduct a post hoc test as this study had only two treatment levels, and consequently, we would already know which treatment levels differed from each other.

Reporting the Results of a One-Way Within-Subjects ANOVA

In a paper, we would indicate the F ratio that was obtained as well as the degrees of freedom used. Specifically, we would report that the fuel additive was not found to affect vehicle mileage ($F(1, 5) = 0.25, p > .05$). Note the direction of the > sign.

PROGRESS CHECK

1. Compared with a one-way between-subjects ANOVA, in a one-way within-subjects ANOVA the denominator of the F ratio is decreased by ____ the variability due to error.

2. The one-way within-subjects ANOVA is a procedure which eliminates ____ subject differences.

3. In a one-way within-subjects ANOVA, the denominator of the F ratio consists only of ____.

Answers: 1. reducing. 2. preexisting. 3. residual error.

A SECOND EXAMPLE

Our next example will show that the one-way within-subjects ANOVA can be used when there are more than two measures from each subject. Anxiety, a sense of apprehension so severe that it interferes with living, is the most prevalent psychological disorder in America. Fortunately, many people who suffer from anxiety report at least some relief by engaging in regular exercise of at least 30 minutes a day. Let us assume that you are a researcher and you are interested in whether exercise of less than 30 minutes a day affects anxiety. You decide to utilize a within-subjects design in which each subject engages in three different levels of exercise (this is a repeated measures design), each for a 2-week period. Your null hypothesis is that exercise will not affect anxiety, and you set α equal to .05. To control for order effects, which occur when a particular sequence of treatments has a unique outcome, you assign the sequence of the treatment levels randomly to each subject. At the end of each 2-week exercise period, you measure each subject's anxiety. The hypothetical scores, squared deviations, treatment level means, and each subject's total are presented in Table 12.7.

Table 12.7 Second Example

Subject	No Exercise			10 Minutes of Exercise			30 Minutes of Exercise			Subject Totals
	X_1	X_1-M_1	$(X_1-M_1)^2$	X_2	X_2-M_2	$(X_2-M_2)^2$	X_3	X_3-M_3	$(X_3-M_3)^2$	$(\sum X_{\text{subject}})$
1	98	4	16	96	3	9	84	2.80	7.84	278
2	96	2	4	95	2	4	81	-0.20	0.04	272
3	95	1	1	95	2	4	82	0.80	0.64	272
4	91	-3	9	91	-2	4	80	-1.20	1.44	262
5	90	-4	16	88	-5	25	79	-2.20	4.84	257
	$\sum X_1 = 470$	$\sum x_1 = 0$	$\sum x_1^2 = 46$	$\sum X_2 = 465$	$\sum x_2 = 0$	$\sum x_2^2 = 46$	$\sum X_3 = 406$	$\sum X_3 = 0$	$\sum x_3^2 = 14.80$	$\sum(\sum x_{\text{subject}}) = 1341$
	$n = 5$			$n = 5$			$n = 5$			
	$M_1 = 470/5$			$M_2 = 465/5$			$M_3 = 406/5$			
	$= 94$			$= 93$			$= 81.20$			

We begin with the same summary table used in our previous example (Table 12.3). As each value is calculated, it is entered into the table. We begin our calculations by finding our SS. Remember,

$$SS_T = SS_{Bet} + SS_W,$$

where $SS_W = SS_{Subjects} + SS_{Residual}$.

As before, we begin by finding SS_T:

$$SS_T = \Sigma(X - M_G)^2,$$

where M_G is the mean of all of the scores, in other words, the grand mean. It is found by using the following equation:

$$M_G = \frac{\Sigma X}{N},$$

where N is the total number of scores.

For our example with a total of 15 scores from 5 subjects, this calculation is shown in Table 12.8.

Table 12.8   Calculation of M_G and SS_T for the Second Example

X	X – M_G	(X – M_G)²
98	8.60	73.96
96	6.60	43.56
95	5.60	31.36
91	1.60	2.56
90	0.60	0.36
96	6.60	43.56
95	5.60	31.36
95	5.60	31.36
91	1.60	2.56
88	−1.40	1.96

X	X – M_G	(X – M_G)^2
84	−5.40	29.16
81	−8.40	70.56
82	−7.40	54.76
80	−9.40	88.36
79	−10.40	108.16
$\Sigma X = 1341$ $N = 15$ $M_G = 1341/15$ $= 89.40$	$\Sigma(X - M_G) = 0$	$\Sigma(X - M_G)^2 = 613.60 = SS_T$

The SS_{Bet} is found as in a between-subjects ANOVA by determining the square of the deviations of each treatment level mean from the grand mean and then multiplying by the number of subjects. Conceptually,

$$SS_{Bet} = \Sigma[(M - M_G)^2 n],$$

where n is the number of subjects.

For our example,

$$SS_{Bet} = (94 - 89.40)^2(5) + (93 - 89.40)^2(5) + (81.20 - 89.40)^2(5)$$

$$= (4.60)^2(5) + (3.60)^2(5) + (-8.20)^2(5)$$

$$= (21.16)(5) + (12.96)(5) + (67.24)(5)$$

$$= 105.80 + 64.80 + 336.20$$

$$= 506.80.$$

Recall that in a within-subjects ANOVA, the variability due to preexisting subject differences is not included in SS_{Bet} as each subject experiences each treatment level.

As SS_T and SS_{Bet} have both been determined, SS_W can be found using the equation $SS_T = SS_{Bet} + SS_W$. Alternatively, SS_W can be found by subtracting each treatment level mean from a score and squaring this deviation. The sum of these squared deviations for all of the scores in each of the treatment levels would be SS_W. Thus, conceptually,

$$SS_W = \Sigma[\Sigma(X - M)^2],$$

where M is the mean of a treatment level.

In other words, with three groups,

$$SS_W = \sum x_1^2 + \sum x_2^2 + \sum x_3^2.$$

Fortunately, we have already calculated these values in Table 12.7.

$$SS_W = 46 + 46 + 14.80$$

$$= 106.80.$$

This value is *not* entered into our ANOVA table, for by using a within-subjects design, we are able to partition it into $SS_{Subjects}$ and $SS_{Residual}$. However, we can check our calculations to this point, as

$$SS_T = SS_{Bet} + SS_W$$

$$613.60 = 506.80 + 106.80$$

$$613.60 = 613.60.$$

The $SS_{Subjects}$ is found by determining the square of the deviations of the mean of each subject's total from the grand mean and then multiplying by the number of treatment levels. Conceptually,

$$SS_{Subjects} = \left[\sum \left(\frac{\sum X_{Subject}}{k} - M_G \right)^2 \right] k,$$

where the subject's total, $\sum X_{Subject}$, is obtained from Table 12.7, the grand mean, M_G, from Table 12.8, and k is the number of treatment levels, in this case 3.

This calculation is shown in Table 12.9.

As you will see, this is the amount that the denominator of the F ratio is being reduced by using a within-subjects design.

As was noted previously, in a one-way within-subjects ANOVA,

$$SS_T = SS_{Bet} + SS_{Subjects} + SS_{Residual}.$$

To determine the $SS_{Residual}$, we subtract the value of $SS_{Subjects}$ from SS_W (remember, $SS_W = SS_{Subjects} + SS_{Residual}$). In our example, this would be $106.8 - 96.3 = 10.5$.

Having calculated the needed SS, we now must calculate the degrees of freedom for between levels, subjects, residual, and total. The degrees of freedom for between levels is equal to the number of treatment levels minus 1. Thus,

$$df_{Bet} = k - 1,$$

Table 12.9 Calculation of SS_{Subjects} for the Second Example

Subject	$\Sigma X_{\text{Subject}}$	$\dfrac{\Sigma X_{\text{Subject}}}{k}$	$\dfrac{\Sigma X_{\text{Subject}}}{k} - M_G$	$\left(\dfrac{\Sigma X_{\text{Subject}}}{k} - M_G\right)^2$
1	278	92.67	3.27	10.69
2	272	90.67	1.27	1.61
3	272	90.67	1.27	1.61
4	262	87.33	−2.07	4.28
5	257	85.67	−3.73	13.91
			$\Sigma\left(\dfrac{\Sigma X_{\text{Subject}}}{k} - M_G\right) = \text{approx.} 0$	$\Sigma\left(\dfrac{\Sigma X_{\text{Subject}}}{k} - M_G\right)^2 = 32.10$

(note there is a small amount of rounding error)

$$SS_{\text{Subjects}} = \left[\Sigma\left(\frac{\Sigma X_{\text{Subject}}}{k} - M_G\right)^2\right] k = (32.10)(3)$$

$$= 96.30$$

where k is the number of treatment levels.

In our example,

$$df_{\text{Bet}} = 3 - 1$$

$$= 2.$$

The degrees of freedom for subjects is equal to the number of subjects minus 1. Thus,

$$df_{\text{Subjects}} = n - 1,$$

where n is the number of subjects.

$$df_{\text{Subjects}} = 5 - 1$$

$$= 4.$$

This is the number of degrees of freedom in the denominator that are lost by using a within-subjects design.

To find the degrees of freedom for residual, we subtract 1 from the total number of subjects and multiply this by the number of levels of the independent variable minus 1. Thus,

$$df_{\text{Residual}} = (n - 1)(k - 1),$$

where n is the number of subjects and k is the number of levels. In our example,

$$df_{\text{Residual}} = (5 - 1)(3 - 1)$$

$$= 4 \times 2$$

$$= 8.$$

To find the degrees of freedom for total, we subtract 1 from the total number of data points. Thus,

$$df_{\text{T}} = N - 1,$$

where N is the total number of data points.

In our example,

$$df_{\text{T}} = 15 - 1$$

$$= 14.$$

As a check on our calculations,

$$df_{\text{T}} = df_{\text{Bet}} + df_{\text{Subjects}} + df_{\text{Residual}}$$

$$14 = 2 + 4 + 8$$

$$14 = 14.$$

For a within-subjects ANOVA, the variability due to preexisting subject differences is removed from both the numerator and the denominator of the F ratio. This occurs in the calculation of SS_{Bet} and by finding SS_{Residual}, which is equivalent to SS_{W} minus the preexisting subject differences (SS_{Subjects}). The F ratio thus consists of MS_{Bet} divided by MS_{Residual}. The MS_{Bet} and the MS_{Residual} are found by dividing the appropriate SS by its df. Thus,

$$MS_{\text{Bet}} = \frac{SS_{\text{Bet}}}{df_{\text{Bet}}}$$

$$= \frac{506.80}{2}$$

$$= 253.40.$$

And,

$$MS_{\text{Residual}} = \frac{SS_{\text{Residual}}}{df_{\text{Residual}}}$$

$$= \frac{10.50}{8}$$

$$= 1.310.$$

(Note that there is a small amount of rounding error.)

Finally, we calculate the F ratio:

$$F = \frac{MS_{\text{Bet}}}{MS_{\text{Residual}}}$$

$$= \frac{253.40}{1.31}$$

$$= 193.44.$$

This value is then entered in our table, and the table is complete (Table 12.10).

To determine whether this F ratio of 193.44 is statistically significant, in the F table, we would locate the column corresponding to the degrees of freedom of our numerator and the row corresponding to the degrees of freedom of our denominator. From Table 12.10, we see that for our F this would be 2 and 8 df, respectively. At the intersection of this column and row in the F table for an α of .05, the critical value is 4.46. As our obtained F of 193.44 is greater than the critical value, we reject the null hypothesis that exercise does not affect anxiety.

Table 12.10	Second Example: Completed Summary Table for the One-Way Within-Subjects ANOVA

Source of Variation	SS	df	MS	F
Between levels	506.80	2	253.40	193.44
Subjects	96.30	4		
Within residual	10.50	8	1.31	
Total	613.60	14		

Note. ANOVA, analysis of variance; *SS*, sum of squares; *df*, degrees of freedom; *MS*, mean square.

While a significant F indicates that the independent variable had an effect, with three or more treatment levels, it does not specify which treatment level means differ. The data obtained from each treatment level of a repeated measures ANOVA are based on the same subjects. Therefore, we do not talk of a difference between samples or groups, as there is only one sample or group of subjects that is being repeatedly tested. Instead, we have differences between treatment levels.

It was noted in Chapter 11 that the number of comparisons between sample (or treatment level) means, called pairwise comparisons, is given by the following equation:

$$\text{Number of pairwise comparisons} = \frac{k(k-1)}{2},$$

where k is the number of samples or treatment levels.

In our case, $k = 3$, so there are $[3(3 - 1)]/2$ pairwise comparisons. These 3 pairwise comparisons are between the mean of treatment Level I and the mean of Level II, the mean of Level II and the mean of Level III, and the mean of Level I and the mean of Level III. Any one, any two, or all three of these comparisons may be significant. The significant F simply indicates that at least one of the treatment level means differs from another. To specify which means differ, we conduct post hoc tests just as we did with the one-way between-subjects ANOVA in Chapter 11.

While there are a number of post hoc tests that can be used after a significant F ratio is found with the one-way within-subjects ANOVA, we will continue to employ Tukey's honestly significant difference (HSD) test. As you will recall from Chapter 11, calculation of Tukey's HSD leads to a critical value that is compared with the differences between each pair of treatment level means. Specifically, for the one-way within-subjects ANOVA,

$$\text{Critical value} = q\sqrt{\frac{MS_{\text{Residual}}}{n}},$$

where q is found from the q table and where $n = $ the number of subjects.

To find the critical value, we now substitute into this equation the value for MS_{Residual}, which is 1.31. The n is equal to 5. The value for q is found in the q table (Appendix J, Table J.5). The column to use is determined by the number of means being compared, in our case 3. The row is determined by the degrees of freedom of the MS_{Residual}, in our case 8. With α equal to .05, q is equal to 4.05. We can now find the critical value:

$$\text{Critical value} = 4.05\sqrt{\frac{1.31}{5}}$$

$$= 4.05\sqrt{0.262}$$

$$= (4.05)(0.512)$$

$$= 2.07.$$

The difference between means for a pairwise comparison must be *as great or greater* than the critical value from Tukey's HSD to be considered significantly different. With large ANOVAs, it is wise to construct a table with all of the pairwise comparisons in order to ensure that none is overlooked. As we are only making three pairwise comparisons, we can dispense with the table and simply list them:

Difference between the means of treatment Level I and Level II = 94 − 93 = 1.

Difference between the means of Level I and Level III = 94 − 81.2 = 12.8.

Difference between the means of Level II and Level III = 93 − 81.2 = 11.8.

It is important to note that when comparing the differences between treatment level means (in our case 1, 12.8, and 11.8) to the critical value, we ignore the sign as this simply indicates the order of the treatment level means in the subtraction. Our critical value is 2.07. Therefore, the difference between the means of treatment Level I and Level II, which is 1, is not statistically significant. The differences between the means of Level I and Level III, which is 12.8, and between the means of Level II and Level III, which is 11.8, are statistically significant.

To ascertain the percentage of variance explained by the treatment with a within-subjects ANOVA, we calculate what is called partial eta squared (η_P^2). It is interpreted in essentially the same manner as eta squared in a between-subjects ANOVA. With a one-way within-subjects ANOVA, the equation for partial eta squared is as follows:

$$\eta_P^2 = \frac{SS_{\text{Bet}}}{SS_{\text{T}} - SS_{\text{Subjects}}},$$

where η_P^2 is the proportion of variance explained by the treatment.

In our example,

$$\eta_P^2 = \frac{506.80}{613.60 - 96.30}$$

$$= \frac{506.80}{517.30}$$

$$= 0.98 \text{ or } 98\%.$$

Reporting the Results of a One-Way Within-Subjects ANOVA

In a paper, we would indicate the *F* ratio that was obtained as well as the degrees of freedom used, which pairwise comparisons were significant, and the measure of effect size. Specifically, we would report,

The treatment level means were found to differ ($F(2, 8) = 193.44$, $p < .05$). Tukey's HSD test indicated that the 30 minutes a day exercise condition led to a decrease in anxiety compared to the control condition, no difference was found between the control and the 10 minutes a day conditions; and the 30 minutes a day exercise condition led to lower anxiety than the 10 minutes condition. A measure of effect size, η_p^2, was found to equal .98.

I want to point out to the readers of this book that the data were created as an example, and an effect size of .98 is much larger than is likely to be found in the real world. It indicates that 98% of the variability in the dependent variable (anxiety) can be explained by the independent variable (exercise condition). Less than 2% of the variability, then, is due to all other factors, which is a very unlikely outcome.

Purpose and Limitations of Using the One-Way Within-Subjects ANOVA

1. *Test for difference:* The null hypothesis is that the treatment does not have an effect. Therefore, if the null is correct, any difference between the means of the treatment levels is due to chance. The alternative hypothesis is that the treatment does have an effect.

2. *Does not provide a measure of effect size:* The one-way within-subjects ANOVA, like the one-way between-subjects ANOVA, is a test of significance. It indicates whether or not an outcome is likely to have occurred by chance if the null hypothesis is correct. If the F test is significant, a measure of effect size, such as partial eta squared (η_p^2), should then be calculated.

3. *Sample size is important:* For the one-way within-subjects ANOVA, if the sample size is 30 or greater, then the assumption that the population is normally distributed can be safely ignored. If the sample size is less than 30, then it is important that the underlying populations be normally distributed. If you cannot collect a larger sample and have reason to believe that the assumption of normality may not have been met, it is best to turn to an alternative test.

4. *Compares two or more treatment level means:* The one-way within-subjects ANOVA is appropriate to use when each subject is assigned to every treatment level.

5. *Does not indicate where the difference is:* With designs with more than two treatment levels, a significant F should be followed with a post hoc procedure such as Tukey's HSD test to identify which treatment level means differ.

Assumptions of the One-Way Within-Subjects ANOVA

1. *Interval or ratio data:* The data are on an interval scale of measurement or a ratio scale of measurement.

2. *Random sample:* The subjects are drawn at random from a population.

3. *Independence within treatment levels:* The data within each treatment level are independent.

4. *Normally distributed populations:* The population at each treatment level is normally distributed.

5. *Population variances are equal:* The populations for each treatment level have equal variances.

6. *No carryover effects:* Having received one treatment level does not affect a subject's response to another treatment level.

Effect of Violating the Assumptions

As has been noted previously, the *F* test has been found to be robust—it often leads to accurate decisions even when an assumption is violated. However, when using a repeated measures design, a researcher should be particularly concerned with carryover effects. Also, if subjects are not randomly drawn, then you have a quasi-experiment and thus less confidence in the interpretation of a statistically significant outcome.

CONCLUSION

The one-way within-subjects ANOVA is a flexible, commonly employed statistical test to determine if treatment level means differ. Though somewhat tedious to calculate by hand, statistical packages such as SPSS make this a most useful statistical procedure.

As both the one-way between-subjects ANOVA and the one-way within-subjects ANOVA compare two or more treatment level means, it is important to understand the advantages and disadvantages of each. As noted at the beginning of this chapter, the one-way within-subjects ANOVA partitions out the $SS_{Subjects}$ from the SS_W. Assuming that $SS_{Subjects}$ is greater than 0, $SS_{Residual}$ will be smaller than SS_W, and thus, all else being equal, the resulting *F* ratio will be larger than if a one-way between-subjects ANOVA had been utilized. As a larger *F* ratio is more likely to be found to be statistically significant, you might wonder why anyone would conduct a one-way between-subjects ANOVA. There are a number of reasons. First, you lose degrees of freedom with the one-way within-subjects ANOVA *F* ratio compared with the one-way between-subjects ANOVA. For instance, in Table 12.10, $df_{Residual}$ is 8. However, if this had been a one-way between-subjects ANOVA, the df_W would have been 12 (remember, $df_W = df_{Subjects} + df_{Residual}$). As an examination of the F table will indicate, this loss of 4 df results in a larger value of F being needed to conclude that a difference is statistically significant. In other words, with a one-way within-subjects ANOVA, the F ratio is likely to be larger than with a one-way between-subjects ANOVA, but as the degrees of freedom will definitely be smaller a larger F ratio will be needed. Whether you gain more with the larger F than you lose due to the smaller degrees of freedom with the one-way within-subjects ANOVA will depend on the specific situation. In addition, with a repeated measures design (which would utilize a one-way within-subjects ANOVA), the experimenter needs to be concerned with treatment order effects. This was mentioned previously in Chapter 10, but the basic idea is that with a repeated measures design, it is being assumed that it does not matter what order subjects are receiving their treatments. In some situations, however, this is unlikely to be the case. For instance, let's assume that in one condition subjects are assigned to run 100 meters and in another condition they run 10,000 meters. If there was not a very substantial rest period between the two conditions, it seems likely that running the long distance first would have a more dramatic effect on subjects' ability to run the short distance than the reverse. Another drawback to the repeated measures design is that subjects may not be willing to commit to repeated testing and thus will drop out of the study. As a consequence of these limitations, the between-subjects design is much more commonly used than the repeated measures design, and thus, the one-way between-subjects ANOVA is more commonly used than the one-way within-subjects ANOVA. However, the repeated measures design, and thus the one-way within-subjects ANOVA, can be very useful, particularly if there are only a limited number of subjects available to be tested.

FINAL THOUGHTS ON THE RELATIONSHIP BETWEEN THE ONE-WAY WITHIN-SUBJECTS ANOVA AND THE DEPENDENT SAMPLES *t* TEST

Though the calculations for the dependent samples t test (reviewed in Chapter 10) and the one-way within-subjects ANOVA with two measures for each subject appear to be quite different, these tests are closely related. In fact, the outcome of the dependent samples t test and the outcome of the one-way within-subjects ANOVA are mathematically related in the same way that the independent t and the one-way between-subjects ANOVA are related:

$$F = t^2.$$

Substituting the value of –0.50 that was found using the dependent samples t test (the data are from Table 10.6), we would have,

$$F = -0.50^2 = 0.25,$$

the same value of F we found in this chapter with the same data (Table 12.6).

Thus, assuming you have interval or ratio data with two measures from each subject, you can consider conducting either a dependent samples t test or a one-way within-subjects ANOVA. Both will always lead to the same decision to retain or reject the null hypothesis.

Chapter Resources

GLOSSARY OF TERMS

Preexisting subject differences: relatively stable subject characteristics. These differences between subjects are a form of error in an ANOVA.

Residual error: changeable subject characteristics. These differences between subjects are a form of error in an ANOVA.

Questions: Chapter 12

(Answers to odd-numbered items are provided in Appendix I.)

1. Compared to the one-way between-subjects ANOVA, the one-way within-subjects ANOVA _____.

   a. reduces the size of the F ratio
   b. eliminates preexisting subject differences
   c. reduces residual error
   d. increases the size of the numerator of the F ratio

2. In the one-way within-subjects ANOVA, the SS_W is partitioned into _____.

   a. $SS_{Subjects}$ and $SS_{Residual}$
   b. SS_T and SS_{Bet}
   c. $SS_{Subjects}$ and SS_{Bet}
   d. SS_T and $SS_{Residual}$

3. M_G is the mean of _____.

   a. the scores in the largest group
   b. the scores in the first experimental condition
   c. the scores in the smallest group
   d. all of the scores

4. If the *F* is *not* significant, we _____.

   a. do not calculate the effect size, partial eta squared η_p^2

   b. can be absolutely certain that our independent variable did not have an effect

   c. should consider conducting the study again, but this time with fewer subjects

5. If the *F* is significant, and we have more than 2 treatment levels for each subject, we would _____.

   a. calculate the effect size, partial eta squared η_p^2

   b. conduct post hoc tests, such as Tukey's HSD

   c. both of the above

   d. none of the above

6. Compared to the one-way between-subjects ANOVA, in a one-way within-subjects ANOVA _____.

   a. there is a loss of *df*

   b. a larger *F* value is needed

   c. it is easier to conduct as there are fewer calculations

   d. both "a" and "b," but not "c"

   e. both "a" and "c," but not "b"

7. Which is more commonly utilized, the one-way between-subjects ANOVA or the one-way within-subjects ANOVA?

   a. One-way between-subjects ANOVA

   b. One-way within-subjects ANOVA

   c. Both are used approximately equally often

8. Eye color is an example of ___ and catching a cold is an example of ___.

   a. residual error; residual error

   b. residual error; preexisting subject differences

   c. preexisting subject differences; preexisting subject differences

   d. preexisting subject differences; residual error

9. The *F* ratio for a one-way within-subjects ANOVA is equal to ___.

   a. MS_{Bet}/MS_W

   b. $MS_{Bet}/MS_{Subjects}$

   c. $MS_{Bet}/MS_{Residual}$

   d. MS_{Bet}/SS_{Total}

10. If your design has 10 treatment levels, how many post hoc pairwise comparisons would there be?

    a. 3

    b. 10

    c. 33

    d. 45

11. If in a paper you read ($F(3, 9) = 61.44$, $p < .05$), what does the number 3 refer to?

    a. df_{Bet}

    b. $df_{Subjects}$

    c. $df_{Residual}$

    d. df_T

12. With a one-way within-subjects ANOVA, partial eta squared is the ___.

    a. proportion of variance explained by the subjects

    b. proportion of variance explained by the treatment

    c. proportion of variance explained by the error

    d. proportion of variance explained by the residual

For Questions 13 to 16, we are going to use the same data as in Chapter 11 except that we now assume there are only a total of six students and each student took different versions of the exam in the quiet, moderately noisy, and noisy environments. Compare each of your answers to the answer you calculated in Chapter 11.

Student	Level of Background Noise		
	Quiet	Moderate	Noisy
1	9	7	6
2	10	9	8
3	8	8	10
4	13	13	7
5	12	11	11
6	14	12	12

13. What is the *SS* for the level of background noise?

    a. 2

    b. 12

    c. 2.432

    d. 6

14. What is the *df* for the level of background noise?

    a. 2

    b. 12

    c. 2.432

    d. 6

15. What is the *MS* for the level of background noise?

    a. 2

    b. 12

    c. 2.432

    d. 6

16. What is the *F* for the level of background noise?

    a. 2

    b. 12

    c. 2.432

    d. 6

Problems 17 to 20 utilize SPSS.

SPSS

USING SPSS WITH THE ONE-WAY WITHIN-SUBJECTS ANOVA

To Begin SPSS

Step 1: The first step, as always, is to activate the program.

   Step 2: Click on "Type in data" and then click on "OK."

   Step 3: Click on "Variable View." We will only be dealing with the columns headed by "Name," "Label," "Values," and "Measure."

   Step 4: Click on the first empty cell under the column heading "Name." You now type the name of the first variable for which you have data. We are going to utilize the same data and labels as were previously employed in Table 12.2. These data dealt with the question of whether a fuel additive changed vehicle mileage. We have called these variables "Milewo" (for mileage without an additive) and "Milew" (for mileage with an additive). Therefore, type "Milewo" in the first empty cell under "Name."

Step 5: Click twice on the first empty cell under the column heading "Label." In this cell, you can type a more extensive description of your variable. In our case, type "Vehicle Mileage Without Additive." Note that to see the entire label, you may need to expand the size of this cell by placing your cursor on the right border of the "Label" heading and moving to the right.

Step 6: Check the first cell under the column heading "Measure." As we are dealing with mileage, be certain that "Scale" is present.

Step 7: Repeat Steps 4 to 7 except that you type "Milew" in the first empty cell under "Name" and "Vehicle Mileage With Additive" for the label. Finally, select "Scale" in the column under the column heading "Measure" as we have interval or ratio data. The result is shown in Figure 12.1.

To Enter Data in SPSS

Step 8: Click on the "Data View" option at the lower left-hand corner of the "Variable View" window. The variables "Milewo" and "Milew" will be evident.

Step 9: Our data consist of two mileages for each of six vehicles. For each vehicle, enter its mileages in the appropriate columns, as is shown in Figure 12.2.

Figure 12.1   Variable View Window

Name	Type	Width	Decimals	Label	Values	Missing	Columns	Align	Measure	Role
Milewo	Numeric	8	2	Vehicle Mileage Without Additive	None	None	8	Right	Scale	Input
Milew	Numeric	8	2	Vehicle Mileage With Additive	None	None	8	Right	Scale	Input

Figure 12.2   Entering Data

Milewo	Milew
12.00	13.00
13.00	15.00
15.00	14.00
17.00	17.00
20.00	24.00
25.00	22.00

To Conduct a One-Way Within-Subjects ANOVA

Step 10: Click the cursor on "Analyze" along the row of SPSS commands above the data you entered, then move to "General Linear Model," then click on "Repeated Measures."

Step 11: A new window will appear. This asks for the "Within-Subject Factor Name." In our case, mileage would be an appropriate name. This is indicated by typing "Mileage" in the box with "Factor 1" in it and "2" for the "Number of Levels." Then click on "Add" (Figure 12.3).

Step 12: Click "Define" and a new window will appear (Figure 12.4). Move each of the labels on the left to the box on the right by clicking on the label and then on the top arrow pointing to the right. The result will appear as is shown in Figure 12.5.

Figure 12.3   Repeated Measures Window

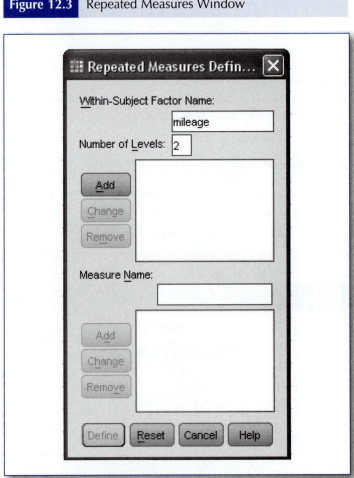

Figure 12.4 Defining the Repeated Measures Variable

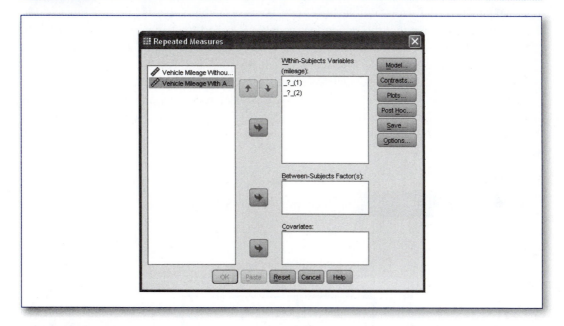

Figure 12.5 Defining the Repeated Measures Variable

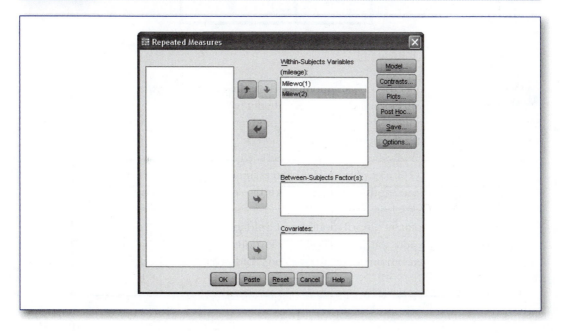

Step 13: Click "OK," and SPSS will conduct the one-way within-subjects ANOVA. The print-out is quite complex. The parts of the output that we are interested in reading have the headings "Within-Subjects Factors" (Table 12.11) and "Tests of Within-Subjects Effects" (Table 12.12). The first table indicates that the dependent variable is called "mileage" and it has two levels, "Milewo" and "Milew." The second table is of more interest. Refer to the two rows labeled "Sphericity Assumed." What you will see is essentially the same result for the ANOVA as we previously created with hand calculations (Table 12.6).

To confirm that you understand how to use SPSS, redo the one-way within-subjects ANOVA that was calculated in the text for the data in Table 12.7, but this time using SPSS. Then redo the ANOVA dealing with level of background noise (Questions 13–16) to check your answers.

Table 12.11   SPSS Output, Within-Subjects Factors

Within   – Subjects Factors

Measure:MEASURE_1

mileage	Dependent Variable
1	Milewo
2	Milew

Table 12.12   SPSS Output, Tests of Within-Subjects Effects

Tests of Within -Subjects Effects
Measure:MEASURE_1

Source		Type III Sum of Squares	df	Mean Square	F	Sig.
mileage	Sphericity Assumed	.750	1	.750	.254	.636
	Greenhouse–Geisser	.750	1.000	.750	.254	.636
	Huynh–Feldt	.750	1.000	.750	.254	.636
	Lower-bound	.750	1.000	.750	.254	.636
Error(mileage)	Sphericity Assumed	14.750	5	2.950		
	Greenhouse–Geisser	14.750	5.000	2.950		
	Huynh–Feldt	14.750	5.000	2.950		
	Lower-bound	14.750	5.000	2.950		

SPSS Problems: Chapter 12

Problems 17 to 20 are based on the same data as was used for Questions 13 to 16 except that we now want to determine the effect of adding a constant (in this case 10) to every score in the noisy condition. (Compare your answers to the Answers for Questions 13 to 16 and the answers in Chapter 11.)

Student	Level of Background Noise		
	Quiet	Moderate	Noisy
1	9	7	16
2	10	9	18
3	8	8	20
4	13	13	17
5	12	11	21
6	14	12	22

17. What is the *SS* for the level of background noise?

   a. 2

   b. 12

   c. 292

   d. 6

18. What is the *df* for the level of background noise?

   a. 2

   b. 12

   c. 2.432

   d. 6

19. What is the *MS* for the level of background noise?

   a. 2

   b. 12

   c. 2.432

   d. 146

20. What is the *F* for the level of background noise?

    a. 2.659

    b. 14.443

    c. 26.5

    d. 59.189

13

FINDING DIFFERENCES WITH INTERVAL AND RATIO DATA—V

The Two-Way Between-Subjects ANOVA

Oh, fancies that might be, oh facts that are!

—Robert Browning

I n Chapter 11, we reviewed the one-way between-subjects ANOVA (analysis of variance). The logic was straightforward: Identify an independent variable (IV), and then, isolate its effect through random assignment of subjects and careful experimental design. Comparison of the control and experimental group(s) then led to a decision concerning the effect of the IV on the dependent variable (DV). This has proven to be a very valuable approach and the one-way between-subjects ANOVA is among the most commonly used of all statistical procedures. In Chapter 12, we reviewed the one-way within-subjects ANOVA, a useful alternative to a between-subjects design. Nevertheless, because these ANOVAs examine the effect of one IV at a time, they are limited. In the real world, we are simultaneously affected by numerous variables. For instance, your comprehension of this chapter will depend on many factors including how much sleep you got last night, whether you are under time pressure, how noisy the background is, and your understanding of previous chapters, to name just a few. In this chapter, we will learn that the ANOVA can be utilized when there is more than one IV. We will only be discussing the situation where there are two IVs. Though the ANOVA can maintain the experiment-wise error rate while simultaneously dealing with an unlimited number of IVs, the analysis quickly becomes difficult to interpret.

TWO-WAY BETWEEN-SUBJECTS ANOVA

In Chapter 11, we learned that when dealing with the ANOVA, each IV is called a factor. Thus, the single-factor or one-way between-subjects ANOVA has only one IV, and if it is a true experiment, each subject is randomly assigned to one level of the IV. ANOVAs with more than one factor are called factorial ANOVAs. If there are two IVs, each with two levels, this would be a 2 × 2 factorial ANOVA. If there were two IVs, one with two levels and the other with three levels, this would be a 2 × 3 factorial ANOVA. If there were three IVs, one with two levels and two with three levels, this would be a 2 × 3 × 3 factorial ANOVA. In this chapter, we will only be dealing with designs with two IVs and where each subject experiences one combination of treatment levels. We will, accordingly, be studying what is called the two-way between-subjects ANOVA or two-factor between-subjects ANOVA. In Table 13.1, the specific procedure that we will be considering is underlined.

With a two-way ANOVA, we can examine the effect of each of the two IVs separately. The two-way ANOVA is, therefore, somewhat like simultaneously conducting two, one-way ANOVAs. In addition, however, with a two-way ANOVA, we can also examine how the two IVs interact with each other. For instance, it has been reported in a number of publications that childhood maltreatment leads to antisocial adult behavior. This effect is sometimes summarized by saying that childhood abuse runs in families. In other words, it has been accepted that there is a relationship between the level of an IV (childhood abuse) and the magnitude of a DV (subsequent degree of antisocial adult behavior). Caspi et al. (2002) reexamined the long-term effects of childhood maltreatment. This study differed from the previous research by including a second IV, the presence or absence in the subjects of a gene encoding the monoamine oxidase A (MAOA) enzyme. It was found that those men with low MAOA levels were much more likely to have a record of antisocial behavior, but only if they had been abused as children. The men with high MAOA levels were not antisocial even if they had been abused as children. This study suggests, therefore, that our previous interpretation was only partially correct. While there is a link between childhood abuse and adult antisocial behavior, this relationship appears to be dependent on the individual's genetic makeup. In other words, Caspi et al. (2002) found that antisocial adult behavior is only enhanced when two factors both occur together. Neither, by itself, is sufficient to lead to elevated rates of adult antisocial behavior. This dependency of an effect on a combination of factors is called an **interaction**.

Interaction: a change in the dependent variable that is due to the presence of a particular combination of independent variables.

We are all familiar with the concept of an interaction. For instance, physicians warn against taking particular combinations of medications. Though each medication may be helpful by itself,

Table 13.1	Overview of Inferential Statistical Procedures for Difference and Interaction Designs

			Type of Data		
	Nominal (Frequency)			**Ordinal** (Ranked)	**Interval/Ratio** (Continuous Measure)

Inferential Statistics (Finding Relationships)

Statistical procedures for difference and interaction designs

	Nominal	Ordinal design	Ordinal	Interval/Ratio
One variable with at least two outcomes	Goodness-of-fit chi-square	**One IV with one sample—one DV**		One-sample *z* score or one-sample *t* test
		One IV with two or more independent samples—one DV	*Kruskal–Wallis H*	One-way between-subjects ANOVA (only two independent samples—independent samples *t* test)
		One IV with one sample having two or more repeated measures—one DV		One-way within-subjects ANOVA (only two repeated measures—dependent samples *t* test)
Two variables, each with at least two outcomes	Chi-square test of independence	**Two IV each with two or more independent samples—one DV**		Two-way between-subjects ANOVA

Notes. IV, independent variable; DV, dependent variable; ANOVA, analysis of variance. Research designs are shown in boldface. The italicized item is reviewed in Appendix A.

the combination may definitely not be. It is also widely known that the combination of two useful household cleaners, ammonia and chlorine bleach, will lead to the production of chlorine gas which is very dangerous. Finally, the author of this book likes to eat pickles and also likes ice cream, but the combination of pickles and ice cream is definitely not appealing. Thus, in an interaction, the combined effect of two factors is not simply the sum of the effects of the two factors alone.

One of the most useful techniques to assist in interpreting interactions is to graph the outcome. Returning to the Caspi et al. (2002) study that examined the long-term effects of childhood maltreatment, we could assign one of our IVs, childhood maltreatment, to the *X* axis, the amount of adult antisocial behavior, the DV, to the *Y* axis, and then plot the outcome for our two levels of the second IV, genetic makeup. The result is illustrated in Figure 13.1.

The advantage of a graph is that the interaction is evident at a glance. The level of adult antisocial behavior is only increased if there was a history of maltreatment and if the individual had low MAOA activity.

Now let us compare what the graph would have looked like if there had not been an interaction. Specifically, if the outcome had been that both IVs had an effect, but there was no interaction between the two factors, we might find an outcome as in Figure 13.2.

Main effect: with a factorial ANOVA, another term used for an independent variable.

In this example, childhood maltreatment would have increased adult antisocial behavior, and low MAOA activity would also have been associated with higher adult antisocial behavior. Thus, in this example, both IVs had an effect. In a two-way ANOVA, each IV is called a **main effect**. However, in this example, there is no interaction as no particular combination of the IVs causes a unique change in the DV. In this case, any outcome is explained by adding the separate effects of each IV.

With a two-way ANOVA, three *F* ratios are calculated. One *F* ratio is calculated for each of the two possible main effects, and a third *F* ratio is calculated to determine if there is an

Figure 13.1   An Example of an Interaction

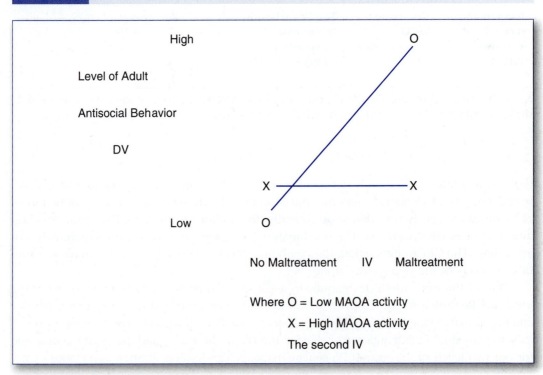

Figure 13.2   An Example of Two Main Effects but No Interaction

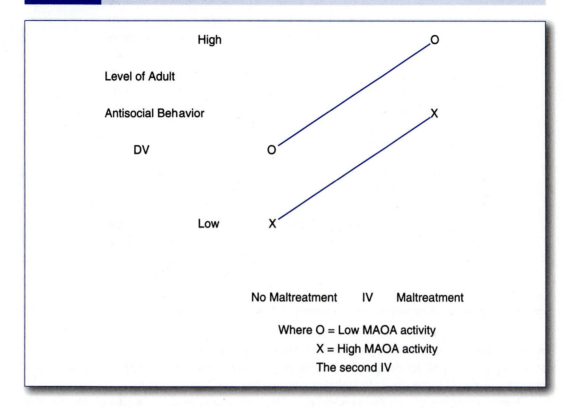

High

Level of Adult

Antisocial Behavior

DV

Low

No Maltreatment   IV   Maltreatment

Where O = Low MAOA activity
X = High MAOA activity
The second IV

interaction. Any combination of these *F* ratios can be significant, and it is possible that none of the three *F* ratios will be significant. In other words, one or both of the main effects might be found to be significant, and the *F* ratio for the interaction could be significant regardless of whether a main effect was found to be significant. For instance, returning to our example of the effects of maltreatment, Figure 13.3 would be an example of a significant interaction, though neither main effect is significant.

If the results had been as shown in Figure 13.3, there would not be a main effect for the maltreatment IV since the overall level of adult antisocial behavior is the same regardless of whether the child was maltreated or not. Similarly, with the results portrayed in Figure 13.3, there is no main effect for the MAOA activity IV since the overall level of adult antisocial behavior is the same regardless of the subject's MAOA activity. However, there is an interaction. As drawn, the results would indicate that there would be an increase in adult antisocial behavior either with no maltreatment and high MAOA activity, or with maltreatment and low MAOA activity. When an interaction is found to be significant, it, not the main effects, becomes the center of our attention. We return now to Figure 13.1, which is a representation of the

| Figure 13.3 | An Example of a Significant Interaction but No Significant Main Effects |

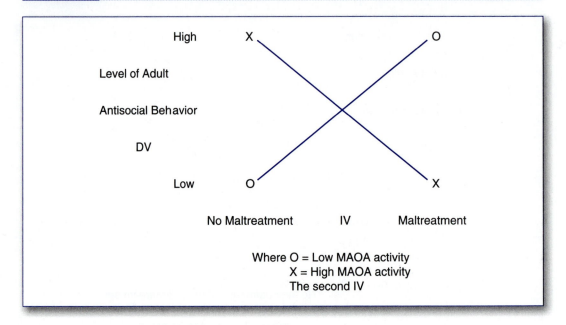

results actually found by Caspi et al. (2002). The interaction suggests that, in addition to trying to reduce the overall level of maltreatment, to counter adult antisocial behavior, we might consider a special focus on male children who exhibit low MAOA activity.

The two-way between-subjects ANOVA can be understood as an extension of the one-way between-subjects ANOVA that was covered in Chapter 11. With the one-way between-subjects ANOVA, we find two estimates of the population variance (σ_X^2). The within-groups estimate is called the mean square within (MS_W). The MS_W is the estimate of σ_X^2 obtained by pooling the variances derived from each score's deviation from its *sample mean*. It is thus based on the variability within each of the samples or experimental groups. Since each subject within an experimental group receives the same level of the treatment, this variability is not a result of the IV and, instead, is due to other sources of variability, which we collectively call error. The other estimate of σ_X^2 in a one-way between-subjects ANOVA is called the mean square between (MS_{Bet}). The MS_{Bet} is the estimate of σ_X^2 based on the deviations of each sample mean from the grand mean (M_G). In other words, it is based on the variability between the samples. Since each experimental group receives a different level of the treatment, this variability is the result of the IV as well as error. Thus, with the one-way between-subjects ANOVA, we have two methods for estimating σ_X^2. If the samples are all drawn from populations with the same mean (in other words, there is no treatment effect), these two estimates of σ_X^2 will be approximately the same. However, if the samples are drawn from populations with different means, which would be true if the IV had an effect, the two estimates of σ_X^2 may differ substantially.

With the one-way between-subjects ANOVA, we calculate one F ratio. If there is no treatment effect, this ratio of $(MS_{Bet})/(MS_W)$ should be approximately 1. If there is a treatment effect, the F ratio will be greater than 1.

With a two-way between-subjects ANOVA, there is still a within-groups estimate of σ_X^2, the MS_W. However, with a two-way between-subjects ANOVA, the SS_{Bet} (sum of squares between), which is the basis for the MS_{Bet}, is partitioned to create an estimate of σ_X^2 from each of the two IVs as well as an estimate from the interaction between the IVs. With ANOVAs, you will recall that IVs are called factors. Therefore, it is customary to say that we partition the SS_{Bet} that is used to create the MS_{Bet} estimate of σ_X^2 into the variability accounted for by Factor A, the variability accounted for by Factor B, and the variability accounted for by the interaction between Factor A and Factor B, which is represented as A × B. The variability accounted for by Factor A is used to create a new estimate of σ_X^2 called the mean square for Factor A (MS_A). The variability accounted for by Factor B is used to create a second estimate of σ_X^2 called the mean square for Factor B (MS_B). (It is important to note that MS_B is not the same as MS_{Bet}.) Finally, the variability accounted for by the interaction of Factor A and Factor B is used to create a third estimate of σ_X^2 called the mean square for the interaction of Factors A and B ($MS_{A \times B}$). We will, therefore, be calculating three F ratios with a two-way between-subjects ANOVA:

$$F_A \text{ (the main effect of Factor A)} = MS_A/MS_W.$$

$$F_B \text{ (the main effect of Factor B)} = MS_B/MS_W.$$

$$F_{A \times B} \text{ (the interaction of Factor A and Factor B)} = MS_{A \times B}/MS_W.$$

If there is no treatment effect for Factor A, then the ratio of $(MS_A)/(MS_W)$ should be approximately 1. If there is a treatment effect, this F ratio should be greater than 1. The same will be true for the F ratio for Factor B and the F ratio for the interaction of Factor A and Factor B.

A FIRST EXAMPLE

For our first example of a two-way between-subjects ANOVA, we will analyze data from a hypothetical experiment on background noise and studying. In our study, the IVs are the subject's history of living in a quiet or loud environment (Factor A) and the presence or absence of background music while studying (Factor B). The DV is the subsequent quiz grade. The null hypothesis for Factor A is that there is no difference in quiz grade between subjects who lived in quiet environments versus those who lived in loud environments. The null hypothesis for Factor B is that there is no difference in quiz grade as a result of studying with or without background music. Finally, our null hypothesis for the interaction of Factor A and Factor B is that there is no unique effect of any combination of treatment levels. As usual, we set our α equal to .05.

While subjects can be randomly assigned to study with or without background music (Factor B), they cannot be randomly assigned to a history of exposure to sound (Factor A). When the levels of a factor cannot be assigned randomly, that factor is not a true IV. Still, the factor is treated as an IV for the purpose of statistical analysis. If there are no true IVs, the design is called a quasi-experimental design. In our example, if the presence of background music while studying is manipulated by the researcher, then that factor is a true independent variable and the study is considered a true experiment.

Cell: *a particular combination of treatment levels in a factorial ANOVA.*

Since our study consists of two levels of Factor A (quiet and loud) and two levels of Factor B (music and no music), this is a 2 × 2 ANOVA, and there are four combinations of the two IVs. These four combinations, along with the initial calculations that will be needed, are shown in Table 13.2. Thus, with a 2 × 2 ANOVA, there are four **cells**. The two-way between-subjects ANOVA requires that there be an approximately equal number of data points in each cell.

The next step is to create a table showing what must be found in the calculation of a two-way between-subjects ANOVA (Table 13.3).

Table 13.2 Example 1: Data and Initial Calculations

Factor A	Factor B		Row Totals
	Music	**No Music**	
Quiet history	X	X	
	4	8	
	4	7	
	3	7	
	$\Sigma X_{cell} = 11$	$\Sigma X_{cell} = 22$	$\Sigma X_{row} = 33$
	$n_{cell} = 3$	$n_{cell} = 3$	$n_{row} = 6$
	$M_{cell} = 3.67$	$M_{cell} = 7.33$	$M_{row} = 5.5$
Loud history	X	X	
	8	4	
	7	3	
	6	2	

Factor A	Factor B		
	Music	**No Music**	**Row Totals**
	$\Sigma X_{cell} = 21$	$\Sigma X_{cell} = 9$	$\Sigma X_{row} = 30$
	$n_{cell} = 3$	$n_{cell} = 3$	$n_{row} = 6$
	$M_{cell} = 7.0$	$M_{cell} = 3.0$	$M_{row} = 5.0$
Column totals	$\Sigma X_{col} = 32$	$\Sigma X_{col} = 31$	$\Sigma X_{total} = 63$
	$n_{col} = 6$	$n_{col} = 6$	$n_{total} = 12$
	$M_{col} = 5.33$	$M_{col} = 5.17$	$M_{total} = 5.25$

Table 13.3 Example 1: Summary Table for the Two-Way Between-Subjects ANOVA

Source of Variation	**SS**	**df**	**MS**	**F**
Factor A	$\underline{SS_A}$	$\underline{df_A}$	$\underline{MS_A}$	F ratio
Factor B	$\underline{SS_B}$	$\underline{df_B}$	$\underline{MS_B}$	F ratio
Interaction A × B	$\underline{SS_{A \times B}}$	$\underline{df_{A \times B}}$	$\underline{MS_{A \times B}}$	F ratio
Within groups	$\underline{SS_W}$	$\underline{df_W}$	$\underline{MS_W}$	
Total	$\underline{SS_T}$	$\underline{df_T}$		

Note. ANOVA, analysis of variance; *SS*, sum of squares; *df*, degrees of freedom; *MS*, mean square.

We then proceed essentially as with the one-way between-subjects ANOVA except that additional calculations are needed to determine Factor A, Factor B, and the interaction A × B. None of these calculations are difficult. However, as a value must be recorded for every entry underlined in Table 13.3, it is time-consuming. Anyone conducting a two-factor or two-way between-subjects ANOVA is strongly encouraged to utilize a statistical package such as SPSS. Accordingly, the outcomes rather than the actual steps of calculating the sums of squared deviations will be presented. Then, the additional steps to complete the ANOVA table will be described.

We begin by noting that we will need five values for *SS*, then, we find five values for *df* (degrees of freedom), four values for *MS*, and finally three *F* ratios.

Recall that in a one-way ANOVA,

$$SS_T = SS_{Bet} + SS_W.$$

With a two-way between-subjects ANOVA, the SS_{Bet} is partitioned, or divided, into three parts:

$$SS_{Bet} = SS_A + SS_B + SS_{A \times B}.$$

Thus, for a two-way between-subjects ANOVA we have,

$$SS_T = SS_A + SS_B + SS_{A \times B} + SS_W.$$

For our data, the values for the five needed SS are as follows:

$$SS_T = 50.25.$$

$$SS_A = 0.75.$$

$$SS_B = 0.09.$$

$$SS_{A \times B} = 44.07.$$

$$SS_W = 5.34.$$

As a check, we note that with a two-way between-subjects ANOVA,

$$SS_T = SS_A + SS_B + SS_{A \times B} + SS_W.$$

$$50.25 = 0.75 + 0.09 + 44.07 + 5.34.$$

$$50.25 = 50.25.$$

These values would then be entered in our table as would the subsequent values we will be calculating.

We now must calculate the values for the degrees of freedom that correspond to each SS:

$$df_A = \text{Number of levels of Factor A} - 1$$

$$= 2 - 1$$

$$= 1.$$

$$df_B = \text{Number of levels of Factor B} - 1$$

$$= 2 - 1$$

$$= 1.$$

$$df_{A \times B} = df_A \times df_B$$

$$= 1 \times 1$$

$$= 1.$$

$$df_w = N - \text{Number of cells,}$$

where N is the total number of subjects in the study.

$$df_w = 12 - 4$$

$$= 8.$$

$$df_T = N - 1,$$

where N is the total number of subjects in the study.

$$df_T = 12 - 1$$

$$= 11.$$

As a check on our calculations,

$$df_T = df_A + df_B + df_{A \times B} + df_w.$$

$$11 = 1 + 1 + 1 + 8.$$

$$11 = 11.$$

The *MS* for Factor A, Factor B, the interaction, and the MS_w are found by dividing the appropriate *SS* by its degrees of freedom. Thus,

$$MS_A = \frac{SS_A}{df_A}$$

$$= \frac{0.75}{1}$$

$$= 0.75.$$

$$MS_B = \frac{SS_B}{df_B}$$

$$= \frac{0.09}{1}$$

$$= 0.09.$$

$$MS_{A \times B} = \frac{SS_{A \times B}}{df_{A \times B}}$$

$$= \frac{44.07}{1}$$

$$= 44.07.$$

$$MS_W = \frac{SS_W}{df_W}$$

$$= \frac{5.34}{8}$$

$$= 0.67.$$

The F ratios for Factor A, Factor B, and the interaction are found by dividing each MS by the MS_W. Thus,

$$F_A = \frac{MS_A}{MS_W}$$

$$= \frac{0.75}{0.67}$$

$$= 1.12.$$

$$F_B = \frac{MS_B}{MS_W}$$

$$= \frac{0.09}{0.67}$$

$$= 0.13.$$

$$F_{A \times B} = \frac{MS_{A \times B}}{MS_W}$$

$$= \frac{44.07}{0.67}$$

$$= 65.78.$$

With the calculation of these three F values, our table is complete (Table 13.4).

Table 13.4	Example 1: Completed Summary Table for the Two-Way Between-Subjects ANOVA

Source of Variation	SS	df	MS	F
Factor A	0.75	1	0.75	1.12
Factor B	0.09	1	0.09	0.13
A × B	44.07	1	44.07	65.78*
Within	5.34	8	0.67	
Total	50.25	11		

Notes. ANOVA, analysis of variance; *SS*, sum of squares; *df*, degrees of freedom; *MS*, mean square. *Asterisk indicates *F* ratio for the interaction is larger than the critical value for an α of .05.

To determine whether any of these *F* ratios is significantly different from a value of 1, which you will recall is what would be expected if there were no effect, we must enter the *F* table. Remember, an *F* ratio is based on two *MS* estimates, each with its degrees of freedom. To find the critical value of *F*, we locate the column in the *F* table corresponding to the degrees of freedom in the numerator of our *F* ratio and the row corresponding to the degrees of freedom in the denominator of the *F* ratio. Because this is a 2 × 2 ANOVA, all three of our *F* ratios are based on the same degrees of freedom. In this example, the degrees of freedom are 1 and 8, respectively. As usual, we continue with an α of .05. At the intersection of our column and row in the *F* table, we find the critical value of 5.32. Only the *F* ratio for the interaction is larger than the critical value for an α of .05. This is indicated with an * (asterisk) in Table 13.4. We therefore conclude that there were no significant main effects, but there was a significant interaction.

The outcome of a 2 × 2 ANOVA can be presented in the form of a figure (Figure 13.4).

While our significant *F* indicates that there was an interaction, it does not specify which cell means differ, or the effect size for the interaction.

As you may recall, the number of comparisons between means, called pairwise comparisons, in an experiment is given by the following equation:

$$\text{Number of pairwise comparisons} = \frac{k(k-1)}{2},$$

where *k* is the number of means being compared.

In our case, *k* = 4 as we are interested in the four cell means. Thus, there are [4(4 − 1)]/2 = 6 pairwise comparisons. The 6 pairwise comparisons between the cell means are shown in

| Figure 13.4 | Example 1: Graph of the Interaction |

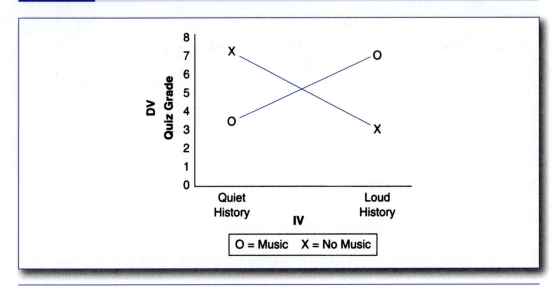

Note. DV, dependent variable; IV, independent variable.

Table 13.5. (Note that the four cell means are listed in the first row and the first column of the table, and the remainder of the table consists of the differences between these cell means. Furthermore, when comparing the differences between these means, we ignore the sign of the difference as this simply indicates the order of the subtraction of the means.)

However, it is important to note that we cannot interpret all 6 of these comparisons. We can only interpret those comparisons in which only one variable is varying. For instance, in the first row of Table 13.5, the difference between the mean of 3.67 and the mean of 7.33 refers to the effect of hearing different levels of background music on subjects who all have a quiet history, and thus, only one variable (level of music) is varying and the comparison can be interpreted. Similarly, the mean of 3.67 can be meaningfully compared with the mean of 7.0 (both groups heard the same level of background music but the groups differed on their history of sound exposure). However, the mean of 3.67 (mean of the group with a quiet history who heard music in the background) cannot be meaningfully compared with the mean of 3.0 (mean of the group with a loud history who did not hear music in the background) as in this case two variables (history and current exposure) are varying. Put another way, if you refer back to Table 13.2, you will see that we can only interpret comparisons of cells when one factor is varying. These are called **unconfounded comparisons**. If a comparison of cell

Unconfounded comparison: comparison of two cell means that involves only one factor that is changing. The comparison can be interpreted.

means involves more than one factor that is changing, this is called a **confounded comparison** and the outcome cannot be interpreted. Put another way, when referring to Table 13.2 any difference between cell means that involves a vertical or horizontal comparison is unconfounded and can be interpreted. Any

Confounded comparison: comparison of two cell means that involves more than one factor that is changing. The comparison cannot be interpreted.

difference between cell means that involves a diagonal comparison is confounded and cannot be interpreted. The two confounded comparisons are indicated in Table 13.5 by the italicized differences.

Of course, we still don't know which of these cell means differ significantly. The significant *F* simply indicates that at least one of the cell means differs from another. To specify which cell means differ, we need to conduct a post hoc test. Fortunately, we can again use Tukey's honestly significant difference (HSD) test, the same post hoc we employed with the one-way between-subjects ANOVA and the one-way within-subjects ANOVA, though it will need to be modified slightly when dealing with a significant interaction.

As you will recall, calculation of Tukey's HSD leads to a critical value that is compared with the difference between each pair of means. Specifically, for a significant interaction,

$$\text{Critical value} = q_i \sqrt{\frac{MS_w}{n}},$$

where q_i is based on the number of unconfounded comparisons of cell means in the interaction and is derived from q (refer to a more advanced statistical text for further details on how to obtain this value), MS_w comes from the ANOVA table, and n = the number of scores for *each* mean (It is important to note that this equation for HSD is only appropriate for designs with an equal n for each cell.)

As there are four unconfounded comparisons of cell means in this example and there are 8 *df* for the MS_w, the value for $q_i = 4.04$ (refer to a more advanced statistical text for further details on how to obtain this value). We can now find the critical value for an α equal to .05.

$$\text{Critical value} = 4.04 \sqrt{\frac{0.67}{3}}$$

$$= 4.04 \sqrt{0.233}$$

$$= (4.04)(0.473)$$

$$= 1.91.$$

Thus, to be considered significant with α equal to .05, Tukey's HSD test indicates that the difference between unconfounded cell means must be *as great or greater* than the critical value of 1.91.

We can also find the critical value for an α equal to .01. In this case, the value for q_i is 5.63:

$$\text{Critical value} = 5.63\sqrt{\frac{0.67}{3}}$$

$$= 5.63\sqrt{0.233}$$

$$= (5.63)(0.473)$$

$$= 2.66.$$

As all of the unconfounded comparisons of cell means have differences greater than 2.66 (Table 13.5), all of the pairwise comparisons of unconfounded cell means are significant at the .05 and at the .01 level. If any comparisons were significant at the .05 level but not at the .01 level, we might differentiate them by using an * for those significant at the .05 but not at the .01 level and a ** for those significant at the .01 level (Table 13.5).

| Table 13.5 | Example 1: Differences Between Cell Means—Significant Post Hoc Comparisons Are Noted (Confounded Comparisons Are Italicized) | | |

	3.67	7.33	7.0	3.0
3.67	—	3.66**	3.33**	*0.67*
7.33		—	*0.33*	4.33**
7.0			—	4.0**
3.0				—

Note. **Double asterisk indicates F ratio for the interaction is larger than the critical value for an α of .01.

To ascertain the percentage of variance explained by the independent variables and the interaction, we calculate an eta squared (η^2) for each F ratio that was found to be significant. With a two-way between-subjects ANOVA, the equations for η^2 are as follows:

$$\eta^2 \text{ for Factor A} = \frac{SS_A}{SS_T}.$$

$$\eta^2 \text{ for Factor B} = \frac{SS_B}{SS_T}.$$

$$\eta^2 \text{ for the interaction} = \frac{SS_{A \times B}}{SS_T}.$$

In our example, only the interaction was found to be significant so we calculate only one η^2:

$$\eta^2 \text{ for the interaction} = \frac{44.07}{50.25}$$

$$= 0.877 \text{ or } 87.7\%,$$

which is a very large η^2.

Reporting the Results of a Two-Way Between-Subjects ANOVA

In a paper, we would indicate the F ratios that were obtained as well as the degrees of freedom used, which F ratio was significant, that Tukey's HSD post hoc was used to determine which pairwise comparisons of cell means were significantly different and the measure of effect size. Specifically, we would report that the main effects for history of exposure, and whether subjects listened to music or not, were not significant ($F(1, 8) = 1.12$, $p > .05$ and $F(1, 8) = 0.13$, $p > .05$, respectively). However, the interaction was found to be significant ($F(1, 8) = 65.78$, $p < .05$). Tukey's HSD test indicated that all four of the unconfounded cell mean comparisons were statistically different. A measure of effect size for the interaction, η^2, was found to equal .88.

The discussion of the results would emphasize that whether background music hinders or enhances studying depends on the subject's history of exposure to sound. Specifically, these hypothetical data would indicate that those subjects with a history of living in a quiet environment find background music disruptive to studying, whereas those subjects with a history of living in an environment with more background sound find a quiet situation disruptive to studying.

PROGRESS CHECK

1. With a two-way between-subjects ANOVA, there are ___ main effects, and a total of ___ F ratios are calculated.

2. If an outcome is due to a particular combination of the independent variables, this is an example of a(an) ___.

3. If we have a statistically significant interaction with a two-way between-subjects ANOVA that has 6 cell means, there would be a total of ___ post hoc pairwise comparisons, but of these only the subset of ___ comparisons could be interpreted.

Answers: 1. two, three. 2. interaction. 3. 15, unconfounded.

A SECOND EXAMPLE

For our second example of a two-way between-subjects ANOVA, we will analyze a hypothetical set of data examining the effect of gender and age on the likelihood of receiving a traffic ticket. In our study, we will treat gender (Factor A) and age (Factor B) as IVs. The DV is the number of traffic tickets received in the preceding 3-year period. The null hypothesis for Factor A is that there is no difference between the number of tickets received by men and women. The null hypothesis for Factor B is that there is no difference between the number of tickets received by three different age-groups of drivers: young, middle aged, and old. Finally, our null hypothesis for the interaction of Factor A and Factor B is that there is no unique effect of any combination of treatment levels. As usual, we set our α equal to .05. As subjects are not being randomly assigned to treatment levels, this is a quasi-experimental design.

Since our study consists of two levels of Factor A (men and women) and three levels of Factor B (young, middle-aged, and old drivers), and each subject receives only one combination of treatment levels, this is a 2×3 between-subjects ANOVA. The data for the six combinations of gender and age, as well as the initial calculations for the ANOVA, are shown in Table 13.6.

Table 13.6   Example 2: Data and Initial Calculations

Factor A	Factor B			
	Young	**Middle Aged**	**Old**	**Row Totals**
Men	X	X	X	
	9	3	6	
	9	3	5	
	8	2	5	
	7	2	4	
	$\Sigma X_{cell} = 33$	$\Sigma X_{cell} = 10$	$\Sigma X_{cell} = 20$	$\Sigma X_{row} = 63$
	$n_{cell} = 4$	$n_{cell} = 4$	$n_{cell} = 4$	$n_{row} = 12$
	$M_{cell} = 8.25$	$M_{cell} = 2.5$	$M_{cell} = 5.0$	$M_{row} = 5.25$
Women	X	X	X	
	6	3	6	
	6	2	5	
	5	2	4	

Factor A	Factor B			
	Young	**Middle Aged**	**Old**	**Row Totals**
	4	2	4	
	$\Sigma X_{cell} = 21$	$\Sigma X_{cell} = 9$	$\Sigma X_{cell} = 19$	$\Sigma X_{row} = 49$
	$n_{cell} = 4$	$n_{cell} = 4$	$n_{cell} = 4$	$n_{row} = 12$
	$M_{cell} = 5.25$	$M_{cell} = 2.25$	$M_{cell} = 4.75$	$M_{row} = 4.08$
Column totals	$\Sigma X_{col} = 54$	$\Sigma X_{col} = 19$	$\Sigma X_{col} = 39$	$\Sigma X_{total} = 112$
	$n_{col} = 8$	$n_{col} = 8$	$n_{col} = 8$	$n_{total} = 24$
	$M_{col} = 6.75$	$M_{col} = 2.375$	$M_{col} = 4.875$	$M_{total} = 4.67$

The next step is to create a table showing what it is that must be calculated. It is the same as for our first example (Table 13.3).

Recall that in a two-way between-subjects ANOVA, the SS_{Bet} is partitioned into SS_A, SS_B, and $SS_{A \times B}$. Therefore, to complete the table, we need to find five values for SS, then the five values for df, the four values for MS, and finally, three F ratios. As with the previous example, we will not actually calculate the SS as this is tedious when done by hand. The results of these calculations are as follows:

$$SS_T = 107.33.$$

$$SS_A = 8.16.$$

$$SS_B = 77.08.$$

$$SS_{A \times B} = 10.09.$$

$$SS_W = 12.00$$

As a check on our calculations, we note that

$$SS_T = SS_A + SS_B + SS_{A \times B} + SS_W.$$

$$107.33 = 8.16 + 77.08 + 10.09 + 12.$$

$$107.33 = 107.33.$$

We now must calculate the degrees of freedom for Factor A, Factor B, the interaction, within groups, and total

$$df_A = \text{Number of levels of Factor A} - 1$$

$$= 2 - 1$$

$$= 1.$$

$$df_B = \text{Number of levels of Factor B} - 1$$

$$= 3 - 1$$

$$= 2.$$

$$df_{A \times B} = df_A \times df_B$$

$$= 1 \times 2$$

$$= 2.$$

$$df_W = N - \text{Number of cells,}$$

where N is the total number of subjects in the study.

$$df_W = 24 - 6$$

$$= 18.$$

$$df_T = N - 1,$$

where N is the total number of subjects in the study.

$$df_T = 24 - 1$$

$$= 23.$$

As a check on our calculations,

$$df_T = df_A + df_B + df_{A \times B} + df_W.$$

$$23 = 1 + 2 + 2 + 18.$$

$$23 = 23.$$

The *MS* for Factor A, Factor B, the interaction, and the *MS* within groups are found by dividing the appropriate *SS* by its degrees of freedom. Thus,

$$MS_A = \frac{SS_A}{df_A}$$

$$= \frac{8.16}{1}$$

$$= 8.16.$$

$$MS_B = \frac{SS_B}{df_B}$$

$$= \frac{77.08}{2}$$

$$= 38.54.$$

$$MS_{A \times B} = \frac{SS_{A \times B}}{df_{A \times B}}$$

$$= \frac{10.09}{2}$$

$$= 5.045.$$

$$MS_W = \frac{SS_W}{df_W}$$

$$= \frac{12}{18}$$

$$= 0.667.$$

The *F* ratios for Factor A, Factor B, and the interaction are found by dividing each *MS* by the *MS*$_W$. Thus,

$$F_A = \frac{MS_A}{MS_W}$$

$$= \frac{8.16}{0.667}$$

$$= 12.23.$$

$$F_B = \frac{MS_B}{MS_W}$$

$$= \frac{38.54}{0.667}$$

$$= 57.78.$$

$$F_{A \times B} = \frac{MS_{A \times B}}{MS_W}$$

$$= \frac{5.045}{0.667}$$

$$= 7.56.$$

With the calculation of these three F values, the table is complete (Table 13.7).

To determine whether any of these F ratios is significantly different from a value of 1, we must enter the F table. Remember, each F ratio is based on two MS estimates, each associated with an SS and a df. To find the critical value of F, we locate the column in the F table corresponding to the df of our numerator and the row corresponding to the df of our denominator. For the F ratio for Factor A, there are 1 and 18 df, respectively. At the intersection of our column and row in the F table, we find the critical value with an α of .05 is 4.41. The critical value of F with an α of .01 is 8.28. Thus, Factor A is statistically significant at the .01 level. For Factor B and the interaction, the df would be 2 and 18, respectively. The critical value for an α of .05 is 3.55. The critical value for an α of .01 is 6.01. Thus, Factor B and the interaction

Table 13.7	Example 2: Completed Summary Table for the Two-Way Between-Subjects ANOVA

Source of Variation	SS	df	MS	F
Factor A	8.16	1	8.16	12.23**
Factor B	77.08	2	38.54	57.78**
A × B	10.09	2	5.045	7.56**
Within	12.00	18	0.667	
Total	107.33	23		

Notes. ANOVA, analysis of variance; *SS*, sum of squares; *df*, degrees of freedom; *MS*, mean square.
**Double asterisk indicates *F* ratio for the interaction is larger than the critical value for an α of .01.

are also statistically significant at the .01 level. Thus, both main effects and the interaction are statistically significant at the .01 level. This is indicated by a ** in Table 13.7.

The outcome of the 2 × 3 between-subjects ANOVA can be presented visually (Figure 13.5).

The *F* for Factor A was significant. This is a main effect as it indicates that an IV had a significant effect. As there are only two levels to Factor A, there is no point in conducting a post hoc test as it is evident that there is a significant difference in the number of traffic tickets given to men and women. We simply compare the means for the two groups and conclude that overall men receive more tickets than women.

There are three levels to Factor B. While our significant *F* indicates that there was an effect for Factor B (this is another main effect), it does not specify which treatment levels of Factor B (column means) differ. The number of main effect pairwise comparisons is given by the following equation:

$$\text{Number of pairwise comparisons} = \frac{k(k-1)}{2},$$

where *k* is the number of means being considered.

With a 2 × 3 ANOVA, *k* (remember we are comparing the column means) equals 3. Thus, there are [3(3 − 1)]/2 = 3, pairwise comparisons. These 3 pairwise comparisons between the column means are indicated in Table 13.8. (The 3 treatment-level (column) means are listed

| **Figure 13.5** | Example 2: Graph of Two Significant Main Effects and a Significant Interaction Between Age and Number of Traffic Tickets |

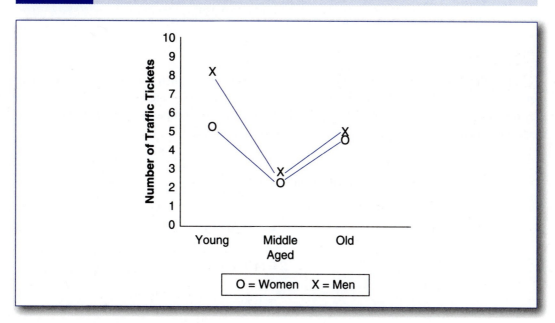

in the first row and the first column of Table 13.8, and the remainder of the table consists of the differences between these means. As before, we ignore the sign of the differences as these simply reflect the order the means were subtracted.) The significant F indicates that at least one of the column means differs from another. To specify which means differ, we will once again use Tukey's HSD test.

For Factor B of the two-way between-subjects ANOVA,

$$\text{Critical value} = q\sqrt{\frac{MS_w}{n}},$$

where $n =$ the number of scores for *each* mean (which equals 8 as we are dealing with column totals) and the MS_w comes from the ANOVA table.

The value for q is found in the q table (Appendix J, Table J.5). (Note that we are not dealing with q_i for we are not dealing with an interaction at this point and, thus, do not have to be concerned with the issue of whether a comparison is confounded or not.) The column to use is determined by the number of means being compared, in our case 3. The row is determined by the degrees of freedom of the MS_w, in our case 18. With α equal to .05, q is equal to 3.62. We can now find the critical value:

$$\text{Critical value} = 3.62\sqrt{\frac{0.667}{8}}$$

$$= 3.62\sqrt{0.833}$$

$$= (3.62)(0.289)$$

$$= 1.05.$$

The difference between column means for a pairwise comparison must be *as great or greater* than the critical value from Tukey's HSD to be considered significantly different. As is evident from an inspection of Table 13.8, all of the pairwise comparisons are statistically significant. In fact, with α equal to .01, q is equal to 4.71, and the

$$\text{Critical value} = 4.71\sqrt{\frac{0.667}{8}}$$

$$= 4.71\sqrt{0.833}$$

$$= (4.71)(0.289)$$

$$= 1.36.$$

Thus, as all of the pairwise comparisons exceed this critical value of 1.36, they are all statistically significant at the .01 level. This is indicated by a ** in Table 13.8.

Table 13.8	Example 2: Differences Between Column Means—Significant Post Hoc Comparisons Are Noted		

	6.75	2.375	4.875
6.75	—	4.375**	1.875**
2.375		—	2.5**
4.875			—

Note. **Double asterisk indicates *F* ratio for the interaction is larger than the critical value for an α of .01.

Our significant *F* also indicates that there was an interaction, though it does not specify which cell means differ. The number of pairwise comparisons between cell means is as follows:

$$\text{Number of pairwise comparisons} = \frac{k(k-1)}{2},$$

where *k* is the number of means being considered.

In our case, $k = 6$ as we are interested in the cell means. Thus, there are $[6(6 - 1)]/2 = 15$, pairwise comparisons. The 15 pairwise comparisons between the cell means are indicated in Table 13.9. The significant *F* for the interaction simply indicates that at least one of the cell means differs from another. To specify which means differ, we once again use Tukey's HSD test. Before doing so, however, we first note that only 9 of the 15 comparisons between cell means are unconfounded and thus can be interpreted (The 6 confounded comparisons are italicized in Table 13.9). Note also that the 6 cell means are listed in the first row and the first column of Table 13.9, and the remainder of the table consists of the differences between these cell means. As before, we ignore whether the difference is positive or negative. For the interaction with the two-way between-subjects ANOVA,

$$\text{Critical value} = q_i \sqrt{\frac{MS_W}{n}},$$

where q_i is based on the number of unconfounded comparisons of cell means in the interaction and is derived from *q* (refer to a more advanced statistical text for further details on how to obtain this value), MS_W comes from the ANOVA table, and n = the number of scores for *each* mean (It is important to note that this equation for HSD is only appropriate for designs with equal *n* for each cell.)

As there are 9 unconfounded comparisons of cell means in the analysis of the significant interaction, and there are 18 *df* for the MS_w, the value for q_i is 4.28 for an α equal to .05. (Refer to a more advanced text to obtain this value.) We can now find the critical value:

$$\text{Critical value} = 4.28\sqrt{\frac{0.667}{4}}$$

$$= 4.28\sqrt{0.167}$$

$$= (4.28)(0.408)$$

$$= 1.75.$$

The difference between means for pairwise comparisons, which are presented in Table 13.9, must be *as great or greater* than the critical value of 1.75 found using Tukey's HSD to be considered significantly different at the .05 level.

With α equal to .01, q_i is equal to 5.38. We can now find the critical value:

$$\text{Critical value} = 5.38\sqrt{\frac{0.667}{4}}$$

$$= 5.38\sqrt{0.167}$$

$$= (5.38)(0.408)$$

$$= 2.20.$$

The unconfounded pairwise comparisons that exceed the critical value at the .01 level are indicated by a ** in Table 13.9. There is no unconfounded comparison only significant at the .05 level. If there was, it would be indicated by an *.

To review the importance of the distinction between confounded and unconfounded comparisons, it is important to note that we cannot interpret all of the differences between cell means. We can only interpret those comparisons in which only one variable is varying. For instance, in the first row of Table 13.9, the difference between the mean of 8.25 and the mean of 2.5 was found to be significant. This refers to the differences of young and middle-aged men, and thus, only one variable (age) is varying and the comparison can be interpreted. Similarly, the mean of 8.25 can be meaningfully compared with the mean of 5.0 (middle-aged men) and the mean of 5.25 (young women), for in each case, only one variable is varying. However, the mean of 8.25 (mean of young men) cannot be meaningfully compared with the mean of 2.25 (mean of middle-aged women) or the mean of 4.75 (mean of old women), for in both of these cases, two variables (age and gender) are varying. Put

Table 13.9	Example 2: Differences Between Cell Means—Significant Post Hoc Comparisons Are Noted (Confounded Comparisons Are Italicized)					

	8.25	2.5	5.0	5.25	2.25	4.75
8.25	—	5.75**	3.25**	3.0**	*6.0*	*3.5*
2.5		—	2.5**	*2.75*	*0.25*	*2.25*
5.0			—	*0.25*	*2.75*	*0.25*
5.25				—	3.0**	*0.5*
2.25					—	2.5**
4.75						—

Note. **Double asterisk indicates *F* ratio for the interaction is larger than the critical value for an α of .01.

another way, if you refer back to Table 13.6, you will see that we can only interpret comparisons of cells that involve only one factor that is changing. As was noted previously, these are called unconfounded comparisons. If a comparison of cell means involves more than one factor that is changing, this is called a confounded comparison and the outcome cannot be interpreted. Thus, when referring to Table 13.6, any difference between cell means that involves a vertical or horizontal comparison is unconfounded and can be interpreted. Any difference between cell means that involves a diagonal comparison is confounded and cannot be interpreted.

To ascertain the percentage of variance explained by the factors, we calculate an eta squared (η^2) for each of the *F* ratios that was found to be significant. With a two-way between-subjects ANOVA with three significant *F* ratios, the equations for η^2 are as follows:

$$\eta^2 \text{ for Factor A} = \frac{SS_A}{SS_T}$$

$$= \frac{8.16}{107.33}$$

$$= 0.076 = 7.6\%.$$

$$\eta^2 \text{ for Factor B} = \frac{SS_B}{SS_T}$$

$$= \frac{77.08}{107.33}$$

$$= 0.718 = 71.8\%.$$

$$\eta^2 \text{ for the interaction} = \frac{SS_{A \times B}}{SS_T}$$

$$= \frac{10.09}{107.33}$$

$$= 0.094 = 9.4\%.$$

Reporting the Results of a Two-Way Between-Subjects ANOVA

In a paper, we would indicate the F ratios that were obtained as well as the degrees of freedom used, and that each F ratio was significant. We would also include the significant post hoc pairwise comparisons and indicate the measure of effect size. Specifically, we would report that both main effects, for gender and age, were significant ($F(1, 18) = 12.23$, $p < .01$ and $F(2, 18) = 57.78$, $p < .01$, respectively). The interaction also was found to be significant ($F(2, 18) = 7.56$, $p < .01$). Tukey's HSD test was conducted to determine which means were statistically different. Finally, a measure of effect size, η^2, was found to equal .08 for gender, .72 for age, and .09 for the interaction of gender and age.

The discussion would emphasize the pattern of cell differences that led to the significant interaction. From Figure 13.5 it is evident, based on these hypothetical data, that being young and male leads to an increased number of tickets. In the discussion section of a paper, it also would be pointed out that, overall, the young and old drivers received more tickets than the drivers who are middle aged.

Purpose and Limitations of Using the Two-Way Between-Subjects ANOVA

1. *Test for difference:* The null hypotheses are that the treatments do not have an effect. Therefore, if the null is correct, any difference between the sample means is due to chance. The alternative hypotheses are that the treatments do have an effect and, therefore, the samples are drawn from populations with different means. The two-way between-subjects ANOVA tests whether there are main effects as well as whether there is an interaction between the IVs.

2. *Does not provide a measure of effect size:* The two-way between-subjects ANOVA, like the one-way between-subjects ANOVA, is a test of significance. It indicates whether an outcome is likely to have occurred by chance. If an F ratio is significant, a measure of effect size, such as eta squared (η^2), should be calculated.

3. *Sample size is important:* As was true for the one-way between-subjects ANOVA, if the sample size is 30 or greater, then the assumption that the population is normal can be

safely ignored. If the sample size is less than 30, then it is important that the underlying population be normally distributed.

4. *Compares two or more sample means for each main effect:* Each factor of the two-way between-subjects ANOVA must have at least two levels or there is no variable. However, there can theoretically be any number of levels greater than two. Of course, a study with a large number of levels for one or both of the factors would be unwieldy to conduct, though the ANOVA would handle the data without difficulty.

5. *Does not indicate where the difference is:* With designs with more than two levels, any significant main effect should be followed up with a post hoc procedure such as Tukey's HSD test. A significant interaction should also be followed up with a post hoc procedure such as Tukey's HSD test, but only the unconfounded comparisons can be interpreted.

Assumptions of the Two-Way Between-Subjects ANOVA

1. *Interval or ratio data:* The data are on an interval scale of measurement or a ratio scale of measurement.

2. *Random samples:* Each sample is drawn at random from a population.

3. *Normally distributed populations:* Each population from which a sample is drawn has a normal distribution of scores.

4. *Population variances are equal:* The populations from which samples are drawn have equal variances.

5. Each cell has an approximately equal number of subjects.

Effect of Violating the Assumptions

The *F* test has been found to be robust so long as the number of subjects in each cell is at least 30 and is approximately equal. However, if these conditions are not met and if the sample distributions have obviously different shapes or the sample variances are clearly not equal, you should not use this test. Also, if samples are not randomly drawn, then you have a quasi-experiment and thus less confidence in the interpretation of a significant outcome.

CONCLUSION

The two-way between-subjects ANOVA is a very flexible test. As you recall, the major advantage of the ANOVA is that it controls the experiment-wise error rate while simultaneously comparing any number of sample means. The specific advantage of conducting a two-way

ANOVA rather than the one-way ANOVA is that you test two IVs instead of one and, in addition, you test whether there is an interaction. Thus, the two-way ANOVA provides additional information, which is why it is such a popular statistical procedure. As you would expect, the assumptions of the two-way between-subjects ANOVA are very similar to those of the one-way between-subjects ANOVA.

Chapter Resources

GLOSSARY OF TERMS

Cell: a particular combination of treatment levels in a factorial ANOVA.

Confounded comparison: comparison of two cell means that involves more than one factor that is changing. The comparison cannot be interpreted.

Interaction: a change in the dependent variable that is due to the presence of a particular combination of independent variables.

Main effect: with a factorial ANOVA, another term used for an independent variable.

Unconfounded comparison: comparison of two cell means that involves only one factor that is changing. The comparison can be interpreted.

Questions: Chapter 13

(Answers to odd-numbered items are provided in Appendix I.)

1. A 2 × 3 × 4 ANOVA has _____ independent variables.

   a. one

   b. two

   c. three

   d. four

2. In a 2 × 3 ANOVA, the number 3 indicates that there are _____.

   a. three independent variables

   b. three levels to an independent variable

   c. three subjects in a condition

   d. none of the above

3. An interaction occurs when _____.

   a. a specific combination of factors determines the value of the dependent variable

   b. a specific combination of factors influences the independent variable

c. more than one experimenter is collecting the data

d. a particularly important finding occurs

4. A main effect occurs when _____.

    a. an interaction occurs

    b. the dependent variable has an effect

    c. an independent variable has an effect

    d. all of the above

5. In a two-way between-subjects ANOVA, we calculate F ratios for _____.

    a. one main effect and two interactions

    b. two main effects and two interactions

    c. two main effects and one interaction

    d. none of the above

6. In a two-way between-subjects ANOVA, we calculate _____ F ratios.

    a. one

    b. two

    c. three

    d. four

7. In a two-way between-subjects ANOVA, each *combination* of treatment levels is a _____.

    a. cell

    b. level

    c. condition

    d. factor

8. Following a significant outcome with a two-way between-subjects ANOVA, you would probably consider _____.

    a. redoing the study with larger sample sizes

    b. increasing the number of independent variables in the study

    c. calculating Tukey's HSD

    d. none of the above

For Questions 9 and 10 assume that we conduct a study comparing the effect of studying (students are randomly assigned to study a little or a great deal) and class in college (freshman, sophomore, junior, and senior).

9. If there was a significant interaction and we compared the cell means for studying a little among freshmen, sophomores, juniors, and seniors, these would be _____.

   a. confounded comparisons

   b. unconfounded comparisons

10. If there was a significant interaction and we compared the cell means for studying a little among freshmen with studying a great deal among sophomores, this would be a _____.

    a. confounded comparison

    b. unconfounded comparison

For Questions 11 to 13 assume that we have conducted a 2 × 5 ANOVA.

11. How many cells means would there be?

    a. 8

    b. 10

    c. 20

    d. 45

12. If the main effect for the factor with 5 treatment levels is found to be statistically significant, but the interaction is not significant, how many post hoc pairwise comparisons would there be?

    a. 8

    b. 10

    c. 20

    d. 45

13. If the interaction is found to be statistically significant, how many post hoc pairwise comparisons would there be?

    a. 8

    b. 10

    c. 20

    d. 45

The data for Problems 14 to 16 are similar to those used in Chapter 11 (Questions 15 to 19) except that we now assume that the original 18 students were 9 males and 9 females. Assume that $SS_{\text{Gender}} = 50$, the $SS_{\text{Background}} = 12$, $SS_{\text{Gender} \times \text{Background}} = 4$, and $SS_{\text{T}} = 96$. Compare your answers to what you calculated in Chapter 11.

Gender	Level of Background Noise		
	Quiet	Moderate	Noisy
Women	9	7	6
	10	9	8
	8	8	10
Men	13	13	7
	12	11	11
	14	12	12

14. What is the value of F for gender?

   a. 50

   b. 20

   c. 0.8

   d. 2.4

15. What is the value of F for background?

   a. 50

   b. 20

   c. 0.8

   d. 2.4

16. What is the value of F for the interaction of gender $\times$ background?

   a. 50

   b. 20

   c. 0.8

   d. 2.4

   Problems 17 to 22 utilize SPSS.

SPSS

USING SPSS WITH THE TWO-WAY BETWEEN-SUBJECTS ANOVA

To Begin SPSS

Step 1: The first step, as always, is to activate the program.

   Step 2: Click on "Type in data," and then, click on "OK."

Step 3: Click on "Variable View." We will only be dealing with the columns headed by "Name," "Label," "Values," and "Measure."

Step 4: Click on the first empty cell under the column heading "Name." You now type the name of the first variable for which you have data. We are going to utilize the same data and labels as were previously employed in Table 13.6. These hypothetical data dealt with the question of whether there is a relationship between gender, age, and the number of traffic tickets received. We have called these variables "Gender," "Age," and "Data." Therefore, type "Gender" in the first empty cell under "Name."

Step 5: Click twice on the first empty cell under the column heading "Label." In this cell, you can type a more extensive description of your variable. In our case, type "Gender of Subject."

Step 6: Click on the first empty cell under the column heading "Values." Then click on the small blue square. A box will appear. In the blank space to the right of "Value," type the number "1"and then "male" in the blank space to the right of "Label." Finally, click on "Add." Your label for a value of 1 will appear in the large white region in the center of the window. Now repeat the above steps in this section for the value "2," which is given the label "female" (Figure 13.6). Then click on "OK."

Step 7: Click on the first empty cell under the column heading "Measure." As we are dealing with labels for groups, select "Nominal" as is shown in Figure 13.7.

Step 8: Repeat Steps 4 to 7 (for the second IV) except that you type "Age" in the first empty cell under "Name," "Age of Subject" for "Label," and you now have three values—"young,"

Figure 13.6 The Value Labels Window

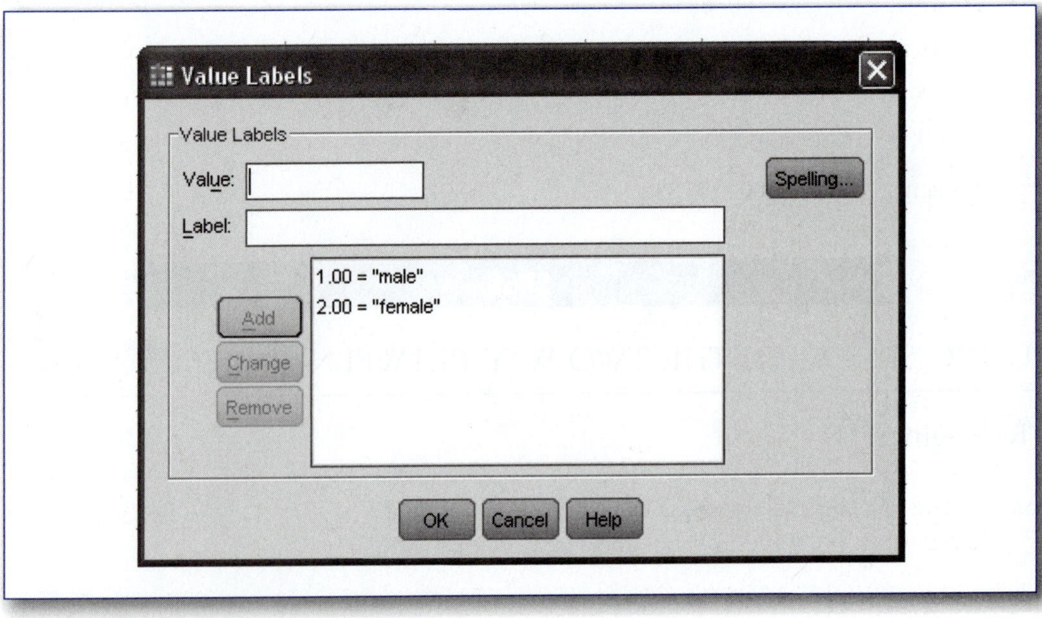

Figure 13.7	The Variable View Window

Name	Type	Width	Decimals	Label	Values	Missing	Columns	Align	Measure	Role
Gender	Numeric	8	2	Gender of Subj...	{1.00, male}...	None	8	≣ Right	♣ Nominal	↘ Input

"middle-aged," and "old." As before, select "Nominal" in the column under the column heading "Measure" as we are dealing with labels for groups. The result is shown in Figure 13.8.

Step 9: Repeat Steps 4 to 7 again for the DV except that you type "Data" in the first empty cell under "Name" and for "Label." Finally, select "Scale" in the column under the column heading "Measure" as we have interval or ratio data. The result is shown in Figure 13.9.

To Enter Data in SPSS

Step 10: Click on the "Data View" option at the lower left-hand corner of the window. The variables "Gender," "Age," and "Data" will be present.

Step 11: For each male subject, type the value of "1" in the column "Gender." Then, in the column "Age," Type "1" if they were young, "2" if they were middle aged, and "3" if they were old. Finally, type the number of tickets each subject received in the third column, "Data" (Figure 13.10). Continue by entering "2" for each female subject along with their age and the number of tickets they received (Figure 13.11).

To Conduct a Two-Way Between-Subjects ANOVA

Step 12: Click the cursor on "Analyze" along the row of SPSS commands above the data you entered, then move to "General Linear Model," then click on "Univariate."

Figure 13.8	Continuing With the Variable View Window

Name	Type	Width	Decimals	Label	Values	Missing	Columns	Align	Measure	Role
Gender	Numeric	8	2	Gender of Subj...	{1.00, male}...	None	8	≣ Right	♣ Nominal	↘ Input
Age	Numeric	8	2	Age of Subject	{1.00, youn...	None	8	≣ Right	♣ Nominal	↘ Input

Figure 13.9	The Completed Variable View Window

Name	Type	Width	Decimals	Label	Values	Missing	Columns	Align	Measure	Role
Gender	Numeric	8	2	Gender of Subj...	{1.00, male}...	None	8	≣ Right	♣ Nominal	↘ Input
Age	Numeric	8	2	Age of Subject	{1.00, youn...	None	8	≣ Right	♣ Nominal	↘ Input
Data	Numeric	8	2	Data	None	None	8	≣ Right	⬦ Scale	↘ Input

Figure 13.10	Entering the Data

Gender	Age	Data
1.00	1.00	9.00
1.00	1.00	9.00
1.00	1.00	8.00
1.00	1.00	7.00
1.00	2.00	3.00
1.00	2.00	3.00
1.00	2.00	2.00
1.00	2.00	2.00
1.00	3.00	6.00
1.00	3.00	5.00
1.00	3.00	5.00
1.00	3.00	4.00

Figure 13.11	The Completed Data Set

Gender	Age	Data
1.00	1.00	9.00
1.00	1.00	9.00
1.00	1.00	8.00
1.00	1.00	7.00
1.00	2.00	3.00
1.00	2.00	3.00
1.00	2.00	2.00
1.00	2.00	2.00
1.00	3.00	6.00
1.00	3.00	5.00
1.00	3.00	5.00
1.00	3.00	4.00
2.00	1.00	6.00
2.00	1.00	6.00
2.00	1.00	5.00
2.00	1.00	4.00
2.00	2.00	3.00
2.00	2.00	2.00
2.00	2.00	2.00
2.00	2.00	2.00
2.00	3.00	6.00
2.00	3.00	5.00
2.00	3.00	4.00
2.00	3.00	4.00

Step 13: A new window will appear. You must now identify the DV and the IVs (each IV is called a factor). In our case, "Data" is the label of the DV. This is indicated by moving "Data" to the box under "Dependent Variable" by placing the cursor over "Data" and then clicking on the top arrow in the box. The result is shown in Figure 13.12. Then select "Gender of Subject" and move it to the box under "Fixed Factor(s)" by clicking on the second arrow. Next, select "Age of Subject" and move it to the box under "Fixed Factor(s)" by clicking on the second arrow. The result will be that each label will move to the appropriate box on the right-hand side of the window, as is shown in Figure 13.13. Then click on "Post Hoc," which is located in the top, right-hand corner of the window.

Step 14: A new window will appear with Gender and Age identified. As the variable "Gender" has only two levels (male and female), there is no need for a post hoc test. However, as the variable "Age" has three levels (young, middle aged, and old), we do have a need for a post hoc in this case. We highlight and move "Age" to the right-hand box. We then note that this window provides a number of statistical options that are available with SPSS. In this course, we will limit ourselves to just Tukey's HSD test. Click on the box next to Tukey. Then click on "Continue." Finally, click on "OK." SPSS calculates the desired two-way ANOVA with Tukey's HSD post hoc test. Table 13.10 provides a count of the number of subjects in each condition as well as the number of data points for each level of the variable "Age." Table 13.11 provides the ANOVA table. SPSS provides extra information in the

Figure 13.12 Defining Variables

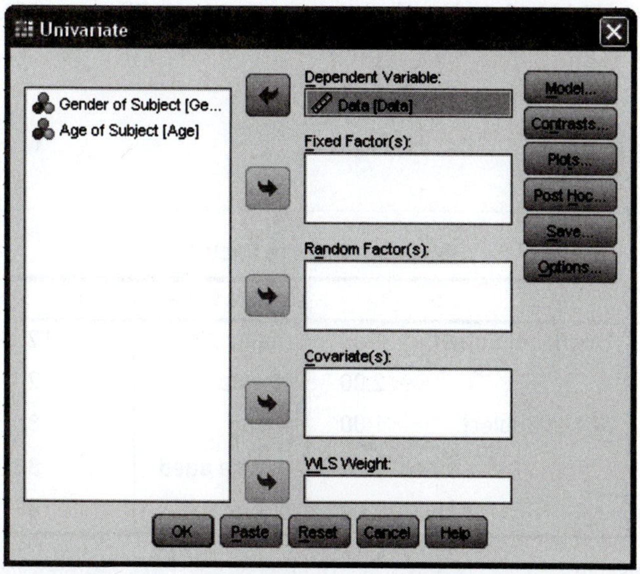

Figure 13.13 Conclusion of Defining Variables

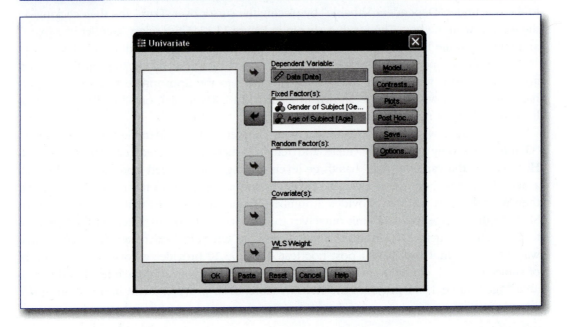

first two rows as well as the next to last row. Otherwise, it is the same outcome as we found earlier, except for rounding error, with hand calculation (Table 13.7). Finally, Table 13.12 shows the results of Tukey's HSD post hoc test, which provides the same information as previously shown in Table 13.8, though the presentation is different. (The final table of the SPSS output is not of interest to us.)

Table 13.10 SPSS Output

Between-Subjects Factors

		Value Label	N
Gender of Subject	1.00	male	12
	2.00	female	12
Age of Subject	1.00	young	8
	2.00	middle aged	8
	3.00	old	8

Table 13.11   SPSS Output, the ANOVA Table

Tests of Between-Subjects Effects

Dependent Variable:Data

Source	Type III Sum of Squares	df	Mean Square	F	Sig.
Corrected Model	95.333[a]	5	19.067	28.600	.000
Intercept	522.667	1	522.667	784.000	.000
Gender	8.167	1	8.167	12.250	.003
Age	77.083	2	38.542	57.813	.000
Gender * Age	10.083	2	5.042	7.563	.004
Error	12.000	18	.667		
Total	630.000	24			
Corrected Total	107.333	23			

a. R Squared = .888 (Adjusted R Squared = .857)

Table 13.12   SPSS Output, Tukey's HSD Post Hoc

Multiple Comparisons

Data
Tukey HSD

(I) Age of Subject	(J) Age of Subject	Mean Difference (I-J)	Std. Error	Sig.	95% Confidence Interval	
					Lower Bound	Upper Bound
young	middle aged	4.3750[*]	.40825	.000	3.3331	5.4169
	old	1.8750[*]	.40825	.001	.8331	2.9169
middle aged	young	-4.3750[*]	.40825	.000	-5.4169	-3.3331
	old	-2.5000[*]	.40825	.000	-3.5419	-1.4581
old	young	-1.8750[*]	.40825	.001	-2.9169	-.8331
	middle aged	2.5000[*]	.40825	.000	1.4581	3.5419

Based on observed means.
The error term is Mean Square(Error) = .667.

*. The mean difference is significant at the 0.05 level.

To confirm that you understand how to use SPSS, redo the two-way between-subjects ANOVA that dealt with level of background noise (Questions 14–16) to check your answers, but this time utilize SPSS.

SPSS Problems: Chapter 13

For Questions 17 to 22, what is the effect of adding a constant, in this case 10, to every score in the noisy condition? Compare your answers with the answers you found for Questions 14 to 16.

Gender	Level of Background Noise		
	Quiet	Moderate	Noisy
Women	9	7	16
	10	9	18
	8	8	20
Men	13	13	17
	12	11	21
	14	12	22

17. What is the F for gender?

   a. 58.4

   b. 0.8

   c. 20

   d. 1.0

18. What is the F for background?

   a. 58.4

   b. 0.8

   c. 20

   d. 1.0

19. What is the F for the interaction of Gender × Background?

   a. 58.4

   b. 0.8

   c. 20

   d. 1.0

For Questions 20 to 22, what is the effect of subtracting 5 from the scores of the first woman subject in each condition? Compare your answers with the answers you found for Questions 17 to 22.

Gender	Level of Background Noise		
	Quiet	Moderate	Noisy
Women	4	2	11
	10	9	18
	8	8	20
Men	13	13	17
	12	11	21
	14	12	22

20. What is the F for gender?

   a. 0.218

   b. 15.927

   c. 12.273

21. What is the F for background?

   a. 0.218

   b. 15.927

   c. 12.273

22. What is the F for the interaction of Gender × Background?

   a. 0.218

   b. 15.927

   c. 12.273

14

IDENTIFYING ASSOCIATIONS WITH NOMINAL AND INTERVAL OR RATIO DATA

The Phi Correlation, the Pearson r Correlation, and the Point Biserial Correlation

> *You can't fix by analysis what you bungled by design.*
>
> —Light, Singer, and Willett (1990, p. viii)

It was pointed out previously that in the broadest sense, scientific observation is undertaken to achieve one of two goals. The goals are to describe situations and events more clearly and to identify relationships. The first chapters of this book dealt with the statistical procedures that are employed when describing data. Together, they are called, appropriately, descriptive statistics. Then, we introduced the concept of inferential statistics. Inferential statistics are the procedures we use to assist us in deciding whether relationships found in samples are likely to generalize to populations. There are two levels of relationships among variables: cause-and-effect relationships and associations. We have just completed our review of some of the most widely used statistical procedures for identifying cause-and-effect relationships. This and the next chapter deal with procedures that are utilized to identify associations among variables.

When we identify an association, we are indicating that two variables **covary**. This means that knowing how one variable changes aids us in predicting how another variable will change. For instance, taller people generally weigh more than shorter people. Knowing a person's height can therefore assist us in predicting the person's weight. While some associations, such as the association between height and weight, seem obvious, others that are commonly accepted may not even exist. For example, even though many Americans take vitamin supplements, a recent study did not find any health benefit for the general population associated with taking multivitamins.

> *Covary: if knowledge of how one variable changes assists you in predicting the value of another variable, the two variables are said to covary.*

> *Correlation: a measure of the degree of association among variables. A correlation indicates whether a variable changes in a predicable manner as another variable changes.*

When variables covary, the variables are related in some way and we say that there is a **correlation** among the variables. In other words, as one variable changes, another variable changes in a predictable manner. Table 14.1, which is a part of the overview table (Appendix K), indicates that the specific statistical procedure that is used when looking for an association will depend on the type of data that are being collected. Specifically, if both variables are nominal and are dichotomous (a score falls in one group or another), then you would use Phi; if both variables consist of ordinal data, you use the Spearman *r* (reviewed in Appendix B); and if you are dealing with two interval or ratio variables, you would employ the Pearson *r*.

Table 14.1	Statistical Procedures for Association Designs

	Type of Data		
	Nominal (Frequency)	**Ordinal (Ranked)**	**Interval or Ratio (Continuous Measure)**
Correlation	Phi	*Spearman r*[a]	Pearson *r*
Regression			Linear regression
			Multiple regression[b]

Note. Italicized items are reviewed in the following appendixes:

a. Appendix B.

b. Appendix C.

Each of these three correlations can vary from −1 through 0 to +1. If we ignore the sign of the correlation, we see that its magnitude goes from 0 to 1. A correlation of 0 indicates that there is no association between the two variables, and in this case, knowing the value of one variable does not assist in predicting the value of the other. For example, eye color and grade average in college are probably unrelated, so we would expect them to have a correlation of 0. A correlation of 1 (either +1 or −1) indicates that there is a perfect association among the variables. In other words, if you know the value of one variable, you can predict the value of the other variable perfectly, without any error. In the real world, correlations of 1 do not usually occur. Instead, we find more modest correlations with values such as .32 (either +.32 or −.32) or .57 (either +.57 or −.57). With correlations of these magnitudes, knowing the value of one variable will be of some assistance in predicting the value of the other variable, but the predictions are not perfect. An example of this is the weather forecast on the nightly news. The forecast is not always correct, but we pay attention because it is much more accurate than simply guessing.

In addition to the magnitude, correlations also have a sign, either + or −. In the case of the phi correlation, the sign simply reflects the order that the variables were entered into an equation. If the order is reversed, the sign will also change. The sign of phi is, therefore, not useful and is not reported when results are published. In contrast, the signs of the Spearman *r* and the Pearson *r* correlations are meaningful. Specifically, the sign indicates the direction of the relationship. For instance, in general, those students who study more get higher grades. This is an example of a **positive correlation**. In a positive correlation, as one variable increases, so does the other (Figure 14.1). Also, as one variable decreases, so does the other. In a **negative correlation**, as one variable increases, the other decreases (Figure 14.2). An example of a negative correlation would be the total mileage of a used car and how much it is worth. In general, the more miles the car has been driven, the less it is worth. That is why some unscrupulous individuals used to roll back odometers before selling their cars. The cars had gone just as many miles, but the buyers were not aware of this and paid more than they would have if they had known the true situation.

> *Positive correlation: a relationship between two variables in which as one variable increases in value, so does the other variable. Also, as one variable decreases in value, so does the other.*

> *Negative correlation: a relationship between two variables in which as one variable increases in value, the other variable decreases in value. Also, as one variable decreases in value, the other increases in value.*

Thus, with a correlation, the sign indicates the direction of the association (except for the phi correlation), while the magnitude indicates the degree to which the two variables covary and, thus, how well we can predict from one variable to another. What a correlation does not provide is the actual equation that would permit a researcher to predict the value of one variable when the value of the other variable is known. In other words, with just a correlation, researchers know that a prediction can be

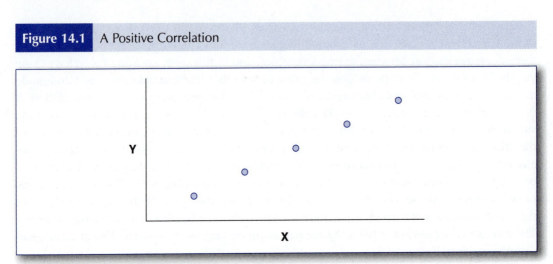

Figure 14.1   A Positive Correlation

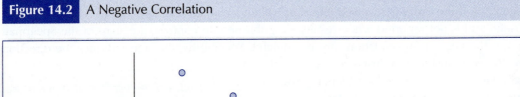

Figure 14.2   A Negative Correlation

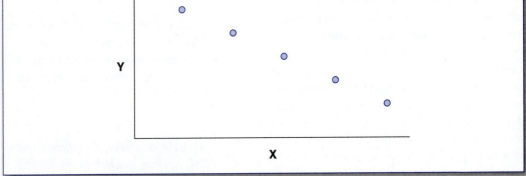

Regression: procedure researchers use to develop an equation that permits the prediction of one variable of a correlation if the value of another variable is known.

made and how well it can be made, but they do not know what the actual prediction would be. To make a prediction, we employ the statistical procedure called **regression**, which is reviewed in Chapter 15.

We have often discussed the concepts of Type I and Type II errors in this book. Each of these errors can also be made with a correlational study. For instance, if we conclude, based on our samples, that a correlation exists when in fact there is no such correlation among the populations, we have made a Type I error. In other words, we have rejected the null hypothesis, which is that the population correlation, called **rho** (ρ; pronounced row), is 0 even though the null hypothesis is actually true. On the other hand, if we conclude that there is no correlation among the variables, when in fact there is, we have made a Type II error. In this case, we have failed to reject the null hypothesis even though it is false.

rho (ρ): symbol used for the population correlation.

In a correlational study, the data are collected, but no independent variable is manipulated by the researcher, and there is no control group. Independent variables and control groups, as you have learned, are characteristics of an experiment. They do not occur in a correlational study. Instead, in a correlational study, the researcher records information concerning naturally occurring variables and later determines whether these variables covary. Correlational studies are generally easier to conduct than experiments, and depending on the design, numerous variables can be examined simultaneously. The studies are, in this sense, efficient. However, there is an important limitation of correlational studies, for their results do not justify reaching cause-and-effect conclusions. For instance, the initial scientific findings linking smoking with cancer were based solely on correlational studies. It quickly was established that an association or linkage existed between smoking and experiencing certain types of cancer. The government responded with warning labels on packages of cigarettes. These labels, however, differed significantly from the current ones. Initially, the warning was that cigarette smoking might cause cancer. Now, the warnings are much stronger and clearly state that smoking cigarettes has been shown to cause a variety of illnesses. The original, correlational studies did not warrant the current stronger, cause-and-effect wording.

The inability to draw strong conclusions from a correlational study is a direct consequence of the lack of control that is characteristic of this form of research. Since correlational studies do not include a control group or the direct manipulation of a variable, it is possible that the association we observe is caused by some unmeasured variable that is changing along with the variables we are measuring. I recall attending a scientific debate concerning how the early studies linking cigarette smoking with cancer should be interpreted. A speaker was adamant that the data did not warrant a strong conclusion. To make his point, the speaker suggested that the relationship between smoking and cancer could be explained by a third factor, genetics. He argued that some people might be destined, due to their genetic makeup, to develop cancer and also to prefer smoking. From this perspective, smoking was not the cause of the cancer, the smoker's genetics were to blame. Since the early studies did not include controls that would preclude this or other explanations, he argued that a strong case could not be made for a causal relationship between smoking and cancer. More recent studies have included the necessary controls, and we now are confident that smoking is a cause of cancer. These controlled studies are what scientists call experiments.

In the mid- to late 19th century, the distinction between experimental and correlational studies had not been clearly made, and the field of statistics was still in its infancy. Francis Galton, who is known for his numerous contributions to science in general, and psychology in particular, is credited with early work on correlation and regression. However, it was

Galton's student, Karl Pearson, who developed a number of the basic equations that we still use. In recognition of this achievement, Pearson's name is associated with a form of correlation. In this chapter, we will begin by reviewing two types of correlations: phi and the Pearson *r*. Each is underlined in Table 14.1, and each is employed with a different type of data. Phi (as well as the Spearman *r*) is actually just a special case of the Pearson *r*.

PHI CORRELATION

For nominal data, phi (ϕ) is a commonly utilized correlation. More precisely, phi (ρ_ϕ) would indicate the population correlation and **phi (r_ϕ)** would signify that we are dealing with samples.

> phi (r_ϕ): correlation used with nominal data. It is a form of Pearson r.

You are familiar with phi from our discussion of effect size in Chapter 8, but we will now be utilizing phi in a different way. This will become clear by referring to a previous example. In Chapter 8, we calculated a 2 × 2 chi-square (χ^2) statistic to test whether there was a *difference* between men and women's views of infidelity. Table 8.7, which includes the marginal totals, is reproduced here in a slightly modified form as Table 14.2. The four cells in the table are labeled *a*, *b*, *c*, and *d*. As the chi-square was found to be statistically significant, we rejected the null hypothesis that there was no difference in the distribution of answers for men and women and accepted the alternative hypothesis that these distributions do differ. More specifically, we concluded that men were more distressed by sexual infidelity, whereas women were more distressed by emotional infidelity. This statistically significant difference indicates that an outcome is unlikely to have occurred by chance. We then used the phi coefficient as a measure of effect size.

If we viewed this as a correlational study, we would not be asking if the distributions or proportions that we have observed were different. Instead, we would be asking if the variables are related or associated. In answering this question we would not, therefore,

Table 14.2   An Example of the Phi Correlation

	Women	Men	Total
More distressed by emotional infidelity	42 (*a*)	12 (*b*)	54 (*a* + *b*)
More distressed by sexual infidelity	17 (*c*)	48 (*d*)	65 (*c* + *d*)
Total	59 (*a* + *c*)	60 (*b* + *d*)	

begin by calculating a chi-square, which is a test of difference. Instead, we would calculate the phi coefficient directly using the following equation:

$$r_\phi = \frac{ad - bc}{\sqrt{(a+b)(c+d)(a+c)(b+d)}}.$$

In our case,

$$r_\phi = \frac{(42 \times 48 - 12 \times 17)}{\sqrt{(54 \times 65 \times 59 \times 60)}}$$

$$= \frac{2016 - 204}{3524.97}$$

$$= \frac{1812}{3524.97}$$

$$= .514.$$

Note that this is the same value that we calculated for phi in Chapter 8. However, now we calculated it directly without first calculating a chi-square value. Remember, if the phi coefficient is negative, change it to positive. The sign simply indicates the order of the columns and rows. For instance, if the proportions for men had been listed in the table before the proportions for women, the phi coefficient would have been negative. Thus, the sign is not meaningful and can be ignored.

As we are dealing with a correlation, the null hypothesis, H_0, usually states that there is no *relationship* between the two variables. In other words, if H_0 is true, the obtained value of phi should not differ significantly from 0. The alternative hypothesis, H_1, states that there is a relationship between the two variables. In other words, if H_1 is true, the obtained value of phi should differ significantly from 0. To test whether the obtained value of phi, in this case, .514, is significantly different from 0, we calculate a chi-square using the following equation:

$$\chi^2 = n(r_\phi)^2,$$

where n = the total number of observations. Thus,

$$n = a + b + c + d$$

and

$$df = (\text{Number of columns} - 1) \times (\text{Number of rows} - 1).$$

Since, we are dealing with a 2 × 2 table, the df is equal to $(2 - 1)(2 - 1) = 1$.

If the obtained value for the chi-square is greater than the critical value listed in the chi-square table, we reject the null hypothesis and accept the alternative. In our case,

$$\chi^2 = (42 + 12 + 17 + 48)(.514)^2$$

$$= (119)(.514)^2$$

$$= (119)(.26)$$

$$= 30.94.$$

This is, except for rounding error, the same value that was obtained when the chi-square was calculated directly for these data in Chapter 8 and is beyond the critical value for the chi-square with 1 df even at α equal to .005. We therefore reject the null hypothesis and accept the alternative that the obtained value of phi is significantly different from 0. If we were reporting this outcome in a journal article, we would conclude that there was a statistically significant relationship between gender and the view of infidelity ($r_\phi = .51$, $p < .005$).

As you recall, phi can vary from 0 to 1, where 0 indicates that there is no correlation between the two variables and 1 indicates that there is a perfect correlation between the two variables. (Remember, with phi, we ignore whether there is a positive or negative sign.) What this means is that if the correlation is 0, then knowing the value of one variable does not assist you in predicting the value of the second variable. For instance, some people have attached ear lobes while others do not. The author of this book does not know, but suspects, that there is no correlation between whether you have attached ear lobes or not and whether you are a psychology major. Thus, knowing whether you have attached ear lobes will not help in predicting whether you are a psychology major. On the other hand, a correlation of 1 permits a perfect prediction from one variable to another. An example of a correlation of 1 based on ratio data would be your height measured in meters and your height measured in centimeters. These two measures are mathematically related. A centimeter is 1/100 of a meter. Therefore, if we know that you are exactly 2 meters tall, we can predict, without error, that you are 200 centimeters tall. As was pointed our earlier, in the real world, we do not commonly find correlations of 1.

Recall that the larger the phi correlation, the better we can predict. Our value of phi was .51. This is on the border between being a medium and a strong correlation. In other words, if we know a person's gender, we would be able to predict quite well how that person views the relative importance of emotional and sexual infidelity.

Coefficient of determination: the square of the correlation. It indicates the proportion of variability in one variable that is explained or accounted for by the variability in the other variable.

The strength of the association can perhaps best be illustrated by finding the square of a correlation. The square of a correlation is called the **coefficient of determination**. In our case, it would be phi², which can also be written as r_ϕ^2. The coefficient of determination measures what proportion of variance in one variable is explained or accounted for by the other variable. In our example, the correlation was equal to .51. Phi^2 or r_ϕ^2 is, therefore, equal to .51^2, which is .26 or 26%. This indicates that knowing whether a subject is a man or a woman will remove or account for 26% of the variability in predicting their view of whether sexual or emotional infidelity is more distressing.

Put another way, there is 74% of the variability in the response to infidelity that is *not* accounted for by knowing whether the subject is a man or a woman. This is determined by subtracting 26%, the percentage of the variability that is known, from 100%, which is the total variability. Alternatively, we could express this in terms of a proportion by subtracting 0.26 from 1.00 to obtain 0.74. This value, which is the proportion of the variability of one variable *not* explained or accounted for by the variability of the other variable is called the **coefficient of nondetermination**. For phi, it is equal to $1 - r_\phi^2$.

> Coefficient of nondetermination: the proportion of the variability of one variable not explained or accounted for by the variability of the other variable. For phi, it is equal to $1 - r_\phi^2$.

Reporting the Results of a Phi Correlation

To provide a complete report of our finding, we would say that there was a significant correlation between gender and view of infidelity ($r_\phi = .51, p < .005$). The coefficient of determination, r_ϕ^2, equaled .26. With this statement, we have indicated to the reader that a phi correlation was conducted, the size of the correlation, and that it was statistically significant. Finally, we have provided a measure of the strength of the association, or effect size, to assist the reader in interpreting our finding.

Remember, the phi coefficient is a correlation. This means that the value of phi is indicative of the magnitude of the relationship evident in the data. It does not indicate whether there is a significant causal relationship between the frequencies or proportions that have been observed. And, if you had wanted to test whether there was a significant difference between the answers of men and women, you would have begun by conducting the chi-square test and then would have used the phi coefficient as a measure of strength of effect, as we did in Chapter 8. This distinction may be made clearer by reviewing how increasing the number of subjects affects the chi-square, but not phi.

In Table 8.9, the data that are included in Table 14.2 were doubled for illustrative purposes. It was shown that doubling the data set did not affect the size of phi. This is because phi is a measure of relationship based on the observed relative proportions. Since doubling each of the frequencies does not affect the relative proportions, phi does not change. Chi-square, on the other hand, is a measure of the likelihood that a set of observed frequencies would occur by chance. Doubling the data set makes us more confident that an outcome is not due to chance, which is reflected in the doubling of the chi-square value.

So which procedure, phi or the chi-square should you begin with? Logically, it should simply be a question of whether your study is a correlation or an experiment. If you have conducted an experiment, which means that you have manipulated a variable and have included appropriate controls, then you should begin with the chi-square as a test of difference and then use phi as a measure of effect size. If, instead, you have conducted a correlational study, you should begin with phi to obtain a measure of the relationship between your variables and then convert this into a chi-square test to ascertain whether the obtained correlation is significantly different from 0. If it is, then proceed to calculate phi^2, which is also written as r_ϕ^2, to determine the percentage of variance explained. However, due to tradition, most researchers immediately turn to a chi-square test when they have nominal data forming two dichotomies regardless of whether they have conducted an experiment or a correlational study. As a result, when a significant chi-square is encountered in the literature, the reader must review the study's design to determine whether the study is an experiment or a correlation. The research design will, in turn, determine how strong a conclusion is warranted. Remember, cause-and-effect conclusions can only be drawn from a properly designed and executed experimental study. Conducting a chi-square test on correlational data will not justify making a stronger conclusion. In other words, *it is the study's design and execution, not the statistical procedure that is subsequently used, that determines the strength of the conclusion that can ultimately be drawn.*

Purpose and Limitations of Using the Phi Correlation

1. *Provides a measure of the association of two dichotomous variables:* The phi coefficient provides a measure of the degree to which two dichotomous variables are associated. As the data are nominal, the data are in the form of frequencies.

2. *Not a measure of cause and effect:* Phi is a type of correlation. Correlational designs lack the level of experimenter control that is needed in order to justify coming to a cause-and-effect conclusion. Thus, all the researcher can conclude is that the two variables are related and to what degree they are related. The researcher cannot conclude that one variable caused a change in the other.

Assumptions of the Phi Correlation

1. *Nominal data:* The data are in the form of frequencies or can be converted to frequencies.

2. *Data are in the form of two dichotomies:* The phi correlation is used when there are two variables, each in the form of a dichotomy.

PEARSON *r* CORRELATION

The **Pearson *r*** correlation, also sometimes called the Pearson product–moment correlation coefficient, is undoubtedly the most commonly used form of correlation. It is located on the same row of Table 14.1 as phi and the Spearman *r* and, like them, is a measure of the association between two variables. Like phi, the Pearson *r* provides a measure of how well you can predict from one variable to the other.

> *Pearson r: correlation used with interval or ratio data.*

With the Pearson *r*, we use the symbol ρ_{XY} to indicate the population correlation between variables *X* and *Y*, and r_{XY} to indicate a sample correlation between *X* and *Y*.

In the case of the Pearson *r*, both variables are measured at the interval or ratio level. As the Pearson *r* is a measure of linear relationship, it only provides an accurate indication of the magnitude of the association if the two variables have a straight line relationship between them. If the relationship is not linear between the variables, the Pearson *r* will underestimate the true degree of the association. In this case, the data can be converted to ranks and the Spearman *r* correlation would then be calculated. (This procedure is reviewed in Appendix B.) Alternatively, you can turn to more advanced texts that include a discussion of curvilinear correlation.

With the Pearson *r*, the sign of the correlation (+ or −) indicates the direction of the relation. When the sign is positive, as one variable increases, so does the other. When the sign is negative, as one variable increases, the other decreases. The magnitude of the correlation, ignoring the sign, indicates the size of the relationship. For instance, if the Pearson *r* is equal to 1, there is no error in predicting from one variable to the other. A graph or scatterplot would show that all of the data points fall along a straight line. If the correlation is +1, the line would rise to the right (Figure 14.3). If the correlation is −1, the line would rise to the left (Figure 14.4). If the magnitude is less than 1 but greater than 0, some degree of prediction is possible. In

---

Figure 14.3   A Correlation of +1

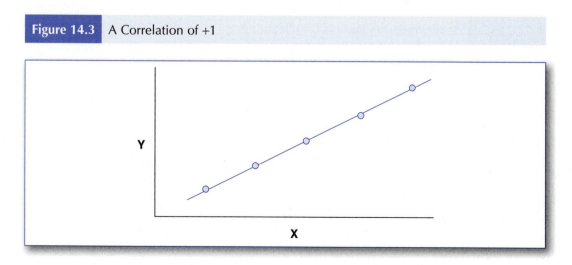

this case, the data points would not all fall directly on a straight line (Figure 14.5). If the Pearson r is equal to 0, knowing the value of one variable does not assist in predicting the value of the other variable (Figure 14.6).

It is important to note that due to a lack of experimental manipulation and control, a significant Pearson r does not justify the researcher coming to a cause-and-effect conclusion. Thus, with a significant Pearson r, you know that it is possible to predict from one variable to the other with some accuracy, but this does not mean that one variable is causing the other to change. For instance, as children age, they attend more school and generally become more proficient in academic disciplines such as mathematics and geography. However, as they age, they also grow taller. There will, accordingly, be a correlation between height and math proficiency. Nevertheless, increased height is presumably not

Figure 14.4   A Correlation of –1

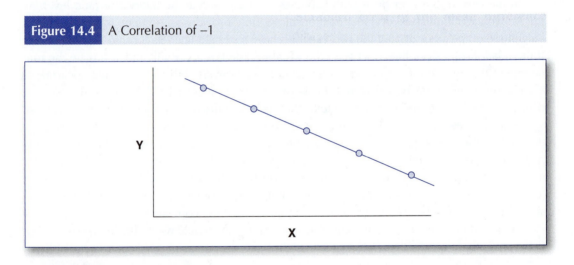

Figure 14.5   An Intermediate, Positive Correlation

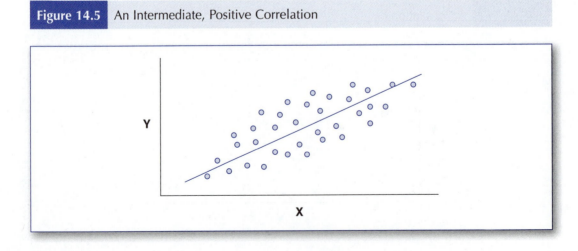

Figure 14.6   A Correlation of 0

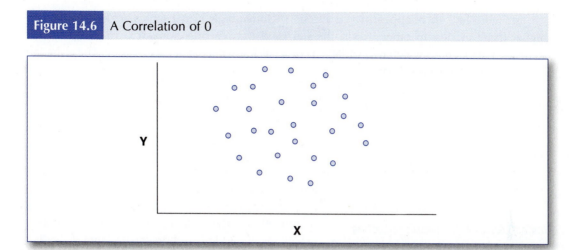

causing the gain in math ability. Instead, the increased math proficiency is due to matura-tion and the experiences that are associated with increasing age.

First Example of a Pearson *r* Correlation

For an example of a Pearson *r*, Table 14.3 includes hypothetical quiz and exam scores for seven students taking a course in statistics. We will set α equal to .05 and utilize a two-tailed test. The null hypothesis (H_0) is that there is no correlation between the two underlying populations. In other words, the null hypothesis is that $\rho_{XY} = 0$. The alternative hypothesis (H_1) is that $\rho_{XY} \neq 0$. These data are graphed in Figure 14.7.

Table 14.3   First Example of a Pearson *r*: Hypothetical Quiz and Exam Scores

Student	Quiz Score (X)	Exam Score (Y)
1	10	92
2	9	98
3	9	84
4	8	87
5	8	81
6	7	72
7	6	76

In Figure 14.7, there appears to be a trend such that higher quiz scores are associated with higher exam grades. In other words, the quiz and exam scores appear to vary together. In statistics, the extent to which two variables covary is known as their **covariance**. The equation for the covariance is as follows:

$$\text{cov}_{XY} = \frac{\sum(X - M_X)(Y - M_Y)}{n - 1},$$

where n is the number of *pairs* of scores.

The equation indicates that each value for X is converted into a deviation from its mean. Similarly, each value for Y is converted into a deviation from its mean. Then, each pair of deviations is multiplied together. Next, all of these multiplied deviations are added, and finally, this sum is divided by the number of pairs of scores minus 1.

Covariance: a statistical measure indicating the extent to which two variables vary together.

On a closer examination of the equation for the covariance, it should be evident that if a value for X is greater than its mean, then $(X - M_X)$ will be positive. Also, if the value for Y that is paired with this X is greater than its mean, then this $(Y - M_Y)$ will also be positive, and their product will thus be positive. Similarly, if a value for X is less than its mean, then $(X - M_X)$ will be negative. Also, if the value for Y that is paired with this X is less than its mean, then this $(Y - M_Y)$ will also be negative, and their product will thus be positive. However, if one of the deviations is positive and the other is negative, then the product will be negative. The sum of all of these pairs of scores, and thus the sign of the covariance, will indicate the direction in which two variables covary.

Figure 14.7	First Example of a Pearson *r*: A Graph of Hypothetical Quiz (*X*) and Exam (*Y*) Scores

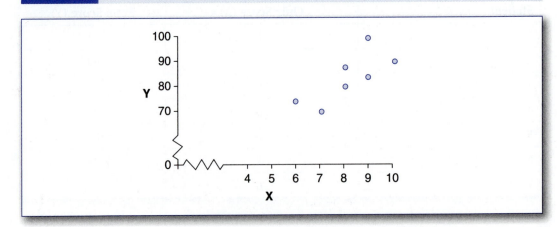

With our example, the individuals with the highest quiz grades tend to also have the highest exam grades. Thus, the greatest positive deviations for the quizzes will tend to be matched with the greatest positive deviations for the exam scores. Similarly, the individuals with the lowest quiz grades tend to also have the lowest exam grades. Thus, the largest negative deviations for the quizzes will tend to be matched with the largest negative deviations for the exam scores. This pairing of positive deviations in one variable with positive deviations in the other, and negative deviations in one variable with negative deviations in the other will lead to a positive value for the covariance. If the positive deviations for the quizzes had tended to be matched with the negative deviations for the exam grades, the covariance would have a negative value. And you will see shortly that the sign of the covariance determines the sign of the Pearson r correlation.

Furthermore, the magnitude of the covariance will be a maximum when the most extreme X and Y scores are paired together. And it will be zero if the two variables are not related and thus do not covary.

Covariation is essential to understanding the Pearson r correlation. To calculate the value of a Pearson r, all that is further needed is to take the magnitude of the standard deviations for the X and Y variables into account. More specifically, the equation for calculating the Pearson r correlation is as follows:

$$r_{XY} = \frac{\text{cov}_{XY}}{s_{XP} s_{YP}}.$$

Conceptually, this equation indicates that the Pearson r is the ratio of a measure of the amount two variables covary or vary together and a measure of their total variability.

To use this equation, it is necessary to determine the value of the covariance and also to calculate the standard deviation of the X scores and the standard deviation of the Y scores. (There are computational equations that are easier to use with large data sets, but the logic for the specific calculations is then not evident. These equations are provided in Appendix F. However, anyone anticipating calculating a Pearson r for a substantial data set is advised to use a computer package instead.) We proceed as shown in Table 14.4.

Substituting the obtained values into the equation for the covariance, we have

$$\text{cov}_{XY} = \frac{\sum (X - M_X)(Y - M_Y)}{n - 1},$$

where n = the number of *pairs* of scores.

$$\text{cov}_{XY} = \frac{57.715}{7 - 1}$$

$$= \frac{57.715}{6}$$

$$= 9.619.$$

Table 14.4	First Example of a Pearson *r*: Initial Steps in the Calculation of the Covariance for Quiz and Exam Scores				

Student	Quiz (X)	Exam (Y)	$X - M_X$	$Y - M_Y$	$(X - M_X)(Y - M_Y)$
1	10	92	1.857	7.714	14.325
2	9	98	0.857	13.714	11.753
3	9	84	0.857	−0.286	−0.245
4	8	87	−0.143	2.714	−0.388
5	8	81	−0.143	−3.286	0.470
6	7	72	−1.143	−12.286	14.043
7	6	76	−2.143	−8.286	17.757
	$\Sigma X = 57$ $M_X = 8.143$	$\Sigma Y = 590$ $M_Y = 84.286$	$\Sigma(X - M_X) =$ approx. 0	$\Sigma(Y - M_Y) =$ approx. 0	$\Sigma(X - M_X)(Y - M_Y) =$ 57.715

To find the value of the Pearson *r* correlation, we now need to calculate the standard deviations for the *X* and *Y* scores (Tables 14.5 and 14.6). Recall that the equation for the standard deviation of a sample as an estimate of the population standard deviation is as follows:

$$s_{XP} = \sqrt{\frac{\Sigma(X - M_X)^2}{n - 1}}.$$

Table 14.5	First Example of a Pearson *r*: Calculation of the Standard Deviation of the Quiz Scores		

Student	Quiz (X)	$X - M_X$	$(X - M_X)^2$
1	10	1.857	3.448
2	9	0.857	0.734
3	9	0.857	0.734
4	8	−0.143	0.020
5	8	−0.143	0.020
6	7	−1.143	1.306
7	6	−2.143	4.592
	$\Sigma X = 57$ $M_X = 8.143$	$\Sigma(X - M_X) =$ approx. 0	$\Sigma(X - M_X)^2 = 10.854$

Substituting the values of $\Sigma(X - M_X)^2$ and n into the equation for the standard deviation of quiz scores, we have

$$s_{XP} = \sqrt{\frac{\Sigma(X - M_X)^2}{n-1}}$$

$$= \sqrt{\frac{10.854}{7-1}}$$

$$= \sqrt{\frac{10.854}{6}}$$

$$= \sqrt{1.809}$$

$$= 1.345.$$

| Table 14.6 | First Example of a Pearson *r*: Calculation of the Standard Deviation of the Exam Scores |

Student	Exam (*Y*)	*Y* – *M*_Y	(*Y* – *M*_Y)²
1	92	7.714	59.506
2	98	13.714	188.074
3	84	−0.286	0.082
4	87	2.714	7.366
5	81	−3.286	10.798
6	72	−12.286	150.946
7	76	−8.286	68.658
	$\Sigma Y = 590$ $M_Y = 84.286$	$\Sigma(Y - M_Y) = $ approx. 0	$\Sigma(Y - M_Y)^2 = 485.430$

Substituting the appropriate values into the equation for the standard deviation of exam scores, we have

$$s_{YP} = \sqrt{\frac{\Sigma(Y - M_Y)^2}{n-1}}$$

$$= \sqrt{\frac{485.430}{7-1}}$$

$$= \sqrt{\frac{485.430}{6}}$$

$$= \sqrt{80.905}$$

$$= 8.995.$$

We are now in a position to calculate the value of the Pearson r correlation. Recall that the equation for the Pearson r correlation is as follows:

$$r_{XY} = \frac{\text{cov}_{XY}}{S_{XP}S_{YP}}$$

Substituting the values just obtained, we have the following:

$$= \frac{9.619}{(1.345)(8.995)}$$

$$= \frac{9.619}{12.098}$$

$$= 0.795.$$

The degrees of freedom(df) for the Pearson $r = n - 2$, where n is the number of *pairs* of scores. In our case, there would be $7 - 2$ or 5 df.

Referring to the Pearson r table (Appendix J, Table J.6), we find that the critical value for 5 df with α equal to .05 is .754 for a two-tailed test. As our obtained Pearson r was .795, we reject the null hypothesis that $\rho_{XY} = 0$ and accept the alternative hypothesis that $\rho_{XY} \neq 0$. We now find the coefficient of determination, $r_{XY}^2 = .795^2$. This, in turn, is equal to .63, or 63%. The coefficient of determination indicates that by knowing the quiz grade, we can eliminate 63% of the variability in predicting the exam grade. This is a very large value.

Reporting the Results of a Pearson *r* Correlation

In an article, we would report, "A positive relationship was found between quiz and exam scores ($r(5) = 0.795, p < .05$)." After reporting the significant r, we would say "r_{XY}^2 was equal to .63."

Second Example of a Pearson *r* Correlation

It is important to understand that the magnitude of the Pearson r of a small set of data can be dramatically affected by the removal of just one or two extreme scores. This is called

restriction of the range. For instance, if we omit subjects 6 and 7 from the above data set, we would have the data shown in Table 14.7.

Proceeding as before, we create Tables 14.8, 14.9, and 14.10.

Restriction of the range: reducing the range of values for a variable will reduce the size of the correlation.

Table 14.7	Second Example of a Pearson *r*: Restricted Range of Hypothetical Quiz and Exam Scores

Student	Quiz (*X*)	Exam (*Y*)
1	10	92
2	9	98
3	9	84
4	8	87
5	8	81

Table 14.8	Second Example of a Pearson *r*: Initial Steps in the Calculation of the Covariance for the Restricted Range of Quiz and Exam Scores

Student	Quiz (*X*)	Exam (*Y*)	*X* − *M*$_X$	*Y* − *M*$_Y$	(*X* − *M*$_X$)(*Y* − *M*$_Y$)
1	10	92	1.200	3.600	4.320
2	9	98	.200	9.600	1.920
3	9	84	.200	−4.400	−.880
4	8	87	−.800	−1.400	1.120
5	8	81	−.800	−7.400	5.920
	Σ*X* = 44 *M*$_X$ = 8.800	Σ*Y* = 442 *M*$_Y$ = 88.400	Σ(*X* − *M*$_X$) = 0	Σ(*Y* − *M*$_Y$) = 0	Σ(*X* − *M*$_X$)(*Y* − *M*$_Y$) = 12.400

Substituting these values into the equation for the covariance, we have

$$\text{cov}_{XY} = \frac{\sum(X - M_X)(Y - M_Y)}{n-1},$$

where n is the number of *pairs* of scores.

$$\text{cov}_{XY} = \frac{12.400}{5-1}$$

$$= \frac{12.400}{4}$$

$$= 3.100.$$

Table 14.9	Second Example of a Pearson r: Calculation of the Standard Deviation of the Quiz Scores for the Restricted Range of Quiz and Exam Scores

Student	Quiz (X)	$X - M_X$	$(X - M_X)^2$
1	10	1.200	1.440
2	9	0.200	0.040
3	9	0.200	0.040
4	8	−0.800	0.640
5	8	−0.800	0.640
	$\Sigma X = 44$ $M_X = 8.800$	$\Sigma(X - M_X) = 0$	$\Sigma(X - M_X)^2 = 2.800$

Substituting these values into the equation for the standard deviation, we have

$$s_{XP} = \sqrt{\frac{\Sigma(X - M_X)^2}{n-1}}$$

$$= \sqrt{\frac{2.800}{5-1}}$$

$$= \sqrt{\frac{2.800}{4}}$$

$$= \sqrt{0.700}$$

$$= 0.837$$

Table 14.10	Second Example of a Pearson r: Calculation of the Standard Deviation of the Exam Scores for the Restricted Range of Quiz and Exam Scores		
Student	**Exam (Y)**	$Y - M_Y$	$(Y - M_Y)^2$
1	92	3.600	12.960
2	98	9.600	92.160
3	84	−4.400	19.360
4	87	−1.400	1.960
5	81	−7.400	54.760
	$\Sigma Y = 442$ $M_Y = 88.400$	$\Sigma(Y - M_Y) = 0$	$\Sigma(Y - M_Y)^2 = 181.200$

Substituting these values into the equation for the standard deviation, we have the following:

$$s_{YP} = \sqrt{\frac{\Sigma(Y - M_Y)^2}{n - 1}}$$

$$= \sqrt{\frac{181.200}{5 - 1}}$$

$$= \sqrt{\frac{181.200}{4}}$$

$$= \sqrt{45.300}$$

$$= 6.731.$$

We are now in a position to calculate the value of the Pearson r correlation. The equation for the Pearson r correlation is as follows:

$$r_{XY} = \frac{\text{cov}_{XY}}{s_{XP} s_{YP}}$$

$$= \frac{3.100}{(0.837)(6.731)}$$

$$= \frac{3.100}{5.634}$$

$$= 0.550.$$

The degrees of freedom for the Pearson $r = n - 2$, where n is the number of *pairs* of scores. In our case, there would be $5 - 2$ or 3 *df*.

Restricting the range by dropping the two lowest quiz scores results in a drop in the size of the correlation from .795 to .550. This is a substantial decline and the resulting correlation would no longer be statistically significant even without the loss of degrees of freedom. If it were significant, r_{XY}^2 would have dropped from 63% to 30%, which indicates that the ability to predict would have been reduced substantially.

Reporting the Results of a Pearson r Correlation

In an article, we would report, "No significant relationship was found between quiz and exam scores $(r(3) = 0.550, p > .05)$."

Purpose and Limitations of Using the Pearson r Correlation

1. *Provides a measure of the association of two interval or ratio variables:* The Pearson r correlation provides a measure of the strength and direction of an association between two interval or ratio variables.

2. *Not a measure of cause and effect:* The Pearson r is a type of correlation. Due to a lack of control in a correlational design, a researcher is not justified in coming to a cause-and-effect conclusion.

3. *Be aware of restriction of the range:* A broad range of X and Y values will increase the size of the Pearson r. Any reduction in the range of these variables will reduce the size of the Pearson r.

4. *Prediction is limited to the range of the original values:* The Pearson r indicates the correlation for a range of X and Y values. The nature of the correlation for these variables is unknown beyond the range included in the original calculations. For instance, if the original correlation of height and weight is based on people with heights between 5 and 6 feet, then we cannot predict the weight for a person 7 feet tall.

Assumptions of the Pearson r Correlation

1. *Interval or ratio data:* The data are on an interval scale of measurement or a ratio scale of measurement.

2. *Data are paired:* The data come as pairs, usually two measures on the same individual.

3. *Linear relationship:* The Pearson *r* correlation assumes that the two variables are linearly related.

4. *Normal distribution for X and Y variables*: The test for significance of the Pearson *r* assumes that the *X* and *Y* variables are normally distributed. However, if the degrees of freedom are greater than 25, this assumption is not critical.

PROGRESS CHECK

1. Another term for the square of a correlation is the ____. It indicates the ____ in one variable that is explained or accounted for by variability in the other variable.

2. With nominal data that consist of two dichotomies, we would use ____ as our correlation. If we had two variables measured at the interval or ratio level we would use the ____ correlation.

3. Assume it was reported that the correlation was .5 between age and reading ability for students selected from grades 1 to 12. We then measure this relationship for grades 6 through 12 and find a smaller correlation. This is an example of ____.

Answers: 1. coefficient of determination, variability.   2. phi, Pearson *r*.   3. restriction of the range.

AN ADDITIONAL CORRELATIONAL TECHNIQUE: THE POINT BISERIAL CORRELATION

This chapter has introduced two of the most commonly used correlational techniques. There are, however, numerous additional correlational procedures that have not been included. For instance, there are correlations that use data from different measurement levels. In the case of the **point biserial (r_{pb})** correlation, one variable is nominal (more specifically, a **true dichotomy**), the other is measured at the interval or ratio level. With a true dichotomy, there is a natural division of scores into two distinctly different categories. Examples would be heads or tails or legally married or not married. A coin lands either heads or tails, and you are either legally married or not married. You are not mostly married or only partially married.

> Point biserial (r_{pb}): correlation used when one variable is nominal (a true dichotomy) and the other consists of interval or ratio data.

> True dichotomy: a natural division of scores into two distinct categories.

The point biserial correlation is not appropriate for use with what might be called an artificial or manufactured dichotomy where there are no distinctly different, natural categories. Examples would be tall or short and thick or thin. In each of these cases, there is an underlying continuum of values that is being split into a dichotomy. Thus, there is no true dichotomy of tall and short people. Instead, a person has a specific height that is being categorized as being within some range that we arbitrarily call tall or short. A point biserial correlation would not be appropriate for these data (instead, you would utilize the biserial correlation, which has almost the same name but is different).

The point biserial correlation is another special case of the Pearson *r*. Therefore, the magnitude can vary from −1 through 0 to +1. However, as with phi, the sign simply indicates the order in which the dichotomy was entered into the calculation. Therefore, the sign does not provide meaningful information concerning the association.

As an example of a point biserial correlation, we will examine the effect of marriage on longevity of male faculty. Research has shown that marriage is associated with increased longevity for men in general, but in a hypothetical study, we will examine whether the effect occurs with male college professors. The results of our hypothetical study are presented in Table 14.11. Specifically, the age of death for 14 faculty members are recorded. Six of these were never married, while eight were married at the time of their death. The married versus not married variable is a true dichotomy, whereas the age of death is measured at the ratio level. As there is no experimental manipulation (we did not either encourage or discourage marriage), this is a correlational design, more specifically a point biserial. The null hypothesis is that there is no correlation between marital

Table 14.11	An Example of the Point Biserial Correlation: Initial Steps in the Calculation of the Covariance for Hypothetical Marital Status and Longevity Data

Subject	Marital Status (X)	Longevity (Y)	$X - M_X$	$Y - M_Y$	$(X - M_X)(Y - M_Y)$
1	0	84	−0.571	9.143	−5.220
2	0	76	−0.571	1.143	−0.653
3	0	72	−0.571	−2.857	1.631
4	0	70	−0.571	−4.857	2.773
5	0	69	−0.571	−5.857	3.344
6	0	65	−0.571	−9.857	5.628
7	1	88	0.429	13.143	5.638

Subject	Marital Status (X)	Longevity (Y)	$X - M_X$	$Y - M_Y$	$(X - M_X)(Y - M_Y)$
8	1	83	0.429	8.143	3.493
9	1	78	0.429	3.143	1.348
10	1	76	0.429	1.143	0.490
11	1	73	0.429	−1.857	−0.797
12	1	72	0.429	−2.857	−1.226
13	1	71	0.429	−3.857	−1.655
14	1	71	0.429	−3.857	−1.655
	$\Sigma X = 8$ $M_X = 0.571$	$\Sigma Y = 1048$ $M_Y = 74.857$	$\Sigma(X - M_X) =$ approx. 0	$\Sigma(Y - M_Y) =$ approx. 0	$\Sigma(X - M_X)(Y - M_Y) =$ 13.139

history and longevity. In other words, the null hypothesis is that $\rho_{pb} = 0$, and the alternative hypothesis is that $\rho_{pb} \neq 0$. Alpha is set to .05.

To conduct a point biserial correlation, an arbitrary value is assigned to each level of the dichotomy. It is customary to assign a value of 0 to one level and a value of 1 to the other, but any two values will work. We will assign a 0 to identify faculty members who never married and a 1 to identify faculty members who were married. Then, the value of the point biserial is calculated using either the Pearson r equation that you just learned or a version of this equation specifically tailored for use with the point biserial. As there is little advantage to the use of a special point biserial equation, we will continue to employ the equation for the Pearson r (Tables 14.11 to 14.13).

Substituting the obtained values into the equation for the covariance, we have the following:

$$\text{cov}_{XY} = \frac{\Sigma(X - M_X)(Y - M_Y)}{n - 1},$$

where n is the number of *pairs* of scores.

$$\text{cov}_{XY} = \frac{13.139}{14 - 1}$$

$$= \frac{13.139}{13}$$

$$= 1.011.$$

Table 14.12	An Example of the Point Biserial Correlation: Calculation of the Standard Deviation of the Marital Status Scores		

Subject	Marital Status (X)	$X - M_X$	$(X - M_X)^2$
1	0	−0.571	0.326
2	0	−0.571	0.326
3	0	−0.571	0.326
4	0	−0.571	0.326
5	0	−0.571	0.326
6	0	−0.571	0.326
7	1	0.429	0.184
8	1	0.429	0.184
9	1	0.429	0.184
10	1	0.429	0.184
11	1	0.429	0.184
12	1	0.429	0.184
13	1	0.429	0.184
14	1	0.429	0.184
	$\Sigma X = 8$ $M_X = 0.571$	$\Sigma(X - M_X) =$ approx. 0	$\Sigma(X - M_X)^2 = 3.428$

Substituting the obtained values into the equation for the standard deviation, we have the following:

$$s_{XP} = \sqrt{\frac{\Sigma(X - M_X)^2}{n - 1}}$$

$$= \sqrt{\frac{3.428}{14 - 1}}$$

$$= \sqrt{\frac{3.428}{13}}$$

$$= \sqrt{0.264}$$

$$= 0.514.$$

Table 14.13	An Example of the Point Biserial Correlation: Calculation of the Standard Deviation of the Longevity Scores		

Subject	Longevity (Y)	Y − M$_Y$	(Y − M$_Y$)^2
1	84	9.143	83.594
2	76	1.143	1.306
3	72	−2.857	8.162
4	70	−4.857	23.590
5	69	−5.857	34.304
6	65	−9.857	97.160
7	88	13.143	172.738
8	83	8.143	66.308
9	78	3.143	9.878
10	76	1.143	1.306
11	73	−1.857	3.448
12	72	−2.857	8.162
13	71	−3.857	14.876
14	71	−3.857	14.876
	$\Sigma Y = 1048$ $M_Y = 74.857$	$\Sigma(Y - M_Y) =$ approx. 0	$\Sigma(Y - M_Y)^2 = 539.708$

Substituting the obtained values into the equation for the standard deviation, we have the following:

$$S_{YP} = \sqrt{\frac{\Sigma(Y - M_Y)^2}{n - 1}}$$

$$= \sqrt{\frac{539.708}{14 - 1}}$$

$$= \sqrt{\frac{539.708}{13}}$$

$$= \sqrt{41.516}$$

$$= 6.443.$$

We are now in a position to calculate the value of the point biserial correlation. The equation we are using for the point biserial correlation is the same as for the Pearson r correlation:

$$r_{pb} = r_{XY} = \frac{COV_{XY}}{S_{XP}S_{YP}}$$

$$= \frac{1.011}{(0.514)(6.443)}$$

$$= \frac{1.011}{3.312}$$

$$= .305.$$

The degrees of freedom for the point biserial $= n - 2$, where n is the number of *pairs* of scores. In our case, there would be $14 - 2$ or 12 *df*.

Referring to the Pearson r table (we also use the Pearson r table with the point biserial correlation), we find that the critical value for 12 *df* with α equal to .05 is .532 for a two-tailed test. If a one-tailed test had been specified, the critical value would be .458. As our obtained point biserial correlation was .305, we do not reject the null hypothesis that $\rho_{pb} = 0$. In other words, with our hypothetical data, it is not evident that marital status is associated with longevity in faculty members. Of course it should be recognized that the data set is very small. If the outcome had been statistically significant, we would have said that there is an association between marital status and longevity, but we could not indicate that there was a causal relationship due to the lack of experimental control. We then would have found r_{pb}^2, a measure of effect size.

Reporting the Results of a Point Biserial Correlation

In an article, we would report, "There was no significant relationship found between marital status of faculty members and their longevity ($r_{pb}(12) = 0.305, p > .05$)."

The data in Table 14.11 could be reconfigured as is shown in Table 14.14. In this form, it should be evident that we have ratio data and two independent groups of faculty members, those who were never married and those who were married. If we had been interested in determining whether there was a difference between the ages of death for the two groups, we would have conducted an independent samples t test (or a one-way between-subjects ANOVA [analysis of variance]) with these data instead of the point biserial correlation. Either of these additional statistical procedures would also be found to be nonsignificant. However, due to the lack of experimental control even if the outcome was significant, we still could not have concluded that it was the marital status that caused the difference in longevity. *Once again, it is important to remember that it is the strength of the study's design and execution that determines the strength of the conclusion that can be drawn, not the statistical procedure employed.*

| Table 14.14 | An Example of the Point Biserial Correlation Reorganized as an Independent Samples *t* Test or a One-Way Between-Subjects ANOVA |

Never Married	Married
84	88
76	83
72	78
70	76
69	73
65	72
	71
	71

Note. ANOVA, analysis of variance.

Final Thoughts Concerning the r_{pb}

As an independent samples *t* test, the one-way between-subjects ANOVA (*F* test) and a r_{pb} can be utilized with the same data, it may not come as a surprise that there is a mathematical relationship between *t*, *F*, and the point biserial

$$r_{pb}^2 = \frac{t^2}{t^2 + df},$$

and

$$r_{pb}^2 = \frac{F}{F + df}.$$

In both of these equations, the degrees of freedom are for the point biserial correlation, the *t* test, or the within-groups component of the *F* test as these are equivalent. Specifically, the degrees of freedom for the point biserial correlation is equal to $n - 2$, where *n* is the number of pairs of scores. The degrees of freedom for the independent samples *t* test and the within-groups *df* of the *F* test are equal to the sum of the number of cases in each group minus 1. In other words, $df_{t \text{ test}}$ and $df_w = (n_1 - 1) + (n_2 - 1)$. This, in turn, is equal to $n_1 + n_2 - 2$, which is equal to $n - 2$, the degrees of freedom for the point biserial correlation.

With the F ratio, we also need the df_{Bet} to find a critical value. The df_{Bet} for a one-way between-subjects ANOVA is equal to $k - 1$, where k is the number of groups. With a point biserial correlation and the independent samples t test, there are always only two groups. With two groups, there is 1 df_{Bet} for the F test.

You are encouraged to confirm that our r_{pb} of .305 and 12 df is equivalent to an independent samples t test of approximately 1.11 with 12 df, and an F of approximately 1.23 with 1 and 12 df.

Purpose and Limitations of Using the Point Biserial Correlation

1. *Provides a measure of the association of one dichotomous and one interval or ratio variable.*

2. *Not a measure of cause and effect*: The point biserial correlation is a type of Pearson r correlation. Due to a lack of control in a correlational design, a researcher is not justified in coming to a cause-and-effect conclusion.

3. *Be aware of restriction of the range*: A broad range of the interval or ratio values will increase the size of the point biserial correlation. Any reduction in the range of this variable will reduce the size of the point biserial correlation.

4. *Prediction is limited to the range of the original values:* The point biserial indicates the correlation for a range of values. The nature of the correlation for this variable is unknown beyond the range included in the original calculations.

Assumptions of the Point Biserial Correlation

1. *One variable is nominal—a true dichotomy—the other consists of interval or ratio data.*

2. *Normal distribution for the interval or ratio variable:* The test for significance of the point biserial correlation assumes that the interval or ratio variable is normally distributed. However, if the degrees of freedom are greater than 25, this assumption is not critical.

CONCLUSION

This chapter has introduced three of the most commonly used correlational techniques—phi, the Pearson r, and the point biserial correlation. Which of these is chosen will depend on the measurement level of the data.

While there are numerous additional correlational procedures, this chapter will end by briefly mentioning an additional two. Each of the correlational techniques that have been reviewed in this chapter employed two variables. In the real world, numerous variables may be associated together. For instance, many variables are associated with a student's SAT score, including their high school grade average, quality of their teachers, physical characteristics of the high school, and level of support at home, to name just a few. With **multiple correlation (R)**, we determine the association between a variable that is of interest to us, in this case SAT score, and a combination of two or more other predictor variables. Thus, with R, we are able to more accurately reflect the true complexity of a situation than we are when we limit ourselves to the association of only two variables.

With partial correlation—the second of our more complex correlational procedures—we can statistically remove the effect of a variable that is *not* of interest to us. For example, as a taxpayer, it should be of interest to you to have some measure of the effectiveness with which your money is spent. If you live within a large

> *Multiple correlation (R): the association between one criterion variable and a combination of two or more predictor variables.*

school district, there may well be a number of high schools. How can you compare the effectiveness of their academic programs? After all, they may differ in many ways—size, age of buildings, years of teaching experience by the faculty, and so on. How can you possibly make a fair decision? One approach is to remove the effect of variables that are suspected of being important, but which are not of interest. For instance, family income level is known to correlate with numerous variables associated with academic success of high school students. Not surprisingly, families with high incomes tend to provide more support at home in the form of computers, the parents tend to be more highly educated and are thus better able to assist their children academically, and these families even move to areas with new schools. Thus, it should come as no surprise that the most academically impressive high schools also tend to have students who come from the most affluent families. However, as a taxpayer, you are probably not willing to simply conclude that those schools with the most affluent students are the most efficient users of your money. As a matter of fact, even though a school with students from less affluent families may not be achieving at the same level as another with students from more affluent families, it may be excelling beyond what would be expected based on the disparity in income. One way to determine whether this is the case is to employ a statistical procedure known as **partial correlation**. With this procedure, we could remove the effect of family income to obtain a better view of which high schools were actually teaching most effectively.

> *Partial correlation: a procedure in which the effect of a variable that is not of interest is removed.*

Chapter Resources

GLOSSARY OF TERMS

Coefficient of determination: the square of the correlation. It indicates the proportion of variability in one variable that is explained or accounted for by the variability in the other variable.

Coefficient of nondetermination: the proportion of the variability of one variable not explained or accounted for by the variability of the other variable. For phi, it is equal to $1 - r_\phi^2$.

Correlation: a measure of the degree of association among variables. A correlation indicates whether a variable changes in a predicable manner as another variable changes.

Covariance: a statistical measure indicating the extent to which two variables vary together.

Covary: if knowledge of how one variable changes assists you in predicting the value of another variable, the two variables are said to covary.

Multiple correlation (R): the association between one criterion variable and a combination of two or more predictor variables.

Negative correlation: a relationship between two variables in which as one variable increases in value, the other variable decreases in value. Also, as one variable decreases in value, the other increases in value.

Partial correlation: a procedure in which the effect of a variable that is not of interest is removed.

Pearson r: correlation used with interval or ratio data.

phi (r_ϕ): correlation used with nominal data. It is a form of Pearson r.

Point biserial (r_{pb}): correlation used when one variable is nominal (a true dichotomy) and the other consists of interval or ratio data.

Positive correlation: a relationship between two variables in which as one variable increases in value, so does the other variable. Also, as one variable decreases in value, so does the other.

Regression: procedure researchers use to develop an equation that permits the prediction of one variable of a correlation if the value of the other variable is known.

Restriction of the range: reducing the range of values for a variable will reduce the size of the correlation.

rho (ρ): symbol used for the population correlation.

True dichotomy: a natural division of scores into two distinct categories.

Questions: Chapter 14

(Answers to odd-numbered items are provided in Appendix I.)

1. When knowledge of the outcome of one event assists in predicting the outcome of another event, then we say _____.
   a. the two events are causally related
   b. the two events are correlated
   c. the two events are independent
   d. the two events are meaningful

2. To use the Pearson r, the data must be either _____.
   a. nominal or ordinal
   b. ordinal or interval
   c. interval or ratio
   d. nominal or ratio

3. The magnitude of the Pearson r indicates the _____ between X and Y.

    a. durability of the relationship

    b. direction of the relationship

    c. degree to which there is a nonlinear relationship

    d. degree to which there is a linear relationship

4. The magnitude of the square of the Pearson r indicates the _____.

    a. percentage of the variance in Y explained by the variance in X

    b. degree to which X and Y are affected by a third variable, Z

    c. degree to which the experimenter has utilized appropriate experimental design

    d. extent to which error occurred in the study

5. If knowing how one variable changes aids us in predicting how another variable will change, we say that the two variables _____.

    a. are causally linked

    b. covary

    c. are identical

    d. should be merged into one variable

6. If you are interested in whether two variables are correlated and if both variables are nominal and are dichotomous (a score falls in one group or another), then you would use _____.

    a. phi

    b. Spearman r

    c. Pearson r

    d. point biserial

7. If you are interested in whether two variables are correlated and if both variables consist of ordinal data, you use _____.

    a. phi

    b. Spearman r

    c. Pearson r

    d. point biserial

8. If you are interested in whether two variables are correlated and if you are dealing with two interval or ratio variables, you would employ _____.

    a. phi

    b. Spearman r

    c. Pearson r

    d. point biserial

9. If you are interested in whether two variables are correlated and if you are dealing with one variable that is a true dichotomy and one variable measured at the interval or ratio level, you would employ _____.

    a. phi

    b. Spearman *r*

    c. Pearson *r*

    d. point biserial

10. A correlation of _____ indicates that there is no association between the two variables.

    a. 0

    b. 1

    c. 2

    d. 3

    e. 4

11. A correlation of _____ indicates that there is a perfect association among the variables.

    a. 0

    b. 1

    c. 2

    d. 3

    e. 4

12. In the case of the _____ correlation, the sign simply reflects the order that the variables were entered into an equation. If the order is reversed, the sign will also change.

    a. phi

    b. Spearman *r*

    c. Pearson *r*

13. In a _____ correlation, as one variable increases, so does the other.

    a. neutral

    b. negative

    c. positive

    d. strong

14. In general, the more flaws a diamond has, the lower its value. This is an example of a _____ correlation.

    a. neutral

    b. negative

    c. positive

    d. strong

15. With a (an)_____ the researchers know that a prediction can be made and how well it can be made, but they do not know what the actual prediction would be. To make a prediction, we employ the statistical procedure called _____.

    a. inferential statistic, correlation

    b. descriptive statistic, correlation

    c. regression, correlation

    d. correlation, regression

16. If we conclude, based on our samples, that a correlation exists when in fact there is no such correlation, we have made a _____.

    a. Type I error

    b. Type II error

    c. Type III error

    d. a correct decision

17. With a (an) _____ design, we are not asking if the distributions or proportions that we have observed are different. Instead, we are asking if the variables are related or associated.

    a. experimental

    b. descriptive statistical

    c. correlational

    d. ANOVA

18. The square of a correlation is called the _____.

    a. Spearman correction

    b. coefficient of determination

    c. covariance

    d. regression equation

19. The _____ measures what proportion of variance in one variable is explained or accounted for by the other variable.

    a. Spearman correction

    b. coefficient of determination

    c. covariance

    d. regression equation

20. The removal of extreme scores usually reduces the size of a correlation. This is called
    _____.

    a. the compression effect

    b. range limitation

    c. deviation control

    d. restriction of the range

Problems Utilizing Phi

Subjects are asked whether they like chicken wings and, then, are asked whether they like pizza. The following data are obtained:

		Like Pizza	
		Yes	No
Like chicken wings	Yes	12	4
	No	5	8

21. What is the value of phi?

    a. .226

    b. .326

    c. .369

    d. .517

Subjects are asked whether they enjoy watching baseball and, then, are asked if they enjoy watching football. The following data are obtained:

		Like Baseball	
		Yes	No
Like football	Yes	15	9
	No	5	12

22. What is the value of phi?

    a. .226

    b. .326

    c. .369

    d. .517

Problem Utilizing Pearson *r*

A group of hypothetical students were asked their high school GPAs and their most recent statistics quiz score:

GPA	Quiz Score
4.0	10
3.75	9
3.5	9
3.25	7
3.0	8
2.5	5

Note. GPA, grade point average.

23. What is the correlation between these two variables?

    a. .932

    b. .950

    c. −.916

    d. .025

(*Note:* It is important to save your work for Problem 23 as it will be needed for Questions 14 and 15 in Chapter 15.)

Problem Utilizing the Point Biserial

Sixteen men and women are asked to indicate their trust in government on a 10-point scale. The following hypothetical data are obtained:

Men	Women
6	10
5	9
5	8
4	8
1	6
3	7
3	7
5	
4	

24. What is the value of the point biserial correlation?

    a. .931

    b. .819

    c. −.926

    d. .034

Problems 25 to 30 utilize SPSS.

SPSS

USING SPSS WITH THE PEARSON r CORRELATION

To Begin SPSS

Step 1: The first step, as before, is to activate the program.

    Step 2: Click on "Type in data," and then click on "OK."

Step 3: Click on "Variable View." We will only be dealing with the columns headed by "Name," "Label," and "Measure."

Step 4: Click on the first empty cell under the column heading "Name." You now type the name of the first variable for which you have data. We are going to utilize the same data and labels as were previously employed in Table 14.3. These data dealt with whether there is a correlation between quiz and exam grades for students in a statistics class. We are calling these variables "Quiz" and "Exam." Therefore, type "Quiz" in the first empty cell under "Name."

Step 5: Click on the first empty cell under the column heading "Label." In this cell, you can type a more extensive description of your variable. In our case, type "Quiz grade."

Step 6: Click on the first empty cell under the column heading "Measure." As we are dealing with interval or ratio data for the quiz grades, select "Scale" as is shown in Figure 14.8.

Step 7: Repeat Steps 4 to 6 except that you type "Exam" in the first empty cell under "Name" and "Exam grade" for the label. As before, select "Scale" in the column under the column heading "Measure" as we have interval or ratio data for the exam grades. The result is shown in Figure 14.8.

Figure 14.8	The Variable View Window for the Pearson *r* Correlation

To Enter Data in SPSS

Step 8: Click on the "Data View" option at the lower left-hand corner of the window. The variables "Quiz" and "Exam" will be present.

Step 9: For each of the seven subjects in the study, type their quiz and exam grades in the appropriate columns (Figure 14.9).

To Conduct a Pearson *r* Correlation

Step 10: Click the cursor on "Analyze" along the row of SPSS commands above the data you entered, then move to "Correlate," then click on "Bivariate" as we are dealing with two variables, the quiz and exam grades.

Step 11: A new window will appear (Figure 14.10). On the left side of this window is a list of all of the variables that have been entered into SPSS. To conduct a Pearson *r*, we must

| Figure 14.9 | Entering Data for the Pearson *r* Correlation |

indicate to SPSS which variables we wish to examine. As we only have two variables, this is accomplished by moving our two variables to the empty box on the right side of the window. To do so, we highlight our first variable, "Quiz grade," and then click on the central arrow, as is shown in Figure 14.11. We then move "Exam grade" to the right side box in the same manner. The result will be that each label will move to the appropriate box on the right-hand side of the window, as is shown in Figure 14.12. Check to be sure that the appropriate options are indicated, in our case "Pearson," "Two-tailed," and "Flag significant correlations." Then click "OK," which is located at the bottom of the window.

Step 12: SPSS calculates the desired Pearson r as shown in Table 14.15. The table takes some practice to get used to. In the left most column, find "Quiz grade." Directly to the right is printed "Pearson Correlation." Continuing in the same row there is a number "1," which indicates that quiz grades are perfectly correlated with quiz grades. Continuing in the same row is the number .795*. This indicates that the Pearson r between quiz grades and exam grades is .795 and the *(asterisk) indicates that this correlation is significant at the .05 level. The next row indicates that the exact probability of a correlation of .795 is .033. The final row in the Quiz grade section is the number of subjects, in this case 7. The same information is then presented again in three rows that begin with "Exam grade." Clearly, if the correlation between quiz and exam grades is .795, then the correlation between exam and quiz grades is also .795. Thus, SPSS essentially presents the results twice. You should verify that this outcome is the same as we found previously.

(*Note:* Save this SPSS data file. It will be used in Chapter 15.)

Figure 14.10 The Bivariate Correlation Window

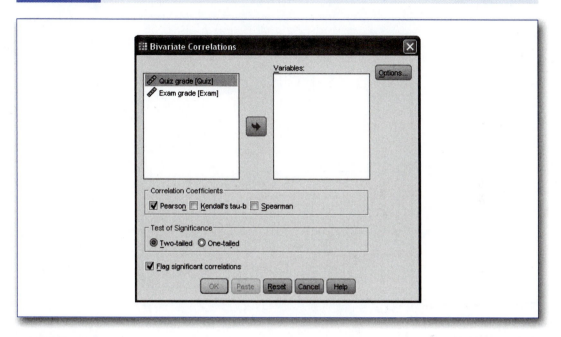

Figure 14.11 The Bivariate Correlation Window (Continued)

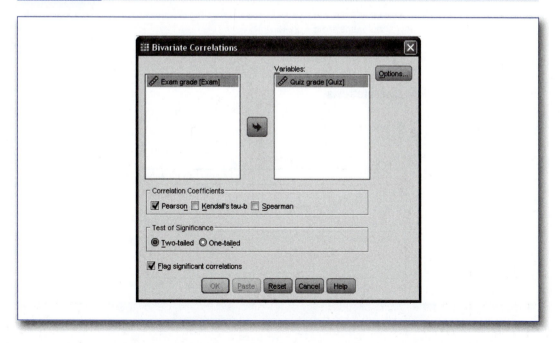

Figure 14.12   The Completed Bivariate Correlation Window

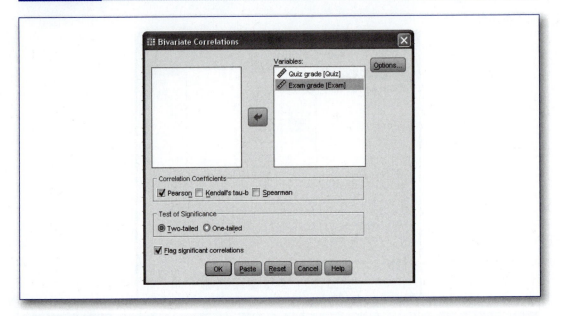

Table 14.15   SPSS Output for the Pearson *r* Correlation

```
CORRELATIONS
  /VARIABLES=Quiz Exam
  /PRINT=TWOTAIL NOSIG
  /MISSING=PAIRWISE.
```

➡ **Correlations**

[DataSet0]

Correlations

		Quiz grade	Exam grade
Quiz grade	Pearson Correlation	1	.795[*]
	Sig. (2-tailed)		.033
	N	7	7
Exam grade	Pearson Correlation	.795[*]	1
	Sig. (2-tailed)	.033	
	N	7	7

*. Correlation is significant at the 0.05 level (2-tailed).

USING SPSS WITH THE POINT BISERIAL CORRELATION

To Begin SPSS

Steps 1 to 3: These are same as for the previous example of a Pearson *r*.

Step 4: Click on the first empty cell under the column heading "Name." You now type the name of the first variable for which you have data. We are going to utilize the same data and labels as were previously employed in Table 14.11. These data dealt with whether there is a correlation between marital status and longevity. We are calling these variables "status" and "age." Therefore, type "status" in the first empty cell under "Name."

Step 5: Click on the first empty cell under the column heading "Label." In this cell, you can type a more extensive description of your variable. In our case, type "Marital status."

Step 6: Click on the first empty cell under the column heading "Values." Then click on the small blue square. A box will appear. In the blank space to the right of "Value," type the number "0." Then, type a brief description of this value of the variable in the blank space to the right of "Label." In our case, type "never married." Finally, click on "Add." Your label for a value of 0 will appear in the large white region in the center of the window. Now repeat the above steps in this section for the value "1," which is given the label "married" (Figure 14.13). Then click "Add" (Figure 14.14) and finally "OK."

Step 7: Click on the first empty cell under the column heading "Measure." As we are dealing with names for conditions, select "Nominal."

Figure 14.13	The Value Labels Window

Figure 14.14	The Completed Value Labels Window

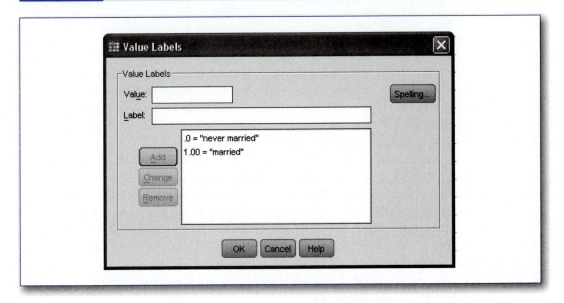

Step 8: Repeat Steps 4 to 7 except that you type "age" in the first empty cell under "Name" and "Age at death" for the label. In this case, select "Scale" in the column under the column heading "Measure" as we have interval or ratio data for the age at which the hypothetical subjects died. The result is shown in Figure 14.15.

To Enter Data in SPSS

Step 9: Click on the "Data View" option at the lower left-hand corner of the window. The variables "status" and "age" will be present.

Step 10: For each of the 14 subjects in the study, type 0 or 1 depending on their marital status and in the next column the age at which they died (Figure 14.16).

Figure 14.15	The Variable View Window for the Point Biserial Correlation

Figure 14.16	Entering Data for the Point Biserial Correlation

File   Edit   View   Data   Transform   Analyze

14 : age   71.00

	status	age
1	.0	84.00
2	.0	76.00
3	.0	72.00
4	.0	70.00
5	.0	69.00
6	.0	65.00
7	1.00	88.00
8	1.00	83.00
9	1.00	78.00
10	1.00	76.00
11	1.00	73.00
12	1.00	72.00
13	1.00	71.00
14	1.00	71.00
15		

To Conduct a Point Biserial *r* Correlation (The Procedure Is Identical to Conducting a Pearson *r* Correlation)

Step 11: Click the cursor on "Analyze" along the row of SPSS commands above the data you entered, then move to "Correlate," then click on "Bivariate" as we are dealing with two variables, marital status and age at death.

Step 12: A new window will appear (Figure 14.17). On the left side of this window is a list of all of the variables that have been entered into SPSS. To conduct a point biserial correlation, we must indicate to SPSS which variables we wish to examine. As we only have two variables, this is accomplished by moving our two variables to the empty box on the right side of the window. To do so, we highlight our first variable, "Marital status," and then click on the central arrow, as is shown in Figure 14.18. We then move "Age at death" to the right side box in the same manner. The result will be that each label will move to the appropriate box on the right-hand side of the window, as is shown in Figure 14.19. Check to be sure that the appropriate options are indicated, in our case "Pearson," "Two-tailed," and "Flag significant correlations." Then click "OK," which is located at the bottom of the window.

Step 13: SPSS calculates the desired point biserial correlation as shown in Table 14.16. The table is the same as for a Pearson *r* correlation. In the left most column, find "Marital status." Directly to the right is printed "Pearson Correlation." Continuing in the same row, there is a number 1, which indicates that marital status is perfectly correlated with itself. Continuing in the same row is the number .306. This indicates that the Pearson *r* between marital status and age at death is .306, and the lack of an * indicates that this correlation is *not* significant at the .05 level. The next row indicates that the exact probability of the correlation of .306 is .288, which is greater than our criterion of .05. The final row in the "Marital status" section is the total number of subjects, in this case 14. The same information is then presented again in three rows that begin with "Age at death." As the correlation between Marital status and Age at death is .306, then the correlation between Age at death and Marital status is also .306. Thus, SPSS essentially presents the results twice. You should verify that this outcome is almost identical to what we found previously.

| Figure 14.17 | The Bivariate Correlation Window |

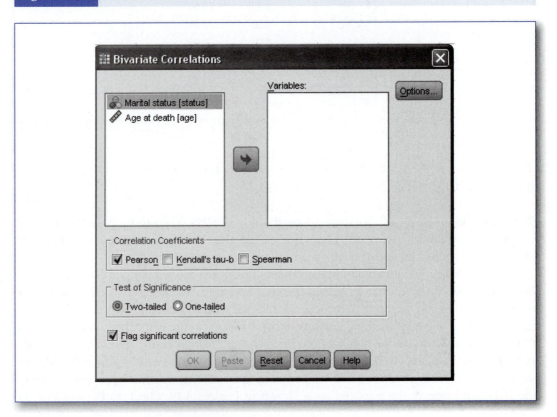

Figure 14.18   The Bivariate Correlation Window (Continued)

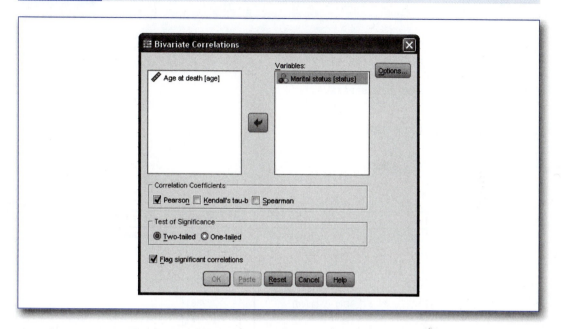

Figure 14.19   The Completed Bivariate Correlation Window

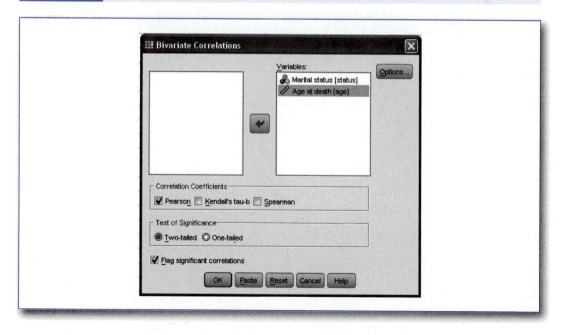

Table 14.16   SPSS Output for the Point Biserial Correlation

```
CORRELATIONS
  /VARIABLES=status age
  /PRINT=TWOTAIL NOSIG
  /MISSING=PAIRWISE.
```

➡ **Correlations**

[DataSet0]

Correlations

		Marital status	Age at death
Marital status	Pearson Correlation	1	.306
	Sig. (2-tailed)		.288
	N	14	14
Age at death	Pearson Correlation	.306	1
	Sig. (2-tailed)	.288	
	N	14	14

SPSS Problems: Chapter 14

A magazine recently listed the horsepower and mileage of sporty cars equipped with a turbo and a manual transmission:

Horsepower	MPG
200	27
265	24
172	33
227	25
197	27
305	21

Note. MPG, miles per gallon.

25. Which correlation would be appropriate for these data?

    a. Phi

    b. Pearson *r*

    c. Point biserial

26. What is the correlation between these two variables?

    a. .932

    b. −.950

    c. −.916

    d. .025

27. Is the correlation statistically significant with alpha equal to .05?

    a. Yes

    b. No

(*Note*: Save the above SPSS data file. It will be used in Chapter 15.)

Seventeen individuals are asked if they voted for Obama for president and their ages. The following hypothetical data are obtained:

	Voted for Obama	
	Yes	No
Ages	18	54
	21	61
	45	36
	62	55
	28	74
	36	84
	74	73
	55	
	24	
	19	

28. Which correlation would be appropriate for these data?

    a. Phi

    b. Pearson *r*

    c. Point biserial

29. What is the correlation between these two variables?

    a. .930

    b. .957

    c. −.912

    d. .567

30. Is the correlation statistically significant with alpha equal to .05?

    a. Yes

    b. No

15

IDENTIFYING ASSOCIATIONS WITH INTERVAL AND RATIO DATA

Linear Regression

It is a capital mistake to theorize before one has data. Insensibly one begins to twist facts to suit theories instead of theories to suit facts.

—Sir Arthur Conan Doyle

I n Chapter 14, we reviewed a number of commonly used correlational procedures. They are used to assist us in deciding whether there is an association or correspondence between two variables. In the case where there are two dichotomous (nominal) variables, we learned to employ phi. If there are two ranked (ordinal) variables, the Spearman r would be appropriate (reviewed in Appendix B). The Pearson r is used when there are two interval or ratio variables. Finally, the point biserial is used when one variable is a true dichotomy and the other is an interval or ratio variable (Table 15.1). All of these are actually forms of the Pearson r, so a value of + or −1 indicates a perfect association, and a value of 0 indicates that there is no association between the variables. In addition, for the Pearson r and the Spearman r, the sign, + or − , indicates the direction of the association. For phi and the point biserial, the sign simply reflects the order in which the dichotomy is entered into the calculation and is thus not meaningful.

Table 15.1   Overview of Correlational Procedures

		Variable A		
		Dichotomous	**Ranked**	**Interval or Ratio**
Variable *B*	**Dichotomous**	Phi	—	Point biserial
	Ranked		*Spearman r*	—
	Interval or ratio			Pearson *r*

Note. The italicized item is reviewed in Appendix B.

A statistically significant correlation indicates that the variables are associated. In other words, if there is a significant correlation, knowing the value of one variable will assist in predicting the value of the other. However, a correlation does not indicate how this prediction is to be made. To actually predict from one variable to another, we use a procedure known as regression.

In this chapter, we will limit our discussion to the situation where there are two interval or ratio variables. It is assumed, therefore, that you have calculated a Pearson *r* and it was found to be significantly different from 0. We know, therefore, that defining the linear relationship between the two variables would permit a better prediction of *Y* than always choosing M_Y. More specifically, if there is a significant Pearson *r*, there is a straight line, as shown in Figure 15.1 or Figure 15.2, that provides a better fit to the data than using M_Y regardless of the value of *X*.

Knowing that two variables are linearly related enhances our ability to predict from one to the other. Let us assume that we are *not* aware that there is an association between height

Figure 15.1   Example of a Positive Linear Relationship Between *X* and *Y*

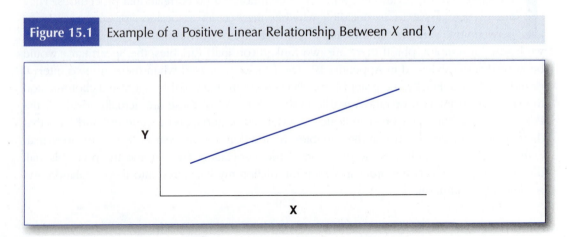

| Figure 15.2 | Example of a Negative Linear Relationship Between *X* and *Y* |

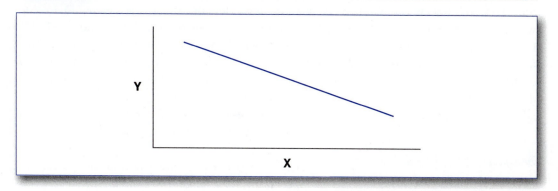

and weight. In this case, regardless of a person's height, our best estimate of their weight would be the mean weight. Thus, regardless of a person's height (X), we would always predict the mean weight (M_y; Figure 15.3). Of course, for tall people, we would tend to underestimate their weights and for short people we would tend to overestimate their weights. Each error in estimation is a deviation from the mean weight, or $Y - M_y$. The sum of the errors would be $\Sigma(Y - M_y)$. This term is not useful, of course, because it will always be equal to 0. However, the sum of the squared deviations from the mean, $\Sigma(Y - M_y)^2$ forms the basis for calculating the standard deviation and variance. In other words, the standard deviation and variance of the Y scores can be thought of as measures of our error of prediction assuming we always chose the mean weight, M_y, regardless of the subject's height (X).

| Figure 15.3 | Example of Error Due to Predicting the Mean of Y (M_y) Regardless of the Value of X |

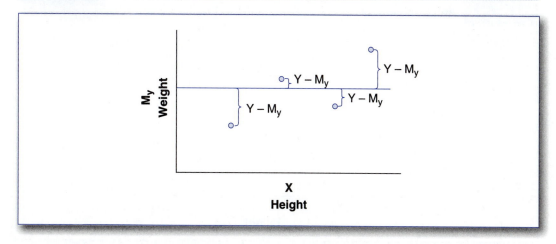

However, if there is a significant correlation between height (X) and weight (Y), then knowing the person's height (X) will assist in predicting that person's weight (Y). Thus, in this situation, we would not choose the mean weight (M_y) regardless of the subject's height (X). Instead, with a positive correlation as the height (X) increases, so does our estimate of the weight (Y). Linear regression is simply the procedure used to derive an equation that enables us to predict from X to Y with better accuracy than choosing M_Y regardless of the value of X. Specifically, for each value of X, we can use our equation to derive a predicted value of Y, for which we use the symbol $\hat{Y}$ (called Y hat). As we are dealing with **linear regression**, all of these $\hat{Y}$ values will fall along a straight line. This line is called the **regression line**. An example is illustrated in Figure 15.4. This example of a regression line rises to the right. This indicates that as the height (X) increases, so does the prediction of the weight ($\hat{Y}$). Specifically, for a height of X_1 the predicted weight is Y_1, and for a height of X_2 the predicted weight is Y_2. Remember, the regression line consists of predicted values of Y. And each predicted value of Y, which we identified as $\hat{Y}$, is paired with a value of X.

Linear regression: procedures used to determine the equation for the regression line.

Regression line: with linear regression, a straight line indicating the value of Y that is predicted to occur for each value of X. The predicted value of Y is called $\hat{Y}$.

In Figure 15.5, all of the actual subject weights fall along the regression line. In this situation, there is no error in predicting from X to the Y values. In other words, if we know the subject's height, we can predict the subject's weight without any error. This would only be the situation if the correlation had a value of + or −1. Of course, this rarely, if ever, occurs in the real world. Instead, while in general taller people weigh more than those who are shorter, there are also individuals who are tall, but who are relatively light, and individuals who are short but relatively heavy. In this more realistic situation, the Pearson r correlation is less than 1.

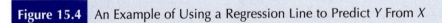

Figure 15.4   An Example of Using a Regression Line to Predict Y From X

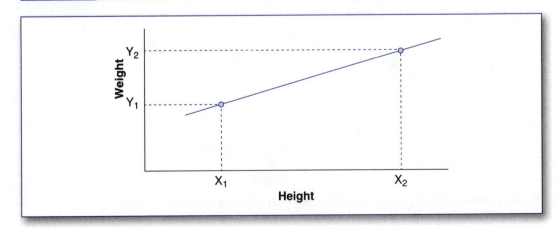

When the correlation is less than 1, all of the observed data points do not fall along the regression line (Figure 15.6). Since the regression line consists of the predicted value of Y for each value of X, any deviation from the line indicates that there was an error of prediction. Thus, the regression line consists of a series of $\hat{Y}$ values, one for each value of X, and each deviation of an actual score (Y) from the predicted value ($\hat{Y}$) is an error of prediction. In other words, when $Y - \hat{Y}$ does not equal zero, there is an error of prediction. As we are just as likely to underestimate as overestimate Y values, the $\Sigma(Y - \hat{Y})$ will be 0. The sum of the squared deviations from the predicted values of Y, which is written as $\Sigma(Y - \hat{Y})^2$, however, can form the basis for calculating a new measure of the standard deviation and variance. These can be thought of as measures of our error of prediction when using the regression line. To prevent confusion, the standard deviation for the error of prediction when using a regression line is called the **standard error of estimate** ($\sigma_{\hat{y}}$).

Standard error of estimate: the standard deviation of Y scores around the regression line. Its symbol is $\sigma_{\hat{Y}}$.

The accuracy of our predictions will depend, first, on how closely the observed data fall along a straight line and, second, how successful we are in defining the equation for the line that best fits our data. The degree to which the data fall along a straight line is an empirical question and is out of our control. However, in those cases in which the Pearson r correlation is large, either + or −, we know the data tend to fall tightly along a straight line. In contrast, in those cases in which the Pearson r correlation is small, the data do not fall as close to a straight line. Regardless, we need an agreed-on method for defining the equation for the line that best fits our data. In statistics, this regression line is defined as the straight line for which the sum of the squared errors of prediction, $\Sigma(Y - \hat{Y})^2$, is a minimum.

Figure 15.5	An Example of a Regression Line Permitting the Prediction of Y From X Without Any Error

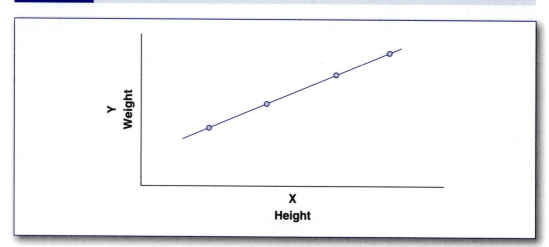

Figure 15.6	An Example of a Regression Line in Which There Is Error in the Prediction of Y From X

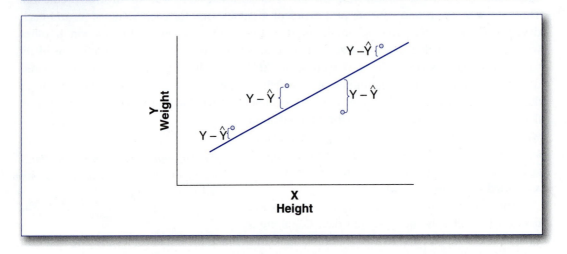

The calculation of maximums and minimums requires the use of calculus. Fortunately, we do not need to actually derive the equations for finding a straight line such that $\Sigma(Y - \hat{Y})^2$ is a minimum. Instead, we will simply make use of the equations that have been derived by others using calculus. However, before doing so, it is important you understand the advantage of using a regression line.

Figure 15.3 is based on the same hypothetical data points used in Figure 15.6. However, instead of showing the errors of prediction from the regression line (Figure 15.6), Figure 15.3 used the mean, M_Y, as the predicted weight for each subject regardless of the subject's height. It is clear that the total error of prediction when using M_Y (Figure 15.3) is greater than the error of prediction when using the regression line (Figure 15.6). This will always be the case when the correlation is statistically significant.

Put another way, when the correlation is statistically significant, the standard deviation based on the deviations of Y scores from M_Y (this is an estimate of σ_Y) will always be greater than the standard error of estimate (the standard deviation based on the deviations of Y scores from the regression line; this is an estimate of $\sigma_{\hat{Y}}$). Thus, the error of prediction when using M_Y, which is an estimate of σ_Y, will be greater than the error of prediction when using the regression line, which is an estimate of $\sigma_{\hat{Y}}$, whenever the correlation is statistically significant. In other words, σ_Y (which is estimated by $\sqrt{\Sigma(Y - M_Y)^2 / (n-1)}$ will be greater than $\sigma_{\hat{Y}}$ (which is estimated by $\sqrt{\Sigma(Y - \hat{Y})^2 / (n-1)}$ whenever the Pearson r is statistically significant. This is evident from the following equation:

$$\sigma_{\hat{Y}} = \sigma_Y \sqrt{(1 - r^2)} \,.$$

So long as $r \neq 0$, and thus r^2 is greater than 0, $\sigma_{\hat{Y}}$ will be less than σ_Y.

If r^2 is equal to 1, then the equation becomes

$$\sigma_{\hat{Y}} = \sigma_Y \sqrt{(1-1)}$$

$$= \sigma_Y \sqrt{(0)}$$

$$= \sigma_Y (0)$$

$$= 0.$$

In other words, when r^2 is equal to 1, the standard error of estimate ($\sigma_{\hat{Y}}$) is equal to 0. This is because when r^2 is equal to 1, then r will equal +1 or −1. When r is equal to +1 or −1, all of the Y scores fall on the regression line, and thus, there is no error when predicting from X to Y, and $\sigma_{\hat{Y}}$ will equal 0.

The same relationship is true, of course, for the variances. Thus, the variance that is estimated by using M_Y (i.e., σ_Y^2) will always be greater than what is called the **error variance** ($\sigma_{\hat{Y}}^2$), which is estimated by using the regression line.

Furthermore, it can be shown that

Error variance: the variance of Y scores around the regression line.

$$r^2 = \frac{\sigma_Y^2 - \sigma_{\hat{Y}}^2}{\sigma_Y^2}.$$

An example will clarify the meaning of this equation. If all of the Y values fall directly along the regression line, the error variance, $\sigma_{\hat{Y}}^2$, is equal to 0. This is the situation illustrated in Figure 15.5, and in this case, there would be no error in prediction. If you know the value of X, you can predict the value of Y without any error. Specifically, in this case,

$$r^2 = \frac{\sigma_Y^2 - 0}{\sigma_Y^2}$$

$$= \frac{\sigma_Y^2}{\sigma_Y^2}$$

$$= 1.$$

It was pointed out previously in this text that r^2 indicates the proportion of variability explained. With regression, r^2 indicates the proportion of the variability that has been accounted for or eliminated by using $\hat{Y}$ (the regression line) as our prediction rather than always choosing M_Y. When the correlation, r, is equal to 1, we can predict perfectly from X to

Y. In other words, for each X value, the corresponding Y value is equal to $\hat{Y}$, and thus, all of the variability has been explained. In this case, r^2 is also equal to 1. Whenever $\sigma_{\hat{Y}}^2$ is small relative to σ_Y^2, it indicates that the predictions using the regression line are considerably more accurate than the predictions using M_Y, and r^2 is therefore large (close to 1). Whenever $\sigma_{\hat{Y}}^2$ approaches the size of σ_Y^2, it indicates that the predictions using the regression line are only marginally better than the predictions using M_Y and as a result, r^2 is small (close to 0).

To this point in the chapter, the discussion has been quite theoretical. The chapter began by explaining that you use linear regression following the determination that a Pearson r is statistically significant. Linear regression enables us to predict the value of Y that corresponds to a value of X. More specifically, it was noted that with a significant Pearson r, we found that the predictions based on linear regression ($\hat{Y}$) are more accurate than if we simply chose the mean of the Y scores regardless of the value of X. In other words, the standard error of estimate ($\sigma_{\hat{Y}}$) is smaller than the standard deviation of Y scores from their mean (σ_Y). Finally, the relationship between linear regression and r^2 was reviewed. We will now conclude with a discussion of how to determine the actual equation for the regression line. It is important to note that if the Pearson r is not statistically significant, then there is no linear relationship between the variables, and thus, there would be no point in identifying a regression equation.

PROGRESS CHECK

1. If we have no idea what the relationship is between two variables, X and Y, then for every value of X, our best estimate of Y would be to choose ____.

2. If the Pearson r correlation is statistically significant, then using the ____ will lead to more accurate predictions than always choosing ____.

3. If the Pearson r correlation is equal to +1 or −1, then the standard error of estimate will equal ____.

Answers: 1. the mean of Y.   2. regression line, the mean of Y.   3. zero.

DETERMINATION OF THE REGRESSION EQUATION

With a significant Pearson r, we know that there is a linear relationship between the X and Y variables as is shown in Figures 15.1 and 15.2. However, the correlation does not tell us the equation of the line that represents that relationship. To predict the value of Y, we need to define the precise relationship between the X and Y variables using the equation for a straight line, which is as follows:

$$Y = bX + a.$$

This equation indicates that the value of Y can be determined once two characteristics of the line are known. These are the **slope of the line,** "b," and the Y intercept, "a." The slope of the line is defined as the ratio of how much the Y variable changes as the X variable changes. It is also called the **regression weight:**

$$b = \frac{\text{Change in } Y}{\text{Change in } X}.$$

Thus, if Y increases by 2 and X increases by 1, the line has a slope of 2. This is shown in Figure 15.7. Similarly, if Y increases by 6 and X increases by 3, the slope is also 2. In each case, the ratio of the change in Y divided by the change in X, which equals "b," remains 2.

Slope of the line: one of the two determinants of the equation for a straight line. It is the ratio of the change in the Y variable divided by the change in the X variable. It has the symbol "b" in the equation Y = bX + a. It is also called the regression weight.

The second determinant of the equation for a straight line, the **Y intercept,** is the value of Y when X is equal to 0. In other words, it is the value of Y when the line crosses the Y axis. In Figure 15.7, "a" is equal to 0.

Regression weight: another term for the slope of the line.

Regression describes the procedure for finding the equation for the straight line that best fits our data. As was noted previously, the best-fitting regression line is defined as the straight line for which the sum of the squared errors of prediction, $\Sigma(Y - \hat{Y})^2$, is a minimum. It was also pointed out that while the calculation of maxima (the plural of maximum) and minima (the plural of minimum) requires the use of calculus, we do not need to perform the derivations of the equations for finding a straight line with $\Sigma(Y - \hat{Y})^2$ as a minimum.

Y intercept: one of the two determinants of the equation for a straight line. It is the value of Y when X is equal to 0. It is, therefore, the value of Y when the line crosses the Y axis. It has the symbol "a" in the equation Y = bX + a.

Instead, we can use the equations that have been found by others. Specifically, the slope of the regression line is as follows:

$$b = r\left[\frac{\sigma_Y}{\sigma_X}\right].$$

If "b" is positive, the regression line will rise or slope upward to the right as in Figure 15.1. If "b" is negative, the regression line will slope downward to the right as in Figure 15.2.

Of course, we usually do not know the population standard deviations (σ_Y and σ_X). However, we can estimate these population standard deviations from the sample data using s_{YP} and s_{XP}. For instance, in Chapter 14, we found a statistically significant Pearson r of .795 for hypothetical quiz and exam scores for seven students taking statistics (Tables 14.3–14.6).

| Figure 15.7 | Example of a Line With a Slope of 2 |

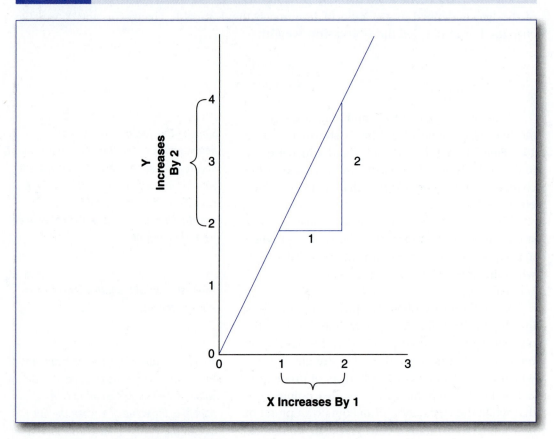

To calculate the Pearson r, we also calculated values for s_{YP} and s_{XP}. We will now proceed to find the regression line for these data.

Substituting the estimates of the standard deviations derived from the sample data, the equation for "b," the slope of the regression line is as follows:

$$b = r \left[\frac{s_{YP}}{s_{XP}} \right]$$

$$= 795 \left[\frac{8.995}{1.345} \right]$$

$$= .795(6.688)$$

$$= 5.317.$$

The equation for "*a*," the *Y* intercept, is as follows:

$$a = M_Y - bM_X$$

The values for the mean of the exam scores (M_Y) and the mean of the quiz scores (M_X) come from Table 14.4. The equation thus becomes,

$$a = 84.286 - 5.317(8.143)$$

$$= 84.286 - 43.296$$

$$= 40.990.$$

The general equation for the regression line is $\hat{Y} = bX + a$. Substituting for "*b*" and "*a*," which were just calculated, we have

$$\hat{Y} = 5.317X + 40.990.$$

This regression line is graphed in Figure 15.8.

Figure 15.8 shows that as the quiz grade increases, so does the exam grade. The relationship between quiz grades and exam grades is also evident from the value of the Pearson *r*, which is .795, but that relationship is now presented graphically. The regression line in Figure 15.8 can be used to obtain a quick estimate of a student's exam grade for any hypothetical quiz grade. For instance, Figure 15.8 indicates that a student with quiz

| Figure 15.8 | The Regression Line for Hypothetical Quiz and Exam Grades |

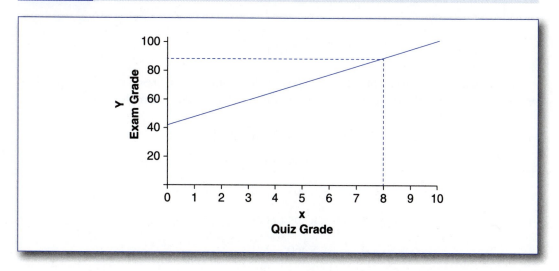

grade of 8 is predicted to obtain an exam grade in the 80s. We can find a more precise prediction by using the regression equation we just determined:

$$\hat{Y} = 5.317X + 40.990.$$

For a quiz grade of 8, we have

$$\hat{Y} = 5.317\ (8) + 40.990$$

$$= 42.536 + 40.990$$

$$= 83.526.$$

The predicted value of 83.526 obtained from the regression equation thus confirms our visual estimation using Figure 15.8 but is, of course, more precise.

If you refer back to Table 14.3, you will find that two students had quiz scores of 8. However, neither of these students obtained an exam grade of 83 or 84. Remember, it is only in the case where the Pearson r is equal to +1 or –1 that you would expect the actual data points to fall exactly along the regression line. Our correlation of .795 is quite large. In other words, there is a good fit between the data points and the regression line. Nevertheless, because the correlation is not 1, we do not have a perfect match between the predicted and actual data.

As you will recall, the calculated regression equation results in the best-fitting line, and thus, there will be less error of prediction using this than any other line or value. For instance, the error of prediction using this line, which is called the standard error of estimate ($\sigma_{\hat{Y}}$), will be less than if the mean of Y was always chosen as the estimate, which would result in an error equal to the standard deviation (σ_Y).

This can be illustrated with the equation for the standard error of estimate ($\sigma_{\hat{Y}}$), which was provided previously:

$$\sigma_{\hat{Y}} = \sigma_Y \sqrt{(1 - r^2)}.$$

In our example from Chapter 14, s_{YP}, which is the estimate of σ_Y based on the sample data, was found to be 8.995. And r was .795. Therefore, for the current example,

$$\sigma_{\hat{Y}} = 8.995\ \sqrt{[1 - (.795)^2]}$$

$$= 8.995\ \sqrt{[1 - .632]}$$

$$= 8.995\ \sqrt{.368}$$

$$= 8.995\ (.607)$$

$$= 5.460.$$

As was previously noted, whenever the Pearson r is statistically significant, the standard error of estimate, $\sigma_{\hat{Y}}$, will be less than the standard deviation, σ_Y. In the present example this is confirmed, for the standard error of estimate is 5.460, while the standard deviation is 8.995.

Reporting the Results of a Pearson *r* followed by Regression

When reporting the results of a correlational study followed by a regression, we would state that the correlation was significant and note that a linear regression was performed. The regression equation would be followed by providing the standard error of estimate and, finally, the coefficient of determination, which was discussed in Chapter 14. Specifically, for our example of quiz (X) and exam (Y) scores, we would state that the Pearson r was found to be significant ($r(5) = .795$, $p < .05$). The regression equation was $\hat{Y} = 5.317X + 40.990$, the standard error of estimate was 5.46 and the coefficient of determination, r^2, was .63.

It is important to note that in our example of the quiz and exam scores, the range of the original quiz scores was from 6 to 10. You should restrict your prediction of exam grades to those future students who have quiz scores between 6 and 10. In other words, even though Figure 15.8 extends from a quiz score of 0 up to a quiz score of 10, and the regression equation we derived will calculate a predicted exam score corresponding to any quiz score, we have no indication of what the relationship would be beyond our original range of quiz scores. You should, therefore, limit any predictions to this range.

Multiple Regression

The previous chapter dealt with correlation, the extent to which two variables are related. And we learned that the ability to predict the value of Y may be enhanced by including more than one predictor variable. For instance, success in college can be predicted with some accuracy by knowing only the student's SAT exam score. However, the prediction can be improved by including other variables such as high school grade point average (GPA) and a measure of the difficulty of the courses that were taken. This is an example of multiple correlation—more than one X variable is used to predict the value of the Y variable.

Just as you can have multiple correlation, you can also have **multiple regression**. With multiple regression, which is covered in more detail in Appendix C, the equation describing the relationship between two or more X variables and one Y variable is determined. The advantage of multiple regression is that it should lead to a more accurate prediction of the value of Y. The disadvantage of multiple regression is that it is more complex

Multiple regression: situation in which several variables (Xs) are used to predict one other variable (Y).

than the procedures that have been reviewed in this chapter. You are strongly encouraged, therefore, to use a computerized statistical package rather than hand computation when using multiple regression.

Purpose and Limitations of Using Regression

1. *Provides an equation so that the value of Y can be predicted:* The Pearson *r* correlation provides a measure of the strength and direction of an association between two interval or ratio variables. Regression provides an equation for this association.

2. *Not a measure of cause and effect:* Regression follows the finding of a statistically significant Pearson *r*. Due to a lack of control in a correlational design, a researcher is not justified in coming to a cause-and-effect conclusion concerning the variables. The regression equation allows the prediction of *Y* from *X* but does not indicate that *X* is causing *Y*.

3. *Prediction is limited to the range of the original values:* The regression equation should not be used for values of *X* that are beyond the range of the original data.

Assumptions of Regression

1. *Interval or ratio data:* The data are on an interval or a ratio scale of measurement.

2. *Data are paired:* the data come as pairs, usually two measures on the same individual.

3. *Linear relationship:* The Pearson *r* correlation and linear regression assume that the two variables are linearly related.

4. *Significant Pearson r:* Regression is only used if the Pearson *r* has been found to be statistically significant.

CONCLUSION

The focus of this chapter has been on linear regression. When there is a statistically significant linear relationship between the *X* and *Y* variables, it is possible to predict, at better than a chance level, the value of *Y* if one knows the value of *X*. Linear regression is utilized to determine the actual equation so we can make these predictions of *Y*.

In addition, multiple regression, a procedure in which two or more *X* variables are used to predict the value of *Y*, was briefly discussed.

Chapter Resources

GLOSSARY OF TERMS

Error variance: the variance of Y scores around the regression line.

Linear regression: procedures used to determine the equation for the regression line.

Multiple regression: situation in which several variables (Xs) are used to predict one other variable (Y).

Regression line: with linear regression, a straight line indicating the value of Y that is predicted to occur for each value of X. The predicted value of Y is called $\hat{Y}$.

Regression weight: another term for the slope of the regression line.

Slope of the line: one of the two determinants of the equation for a straight line. It is the ratio of the change in the Y variable divided by the change in the X variable. It has the symbol "b" in the equation $Y = bX + a$.

Standard error of estimate: the standard deviation of Y scores around the regression line. Its symbol is $\sigma_{\hat{Y}}$

Y intercept: one of the two determinants of the equation for a straight line. It is the value of Y when X is equal to 0. It is, therefore, the value of Y when the line crosses the Y axis. It has the symbol "a" in the equation $Y = bX + a$.

Questions: Chapter 15

(Answers to odd-numbered items are provided in Appendix I.)

1. The greater the correlation, ignoring the sign, between X and Y, the _____.

    a. farther the data points are from the regression line

    b. closer the data points are to the regression line

    c. more closely the data points around the regression line look like a circle

    d. the lower the ability to predict from X to Y

2. To actually predict from one variable to another, we use a procedure known as _____.

    a. regression

    b. correlation

    c. dependency analysis

    d. post hoc testing

3. The sum of the errors, $\Sigma(Y - M_Y)$, will always be equal to _____.

    a. 0

    b. 1

    c. 2

    d. 3

    e. none of the above

4. If you don't have any other information, your best prediction of Y would be _____ for every value of X.

    a. mean of X

    b. mean of Y

    c. mean of $X + Y$

    d. mean of Y^2

5. The standard deviation for the error of prediction when using a regression line is called the _____.

    a. standard deviation of estimate

    b. standard deviation of error

    c. standard error of estimate

    d. standard variation of estimate

6. When the correlation is 1, all of the observed data points fall along the _____.

    a. X axis

    b. Y axis

    c. horizontal line for the mean of Y

    d. regression line

7. The regression line is defined as the straight line for which the sum of the squared errors of prediction, $\Sigma(Y - \hat{Y})^2$, is a _____.

    a. minimum

    b. maximum

    c. mean of the minimum and maximum

    d. none of the above

8. Whenever the Pearson r is significant _____.

    a. $\sqrt{(Y - M_Y)^2 / (n - 1)}$ will be greater than $\sqrt{(Y - \hat{Y})^2 / (n - 1)}$

    b. $\sqrt{(Y - M_Y)^2 / (n - 1)}$ will equal $\sqrt{(Y - \hat{Y})^2 / (n - 1)}$

    c. $\sqrt{(Y - M_Y)^2 / (n - 1)}$ will be less than $\sqrt{(Y - \hat{Y})^2 / (n - 1)}$

9. When r^2 is equal to 1, the standard error of estimate ($\sigma_{\hat{y}}$) is equal to _____.

    a. 0

    b. 1

    c. 2

    d. 3

10. We are more accurate in making predictions when r^2 is _____.
    a. small
    b. of intermediate size
    c. large
    d. It depends on the specific question being asked.

11. In the general equation for a straight line, $Y = bX + a$, the slope is indicated by _____.
    a. "b"
    b. "X"
    c. "a"
    d. none of the above

12. The procedure for finding the equation for the straight line that best fits our data is called _____.
    a. correlation
    b. linear maximization
    c. finding the Y intercept
    d. regression

13. If the correlation between X and Y is zero, then for any value of X, the best prediction for the value of Y would be the _____.
    a. standard error of estimate
    b. minimum value of Y
    c. maximum value of Y
    d. mean value of Y

14. In Problem 23 in Chapter 14 that involved GPA and quiz grades, what is the value of the constant in the regression equation?
    a. 3.086
    b. −0.075
    c. −2.286
    d. 43.152

15. Problem 23 in Chapter 14 involved GPA and quiz grades. What is the value of the slope of the regression line for these data?
    a. 3.086
    b. −0.075
    c. −2.286
    d. 43.152

Problems 16 to 20 utilize SPSS.

SPSS

USING SPSS FOR LINEAR REGRESSION

We will use the data from Table 14.3 to illustrate how SPSS can be used to calculate a linear regression.

Step 1: Retrieve the SPSS data file that was created at the end of Chapter 14 for the data in Table 14.3. (If you did not save this file, you will need to go back to the SPSS section of Chapter 14 and follow the steps to enter the data.)

Step 2: Click on "Analyze," then on "Regression," and finally on "Linear Regression." A new window appears. As we are trying to predict exam grades from quiz grades, highlight "Exam grade" and click on the top arrow. "Exam grade" will move to the box under "Dependent" (Figure 15.9).

Step 3: Highlight "Quiz grade" and click on the second arrow. "Quiz grade" will move to the box under "Independent(s)."

Step 4: Click on "OK" and the SPSS linear regression analysis will appear. We are only interested in the last three of the four sections of the output. Table 15.2 indicates the value of the linear regression is .795. As we have only two variables, this value of *R* is the same as was

| **Figure 15.9** | The Linear Regression Window |

calculated for *r* in Chapter 14. In addition, Table 15.2 shows that 63.2% of the variability in the exam scores can be accounted for by the differences in the quiz scores. Furthermore, a value for the "Adjusted R Square" is given, but this statistic is rarely used. Finally, the standard error of estimate is provided. Approximately 68% of the estimated exam grades will fall within plus or minus one standard error of estimate, in this case 5.97715, and approximately 95% of the exam grades will fall within plus or minus two standard errors of estimate.

Table 15.3 provides a statistical test of whether the regression line provides a better estimate of the dependent variable (exam grades) than if the researcher always chose the mean value for the dependent variable (exam grades) regardless of the value of the independent variable (quiz grades). As the significance level is reported to be .033, which is less than .05, the conclusion based on the analysis of variance (ANOVA) is that the regression equation provides a better estimate.

Table 15.2   The SPSS Output: *R* and *R²*

Model Summary

Model	R	R Square	Adjusted R Square	Std. Error of the Estimate
di 1 me nsi on 0	.795ᵃ	.632	.558	5.97715

a. Predictors: (Constant), Quiz grade

Table 15.3   The SPSS Output: Test of Significance

ANOVA ᵇ

Model		Sum of Squares	df	Mean Square	F	Sig.
1	Regression	306.797	1	306.797	8.587	.033ᵃ
	Residual	178.632	5	35.726		
	Total	485.429	6			

a. Predictors: (Constant), Quiz grade
b. Dependent Variable: Exam grade

Table 15.4   The SPSS Output: Regression Coefficients

Coefficients[a]

Model		Unstandardized Coefficients		Standardized Coefficients		
		B	Std. Error	Beta	T	Sig.
1	(Constant)	41.000	14.943		2.744	.041
	Quiz grade	5.316	1.814	.795	2.930	.033

a. Dependent Variable: Exam grade

Table 15.4 provides the actual regression coefficients. In this chapter, we have learned that the equation for the regression line is provided by the equation $\hat{Y} = bX + a$. The values for "a" and "b" are listed in the column with the heading "B." Specifically, the value for the constant "a" is 41.000 and the value for the slope "b" is 5.316. These are the same values that we previously found for "a" and "b" in the regression equation (illustrated in Figure 15.8) except for slight discrepancies due to rounding error when the calculations were completed by hand. We do not need to be concerned with the remainder of Table 15.4.

Caution: Which variable you identify as the dependent variable and which as the independent variable is critical as the values for "a" and "b" will be affected.

SPSS Problems: Chapter 15

For the following problems, utilize the data previously entered for Questions 25 to 27 in Chapter 14 that dealt with the association between horsepower and miles per gallon.

16. What is the value of the Y intercept in the regression line?

   a. 3.086

   b. −0.075

   c. −2.286

   d. 43.152

17. What is the value of the slope of the regression line?

   a. 3.086

   b. −0.075

   c. −2.286

   d. 43.152

18. Calculate the predicted miles per gallon for a car with 300 horsepower.

    a. 20.65

    b. 22.39

    c. 23.45

    d. 24.60

19. Calculate the predicted miles per gallon for a car with 400 horsepower.

    a. 16.92

    b. 13.15

    c. A value should not be calculated as 400 horsepower is beyond the range of the original data

    d. Less than 10

20. Finally, calculate the predicted miles per gallon for a car with 200 horsepower.

    a. 27.33

    b. 28.15

    c. 29.25

    d. 30.67

CONGRATULATIONS: THE BIG PICTURE AND NEXT STEPS

Recapitulation and Final Considerations

The science of statistics is the chief instrumentality through which the progress of civilization is now measured, and by which its development hereafter will be largely controlled.

—S. N. D. North

GENERAL REVIEW

You are to be congratulated! This is the final chapter of a demanding book. It is the author's hope that you have not only mastered the techniques that have been presented but that you have also gained an appreciation of the usefulness of statistical analysis of data.

As you are quite aware, there are numerous statistical procedures, each appropriate for a different situation. The text in each chapter was organized around an overview table (also see complete overview table in Appendix K) to assist you in seeing how the various tests and procedures are related and so that you would be better able to understand the broader context within which statistical procedures are used. At the broadest level, there are two types of statistics, descriptive and inferential. As you learned, descriptive statistics consist of those procedures that are used to summarize a set of data. Measures of central tendency, such as the mean, as well as measures of variability, including the range and standard deviation, are examples of descriptive statistics. Most of the text, however, was devoted to a review of inferential statistics. These are the procedures used with correlational, quasi-experimental, and experimental designs. Inferential statistics enable us to identify relationships in the data. Examples include the Pearson *r*, chi-square, and analysis of variance (ANOVA).

Of course, as the overview table (Appendix K) indicates, the specific descriptive or inferential procedure that is appropriate will depend, in part, on the type of data that have been collected. Statistical procedures deal with data measured at the nominal, ordinal, interval, or ratio levels. The nature of the research question that is being examined will usually determine a specific level of measurement. Once the question is identified, there is often little choice in the level of measurement that will be employed. However, since the amount of information conveyed by the data differs with the level of measurement, the power of the statistical tests that are matched with the various levels of measurement will also differ. Thus, the power of the statistical tests that are used with interval and ratio data is greater than the power of the tests appropriate for ordinal or nominal data. As a result, fewer subjects will be needed when collecting interval or ratio data compared with ordinal or nominal data. For instance, a two-way between-subjects ANOVA is more powerful, and thus more efficient, than a chi-square test of independence.

Regardless of the inferential statistical procedures used, their strength is in enabling us to predict. Properly employed statistical procedures enable us to generalize findings from our sample to a population and, accordingly, to predict the likelihood of future occurrences. This has proven to be incredibly valuable. With the assistance of statistics, we are able to predict the success in college of students who have not yet finished high school, we can predict the effectiveness of medical treatment options, and we can predict economic outcomes, to name just a few uses. In other words, statistics are immensely practical. Because of this, they are also ubiquitous. Since you cannot hide from them, a better approach is to learn about statistics so that you can benefit from their potential. Hopefully, this book has assisted you in achieving this goal.

FUTURE DIRECTIONS

I had a number of purposes in writing this book. A major goal, of course, was to provide an introduction to the most essential statistical procedures. This book should have provided you with the background needed to understand much of the research in your specific field of interest. I also aspired to provide an introduction to statistics organized in such a way that the relationships between different statistical procedures would be evident. This perspective should provide a good foundation for those of you who plan to learn more about statistics in the future. In fact, if this text has served to enhance your interest in this field and, as a result, you are excited about continuing to explore the field of statistics, or research methodology, then I am most gratified. If, on the other hand, you see this as your last formal exposure to statistics, I hope that you have gained an appreciation of the usefulness of statistical analysis and the knowledge that you have mastered many of the field's intricacies. However, regardless of whether this is your last, or just your first, course in statistics, you should be aware that due to time limitations, there are numerous statistical procedures that could not be included.

At the nominal level of measurement, a very useful procedure is Fisher's exact test. It is an alternative to the 2 × 2 chi-square test of independence and provides either a test of significance or an exact probability for the obtained outcome. The test of significance is easy to calculate, but as the number of subjects increases the table's length expands dramatically. The calculation of an exact probability is more involved, particularly as the number of subjects increases. As a result, use of Fisher's exact test is usually limited to 2 × 2 studies with small data sets.

There are numerous additional procedures for use with interval or ratio data that you may see in the literature. For instance, factor analysis permits the identification of which variables, out of a set of predictor variables, statistically group together. The resulting groups of related variables are called factors. This technique was developed by Spearman and Burt in the 1930s to try to ascertain whether intelligence consisted of a series of largely independent characteristics or whether there was some shared component underlying the more specific attributes. Factor analysis involves highly complex calculations and is, therefore, reliant on computer-assisted data analysis.

You are also likely to see larger ANOVAs than were covered in this text. We discussed one-and two-way designs. Three-way and even larger ANOVAs are commonly encountered in the literature. There is no theoretical limit to the number of independent variables that can be included in an ANOVA, but the interpretation of the interactions quickly becomes problematic. Also, the author did not have time to cover what is called the mixed or split-plot ANOVA. This is a very useful, two-factor design in which there is one between-subjects and one within-subjects factor.

Just as we learned that ANOVAs can be expanded so that two or more independent variables can be simultaneously analyzed, a technique known as multivariate analysis of variance (or MANOVA) permits the simultaneous analysis of more than one dependent variable. This can be essential to analyzing some research designs, but once again the output can become overwhelming, and the calculation is definitely best left to a computer.

This by no means exhausts the additional statistical options. It may be helpful to think of each statistical procedure as a tool. You have now acquired a basic, general tool kit, such as initial buyers of a home or car often purchase. You have the equivalent of a hammer, a few pliers, and a couple of screwdrivers. The more you learn in the field, the more tools you acquire. Many are quite specialized. But as with the tools of a master mechanic, each has its purpose. The more techniques you learn, the more flexible you become in analyzing data.

OVERVIEW: THIS STATISTICS BOOK MAKES USE OF MATHEMATICS BUT IS NOT A MATHEMATICS BOOK

It may have occurred to you that while this statistics book uses a great deal of mathematics, it is different from other mathematics texts you have studied. That is because this is not truly a mathematics book. By this it is meant that this statistics book has a different orientation than one written by mathematicians. Mathematicians generally seek universal solutions through

Deduction: a method of thinking in which conclusions are logically derived from general statements that are assumed to be true.

logical analysis. In this text, we have not developed any such general solutions. We have not, therefore, been functioning as mathematicians. Instead, we have been the beneficiaries of their efforts. Fundamentally, in this text, we have learned how to employ the solutions developed by mathematicians. To employ the solutions correctly, we have had to learn, first, to recognize what type of research problem we were facing and, second, to then use the appropriate solution correctly. What I have not attempted to do is to explain the underlying logic of any of the statistical procedures in depth.

This distinction between a mathematician's analysis of a statistical problem and our use of statistical procedures is evident at a number of levels. Most significantly, mathematicians find "truth" through a method called **deduction**.

CONTRIBUTIONS OF THE GREEKS

Deduction was developed by the Greeks and is the fundamental method used by mathematicians. This method emphasizes human reason, or rationalism. Before the Greeks, the Egyptian and Babylonian civilizations had found solutions for mathematical operations and used basic algebra. They also had determined how to find areas and volumes and thus had a value for π that was accurate enough for their purposes. For the Egyptians, this was 3.16, while for the Babylonians, it was simply 3, the same value as is found in the Bible. Thus, for the Egyptians and Babylonians, mathematics was simply a tool. They used mathematics practically, for measurement, finance, and astronomy. Their mathematics was useful but limited.

Rationalism: a method for finding truth that emphasizes logical thinking rather than observation.

While the Greeks acknowledged their debt to other civilizations, especially to the Egyptians, they proceeded to revolutionize mathematics and many other fields with their emphasis on human reasoning. In their view, the senses are inadequate to find truth, and thus, one should emphasize the human capacity for logic. The immediate consequence was that the Greek civilization created Western philosophy, political analysis, much of what we call literature, as well as our conception of mathematics. A mathematician begins with some basic assumptions, called axioms, and from them develops theorems. So long as the initial axioms are correct, deductions based on logical thinking will lead to general solutions that we can be completely confident are correct. Thus, a mathematician seeks definite knowledge through a rational process.

The results of this emphasis on reason were impressive. By 300 BCE, Greeks such as Thales and Pythagoras had made significant advances, especially in geometry. This effort culminated with Euclid's *Elements* in which 467 theorems are deduced from an initial set of 10 axioms.

Throughout the Middle Ages, the Renaissance, and for several subsequent centuries, Euclid's *Elements* served as the foundation for a Western education in logical thinking. It is undoubtedly one of the most significant and influential books ever written.

The emphasis of Greek thinking was not on practical gain. They were, instead, interested in the acquisition of pure knowledge. Nevertheless, their emphasis on human reason, and particularly their reliance on deduction in mathematics, has had an enormous practical as well as theoretical legacy. For instance, it is a commonly repeated myth that Columbus, to get support for his proposal to reach China by sailing west, had to first convince the king and queen of Spain that the earth was round rather than flat. The truth is that the royalty of Spain were quite aware that the earth was essentially a sphere and, in fact, had an estimate of its size. This estimate of the earth's circumference came from Eratosthenes (275–194 BCE), a Greek scholar who resided in Alexandria, Egypt.

Eratosthenes had heard that on the summer solstice the sun's rays reached all the way to the bottom of a deep well at Syene, which was 500 miles (using one of today's units of measurement) due south of Alexandria. He realized that this meant that the sun had to be positioned directly over the well on this day (Figure 16.1). He also understood that this information, along with his training in geometry, would permit him to estimate the earth's circumference. Specifically, on the day of the summer solstice, he placed a stick vertically into the ground at Alexandria. He then carefully measured the angle between the direction of the stick and the direction to the sun, which was 7.5° (Figure 16.2). The rest was geometry. We will call the angle between the stick and the sun's rays "*a*." Since this is known to be 7.5°, we also know that several other angles have the same value. We will call these equivalent angles "*A*" (Figure 16.3). Hence, the angle between the line from Alexandria to the center of the earth and the line from Syene to the center of the earth is also 7.5°. Thus, the distance of 500 miles (the distance from Syene to Alexandria) corresponds to 7.5/360 or 1/48 of the circumference of the earth since there are 360° in a circle. Eratosthenes noted that the circumference of the earth is, therefore, 48 × 500 miles, which is 24,000 miles. We now know that the circumference is approximately 24,888 miles. In other words, Eratosthenes had an error of only 888 miles, or less than 4%. I think you will agree that this is a remarkable achievement considering it was accomplished more than 2,000 years ago using only a few simple measurements. Of course, Eratosthenes also benefited from a long history of mathematical progress that was a direct result of the Greek emphasis on deduction.

And what about Columbus? The royalty of Spain had an approximate idea how far to the east China was from Spain, for travelers had walked there and back. They also knew that if Eratosthenes's estimate of the earth's circumference was correct, no sailor could hope to survive a voyage to China by sailing west. The distance was simply too great for the ships then available. Columbus convinced the Spanish royalty that Eratosthenes's estimate of the earth's circumference was far too great and thus a voyage from Spain west to China was feasible. We now

(Continued)

(Continued)

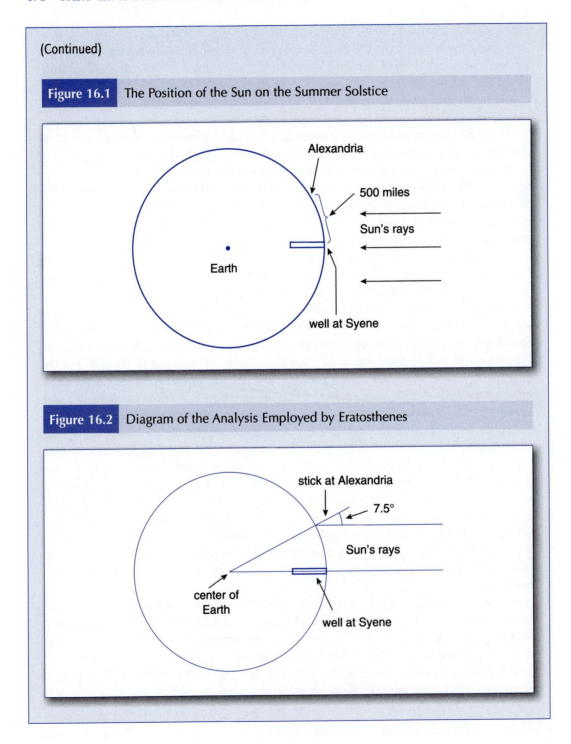

Figure 16.1   The Position of the Sun on the Summer Solstice

Figure 16.2   Diagram of the Analysis Employed by Eratosthenes

Figure 16.3 Eratosthenes's Geometric Analysis

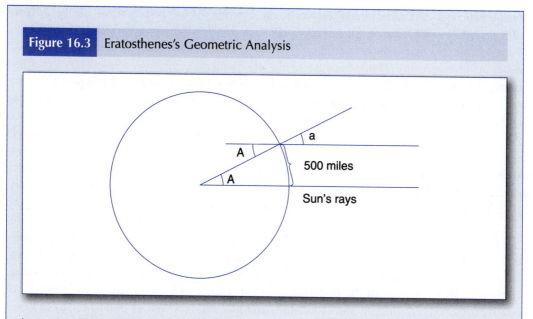

know that Eratosthenes had actually slightly *underestimated* the earth's circumference. As a glance at a globe will indicate, Columbus and the crews of his three little ships were very fortunate indeed that two unknown continents lay between Spain and China. Otherwise Columbus and his crews would probably have never been heard of again. Some people are just lucky! But Eratosthenes will always have the last laugh because he was essentially correct.

We, as users of statistics, function quite differently. In contrast to the mathematicians' or the ancient Greeks' use of deduction, we rely more on **induction**. We begin with a limited sample of data and attempt to generalize the outcome to some population. Thus, instead of beginning with axioms that are assumed to be true, we start with hypotheses and then use observations and statistical analyses to determine their likelihood. We understand that the outcome of this process is not the definite knowledge that a mathematician seeks but rather a probabilistic statement. While the statistical procedures developed by the mathematician will always be correct so long as the initial assumptions are met, the specific outcomes we obtain by using these statistical procedures will only have a probability of leading to a correct conclusion. For example, if the overview table (Appendix K) indicates that an ANOVA is the appropriate test, we can be confident that the equations used are correct because they are based on the

Induction: a method of thinking in which conclusions are derived from generalizations based on limited statements or observations that are assumed to be true. Induction is fundamental to science, as observations are used to develop general laws of nature.

mathematicians' deductive efforts. However, the outcome of using an ANOVA will be in terms of a probability. We learned, for instance, that with $\alpha = .05$, there is a 5% chance of making a Type I error. No matter how carefully the study is conducted, or the data analyzed, we will never achieve certainty. This is because unlike the mathematician, who approaches a problem from a rational perspective, we approach our problems from an empirical perspective.

With **empiricism**, we gain knowledge through observation. Everyone is at some level an empiricist. You choose your friends based on your observations of their behavior, perhaps you choose your car after reading reviews, and you will receive grades based on your professors' observations of your work. In this text, you have been introduced to sophisticated methods of empirical inquiry. These are the correlational, quasi-experimental, and experimental designs. Used correctly, these procedures, paired with the appropriate statistical analyses, greatly enhance the likelihood of gaining knowledge through observation. Nevertheless, empiricism is always based on limited observations and, thus, will never permit the absolute confidence that comes with the deductive method employed by mathematicians. Science, of course, uses both empiricism and rationalism and induction as well as deduction, in its quest for truth.

> Empiricism: a method for finding truth that emphasizes observation rather than the logical thinking of rationalism.

Though statistical analysis does not lead to certainty, it does lead to a probabilistic understanding of situations that has revolutionized many fields of study. In fact, it is not an exaggeration to say that statistical thinking is largely responsible for the transformation of fields such as economics, sociology, and psychology into sciences; and it has dramatically affected others such as anthropology, political science, and history. This is an amazing outcome for an offshoot of mathematics that began with the analysis of games of chance.

CAUTIONS IN USING STATISTICS

Statistics are no substitute for judgment.

—Henry Clay

Like any powerful tool, statistical analysis must be used intelligently. While statistics is based on samples, we are usually interested in generalizing from the sample to a population. It is essential to recognize that our confidence in doing so is dependent, in large part, on the manner in which the sample was chosen. A biased sample does not provide the necessary basis for confidently making such a generalization. In this text, we have repeatedly emphasized the importance of randomly selecting the subjects who will be included in the sample. In fact, the statistical procedures assume that the samples have been randomly selected. Nevertheless, many studies, perhaps most, do not use random sampling. This is not because the researchers are ignorant of the need for random sampling. Instead, it is a consequence of the difficulty of obtaining random samples in a real-world setting. For instance, researchers at a college might want to generalize the results of their study to the entire population of Americans. To do so, they recognize that their sample should be a random selection of everyone residing in the United States. How could they practically collect such a sample? Yet if they don't, how justified are they in claiming that their findings will generalize?

In psychology, many studies are conducted with samples drawn from students taking an introductory college course. To what population would it be appropriate to generalize the results? Not only are the subjects all in college and thus likely to be more intelligent than the American population in general, they also are more likely to be young and female. Clearly, not only is this not a random sample, it is not even remotely representative of the American population. Instead it is what is often called a **sample of convenience**.

> *Sample of convenience: a sample that is chosen because it is easily available rather than because it is optimal.*

The researchers are aware that they do not have a random sample, but what are they to do? Texts such as this one often make it sound like selecting the sample is relatively straightforward. Actually, selecting an appropriate sample can be extremely challenging.

At least researchers are aware of the problem of selecting an appropriate sample. They are, however, commonly not aware of their own biases. There are numerous examples of researchers finding what they were looking for. Some striking instances are reviewed in the *Mismeasure of Man* by Stephen J. Gould (1981). In this book, Gould explains how numerous, competent researchers of the 19th century published findings of skull volumes supporting the commonly held view that women and minorities were intellectually inferior to white males. As Gould is careful to point out, this was usually not the result of any conscious manipulation of the data. In other words, in the vast majority of cases, there is no evidence that fraud was involved. Instead, the researchers apparently were convinced of what the findings would be before they collected the data and, not surprisingly, interpreted their findings according to these preconceived views. Biases such as these are, in some respects, more problematic than outright dishonesty. Hopefully, none of us is ever going to publish a fraudulent paper. However, any of us could unknowingly publish results or conclusions affected by biases that we are not even aware we have.

To control against such biases, the researcher can conduct what is called a **"blind" study**. There are a number of variants, but the essential idea is that neither the subject nor the researcher knows to which group the subject is assigned when the data are collected. If properly used, this technique will prevent biased observation. However, "blind" studies are more difficult to conduct and, in some cases, are not feasible. For instance, if a study involves a comparison

> *"Blind" study: a study in which the data are collected in such a way that the subject's assignment to the control or experimental condition is not known. There are several variations of "blind" procedures. They are all employed to reduce bias.*

of men and women in face-to-face interactions, without careful precautions it is difficult to imagine that the individual collecting the data won't be aware of the subjects' genders.

A FINAL THOUGHT

We have just reviewed some very important philosophical issues—rationalism and empiricism, deduction and induction, and the danger of bias. What may not be clear is that this book was written from a particular perspective that is fundamental to the field of statistics. This perspective, or assumption, is so basic that it may seem obvious. Use of statistical procedures presupposes that facts matter. Put another way, it has been assumed throughout this book that an emphasis on data is critical to understanding the world and people. This is, clearly, an empirical view. This view was discussed previously and, I suspect, the vast majority of readers accepted it uncritically. However, I believe that on closer inspection, you will agree that some people seem immune to feedback—they seem to hold views that are simply not open to being changed no matter how much data are presented.

In addition, this book assumes that facts should modify our opinions, and not the reverse. But once again I think you will agree that many, perhaps all, people seem to see what they want to see, and they ignore what is uncomfortable or threatening to their views and values.

This book has presented a variety of tools to help you see the world more clearly and to improve the quality of your decisions. It is likely that you have spent much of your time learning the details of the many statistical procedures that were presented. This is common in a first exposure to statistics. I have tried to also assist you in gaining a broader perspective by emphasizing an understanding of the overview table (Appendix K). What I am now suggesting is that this is fundamentally a book on critical thinking. And if you now question the basis for the decisions that others as well as you make, then this will have been a particularly valuable experience.

CONCLUSION

The most useful skill we could teach is the habit of asking oneself and others, how do you know? If knowledge comes from intuition or anecdote, it is likely wrong.

—Sharon Begley

You have now completed this introduction to statistics. Statistical procedures are powerful tools in our quest to understand the world we live in. Used correctly, statistics can be extremely valuable. Though an incorrect conclusion is always possible, properly used statistical analysis will lessen the likelihood of making errors and will greatly enhance our ability to predict relationships among variables. Used incorrectly, statistics can be quite detrimental, as the "cooked" books at failed companies such as Enron indicate. Like any capability, your knowledge of statistics needs to be paired with integrity and judgment. Finally, in research, it is important to keep focused on the big picture. Quality studies require an insightful research idea, careful implementation of procedures, and correct statistical analysis of the resulting data. And always remember,

Not everything that can be counted counts, and not everything that counts can be counted.

—George Gallup

Chapter Resources

GLOSSARY OF TERMS

"Blind" study: a study in which the data are collected in such a way that the subject's assignment to the control or experimental condition is not known. There are several variations of "blind" procedures. They are all employed to reduce bias.

Deduction: a method of thinking in which conclusions are logically derived from general statements that are assumed to be true.

Empiricism: a method for finding truth that emphasizes observation rather than the logical thinking of rationalism.

Induction: A method of thinking in which conclusions are derived from generalizations based on limited statements or observations that are assumed to be true. Induction is fundamental to science, as observations are used to develop general laws of nature.

Rationalism: a method for finding truth that emphasizes logical thinking rather than observation.

Sample of convenience: a sample that is chosen because it is easily available rather than because it is optimal.

Questions: Chapter 16

(Answers to odd-numbered items are provided in Appendix I.)

1. Which of the following is the correct order for the power of tests, from those with the least to those with the most power?

   a. Ordinal, nominal, interval/ratio

   b. Interval/ratio, nominal, ordinal

   c. Nominal, interval/ratio, ordinal

   d. Nominal, ordinal, interval/ratio

2. _____ permits the identification of which predictor or independent variables group together.

   a. Kruskal–Wallis

   b. ANOVA

   c. Spearman

   d. Factor analysis

3. A method of thinking in which conclusions are logically derived from general statements that are assumed to be true.

   a. Empiricism

   b. Deduction

   c. Induction

   d. None of the above

4. A method for finding truth that emphasizes logical thinking rather than observation.

   a. Empiricism

   b. Induction

   c. Rationalism

   d. None of the above

5. Euclid's *Elements* dealt with _____.

   a. statistics

   b. algebra

   c. geometry

   d. history

6. Instead of beginning with axioms that are assumed to be true, in statistics, we begin with data that have been observed. This is the process of _____.

   a. induction

   b. deduction

   c. rationalism

   d. thought for which the ancient Greeks are famous

7. Statistical analysis does not lead to certainty, instead it leads to a (an) _____.

   a. absolute truth

   b. probabilistic understanding

   c. inability to predict the future

   d. unsubstantiated opinion

8. Scientists would prefer to have a _____sample, but they often must employ a _____ sample.

   a. convenience, random

   b. biased, unbiased

   c. random, convenience

   d. none of the above

9. The essential idea of a (an) _____ study is that which group the subject is assigned to is not known by the researcher when the data are collected.

   a. well-controlled

   b. experimental

   c. correlational

   d. blind

For each of the following questions indicate the appropriate statistical procedure to employ.

10. Each subject is randomly assigned to one of five levels of studying and then their exam grades are compared.

    a. Goodness-of-fit chi-square

    b. One-way between-subjects ANOVA

    c. Pearson *r*

11. We measure how tall each person is and then look to see if there is an association with how high they can jump.

    a. Two-way between-subjects ANOVA

    b. One-way between-subjects ANOVA

    c. Pearson *r*

12. We compare the GPA (grade point average) of men versus women who have, or have not, studied abroad.

    a. Two-way between-subjects ANOVA

    b. One-way between-subjects ANOVA

    c. Pearson *r*

13. We check the claim that a person can flip a coin so it tends to land heads.

    a. Goodness-of-fit chi-square

    b. One-way between-subjects ANOVA

    c. Pearson *r*

14. We compare the frequencies of social science majors and humanities majors, and their choice of political party preference (Democratic, Republican, and other).

   a. Chi-square test of independence

   b. One-way between-subjects ANOVA

   c. Point biserial correlation

15. We examine if there is an association between whether a student is married or not and how happy the student reports he or she is on a 25-item scale.

   a. Pearson r

   b. One-way between-subjects ANOVA

   c. Point biserial correlation

16. A researcher is interested in whether there is an association between a person's gender and whether the person votes Democratic or Republican.

   a. Pearson r

   b. Phi

   c. Chi-square test of independence

17. A researcher examines whether living at high altitudes affects intelligence quotient. She compares the intelligence quotient data from 500 people who live at high altitudes to the known mean and standard deviation for the general population.

   a. One-way between-subjects ANOVA

   b. One-sample z

   c. One-sample t

18. We compare the age of death for people who had a pet versus those who did not have a pet.

   a. Pearson r

   b. Two-way between-subjects ANOVA

   c. Independent samples t test or one-way between-subjects ANOVA

19. A study for a car magazine examines whether there is an association between the weight of a car and how many feet it takes for it to stop from 60 miles/hour. Data are collected from 30 cars of various weights.

   a. Pearson r

   b. One-way between-subjects ANOVA

   c. Phi

20. From past history it is known that with a particular manufacturing process, 10% of the product has been defective. A new process is instituted, and for the first 100 items, there are only 6 that are defective. Has the frequency of defective product been reduced?

   a. One-sample *t*

   b. Pearson *r*

   c. Goodness-of-fit chi-square

21. A teacher is interested in whether there is an association between gender (male or female) and openness to experience (measured on a 25-point scale).

   a. Phi

   b. Pearson *r*

   c. Point biserial

22. A restaurant wants to determine whether the quality of their five most popular offerings differ according to reviewers. Ten food tasters are invited to give each dish a rating from 1 to 10.

   a. One-way between-subjects ANOVA

   b. One-way within-subjects ANOVA

   c. Two-way between-subjects ANOVA

23. A physical education instructor compares males and females and whether they prefer playing basketball or volleyball.

   a. Chi-square test of independence

   b. Phi

   c. One-way between-subjects ANOVA

24. We compare males and females who are judged to be either attractive or not on how outgoing they are (measured on a 15-point scale).

   a. One-way between-subjects ANOVA

   b. One-way within-subjects ANOVA

   c. Two-way between-subjects ANOVA

25. A newspaper examines whether there is an association between age and the number of speeding tickets received by 100 drivers over the previous 3 years.

   a. Phi

   b. Pearson *r*

   c. Point biserial

26. A researcher checks to see if there is an association between handedness (either left or right) and GPA.

    a. Phi

    b. Pearson r

    c. Point biserial

27. A study is conducted that examines whether there is a difference in the type of car (domestic or foreign) driven by Republicans and Democrats.

    a. Phi

    b. Chi-square test of independence

    c. One-way between-subjects ANOVA

28. At a college, a study is conducted that compares whether appreciation of the liberal arts (measured on a 20-item scale) is affected by major (art or science) and class in college (freshman, sophomore, junior, or senior).

    a. One-way between-subjects ANOVA

    b. One-way within-subjects ANOVA

    c. Two-way between-subjects ANOVA

Appendixes

Appendixes

APPENDIX A

KRUSKAL–WALLIS *H* TEST

Difference Design With One Independent Variable, Two or More Independent Samples, and Ordinal Data

Nothing has such power to broaden the mind as the ability to investigate systematically and truly all that comes under thy observation in life.

—Marcus Aurelius

In Table A.1, you will see that the Kruskal–Wallis *H* test, which is underlined and italicized, is on the same *row* as the one-way between-subjects ANOVA (analysis of variance). Thus, this test is appropriate when you have one independent variable and two or more independent samples. While the one-way between-subjects ANOVA is used when you have interval or ratio data, the Kruskal–Wallis *H* test is used with ordinal data or when results have been converted into ordinal data.

As an example, let us compare the order in which the first 19 football players might be chosen in the first round of a fictitious NFL (National Football League) draft. More specifically, we will compare the order in which offensive players (Sample 1) were chosen with the order in which defensive players (Sample 2) were chosen, and the order in which special team's players were chosen (Sample 3). These fictitious ranks, as well as totals needed

Table A.1	Overview of Inferential Statistical Procedures for Difference and Interaction Designs

	Type of Data		
	Nominal (Frequency)	**Ordinal** (Ranked)	**Interval/Ratio** (Continuous Measure)

Inferential Statistics (Finding Relationships)

Statistical procedures for difference and interaction designs

	Nominal (Frequency)	**Ordinal** (Ranked)	**Interval/Ratio** (Continuous Measure)
One variable with at least two outcomes	Goodness-of-fit chi-square	**One IV with one sample—one DV**	One-sample z score or one-sample t test
		One IV with two or more independent samples—one DV *Kruskal–Wallis H*	One-way between-subjects ANOVA (only two independent samples— independent samples t test)
		One IV with one sample having two or more repeated measures—one DV	One-way within-subjects ANOVA (only two repeated measures— dependent samples t test)
Two variables, each with at least two outcomes	Chi-square test of independence	**Two IV each with two or more independent samples—one DV**	Two-way between-subjects ANOVA

Note. IV, independent variable; DV, dependent variable; ANOVA, analysis of variance.

for the computation of the Kruskal–Wallis H test, are shown in Table A.2. The null and alternative hypotheses are as follows:

H_0: The ranks for the three groups are the same.

H_1: The ranks for the three groups are not the same.

Note that the number of individuals in the samples do not have to be equal. To calculate the Kruskal–Wallis H statistic, we use the following equation:

$$H = \left[\frac{12}{N(N+1)} \right] \left[\Sigma \left(\frac{T^2}{n} \right) \right] - 3(N+1),$$

Table A.2	Example 1: Order Players Were Chosen in a Fictitious NFL Draft		

Sample 1	**Sample 2**	**Sample 3**	
1	2	12	
3	4	14	
6	5	16	
8	7	17	
9	11	18	
10	15	19	
13			
Total (*T*) = 50	*T* = 44	*T* = 96	
n = 7	*n* = 6	*n* = 6	*N* = 19

Note. NFL, National Football League.

where N = the total number of subjects, T = the total of the ranks for a sample, and n = the sample size.

This equation may be intimidating at first, but once you examine it carefully you will find it is actually quite easy to use.

The constants in the equation, 12 and 3, are not specific to this problem, they are part of the general equation for the Kruskal–Wallis H statistic. For our example, we would substitute and obtain

$$
\begin{aligned}
H &= \left[\frac{12}{(19)(19+1)} \right]\left[\left(\frac{50^2}{7}\right) + \left(\frac{44^2}{6}\right) + \left(\frac{96^2}{6}\right) \right] - 3(19+1) \\
&= \left[\frac{12}{380} \right]\left[\left(\frac{2500}{7}\right) + \left(\frac{1936}{6}\right) + \left(\frac{9216}{6}\right) \right] - 60 \\
&= (0.0316)(2215.813) - 60 \\
&= 10.02.
\end{aligned}
$$

The degrees of freedom for the Kruskal–Wallis H statistic are equal to the number of samples minus one. In our case, this would be 3 − 1, which equals 2. Referring to the chi-square table (Appendix J, Table J.2), which is also used with the Kruskal–Wallis H test, we find a critical value of 5.99 with 2 *df* and alpha set at .05. As our obtained value of 10.02 is greater than the critical value, we reject the null and accept the alternative hypothesis. In other words, we conclude that the ranks for the three groups are not the same.

We are still faced with two issues. First, we have not yet calculated a measure for effect size. Second, while the significant Kruskal–Wallis H statistic indicates that at least one of the sample's ranks differs from another sample's ranks, or a combination of sample ranks, the test does not indicate which, or how many, of these sample ranks differ. In other words, just as with the chi-square test of independence and the ANOVA, the Kruskal–Wallis H statistic provides an overall test of significance for the entire study, but does not indicate where the significant difference(s) is (are). We will examine the issue of effect size first, and then, describe a procedure for specifying where a difference within a significant Kruskal–Wallis H test is located.

Eta squared (η^2) is a measure of effect size for the Kruskal–Wallis H test. It is easily found once the Kruskal–Wallis H statistic is computed, as the following equation indicates:

$$\text{Eta squared}(\eta^2) = \frac{H}{N-1},$$

where H is the value of the Kruskal–Wallis statistic and N is the total number of ranks.

$$= \frac{10.02}{19-1}$$
$$= 0.56.$$

Eta squared (η^2) is an example of what is called a coefficient of determination, which was discussed in Chapter 14. A coefficient of determination indicates what proportion of variability in one variable is accounted for by the variability in another variable. In our case, $\eta^2 = .56$. Therefore, 56% of the variability in the hypothetical rankings is accounted for by knowing whether the choice in the draft involves an offensive, defensive, or special team's player.

Next, we return to the question of which sample ranks differ significantly. We rejected the null hypothesis, and therefore concluded that there exists at least one difference in the rankings between samples or of combinations of samples. However, we do not know where this (these) difference(s) may be. As with the chi-square test of independence and the ANOVA, we now need to perform post hoc tests to ascertain which specific comparisons are statistically significant. And, just as with the chi-square test and the ANOVA, we will simplify the situation by limiting ourselves to comparisons of the original samples and omit comparisons where samples are combined. We are, therefore, making what are called pairwise comparisons. There are $k(k-1)/2$ possible pairwise comparisons, where k = the number of samples. In our example, there are three independent samples, and there would be $3(3-1)/2$, or 3 comparisons. These pairwise comparisons would be between Sample 1 and Sample 2, between Sample 1 and Sample 3, and between Sample 2 and Sample 3, respectively. Any one, any two, or all three of these comparisons could be statistically significant. Just as with the chi-square test and the ANOVA, a significant Kruskal–Wallis H test simply indicates that there is at least one comparison between samples that is significant.

A number of post hoc procedures have been developed for use with the Kruskal–Wallis H test. The easiest alternative is to conduct a series of tests appropriate for use with a two-sample difference design and then utilize the Bonferroni method that was introduced in Chapter 8 to control the experiment-wise error. As we have ordinal data, inspection of the overview table (Appendix K) indicates that our post hoc would be further Kruskal–Wallis H tests (there are other alternatives).

As you recall, the Bonferroni method maintains the experiment-wise error by dividing the alpha level by the number of comparisons being made. In the present case, there are three comparisons, so we would divide our alpha of .05 by 3 to obtain .0167. Because this specific alpha level is not included in most chi-square tables, we turn to a table that includes more levels of alpha, or to a computer program. The degrees of freedom for each comparison are equal to the number of samples in the comparison minus one. In our case, as we are making pairwise comparisons this would be 2 – 1, which equals 1. With an alpha of .0167 and 1 *df*, our critical value becomes 5.73. We now proceed with our first post hoc comparison, a comparison of Sample 1 and Sample 2. For the post hoc, we treat Sample 1 and Sample 2 as a complete set of data. The first step, therefore, is to re-rank the data for these two samples, as is shown in Table A.3.

Table A.3   Example 1: Post Hoc Analysis for Sample 1 and Sample 2

Sample 1	Sample 2	
1	2	
3	4	
6	5	
8	7	
9	11	
10	13	
12		
$T = 49$	$T = 42$	
$n = 7$	$n = 6$	$N = 13$

To calculate the Kruskal–Wallis H statistic, we use the same equation as previously

$$H = \left[\frac{12}{N(N+1)}\right]\left[\Sigma\left(\frac{T^2}{n}\right)\right] - 3(N+1).$$

For our example, we would substitute and obtain

$$H = \left[\frac{12}{(13)(13+1)}\right]\left[\left(\frac{49^2}{7}\right)+\left(\frac{42^2}{6}\right)\right] - 3(13+1)$$

$$= \left[\frac{12}{182}\right]\left[\left(\frac{2401}{7}\right)+\left(\frac{1764}{6}\right)\right] - 42$$

$$= (0.066)(637) - 42$$

$$= 0.042.$$

The re-ranking for the comparison between Sample 1 and Sample 3, is shown in Table A.4.

Table A.4   Example 1: Post Hoc Analysis for Sample 1 and Sample 3

Sample 1	Sample 3	
1	7	
2	9	
3	10	
4	11	
5	12	
6	13	
8		
$T = 29$	$T = 62$	
$n = 7$	$n = 6$	$N = 13$

To calculate the Kruskal–Wallis H statistic, we would substitute these values and obtain

$$H = \left[\frac{12}{(13)(13+1)}\right]\left[\left(\frac{29^2}{7}\right) + \left(\frac{62^2}{6}\right)\right] - 3(13+1)$$

$$= \left[\frac{12}{182}\right]\left[\left(\frac{841}{7}\right) + \left(\frac{3844}{6}\right)\right] - 42$$

$$= (0.066)(760.81) - 42$$

$$= 8.21.$$

The re-ranking for the comparison between Sample 2 and Sample 3 is shown in Table A.5.

To calculate the Kruskal–Wallis H statistic, we would substitute these values and obtain

$$H = \left[\frac{12}{(12)(12+1)}\right]\left[\left(\frac{23^2}{6}\right) + \left(\frac{55^2}{6}\right)\right] - 3(12+1)$$

$$= \left[\frac{12}{156}\right]\left[\left(\frac{529}{6}\right) + \left(\frac{3025}{6}\right)\right] - 39$$

$$= (0.077)(592.33) - 39$$

$$= 6.61.$$

Table A.5   Example 1: Post Hoc Analysis for Sample 2 and Sample 3

Sample 2	Sample 3	
1	6	
2	7	
3	9	
4	10	
5	11	
8	12	
$T = 23$	$T = 55$	
$n = 6$	$n = 6$	$N = 12$

As the critical value, based on the Bonferroni method, is 5.73, the comparison between Sample 1 and Sample 3, as well as the comparison between Sample 2 and Sample 3, are statistically significant. The comparison between Sample 1 and Sample 2 is not statistically significant.

Reporting the Results of a Kruskal–Wallis H Test

In a paper, we would indicate that the overall statistical test was significant and which specific group comparisons were found to differ. Specifically, we would say that the overall Kruskal–Wallis H test was significant (2, $N = 19$) = 10.02, $p < .05$, with η^2 equal to .59. Furthermore, pairwise comparisons using the Bonferroni method for control indicated that the comparison between Sample 1 and Sample 3 [$H(1, N = 13) = 8.21$], as well as the comparison between Sample 2 and Sample 3 [$H(1, N = 12) = 6.61$], were statistically significant. The comparison between Sample 1 and Sample 2 was not statistically significant [$H(1, N = 13) = .042$].

It is important to note that the Bonferroni method is quite conservative. This means that the probability of making a Type I error is somewhat less than the value the experimenter has chosen, in this case .05. However, this also results in an increase in the probability of making a Type II error. In other words, while the Bonferroni method is very effective at preventing us from rejecting the null hypothesis when it is in fact correct, it also increases the likelihood that we will fail to reject the null hypothesis when it is in fact false. With a small number of comparisons the Bonferroni method is appropriate, but as the number of comparisons increases it becomes increasingly conservative and, therefore, there is an increased risk of making a Type II error. The rule of thumb is to use the Bonferroni method when there are five or fewer comparisons. If you need to conduct post hoc tests from a Kruskal–Wallis H with a larger number of groups then you should consult a more advanced statistics text to determine the appropriate procedure.

In our first example of the Kruskal–Wallis H test, we utilized data that were collected as ranks. The Kruskal–Wallis H test is also commonly used with data that were originally collected at the interval or ratio level of measurement, but which were then converted to ranks. Since interval or ratio data include more information than ranked data, the statistical tests that use the interval or ratio levels of measurement are more efficient than tests that rely on levels of measurement that include less information. What this means is that a test that utilizes data at the interval or ratio level of measurement will, all else being equal, not need as much data to find a difference. Put another way, with interval or ratio data, we do not need to collect data from as many subjects as we will have to if we use ordinal data. Similarly, with ordinal data, we do not need to collect data from as many subjects as we will have to if we use nominal data. So, you may ask, Why would anyone convert interval or ratio data to ordinal data since this leads to a loss of information and, therefore, a loss of statistical power? The answer, fortunately, is quite simple.

The tests that utilize interval or ratio data are called parametric tests because they make assumptions about population parameters and they assume normal distributions. However, these assumptions may not be met. For instance, let us assume that we have collected data of a class exam. For this to be suitable for parametric analysis, the data should be normally distributed. This means that there are many scores in the middle of the distribution and progressively fewer scores the farther we move, in either direction, from the middle. But what if the students in the class found the exam to be very easy? In this case, most students will have done well. We may get what is called a ceiling effect, with many scores clustered in the high 90s. However, some students may not have found the test to be easy, and they may have scored much lower. If so, the distribution will not be normal. It will be negatively skewed. In this case, it would not be appropriate to use a test that assumes normality even though the data are measured at the interval or ratio level. Instead, one option is to convert the scores to ranks and utilize a nonparametric procedure, such as the Kruskal–Wallis *H* test. An example follows.

Let us assume that a physician is interested in how quickly two different types of anesthesia take effect. Subjects undergoing surgery are randomly assigned to receive one type of the anesthesia. The time to reach a standard state of relaxation, in seconds, for each patient is indicated in Table A.6.

Time is a measurement scale where the size of the intervals between numbers is meaningful and there is a true zero. Therefore, this is an example of ratio data. Referring

Table A.6	Example 2: Time for Two Different Types of Anesthesia to Take Effect

Anesthesia A	Anesthesia B
12	15
13	16
14	17
20	18
24	18
29	19
36	21
61	
92	

to Table A.1 or the overview table (Appendix K) will indicate that with two independent samples, we would initially consider using either the independent samples t test or the one-way between-subjects ANOVA. However, these are parametric tests that assume that the samples are drawn from populations that are normally distributed and have equal variability. Both of these assumptions are suspect with our data. Sample 2 (Anesthesia B) appears to have a bell-shaped distribution as we would expect if the population from which it came was normally distributed. However, Sample 1 (Anesthesia A) does not appear to have a bell-shaped distribution, and clearly, the variability of the two samples is quite different. The scores for the subjects who received Anesthesia B are clustered tightly together while the scores for the subjects who received Anesthesia A exhibit much more variability. It is, accordingly, inappropriate to conduct either an independent samples t test or an ANOVA with these data. Instead, we can convert the scores to ranks and conduct a nonparametric test such as the Kruskal–Wallis H test with two samples (there are other appropriate tests). The ranked data are presented in Table A.7, as well as totals needed for the computation of the Kruskal–Wallis H test. Note that when two scores are tied, the mean of the two ranks involved is assigned to each of the scores. In our example, the scores for Ranks 7 and 8 were tied in the second group so each was given the Rank of 7.5. As the 7th and 8th scores have already been ranked, the next rank in the table is 9.

Table A.7   Example 2: Conversion of Data to Ranks

Anesthesia A	Anesthesia B	
1	4	
2	5	
3	6	
10	7.5	
12	7.5	
13	9	
14	11	
15		
16		
$T = 86$	$T = 50$	
$n = 9$	$n = 7$	$N = 16$

Now that the data are ranked, the Kruskal–Wallis *H* test is conducted as before

$$H = \left[\frac{12}{N(N+1)}\right]\left[\Sigma\left(\frac{T^2}{n}\right)\right] - 3(N+1)$$

$$= \left[\frac{12}{(16)(16+1)}\right]\left[\left(\frac{86^2}{9}\right) + \left(\frac{50^2}{7}\right)\right] - 3(16+1)$$

$$= \left[\frac{12}{272}\right]\left[\left(\frac{7396}{9}\right) + \left(\frac{2500}{7}\right)\right] - 51$$

$$= (0.044)(1178.92) - 51$$

$$= 0.88.$$

The degrees of freedom are equal to the number of samples minus one. In our case, this would be 2 − 1 = 1. Referring to the chi-square table, we find a critical value of 3.84 with alpha set at .05. As our obtained value of 0.88 is less than the critical value, we retain the null hypothesis that there is no difference in the delay of the two types of anesthesia to take effect.

Purpose and Limitations of Using the Kruskal–Wallis *H* Test

1. *This is a test for equality of ranks.* The null hypothesis is that the distribution of observed ranks in each sample is equal. In other words, any difference in the distribution of the ranks is due to chance.

2. *This is an overall test of significance.* In designs with more than two samples, a statistically significant outcome indicates that a difference in the rankings exists between the samples, but the initial Kruskal–Wallis *H* test does not indicate where that difference(s) is (are). Post hoc tests would need to be conducted to identify the specific groups that differ.

3. *The test does not provide a measure of effect size.* The Kruskal–Wallis *H* is a test of significance. It indicates whether or not an outcome is likely to have occurred by chance. If the Kruskal–Wallis *H* statistic is significant, a measure of effect size, such as eta squared, should then be calculated.

4. *The sample size should not be too small.* As a general rule, no sample should have fewer than six subjects.

Assumptions of the Kruskal–Wallis *H* Test

1. *You have ordinal data.* The data are in the form of ranks or can be converted into ranks.

2. *The observations are independent.* Each subject provides only one datum and no subject is matched with another subject during assignment to samples.

CONCLUSION

We have now completed our introduction to the Kruskal–Wallis H statistic. Before moving on to other tests it might be valuable to review how the Kruskal–Wallis H statistic is related to other procedures. By referring to TableA.1, you will see that the Kruskal–Wallis H test is on the same *row* as the one-way between-subjects ANOVA. Each of these tests is used with a different level of measurement, the Kruskal–Wallis H test for ordinal data and the ANOVA for interval or ratio data. In other respects, they are quite similar. Each is used when you have a design with two or more independent samples, each provides an overall test of whether there is a difference but with more than two samples they do not indicate what the specific basis of this difference is, and, if significant, each should be followed by a measure of effect size.

Questions: Appendix A

(Answers to odd-numbered items are provided in Appendix I.)

1. The Kruskal–Wallis H test is used with _____ data.
   a. nominal
   b. ordinal
   c. interval/ratio
   d. it can be used with any scale of measurement.

2. The Kruskal–Wallis H test is appropriate when you have _____.
   a. two or more independent samples
   b. repeated measures
   c. one group compared with a known population parameter
   d. one independent sample and one repeated measures sample

3. The degrees of freedom for the Kruskal–Wallis H statistic are equal to _____.
   a. the number of subjects minus one
   b. the number of subjects minus the number of samples
   c. the number of samples plus the number of subjects
   d. the number of samples minus one

4. The table used with the Kruskal–Wallis H test is also used with the _____.

   a. ANOVA

   b. independent samples t test

   c. chi-square test

   d. z score

5. The measure of effect size for the Kruskal–Wallis H test is _____.

   a. eta squared (η^2)

   b. the square of r

   c. not defined

   d. difficult to calculate

6. The _____ indicates what proportion of variability in one variable is accounted for by the variability in another variable.

   a. value of the Kruskal–Wallis H test

   b. number of the degrees of freedom minus one

   c. coefficient of determination

   d. coefficient of nondetermination

7. Following a significant overall Kruskal–Wallis H test with three or more samples, further pairwise comparisons using the _____ for control would be used.

   a. Bonferroni method

   b. Tukey's HSD

   c. chi-square

   d. any of the above

A banker wanted to compare the incomes of people living in two sections of a city. To do so he conducted a questionnaire study. He noted that the ratio data were positively skewed and, thus, converted them to ranks.

Group 1	Group 2
2	1
3	6
4	9
5	10
7	13
8	14
11	15
12	16
	17

8. What is the value of the *H* test?

 a. 1.774

 b. 2.673

 c. 3.68

 d. 4.51

9. What is the critical value ($\alpha = .05$, two-tailed test)?

 a. 1.96

 b. 2.58

 c. 3.16

 d. 3.84

10. Do the ranks of the two groups differ statistically?

 a. Yes

 b. No

11. What is the value of eta squared?

 a. .212

 b. .28

 c. Eta squared should not be calculated as the *H* test was not significant.

The following problem examines the effect of making one switch in the rankings of each of the above groups:

Group 1	Group 2
2	<u>11</u>
3	6
4	9
5	10
7	13
8	14
<u>1</u>	15
12	16
	17

12. What is the value of the *H* test?

    a. 1.77

    b. 2.67

    c. 3.76

    d. 7.99

13. What is the critical value (α = .05, two-tailed test)?

    a. 1.96

    b. 2.58

    c. 3.16

    d. 3.84

14. Do the ranks of the two groups differ statistically?

    a. Yes

    b. No

15. What is the value of eta squared?

    a. .21

    b. .50

    c. Eta squared should not be calculated as the *H* test was not significant.

APPENDIX B

SPEARMAN *r* CORRELATION

Association Design With Ordinal Data

The fewer the facts, the stronger the opinion.

—Arnold H. Glasow

The Spearman *r* correlation, also sometimes called the Spearman rank order correlation coefficient, is a commonly used statistic. It is located on the same *row* as phi and the Pearson *r* (Table B.1) and is italicized and underlined in the table. Remember, each of these correlations provides a measure of the association between two sets of numbers. Thus, when using these statistics, we are not asking if samples differ. Instead, we are asking if the samples show evidence of being related.

With the Spearman *r*, we employ symbols that are similar to those that were used for phi and the Pearson correlation. More precisely, the symbol ρ_s indicates the population correlation and r_s signifies that we are dealing with samples.

In the case of the Spearman *r*, both variables will have been measured at the ordinal level or, more commonly, will have been converted from an interval or ratio level into ordinal form. Conversion into an ordinal level is usually undertaken because an assumption of the preferred correlation for interval or ratio data, the Pearson *r*, has not been met. For instance, the Pearson *r* is a measure of linear relationship. It only provides an accurate measure if the two interval or ratio variables have a straight-line relationship between them. The heights of the members of a club or class measured in both inches and centimeters would form a linear relationship. However, there is no linear relationship between the height and weight of children, as is indicated

Table B.1	Overview of Inferential Statistical Procedures for Association Designs

	Type of Data		
	Nominal (Frequency)	**Ordinal (Ranked)**	**Interval or Ratio (Continuous Measure)**
Correlation	Phi		*Spearman r*	Pearson *r*
Regression				Linear regression
				Multiple regression

in Figure B.1. If a Pearson *r* is calculated for these data, it will underestimate the true degree of the relationship.

One solution would be to convert the heights and weights, which are ratio data, into ordinal data and then conduct a Spearman *r* correlation. This will give you a measure of the consistency of the rankings between your two variables. In other words, with the Pearson *r* correlation, we are asking "As one variable gets larger, does the other variable either increase

Figure B.1	Example 1: A Nonlinear Relationship for Height and Weight

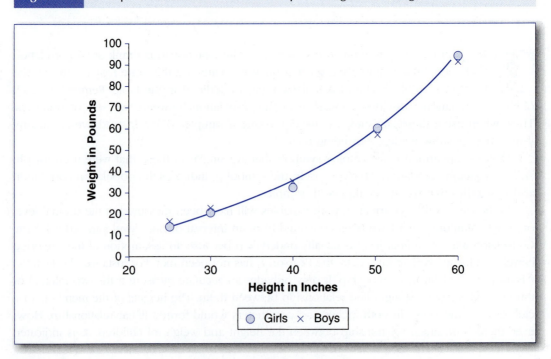

or decrease in a straight line fashion?" With the Spearman r correlation, we drop the requirement for a straight-line relationship. We are simply interested in knowing whether there is a reliable or consistent relationship between the order of the changes in the two variables, regardless if it is linear or not.

An example of converting ratio scores into ordinal data and then using the Spearman r correlation comes from the history of aviation. Before jet engines, planes were powered by piston engines, as are most cars today. Figure B.2 is a graph of the relationship between the power of the airplane's engine (measured in horsepower) and the plane's maximum speed (measured in miles per hour) for a number of historically significant airplanes.

It is evident that as the horsepower increases, so does the speed. However, it is also evident that with increased horsepower, a plateau is reached. In other words, there is not a linear relationship between power and speed. It would, therefore, be inappropriate to calculate a Pearson r. Instead, we convert the data in Table B.2 into ranks, as shown in Table B.3, and then conduct a Spearman r correlation. The null hypothesis is that there is no association between the rank of horsepower and the rank of speed. The alternative hypothesis is that there is an association. We set $\alpha = .05$.

Note that the sum of the differences between pairs of ranks (the column headed by *Difference*) should always equal zero.

Figure B.2   Example 2: A Nonlinear Relationship for Horsepower and Maximum Speed

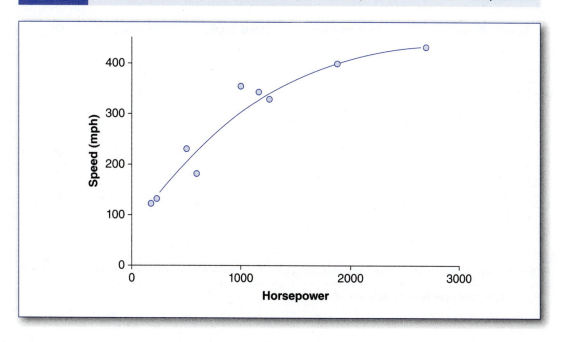

Table B.2 Example 2: Power and Maximum Speed of Select Planes

Type of Plane	Horsepower	Speed (mph)
Fokker D VII	185	125
Spad XIII	235	133
Boeing P–26	500	234
Curtis P–6A Hawk	600	179
Spitfire IA	1,030	362
P–40 C	1,150	345
Hurricane II C	1,260	329
FW–190 A–6	1,800	398
F8F Bearcat	2,700	434

Note. mph, miles per hour (1 mile = 1.60 kilometers).

Table B.3 Example 2: Ranks of Power and Maximum Speed of Select Planes

Type of Plane	Horsepower	Speed (mph)	Difference	D^2
Fokker D VII	1	1	0	0
Spad XIII	2	2	0	0
Boeing P–26	3	4	−1	1
Curtis P–6A Hawk	4	3	1	1
Spitfire IA	5	7	−2	4
P–40 C	6	6	0	0
Hurricane II C	7	5	2	4
FW–190 A–6	8	8	0	0
F8F Bearcat	9	9	0	0
			$\Sigma D = 0$	$\Sigma D^2 = 10$

Note. mph, miles per hour (1 mile = 1.60 kilometers).

The equation for the Spearman r is as follows:

$$r_s = 1 - \frac{6\Sigma D^2}{n(n^2 - 1)},$$

where D is the difference between a pair of ranks and n is the number of pairs of data, in our case, 9. Note that the Number 6 is a constant in the equation and is not related to our specific example.

Substituting, we find

$$\text{the Spearman } r = 1 - \frac{6 \times 10}{9(81 - 1)}$$
$$= 1 - \frac{60}{9(80)}$$
$$= 1 - \frac{60}{720}$$
$$= 1 - .083$$
$$= .92.$$

To determine if the Spearman correlation that we just calculated is statistically different from 0, we consult the Spearman r table (Appendix J, Table J.7). There are two characteristics of this table that you must be aware of. First, unlike most other tables of critical values, *the Spearman r table is not based on degrees of freedom but rather is based directly on n, in this case, the number of pairs of data*. Thus, we do not calculate degrees of freedom before consulting the Spearman r table. And second, *to be significant, the obtained value must be equal to or greater than the value listed in the table*. With most other statistical procedures, the obtained value has to be greater than the critical value in the table.

For our example, we refer to the row for an n of 9. With alpha equal to .05, we would need an outcome equal to or greater than 0.683 if we did not specify a predicted direction for the relationship before the data were collected, for this would be a two-tailed test. However, if we had specified that increased horsepower would lead to increased speed before the data were collected, this would be a one-tailed test, and our critical value would instead be 0.60.

An appropriate time to have used the one-tailed test would have been with our airplane data. After all, it would have been reasonable to assume before any data were collected that more powerful engines would have resulted in faster planes. However, we did not specify this direction before we collected the data, so we will use the two-tailed critical value of 0.683. As our obtained value is 0.92, we reject the null that there is no relationship between power and speed and accept the alternative that there is a relationship. In fact, this outcome is significant at even the .01 level.

Inspection of the data indicates that as the engine power increases, so does the speed. This is also what the positive sign of the correlation indicates. When a Spearman r correlation has a positive sign, it indicates that as the ranks for one variable increase, so do the ranks for the other variable. A graph of our ranks for the power and speed of planes is shown in Figure B.3. Note that if a Spearman r correlation is positive, it also indicates that as the ranks of one variable *decrease,* so do the ranks of the other. In other words, with a positive correlation the graph will rise to the right.

It is also important to note that in the Spearman r table there are no negative numbers. The table indicates how large a Spearman r correlation must be to reject the null hypothesis *without regard to its sign.* Thus, if we had found a correlation of −0.92, we would ignore the sign and look up 0.92 in the table. Of course, with a two-tailed test, the sign doesn't matter in determining whether to reject the null hypothesis. However, with a one-tailed prediction,

Figure B.3	Example 2: Relationship of the Ranks of Aircraft Horsepower and Maximum Speed

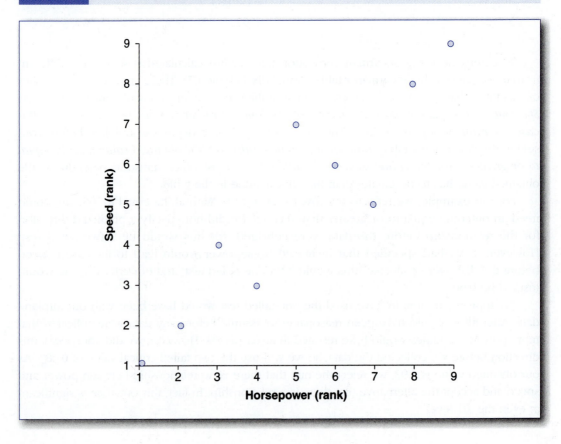

the sign does matter. The table will indicate the magnitude of the correlation that is needed to reject the null hypothesis. The researcher would then have to check that the outcome was in the predicted direction.

To this point, we have taken a set of ratio data, converted it to ranks, calculated a Spearman r correlation, and determined that it is statistically significant. Just as with phi and the Pearson r, we would also like to have a measure of strength of the association to help us interpret what our significant outcome means. With the Spearman r correlation, as with phi and the Pearson r, a commonly used measure of effect size is the coefficient of determination. It is simply the square of the correlation, in this case, r_s^2.

In the case of the Spearman r correlation, the coefficient of determination indicates how much of the variability in one set of ranks is explained by the variability in the other set of ranks. In our case, the Spearman r equals 0.92 and r_s^2 equals .85. Thus, by knowing the rank of the aircraft's engine power, we have explained 85% of the variability in the rank of the aircraft's speed. In the social sciences, any coefficient of determination that is greater than .25 would be considered to be large.

Put another way, our analysis indicates that there is only 15% of the variability in the ranks of the aircraft's speed that is *not* accounted for by knowing the rank of the aircraft's horsepower. This value, if you recall, which is the proportion of the variability of one variable not explained or accounted for by the variability of the other variable, is called the coefficient of nondetermination. For the Spearman r, it is equal to $1 - r_s^2$.

Reporting the Results of a Spearman *r* Correlation

To report our finding, we would say that there was a significant correlation between the ranked power and ranked speed of a series of aircraft [$r_s(9) = .92, p < .01$]. The coefficient of determination, r_s^2, equaled .85. With this statement, we have indicated to the reader that the data were ranked, the number of pairs of scores, the size of the Spearman r correlation, and that it was statistically significant. Finally, we have provided a measure of the strength of the association, or effect size, to assist the reader in interpreting the size of the effect.

Purpose and Limitations of Using the Spearman *r* Correlation

1. *Provides a measure of the association of two ranked variables:* The Spearman r correlation provides a measure of the strength and direction of an association between two ranked variables.

2. *Not a measure of cause and effect:* The Spearman r is a type of correlation. Due to a lack of control in a correlational design, a researcher is not justified in coming to a cause-and-effect conclusion.

Assumptions of the Spearman r Correlation

1. *Ordinal data:* The data are in the form of ranks or have been converted to ranks.

2. *Data are paired:* The data come as pairs, usually two measures on the same individual.

3. *No tied ranks:* The Spearman r correlation assumes that there are no tied ranks. If there are only a few, the Spearman r will remain reasonably accurate. However, if there are a substantial number of tied ranks the Spearman r should not be employed.

CONCLUSION

The Spearman r correlation is a commonly utilized, easy to calculate measure of the relationship between two ranked variables. It is a form of Pearson r and, like the Pearson r, the sign of the Spearman r indicates the direction of the relationship, and the square of the Spearman r provides a measure of effect size.

Questions: Appendix B

(Answers to odd-numbered items are provided in Appendix I.)

1. The Spearman r correlation is used with _____ data.

   a. nominal

   b. ordinal

   c. interval or ratio

   d. any of the above

2. The Spearman r correlation _____ assume a linear relationship between the variables.

   a. does

   b. does not

3. Following the calculation of the Spearman r correlation, we use _____ when referring to the table to determine if the outcome is significant.

   a. the sample size, n

   b. df

   c. $n - 1$

   d. we do not refer to a table to determine the significance of the outcome

4. If a Spearman *r* correlation is positive, _____.
   a. as the ranks of one variable *increase*, so do the ranks of the other
   b. as the ranks of one variable *decrease*, so do the ranks of the other
   c. as the ranks of one variable increase, the ranks of the other decrease
   d. both "a" and "b," but not "c"

5. With the Spearman *r* correlation a commonly used measure of effect size is _____.
   a. the coefficient of determination
   b. the square root of the correlation
   c. r_S^2
   d. both "a" and "b," but not "c"
   e. both "a" and "c," but not "b"

6. The proportion of the variability of one variable *not* explained or accounted for by the variability of the other variable, is called the _____.
   a. coefficient of determination
   b. coefficient of nondetermination
   c. r_S^2
   d. both "b" and "c"

7. If there are a substantial number of tied ranks, the Spearman *r* _____.
   a. should not be employed
   b. can still be employed
   c. will become equivalent to a Pearson *r*

To determine the relationship between studying and grades, a professor gave an exam and asked how many hours students had studied for it. The data were as follows:

Student	Exam Grade	Hours Studied
1	96	12
2	94	6
3	90	6
4	85	5
5	80	3
6	71	2
7	68	4

8. What is the Spearman r for these data?

   a. .443

   b. .741

   c. .884

   d. .968

9. What is the critical value assuming alpha equals .05 and this was a *one*-tailed test?

   a. .886

   b. .829

   c. .786

   d. .714

   e. .893

10. Is the outcome statistically significant assuming it is in the predicted direction?

   a. Yes

   b. No

11. What is the coefficient of determination?

   a. .781

   b. .714

   c. .843

   d. .662

APPENDIX C

MULTIPLE REGRESSION

The difficulty lies, not in the new ideas, but in escaping the old ones.

—John Maynard Keynes

Multiple regression (italicized and underlined in Table C.1) is a commonly utilized extension of linear regression. In linear regression, which was covered in Chapter 15, a statistically significant Pearson r correlation is followed by the determination of the equation for the regression line. This equation, which can be written as $\hat{Y} = bX + a$, permits the prediction of Y (the criterion) from X (the predictor). It is defined as the line such that the sum of the squared errors of estimate is a minimum. So long as the Pearson r correlation is statistically significant, predictions based on the regression equation will be more accurate than simply choosing the mean of Y regardless of the value of X. In other words, the standard error of estimate will be less than the standard deviation (refer to Chapter 15 for a review).

Table C.1   Overview of Inferential Statistical Procedures for Association Designs

	Type of Data		
	Nominal (Frequency)	**Ordinal (Ranked)**	**Interval/Ratio (Continuous Measure)**
Correlation	Phi	*Spearman r*	Pearson *r*
Regression			Linear regression
			Multiple regression

The logic of linear regression can be extended to situations in which there is more than one predictor of Y. For example, if we were interested in predicting students' college grade point averages (GPA; Y) based on their high school GPA (X), we would use linear regression assuming the assumptions were met. However, there are other reasonable predictors, including a student's SAT score and a measure based on their letters of recommendation. With multiple regression, we can combine any number of predictors into one equation to estimate the value of a criterion variable. By doing so, our ability to predict Y is likely to be improved. The equation for multiple regression with two predictors can be written in a number of ways. One form of the equation is as follows:

$$\hat{Y} = B_1 X_1 + B_2 X_2 + B_0,$$

where $\hat{Y}$ is the predicted value of the criterion variable, B_1 is the regression weight associated with the first predictor variable, X_1, B_2 is the regression weight associated with the second predictor variable, X_2, and B_0 is a constant, the value of the Y intercept.

The equation for multiple regression with three predictors could be written as

$$\hat{Y} = B_1 X_1 + B_2 X_2 + B_3 X_3 + B_0,$$

where each term is defined as before and where B_3 is the regression weight associated with the third predictor variable, X_3.

While these equations may appear "new," they are actually just more involved forms of the equation we employed for linear regression, $\hat{Y} = bX + a$. As we are now dealing with multiple regression, and thus additional predictors, the equation has additional terms. Two other things to note are that while the slope of the line in linear regression (also called the regression weight) is usually indicated by the letter "b," in multiple regression, an equivalent regression weight is often signified with a capital letter "B." And, while the Y intercept in linear regression is commonly indicated by the letter "a," in multiple regression, it is often indicated by the symbol B_0. Nevertheless, while the multiple regression equation is more complex than the linear regression equation, it should be evident that it is a straightforward extension of the simpler equation.

As was noted previously, there is no theoretical limit to the number of possible predictors in multiple regression. However, the computations quickly become tedious, and thus, anyone who will be utilizing multiple regression is strongly encouraged to employ a computer-based statistical package. Finally, while there is only one type of linear regression, there are a number of approaches to multiple regression.

Simple multiple regression: a form of multiple regression in which all of the predictor variables are assessed simultaneously. All predictors that do not significantly enhance the overall prediction are dropped.

In **simple multiple regression,** all of the predictor variables are assessed simultaneously, without any consideration of theoretical importance or prior findings. All predictors that do not significantly enhance the overall prediction are dropped.

With **hierarchical multiple regression,** the researcher specifies the order in which predictor variables are entered into the regression equation. Only those variables that provide a statistically significant improvement in the ability to predict Y are maintained in the equation. This approach to multiple regression is best suited to situations where there is a theoretical basis for the order in which predictor variables are to be considered.

In **forward stepwise multiple regression**, predictor variables are entered into the regression equation based on their individual correlation with Y. Thus, the predictor variable with the strongest individual correlation with Y is entered first. Then, the variable that accounts for the greatest proportion of the remaining variability is entered. This process continues until there is no longer a statistically significant improvement in the ability to predict Y.

With **backward stepwise multiple regression,** all of the predictor variables are assessed simultaneously as in simple multiple regression. Then, however, instead of dropping all of the predictors that do not significantly enhance the prediction, only the predictor variable with the weakest individual correlation with Y is eliminated and the regression equation is recalculated. If there is no significant decrease in the ability to predict Y, this predictor variable is eliminated. This process continues until there is a significant effect of dropping a predictor variable.

So which approach to multiple regression should you employ? It has been found that both the forward and backward stepwise multiple regression techniques are likely to be affected by chance factors related to sample selection, and thus, their results are less stable. As a consequence, these approaches are less commonly used. Hierarchical multiple regression is appropriate if the researcher has a theoretical reason for controlling the order in which variables are

Hierarchical multiple regression: a form of multiple regression in which the researcher specifies the order in which predictor variables are entered into the regression equation. Only those variables that provide a statistically significant improvement in the ability to predict Y are maintained in the equation.

Forward stepwise multiple regression: a form of multiple regression in which predictor variables are entered into the regression equation based on their individual correlation with Y. To begin, the predictor variable with the strongest individual correlation with Y is entered first. Then, the variable that accounts for the greatest proportion of the remaining variability is entered. This process continues until there is no longer a statistically significant improvement in the ability to predict Y.

Backward stepwise multiple regression: a form of multiple regression in which all of the predictor variables are assessed simultaneously as in simple multiple regression. Then, however, instead of dropping all of the predictors that do not significantly enhance the prediction, only the predictor variable with the weakest individual correlation with Y is eliminated, and the regression equation is recalculated. If there is no significant decrease in the ability to predict Y, this predictor variable is eliminated. This process continues until there is a significant effect of dropping a predictor variable.

entered into the regression equation. Otherwise, simple multiple regression is the procedure that is best suited for most researchers.

To conduct a multiple regression analysis, the first step is to ensure that the assumptions have been met (these are reviewed later in this section). Next, any outliers are identified, and either the data from those subjects are omitted or the data are transformed (reviewed in more advanced statistical texts). Assuming the assumptions have been met, and there are no outliers, the analysis is then conducted, presumably with a computer package such as SPSS.

Table C.2 presents the SPSS output of a simple multiple regression analysis. The data come from a study by Norvilitis and Reid (2011) which, in part, examined four possible predictors of academic adjustment in college students. The four predictors consisted of (1) a measure of study skills, "studytot," (2) the outcome of the 15-item Appreciation of the Liberal Arts scale (ALAS), "alastot," (3) the hyperactivity component of ADHD (attention-deficit/hyperactivity disorder), "adhdhyp," and (4) finally, the inattention component of ADHD, "adhdatt." These variables are listed in the first section of the output.

The second section of the output, which has the heading "Model Summary," indicates that the value of the multiple regression, R, is .731. Recall that with only one predictor, as was reviewed in Chapter 15, we calculate a Pearson r correlation. With multiple predictors, we calculate a multiple correlation based on all of the predictor variables. This correlation is symbolized by the letter R. Furthermore, in linear regression, which has only one predictor, if we have a statistically significant r we then calculate r^2 to determine the proportion of variance in Y explained by the correlation. Similarly, in a multiple regression analysis, we calculate R^2, the proportion of variance in Y explained by all of the predictors. In this example, the value of R^2 is .534 (in SPSS this is called R Square). In other words, over half of the variability in the academic adjustment scores is accounted for by the four predictor variables. However, it has been found that R^2 slightly overestimates the proportion of variance that has been explained. Consequently, SPSS provides an adjusted R^2 that corrects for this overestimate. In this case, the value of the Adjusted R Square is .515, but this correction is not commonly reported in research papers. Finally, a measure of variability is given. The smaller the standard error of estimate, the more accurately you can predict Y.

The third section of the output, labeled "ANOVA," provides a test of the statistical significance of the multiple regression. If the ANOVA is not significant, there is no point in reviewing the remainder of the output, for there is no significant relationship between your set of predictors and the criterion variable, Y. However, in this case, the value of the F ratio is 27.231, which indicates this regression value of .731 has a probability of less than 1 in 1,000 of having occurred by chance if the true value was zero. As the ANOVA is statistically significant, you proceed to the remaining portion of the output.

The fourth section of the output, with the heading "Coefficients," consists of six columns. The first column consists of the labels for each of the predictors in the regression equation as well as the word (Constant). The next column has the heading "B." It consists of the values for B in the regression equation, beginning with the value for the constant, which has the symbol B_0 in the regression equation, followed by the regression weights of the predictors

Table C.2   SPSS Output for a Simple Multiple Regression

Variables Entered/Removed[b]

Model	Variables Entered	Variables Removed	Method
1	adhdhyp, studytot, alastot, adhdatt[a]	.	Enter

a. All requested variables entered.
b. Dependent Variable: sacqacad

Model Summary

Model	R	R Square	Adjusted R Square	Std. Error of the Estimate
1	.731[a]	.534	.515	9.67358

a. Predictors: (Constant), adhdhyp, studytot, alastot, adhdatt

ANOVA[b]

Model		Sum of Squares	df	Mean Square	F	Sig.
1	Regression	10193.061	4	2548.265	27.231	.000[a]
	Residual	8889.929	95	93.578		
	Total	19082.990	99			

a. Predictors: (Constant), adhdhyp, studytot, alastot, adhdatt
b. Dependent Variable: sacqacad

Coefficients[a]

Model		Unstandardized Coefficients		Standardized Coefficients		
		B	Std. Error	Beta	t	Sig.
1	(Constant)	119.296	11.405		10.460	.000
	Studytot	−.977	.164	−.479	−5.947	.000
	Alastot	−.557	.125	−.323	−4.447	.000
	Adhdatt	.759	.382	.178	1.989	.050
	Adhdhyp	.098	.369	.022	.266	.791

a. Dependent Variable: sacqacad

(B_1, etc.). The third column provides a measure of variability for each of these values of B. The fourth column provides measures of standardized coefficients. These are the values in the regression equation that would be obtained if all of the data had initially been converted to z scores (in other words, standardized), as was reviewed in Chapter 4. **Beta** is the term used in multiple regression for a regression weight based on standardized scores (note that beta can also refer to the size of Type II error, which is a different concept). Essentially, the use of standardized scores takes the variability of the predictor measures into account (standardizes them) and thus permits the researcher a more accurate perspective of the effect of each of the predictors.

Beta: the term used in multiple regression for a regression weight based on standardized scores.

In this case, note that the absolute value of Beta for adhdhyp is considerably smaller than the other variables' values for Beta and, in fact, is only .022, which is close to zero. We will discuss the meaning of this in a moment. The entries in the fifth column are t values (refer to Chapter 10 for a discussion of the t test). The predictors are listed in order based on the absolute value of their t statistic. More specifically, the t statistic provides a test of whether the value listed in the second column, with the heading B, is significantly different from zero. The actual significance levels of these t statistics are provided in the last column, which has the heading "Sig." This column indicates that the B values for constant, studytot, and alastot all have a probability of less than 1 in 1,000 of having occurred by chance if their actual value for B was zero. The predictor, adhdatt, has a probability of .05. In other words, the probability is only 1 in 20 of this value of B occurring by chance if the actual value was zero. Thus, three of the four predictors (alastot, studytot, and adhdatt) have B values statistically different from zero. However, the predictor adhdhyp has a B value of only .098. This B value is associated with a t statistic of .266, which indicates that a B value of this magnitude has a probability of occurring by chance approximately 79 times out of 100 if the actual value of B was zero. This is not statistically significant, and thus, adhdhyp, the hyperactivity component of ADHD, is not a significant predictor of academic adjustment in these college students.

Multicollinearity: In multiple regression, a concern that arises when the predictors in the multiple regression equation are highly correlated with each other. If they are, then the results of the multiple regression analysis are likely to vary dramatically between samples. This is an undesirable characteristic.

A more complete output would provide information concerning what is known as **multicollinearity**. Essentially, this concept deals with whether the predictors in the multiple regression equation are highly correlated with each other. If they are, then the results of the multiple regression analysis are likely to vary dramatically between samples. This is an undesirable characteristic. For a more detailed discussion, you should turn to a more advanced text. I will just point out that so long as the values for the variance inflation factors are less than 2, as is the case with these data, multicollinearity is not considered to be a problem.

Reporting the Results of a Multiple Regression Analysis

Clearly, the SPSS output provides a great deal of information. Table C.3 presents a summary of how the results of this regression analysis would be presented in a paper.

Table C.3 Summary of the Regression Analysis Predicting Academic Adjustment

Predictor Variable	B	SE B	β	T	α
Study skills	−.98	.16	−.48	−5.95	<.001
ALAS	−.56	.13	−.32	−4.45	<.001
Inattention	.76	.38	.18	1.99	.05
Hyperactivity	.10	.37	.02	.27	.79

The multiple regression equation for these data would therefore be

$$\hat{Y} = (-.98)X_1 + (-.56)X_2 + (.76)X_3 + 119.296,$$

where X_1 is the score for Study skills, X_2 is the ALAS score, and X_3 is the Inattention score. Note that the variable Hyperactivity has been dropped as it did not significantly enhance the overall prediction. The value of the constant, 119.296, comes from the previous table with the heading "Coefficients."

Purpose and Limitations of Using Multiple Regression

1. *Provides an equation so that the value of Y can be predicted:* The multiple correlation, *R*, provides a measure of the strength of an association between multiple predictor variables (*X* variables) and a single criterion variable (*Y*). Multiple regression provides an equation for this association that enables *Y* to be predicted.

2. *May not be a measure of cause and effect:* Multiple regression follows the finding of a statistically significant multiple correlation, *R*. If the study was based on a correlational design, the researcher is not justified in coming to a cause-and-effect conclusion due to the lack of experimental control. In this case, the multiple regression equation would allow the prediction of *Y* from a series of *X* variables, but would not indicate that the *X* variables are causing changes in the *Y* variable. However, if the study had incorporated appropriate experimental controls, then cause-and-effect conclusions would be warranted.

3. *Prediction is limited to the range of the original values:* The multiple regression equation should not be used for values of the predictor variables that are beyond the range of the original data.

Assumptions of Multiple Regression

1. *Interval or ratio data:* The data are on an interval or a ratio scale of measurement.

2. *Data are associated:* The data are usually multiple measures on the same individual.

3. *Linear relationship:* It is assumed that all of the variables are linearly related.

4. *Significant multiple correlation, R:* A multiple regression analysis will only be undertaken if the multiple correlation, R, has been found to be statistically significant.

CONCLUSION

Multiple regression is an extension of linear regression to situations in which there is more than one predictor variable. There are four basic types of multiple regression. For most purposes, simple multiple regression is preferable to hierarchical, forward stepwise, or backward stepwise multiple regression.

Appendix C Resources

GLOSSARY OF TERMS

Backward stepwise multiple regression: a form of multiple regression in which all of the predictor variables are assessed simultaneously as in simple multiple regression. Then, however, instead of dropping all of the predictors that do not significantly enhance the prediction, only the predictor variable with the weakest individual correlation with Y is eliminated and the regression equation is recalculated. If there is no significant decrease in the ability to predict Y, this predictor variable is eliminated. This process continues until there is a significant effect of dropping a predictor variable.

Beta: the term used in multiple regression for a regression weight based on standardized scores.

Forward stepwise multiple regression: a form of multiple regression in which predictor variables are entered into the regression equation based on their individual correlation with Y. To begin, the predictor variable with the strongest individual correlation with Y is entered first. Then, the variable that accounts for the greatest proportion of the remaining variability is entered. This process continues until there is no longer a statistically significant improvement in the ability to predict Y.

Hierarchical multiple regression: a form of multiple regression in which the researcher specifies the order in which predictor variables are entered into the regression equation. Only those variables that provide a statistically significant improvement in the ability to predict Y are maintained in the equation.

Multicollinearity: in multiple regression, a concern that arises when the predictors in the multiple regression equation are highly correlated with each other. If they are, then the results of the multiple regression analysis are likely to vary dramatically between samples. This is an undesirable characteristic.

Simple multiple regression: a form of multiple regression in which all of the predictor variables are assessed simultaneously. All predictors that do not significantly enhance the overall prediction are dropped.

Questions: Appendix C

(Answers to odd-numbered items are provided in Appendix I.)

1. If the Pearson r is statistically significant, then in simple linear regression the _____ will be less than the _____.

   a. mean of Y; mean of X

   b. mean of X; mean of Y

   c. standard error of estimate; standard deviation

   d. standard deviation; standard error of estimate

2. With linear regression, there is (are) always _____ predictor(s) while in multiple regression there is (are) always _____ predictor(s).

   a. one; two

   b. one; two or more

   c. two; one

   d. two or more; one

3. In the linear regression equation, the Y intercept is commonly indicated by _____ while in the multiple regression equation the Y intercept is commonly indicated by _____.

   a. B_1; B_0

   b. a; B_0

   c. B_0; B_1

   d. B_0; a

4. In _____ all of the predictor variables are assessed simultaneously, without any consideration of theoretical importance or prior findings. All predictors that do not significantly enhance the overall prediction are dropped.

   a. simple multiple regression

   b. hierarchical multiple regression

   c. forward stepwise multiple regression

   d. backward stepwise multiple regression

5. This approach to multiple regression is best suited to situations where there is a theoretical basis for the order in which predictor variables are to be considered.

   a. Simple multiple regression

   b. Hierarchical multiple regression

   c. Forward stepwise multiple regression

   d. Backward stepwise multiple regression

6. It has been found that this (these) multiple regression technique(s) is (are) likely to be affected by chance factors related to sample selection, and thus, its (their) results are less stable. As a consequence, this (these) approach(es) is (are) less commonly used.

   a. Simple multiple regression

   b. Hierarchical multiple regression

   c. Forward stepwise multiple regression

   d. Backward stepwise multiple regression

   e. Both "c" and "d"

7. In linear regression, if we have a statistically significant r, we then calculate _____ to determine the proportion of variance in Y explained by the correlation. In multiple regression, if we have a statistically significant R, we then calculate _____ to determine the proportion of variance in Y explained by the multiple correlation.

   a. R; r

   b. a; B_0

   c. r^2; R^2

   d. B_0; a

8. _____ is the symbol or term used in multiple regression for a regression weight based on standardized scores.

   a. B_0

   b. B_1

   c. R^2

   d. Beta

9. This concept deals with whether the predictors in the multiple regression equation are highly correlated with each other.

    a. Multicollinearity

    b. Beta

    c. Hierarchical multiple regression

    d. Backward stepwise multiple regression

10. With multiple regression which scale of measurement do we have for the predictors and the criterion?

    a. Always interval

    b. Either interval or ratio

    c. At least ordinal

    d. Any scale of measurement is appropriate.

APPENDIX D

AN INTRODUCTION TO POWER ANALYSIS

Minimum Appropriate Sample Sizes

A few observations and much reasoning lead to error; many observations and a little reasoning to truth.

—Alexis Carrel

This text, like all introductory statistical texts, has emphasized the understanding of Type I error, which is the probability of incorrectly rejecting a true null hypothesis. Type I error is called alpha and has the symbol α. As was previously discussed, in most experiments the alpha level is set by the researcher at .05, or 1 chance in 20, though another value such as .01 is sometimes chosen.

This appendix will emphasize the importance of Type II error, which is the probability of failing to reject a false null hypothesis. Type II error is called beta (note that beta has a different definition in multiple regression, which is discussed in Appendix C) and has the symbol β. As was noted in Chapter 6, the value of beta is not usually known. Nevertheless, an understanding of beta is important, in part because beta is related to the concept of statistical power, which is defined as $1 - \beta$. Power is thus the probability of correctly rejecting a false null hypothesis, which is what an experimenter is attempting to accomplish when conducting a study. Alternatively, if we assume that an independent variable has had an effect on a dependent variable, then power can be thought of as indicating how well the researcher can detect that this has occurred. An example may be helpful.

Table 7.2 (reproduced in part here as Table D.1) summarizes the results of tossing a coin. The question raised in Chapter 7 was whether, with 10 tosses of a coin, an outcome of 7 heads and 3 tails was different enough from the expected outcome of 5 heads and 5 tails to warrant rejecting the null hypothesis that the coin was fair. A chi-square value of 1.6 was obtained which, with 1 degree of freedom, was not statistically significant, and thus, the null hypothesis was not rejected. Of course, this does not "prove" that the coin was fair, just that there was not sufficient evidence to conclude that the coin was not fair. But this raises a question, if the coin was actually unfair, Would the researcher have been likely to recognize this? In other words, did the study have enough power to enable the research to detect that the coin was unfair?

Table D.1	Outcome of Tossing a Coin 10 Times	
Values	f_o	f_e
Heads	7	5
Tails	3	5

Steps to increase the power of an experiment were reviewed in Chapter 6. One of these steps is to increase the sample size(s) in the study. Thus, when conducting a study, a larger sample is, generally speaking, better than a smaller one. However, this advice is of only modest practical value as every experimenter has time and material constraints that will limit how many subjects they can test. What an experimenter needs to know is what the minimum acceptable sample size is for their particular situation, and in Chapter 6, there was no discussion concerning this issue. Furthermore, as this is an introductory text, an important consideration in creating examples was that the calculations be kept to a minimum. To do so, the data were frequently created so that significant outcomes would occur with very small samples. An unfortunate consequence is that a reader may have come to an incorrect view as to the sample size that is likely to be needed in actual research. Determination of how large a sample an experimenter should choose in order to have confidence that they can reasonably expect to reject a false null hypothesis is an example of what is called **power analysis**. The four variables that are involved in power analysis are the desired value for statistical power, the alpha level chosen by the researcher, the effect size, and the sample size.

Power analysis: detailed examination of the statistical power of a study. The current text emphasizes how this examination can assist the researcher in determining the minimum sample size that is needed.

As noted previously, power is the probability of correctly rejecting a false null hypothesis, and its value is linked to the value of beta. It has been suggested (Cohen, 1988) that a reasonable level of power for a study would be .80. With this value of power, the experimenter would be able to reject a false null hypothesis 80% of the time. Put another way, if the power of a study is .80, then the beta for the study is .20. This is generally seen as a reasonable level for beta. However, a number of published papers have noted that many studies have too little power. In other words, in many studies beta is greater than .20, sometimes much greater, and thus, it is unlikely that the null hypothesis could be rejected in these studies even if it was false. What this means is that these experimenters essentially wasted their time conducting their studies. But the damage is not limited to these researchers. Readers of this research may interpret a failure to reject the null hypothesis as evidence that the independent variable in question did not have an effect. If so, they will be less likely to explore this issue in the future, and thus, a promising direction for research may be overlooked. As many studies are underpowered, the cumulative effect can bias the direction or rate of development of an entire field of study (Maxwell, 2004)!

The levels of beta and alpha are linked. Recall that the alpha level is defined as the probability of making a Type I error. It is usually set by the experimenter at .05. Choosing a smaller level of alpha, such as .01, will reduce the probability of making a Type I error but will, of course, simultaneously increase the probability of making a Type II error (refer to Chapter 6 for a review). And, as Type II error (β) increases, the power of the experiment decreases (remember, power is defined as $1 - \beta$).

The effect size is also an important component of power analysis. The effect size is a measure of the strength of the independent variable. It can be thought of as the impact that an independent variable has on a dependent variable. Thus, in a simple two-group study, if the effect size is large, then the mean of the experimental group is likely to differ substantially from that of the control group and, all else being equal, larger differences are easier to detect than smaller differences.

The final variable in a power analysis is the number of subjects in the study. Intuitively, larger samples provide better estimates of population parameters than do smaller samples. Thus, as a general rule larger samples are better than smaller ones. Furthermore, if the values of the other three variables in a power analysis (power, the alpha level, and the effect size) are known, then the minimum sample size that is required for a study can also be determined. For instance, it was just noted that a reasonable level of statistical power for a study would be .80. Furthermore, the experimenter sets the value of alpha, usually at .05, so this is a known value. However, determining the effect size is more problematical. A review of previous studies may provide a reasonable estimate. If you do have values for power, alpha, and the effect size, there are websites that you can use to calculate the needed minimum sample size for your study. Alternatively, you can refer to the following tables to provide an estimate of your needed sample size. These tables are based on Cohen (1988), and you are encouraged to refer to this reference, or a shorter "primer" (Cohen, 1992) for a more in-depth discussion of this topic.

The following tables give the minimum sample sizes needed for studies utilizing the chi-square test of independence (Table D.2), one-way between-subjects ANOVA (analysis of variance) or independent samples *t* test (Table D.3), and the Pearson *r* correlation (Table D.4). The tables assume that power has been set as .80 and that the experimenter is utilizing a two-tailed test with the alpha level equal to .05. Furthermore, each table includes three esti-mates for the effect size (small, medium, or large). Cohen (1988) provides more extensive tables. However, the current tables provide an easy-to-understand introduction to power analysis and should be useful in determining approximate sample sizes for these commonly utilized statistical procedures.

Table D.2 indicates the total number of subjects needed in a study that utilizes a chi-square test of independence and which has the previously defined values for power and alpha. Cohen's (1988, 1992) tables were based on the statistic w as the measure of effect size. In this text, you were taught to use phi and Cramer's V as measures of effect size with a chi-square test. For a 2 × 2 table, phi is equal to w. For larger tables, Cramer's V is equal to $w / \sqrt{(r-1)}$, where r is the smaller of the rows and columns. Following the suggestion of Cohen (1988, 1992), a small effect size would have a w equal to .10, a medium effect size would have a w equal to .30, and a large effect size would have a w equal to .50.

It is important to note that in Table D.2, the needed minimum total number of subjects or cases increases as the degrees of freedom increases. This should be intuitively obvious, for it is reasonable that as the number of cells in a design increases, so would the necessary size of the total sample. In addition, as the effect size become larger, the needed sample size decreases dramatically. This is simply an indication that a large difference is easier to detect than a small difference. Finally, it should be noted that the number in Table D.2 for the minimum total sample size should be divided as evenly as possible among the cells in the chi-square. In addition, you must meet the assumptions of the test for minimum sample size for each cell and, to the extent that the sample sizes of the cells are uneven, the overall sample size will need to be increased.

Table D.1 summarized the outcome of tossing a coin 10 times. It was concluded that the results did not warrant rejecting the null hypothesis that the coin was fair. This was based on

Table D.2	Determination of the Minimum Number of Subjects Needed for a Chi-Square Test of Independence

	Effect Size		
df	**Small**	**Medium**	**Large**
1	785	87	31
2	964	107	39
3	1,090	121	44
4	1,194	133	48
5	1,283	143	51

the calculation of a chi-square, with 1 *df*, of 1.6. However, as Table D.2 indicates, even if the effect size was expected to be large, the study would have required a minimum sample size of 31. And if a medium effect size was anticipated, the minimum sample size would have increased to 87. With a sample size of only 10, the results in Table D.1 are an example of a woefully underpowered study.

Table D.3 indicates the number of subjects needed in each sample in a study that utilizes a one-way between-subjects ANOVA or independent samples t *test* with the previously defined values for power and alpha. The current text utilized η^2 as the measure of effect size with ANOVA. The measure of effect size utilized by Cohen (1988, 1992) was the statistic *f*. The conversion between these measures of effect size is straightforward: $\eta^2 = f^2/(1 + f^2)$. Thus, for small effect sizes η^2 is essentially equal to f^2. Following Cohen's (1988, 1992) suggestion, a small effect size would have an *f* equal to .10, a medium effect size would have an *f* equal to .25, and a large effect size would have an *f* equal to .40. The corresponding values of η^2 would therefore be .01 for a small effect size, .06 for a medium effect size, and .14 for a large effect size.

It is important to note that numbers in Table D.3 are for the minimum number of subjects needed in each sample of the study. Thus, while this number decreases with increasing degrees of freedom, the total number of subjects or cases needed in the entire study still increases as the degrees of freedom increases. In addition, as the effect size become larger, the number of subjects needed in each sample decreases dramatically. Once again, this is simply an indication that it is easier to detect a large difference than a small difference. Finally, it was pointed out in this text that the independent samples *t* test is closely related to an ANOVA. The number of subjects needed in each sample of the independent samples *t* test is the same as for a one-way between-subjects ANOVA with 1 df_{Bet}.

Table D.3	Determination of the Minimum Sample Size for a One-Way Between-Subjects ANOVA		

	Effect Size		
df_{Bet}	**Small**	**Medium**	**Large**
1	393	64	26
2	322	52	21
3	274	45	18
4	240	39	16
5	215	35	14

Note. ANOVA, analysis of variance; df_{Bet}, degrees of freedom between.

Table D.4 indicates the number of pairs of observations needed in a study that utilizes a Pearson r *correlation* with the previously defined values for power and alpha. Cohen's (1988, 1992) measure of effect size was based on the statistic r. This text utilized r^2 as the measure of effect size, so the conversion between these measures is straightforward. Following Cohen's (1988, 1992) suggestion, a small effect size would have an r equal to .10, a medium effect size would have an r equal to .30, and a large effect size would have an r equal to .50. These would correspond to r^2 values of .01, .09, and .25, respectively.

Table D.4	Determination of the Minimum Number of Pairs of Observations for a Pearson r Correlation

Effect Size		
Small	**Medium**	**Large**
783	85	28

It is important to note that the entries in Table D.4 are for the number of pairs of observations needed in the study. And as the effect size becomes larger, the number of pairs of observations needed in the study decreases dramatically. Once again, this is simply an indication that it is easier to detect a large effect than a small effect.

The previous examples are not meant to be comprehensive. However, even a brief review of the tables provided in this appendix will indicate that substantial sample sizes will frequently be needed for a study to have adequate power. This is a critical piece of information when designing your research, or when reviewing the research of others.

PURPOSE AND LIMITATIONS OF USING POWER ANALYSIS WHEN CHOOSING APPROPRIATE SAMPLE SIZES

1. Provides an estimate of the minimum number of subjects that is needed for a study.

2. Estimate of the minimum number of subjects needed is dependent on the values utilized for power, alpha, and effect size. The estimates for power, alpha, and effect size are all either based on convention (power and alpha) or on previous findings (effect size). While there is a solid logical basis for the conventions that underlie choices for values of power and alpha, there is still the possibility that for a particular study different values would have been appropriate. Furthermore, while the determination of effect size is based on the previous literature, in many cases this record is likely to be limited. All of these factors could affect the accuracy of the estimate of the minimum number of subjects that is needed.

ASSUMPTIONS OF POWER ANALYSIS WHEN IT IS BEING USED TO CHOOSE APPROPRIATE SAMPLE SIZES

Values of power, alpha, and effect size are either known or can be estimated.

CONCLUSION

Power analysis provides guidelines for determining the number of subjects that are needed in a study to maintain the Type II error rate at a reasonable level. Without an adequate number of subjects, it is likely that a false null hypothesis will not be rejected, a situation which has been found to commonly occur in reviews of research.

Appendix D Resources

GLOSSARY OF TERMS

Power analysis: detailed examination of the statistical power of a study. The current text emphasizes how this examination can assist the researcher in determining the minimum sample size that is needed.

Questions: Appendix D

(Answers to odd-numbered items are provided in Appendix I.)

1. The probability of incorrectly rejecting a true null hypothesis is the definition of _____.
   a. Type I error
   b. Type II error
   c. beta
   d. power
   e. both "b" and "c"

2. The probability of failing to reject a false null hypothesis is the definition of _____.
   a. Type I error
   b. Type II error
   c. beta
   d. power
   e. both "b" and "c"

3. The probability of correctly rejecting a false null hypothesis is the definition of _____.

   a. Type I error

   b. Type II error

   c. beta

   d. power

   e. both "b" and "c"

4. This statistical concept is defined as $1 - \beta$.

   a. Type I error

   b. Type II error

   c. beta

   d. power

   e. both "b" and "c"

5. If the power of a study is .70, then the beta for the study is _____.

   a. .10

   b. .20

   c. .30

   d. .40

   e. cannot be determined

6. Cohen suggested that a reasonable level of power for a study would be _____.

   a. .05

   b. .80

   c. .20

   d. .01

   e. .50

7. As the probability of making a Type I error increases, the probability of making a Type II error _____ and the power of the experiment _____.

   a. decreases, increases

   b. decreases, decreases

   c. increases, decreases

   d. increases, increases

8. Assuming that Cohen's recommendation for the size of power has been followed, and alpha has been set at .05, what is the minimum number of subjects that a researcher

should plan to include in their chi-square study, if there are 4 *df* and the expected effect size is large?

a. 31

b. 133

c. 48

d. 1,194

9. Assuming that Cohen's recommendation for the size of power has been followed, and alpha has been set at .05, what is the minimum number of subjects that a researcher should plan to include in each level of their one-way ANOVA study, if there are 5 *df* and the expected effect size is medium?

a. 35

b. 14

c. 215

d. 16

10. Assuming that Cohen's recommendation for the size of power has been followed, and alpha has been set at .05, what is the minimum number of pairs of subjects that a researcher should plan to include in their Pearson *r* study if the expected effect size is small?

a. 1,012

b. 783

c. 85

d. 28

APPENDIX E

STATISTICAL SYMBOLS USED IN THIS TEXT

(And Commonly Used Alternatives)

CHAPTER 1: INTRODUCTION

ΣX	sum each of the scores, it is read as sum of X
ΣX^2	sum each of the squared scores, it is read as sum of X squared
$(\Sigma X)^2$	the square of the sum of scores, it is read as sum of X, quantity squared
< and >	less than and greater than, respectively

CHAPTER 3: MEAN AND VARIABILITY WITH INTERVAL AND RATIO DATA

μ	population mean
M	sample mean ($\bar{X}$)
σ^2	variance of a population
σ	standard deviation of a population

CHAPTER 4: VARIABILITY WITH INTERVAL AND RATIO DATA

s^2	variance of a sample
s	standard deviation of a sample
z	z score
α	alpha level

CHAPTER 7: CHI-SQUARE

χ^2	chi-square
f_o	frequency observed
f_e	frequency expected

CHAPTER 8: CHI-SQUARE

ϕ	phi

CHAPTER 9: ONE SAMPLE z AND t TESTS

σ_M	population standard error ($\sigma_{\bar{x}}$)
z_c	critical value of z
$\leq$	less than or equal to
t	t score
s_{XP}	estimate of the population standard deviation based on sample data (s_x)
s_M	estimate of the population standard error based on sample data ($s_{\bar{x}}$)
df	degrees of freedom
η^2	eta squared
t_c	critical value of t

CHAPTER 10: INDEPENDENT SAMPLES *t* AND DEPENDENT SAMPLES *t*

M_1	mean of sample one
M_2	mean of sample two
$s_{(M_1 - M_2)}$	standard error of the difference between sample means
D	difference between two scores
M_D	mean of a set of difference scores
s_{M_D}	standard error of the mean difference

CHAPTER 11: ONE-WAY BETWEEN-SUBJECTS ANOVA

F	*F* ratio in an ANOVA
SS_T	sum of squares total
SS_{Bet}	sum of squares between
SS_W	sum of squares within
df_T	degrees of freedom total
df_{Bet}	degrees of freedom between
df_W	degrees of freedom within
MS_{Bet}	mean square between
MS_W	mean square within
k	number of samples or groups
q	value obtained from Tukey's HSD (honestly significant difference) table

CHAPTER 12: ONE-WAY WITHIN-SUBJECTS ANOVA

$SS_{Subjects}$	sum of squares subjects
$SS_{Residual}$	sum of squares residual
$df_{Subjects}$	degrees of freedom subjects

$df_{Residual}$ degrees of freedom residual

$MS_{Residual}$ mean square residual

CHAPTER 13: TWO-WAY BETWEEN-SUBJECTS ANOVA

F_A	main effect of Factor A
F_B	main effect of Factor B
$F_{A \times B}$	interaction of Factor A and Factor B
df_A	degrees of freedom Factor A
df_B	degrees of freedom Factor B
$df_{A \times B}$	degrees of freedom for interaction
df_W	degrees of freedom within
MS_A	mean square Factor A
MS_B	mean square Factor B
$MS_{A \times B}$	mean square for interaction
MS_W	mean square within

CHAPTER 14: ASSOCIATIONS WITH NOMINAL AND INTERVAL OR RATIO DATA: PHI, PEARSON r, AND POINT BISERIAL CORRELATION

r_ϕ	phi correlation
r_ϕ^2	with phi correlation, the proportion of variance in one variable that is explained or accounted for by the other variable
r_{XY}	Pearson r correlation with X predicting Y
r_{XY}^2	with Pearson r correlation, the proportion of variance in one variable (Y) that is explained or accounted for by the other variable (X)
r_{pb}	point biserial correlation
r_{pb}^2	with point biserial correlation, the proportion of variance in the continuous variable that is explained or accounted for by the dichotomous variable

CHAPTER 15: LINEAR REGRESSION

M_X	mean of the scores of variable X ($\bar{X}$)
M_Y	mean of the scores of variable Y ($\bar{Y}$)
$\hat{Y}$	predicted value of Y
$\sigma_{\hat{Y}}$	standard error of estimate—standard deviation of Y scores around the regression line
$\sigma_{\hat{Y}}^2$	error variance—variance of Y scores around the regression line
b	slope of a line, also called the regression weight
a	Y intercept of a line

APPENDIX C: MULTIPLE REGRESSION

B	regression weight in multiple regression
R	symbol for multiple correlation
R^2	in multiple correlation, the proportion of variance in the Y variable that is explained or accounted for by the predictor variables

APPENDIX F

DEFINITIONAL EQUATIONS AND, WHERE APPROPRIATE, THEIR COMPUTATIONAL EQUATION EQUIVALENTS

CHAPTER 3: MEAN AND VARIABILITY WITH INTERVAL AND RATIO DATA

$$M = \frac{\sum X}{n}$$

Definitional Equations	Computational Equations
$\sigma^2 = \dfrac{\sum (X - \mu)^2}{N}$	$\sigma^2 = \dfrac{\sum X^2 - \dfrac{(\sum X)^2}{N}}{N}$
$\sigma = \sqrt{\dfrac{\sum (X - \mu)^2}{N}}$	$\sigma = \sqrt{\dfrac{\sum X^2 - \dfrac{(\sum X)^2}{N}}{N}}$

CHAPTER 4: VARIABILITY WITH INTERVAL OR RATIO DATA

Definitional Equations	Computational Equations
$s^2 = \dfrac{\Sigma(X-M)^2}{n}$	$s^2 = \dfrac{\Sigma X^2 - \dfrac{(\Sigma X)^2}{n}}{n}$
$s = \sqrt{\dfrac{\Sigma(X-M)^2}{n}}$	$s = \dfrac{\Sigma X^2 - \dfrac{(\Sigma X)^2}{n}}{n}$
	$z = \dfrac{X - \mu}{\sigma}$

CHAPTER 7: CHI-SQUARE

$$\chi^2 = \Sigma \frac{(f_o - f_e)^2}{f_e}.$$

CHAPTER 8: CHI-SQUARE

$$\phi = \sqrt{\frac{\chi^2}{n}}$$

$$\text{Cramer's } V = \sqrt{\frac{\chi^2}{n(df)}},$$

where df = the smaller of $(r - 1)$ and $(c - 1)$.

CHAPTER 9: ONE SAMPLE z AND t TESTS

$$z = \frac{M - \mu}{\sigma_M},$$

where $\sigma_M = \sigma/\sqrt{n}$.

This equation may be clearer if we substitute σ_X for σ:

$$\sigma_M = \frac{\sigma_X}{\sqrt{n}}.$$

Confidence interval for z

$$M - z_c\,(\sigma_M) \leq \mu \leq M + z_c\,(\sigma_M),$$

where z_c is the critical value for z obtained from the z table (Appendix J, Table J.1)

$$t = \frac{M - \mu}{s_M},$$

where $s_M = s_{XP}\,/\,\sqrt{n}.$

$df = n - 1$, where n = the number of data points.

$$\eta^2 = \frac{t^2}{t^2 + df}.$$

Definitional Equations	Computational Equations
$s_{XP}^2 = \dfrac{\sum(X - M)^2}{n-1}$	$s_{XP}^2 = \dfrac{\sum X^2 - \dfrac{(\sum X)^2}{n}}{n-1}$
$s_{XP} = \sqrt{\dfrac{\sum(X - M)^2}{n-1}}$	$s_{XP} = \sqrt{\dfrac{\sum X^2 - \dfrac{(\sum X)^2}{n}}{n-1}}$

Confidence interval for t

$$M - t_c\,(s_M) \leq \mu \leq M + t_c\,(s_M).$$

Note that t_c for the confidence interval utilizes the value of t for a two-tailed test even if the original design utilized a one-tailed test.

CHAPTER 10: INDEPENDENT SAMPLES t AND DEPENDENT SAMPLES t TESTS

Independent Samples t Test

$$t = \frac{(M_1 - M_2) - (\mu_1 - \mu_2)}{s_{(M_1 - M_2)}},$$

where

$$s_{(M_1-M_2)} = \sqrt{\frac{(n_1-1)\, s_{XP_1}^2 + (n_2-1)\, s_{XP_2}^2}{n_1 + n_2 - 2}\left(\frac{1}{n_1}+\frac{1}{n_2}\right)},$$

and where $df = n_1 + n_2 - 2$.

$$\eta^2 = \frac{t^2}{t^2 + df}.$$

Confidence interval

$$\left[(M_1 - M_2) - t_c\left(s_{(M_1-M_2)}\right)\right] \le (\mu_1 - \mu_2) \le \left[(M_1 - M_2) + t_c\left(s_{(M_1-M_2)}\right)\right].$$

Dependent Samples t Test

$$t = \frac{M_D - \mu_D}{s_{M_D}},$$

where the mean difference, $M_D = \sum D / n$; the standard error, $s_{M_D} = s_{DP} / \sqrt{n}$; the standard deviation of the differences, $s_{DP} = \sqrt{\sum(D - M_D)^2 / (n - 1)}$; and n is equal to the number of *pairs* of scores. The df is equal to $n - 1$.

If the null hypothesis is that the difference between population means (μ_D) is zero,

$$t = \frac{M_D}{s_{M_D}}.$$

$$\eta^2 = \frac{t^2}{t^2 + df}.$$

Confidence interval: $M_D - t_c(s_{M_D}) \le \mu_D \le M_D + t_c(s_{M_D})$.

CHAPTER 11: ONE-WAY BETWEEN-SUBJECTS ANOVA

Likelihood of at least one Type I error $= 1 - (1 - \alpha)^c$,

where c is the number of pairwise comparisons.

$$\text{Number of pairwise comparisons} = \frac{k(k-1)}{2},$$

where k is the number of samples or groups.

$$F = \frac{\text{(Between groups estimate of } \sigma_X^2)}{\text{(Within groups estimate of } \sigma_X^2)}.$$

$$SS_T = SS_{Bet} + SS_W.$$

$$SS_T = \Sigma(X - M_G)^2,$$

where $M_G = \Sigma X / N$, and N is the total number of subjects in all the groups or samples.

$$SS_{Bet} = \Sigma\left[(M - M_G)^2 n\right],$$

where M is the mean of a group and n is the sample size.

$$SS_W = \Sigma\left[\Sigma(X - M)^2\right].$$
$$df_T = df_{Bet} + df_W.$$
$$df_T = N - 1.$$
$$df_{Bet} = k - 1,$$

where k is the number of groups or treatment levels.

$$df_W = \Sigma(n - 1),$$

where n is the number of subjects in each group or sample.

$$F = \frac{MS_{Bet}}{MS_W}$$

$$= \frac{\text{Estimate of } \sigma_X^2 \text{ based on treatment } + \text{ Error}}{\text{Estimate of } \sigma_X^2 \text{ based only on error}}.$$

$$MS_{Bet} = \frac{SS_{Bet}}{df_{Bet}}.$$

$$MS_W = \frac{SS_W}{df_W}.$$

$$\text{Tukey HSD critical value} = q\sqrt{\frac{MS_W}{n}},$$

where q is found from the q table (Appendix J, Table J.5) and n is the number of subjects in *each* sample if the sample size is the same for all of the samples. Or

$$n = \frac{\text{Number of means}}{\sum \dfrac{1}{\text{Number of subjects in each sample}}},$$

if the sample size is not the same for all of the samples.

$$\eta^2 = \frac{SS_{Bet}}{SS_T}.$$

$$t^2 = F.$$

CHAPTER 12: ONE-WAY WITHIN-SUBJECTS ANOVA

$$SS_T = SS_{Bet} + SS_{Subjects} + SS_{Residual}.$$

$$SS_T = \sum (X - M_G)^2,$$

where $M_G = \sum X / N$ and N is the total number of subjects in all of the samples.

$$SS_{Bet} = \sum [(M - M_G)^2 n],$$

where $n =$ the number of subjects in the sample.

$$SS_{Residual} = SS_W - SS_{Subjects}.$$

$$SS_W = \sum \left[\sum (X - M)^2 \right],$$

where M is the mean of a group.

$$SS_{Subjects} = \left[\sum \left(\frac{\sum X_{Subject}}{k} - M_G \right)^2 \right] k,$$

where k is the number of treatment levels.

$$df_T = df_{Bet} + df_{Subjects} + df_{Residual}$$

$$df_T = N - 1,$$

where $N =$ the total number of data points.

$$df_{\text{Bet}} = k - 1.$$

$$df_{\text{Subjects}} = n - 1.$$

$$df_{\text{Residual}} = (n - 1)(k - 1),$$

$$MS_{\text{Bet}} = \frac{SS_{\text{Bet}}}{df_{\text{Bet}}}.$$

$$MS_{\text{Residual}} = \frac{SS_{\text{Residual}}}{df_{\text{Residual}}}.$$

$$F = \frac{MS_{\text{Bet}}}{MS_{\text{Residual}}}.$$

$$\text{Number of pairwise comparisons} = \frac{k(k-1)}{2}.$$

$$\text{Tukey HSD critical value} = q\sqrt{\frac{MS_{\text{Residual}}}{n}},$$

where q is found from the q table (Appendix J, Table J.5), MS_{Residual} comes from the ANOVA summary table (for example, see Table 12.3), and n is the number of subjects.

$$\eta_P^2 = \frac{SS_{\text{Bet}}}{SS_T - SS_{\text{Subjects}}}.$$

CHAPTER 13: TWO-WAY BETWEEN-SUBJECTS ANOVA

There are three F ratios:

F_A, the main effect of Factor A

F_B, the main effect of Factor B

$F_{A \times B}$, the interaction of Factor A and Factor B

$$df_T = df_A + df_B + df_{A \times B} + df_W.$$

$$df_T = N - 1,$$

where N is the total number of subjects in the study.

$$df_A = \text{Number of levels of Factor A} - 1.$$

$$df_B = \text{Number of levels of Factor B} - 1.$$

$$df_{A \times B} = df_A \times df_B.$$

$$df_w = N - \text{Number of cells.}$$

$$MS_A = \frac{SS_A}{df_A}.$$

$$MS_B = \frac{SS_B}{df_B}.$$

$$MS_{A \times B} = \frac{SS_{A \times B}}{df_{A \times B}}.$$

$$MS_w = \frac{SS_w}{df_w}.$$

$$F_A = \frac{MS_A}{MS_w}.$$

$$F_B = \frac{MS_B}{MS_w}.$$

$$F_{A \times B} = \frac{MS_{A \times B}}{MS_w}.$$

$$\text{Number of pairwise comparisons} = \frac{k(k-1)}{2},$$

where k is the number of means being compared.

$$\text{Tukey HSD critical value} = q\sqrt{\frac{MS_w}{n}},$$

where q is found from the q table (Appendix J, Table J.5), MS_w comes from the ANOVA summary table (for example, see Table 13.3), and n = the number of scores for *each* mean.

Eta squared (η^2) is calculated for each F ratio that was found to be significant:

$$\eta^2 \text{ for Factor A} = \frac{SS_A}{SS_T}.$$

$$\eta^2 \text{ for Factor B} = \frac{SS_B}{SS_T}.$$

$$\eta^2 \text{ for the Interaction} = \frac{SS_{A \times B}}{SS_T}.$$

CHAPTER 14: ASSOCIATIONS WITH NOMINAL AND INTERVAL/RATIO DATA: PHI, PEARSON *r*, AND POINT BISERIAL CORRELATION

Phi Correlation

$$r_\phi = \frac{ad - bc}{\sqrt{(a+b)(c+d)(a+c)(b+d)}}.$$

$$\text{Chi-square} = (n)\,(r_\phi)^2.$$

where n = the total number of observations = $a + b + c + d$ and the df = (Number of columns − 1) × (Number of rows − 1).

Proportion of variance in one variable that is explained or accounted for by the other variable is phi^2 or r_ϕ^2

$$\text{The coeffecient of nondetermination} = 1 - r_\phi^2.$$

Pearson *r* Correlation

$$\text{cov}_{XY} = \frac{\Sigma(X - M_X)(Y - M_Y)}{(n-1)},$$

where n is the number of *pairs* of scores.

$$r_{XY} = \frac{\text{cov}_{XY}}{s_{XP}s_{YP}}.$$

df for the Pearson $r = n - 2$,

where n is the number of *pairs* of scores.

r_{XY}^2 is the proportion of variance in one variable that is explained or accounted for by the other variable.

Point Biserial Correlation

r_{pb} is calculated using the same equations as used with the Pearson *r*

$$r_{pb}^2 = \frac{t^2}{t^2 + df} \quad \text{and} \quad r_{pb}^2 = \frac{F}{F + df}.$$

CHAPTER 15: LINEAR REGRESSION

$$\sigma_{\hat{Y}} = \sigma_Y \sqrt{1-r^2}.$$

$$r^2 = \frac{\sigma_Y^2 - \sigma_{\hat{Y}}^2}{\sigma_Y^2}.$$

$$\hat{Y} = bX + a,$$

where

$$b = \frac{\text{Change in } Y}{\text{Change in } X}.$$

$$b = r\left(\frac{S_{YP}}{S_{XP}}\right).$$

$$a = M_Y - bM_X.$$

Definitional Equations	Computational Equations
$b = r\left(\dfrac{\sigma_Y}{\sigma_X}\right)$	$b = \dfrac{N\sum XY - \sum X \sum Y}{N\sum X^2 - (\sum X)^2}$

APPENDIX A: KRUSKAL–WALLIS H TEST

$$H = \left[\frac{12}{N(N+1)}\right]\left[\sum\left(\frac{T^2}{n}\right)\right] - 3(N+1),$$

where N = the total number of subjects, T = the total of the ranks for a sample, n = the sample size, and df = number of samples − 1.

$$\text{Number of possible pairwise comparisons} = \frac{k(k-1)}{2},$$

where k = the number of samples.

$$\text{Eta squared } (\eta^2) = \frac{H}{N-1}.$$

APPENDIX B: SPEARMAN r CORRELATION

$$r_S = 1 - \frac{6\sum D^2}{n(n^2 - 1)},$$

where D is the difference between a pair of ranks and n is the number of *pairs* of data.

The Spearman r table (Appendix J, Table J.7) is not based on degrees of freedom but rather is based directly on n, the number of pairs of data.

The coeffecient of determination $= r_S^2$.

The coeffecient of nondetermination $= 1 - r_S^2$.

APPENDIX C: MULTIPLE REGRESSION

The equation for multiple regression with two predictors is as follows:

$$\hat{Y} = B_1 X_1 + B_2 X_2 + B_0,$$

where $\hat{Y}$ is the predicted value of the criterion variable, B_1 is the regression weight associated with the first predictor variable, X_1, B_2 is the regression weight associated with the second predictor variable, X_2, and B_0 is a constant, the value of the Y intercept.

The equation for multiple regression with three predictors could be written as follows:

$$\hat{Y} = B_1 X_1 + B_2 X_2 + B_3 X_3 + B_0,$$

where each term is defined as before and where B_3 is the regression weight associated with the third predictor variable, X_3.

APPENDIX G

INFERENTIAL STATISTICAL PROCEDURES AND THEIR MEASURES OF EFFECT SIZE

Statistical Procedure	Measure of Effect Size
For difference and interaction designs (presented in order of coverage)	
Chi-square goodness-of-fit	None
Chi-square test of independence	Phi or Cramer's *V*
One-sample *t* test	Eta squared
Independent samples *t* test	Eta squared
Dependent samples *t* test	Eta squared
One-way between-subjects ANOVA	Eta squared
One-way within-subjects ANOVA	Eta squared
Two-way between-subjects ANOVA	Eta squared
Kruskal–Wallis *H* Test	Eta squared
For association designs (presented in order of coverage)	
Phi correlation	Phi squared
Pearson *r* correlation	Pearson *r* squared
Point biserial correlation	Point biserial squared
Spearman *r* correlation	Spearman *r* squared

APPENDIX H

GLOSSARY OF TERMS

Absolute value: the magnitude of a number irrespective of whether it is positive or negative.

Alpha: another term for Type I error. Its symbol is α.

Alpha level: criterion set for rejecting the null hypothesis. This is usually .05.

Alternative hypothesis (H_1): when used with a difference design, the statement that the treatment does have an effect.

Area of rejection: area of the distribution equal to the alpha level. It is also called the critical region.

Association design: research undertaken to determine whether an observed association is likely to generalize.

Backward stepwise multiple regression: a form of multiple regression in which all of the predictor variables are assessed simultaneously as in simple multiple regression. Then, however, instead of dropping all of the predictors that do not significantly enhance the prediction, only the predictor variable with the weakest individual correlation with Y is eliminated and the regression equation

is recalculated. If there is no significant decrease in the ability to predict Y, this predictor variable is eliminated. This process continues until there is a significant effect of dropping a predictor variable.

Bar graph: a graph in which the frequency of each category or class of observation is indicated by the length of its associated bar.

Bell-shaped curve: a symmetrical distribution in which the highest frequency scores are located near the middle, and the frequency drops the farther a score is from middle.

Beta: another term for Type II error. Its symbol is β. Also, the term used in multiple regression for a regression weight based on standardized scores.

Between-subjects design: with an ANOVA, those designs in which each subject receives a single level of a factor.

Biased estimator: an estimator that does not accurately predict what it is intended to because of systematic error.

Bimodal: a descriptive term for a distribution that has two modes.

"Blind" study: a study in which the data are collected in such a way that the subject's assignment to the control or experimental condition is not known. There are several variations of "blind" procedures. They are all employed to reduce bias.

Bonferroni method: a procedure to control the Type I error rate when making numerous comparisons. In this procedure, the alpha level that the experimenter sets is divided by the number of comparisons.

Carryover effect: a treatment or intervention at one point in time may affect or carryover to another point in time.

Cell: a particular combination of treatment levels in a factorial ANOVA.

Central limit theorem:

—with increasing sample sizes, the shape of the distribution of sample means (sampling distribution of the mean) rapidly approximates the normal distribution irrespective of the shape of the population from which it is drawn.

—the mean of the distribution of sample means is an unbiased estimator of the population mean.

—the standard deviation of the distribution of sample means (σ_M) will equal $\sigma_x/\sqrt{n}$.

Coefficient of determination: the square of the correlation. It indicates the proportion of variability in one variable that is explained or accounted for by the variability in the other variable.

Coefficient of nondetermination: the proportion of the variability of one variable not explained or accounted for by the variability of the other variable. For phi, it is equal to $1 - r_\phi^2$.

Computational equations: equations developed to aid in statistical calculations.

They were particularly useful with large data sets, but now researchers would employ computer software packages instead.

Confidence interval: the range of values that has a known probability of including the population parameter, usually the mean.

Confounded comparison: comparison of two cell means that involves more than one factor that is changing. The comparison cannot be interpreted.

Control group: in a between-groups design, the group of subjects that does not receive the treatment.

Correlation: a measure of the degree of association among variables. A correlation indicates whether a variable changes in a predicable manner as another variable changes.

Correlational study: a study in which the researcher does not randomly assign the subjects and does not manipulate the value of a variable. As a result, at the conclusion of the study the researcher has little confidence that there is a cause-and-effect relationship between the variables.

Counterbalancing: a method used to control for carryover effects. In counterbalancing, the order of the treatments or interventions is balanced so that an equal number of subjects will experience each order of presentation.

Covariance: a statistical measure indicating the extent to which two variables vary together.

Covary: if knowledge of how one variable changes assists you in predicting the value of another variable, the two variables are said to covary.

Critical region: area of the distribution equal to the alpha level. It is also called the area of rejection.

Data (plural of datum): factual information, often in the form of numbers.

Data view: SPSS window in which the data are displayed.

Deduction: a method of thinking in which conclusions are logically derived from general statements that are assumed to be true.

Degrees of freedom (*df*): the number of observations out of the total that are free to vary.

Dependent: two events, samples or variables are dependent if knowing the outcome of one enhances our prediction of the other.

Dependent variable (DV): in an experiment, the variable whose value is not directly controlled by the researcher. Its value may be changed by the independent variable (IV).

Descriptive statistics: techniques that are used to summarize a set of numbers.

Deviation: the difference between a score and some measure, usually the mean. Thus, with population data the deviation equals $X - \mu$.

Difference design: research undertaken to determine whether an observed difference is likely to generalize.

Effect size: a measure of how strong a statistically significant outcome is.

Empiricism: a method for finding truth that emphasizes observation rather than the logical thinking of rationalism.

Error variance: the variance of Y scores around the regression line.

Expected frequencies: with nominal data, the outcome that would be expected if the null hypothesis were true.

Experimental group: in a between-groups design, the group of subjects that does receive the treatment.

Experiment-wise error: the likelihood of making at least one Type I error with any of the experiment's comparisons.

Factor: with an ANOVA, the term *factor* is used instead of independent variable.

Factorial ANOVA: an ANOVA with more than one factor.

Forward stepwise multiple regression: a form of multiple regression in which predictor variables are entered into the regression equation based on their individual correlation with Y. To begin, the predictor variable with the strongest individual correlation with Y is entered first. Then the variable that accounts for the greatest proportion of the remaining variability is entered. This process continues until there is no longer a statistically significant improvement in the ability to predict Y.

Frequency distribution: a listing of the different values or categories of the observations along with the frequency with which each occurred.

Frequency polygon: a graphic presentation for use with interval or ratio data. It is similar to a histogram except that the frequency is indicated by the height of a point rather than the height of a bar. The points are connected by straight lines.

Gambler's fallacy: the incorrect assumption that if an event has not occurred recently, then the probability of it occurring in the future increases.

Grand mean (M_G): the mean of all of the scores.

Hierarchical multiple regression: a form of multiple regression in which the researcher specifies the order in which predictor variables are entered into the regression equation. Only those variables that provide a statistically significant improvement in the ability to predict Y are maintained in the equation.

Histogram: a graph used with interval or ratio data. As with the bar graph, frequencies are indicated by the length of the associated bars. However, as there are no distinct categories in a histogram, the bars are positioned side by side.

Independent: two events, samples, or variables are independent if knowing the outcome of one does not enhance our prediction of the other.

Independent variable (IV): in an experiment, the variable the experimenter manipulates or directly controls.

Induction: a method of thinking in which conclusions are derived from generalizations based on limited statements or observations that are assumed to be true. Induction is fundamental to science, as observations are used to develop general laws of nature.

Inferential statistics: techniques that are used in making decisions based on data.

Inflection point: a point on a graph where the curvature changes from concave to convex or from convex to concave.

Interaction: a statistical term indicating that the effects of two or more variables are not independent. Also, a change in the dependent variable that is due to the presence of a particular combination of independent variables.

Interval scale of measurement: a measurement scale in which the magnitude of the difference between numbers is meaningful, and thus, addition and subtraction are

possible. However, there is no true zero, and thus, multiplication and division are not meaningful.

Intrinsic plausibility: decision-making process in which the alternative that seems most reasonable is accepted as being true.

Law of large numbers: the larger the sample size, the better the estimate of population parameters such as μ.

Level: with an ANOVA, the number of values of the independent variable.

Linear regression: procedures used to determine the equation for the regression line.

Longitudinal study: a study in which subjects are measured repeatedly across time. A repeated measures design is a type of longitudinal study.

Main effect: with a factorial ANOVA, another term used for an independent variable.

Mean: sum of the scores divided by the total number of scores. Also, a measure of central tendency for use with interval or ratio data. It is what is commonly called an average, but in statistics, the term *average* can refer to a mean, median, or mode.

Mean square between (MS_{Bet}): the estimate of σ_X^2 obtained from the deviations of the sample means from M_G. It is thus based on the variability between the samples.

Mean square within (MS_W): the estimate of σ_X^2 obtained by pooling the variances of the scores from their sample means. It is thus based on the variability within each of the samples.

Measure of central tendency: a single number that is chosen to best summarize an entire set of numbers.

Median: a measure of central tendency. It is the midmost score in a distribution. In other words, the median splits a distribution in half, with just as many scores above it as below it. It is at the 50th percentile.

Mode: a measure of central tendency. It is the most common category or score.

Multicollinearity: in multiple regression a concern that arises when the predictors in the multiple regression equation are highly correlated with each other. If they are, then the results of the multiple regression analysis are likely to vary dramatically between samples. This is an undesirable characteristic.

Multiple correlation (R): the association between one criterion variable and a combination of two or more predictor variables.

Multiple regression: situation in which several variables (Xs) are used to predict one other variable (Y)

Negative correlation: a relationship between two variables in which as one variable increases in value, the other variable decreases in value. Also, as one variable decreases in value, the other increases in value.

Negatively skewed: a nonsymmetrical distribution in which the tail pointing to the left is larger than the tail pointing to the right.

Nominal scale of measurement: a measurement scale in which numbers serve as names of categories. In this level of measurement, the magnitude of the number is arbitrary.

Normal distribution: a specific, bell-shaped distribution. Many statistical procedures assume that the data are distributed normally.

Null hypothesis (H_0): when used with a difference design, the statement that the treatment does not have an effect.

Observed frequencies: with nominal data, the actual data that were collected.

One-tailed or directional test: an analysis in which the null hypothesis will be rejected if an extreme outcome occurs in only one direction. In such a test, the single area of rejection is equal to alpha.

Ordinal scale of measurement: a measurement scale in which the magnitude of the numbers indicates the order in which events occurred. In this level of measurement, the magnitude of the number is meaningful.

Pairwise comparison: comparison between two sample means.

Pairwise error rate: the likelihood of making a Type I error for a single comparison between sample means. This is equal to α, which is usually .05 or .01.

Parameter: a measure of a characteristic of a population, such as its mean or its variance.

Partial correlation: a procedure in which the effect of a variable that is not of interest is removed.

Pearson r: correlation used with interval or ratio data.

Percentile rank: the percentage of the data at or below a category or score.

Phi (r_ϕ): —Correlation used with nominal data. It is a form of Pearson r.

Pie chart: a presentation of categorical data in which the area of a slice of a circle is indicative of the relative frequency with which the category occurs.

Point biserial (r_{pb}): correlation used when one variable is nominal (a true dichotomy) and the other consists of interval or ratio data.

Population: the entire group that is of interest.

Positive correlation: a relationship between two variables in which as one variable increases in value, so does the other variable. Also, as one variable decreases in value, so does the other.

Positively skewed: a nonsymmetrical distribution in which the tail pointing to the right is larger than the tail pointing to the left.

Post hoc comparisons: statistical procedures utilized following an initial, overall test of significance to identify the specific samples that differ.

Power: the probability of correctly rejecting a false null hypothesis. This probability is $1 - \beta$.

Power analysis: detailed examination of the statistical power of a study. The current book emphasizes how this examination can assist the researcher in determining the minimum sample size that is needed.

Preexisting subject differences: relatively stable subject characteristics. These differences between subjects are a form of error in an ANOVA.

Quasi-experiment: an experiment in which the researcher manipulates the value of the independent variable but does not randomly assign the subjects. As a result, at the conclusion of the study, the researcher has less confidence in concluding that there is a cause-and-effect relationship between the independent and dependent variables than with a true experiment.

Random sample: a sample in which every member or subset of the population has an equal chance of being chosen.

Range: a measure of variability for ordinal data. Also, a measure of variability for interval or ratio data. With interval or ratio data, it equals the difference between the upper real limit of the highest score or category and the lower real limit of the lowest score or category.

Ratio scale of measurement: a measurement scale in which the magnitude of the difference between numbers is meaningful, and there is a true zero. Thus, multiplication and division as well as addition and subtraction are meaningful.

Rationalism: a method for finding truth that emphasizes logical thinking rather than observation.

Raw score: your data as they are originally measured, before any transformation.

Real limits: with interval or ratio data, the actual limits used in assigning a measurement. These are halfway between adjacent scores. Each score thus has an upper and a lower real limit.

Regression: procedure researchers use to develop an equation that permits the prediction of one variable of a correlation if the value of the other variable is known.

Regression line: with linear regression, a straight line indicating the value of Y that is predicted to occur for each value of X. The predicted value of Y is called $\hat{Y}$.

Regression weight: another term for the slope of the regression line.

Relative frequency: the frequency of a category divided by the total frequency.

Residual error: changeable subject characteristics. These differences between subjects are a form of error in an ANOVA.

Restriction of the range: reducing the range of values for a variable will reduce the size of the correlation.

Rho (ρ): symbol used for the population correlation.

Sample: a subset of a population.

Sample of convenience: a sample that is chosen because it is easily available rather than because it is optimal.

Sampling distribution of the mean: a theoretical probability distribution of sample means. The samples are all of the same size and are randomly selected from the same population.

Scientific method: an approach to understanding that emphasizes rigorous logic and that careful observation is the ultimate authority for determining truth. It is a self-correcting approach that limits bias.

Significant: in statistics, a measure of how unlikely it is that an event occurred by chance.

Simple multiple regression: a form of multiple regression in which all of the predictor variables are assessed simultaneously. All predictors that do not significantly enhance the overall prediction are dropped.

Slope of the line: one of the two determinants of the equation for a straight line. It is the ratio of the change in the Y variable divided by the change in the X variable. It has the symbol "b" in the equation $Y = bX + a$.

SPSS: a powerful, commonly used statistical computer package.

Standard deviation: a measure of variability—the average deviation of scores within a distribution. It is defined as the square root of the variance. The symbol for the population standard deviation is σ.

Standard error: the standard deviation of the sampling distribution of a statistic. Thus, the standard error of the mean is the standard deviation of the sampling distribution of means.

Standard error of the difference between sample means ($S_{(M_1-M_2)}$): the standard deviation of the sampling distribution of the difference between sample means.

Standard error of estimate: the standard deviation of Y scores around the regression line. Its symbol is $\sigma_{\hat{Y}}$.

Standard error of the mean difference (s_{M_D}): the standard deviation of the sampling distribution of the mean difference between measures.

Statistic: a measure of a characteristic of a sample, such as its mean.

Sum of the squared deviations: for a population, it is equal to $\Sigma(X - \mu)^2$ or Σx^2. It is often abbreviated as "sum of squares," which is shortened even further to SS.

Symmetrical distribution: a distribution in which the right half is the mirror image of the left half. In such a distribution, there is a high score corresponding to each low score.

True dichotomy: a natural division of scores into two distinct categories.

True experiment: an experiment in which the researcher randomly assigns the subjects and also manipulates the value of the independent variable. As a result, at the conclusion of the study, the researcher is justified in reaching a cause-and-effect conclusion concerning the relationship between the independent and dependent variables.

Two-tailed or nondirectional test: an analysis in which the null hypothesis will be rejected if an extreme outcome occurs in either direction. In such a test, the alpha level is divided into two equal parts.

Type I error: the probability of rejecting the null hypothesis when it is in fact true. This probability is equal to alpha, α, which is usually 5%.

Type II error: the probability of retaining the null hypothesis when it is in fact false.

The probability is equal to beta, β, which is usually not known.

Unconfounded comparison: comparison of two cell means that involves only one factor that is changing. The comparison can be interpreted.

Unimodal distribution: a distribution with only one mode.

Unstable: a term used to describe a measure, such as of central tendency, that can vary significantly with only a few changes to the original set of data. This is seen as an undesirable quality.

Variability: how much scores of a sample or population differ or deviate from each other.

Variable view: SPSS window in which experimental variables are defined.

Variance: a measure of variability—the average of the sum of the squared deviations of scores from their mean. The symbol for the population variance is σ^2.

x: the symbol for a deviation. Thus, $x = (X - \mu)$ if we are dealing with a population.

***Y* intercept:** one of the two determinants of the equation for a straight line. It is the value of Y when X is equal to 0. It is, therefore, the value of Y when the line crosses the Y axis. It has the symbol "a" in the equation $Y = bX + a$.

***z* score:** a conversion of raw data so that the deviation is measured in standard deviation units, and the sign, positive or negative, indicates the direction of the deviation.

APPENDIX I

ANSWERS TO CHAPTER PROBLEMS

Chapter 1

1. c	8.	15. b
2.	9. b	16.
3. a	10.	17. d
4.	11. c	18.
5. c	12.	19. c
6.	13. a	20.
7. b	14.	

Chapter 2

1. d	5. a	9. a
2.	6.	10.
3. d	7. b	11. c
4.	8.	12.

13. a

14.

15. c

16.

17. c

18.

19. c

20.

Chapter 3

1. c

2.

3. b

4.

5. c

6.

7. b

8.

9. c

10.

11. d

12.

13. d

14.

15. c

16.

17. d

18.

19. c

20.

21. b

22.

23. b

24.

25. b

Chapter 4

1. a

2.

3. b

4.

5. a

6.

7. d

8.

9. a

10.

11. b

12.

13. d

14.

15. a

16.

17. b

18.

19. a

20.

Chapter 5

1. b

2.

3. a

4.

5. a

6.

Chapter 6

1. c	8.	15. b
2.	9. c	16.
3. a	10.	17. a
4.	11. d	18.
5. a	12.	19. c
6.	13. d	20.
7. c	14.	

Chapter 7

1. a	13. b	25. c
2.	14.	26.
3. a	15. c	27. b
4.	16.	28.
5. c	17. e	29. c
6.	18.	30.
7. c	19. a	31. c
8.	20.	32.
9. b	21. b	33. c
10.	22.	34.
11. d	23. e	
12.	24.	

Chapter 8

1. b	4.	7. e
2.	5. b	8.
3. e	6.	9. a

10.	15. b	20.
11. c	16.	21. c
12.	17. b	22.
13. a	18.	23. a
14.	19. a	

Chapter 9

1. d	14.	27. b
2.	15. b	28.
3. b	16.	29. b
4.	17. b	30.
5. c	18.	31. c
6.	19. a	32.
7. c	20.	33. e
8.	21. d	34.
9. a	22.	35. a
10.	23. b	36.
11. d	24.	37. a
12.	25. b	38.
13. a	26.	39. a

Chapter 10

1. c	7. a	13. a
2.	8.	14.
3. a	9. c	15. b
4.	10.	16.
5. c	11. b	17. a
6.	12.	18.

19. c	27. b	35. b
20.	28.	36.
21. c	29. b	37. c
22.	30.	38
23. b	31. b	39. a
24.	32.	40.
25. b	33. b	41. b
26.	34.	

Chapter 11

1. c	10.	19. b
2.	11. b	20.
3. b	12.	21. a
4.	13. d	22.
5. b	14.	23. c
6.	15. b	24.
7. c	16.	25. b
8.	17. a	26.
9. a	18.	

Chapter 12

1. b	8.	15. d
2.	9. c	16.
3. d	10.	17. c
4.	11. a	18.
5. c	12.	19. d
6.	13. b	20.
7. a	14.	

Chapter 13

1. c	9. b	17. c
2.	10.	18.
3. a	11. b	19. b
4.	12	20.
5. c	13. d	21. b
6.	14.	22.
7. a	15. d	
8.	16.	

Chapter 14

1. b	11. b	21. c
2.	12.	22.
3. d	13. c	23. a
4.	14.	24.
5. b	15. d	25. b
6.	16.	26.
7. b	17. c	27. a
8.	18.	28.
9. d	19. b	29. d
10.	20.	30.

Chapter 15

1. b	5. c	9. a
2.	6.	10.
3. a	7. a	11. a
4.	8.	12.

13. d

14.

15. a

16.

17. b

18.

19. c

20.

Chapter 16

1. d

2.

3. b

4.

5. c

6.

7. b

8.

9. d

10.

11. c

12.

13. a

14.

15. c

16.

17. b

18.

19. a

20.

21. c

22.

23. a

24.

25. b

26.

27. b

28.

Appendix A

1. b

2.

3. d

4.

5. a

6.

7. a

8.

9. d

10.

11. c

12.

13. d

14.

15. b

Appendix B

1. b

2.

3. a

4.

5. e

6.

7. a

8.

9. d

10.

11. a

Appendix C

1. c	5. b	9. a
2.	6.	10.
3. b	7. c	
4.	8.	

Appendix D

1. a	5. c	9. a
2.	6.	10.
3. d	7. a	
4.	8.	

APPENDIX J

STATISTICAL TABLES

Table J.1 Proportions of Area Under the Standard Normal Curve: The Unit Normal Table

Column (A) lists z score values. Column (B) lists proportion of the area between the mean and the z score value. Column (C) lists the proportion of the area beyond the z score in the tail of the distribution. (Note: Because the normal distribution is symmetrical, areas for negative z scores are the same as those for positive z scores.)

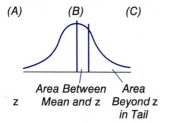
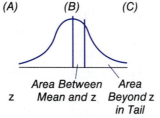
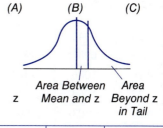

(A) z	(B) Area Between Mean and z	(C) Area Beyond z in Tail	(A) z	(B) Area Between Mean and z	(C) Area Beyond z in Tail	(A) z	(B) Area Between Mean and z	(C) Area Beyond z in Tail
0.00	.0000	.5000	0.03	.0120	.4880	0.06	.0239	.4761
0.01	.0040	.4960	0.04	.0160	.4840	0.07	.0279	.4721
0.02	.0080	.4920	0.05	.0199	.4801	0.08	.0319	.4681

(Continued)

Table J.1 (Continued)

(A) z	(B) Area Between Mean and z	(C) Area Beyond z in Tail	(A) z	(B) Area Between Mean and z	(C) Area Beyond z in Tail	(A) z	(B) Area Between Mean and z	(C) Area Beyond z in Tail
0.09	.0359	.4641	0.37	.1443	.3557	0.65	.2422	.2578
0.10	.0398	.4602	0.38	.1480	.3520	0.66	.2454	.2546
0.11	.0438	.4562	0.39	.1517	.3483	0.67	.2486	.2514
0.12	.0478	.4522	0.40	.1554	.3446	0.68	.2517	.2483
0.13	.0517	.4483	0.41	.1591	.3409	0.69	.2549	.2451
0.14	.0557	.4443	0.42	.1628	.3372	0.70	.2580	.2420
0.15	.0596	.4404	0.43	.1664	.3336	0.71	.2611	.2389
0.16	.0636	.4364	0.44	.1700	.3300	0.72	.2642	.2358
0.17	.0675	.4325	0.45	.1736	.3264	0.73	.2673	.2327
0.18	.0714	.4286	0.46	.1772	.3228	0.74	.2704	.2296
0.19	.0753	.4247	0.47	.1808	.3192	0.75	.2734	.2266
0.20	.0793	.4207	0.48	.1844	.3156	0.76	.2764	.2236
0.21	.0832	.4168	0.49	.1879	.3121	0.77	.2794	.2206
0.22	.0871	.4129	0.50	.1915	.3085	0.78	.2823	.2177
0.23	.0910	.4090	0.51	.1950	.3050	0.79	.2852	.2148
0.24	.0948	.4052	0.52	.1985	.3015	0.80	.2881	.2119
0.25	.0987	.4013	0.53	.2019	.2981	0.81	.2910	.2090
0.26	.1026	.3974	0.54	.2054	.2946	0.82	.2939	.2061
0.27	.1064	.3936	0.55	.2088	.2912	0.83	.2967	.2033
0.28	.1103	.3897	0.56	.2123	.2877	0.84	.2995	.2005
0.29	.1141	.3859	0.57	.2157	.2843	0.85	.3023	.1977
0.30	.1179	.3821	0.58	.2190	.2810	0.86	.3051	.1949
0.31	.1217	.3783	0.59	.2224	.2776	0.87	.3078	.1922
0.32	.1255	.3745	0.60	.2257	.2743	0.88	.3106	.1894
0.33	.1293	.3707	0.61	.2391	.2709	0.89	.3133	.1867
0.34	.1331	.3669	0.62	.2324	.2676	0.90	.3159	.1841
0.35	.1368	.3632	0.63	.2357	.2643	0.91	.3186	.1814
0.36	.1406	.3594	0.64	.2389	.2611	0.92	.3212	.1788

(A) z	(B) Area Between Mean and z	(C) Area Beyond z in Tail	(A) z	(B) Area Between Mean and z	(C) Area Beyond z in Tail	(A) z	(B) Area Between Mean and z	(C) Area Beyond z in Tail
0.93	.3238	.1762	1.21	.3869	.1131	1.49	.4319	.0681
0.94	.3264	.1736	1.22	.3888	.1112	1.50	.4332	.0668
0.95	.3289	.1711	1.23	.3907	.1093	1.51	.4345	.0655
0.96	.3315	.1685	1.24	.3925	.1075	1.52	.4357	.0643
0.97	.3340	.1660	1.25	.3944	.1056	1.53	.4370	.0630
0.98	.3365	.1635	1.26	.3962	.1038	1.54	.4382	.0618
0.99	.3389	.1611	1.27	.3980	1020	1.55	.4394	.0606
1.00	.3413	.1587	1.28	.3997	.1003	1.56	.4406	.0594
1.01	.3438	.1562	1.29	.4015	.0985	1.57	.4418	.0582
1.02	.3461	.1539	1.30	.4032	.0968	1.58	.4429	.0571
1.03	.3485	.1515	1.31	.4049	.0951	1.59	.4441	.0559
1.04	.3508	.1492	1.32	.4066	.0934	1.60	.4452	.0548
1.05	.3531	.1469	1.33	.4082	.0918	1.61	.4463	.0537
1.06	.3554	.1446	1.34	.4099	.0901	1.62	.4474	.0526
1.07	.3577	.1423	1.35	.4115	.0885	1.63	.4484	.0516
1.08	.3599	.1401	1.36	.4131	.0869	1.64	.4495	.0505
1.09	.3621	.1379	1.37	.4147	.0853	1.65	.4505	.0495
1.10	.3643	.1357	1.38	.4162	.0838	1.66	.4515	.0485
1.11	.3665	.1335	1.39	.4177	.0823	1.67	.4525	.0475
1.12	.3686	.1314	1.40	.4192	.0808	1.68	.4535	.0465
1.13	.3708	.1292	1.41	.4207	.0793	1.69	.4545	.0455
1.14	.3729	.1271	1.42	.4222	.0778	1.70	.4554	.0446
1.15	.3749	.1251	1.43	.4236	.0764	1.71	.4564	.0436
1.16	.3770	.1230	1.44	.4251	.0749	1.72	.4573	.0427
1.17	.3790	.1210	1.45	.4265	.0735	1.73	.4582	.0418
1.18	.3810	.1190	1.46	.4279	.0721	1.74	.4591	.0409
1.19	.3830	.1170	1.47	.4292	.0708	1.75	.4599	.0401
1.20	.3849	.1151	1.48	.4306	.0694	1.76	.4608	.0392

(Continued)

Table J.1   (Continued)

(A) z	(B) Area Between Mean and z	(C) Area Beyond z in Tail	(A) z	(B) Area Between Mean and z	(C) Area Beyond z in Tail	(A) z	(B) Area Between Mean and z	(C) Area Beyond z in Tail
1.77	.4616	.0384	2.04	.4793	.0207	2.31	.4896	.0104
1.78	.4625	.0375	2.05	.4798	.0202	2.32	.4898	.0102
1.79	.4633	.0367	2.06	.4803	.0197	2.33	.4901	.0099
1.80	.4641	.0359	2.07	.4808	.0192	2.34	.4904	.0096
1.81	.4649	.0351	2.08	.4812	.0188	2.35	.4906	.0094
1.82	.4656	.0344	2.09	.4817	.0183	2.36	.4909	.0091
1.83	.4664	.0336	2.10	.4821	.0179	2.37	.4911	.0089
1.84	.4671	.0329	2.11	.4826	.0174	2.38	.4913	.0087
1.85	.4678	.0322	2.12	.4830	.0170	2.39	.4916	.0084
1.86	.4686	.0314	2.13	.4834	.0166	2.40	.4918	.0082
1.87	.4693	.0307	2.14	.4838	.0162	2.41	.4920	.0080
1.88	.4699	.0301	2.15	.4842	.0158	2.42	.4922	.0078
1.89	.4706	.0294	2.16	.4846	.0154	2.43	.4925	.0075
1.90	.4713	.0287	2.17	.4850	.0150	2.44	.4927	.0073
1.91	.4719	.0281	2.18	.4854	.0146	2.45	.4929	.0071
1.92	.4726	.0274	2.19	.4857	.0143	2.46	.4931	.0069
1.93	.4732	.0268	2.20	.4861	.0139	2.47	.4932	.0068
1.94	.4738	.0262	2.21	.4864	.0136	2.48	.4934	.0066
1.95	.4744	.0256	2.22	.4868	.0132	2.49	.4936	.0064
1.96	.4750	.0250	2.23	.4871	.0129	2.50	.4938	.0062
1.97	.4756	.0244	2.24	.4875	.0125	2.51	.4940	.0060
1.98	.4761	.0239	2.25	.4878	.0122	2.52	.4941	.0059
1.99	.4767	.0233	2.26	.4881	.0119	2.53	.4943	.0057
2.00	.4772	.0228	2.27	.4884	.0116	2.54	.4945	.0055
2.01	.4778	.0222	2.28	.4887	.0113	2.55	.4946	.0054
2.02	.4783	.0217	2.29	.4890	.0110	2.56	.4948	.0052
2.03	.4788	.0212	2.30	.4893	.0107	2.57	.4949	.0051

(A) z	(B) Area Between Mean and z	(C) Area Beyond z in Tail	(A) z	(B) Area Between Mean and z	(C) Area Beyond z in Tail	(A) z	(B) Area Between Mean and z	(C) Area Beyond z in Tail
2.58	.4951	.0049	2.84	.4977	.0023	3.10	.4990	.0010
2.59	.4952	.0048	2.85	.4978	.0022	3.11	.4991	.0009
2.60	.4953	.0047	2.86	.4979	.0021	3.12	.4991	.0009
2.61	.4955	.0045	2.87	.4979	.0021	3.13	.4991	.0009
2.62	.4956	.0044	2.88	.4980	.0020	3.14	.4992	.0008
2.63	.4957	.0043	2.89	.4981	.0019	3.15	.4992	.0008
2.64	.4959	.0041	2.90	.4981	.0019	3.16	.4992	.0008
2.65	.4960	.0040	2.91	.4982	.0018	3.17	.4992	.0008
2.66	.4961	.0039	2.92	.4982	.0018	3.18	.4993	.0007
2.67	.4962	.0038	2.93	.4983	.0017	3.19	.4993	.0007
2.68	.4963	.0037	2.94	.4984	.0016	3.20	.4993	.0007
2.69	.4964	.0036	2.95	.4984	.0016	3.21	.4993	.0007
2.70	.4965	.0035	2.96	.4985	.0015	3.22	.4994	.0006
2.71	.4966	.0034	2.97	.4985	.0015	3.23	.4994	.0006
2.72	.4967	.0033	2.98	.4986	.0014	3.24	.4994	.0006
2.73	.4968	.0032	2.99	.4986	.0014	3.25	.4994	.0006
2.74	.4969	.0031	3.00	.4987	.0013	3.30	.4995	.0005
2.75	.4970	.0030	3.01	.4987	.0013	3.35	.4996	.0004
2.76	.4971	.0029	3.02	.4987	.0013	3.40	.4997	.0003
2.77	.4972	.0028	3.03	.4988	.0012	3.45	.4997	.0003
2.78	.4973	.0027	3.04	.4988	.0012	3.50	.4998	.0002
2.79	.4974	.0026	3.05	.4989	.0011	3.60	.4998	.0002
2.80	.4974	.0026	3.06	.4989	.0011	3.70	.4999	.0001
2.81	.4975	.0025	3.07	.4989	.0011	3.80	.4999	.0001
2.82	.4976	.0024	3.08	.4990	.0010	3.90	.49995	.00005
2.83	.4977	.0023	3.09	.4990	.0010	4.00	.49997	.00003

Source. J. E. Freund, *Modern Elementary Statistics* (11th edition). Pearson Prentice Hall, 2004.

Table J.2	Critical Values of Chi-Square (χ^2)

	Level of Significance	
df	$\alpha = .05$	$\alpha = .01$
1	3.84	6.64
2	5.99	9.21
3	7.81	11.34
4	9.49	13.28
5	11.07	15.09
6	12.59	16.81
7	14.07	18.48
8	15.51	20.09
9	16.92	21.67
10	18.31	23.21
11	19.68	24.72
12	21.03	26.22
13	22.36	27.69
14	23.68	29.14
15	25.00	30.58
16	26.30	32.00
17	27.59	33.41
18	28.87	34.80
19	30.14	36.19
20	31.41	37.47
21	32.67	38.93
22	33.92	40.29
23	35.17	41.64
24	36.42	42.98
25	37.65	44.31
26	38.88	45.64
27	40.11	46.96
28	41.34	48.28
29	42.56	49.59
30	43.77	50.89
40	55.76	63.69
50	67.50	76.15
60	79.08	88.38
70	90.53	100.42

Source. (1965), Fisher, R. A., and F. Yates: Statistical tables for biological, agricultural and medical research. 6. Aufl. Oliver & Boyd, London 1963. 146 S. Preis 30 s. Biometrische Zeitschrift, 7: 124–125. doi: 10.1002/bimj.19650070219 http://onlinelibrary.wiley.com/doi/10.1002/bimj.19650070219/abstract

Table J.3 Critical Values of the Student *t* Distribution

	Level of Significance for One-Tailed Test					
	0.10	0.05	0.025	0.010	0.005	0.0005
	Level of Significance for Two-Tailed Test					
Df	0.20	0.10	0.05	0.02	0.01	0.001
1	3.078	6.314	12.706	31.821	63.657	636.619
2	1.886	2.920	4.303	6.965	9.925	31.599
3	1.638	2.353	3.182	4.541	5.841	12.924
4	1.533	2.132	2.776	3.747	4.604	8.610
5	1.476	2.015	2.571	3.365	4.032	6.869
6	1.440	1.943	2.447	3.143	3.707	5.959
7	1.415	1.895	2.365	2.998	3.499	5.408
8	1.397	1.860	2.306	2.896	3.355	5.041
9	1.383	1.833	2.262	2.821	3.250	4.781
10	1.372	1.812	2.228	2.764	3.169	4.587
11	1.363	1.796	2.201	2.718	3.106	4.437
12	1.356	1.782	2.179	2.681	3.055	4.318
13	1.350	1.771	2.160	2.650	3.012	4.221
14	1.345	1.761	2.145	2.624	2.977	4.140
15	1.341	1.753	2.131	2.602	2.947	4.073
16	1.337	1.746	2.120	2.583	2.921	4.015
17	1.333	1.740	2.110	2.567	2.898	3.965
18	1.330	1.734	2.101	2.552	2.878	3.922
19	1.328	1.729	2.093	2.539	2.861	3.883
20	1.325	1.725	2.086	2.528	2.845	3.850
21	1.323	1.721	2.080	2.518	2.831	3.819
22	1.321	1.717	2.074	2.508	2.819	3.792
23	1.319	1.714	2.069	2.500	2.807	3.768
24	1.318	1.711	2.064	2.492	2.797	3.745
25	1.316	1.708	2.060	2.485	2.787	3.725
28	1.313	1.701	2.048	2.467	2.763	3.674

(Continued)

Table J.3	(Continued)

	Level of Significance for One-Tailed Test					
	0.10	0.05	0.025	0.010	0.005	0.0005
	Level of Significance for Two-Tailed Test					
Df	0.20	0.10	0.05	0.02	0.01	0.001
29	1.311	1.699	2.045	2.462	2.756	3.659
30	1.310	1.697	2.042	2.457	2.750	3.646
40	1.303	1.684	2.021	2.423	2.704	3.551
60	1.296	1.671	2.000	2.390	2.660	3.460
120	1.289	1.658	1.980	2.358	2.617	3.373
∞	1.282	1.645	1.960	2.327	2.576	3.291

Source. Ha and Ha. Integrative Statistics for the Social and Behavioral Sciences. 2012. SAGE. Table B page 384.

Table J.4	Table entries indicate critical values for the *F*-distribution.

Critical values at a .05 level of significance are given in lightface type.

Critical values at a .01 level of significance are given in boldface type.

		Degrees of Freedom Numerator											
		1	2	3	4	5	6	7	8	9	10	20	∞
Degrees of Freedom Denominator	1	161 **4052**	200 **5000**	216 **5403**	225 **5625**	230 **5764**	234 **5859**	237 **5928**	239 **5928**	241 **6023**	242 **6056**	248 **6209**	254 **6366**
	2	18.51 **98.49**	19.00 **99.00**	19.16 **99.17**	19.25 **99.25**	19.30 **99.30**	19.33 **99.33**	19.36 **99.34**	19.37 **99.36**	19.38 **99.38**	19.39 **99.40**	19.44 **99.45**	19.5 **99.5**
	3	10.13 **34.12**	9.55 **30.92**	9.28 **29.46**	9.12 **28.71**	9.01 **28.24**	8.94 **27.91**	8.88 **27.67**	8.84 **27.49**	8.81 **27.34**	8.78 **27.23**	8.66 **26.69**	8.5 **26.1**
	4	7.71 **21.20**	6.94 **18.00**	6.59 **16.69**	6.39 **15.98**	6.26 **15.52**	6.16 **15.21**	6.09 **14.98**	6.04 **14.80**	6.00 **14.66**	5.96 **14.54**	5.80 **14.02**	5.6 **13.5**
	5	6.61 **16.26**	5.79 **13.27**	5.41 **12.06**	5.19 **11.39**	5.05 **10.97**	4.95 **10.67**	4.88 **10.45**	4.82 **10.27**	4.78 **10.15**	4.74 **10.05**	4.56 **9.55**	4.37 **9.02**
	6	5.99 **13.74**	5.14 **10.92**	4.76 **9.78**	4.53 **9.15**	4.39 **8.75**	4.28 **8.47**	4.21 **8.26**	4.15 **8.10**	4.10 **7.98**	4.06 **7.87**	3.87 **7.39**	3.67 **6.88**

		\multicolumn{12}{c}{**Degrees of Freedom Numerator**}
		1	**2**	**3**	**4**	**5**	**6**	**7**	**8**	**9**	**10**	**20**	**∞**
	7	5.59 **13.74**	4.74 **9.55**	4.35 **8.45**	4.12 **7.85**	3.97 **7.46**	3.87 **7.19**	3.79 **7.00**	3.73 **6.84**	3.68 **6.71**	3.63 **6.62**	3.44 **6.15**	3.23 **5.65**
	8	5.32 **11.26**	4.46 **8.65**	4.07 **7.59**	3.84 **7.01**	3.69 **6.63**	3.58 **6.37**	3.50 **6.19**	3.44 **6.03**	3.39 **5.91**	3.34 **5.82**	3.15 **5.36**	2.93 **4.86**
	9	5.12 **10.56**	4.26 **8.02**	3.86 **6.99**	3.63 **6.42**	3.48 **6.06**	3.37 **5.80**	3.29 **5.62**	3.23 **5.47**	3.18 **5.35**	3.13 **5.26**	2.93 **4.80**	2.71 **4.31**
	10	4.96 **10.04**	4.10 **7.56**	3.71 **6.55**	3.48 **5.99**	3.33 **5.64**	3.22 **5.39**	3.14 **5.21**	3.07 **5.06**	3.02 **4.95**	2.97 **4.85**	2.77 **4.41**	2.54 **3.91**
	11	4.84 **9.65**	3.98 **7.20**	3.59 **6.22**	3.36 **5.67**	3.20 **5.32**	3.09 **5.07**	3.01 **4.88**	2.95 **4.74**	2.90 **4.63**	2.86 **4.54**	2.65 **4.10**	2.40 **3.60**
	12	4.75 **9.33**	3.89 **6.93**	3.49 **5.95**	3.26 **5.41**	3.11 **5.06**	3.00 **4.82**	2.92 **4.65**	2.85 **4.50**	2.80 **4.39**	2.76 **4.30**	2.54 **3.86**	2.30 **3.36**
	13	4.67 **9.07**	3.80 **6.70**	3.41 **5.74**	3.18 **5.20**	3.02 **4.86**	2.92 **4.62**	2.84 **4.44**	2.77 **4.30**	2.72 **4.19**	2.67 **4.10**	2.46 **3.67**	2.21 **3.17**
	14	4.60 **8.86**	3.74 **6.51**	3.34 **5.56**	3.11 **5.03**	2.96 **4.69**	2.85 **4.46**	2.77 **4.28**	2.70 **4.14**	2.65 **4.03**	2.60 **3.94**	2.39 **3.51**	2.13 **3.00**
	15	4.54 **8.68**	3.68 **6.36**	3.29 **5.42**	3.06 **4.89**	2.90 **4.56**	2.79 **4.32**	2.70 **4.14**	2.64 **4.00**	2.59 **3.89**	2.55 **3.80**	2.33 **3.36**	2.07 **2.87**
	16	4.49 **8.53**	3.63 **6.23**	3.24 **5.29**	3.01 **4.77**	2.85 **4.44**	2.74 **4.20**	2.66 **4.03**	2.59 **3.89**	2.54 **3.78**	2.49 **3.69**	2.28 **3.25**	2.01 **2.75**
	17	4.45 **8.40**	3.59 **6.11**	3.20 **5.18**	2.96 **4.67**	2.81 **4.34**	2.70 **4.10**	2.62 **3.93**	2.55 **3.79**	2.50 **3.68**	2.45 **3.59**	2.23 **3.16**	1.96 **2.65**
	18	4.41 **8.28**	3.55 **6.01**	3.16 **5.09**	2.93 **4.58**	2.77 **4.25**	2.66 **4.01**	2.58 **3.85**	2.51 **3.71**	2.46 **3.60**	2.41 **3.51**	2.19 **3.07**	1.92 **2.57**
	19	4.38 **8.18**	3.52 **5.93**	3.13 **5.01**	2.90 **4.50**	2.74 **4.17**	2.63 **3.94**	2.55 **3.77**	2.48 **3.63**	2.43 **3.52**	2.38 **3.43**	2.15 **3.00**	1.88 **2.49**
	20	4.35 **8.10**	3.49 **5.85**	3.10 **4.94**	2.87 **4.43**	2.71 **4.10**	2.60 **3.87**	2.52 **3.71**	2.45 **3.56**	2.40 **3.45**	2.35 **3.37**	2.12 **2.94**	1.84 **2.42**
	21	4.32 **8.02**	3.47 **5.78**	3.07 **4.87**	2.84 **4.37**	2.68 **4.04**	2.57 **3.81**	2.49 **3.65**	2.42 **3.51**	2.37 **3.40**	2.32 **3.31**	2.09 **2.88**	1.81 **2.36**
	22	4.30 **7.94**	3.44 **5.72**	3.05 **4.82**	2.82 **4.31**	2.66 **3.99**	2.55 **3.76**	2.47 **3.59**	2.40 **3.45**	2.35 **3.35**	2.30 **3.26**	2.07 **2.83**	1.78 **2.31**
	23	4.28 **7.88**	3.42 **5.66**	3.03 **4.76**	2.80 **4.26**	2.64 **3.94**	2.53 **3.71**	2.45 **3.54**	2.38 **3.41**	2.32 **3.30**	2.28 **3.21**	2.04 **2.78**	1.76 **2.26**

Degrees of Freedom Denominator (row label, left side)

(Continued)

Table J.4 (Continued)

		\multicolumn{12}{c}{Degrees of Freedom Numerator}
		1	2	3	4	5	6	7	8	9	10	20	∞
24		4.26	3.40	3.01	2.78	2.62	2.51	2.43	2.36	2.30	2.26	2.02	1.73
		7.82	5.61	4.72	4.22	3.90	3.67	3.50	3.36	3.25	3.17	2.74	2.21
25		4.24	3.38	2.99	2.76	2.60	2.49	2.41	2.34	2.28	2.24	2.00	1.71
		7.77	5.57	4.68	4.18	3.86	3.63	3.46	3.32	3.21	3.13	2.70	2.17
26		4.22	3.37	2.98	2.74	2.59	2.47	2.39	2.32	2.27	2.22	1.99	1.69
		7.72	5.53	4.64	4.14	3.82	3.59	3.42	3.29	3.17	3.09	2.66	2.13
27		4.21	3.35	2.96	2.73	2.57	2.46	2.37	2.30	2.25	2.20	1.97	1.67
		7.68	5.49	4.60	4.11	3.79	3.56	3.39	3.26	3.14	3.06	2.63	2.10
28		4.20	3.34	2.95	2.71	2.56	2.44	2.36	2.29	2.24	2.19	1.96	1.65
		7.64	5.45	4.57	4.07	3.76	3.53	3.36	3.23	3.11	3.03	2.60	2.07
29		4.18	3.33	2.93	2.70	2.54	2.43	2.35	2.28	2.22	2.18	1.94	1.63
		7.60	5.42	4.54	4.04	3.73	3.50	3.33	3.20	3.08	3.00	2.57	2.04
30		4.17	3.32	2.92	2.69	2.53	2.42	2.34	2.27	2.21	2.16	1.93	1.61
		7.56	5.39	4.51	4.02	3.70	3.47 -	3.30	3.17	3.06	2.98	2.55	2.01
31		4.16	3.30	2.91	2.68	2.52	2.41	2.32	2.25	2.20	2.15	1.92	1.60
		7.53	5.36	4.48	3.99	3.67	3.45	3.28	3.15	3.04	2.96	2.53	1.89
32		4.15	3.29	2.90	2.67	2.51	2.40	2.31	2.24	2.19	2.14	1.91	1.59
		7.50	5.34	4.46	3.97	3.65	3.43	3.26	3.13	3.02	2.93	2.51	1.88
33		4.14	3.28	2.89	2.66	2.50	2.39	2.30	2.23	2.18	2.13	1.90	1.58
		7.47	5.31	4.44	3.95	3.63	3.41	3.24	3.11	3.00	2.91	2.49	1.87
34		4.13	3.28	2.88	2.65	2.49	2.38	2.29	2.23	2.17	2.12	1.89	1.57
		7.44	5.29	4.42	3.93	3.61	3.39	3.22	3.09	2.98	2.89	2.47	1.86
35		4.12	3.27	2.87	2.64	2.49	2.37	2.29	2.22	2.16	2.11	1.88	1.56
		7.42	5.27	4.40	3.91	3.59	3.37	3.20	3.07	2.96	2.88	2.45	1.85
36		4.11	3.26	2.87	2.63	2.48	2.36	2.28	2.21	2.15	2.11	1.87	1.55
		7.40	5.25	4.38	3.89	3.57	3.35	3.18	3.05	2.95	2.86	2.43	1.84
37		4.11	3.25	2.86	2.63	2.47	2.36	2.27	2.20	2.14	2.10	1.86	1.54
		7.37	5.23	4.36	3.87	3.56	3.33	3.17	3.04	2.93	2.84	2.42	1.83
38		4.10	3.24	2.85	2.62	2.46	2.35	2.26	2.19	2.14	2.09	1.85	1.53
		7.35	5.21	4.34	3.86	3.54	3.32	3.15	3.02	2.92	2.83	2.40	1.82
39		4.09	3.24	2.85	2.61	2.46	2.34	2.26	2.19	2.13	2.08	1.84	1.52
		7.33	5.19	4.33	3.84	3.53	3.30	3.14	3.01	2.90	2.81	2.39	1.81
40		4.08	3.23	2.84	2.61	2.45	2.34	2.25	2.18	2.12	2.07	1.84	1.51
		7.31	5.18	4.31	3.83	3.51	3.29	3.12	2.99	2.88	2.80	2.37	1.80

Degrees of Freedom Denominator

						Degrees of Freedom Numerator							
		1	**2**	**3**	**4**	**5**	**6**	**7**	**8**	**9**	**10**	**20**	**∞**
Degrees of Freedom Denominator	42	4.07	3.22	2.83	2.59	2.44	2.32	2.24	2.17	2.11	2.06	1.82	1.50
		7.27	**5.15**	**4.29**	**3.80**	**3.49**	**3.26**	**3.10**	**2.96**	**2.86**	**2.77**	**2.35**	**1.78**
	44	4.06	3.21	2.82	2.58	2.43	2.31	2.23	2.16	2.10	2.05	1.81	1.49
		7.24	**5.12**	**4.26**	**3.78**	**3.46**	**3.24**	**3.07**	**2.94**	**2.84**	**2.75**	**2.32**	**1.76**
	60	4.00	3.15	2.76	2.53	2.37	2.25	2.17	2.10	2.04	1.99	1.75	1.39
		7.08	**4.98**	**4.13**	**3.65**	**3.34**	**3.12**	**2.95**	**2.82**	**2.72**	**2.63**	**2.20**	**1.60**
	120	3.92	3.07	2.68	2.45	2.29	2.18	2.09	2.02	1.96	1.91	1.66	1.25
		6.85	**4.79**	**3.95**	**3.48**	**3.17**	**2.96**	**2.79**	**2.66**	**2.56**	**2.47**	**2.03**	**1.38**
	∞	3.84	3.00	2.60	2.37	2.21	2.10	2.01	1.94	1.88	1.83	1.57	1.00
		6.63	**4.61**	**3.78**	**3.32**	**3.02**	**2.80**	**2.64**	**2.51**	**2.41**	**2.32**	**1.88**	**1.00**

Source. Privitera, Statistics for the Behavioral Sciences, 2012. SAGE Table B.3 page 634.

Table J.5 The Studentized Range Statistic (*q*)

The critical values for q correspond to alpha = .05 (lightface type) and alpha = .01 (boldface type)

df_E	Range								
	2	**3**	**4**	**5**	**6**	**7**	**8**	**9**	**10**
5	3.64	4.60	5.22	5.67	6.03	6.33	6.58	6.80	6.99
	5.70	**6.98**	**7.80**	**8.42**	**8.91**	**9.32**	**9.67**	**9.97**	**10.24**
6	3.46	4.34	4.90	5.30	5.63	5.91	6.13	6.32	6.50
	5.24	**6.32**	**7.02**	**7.55**	**7.98**	**8.33**	**8.62**	**8.87**	**9.10**
7	3.34	4.17	4.68	5.06	5.36	5.60	5.82	5.99	6.15
	4.95	**5.91**	**6.54**	**7.00**	**7.38**	**7.69**	**7.94**	**8.17**	**8.38**
8	3.26	4.05	4.53	4.89	5.17	5.41	5.60	5.78	5.93
	4.75	**5.64**	**6.21**	**6.63**	**6.97**	**7.26**	**7.47**	**7.70**	**7.89**
9	3.20	3.95	4.42	4.76	5.03	5.24	5.43	5.60	5.74
	4.60	**5.43**	**5.95**	**6.34**	**6.67**	**6.91**	**7.13**	**7.33**	**7.50**
10	3.15	3.88	4.33	4.66	4.92	5.12	5.30	5.46	5.60
	4.48	**5.27**	**5.77**	**6.14**	**6.43**	**6.67**	**6.89**	**7.06**	**7.22**
11	3.11	3.82	4.27	4.59	4.83	5.03	5.21	5.36	5.49
	4.38	**5.16**	**5.63**	**5.98**	**6.25**	**6.48**	**6.69**	**6.85**	**7.01**

(Continued)

Table J.5   (Continued)

df_E	Range								
	2	**3**	**4**	**5**	**6**	**7**	**8**	**9**	**10**
12	3.08	3.78	4.20	4.51	4.75	4.96	5.12	5.26	5.39
	4.32	**5.05**	**5.50**	**5.84**	**6.10**	**6.32**	**6.52**	**6.67**	**6.82**
13	3.05	3.73	4.15	4.47	4.69	4.88	5.06	5.21	5.33
	4.26	**4.97**	**5.41**	**5.74**	**5.98**	**6.19**	**6.39**	**6.53**	**6.68**
14	3.03	3.70	4.11	4.41	4.64	4.83	4.99	5.13	5.25
	4.21	**4.90**	**5.33**	**5.64**	**5.88**	**6.10**	**6.28**	**6.41**	**6.56**
15	3.01	3.68	4.09	4.38	4.59	4.79	4.95	5.09	5.21
	4.17	**4.84**	**5.26**	**5.56**	**5.80**	**6.01**	**6.18**	**6.31**	**6.46**
16	2.99	3.65	4.05	4.33	4.56	4.74	4.89	5.03	5.15
	4.13	**4.79**	**5.19**	**5.50**	**5.72**	**5.94**	**6.10**	**6.23**	**6.37**
17	2.98	3.63	4.02	4.30	4.52	4.70	4.85	4.99	5.11
	4.10	**4.75**	**5.15**	**5.44**	**5.66**	**5.86**	**6.02**	**6.14**	**6.28**
18	2.97	3.62	4.01	4.29	4.49	4.68	4.84	4.97	5.08
	4.07	**4.71**	**5.10**	**5.39**	**5.60**	**5.80**	**5.95**	**6.08**	**6.21**
19	2.96	3.59	3.98	4.26	4.47	4.65	4.80	4.93	5.04
	4.05	**4.68**	**5.05**	**5.35**	**5.56**	**5.75**	**5.91**	**6.03**	**6.15**
20	2.95	3.58	3.96	4.24	4.45	4.63	4.78	4.91	5.01
	4.02	**4.64**	**5.02**	**5.31**	**5.51**	**5.71**	**5.86**	**5.98**	**6.09**
22	2.94	3.55	3.93	4.20	4.41	4.58	4.72	4.85	4.96
	3.99	**4.59**	**4.96**	**5.27**	**5.44**	**5.62**	**5.76**	**5.87**	**6.00**
24	2.92	3.53	3.91	4.17	4.37	4.54	4.69	4.81	4.92
	3.96	**4.55**	**4.92**	**5.17**	**5.37**	**5.55**	**5.70**	**5.81**	**5.93**
26	2.91	3.52	3.89	4.15	4.36	4.53	4.67	4.79	4.90
	3.94	**4.51**	**4.87**	**5.13**	**5.33**	**5.49**	**5.63**	**5.74**	**5.86**
28	2.90	3.50	3.87	4.12	4.33	4.49	4.63	4.75	4.86
	3.91	**4.48**	**4.83**	**5.09**	**5.28**	**5.45**	**5.58**	**5.69**	**5.81**
30	2.89	3.49	3.85	4.10	4.30	4.47	0.60	4.73	4.84
	3.89	**4.45**	**4.80**	**5.05**	**5.24**	**5.40**	**5.54**	**5.64**	**5.76**
40	2.86	3.45	3.79	4.05	4.23	4.39	4.52	4.65	4.73
	3.82	**4.37**	**4.70**	**4.93**	**5.11**	**5.26**	**5.39**	**5.49**	**5.60**

df_E	Range								
	2	**3**	**4**	**5**	**6**	**7**	**8**	**9**	**10**
60	2.83 **3.76**	3.41 **4.28**	3.75 **4.60**	3.98 **4.82**	4.16 **4.99**	4.31 **5.13**	4.44 **5.25**	4.56 **5.36**	4.65 **5.45**
100	2.81 **3.72**	3.36 **4.22**	3.70 **4.52**	3.93 **4.74**	4.11 **4.90**	4.26 **5.04**	4.39 **5.15**	4.50 **5.23**	4.59 **5.34**
∞	2.77 **3.64**	3.31 **4.12**	3.63 **4.40**	3.86 **4.60**	4.03 **4.76**	4.17 **4.88**	4.28 **4.99**	4.39 **5.08**	4.47 **5.16**

Source. Adapted from Privitera, Statistics for the Behavioral Sciences, 2012. SAGE Table B.4 page 637 and Ha and Ha. Integrative Statistics for the Social and Behavioral Sciences. 2012. SAGE. Table B page 384.

Table J.6	Critical Values for the Pearson Correlation*

*To be significant, the sample correlation, r, must be greater than or equal to the critical value in the table.

	Level of Significance for One-Tailed Test			
	.05	**.025**	**.01**	**.005**
	Level of Significance for Two-Tailed Test			
$df = n - 2$	**.10**	**.05**	**.02**	**.01**
1	.988	.997	.9995	.99999
2	.900	.950	.980	.990
3	.805	.878	.934	.959
4	.729	.811	.882	.917
5	.669	.754	.833	.874
6	.622	.707	.789	.834
7	.582	.666	.750	.798
8	.549	.632	.716	.765

(Continued)

Table J.6 (Continued)

	Level of Significance for One-Tailed Test			
	.05	.025	.01	.005
	Level of Significance for Two-Tailed Test			
$df = n - 2$	.10	.05	.02	.01
9	.521	.602	.685	.735
10	.497	.576	.658	.708
11	.476	.553	.634	.684
12	.458	.532	.612	.661
13	.441	.514	.592	.641
14	.426	.497	.574	.623
15	.412	.482	.558	.606
16	.400	.468	.542	.590
17	.389	.456	.528	.575
18	.378	.444	.516	.561
19	.369	.433	.503	.549
20	.360	.423	.492	.537
21	.352	.413	.482	.526
22	.344	.404	.472	.515
23	.337	.396	.462	.505
24	.330	.388	.453	.496
25	.323	.381	.445	.487
26	.317	.374	.437	.479
27	.311	.367	.430	.471
28	.306	.361	.423	.463
29	.301	.355	.416	.456
30	.296	.349	.409	.449

df = n − 2	Level of Significance for One-Tailed Test			
	.05	**.025**	**.01**	**.005**
	Level of Significance for Two-Tailed Test			
	.10	**.05**	**.02**	**.01**
35	.275	.325	.381	.418
40	.257	.304	.358	.393
45	.243	.288	.338	.372
50	.231	.273	.322	.354
60	.211	.250	.295	.325
70	.195	.232	.274	.302
80	.183	.217	.256	.283
90	.173	.205	.242	.267
100	.164	.195	.230	.254

Source. Ha and Ha. Integrative Statistics for the Social and Behavioral Sciences. 2012. SAGE. Table E page 391.

Table J.7 Spearman's Correlation

Number of Pairs (n)	Level of Significance for a One-Tailed Test			
	.05	**.025**	**.01**	**.005**
	Level of Significance for a Two-Tailed Test			
	.10	**.05**	**.02**	**.01**
5	0.900	1.000	1.000	—
6	0.829	0.886	0.943	1.000
7	0.714	0.786	0.893	0.929
8	0.643	0.738	0.833	0.881
9	0.600	0.683	0.783	0.833

(Continued)

Table J.7   (Continued)

Number of Pairs (n)	Level of Significance for a One-Tailed Test			
	.05	.025	.01	.005
	Level of Significance for a Two-Tailed Test			
	.10	.05	.02	.01
10	0.564	0.648	0.746	0.794
12	0.506	0.591	0.712	0.777
14	0.456	0.544	0.645	0.715
16	0.425	0.506	0.601	0.665
18	0.399	0.475	0.564	0.625
20	0.377	0.450	0.534	0.591
22	0.359	0.428	0.508	0.562
24	0.343	0.409	0.485	0.537
26	0.329	0.392	0.465	0.515
28	0.317	0.377	0.448	0.496
30	0.306	0.364	0.432	0.478

Source. Ha and Ha. Integrative Statistics for the Social and Behavioral Sciences. 2012. SAGE. Table I page 398.

Note. Reject the null hypothesis if the derived Spearman coefficient is equal to or greater than the tabled Spearman coefficient value.

APPENDIX K

OVERVIEW OF STATISTICAL PROCEDURES COVERED IN THIS TEXT

	Type of Data		
	Nominal (Frequency)	**Ordinal** (Ranked)	**Interval/Ratio**[a] (Continuous Measure)
Descriptive Statistics (Summarizing Data)			
Frequency distribution	Bar graph or pie chart	Bar graph	Histogram or frequency polygon
Central tendency	Mode	Median	Mean
Variability		Range	Standard deviation and z score
Inferential Statistics (Finding Relationships)			
Statistical procedures for difference and interaction designs			
One variable with at least two outcomes	Goodness-of-fit chi-square	**One IV with one sample—one DV**	One-sample z score or one-sample t test

(Continued)

(Continued)

	Type of Data			
	Nominal (Frequency)		**Ordinal** (Ranked)	**Interval/Ratio** (Continuous Measure)
		One IV with two or more independent samples—one DV	*Kruskal–Wallis H*	One-way between-subjects ANOVA (only two independent samples—independent samples *t* test)
		One IV with one sample having two or more repeated measures—one DV[b]		One-way within-subjects ANOVA (only two repeated measures—dependent samples *t* test)
Two variables, each with at least two outcomes	Chi-square test of independence	**Two IV each with two or more independent samples—one DV**		Two-way between-subjects ANOVA
Statistical procedures for association designs				
Correlation	Phi		*Spearman r*	Pearson *r*
Regression				Linear regression *Multiple regression*

Notes. IV, independent variable (to be a true experiment, the subjects are randomly assigned to the treatment conditions; in quasi-experiments, the subjects effectively assign themselves to the treatment conditions); DV, dependent variable; ANOVA, analysis of variance. The italicized items in the Type of Data columns are reviewed in the following appendixes:

Kruskal–Wallis H in Appendix A

Spearman r in Appendix B

Multiple regression in Appendix C

a. If data are normally distributed and meet parametric assumptions, use statistical procedures listed in this column. If not, it may be appropriate to use procedures listed under ordinal data.

b. Alternatively, this design could have two or more related or matched samples in which case each subject would provide one score.

REFERENCES

Bandura, A., Ross, D., & Ross, S. A. (1961). Transmission of aggression through imitation of aggressive models. *Journal of Abnormal and Social Psychology, 63,* 575–582.

Caspi, A., McClay, J., Moffitt, T., Mill, J., Martin, J., Craig, I. W., . . . Poulton, R. (2002). Role of genotype in the cycle of violence in maltreated children. *Science, 297,* 851–854.

Chou, K. L., Ho, A. H. Y., & Chi, I. (2006). Living alone and depression in Chinese older adults. *Aging & Mental Health, 10*(6), 583–591.

Cohen, J. (1988). *Statistical power analysis for the behavioral sciences* (2nd ed.). Hillsdale, NJ: Lawrence Erlbaum.

Cohen, J. (1992). A power primer. *Psychological Bulletin, 112*(1), 155–159.

Gazzaniga, M. S. (1967). The split brain in man. *Scientific American, 217*(2), 24–29.

Gould, S. J. (1981). *The mismeasure of man.* New York, NY: W. W. Norton.

Graunt, J. (1981). *Natural and political observations upon bills of mortality.* London, England: John Martin & James Allestry. (Original work published 1662)

Light, R. J., Singer, J. D., & Willott, J. B. (1990). *By design: Planning research on higher education.* Cambridge, MA: Harvard University Press.

Mathes, E. (2003). Are sex differences in sexual vs emotional jealousy explained better by differences in sexual strategies or uncertainty of paternity. *Psychological Reports, 93*(3), 895–906.

Maxwell, S. E. (2004). The persistence of underpowered studies in psychological research: Causes, consequences, and remedies. *Psychological Methods, 9*(2), 147–163.

Norvilitis, J. M., & Reid, H. M. (2011, March). *College success: The relations between appreciation of the liberal arts, symptoms of ADHD and study skills.* Poster presented at the Eastern Psychological Association Convention, Cambridge, MA.

Perfect, T. (2003). Local processing bias impairs lineup performance. *Psychological Reports, 93*(2), 393–394.

Riniolo, T. C., Koledin, M., Drakulic, G. M., & Payne, R. A. (2003). An archival study of eyewitness memory of the Titanic's final plunge. *Journal of General Psychology, 130*(1), 89–95.

Sandson, T. A., Bachna, K. J., & Morin, M. D. (2000). Right hemisphere dysfunction in ADHD: Visual hemispatial inattention and clinical subtype. *Journal of Learning Disabilities, 33*(1), 83–90.

INDEX

⑨SAGE researchmethods

The essential online tool for researchers from the world's leading methods publisher

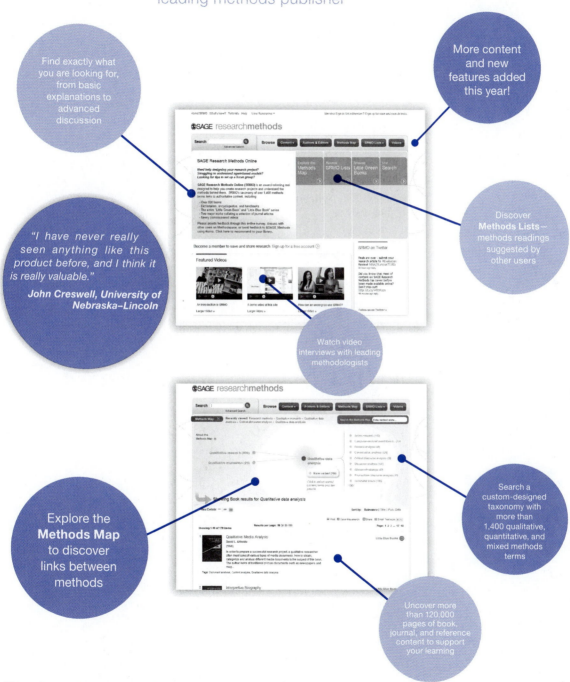

Find exactly what you are looking for, from basic explanations to advanced discussion

More content and new features added this year!

Discover **Methods Lists**—methods readings suggested by other users

"I have never really seen anything like this product before, and I think it is really valuable."

John Creswell, University of Nebraska–Lincoln

Watch video interviews with leading methodologists

Explore the **Methods Map** to discover links between methods

Search a custom-designed taxonomy with more than 1,400 qualitative, quantitative, and mixed methods terms

Uncover more than 120,000 pages of book, journal, and reference content to support your learning

Find out more at
www.sageresearchmethods.com